S0-EAY-601

2023–2024
OREGON BLUE BOOK

Compiled and
published by

Shemia Fagan
Secretary of State

Carla Axtman, Managing Editor
Phil Wiebe, Copy Editor
Brett Fuller & Gary Halvorsen, Web Editors
Kierrah Byrd, Jeffery Plummer & Ben Zeiner, Designers
Archives Division
Office of the Secretary of State
Salem, Oregon 97310
bluebook.oregon.gov

Acknowledgements and special thanks to the following people:

Office of the Secretary of State:
    Archives Division, Stephanie Clark, State Archivist
        Fact gathering/verification: Kimberly Gorman, Dani Morley, Theresa Rae and Todd Shaffer
        Proofreader: Sue White
        Section review: Stephanie Clark, Mary McRobinson, Kate Dunn, Brett Fuller and
            Christina Pellegrino
    Business Services Division: Blue Book order processing and fulfillment, Steve Bergmann, Director;
        Michael Hickam, Manager; Aubrey Gesner, Karla Willmschen, Don Stewart and
        Debra Wikel
    Elections Division: Lydia Plukchi

Department of Administrative Services, Chief Financial Office and Geospatial Enterprise Office, Maps
Department of Administrative Services Publishing & Distribution: Julie Monk, Keith Whittier
Employment Department, Research Division: Nick Beleiciks, State Employment Economist;
        Erik Knoder, Gail Krumenauer,

Office of the State Court Administrator: Kim Blanding, Judicial Section
Oregon State Legislature: Carol Suzuki and Mandi McGowan

Oregon Department of Education: Peter Rudy and Jon Wiens, Research, Education Section
Higher Education Coordinating Commission: Endi Hartigan, Education Section

bluebook.oregon.gov

Orders:

Office of the Secretary of State
Oregon Blue Book
255 Capitol St. NE, Suite 180
Salem, OR 97310
503-986-2201

Copyright 2023 by the Office of the Secretary of State, pursuant to ORS 177.120
ISBN 978-0-924540-07-3
ISSN 0196-4577
Library of Congress Catalog Card No. sn 79-19170
Printed by Sheridan Books, Inc., Ann Arbor, Michigan

TABLE OF CONTENTS

Introduction and Dedication by Shemia Fagan, Secretary of State
Foreword by Governor Tina Kotek

Color illustrations, photographs and information following page 232

Shemia Fagan
SECRETARY OF STATE

STATE OF OREGON
SECRETARY OF STATE

136 STATE CAPITOL
SALEM, OREGON 97310-0722
sos.oregon.gov

March 2023

Fellow Oregonians,

In this introduction to Oregon's 2023-24 Oregon Blue Book — Oregon's biannual publication of our history, economy, government and cultures — I once again find myself writing during a tumultuous time. Would it surprise you to hear that I'm optimistic?

Like many Oregonians (and Americans in general) I'm frustrated by the unequal economy, the climate crisis, and the undemocratic roll-back of women's rights by the U.S. Supreme Court last year. I hate it when big corporations get bailed out but solutions for working families always seem out of reach. As a mom of two young kids, I worry about the future we are leaving for them.

What I don't buy is the narrative that we're too divided to solve these problems. Maybe it's the Oregonian in me. After living my whole life in Oregon and serving the people of Oregon for more than a decade, I know we can put our differences aside and do big, meaningful things.

Look at the Oregon Reproductive Health Equity Act. When the U.S. Supreme Court eliminated the constitutional right to an abortion over the objection of most Americans, Oregonians could rest assured that our state laws protect a woman's right to make her own reproductive health care decisions.

Look at our vote-by-mail system. Republicans and Democrats in Oregon came together over the last two decades to build the gold-standard for modern, secure and transparent elections systems. That's why we don't see voter disenfranchisement, attacks on democratic values or highly politicized legal battles in Oregon the way we do in other states.

Oregon is special. But if we can overcome obstacles and do big things, so can this country. We need leaders who will put their heads down and do the hard work of building us up and bringing us together.

I know it feels like we don't have those leaders right now. But through the darkness there are glimmers of light. Unemployment continues to fall, nearing the historic lows we saw before the pandemic. Record numbers of new businesses started in 2020 and 2021, showcasing Oregon's entrepreneurial spirit. And Oregon remains an attractive place to live, with positive net migration last year.

In August of 2022, President Biden signed the Inflation Reduction Act into law. The bill will lower the cost of prescription drugs, require tax-dodging corporations to pay a minimum federal tax, and make the largest investment in clean energy by any nation ever.

We are in a storm, no doubt about it. But as we enter 2023 not knowing what the future holds, let us once again commit ourselves to bringing our loved ones, our neighbors and our fellow Oregonians through these challenging times.

My promise to Oregonians is that as your Secretary of State, I will always work to build us all up. I will never use my position to tear us down or split us apart.

Shemia Fagan
Oregon Secretary of State

Dedication

The 2023-2024 Blue Book is dedicated to Governor Kate Brown in gratitude for over 30 years of public service to the people of Oregon.

First elected in 1992, Gov. Brown served in both the State House and Senate. In 2004, she became the first woman to serve as Senate majority leader. In 2008, Brown was elected as Oregon's 24th Secretary of State, serving two terms. After Governor John Kitzhaber resigned in 2015, Brown was sworn in as Oregon's 38th Governor. She was elected on November 8, 2016 to finish out Governor Kitzhaber's first term and was reelected in 2018 to a second term.

Governor Brown served during an unprecedented worldwide pandemic that required her to take decisive actions. She relied on science, data, and the advice of health experts, to make tough choices that saved lives. Thanks to her leadership, Oregon's pandemic performance ranked near the top as measured by vaccination, hospitalization and mortality rates. Governor Brown also worked to ensure that Oregon has had a strong and equitable economic recovery from the pandemic, focusing on the hardest hit communities. She established Oregon's Racial Justice Council to, for the first time, truly center equity in state government by bringing community voices directly to decision-making tables.

In addition to her leadership during these most challenging times, Governor Brown has worked to make historic investments in addressing climate change, education, transportation, and affordable housing, and expand the Oregon Health Plan to cover 94% of adults and every single child in Oregon. Under her leadership, Oregon has:

• Dramatically increased access to the ballot box, as the first state in the country with automatic voter registration;

•Made historic investments in Oregon education with the passage of the Student Success Act, which prioritized access and opportunities for students who have been historically underserved by the education system;

• Set some of the most ambitious goals in the nation to comprehensively address climate change, reduce carbon emissions, and move to 100% clean energy sources;

•Invested more in affordable housing and homelessness prevention during her tenure than under any previous Oregon governor;

• Enhanced protections against discrimination for the LGBTQIA+ community;

•Led the nation by passing the Reproductive Health Equity Act, the first bill of its kind in the nation, to expand and ensure access to reproductive health services for all Oregonians;
• Negotiated a historic agreement between timber, environmental, and fishing interests to update the Forest Practices Act.

We are thankful to Governor Brown for her service to the people of Oregon.

Tina Kotek
Governor

STATE OF OREGON
GOVERNOR
254 STATE CAPITOL
SALEM, OREGON 97301-4047
(503) 378-3111
oregon.gov

January 2023

Dear Oregon,

Oregon faces major challenges, but I know that we can make things better, fix what's not working, and come together to turn things around.

In my first year as Oregon's Governor, I will work tirelessly to deliver results on issues of shared concern across our state: housing and homelessness, access to mental health and addiction treatment, and successful schools.

I ask my fellow Oregonians – no matter who you voted for – to believe in our state and its future. Please be engaged so we can help solve problems together.

The Oregon Blue Book is a fantastic resource to help you learn more about the history of our great state, the mechanics of how our government works, and the arts and cultural institutions that are unique to Oregon. I encourage you to read through these pages, use the information to help guide the projects you care about, and share something interesting that you learn with your friends and family.

Oregonians don't back down when things get hard. We dig in, we think outside the box, and we get the job done. I'm looking forward to moving Oregon forward together.

Sincerely,

Tina Kotek
Governor

New in this Edition . . .

Introducing Oregon's Four National Monuments

The featured exhibit in this edition of the *Oregon Blue Book* shows off our state's four national monuments: John Day Fossil Beds, Newberry Volcanic, Oregon Caves and Cascade-Siskiyou. The exhibit uses images, designed artwork and words to highlight and introduce these special places.

Oregon's four national monuments represent some of our most unique and varied landscapes, yet many Oregonians don't know about them. We hope this exhibit feeds your curiosity and gets you out there for a visit.

You can find this exhibit in the color insert located after page 232. An expanded version is available online at bluebook.oregon.gov.

Tribal Cultural Heritage and the Geologic History of Oregon's National Monuments

We've extended our national monument theme with two thoughtful and informative featured essays that begin on page 314.

The first is by Portland State University Professor Douglas Deur, who explores the long-held tribal cultural and heritage connections to these special places.

The second essay features the fascinating geologic history of the monuments. It's written by Jason McClaughry, a registered geologist with the Oregon Department of Geology and Mineral Industries (DOGAMI).

These must-read pieces provide a helpful introduction to the monuments and the people who've called these areas home for time immemorial.

Student Essays About Living in the Time of COVID

The COVID-19 pandemic has been a challenging time for Oregonians. Students from around the state crafted incredibly thoughtful essays about their own pandemic experience, how it impacted their lives and the ways they're looking toward the future. We've selected ten of the submitted student essays to print in this edition, including one specially selected by Oregon Secretary of State Shemia Fagan.

See the selected essays, which are shown as submitted, on pages viii, 80, 106, 144, 153, 154, 158, 180, 181 and 232 . You can read all of the submitted essays online at bluebook.oregon.gov.

As Oregon changes, we change with it

Our team emailed and called hundreds of government offices, newspapers, cultural institutions and others to gather the most up-to-date and comprehensive information for this edition of the *Oregon Blue Book*.

The Arts, History and Science section has been revamped so we could incorporate many more arts and cultural organizations from all over Oregon. Also look for changes in the Economy, Government Finance and Education sections.

As always, our online *Oregon Blue Book* is where we continually add new information as we receive it throughout the year. Visit us at bluebook.oregon.gov or use this QR code with your mobile device to navigate there now.

STUDENT ESSAY CONTEST WINNER - SECRETARY'S CHOICE

My Pandemic Experience

Ashlyn Huang
Desiree Chiu's 6th Grade Class
Corbett Grade School, Corbett

This drawing by Ashlyn Huang shows what she'd like people to know about her COVID-19 experience.

Life isn't always fair. Sometimes that's the case with those who are being treated differently. Being paid less, or being assaulted. But sometimes, it's seen and dismissed. It's hidden in the classrooms. Hidden in the laughs in the cafeteria. In April, 2020, I was in the cafeteria.

"Have you heard of the Coronavirus?" The kids chattered. Kids would walk around the cafeteria. "Wanna join me at Recess?" I'd watch from the swings. They scampered around. They chased each other, and tagged each other. It was Covid Tag. How could they make it a game? That was only the start.

Asian hate crimes rose after the start of the Pandemic. According to the NYPD, Anti-AAPI hate crimes rose by 1900% in the last year. Many Asian people stayed home in fear …what if they got hurt? My great grandmother is one of these people. She feared being attacked. Through media and personal stories, we've learned about the hardships that people face for their race. How can our society improve?

I know that most people aren't racist, even though they seem like they are. It's only ignorance. I understand that. I've been told to go back to my country, I've been asked if I really ate bats or not, I've been looked at whenever someone mentions the Coronavirus, I've been told by other people about the "China virus", and I've been mocked for speaking Chinese. I know it's not much, but people can do better and be more considerate. My parents have always told me, "You're lucky that you can experience two cultures." I try to remember this when people are thoughtless.

I have come to realize that the obstacles I have faced make me stronger. I desire to celebrate my roots, to bring my culture out into the open. I want to learn Chinese, to help translate English to Chinese for people who need help. The pandemic taught me to embrace sharing my culture. I feel like it's important to teach this to students. People need to learn it. Awareness can change things, and make people more understanding.

ALMANAC

Facts, like maps, help us envision a complete picture of Oregon. This section includes an almanac with interesting statistics and general information about Oregon, a list of Oregon Olympic Games medal winners, "Oregon, My Oregon"— our state song and a map of Oregon showing counties and major roads.

For entries with an asterisk (*), see related photo in the color insert pages.

Abbreviation, Oregon: OR (postal)

Alternative Energy
Geothermal (2021)
33 Megawatts Total Capacity
99 Megawatts Planned Capacity
192,101 Megawatt Hours Generated (2020)
Solar (2021)
726 Megawatts Total Capacity
Over 20,000 residential solar projects
1,077,902 Megawatt Hours Generated (2020)
Wind (2021)
3,772 Megawatts Total Capacity
51 operating facilities
8,777,254 Megawatt Hours Generated (2020)

Altitudes
Highest: Mt. Hood (11,239')
Lowest: Pacific Ocean (sea level)

Amusement Park, Oldest
Oaks Amusement Park, Portland. Opened in May, 1905, it is one of the oldest continuously operating amusement parks in the United States.

Animal, State*
The 1969 Legislature named the American Beaver *(Castor canadensis)* the Oregon state animal. Prized for its fur, the beaver was overtrapped by early settlers and eliminated from much of its original range. Through management and protection, the beaver has been reestablished in waterways throughout the state. The beaver has been referred to as "nature's engineer," and its dam-building activities are important to natural water flow and erosion control. Oregon is known as the "Beaver State." The beaver is Oregon State University's mascot.

Apportionment, U.S. House of Representatives
(number of U.S. Representatives from Oregon)

1860–1880	1	1940–1970	4
1890–1900	2	1980–2021	5
1910–1930	3	2022–Present	6

Awards (Nobel, Pulitzer)
1934: William P. Murphy, Nobel, Medicine
1934: Medford *Mail Tribune,* Pulitzer, Journalism
1939: Ronald Callvert, *The Oregonian,* Pulitzer, Editorial Writing
1954: Linus Pauling, Nobel, Chemistry
1956: Walter H. Brattain, Nobel, Physics
1957: Wallace Turner and William Lambert, *The Oregonian,* Pulitzer, Local Reporting
1962: Linus Pauling, Nobel, Peace
1990: Nicholas D. Kristof, Sheryl WuDunn, *The New York Times,* Pulitzer, International Reporting
1999: Richard Read, *The Oregonian,* Pulitzer, Explanatory Writing
2001: Carl Weiman, Nobel, Atomic Physics
2001: *The Oregonian,* Pulitzer, Public Service
2001: Tom Hallman, Jr., *The Oregonian,* Pulitzer, Feature Writing
2005: Nigel Jaquiss, *Willamette Week,* Pulitzer, Investigative Reporting
2006: Rick Attig and Doug Bates, *The Oregonian,* Pulitzer, Editorial Writing
2006: Nicholas D. Kristof, *The New York Times,* Pulitzer, Commentary
2007: *The Oregonian,* Pulitzer, Breaking News Reporting
2010: Dale T. Mortensen, Nobel, Economics
2014: *The Oregonian,* Pulitzer, Editorial Writing
2021: Mitchell S. Jackson, Pulitzer, Feature Writing

Beverage, State
Milk was designated Oregon's state beverage in 1997. The Legislature recognized that milk production and the manufacture of dairy products are major contributors to the economic well-being of Oregon agriculture.

Birds, State*
Songbird: Distinctive for its flute-like song, the Western Meadowlark *(Sturnella neglecta)* was chosen to be the state bird by the Oregon Audubon Society-sponsored schoolchildren's 1927 election. The selection was proclaimed by Governor

Patterson in July, 1927, and the 2017 Legislature declared the Western Meadowlark to be the State Songbird. Native to western North America, the bird has brown plumage with buff and black markings. Its underside is bright yellow with a black V-shape on the breast. Outer tail feathers are mainly white and are easily visible when it flies.

Raptor: The Osprey (*Pandion haliaetus*) was designated state raptor by the 2017 Legislature, declaring the large bird with its striking markings to be a fitting symbol of Oregon's rugged independence, strength and resilience, evoking Oregon's lakes, rivers, streams and ocean.

Births: 40,847 (2021)

Borders and Boundaries
Washington on the north; California on the south; Idaho on the east; Pacific Ocean on the west; Nevada on the southeast.

Bridges
Highest: Thomas Creek Bridge, north of Brookings, 345'
Longest: Astoria-Megler Bridge, Astoria, 21,474'
Covered bridges: 51; 33 are located in the Willamette Valley

Buildings, Tallest (Portland)
1. Wells Fargo Tower (1972), 546', 40 floors
2. Park Avenue West (2016), 537', 30 floors
3. U.S. Bancorp Tower (1983), 536', 42 floors

Cities, Total Incorporated: 241
Largest Populations (2021)
1. Portland (658,773)
2. Salem (177, 694)
3. Eugene (175,626)

Counties, Total: 36
Largest Area, Square Miles
1. Harney (10,133)
2. Malheur (9,888)
3. Lake (8,139)
Smallest Area, Square Miles
1. Multnomah (431)
2. Hood River (522)
3. Columbia (657)
Largest Populations (2021)
1. Multnomah (820,672)
2. Washington (605,036)
3. Clackamas (425,316)

Craft Brewing Industry (2021)
310 craft breweries (ranks 12th nationally)
Barrels of craft beer produced per year: 897,473 (ranks 9th nationally)

Crustacean, State*
The 2009 Legislature designated the Dungeness Crab (*Metacarcinus magister*) as the official state crustacean. The action followed petitioning by the fourth grade class of Sunset Primary School in West Linn. Common to the Pacific coastline from the Alaskan Aleutian Islands to Santa Cruz, California,

Dungeness Crab is considered the most commercially important crab in the Pacific Northwest.

Dance, State
In 1977, the Legislature declared the Square Dance to be Oregon's state dance. The dance is a combination of various steps and figures with four couples grouped in a square. The pioneer origins of the dance and the characteristic dress are deemed to reflect Oregon's heritage. The lively spirit of the dance exemplifies the friendly, free nature and enthusiasm that are part of the Oregon character.

Deaths: 40,226 (2020)

Divorces: 10,978 (2020)

Electoral Votes for U.S. President: 8

Fair, Oregon State: Early History
1858: The State Fair was unofficially started by a group of farmers known as the Oregon Fruitgrowers Association.
1861: The first official Oregon State Fair was held along the Clackamas River in the Gladstone/Oregon City area.
1862: The second State Fair took place in Salem, at the same location where it is held today.

Fish, State*
The Chinook Salmon (*Oncorhynchus tshawytscha*), also known as the spring, king or tyee salmon, is the largest of the Pacific salmons and the most highly prized for the fresh fish trade. Declared the Oregon state fish by the 1961 Legislature, the Chinook Salmon is found from southern California to the Canadian Arctic.

Flag, State*
The state flag, adopted in 1925, is blue with gold lettering and symbols. Blue and gold are the state colors. On the flag's face the legend "STATE OF OREGON" is written above a shield, which is surrounded by 33 stars. Below the shield, which is part of the state seal, is written "1859," the year of Oregon's admission to The Union as the 33rd state. The flag's reverse side depicts a beaver. Oregon has the distinction of being the only state in The Union whose flag has different patterns on each side. The utility flag has a plain border, and the dress or parade flag has gold fringe.

Flower, State*
The Legislature designated the Oregon Grape (*Mahonia aquifolium*) as the state flower by resolution in 1899. A low-growing plant, the Oregon Grape is native to much of the Pacific Coast and is found sparsely east of the Cascades. Its year-round foliage of pinnated, waxy green leaves resemble holly. The plant bears clusters of small yellow flowers in early summer and dark blue berries that ripen in the fall. The fruit can be used in cooking.

Fossil, State*
The Legislature designated the Metasequoia, or Dawn Redwood (Metasequoia glyptostroboides),

as the state fossil by resolution in 2005. The Metasequoia flourished in the Miocene Epoch of 25 to 5 million years ago and left its record embedded in rocks across Oregon's landscape. While long extinct in Oregon, paleontologists discovered living 100-foot Metasequoia trees in a remote area of China in the 1940s and brought specimens back to the United States for propagation to ensure Metasequoia trees can be found today.

Fruit, State*

The Legislature designated the pear *(Pyrus communis)* as the state fruit by resolution in 2005. Oregon produces a variety of pears, including Comice, Anjou, Bosc and Bartlett. The pear ranks as the top-selling tree fruit crop in the state and grows particularly well in the Rogue River Valley and in the area between the Columbia River and Mt. Hood.

Gemstone, State*

The 1987 Legislature designated the Oregon Sunstone as the state gemstone. Uncommon in its composition, clarity and colors, it is a large, brightly colored transparent gem in the feldspar family. The Oregon Sunstone attracts collectors and miners and has been identified as a boon to tourism and economic development in southeastern Oregon counties.

Geographic Center

Oregon's geographic center lies in Crook County, 25 miles south-southeast of Prineville.

Gorge, Deepest

Hells Canyon, Wallowa County, Snake River: At up to 7,913' deep, it is the deepest gorge in North America.

Highways, Special Designation

Historic Columbia River Highway: The 74-mile stretch of the Columbia River Highway from Troutdale to The Dalles was built from 1913 to 1922. For many years, it was designated U.S. 30. Beginning in the 1950s, Interstate 84 replaced the historic highway as the main route through the Columbia Gorge. The historic highway became a National Scenic Byway All-American Road in 1999. In 2000, the U.S. Secretary of the Interior designated it a National Historic Landmark, which recognized the highway as a significant national heritage resource. The route became the first highway in the country to be given either of these national designations.

Oregon 99: Originally known as the Pacific Highway, Oregon 99 runs from the Oregon/California border north to Junction City, where it splits into Oregon 99E and Oregon 99W. The Pacific Highway, once designated as U.S. 99, U.S. 99E and U.S. 99W, was the main north–south highway in Oregon from the 1920s until Interstate 5 replaced it in 1964.

U.S. 101: Completed in the 1930s, the Oregon Coast Highway (U.S. 101) runs the length of Oregon's Pacific Coast from Astoria on the Columbia River to the Oregon/California border. The highway was designated an Oregon Scenic Byway in 1991 and a National Scenic Byway All-American Road in 2002.

Veterans Memorial Highways: 479,600 Oregon veterans have served our nation during five major wars—WWI, WWII, Korea, Vietnam, Persian Gulf/Afghanistan/ Iraq. Over 6,000 lost their lives and 15,000 were wounded during those wars. Five border-to-border highways were designated by the Legislature and three governors to honor these veterans:

WWI Veterans Memorial Highway: U.S. 395,

WWII Veterans Historic Highway: U.S. 97,

Oregon Nisei Veterans WWII Memorial Highway: S.R. 35,

Korean War Veterans Memorial Highway: Interstate 5,

Vietnam Veterans Memorial Highway: Interstate 84,

Persian Gulf, Afghanistan and Iraq Veterans Memorial Highway: U.S. 101,

POW/MIA Memorial Highway: U.S. 26,

Atomic Veterans and Atomic Cleanup Veterans Memorial Highway: Interstate 5 from Albany to Salem,

Oregon Medal of Honor Highway: US 20

Purple Heart Trail: Interstate 5,

Warm Springs Veterans Memorial Highway: US 26 within the Warm Springs Reservation.

The Historic Columbia River Highway has been designated as a National Historical Landmark. (Oregon State Archives scenic photo)

Hops Production (2021)

Acres harvested: 7,395

Yield per acre: 1,705 pounds

Oregon accounted for 11% of the United States' hop crop in 2021.

Top varieties grown in Oregon: Nugget, Cascade, Citra, and Willamette, accounting for 50% of the state's hop production.

Hydropower (2021)

8,888 Megawatts Total Capacity

94 hydropower facilities
Smallest: 0.025 megawatt
Largest: 2,160 megawatts (John Day Dam, Columbia River)
31,920,334 Megawatt Hours Generated (2020)
Oregon is the second highest hydropower-producing state in the nation, behind only Washington.

Insect, State*

In 1979, the Legislature designated the Oregon Swallowtail Butterfly *(Papilio oregonius)* as the state insect. A true native of the Northwest, the Oregon Swallowtail is at home in the lower sagebrush canyons of the Columbia River and its tributaries, including the Snake River watershed. This strikingly beautiful butterfly has a wingspan of 2-1/2 to 3 inches and is bright yellow and black with a reddish-orange hindspot.

Judicial Districts: 27

Lakes

Deepest: Crater Lake, 1,943' (deepest in the United States)

Largest:
Upper Klamath Lake, 61,543 surface acres
Malheur Lake, 49,700 surface acres
Note: Sizes may vary depending on seasons and precipitation. At times, Malheur Lake may have a larger surface area than Upper Klamath Lake.

Legal Holidays

New Year's Day (observed)
1/2/23, 1/1/24, 1/1/25
Martin Luther King, Jr.'s Birthday (observed)
1/16/23, 1/15/24, 1/20/25
Presidents' Day
2/20/23, 2/19/24, 2/17/25
Memorial Day
5/29/23, 5/27/24, 5/26/25
Juneteenth
6/19/23, 6/19/24, 6/19/25
Independence Day (observed)
7/4/23, 7/4/24, 7/4/25
Labor Day
9/4/23, 9/2/24, 9/1/25
Indigenous Peoples' Day
10/9/23, 10/14/24, 10/13/25
Veterans Day (observed)
11/10/23, 11/11/24, 11/11/25
Thanksgiving Day
11/23/23, 11/28/24, 11/27/25
Christmas Day (observed)
12/25/23, 12/25/24, 12/25/25
When a holiday falls on a Sunday, the following Monday shall be observed as the holiday. When a holiday falls on a Saturday, the preceding Friday shall be observed as the holiday.

Lighthouses

Cape Arago Lighthouse, Coos Bay: lighted 1934; deactivated 2006 (not accessible to the public)

Cape Blanco Lighthouse, Port Orford: lighted 1870

Cape Meares Lighthouse, Tillamook: lighted 1890; deactivated 1963

Cleft of the Rock Lighthouse, Yachats (privately owned, not open to the public): lighted 1976

Coquille River Lighthouse, Bandon: lighted 1896; deactivated 1939

Heceta Head Lighthouse, Florence: lighted 1893

Port of Brookings Lighthouse, Brookings (privately owned, not open to the public): lighted 1999

Tillamook Rock Lighthouse, Cannon Beach: lighted 1881; deactivated 1957 (privately owned, not open to the public)

Umpqua River Lighthouse, Reedsport: lighted 1894

The Coquille River Lighthouse in Bandon guided vessels past dangerous shifting sandbars until 1939. (Oregon State Archives scenic photo)

Yaquina Bay Lighthouse, Newport: lighted 1871–74; reactivated 1996

Yaquina Head Lighthouse, Newport: lighted 1873

Marriages: 24,080 (2021—preliminary data)

Microbe, State

In 2013, the Oregon Legislature designated *Saccharomyces cerevisiae* as the state microbe. The yeast converts sugar into carbon dioxide and ethanol, an essential process for leavening bread and brewing alcoholic beverages, making Oregon an internationally recognized hub of craft brewing.

Motto, State

"She Flies With Her Own Wings" was adopted by the 1987 Legislature as the Oregon state motto. The phrase originated with Judge Jessie Quinn Thornton and was pictured on the territorial seal in Latin: *Alis Volat Propriis.* The new motto replaced "The Union," which was adopted in 1957.

Mountains, Major

Blue Mountains: This northeastern Oregon mountain chain is part of the Columbia Plateau, which extends into southeastern Washington. Lava flows cover much of the surface, and the upper, wooded slopes have been used for lumbering. Today, recreation and livestock grazing are the principal economic uses. The highest elevation is Rock Creek Butte (9,105'), located on the Elkhorn Ridge a few miles west of Baker City.

Cascade Range: This lofty mountain range extends the entire north–south length of Oregon east of the Willamette Valley. It lies about 100 to 150 miles inland from the coastline and forms an important climatic divide, with the western slopes receiving abundant precipitation but the eastern slopes very little. The western slopes are heavily wooded, with the eastern section mainly covered by grass and scrub plants. Many lakes and several large rivers are in the mountains, the latter harnessed for hydroelectric power. The range is used frequently for outdoor recreation. The highest elevations are Mt. Hood (11,237'), located in Clackamas and Hood River Counties, and Mt. Jefferson (10,495'), located in Jefferson, Linn and Marion Counties.

Coast Range: The Coast Range runs the length of the state along the western coastline, from the Columbia River in the north to the Rogue River in the south. These mountains contain dense softwood forests, which historically made lumbering an important economic activity. Their eastern slopes mark the western edge of the Willamette Valley. The highest elevations are Mt. Bolivar (4,319') in Coos and Curry Counties; and Mary's Peak (4,097') in Benton County.

Klamath Mountains: The Klamath Mountains in southwestern Oregon are sometimes included as part of the Coast Range. These mountains include numerous national forest and wildlife preserves and contain scenic portions of the Klamath River. The highest elevation is Mt. Ashland (7,532') in Jackson County.

Steens Mountain: This is a massive, 30-mile-long mountain in the Alvord Valley, featuring valleys and U-shaped gorges that were cut by glaciers one million years ago. Located in Harney County in southeastern Oregon, it is 9,773' in elevation.

Mushroom, State*

The 1999 Legislature recognized the Pacific Golden Chanterelle *(Cantharellus formosus)* as the state mushroom. This mushroom is a wild, edible fungus of high culinary value that is unique to the Pacific Northwest. More than 500,000 pounds of Pacific Golden Chanterelles are harvested annually, representing a large portion of the commercial mushroom business.

Name of Oregon

The first written record of the name "Oregon" comes from a 1765 proposal for a journey written by Major Robert Rogers, an English army officer. It reads, "The rout . . . is from the Great Lakes towards the Head of the Mississippi, and from thence to the River called by the Indians Ouragon." His proposal rejected, Rogers reapplied in 1772, using the spelling "Ourigan." The first printed use of the current spelling appeared in Captain Jonathan Carver's 1778 book, *Travels Through the Interior Parts of North America 1766, 1767 and 1768.* He listed the four great rivers of the continent, including "the River Oregon, or the River of the West, that falls into the Pacific Ocean at the Straits of Annian."

While no definitive pronunciation of "Oregon" is given in *Oregon Geographic Names,* the most common pronunciation by long-time Oregonians is "OR-ih-gun."

National Cemeteries

Willamette, Portland (1950); Eagle Point (1973); Roseburg (1973); Fort Stevens (2020)

National Fish Hatcheries

Eagle Creek, Estacada (1956); Warm Springs (1966)

National Forests

Deschutes (1908); Fremont-Winema (combined 2002: Fremont est. 1908, Winema 1961); Malheur (1908); Mt. Hood (1908); Ochoco (1911); Rogue River-Siskiyou (combined 2004; Rogue River est. 1908, Siskiyou 1907); Siuslaw (1908); Umatilla (1908); Umpqua (1908); Wallowa-Whitman (combined 1954: both est. 1908); Willamette (1933)

National Grassland

Crooked River National Grassland, near Madras (1960)

National Historic Landmarks

Bonneville Dam Historic District, Multnomah County and Skamania County, Washington (1987)

Crater Lake Superintendent's Residence, Klamath County (1987)

Columbia River Highway, Multnomah, Hood River and Wasco Counties (2000)

Deady and Villard Halls, University of Oregon, Lane County (1977)

Fort Astoria Site, Clatsop County (1961)

Fort Rock Cave, Lake County (1961)

Kam Wah Chung Company Building, Grant County (2005)

Jacksonville Historic District, Jackson County (1966)

Lightship WAL-604 "Columbia," Clatsop County (1989)

Lower Klamath Wildlife Refuge, Klamath County and Siskiyou County, California (1965)

Oregon Caves Chateau, Josephine County (1987)

Pioneer Courthouse, Multnomah County (1977)

Skidmore/Old Town Historic District, Multnomah County (1977—Updated documentation approved 2008)

Sunken Village Archeological Site, Multnomah County (1989)

Timberline Lodge, Clackamas County (1977)

Wallowa Lake Site, Wallowa County (1989)

Watzek Aubrey House, Multnomah County (2011)

National Monuments

Cascade-Siskiyou, near Ashland (2000); John Day Fossil Beds, located in three units near Kimberly, Mitchell and Fossil (1975); Newberry National Volcanic Monument, near Bend (1990); Oregon Caves, near Cave Junction (1909)

National Parks

Crater Lake (1902); Lewis and Clark National Historical Park in Oregon/Washington (1958); Nez Perce National Historical Park in Oregon/Idaho/Montana/Washington (1965)

National Recreation Areas

Hells Canyon National Recreation Area in Oregon/Idaho (1975); Oregon Dunes National Recreation Area (1972)

National Scenic Areas

Columbia River Gorge National Scenic Area (1986); Cascade Head Scenic Research Area (1974)

National Wildlife Refuges

Ankeny, near Jefferson (1965); Bandon Marsh, near Bandon (1983); Baskett Slough, near Dallas (1965); Bear Valley, near Klamath Falls (1978); Cape Meares, near Tillamook (1938); Cold Springs, near Hermiston (1909); Hart Mountain National Antelope Refuge, near Lakeview (1936); Klamath Marsh, near Klamath Falls (1958); Lewis and Clark (1972); Malheur, near Burns (1908); McKay Creek, near Pendleton (1927); Nestucca Bay, near Pacific City (1991); Oregon Islands, off southern Oregon coast (1935); Siletz Bay, near Lincoln City (1991); Three Arch Rocks, off coast near Oceanside (1907); Tualatin River, near Sherwood (1992); Umatilla, near Irigon (1969); Upper Klamath, near Klamath Falls (1928); Wapato Lake, near Gaston (2013); William L. Finley, near Corvallis (1964)

Nut, State*

The hazelnut, or filbert, *(Corylus avellana)* was named the state nut by the 1989 Legislature. Oregon grows 99% of the entire U.S. commercial crop. The Oregon hazelnut, unlike wild varieties, grows on single-trunked trees up to 40 feet tall. Adding a unique texture and flavor to recipes and products, hazelnuts are preferred by chefs, bakers, confectioners, food manufacturers and homemakers worldwide.

Outdoor Pageant, State

The 2011 Legislature designated Pendleton's Happy Canyon Indian Pageant and Wild West Show the official outdoor pageant. Presented annually since 1911, local area tribal members worked up the depiction of native village life seen in the present-day script. Acted by a cast of members of local area tribes and local community volunteer actors, the show moves from a depiction of early tribal culture into historic and cultural events such as the coming of Lewis and Clark and the settling of the American West. A live orchestra of Pacific Northwest professional musicians accompanies the show.

Parks, State

259 parks totaling over 113,000 acres; day use attendance of 50 million per year; 8 scenic and 4 regional trails; 52 campgrounds

Physical Dimensions

United States rank in total area: 9th

Land area: 95,988 square miles

Water area: 2,391 square miles

Total area: 98,379 square miles

Coastline: 362 miles

Pie, State

Marionberry pie was designated Oregon's official pie by the 2017 Legislature. The Marionberry was an Oregon State University blackberry breeding program's 1950s cross between the "Chehalem" and "Olallieberry." It was named for Marion County where extensive testing found it to have a greater yield and earlier harvest season than the more well-known Boysenberry.

Poet Laureate

In 2020, Governor Kate Brown named Anis Mojgani Oregon's 10th Poet Laureate. Born in New Orleans to Black and Iranian parents, Mojgani earned a BFA in Sequential Art from the Savannah College of Art and Design. He has been awarded artist and writer residencies from the Vermont Studio Center, AIR Serenbe, Bloedel Nature Reserve, Sou'wester, and the Oregon Literary Arts Writers in the Schools. Mojgani came to Oregon in 2004. He has authored five books of poetry, serves on the board of directors of Literary Arts and lives in Portland.

Population

Oregon is ranked 39th in population density with 42 inhabitants per square mile.

1850	12,093	1940	1,089,684
1860	52,465	1950	1,521,341
1870	90,923	1960	1,768,687
1880	174,768	1970	2,091,533
1890	317,704	1980	2,633,156
1900	413,536	1990	2,842,321
1910	672,765	2000	3,421,399
1920	783,389	2010	3,837,300
1930	953,786	2020	4,237,256

Precipitation

Record 24-hour maximum rainfall: 14.3" on November 6, 2006, at Lees Camp in the Tillamook County Coast Range

Average yearly precipitation at Salem: 40.08"

Record 24-hour snowfall: 47" on January 9, 1980, at the Hood River Experimental Station

Record snow depth: 252" in 1950 at Crater Lake National Park Headquarters

Reservoir, Longest: Lake Owyhee, 53 miles

Rivers, Longest

Partially in the State of Oregon:
Columbia River: 1,249 miles; Snake River: 1,040 miles

Entirely in the State of Oregon:
John Day River: 284 miles; Deschutes River: 252 miles

Rock, State*

The thunder egg (geode) was named the Oregon state rock by the 1965 Legislature after rockhounds throughout Oregon voted it as their favorite rock. Thunder eggs range in diameter from less than one inch to over four feet. Nondescript on the outside, they reveal exquisite designs in a wide range of colors when cut and polished. They are found chiefly in Crook, Jefferson, Malheur, Wasco and Wheeler Counties.

Franklin High School in southeast Portland is one of many architecturally significant public schools in Oregon. (Oregon State Archives scenic photo)

Schools, Public

Education Service Districts	19
Schools	over 1,200
School Districts	197
Student population (2021–2022)	553,012

Seal, State*

On September 17, 1857, the Constitutional Convention adopted a resolution that authorized the U.S. president to appoint a committee of three—Benjamin F. Burch, L. F. Grover and James K. Kelly—to report on a proper seal for the State of Oregon. Harvey Gordon created a draft, to which the committee recommended additions. The state seal consists of a shield, supported by 33 stars and divided by a ribbon with the inscription "The Union." Above the ribbon are the mountains and forests of Oregon, an elk with branching antlers, a covered wagon and ox team, the Pacific Ocean with setting sun, a departing British man-of-war ship signifying the departure of British influence in the region, and an arriving American merchant ship, signifying the rise of American power. Below the ribbon is a quartering with a sheaf of wheat, plow and pickax, representing Oregon's mining and agricultural resources. The crest is the American Eagle and around the perimeter of the seal is the legend "State of Oregon 1859."

Seashell, State*

In 1848, conchologist John Howard Redfield named the *Fusitriton oregonensis* after the Oregon Territory. Commonly called the Oregon hairy triton, the shell is one of the largest found in the state, reaching lengths up to five inches. The shells are found from Alaska to California and wash up on the Oregon coast at high tide. The Legislature designated it the state shell in 1989.

Shoes, Oldest

Sandals that are 9,300 years old, made of sagebrush and bark, were found at Fort Rock Cave in Central Oregon in 1938 by archaeologist Luther Cressman.

Soil, State

The Legislature designated Jory soil as Oregon's state soil in 2011. Jory soil is distinguished by its brick-red, clayish nature, developed on old volcanic rocks through thousands of years of weathering. It is estimated to exist on more than 300,000 acres of western Oregon hillsides and is named after Jory Hill in Marion County.

Jory soil supports forest vegetation such as Douglas fir and Oregon white oak. Many areas with the soil have been cleared and are now used for agriculture. Jory soil, coupled with Willamette Valley climate, provides an ideal setting for various crops, including wine grapes, wheat, Christmas trees, berries, hazelnuts and grass seed.

Song, State

J. A. Buchanan of Astoria and Henry B. Murtagh of Portland wrote "Oregon, My Oregon," in 1920. With this song, Buchanan and Murtagh won a statewide competition sponsored by the Society of Oregon Composers. The song became the Oregon state song in 1927. In 2021, the Oregon Legislature approved new lyrics to the song written by Amy Shapiro of Beaverton. The updated lyrics are meant to be more inclusive and removed racist language.

Standard of Time

The standard time zones were established by Congress in 1918. Oregon lies within the Pacific Standard Time zone with the exception of most of Malheur County along the Idaho border, which is on Mountain Standard Time. Daylight Saving Time is in effect from March to November.

Clocks "spring forward" one hour at 2:00 a.m. on the second Sunday of March: 3/12/23, 3/10/24 3/9/25

Clocks "fall back" one hour at 2:00 a.m. on the first Sunday of November: 11/5/23, 11/3/24,11/2/25

Tartan, State

Tartan, registration number 36406 was designated Oregon's official tartan by the 2017 Legislature. With colors symbolizing the distinctive features of the state, its blue, gold, green, black, white, taupe, crimson and azure represent the water, mountains, forests, grasslands and volcanic past of our state.

Temperatures, Records and Averages

Highest: 119°F on August 10, 1898, in Pendleton and on July 29, 1898, in Prineville

Lowest: -54°F on February 9, 1933, in Ukiah (50 miles south of Pendleton) and on February 10, 1933, in Seneca (105 miles southwest of Baker City)

Average January/July Temperatures:

Burns .... January 26.5°F/July 68.6°F
Grants Pass .... January 41.5°F/July 73.4°F
North Bend ....January 47.3°F/July 59.8°F
Redmond .... January 34.8°F/July 73.4°F
Salem................. January 42.1°F/July 69.3°F

Travel and Tourism (2021)

Total direct spending: $10.9 billion
Overnight visitors: 14 million
Travel-generated employment: 100,000

Tree, State*

The Douglas fir *(Pseudotsuga menziesii)*, named for David Douglas, a 19th century Scottish botanist, was designated the Oregon state tree in 1939. Great strength, stiffness and moderate weight make it an invaluable timber product said to be stronger than concrete. Averaging up to 200' in height and six feet in diameter, heights of 325' and diameters of 15' can also be found.

Waterfall, Highest

Multnomah Falls, 620'

Wine Industry Production (2020)

Grape production value: $157.9 million.
Number of vineyards: 1,370
Number of wineries: 995
Total planted acreage: 39,531 acres
Leading variety: Pinot Noir—59% of all planted acreage and 49% of wine grape production

---

Olympic Games Medalists from Oregon (1906–2021)

Note: The 2020 games were rescheduled due the COVID-19 pandemic.

1906		
Kerrigan, H.W. (Bert)	High Jump	Bronze
1908		
Gilbert, Alfred C.	Pole Vault	Gold
Kelly, Dan	Broad Jump	Silver
Smithson, Forrest	Hurdles	Gold
1912		
Hawkins, Martin	Hurdles	Bronze
1920		
Balbach, Louis J.	Diving	Bronze
Kuehn, Louis (Hap)	Diving	Gold
Ross, Norman	Swimming	Gold (3)
Sanborn-Payne, Thelma	Diving	Bronze
Sears, Robert	Fencing	Bronze
1924		
Newton, Chester	Wrestling	Silver
Reed, Robin	Wrestling	Gold
1928		
Hamm, Edward B.	Broad Jump	Gold
1932		
Graham, Norris	Rowing	Gold
Hill, Ralph	5000m	Silver
LaBorde, Henri J.	Discus	Silver
1936		
Robinson, Mack	200m	Silver

1948		
Beck, Lewis W. Jr.	Basketball	Gold
Brown, David P.	Rowing	Gold
Gordien, Fortune	Discus	Bronze
Helser (de Morelos), Brenda	Swimming	Gold
Zimmerman-Edwards, Suzanne	Swimming	Silver
1952		
Proctor, Hank	Rowing	Gold
Smith, William T.	Wrestling	Gold
1956		
Fifer, James	Rowing	Gold
Gordien, Fortune	Discus	Silver
1960		
Davis, Otis	400m	Gold (2)
Dischinger, Terry G.	Basketball	Gold
Imhoff, Darrall	Basketball	Gold
Wood, Carolyn	Swimming	Gold
1964		
Carr, Ken	Basketball	Gold
Counts, Mel G.	Basketball	Gold
Dellinger, William S.	Track and Field	Bronze
Freeman, Kevin	Equestrian	Silver
Saubert, Jean M.	Skiing	Silver/Bronze
Schollander, Don	Swimming	Gold (4)

1968

Fosbury, Richard D.	High Jump	Gold
Freeman, Kevin	Equestrian	Silver
Garrigus, Thomas I.	Trapshooting	Silver
Johnson Bailes, Margaret	4x100m Relay	Gold
Sanders, Richard J.	Wrestling	Silver
Schollander, Don	Swimming	Gold/Silver

1972

Freeman, Kevin	Equestrian	Silver
Peyton McDonald, Kim	Swimming	Gold
Sanders, Richard J.	Wrestling	Silver

1976

Peyton McDonald, Kim	Swimming	Gold
Wilkins, Mac M.	Discus	Gold

1984

Burke, Douglas L.	Water Polo	Silver
Herland, Douglas J.	Rowing	Bronze
Huntley (Ruete), Joni	High Jump	Bronze
Johnson, William D.	Skiing	Gold
King (Brown), Judith	400m Hurdles	Silver
Menken-Schaudt, Carol	Basketball	Gold
Schultz, Mark P.	Wrestling	Gold
Wilkins, Mac M.	Discus	Silver

1988

Brown, Cynthia L.	Basketball	Gold
Lang, Brent	Swimming	Gold

1992

Johnson, Dave	Decathlon	Bronze
Jorgenson, Dan	Swimming	Bronze

1994

Street, Picabo	Skiing	Silver

1996

Deal, Lance	Hammer	Silver
MacMillan, Shannon	Soccer	Gold
Milbrett, Tiffany	Soccer	Gold
O'Brien, Dan	Decathlon	Gold
Schneider, Marcus	Rowing	Bronze
Steding, Katy	Basketball	Gold

1998

Street, Picabo	Skiing	Gold

2000

French, Michelle	Soccer	Silver
Kinkade, Mike	Baseball	Gold
Lindland, Matt	Wrestling	Silver
MacMillan, Shannon	Soccer	Silver
Milbrett, Tiffany	Soccer	Silver
Thompson, Chris	Swimming	Bronze

2002

Steele, Dan	Bobsled	Bronze
Klug, Chris	Snow Board	Bronze

2004

Hansen, Joey	Rowing	Gold
Johnson, Kate	Rowing	Silver
Zagunis, Mariel	Fencing	Gold

2008

Cox, Stephanie Lopez	Soccer	Gold
Inman, Josh	Rowing	Bronze
Ward, Rebecca	Fencing	Bronze (2)
Windes, Elsie	Water Polo	Silver
Zagunis, Mariel	Fencing	Gold/Bronze

2012

Eaton, Ashton	Decathlon	Gold
Rupp, Galen	10,000m	Silver
Windes, Elsie	Water Polo	Gold

2016

Crouser, Ryan	Shot Put	Gold
Eaton, Ashton	Decathlon	Gold
Hill, Kim	Volleyball	Bronze
Rupp, Galen	10,000m	Bronze
Zagunis, Mariel	Fencing	Bronze

2021

Chiles, Jordan	Gymnastics	Silver
Crouser, Ryan	Shot Put	Gold
Grant, Jeremi	Basketball	Gold
Hill, Kimberly	Volleyball	Gold
Lillard, Damian	Basketball	Gold

Olympic Games medal information courtesy of Jack Elder, Olympian, Luge 1972

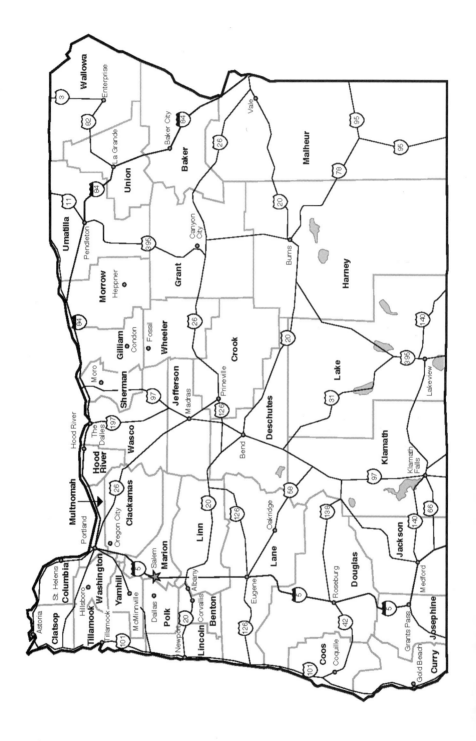

Executive

Oregonians elect five officials for statewide office to manage the executive branch of government: governor, secretary of state, treasurer, attorney general, and bureau of labor and industries commissioner. This section introduces these officials and covers their responsibilities. It also describes the agencies that make up the Executive Branch and the services they provide.

OFFICE OF THE GOVERNOR

Tina Kotek, Governor

Address: State Capitol Bldg., 900 Court St. NE, Suite 254, Salem 97301
Phone: 503-378-4582
Web: oregon.gov/gov/pages/index.aspx
Tina Kotek, Portland; Democrat; elected 2022; term expires January 2027.

The governor is elected to a four-year term and is limited to two consecutive terms in office during any 12-year period. The governor must be a U.S. citizen, at least 30 years old and an Oregon resident for three years before taking office.

Statutory Authority: ORS Chapter 176
Bio: Governor Tina Kotek began her public service career as a policy advocate for Oregon Food Bank, working to eliminate hunger for every Oregonian. She went on to serve as the policy director for Children First for Oregon, and stepped up to run for the Oregon House of Representatives to do more to help working families. She was first elected to represent North Portland in 2006.

In 2013, she became the first openly lesbian speaker of any state house in the nation. Then-Speaker Kotek worked tirelessly to respond to the immediate crises facing Oregonians — delivering pandemic relief, funding wildfire recovery, protecting renters from eviction, making historic investments to increase affordable housing construction, passing a first-in-the-nation statewide rent stabilization law and advocating for more equitable policing and a fairer criminal justice system. When she left office in January 2022, she was the longest serving Speaker of the House in Oregon history.

She was elected governor on November 8, 2022, and sworn in as Oregon's 39th governor on January 9, 2023. Governor Kotek and her wife Aimee Kotek Wilson, a social worker, have been together for 19 years and have two dogs.

Duties and Responsibilities: The governor is the chief executive of Oregon. The Oregon Constitution charges the governor with faithfully executing the laws, making recommendations to the Legislature and transacting all necessary business of state government.

The governor provides leadership, planning and coordination for the executive branch of state government. She appoints many department and agency heads within the executive branch and members to nearly 300 policymaking, regulatory and advisory boards and commissions. The governor proposes a two-year budget to the Legislature, recommends a legislative program each regular session and may also call special sessions. She reviews all bills passed by the Legislature, may veto measures she believes are not in the public interest and shall fill vacancies by appointment.

The governor chairs the State Land Board, which manages state-owned lands, acts as the superintendent of public instruction, directs state government coordination with local and federal governments and is commander-in-chief of the state's military forces.

The governor appoints judges to fill vacancies in judicial office, has extradition authority and may grant reprieves, commutations and pardons of criminal sentences.

If the office of governor becomes vacant, the office passes, in order, to the secretary of state, state treasurer, president of the Senate and speaker of the House of Representatives. There is no lieutenant governor in Oregon.

Constituent Services

Address: State Library Bldg., 250 Winter St.NE, 3rd Floor, Salem 97301

Mail: State Capitol Bldg., 900 Court St. NE, Suite 254, Salem 97301

Phone: 503-378-4582

Fax: 503-378-6827

Web: oregon.gov/gov/Pages/request-assistance.aspx

Duties and Responsibilities: The Governor's Constituent Services office assists Oregonians in navigating state services, helping citizens obtain benefits or resolve their problems with government agencies. This team works with individuals and constituency groups to ensure the governor is aware of their concerns, reporting regularly to the governor and policy advisors. The office seeks to treat all inquiries fairly, to examine each situation objectively, and to respond in a clear and helpful way.

Policy Advisors & Governor's Office Staff

The mailing address for all members of the Governor's Office Staff is State Capitol Bldg., 900 Court St. NE, Room 254, Salem, OR 97301. The full staff directory is available at: oregon.gov/gov/Pages/staff.aspx.

OFFICE OF THE SECRETARY OF STATE

Shemia Fagan, Secretary of State

Address: 136 State Capitol Bldg., Salem 97310-0722

Phone: 503-986-1523

Fax: 503-986-1616

Email: oregon.sos@sos.oregon.gov

Web: sos.oregon.gov

Shemia Fagan, Clackamas; Democrat; elected 2020; term expires January 2025; Oregon's 28th secretary of state.

The secretary of state is one of three constitutional officers of the executive branch elected statewide. The secretary is elected to a four-year term and is limited to two consecutive terms in office during any 12-year period.

Bio: Secretary of State Shemia Fagan is mom to two young children and a proud lifelong Oregonian. Secretary Fagan was raised by her dad and two older brothers in small towns in Wasco county. Secretary Fagan has always been open with Oregonians about the challenges her family overcame — Fagan's dad struggled as a single parent and her mom battled addiction and homelessness during Fagan's childhood. But Secretary Fagan was encouraged by loving members of her community and the dedicated educators who would not give up on her.

After graduating from The Dalles High School in 1999, Fagan earned a scholarship to play soccer for Northwest Nazarene University in Nampa, Idaho where she earned her B.A. in Philosophy and Religion. Following college, Fagan worked to save money before attending law school at Willamette University College of Law and earning her J.D. at Lewis and Clark Law School. While working as an attorney at Ater Wynne LLP and later at HKM Employment Attorneys LLP, Fagan received training on campaigning for public office from the Emerge Oregon program. Fagan first entered public service in 2011 when she was elected to the David Douglas School Board. Later, Secretary Fagan served in the Oregon House and Senate before she was elected Oregon's 28th secretary of state in 2020. Secretary Fagan is a strong defender of the nation's most successful vote by mail system and committed to building on Oregon's tradition of secure and accessible elections.

Duties and Responsibilities: The secretary of state is one of three constitutional offices established at statehood and is the auditor of public accounts, chief elections officer, public records administrator and custodian of the State Seal. As an independent constitutional officer, the secretary of state answers directly and solely to the people of Oregon.

The secretary interprets and applies state election laws, compiles and publishes the *Voters' Pamphlet* and supervises all elections, local and statewide.

She examines and audits accounts of all publicly funded boards, commissions and agencies.

She keeps public records of businesses authorized to transact business in Oregon, nonprofit corporations and trade and service marks. Other public business records include notices of security interests in movable and personal property, statutory liens and warrants.

As the public records administrator, the secretary houses and provides access to the permanently valuable records of state government through the Archives Division and manages all public records for retention and disposition.

The secretary shares responsibility with the governor and treasurer for supervising and managing state-owned lands and chairs the Oregon Sustainability Board which works to optimize organizations' financial, environmental and social performance. She also regulates Oregon notaries public and publishes the *Oregon Blue Book*.

Oregon does not have a lieutenant governor. If the office of governor becomes vacant, the office passes to the secretary of state.

Legal Authority: Oregon Constitution, Article VI, Section 2; ORS Chapters 177, 240

Archives Division

Address: 800 Summer St. NE, Salem 97310
Phone: 503-373-0701
Fax: 503-378-4118
Email: reference.archives@sos.oregon.gov
Web: sos.oregon.gov/archives
Contact: Stephanie Clark, State Archivist
Statutory Authority: ORS 177.120, Chapter 183, 192.001–192.170, 357.805–357.885
Duties and Responsibilities: The state archives manages the state's public records from creation until final disposition, and identifies, preserves and provides access to the permanently valuable public records of the state. In addition, the division is responsible for filing, codifying and publishing Oregon's Administrative Rules; compiling and publishing the Oregon Blue Book; filing Official Documents; providing advice and assistance on a variety of public records issues; and managing the State Records Center for non-permanent, paper records storage and the Security Copy Depository for microfilm.

The state archives is home to the original Oregon Constitution.

State Historical Records Advisory Board
Address: 800 Summer St. NE, Salem 97310
Phone: 503-378-4972
Fax: 503-378-4118
Contact: Mary McRobinson, State Coordinator

Audits Division

Address: Public Service Bldg., 255 Capitol St. NE, Suite 180, Salem 97310
Phone: 503-986-2255; Hotline: 1-800-336-8218
Fax: 503-378-6767
Email: audits.sos@sos.oregon.gov
Web: sos.oregon.gov/audits
Contact: Kip Memmott, Director
Statutory Authority: ORS 177.170–177.180, Chapter 297
Duties and Responsibilities: This division conducts audits to protect the public interest while helping improve Oregon government.

Auditors ensure public funds are spent as legally required, used to their best advantage and properly accounted for. Audits are conducted in compliance with stringent professional standards and use modern analytical tools to examine millions of records and be as meticulous as possible. All reports are publicly available.

Financial audits are a core focus. The division, meanwhile, has pushed performance audits to new levels. The aim is to increase the efficiency of state and local government while generating savings.

Corporation Division

Address: Public Service Bldg., 255 Capitol St. NE, Suite 151, Salem 97310
Phone: 503-986-2200
Fax: 503-986-6355
Web: sos.oregon.gov/business
Contact: Eloisa Miller, Director
Statutory Authority: ORS Chapters 56, 58, 60, 62, 63, 65, 67, 68, 79, 80, 87, 128, 194, 554, 647, 648
Duties and Responsibilities: The division helps entrepreneurs start a business in Oregon by ensuring state government registration processes are as fast and easy as possible. Specifically, it assists the public in registering business entities and filing public notice of records of debt, commissions notaries public and provides certification of records and notarized documents. The division provides access to public records in the form of copies, certificates, lien searches, computer reports and online database access. This allows the public and businesses to know with whom they are doing business.

The Office of Small Business Assistance helps businesses who experience difficulty in their interactions with a state agency and connects businesses with state and non-state resources. The office acts as an ombudsman to help resolve problems between businesses and state agencies.

Elections Division

Address: Public Service Bldg., 255 Capitol St. NE, Suite 126, Salem 97310-0722
Phone: 503-986-1518
Fax: 503-373-7414
Email: elections.sos@sos.oregon.gov
Web: sos.oregon.gov/voting-elections
Contact: Molly Woon, Director
Statutory Authority: ORS Chapters 246–260
Duties and Responsibilities: Voting is central to democracy. The division oversees state elections, ensuring that voting reflects the will of the citizenry. It is also in charge of the initiative, referendum and referral process.

By interpreting and applying election laws, the division helps uphold the democratic process. By logging data on past elections, it serves as chronicler and statistician.

The secretary of state prioritizes modernizing the election process and streamlining voter registration. The Elections Division has led the way with vote by mail and moving registration online. It is also a leader in bringing transparency to campaign funding through the development of the ORESTAR online application, which provides transparency for all money raised and spent during political campaigns.

Internal Support:

Business Services Division
Steve Bergmann, Director

Human Resources Division
Tasha Petersen, Director

Information Systems Division
Chris Molin, Director

OFFICE OF THE STATE TREASURER
Tobias Read, State Treasurer

Address: 159 State Capitol Bldg., 900 Court St. NE, Salem 97301
Phone: 503-378-4329
Email: oregon.treasurer@ost.state.or.us
Web: oregon.gov/treasury
Tobias Read, Beaverton; Democrat; elected 2016; reelected 2020; term expires January 2025.

The state treasurer is elected to a four-year term and is limited to two consecutive terms in office during any 12-year period.

Bio: Tobias Read is Oregon's 29th state treasurer. Born in Montana and raised in Idaho, he moved to Salem, Oregon to attend Willamette University before earning his Master of Business Administration degree at the University of Washington. He brings a wide range of public-sector and private-sector experience to the office. He worked for two U.S. Treasury secretaries, the Nike Corporation and

has most recently served as a state representative in Oregon for a decade.

As a state representative, Tobias was known for focusing on the issues that contribute to a growing economy—a high-quality education, innovation, and funding for our roads and bridges. He strove to fund full-day kindergarten and give all districts the opportunity to offer it. In 2015, he was a chief sponsor of the Oregon Retirement Savings Plan, which in 2017 became the first operating state-sponsored retirement program. Known as OregonSaves, the program enrolls Oregon workers who lack access to a retirement savings option through their employers, allowing hundreds of thousands more Oregonians to retire with dignity after a lifetime of work.

As state treasurer, Tobias' first priority is to focus on managing Oregon's money responsibly and with transparency. He is also working hard to help Oregonians save for college and retirement so that everyone in Oregon has a chance to succeed.

Tobias lives in Beaverton with his wife Heidi and their two children

Duties and Responsibilities: The state treasurer is a constitutional officer and a statewide elected official. The treasurer serves as the chief financial officer for the state and is responsible for the prudent management of billions of taxpayer dollars.

The treasurer serves as the state's chief investment officer and has the duty of investing the monies of numerous funds such as the Public Employees Retirement Fund, the State Accident Insurance Fund and the Common School Fund.

The treasurer serves on a variety of state financial boards and on the State Land Board, which has a fiduciary duty to manage state trust lands for the benefit of the Common School Fund.

The treasurer's financial responsibilities include managing the investment of state funds, issuing state bonds, serving as the central bank for state agencies and administering the Oregon 529 Savings Network, Oregon Retirement Savings Plan, the Oregon Investment Council and State Debt Policy Advisory Commission.

Statutory Authority: ORS Chapter 178

Executive Division
Address: 867 Hawthorne Ave SE, Salem 97301-5241
Phone: 503-378-4000
Contact: Michael Kaplan, Deputy State Treasurer
Duties and Responsibilities: The division coordinates agency-wide business services including strategic planning, internal auditing and accounting, human resource functions, project management, procurement and communications.

Debt Management Division

Address: 867 Hawthorne Ave SE Salem, 97301-5241
Phone: 503-378-3561
Contact: Jacqueline Knights, Director
Duties and Responsibilities: The division oversees the sale, issuance and ongoing management of all state bonds, serves as a resource for debt-issuing local governments and serves as the state's liaison to rating agencies and investors with regard to the state's financial condition. The division's work intersects with and is supported by the following three groups:

Municipal Debt Advisory Commission

Statutory Authority: ORS 287.030
Duties and Responsibilities: The commission collects and reports information related to Oregon local government debt and provides policy input to the Legislature on debt matters of local governments.

Private Activity Bond Committee

Duties and Responsibilities: The committee allocates tax-exempt private activity bond allotments provided to the state under federal tax law.

State Debt Policy Advisory Commission

Statutory Authority: ORS 286.550–286.555
Duties and Responsibilities: The commission, chaired by the state treasurer, prepares annual reports regarding outstanding tax-supported and non-tax-supported debt and makes recommendations to the governor and Legislature regarding affordable levels of state indebtedness.

Facilities Authority, Oregon

Address: 1600 Pioneer Tower, 888 SW Fifth Ave., Portland 97204
Phone: 503-802-2102
Contact: Gwendolyn Griffith, Executive Director
Statutory Authority: ORS 289.100
Duties and Responsibilities: The authority was created in 1989 and is empowered to issue low-cost bonds to assist nonprofit organizations with the financing of property and facilities for health, housing, education and culture. The authority reviews proposed projects and makes recommendations to the state treasurer about the issuance of bonds.

Finance Division

Address: 867 Hawthorne Ave SE, Salem 97301-5241
Phone: 503-378-4633
Contact: Cora Parker, Director

Duties and Responsibilities: The division provides cash management services to all Oregon state agencies and hundreds of Oregon local government entities, including cities, counties, schools and special districts. The division also helps protect public funds deposited at private banks and credit unions through collateralization requirements governed by ORS chapter 295. As the central bank for state agencies, the division manages millions of financial transactions annually, including cash deposits, electronic fund transfers and check issuance. The division also administers the Local Government Investment Pool, which provides a short-term investment vehicle for local governments for the period between when revenue is received and when it is needed to pay public bills.

Short Term Fund Board

Address: 867 Hawthorne Ave SE, Salem 97301-5241
Phone: 503-431-7900
Fax: 503-378-2870
Contact: Heidi Rawe
Statutory Authority: ORS 294.885
Duties and Responsibilities: The board advises the state treasurer and the Oregon Investment Council in the management and investments of the Oregon Short Term Fund and the Local Government Investment Pool. The treasurer serves as an ex officio member and appoints three members to the board. The governor appoints the remaining three members.

Investment Division

Address: 16290 SW Upper Boones Ferry Rd., Tigard 97224
Phone: 503-431-7900
Contact: Rex Kim, Chief Investment Officer
Duties and Responsibilities: The division manages the financial and real asset portfolios comprised by the Public Employees Retirement Fund, State Accident Insurance Fund, Oregon Short Term Fund, Common School Fund and numerous other state and agency accounts. On December 31, 2021 the combined market value of these funds totaled $139.1 billion. Each managed fund has a unique risk and return profile and is broadly diversified across asset class, geography and investment strategy. The division also manages the investment program for the state's deferred compensation plan, serves as staff for the Oregon Investment Council and strives to save taxpayers and beneficiaries money by meeting each fund's specific investment objective at the lowest possible net cost.

Investment Council, Oregon

Address: 16290 SW Upper Boones Ferry Rd., Tigard 97224
Phone: 503-378-4000
Contact: Rex Kim, Chief Investment Officer
Statutory Authority: ORS 293.706

Duties and Responsibilities: The council sets policy for all state investment trust funds and discharges its responsibilities consistent with state law and governing fiduciary standards. The state treasurer and director of the Public Employees Retirement System are ex officio council members, and the governor appoints four members whose service is subject to Senate confirmation. The council approves guidelines for all state investment activities and delegates day-to-day management authority to the Office of the State Treasurer's Investment Division.

Oregon Savings Network

Address: 867 Hawthorne Ave SE, Salem 97301-5241

Phone: 503-373-1903

Web: oregontreasurysavingsnetwork.com

Contact: Michael Parker, Director

Statutory Authority: ORS 348.841

Duties and Responsibilities: The Oregon Savings Network was created to increase the ability of Oregonians to save for a variety of significant future needs, including college, disability-related expenses and retirement. The network offers a number of unique financial tools and investment options that can provide state and federal tax advantages and more flexibility than many other savings vehicles. Oregon offers two 529 college savings plans: the Oregon College Savings Plan, which is sold directly to investors, and the MFS 529 Savings Plan, sold exclusively through financial advisors. Both plans operate independently of each other but are governed by the same state and federal laws.

The Oregon ABLE (Achieving a Better Life Experience) Savings Plan was launched in 2016 and gives disabled Oregonians the ability to save and receive the same tax benefits. In addition, under federal law, as much as $100,000 in assets may be saved in ABLE accounts and not jeopardize eligibility for vital public assistance programs.

OregonSaves is a convenient, simple way for Oregonians to save for retirement at work. Employees contribute part of their paycheck into their own personal IRAs that stay with them throughout their careers. The program also benefits employers who don't offer a qualified retirement plan by helping them compete with businesses that do. The program is overseen by the Oregon Retirement Savings Board and administered by a program service provider.

BUREAU OF LABOR AND INDUSTRIES

Christina Stephenson, Commissioner of the Bureau of Labor and Industries

Address: 800 NE Oregon St., Suite 1045, Portland 97232

Phone: 971-245-3844; Oregon Relay System TTY: 711

Fax: 971-317-8364

Web: oregon.gov/boli

Salem: 3865 Wolverine St. NE, Bldg. E-1, Salem 97305

Eugene: 1400 Executive Pkwy., Suite 200, Eugene 97401

Christina Stephenson, Washington County; nonpartisan; elected Nov 2022; term expires January 2027.

Chief executive of the Bureau of Labor and Industries and the Chair of the Oregon State Apprenticeship and Training Council. The term of the commissioner is four years.

Bio: Oregon's statewide Labor Commissioner Christina Stephenson was previous a small business owner and civil rights attorney. Stephenson has dedicated many pro-bono hours to helping draft and pass laws in Oregon. She lives in unincorporated Washington County, Oregon with her husband, son and cats.

Statutory Authority: ORS Chapter 651

Duties and Responsibilities: The Bureau of Labor and Industries' (BOLI) mission is to protect employment rights, advance employment opportunities and protect access to housing and public accommodations that are free from unlawful discrimination.

The commissioner enforces state laws prohibiting discrimination in employment, housing, public accommodation and vocational, professional and trade schools. The commissioner has the authority to initiate a "commissioner's complaint" on behalf of victims of discrimination.

Through the Wage and Hour Division, the commissioner administers state laws relating to wages, hours of employment, basic working conditions, child labor and prevailing wage rates, and licenses certain labor contractors to protect the workers they employ. The division oversees the Wage Security Fund that covers workers for unpaid wages in certain business closures and enforces group health insurance termination notification provisions.

The commissioner also directs the state's registered apprenticeship training system that gives workers the opportunity to learn a job skill while earning a living. The program benefits employers by providing a pool of skilled workers to meet business and industry demands.

The agency works to support and train employers so that they can more easily comply with frequently complex state and federal employment law. The Administrative Prosecution Unit prosecutes the agency's contested wage and hour and civil rights complaints. The commissioner issues final orders in all contested cases, except commissioner's complaints.

BOLI employs nearly 100 professionals and is headquartered in Portland. Regional offices are located in Eugene and Salem.

Commissioner's Office and Program Services Division

Contact: Jessica Giannettino Villatoro, Deputy Labor Commissioner
Statutory Authority: ORS Chapter 651
Duties and Responsibilities: The office develops legislative initiatives, oversees communications for the agency and manages constituent correspondence and public engagement. The office also oversees legislatively directed reporting and serves as staff for legislative workgroups and the Oregon Council on Civil Rights. Other duties include intergovernmental relations, strategic planning and budget management. The Administrative Prosecution Unit convenes administrative law hearings in contested cases for both wage and hour and civil rights determinations.

Apprenticeship and Training Division

Contact: Lisa Ransom, Administrator
Statutory Authority: ORS Chapter 660
Duties and Responsibilities: The division promotes apprenticeship in a variety of trades by working with business, labor, government and educational organizations to increase training and employment opportunities throughout the state. Apprenticeship is occupational training that includes on-the-job experience with classroom learning. The division registers occupational skills standards and agreements between apprentices and employers and works with local apprenticeship committees to ensure quality training and equal opportunity, especially for women and people of color, in technical craft jobs.

State Apprenticeship and Training Council

Contact: Lisa Ransom, Secretary
Statutory Authority: ORS Chapter 660
Duties and Responsibilities: The council oversees apprenticeship committees, programs and policies and approves apprenticeship committee members. The BOLI commissioner serves as the chairperson,

and the director of the Apprenticeship and Training Division serves as its secretary.

Civil Rights Division

Contact: Leila Wall, Interim Administrator
Statutory Authority: ORS 25.337–25.424, 171.120–171.125, 345.240, 399.230, 399.235, 408.230, 408.237, 441.178. 476.576, 654.062, Chapter 659A
Duties and Responsibilities: The division defends the rights of all Oregonians to equal opportunity in employment, housing, public accommodations and career schools. It protects employment rights, advances employment opportunities and protects access to housing and public accommodations free from discrimination. The division enforces whistleblower and retaliation laws, including those filed in relation to OSHA and Workers Compensation claims.

Wage and Hour Division

Contact: Laura van Enckevort, Administrator
Statutory Authority: ORS 279C.800–279C.870, Chapters 652, 653, ORS 654.251, Chapter 658
Duties and Responsibilities: The division enforces laws covering state minimum wage and overtime requirements, working conditions, child labor, farm, forest, construction, janitorial, labor contracting and wage collection. The division enforces the payment of prevailing wage rates required to be paid to construction workers on public works projects. BOLI determines and publishes prevailing wage rates based on an annual construction industry survey.

Prevailing Wage Advisory Committee

Contact: Jessica Ponaman, Operations Manager
Statutory Authority: ORS 279C.820
Duties and Responsibilities: The committee was legislatively established in 2003 to assist the BOLI commissioner in the administration of the Prevailing Wage Rate Law.

Employer Assistance

Contact: Dylan Morgan, Manager
Duties and Responsibilities: The program offers guidance to Oregon businesses and organizations, so they can understand Oregon employment law and stay in compliance. The program holds employment law seminars throughout the state and publishes employer handbooks on wage and hour, civil rights, family leave laws and other important topics. The staff fields daily calls from Oregon employers seeking guidance on employment-related matters.

Administrative Prosecution Unit

Contact: Adam Jeffries, Manager
Statutory Authority: ORS chapter 183; ORS
279C.800 to 279C.870; ORS 651.060(4); ORS
chapters 652, 653, 659, and 659A
Duties and Responsibilities: The Administrative
Prosecution Unit prepares and presents cases at
contested case hearings to achieve compliance with
laws enforced by BOLI through equitable regulation and enforcement. The unit prosecutes and
resolves cases involving civil rights laws, wage and
hour laws and certain laws regarding licensed and
regulated occupations.

OFFICE OF THE ATTORNEY GENERAL

Ellen F. Rosenblum, Attorney General

Address: 1162 Court St. NE, Salem 97301-4096
Phone: 503-378-4402
Web: doj.state.or.us/oregon-department-of-jus-
tice/office-of-the-attorney-general/ellen-f-
rosenblum-attorney-general
Contact: Lisa M Udland, Deputy Attorney
General
Ellen F. Rosenblum, Portland; Democrat; appointed June 2012; elected November 2012; reelected
2016; reelected 2020; term expires January 2025.
The term of office for attorney general is four
years.
Bio: Attorney General Rosenblum began her legal
career as a small firm lawyer in Eugene and later
served as a federal prosecutor and state trial and
appellate court judge. She is the first woman to
serve as Oregon attorney general.

Her priorities as attorney general include consumer protection and civil rights—advocating for
and protecting Oregon's children and families, students, seniors, immigrants and refugees, crime
victims and survivors. As attorney general, she has
established a criminal elder abuse unit and a
statewide hate crimes and bias incident response
program. She has successfully led statewide task
forces on police profiling, hate crimes, public
records and consumer privacy. She is committed to

supporting law enforcement in investigating and
prosecuting complex crimes and to holding corporations accountable when they violate the law.

Attorney General Rosenblum attended the University of Oregon, where she received both her
undergraduate degree in sociology and her J.D.
(law degree). Rosenblum is currently the vice president of the National Association of Attorneys
General. She has previously served as chair of the
Conference of Western Attorneys General, and co-
chair of the Democratic Attorneys General Association. She has also served as secretary of the
American Bar Association (ABA) and as chair of
the ABA Section of State and Local Government
Law.
Duties and Responsibilities: The Legislature created the Office of Attorney General in 1891. The
Department of Justice was later established by the
Legislature in 1947 and is the equivalent of the
state's law firm. The attorney general is the chief
law officer of the state and heads the Department
of Justice. The agency has a staff of approximately 1,300 with 10 legal and 13 child support offices
throughout the state.

The attorney general appears in and represents
the state in all court actions and legal proceedings
in which the state of Oregon is a party or has an
interest. This includes proceedings involving elected and appointed state officials, state agencies,
boards and commissions. She appoints assistant
attorneys general to act as counsel for state agencies, boards and commissions.

When requested by the governor, any state
agency official, or any member of the Legislature,
the attorney general gives legal opinions upon any
question of law in which the state or any public subdivision may have an interest. Unless expressly
authorized by law, the attorney general and
her assistant attorneys general may not render opinions or give legal advice to any other persons or
agencies.

The attorney general writes ballot titles for measures to be voted upon by the people of Oregon and
defends them in the Oregon Supreme Court.

The department advocates for and protects all
Oregonians, especially the most vulnerable, such as
children and seniors. More than 350 state laws con-
fer numerous responsibilities and authorities to the
attorney general. Those responsibilities include
supervision of charities, enforcement of antitrust
laws, assistance to the state's district attorneys,
administration of the state's Crime Victims' Compensation Program, investigations of organized
crime and public corruption, and the establishment
and enforcement of child support obligations for
Oregon families.
Statutory Authority: ORS Chapter 180

Appellate Division

Address: 1162 Court St. NE, Salem 97301-4096
Phone: 503-378-4402
Web: doj.state.or.us/oregon-department-of-justice/divisions/appellate-division
Contact: Benjamin Gutman, Solicitor General
Duties and Responsibilities: The division represents the State of Oregon in all cases in the United States federal courts, Oregon Supreme Court and Oregon Court of Appeals. Lawyers in the division work on civil and administrative appeals such as tort claims, contract disputes and child welfare cases; defense of criminal convictions in direct criminal appeals; and defense of criminal convictions involving challenges to the validity of convictions or sentences after direct appeals are complete. The division also supports district attorneys throughout the state by providing advice and training on legal issues.

Child Support, Division of

Address: 1215 State St., Salem 97301;
Mail: 1162 Court St. NE, Salem 97301-4096
Phone: 503-947-4388
Web: doj.state.or.us/child-support
Contact: Kate Cooper Richardson,
Administrator
Duties and Responsibilities: The division administers the child support program for the state, providing free child support services to Oregonians. Services include locating absent parents, establishing paternity, assisting with child and medical support orders, modifying and enforcing support orders and receiving and distributing child and medical support payments. Child support services are provided to all parents. The division maintains local branches around the state and works in partnership with district attorneys' offices to deliver child support services through the Oregon Child Support Program. The program collects and distributes more than $394 million in child support annually, helping to ensure the well-being of Oregon families.

Civil Enforcement Division

Address: 1162 Court St. NE, Salem 97301
Phone: 503-947-4400
Web: doj.state.or.us/oregon-department-of-justice/divisions/civil-enforcement
Contact: Claudia Groberg, Co-Chief Counsel;
Joanne Southey, Co-Chief Counsel
Duties and Responsibilities: The Charitable Activities Section enforces laws regarding charitable trusts and solicitations and regulates charitable gaming activities, such as bingo and raffle operations.

The Civil Recovery Section is responsible for obtaining judgments and collecting debts owed to state agencies. It also provides legal services to the Division of Child Support.

The Consumer Protection Section protects Oregon consumers by enforcing the Unlawful Trade Practices Act, commonly known as Oregon's consumer protection law. The Section also educates consumers and businesses and enforces antitrust and false claims laws.

The division's Medicaid Fraud Unit is part of a federally subsidized program for deterring fraud committed by Medicaid health care service providers. It also handles cases involving physical or financial abuse/neglect of residents of Medicaid-funded facilities.

The Child Advocacy Section helps protect abused, neglected and abandoned children. Child Advocacy attorneys provide a wide range of legal advice to Oregon Department of Human Services (DHS) child welfare workers and often represent DHS in contested juvenile and circuit court hearings and help achieve safe and permanent placement for children.

Crime Victim and Survivor Services Division

Address: 1162 Court St. NE, Salem 97301
Phone: 503-378-5348, Toll-free 1-800-503-7983
Fax: 503-378-5738
Email: cvssd@doj.state.or.us
Web: doj.state.or.us/crime-victims
Contact: Shannon Sivell, Director
Duties and Responsibilities: The Crime Victim and Survivor Services Division (CVSSD) helps to compensate victims for crime-related costs, protects victims' rights and helps fund local victim service providers. Through trainings, advisory committees, and partnerships, CVSSD helps shape best practices statewide and brings a diverse collection of voices to the issue of victim and survivors' rights. The division connects many different programs with a single goal: to serve victims and survivors effectively and compassionately. CVSSD also houses the Civil Rights Unit (CRU), which manages the Oregon Bias Response Hotline.

Criminal Justice Division

Address: 1162 Court St. NE, Salem 97301-4096
Phone: 503-378-6347
Fax: 503-373-1936
Web: doj.state.or.us/oregon-department-of-justice/divisions/criminal-justice
Contact: Michael Slauson, Chief Counsel
Duties and Responsibilities: The division provides investigative, analytical, prosecution and training support to Oregon's district attorneys and law enforcement agencies. The division also leads or participates in several important criminal information sharing and analysis programs. The division

consists of three sections: District Attorney Assistance, Organized Crime and the Analytical Criminal Information Services section.

General Counsel Division

Address: 1162 Court St. NE, Salem 97301-4096
Phone: 503-947-4540
Web: doj.state.or.us/oregon-department-of-justice/divisions/general-counsel
Contact: Renee Stineman, Chief Counsel
Duties and Responsibilities: The division acts as the state's in-house counsel and provides a broad range of legal services to state agencies, boards and commissions. This includes day-to-day legal advice and representing state agencies in administrative hearings. The division is composed of the following sections: Business Activities, Business Transactions, Government Services, Health and Human Services, Labor and Employment, Natural Resources and Tax and Finance.

Trial Division

Address: 158 12th St. NE, Salem 97301;
Mail: 1162 Court St. NE, Salem 97301
Phone: 503-947-4700
Web: doj.state.or.us/oregon-department-of-justice/divisions/trial
Contact: Steve Lippold, Chief Trial Counsel
Duties and Responsibilities: The division defends the state, its agencies, employees and officers in civil lawsuits brought in state and federal courts. The division is divided into three sections.

The Civil Litigation Section (CLS) handles a wide variety of cases in state and federal courts. These cases involve disputes over agency orders, tort claims, civil rights, employment and other civil cases involving the state.

The Criminal and Collateral Remedies Section handles cases filed by a convicted person seeking a new trial or a re-sentencing from a trial court. This Section seeks to uphold the convictions won by a district attorney when a case reaches the state post-conviction and federal habeas corpus stage.

The Special Litigation Unit defends state statutes and policies against constitutional challenges in state and federal courts. This unit also defends the state in complex litigation involving elections law, class action lawsuits and environmental cases.

STATE BUILDINGS*

Agriculture Building (1966)
635 Capitol St. NE, Salem 97301

Barbara Roberts Human Services Bldg. (1992)
550 Summer St. NE, Salem 97301

Capitol Mall Parking Structure (1991)
900 Chemeketa St. NE, Salem 97301

Cecil Edwards Archives Building (1991)
800 Summer St. NE, Salem 97310

Commerce Building (1931)
158 12th St. NE, Salem 97301

Commission for the Blind (1977)
535 SE 12th Ave., Portland 97204

Employment Building (1974)
875 Union St. NE, Salem 97311

Executive Building (1979)
155 Cottage St. NE, Salem 97301

Fish and Wildlife Building (2013)
4034 Fairview Industrial Dr. SE, Salem 97302

550 Building (1992, formerly PUC Building)
550 Capitol St. NE, Salem 97301

Forestry Buildings (1938)
2600 State St., Salem 97310

General Services Building (1954)
1225 Ferry St. SE, Salem 97301

General Services Building Annex (1967)
1257 Ferry St. SE, Salem 97301

Justice Building (1930)
1162 Court St. NE, Salem 97301

Labor and Industries Building (1961)
350 Winter St. NE, Salem 97301

Liquor and Cannabis Commission Building (1955)
9201 SE McLoughlin Blvd., Milwaukie 97222

North Mall Office Building (2003)
725 Summer St. NE, Salem 97301

North Valley Campus (2019)
26755 SW 95th Avenue, Wilsonville, 97070

Property Distribution Center (1974)
1655 Salem Industrial Dr NE, Salem, 97301

Public Employees' Retirement System Building (1998)
11410 SW 68th Pkwy., Tigard 97281

Public Service Building (1949)
255 Capitol St. NE, Salem 97310

Real Estate Building (1990)
1177 Center St. NE, Salem 97301

Revenue Building (1981)
955 Center St. NE, Salem 97301

State Capitol Building (1938)
900 Court St. NE, Salem 97301

State Fair Buildings, State Fairgrounds
2330 17th St. NE, Salem 97303

State Hospital Building (1883)
2600 Center St. NE, Salem 97301

State Lands Building (1990)
775 Summer St. NE, Salem 97301

State Library (1939)
250 Winter St. NE, Salem 97301

State Lottery Building (1996)
500 Airport Rd. SE, Salem 97301

continued on page 23

DISTRICT ATTORNEYS

Oregon's 36 District Attorneys (DAs) are responsible for safeguarding the rights of all Oregonians, including both victims and defendants in criminal cases. As set forth in the Oregon Constitution, DAs represent the public in criminal matters by filing criminal charges where warranted by the law and available evidence. The DA is responsible for seeking justice for crime victims while also protecting a defendant's right to due process and a fair trial.

Oregon's DAs enforce child support orders, represent the community in juvenile matters and inquiries into the cause and manner of deaths.

Oregon DAs are elected in every county and are required to stand for election every four years, thereby maintaining accountability to the public they serve. Although Oregon's DAs are elected by and accountable to the people in their respective counties, they are considered state officers whose salaries are paid by the state.

Baxter, Greg M.
Baker County DA

Haroldson, John
Benton County DA

Wentworth, John D.
Clackamas County DA

Brown, Ron L.
Clatsop County DA

Auxier, Jeffrey D.
Columbia County DA

Frasier, R. Paul
Coos County DA

Hathorn, Kari
Crook County DA

Spansail, Joshua A.
Curry County DA

Gunnels, Steve
Deschutes County DA

Wesenberg, Rick
Douglas County DA

Weatherford, Marion
Gilliam County DA

Carpenter, Jim
Grant County DA

Hughes, Ryan P.
Harney County DA

Rasmussen, Carrie
Hood River Co. DA

Heckert, Beth
Jackson County DA

Lariche, Steven F.
Jefferson County DA

Eastman, Joshua J.
Josephine County DA

Photo
Not
Submitted

Vacant
Klamath County DA

Photo
Not
Submitted

Martin, Ted K.
Lake County DA

Perlow, Patricia W.
Lane County DA

Danforth, Lanee
Lincoln County DA

Marteeny, Doug
Linn County DA

Goldthorpe, David M.
Malheur County DA

Clarkson, Paige E.
Marion County DA

Nelson, Justin
Morrow County DA

Schmidt, Mike
Multnomah Co. DA

Felton, Aaron
Polk County DA

McLeod, Wade
Sherman County DA

Porter, William
Tillamook County DA

Primus, Daniel R.
Umatilla County DA

McDaniel, Kelsie
Union County DA

Frolander, Rebecca
Wallowa County DA

Ellis, Matthew
Wasco County DA

Barton, Kevin
Washington Co. DA

Photo Not Submitted

Ladd, Gretchen M.
Wheeler County DA

Berry, Brad
Yamhill County DA

continued from page 20

State Office Building, Eugene (1961)
165 E 7th Ave., Eugene 97401

State Office Building, Pendleton (1963)
700 SE Emigrant St., Pendleton 97801

State Office Building, Portland (1992)
800 NE Oregon St., Portland 97232

State Police Salem Headquarters (2016)
3565 Trelstad Ave. SE, Salem 97317

State Printing Plant (1980)
550 Airport Rd. SE, Salem 97301

State Treasury Building (2021)
867 Hawthorne Ave. SE, Salem, OR 97301

Supreme Court Building (1914)
1163 State St., Salem 97301

Transportation Building (1951)
355 Capitol St. NE, Salem 97301

Veterans' Building (1984)
700 Summer St. NE, Salem 97301

*Year is the date the building was constructed, purchased or occupied by the state.

OTHER STATE AGENCIES, BOARDS AND COMMISSIONS

The following section describes agencies, boards, commissions and programs that carry out executive branch duties. Descriptions include basic contact information and a summary of the entity's duties and responsibilities.

Agencies are listed alphabetically by substantive name. For example, the Department of Human Services appears as "Human Services, Department of." Programs under the main agency are listed under that agency's heading. Thus, the Child Welfare Division would appear within the larger entry for Department of Human Services. The *Blue Book* Index is helpful for locating individual agencies, boards, commissions and programs.

ACCOUNTANCY, OREGON BOARD OF

Address: 200 Hawthorne Ave. SE, Suite D450, Salem 97301-5289
Phone: 503-378-4181
Fax: 503-378-3575
Web: oregon.gov/boa
Contact: Martin Pittioni, Executive Director; Nancy Young-Oliver, CPA, CISA, CFE, Board Chair
Statutory Authority: ORS Chapter 673
Duties and Responsibilities: The board regulates approximately 8,500 Certified Public Accountants (CPAs) and Public Accountants (PAs), as well as approximately 1,000 public accounting firms. Applicants for licensure must meet minimum standards in terms of education, work experience and successful completion of the national CPA exam. Thereafter, licensees must renew their license

by demonstrating professional accounting competency every two years through 80 hours of education for active licensees.

The board holds licensees accountable for adhering to all professional and ethical standards that apply to their practice. Complaints can be submitted to the board from members of the public, other sources or may be self-initiated by the board. A complaint form can be found on the board's website. If an investigation finds a violation of board statutes or rules, licensees are held accountable for their conduct through disciplinary action. The public can verify the status and disciplinary history of an Oregon licensee or public accounting firm on the board's website or by calling the board office. Seven staff members support the board.

ADMINISTRATIVE HEARINGS, OFFICE OF

Address: 4600 25th Ave. NE, Suite 140, Salem 97301; Mail: PO Box 14020, Salem 97309-4020
Phone: 503-947-1918
Email: rema.a.bergin@oregon.gov
Web: oregon.gov/oah
Contact: Rema Bergin, Executive Assistant to Chief Administrative Law Judge
Statutory Authority: ORS 183.605
Duties and Responsibilities: The office provides an independent and impartial forum for citizens and businesses to dispute state agency actions against them. A Chief Administrative Law Judge is appointed by the governor and has independent statutory authority to manage the office. Sixty-four professional administrative law judges hold more than 24,000 hearings a year for approximately 70 state agencies. By statute, all administrative law judges are required to be "impartial in the performance of [their] duties and shall remain fair in all hearings." Oregon is one of 22 states with an independent central panel of administrative law judges.

ADMINISTRATIVE SERVICES, DEPARTMENT OF

Address: 155 Cottage St. NE, Salem 97301-3972
Phone: 503-378-3104
Email: oregon.info@das.oregon.gov
Web: oregon.gov/das
Contact: Berri Leslie, Chief Operating Officer and Director
Statutory Authority: ORS 184.305
Duties and Responsibilities: The Department of Administrative Services (DAS) implements the policy and financial decisions made by the governor

and the Oregon Legislature, DAS manages and coordinates projects involving multiple state agencies and serves as a catalyst for innovation and improvement across all of state government. DAS serves Oregonians by supporting the state agencies, boards and commissions they rely on each day. DAS employs about 900 people, with offices primarily in the Salem area.

Chief Operating Officer, Office of the

Address: 155 Cottage St. NE, Salem 97301-3965
Phone: 503-378-3104
Email: oregon.info@das.oregon.gov
Web: oregon.gov/das
Contact: Berri Leslie, Chief Operating Officer and Director
Statutory Authority: ORS 184.315
Duties and Responsibilities: The office provides leadership and policy direction to the department and all other state executive branch agencies. It oversees DAS public affairs, internal audits, economic analysis, legislation and cultural change efforts. The office is headed by the Chief Operating Officer, who is appointed by the governor. Staff also provides support to state government's Enterprise Leadership Team, which is comprised of state agency leaders and serves as an advisory board to the governor and the office on long-term strategic policies and statewide initiatives.

Chief Financial Office

Address: 155 Cottage St. NE, U10, Salem 97301-3965
Phone: 503-378-3106
Email: cfo.info@das.oregon.gov
Web: oregon.gov/das/financial
Contact: George Naughton, Chief Financial Officer
Statutory Authority: ORS 184.335
Duties and Responsibilities: The Chief Financial Office (CFO) provides statewide comprehensive fiscal policy, budget development and financial oversight for the Executive Branch, as well as statewide financial reporting. The CFO prepares the governor's biennial budget and compiles the state's Annual Comprehensive Financial Report. The program also maintains state government's budget system, monitors agency spending for compliance with applicable budgetary laws and intent and works with agencies to resolve issues between legislative sessions, including appearances before the Emergency Board and Interim Joint Ways and Means Committee. Additionally, the Capital Finance and Planning section is responsible for the administration of various statewide financial programs including Article XI-Q bonds, Lottery Revenue Bonds, Tax Anticipation Notes, Seismic

Rehabilitation Bonds, Pension Obligation Bonds and others. The section also ensures the statewide capital planning process considers current conditions of the facilities and future project needs.

Chief Human Resources Office

Address: 155 Cottage St. NE, U30, Salem 97301-3967
Phone: 971-707-0880
Fax: 503-373-7684
Email: chro.hr@das.oregon.gov
Web: oregon.gov/das/hr
Contact: VACANT, Chief Human Resources Officer
Statutory Authority: ORS 240.055
Duties and Responsibilities: The office is responsible for statewide human resource systems, policies and initiatives. This includes human resource management and consultation; establishing and maintaining classification and compensation plans; training and development; administering and maintaining the central state human resources system. DAS Human Resources also oversees employee recruitment, labor relations and workforce development.

DAS Business Services

Address: 155 Cottage St. NE, U90, Salem 97301-3972
Phone: 503-373-7607
Email: janet.e.savarro@das.oregon.gov
Web: oregon.gov/das/financial/pages/dbs.aspx
Contact: Janet Savarro, Administrator
Statutory Authority: ORS 184.335
Duties and Responsibilities: This program provides budget, business continuity, performance management and data analysis services for the agency. The program is also responsible for DAS records management and administrative rules. It coordinates rate development, calculates rates, fees and assessments, performs financial analysis for DAS divisions, develops the statewide price list of goods and services and prepares and monitors DAS's biennial budget.

Enterprise Asset Management

Address: 1225 Ferry St. SE, U100, Salem 97301-4281
Phone: 503-428-3362
Email: fac.info@das.oregon.gov
Web: oregon.gov/das/Pages/eam.aspx
Contact: Shannon Ryan, Administrator
Statutory Authority: ORS Chapters 270, 276, 279, 279A, 279B, 279C, 283
Duties and Responsibilities: This program provides services to state government, such as motor pool and surplus property, acquiring and maintaining space for state agencies, property management, real property transaction services (buy, sell and lease), project management, space planning, state building operations and maintenance and landscape maintenance. It also manages parking and commuter programs for state employees in Salem and Portland.

Enterprise Goods and Services

Address: 1225 Ferry St. SE, Salem 97301
Phone: 503-378-4642
Fax: 503-373-1626
Email: debbie.dennis@das.oregon.gov
Web: oregon.gov/das/Pages/egs.aspx
Contact: Debbie Dennis, Administrator
Statutory Authority: ORS 184.305, ORS Chapters 278, 279, 282, 283
Duties and Responsibilities: This program provides accounting, payroll, mail distribution, printing, procurement, insurance programs with risk consulting and claim adjusting, and financial system management to Executive Branch agencies.

Enterprise Information Services

Address: 550 Airport Rd. SE, Salem 97301
Phone: 503-378-3175
Email: oscio.info@das.oregon.gov
Web: oregon.gov/das/oscio
Contact: Terrence Woods, State Chief Information Officer
Statutory Authority: ORS Chapter 276A
Duties and Responsibilities: Oregon's State Chief Information Officer (State CIO) is an independent official directly responsible to the governor. The State CIO operates as the governor's primary advisor for statewide enterprise technology and telecommunication projects and programs. The State CIO also advises on implementation of the Information Technology (IT) Governance framework and establishment of Oregon's long-term IT strategy using the Enterprise Information Services (EIS) Strategic Framework. EIS includes the following sections: Data Center Services, Cyber Security Services, Project Portfolio Performance, Shared Services, Strategy and Design, Data Governance and Transparency and Administrative Services.

Other Groups:

Economic Analysis, Office of

Address: 155 Cottage St. NE, U20, Salem 97301-3966
Phone: 503-378-3405
Fax: 503-373-7643
Email: OEA.info@oregon.gov
Web: oregon.gov/das/oea
Contact: Mark McMullen, State Economist
Duties and Responsibilities: The office prepares state economic and revenue forecasts and long-term population and employment forecasts. It assesses long-term economic and demographic trends, evaluates their implications and conducts special economic and demographic studies. The office also

prepares state criminal and juvenile population forecasts and manages the Highway Cost Allocation Study.

Governor's Council of Economic Advisors
Address: 155 Cottage St. NE, U20, Salem 97301-3966
Phone: 503-378-3405
Fax: 503-373-7643
Contact: Joseph Cortright, Chair
Duties and Responsibilities: The council is a group of 12 economists from academia, finance, utilities and industry. It works in conjunction with the Office of Economic Analysis.

Public Lands Advisory Committee
Address: 155 Cottage St. NE, U10, Salem 97301-3965
Phone: 503-559-1401
Fax: 503-373-7210
Email: res.info@das.oregon.gov
Web: oregon.gov/das/facilities/pages/resplacprofile.aspx
Contact: John H. Brown, Chair
Statutory Authority: ORS 270.100(1)(d), 270.120
Duties and Responsibilities: The committee's primary role is to advise and give consent to DAS for all real property acquisitions, exchanges or terminal dispositions valued at $100,000 or more.

Public Officials Compensation Commission
Address: 155 Cottage St. NE, U30, Salem 97301-3967
Phone: 503-378-2065
Email: oregon.pocc@oregon.gov
Web: oregon.gov/das/hr/pages/pocc.aspx
Statutory Authority: ORS 292.036
Duties and Responsibilities: The commission's primary role is to review and make recommendations to the Legislature on the amount of annual salary to be paid to the governor, secretary of state, treasurer, attorney general, commissioner of the Bureau of Labor and Industries, members of the Legislature, chief justice and judges of the Supreme Court, and judges of the Court of Appeals, Circuit Courts and Tax Courts.

ADVOCACY COMMISSIONS OFFICE, OREGON

Address: 421 SW Oak St., Suite 770, Portland 97204
Phone: 503-302-9725
Email: oaco.mail@oregon.gov
Web: oregon.gov/oac
Contact: Albert Lee, Executive Director
Statutory Authority: ORS 185.005–185.025

Duties and Responsibilities: The office supports Oregon's Commissions on Asian and Pacific Islander Affairs, Black Affairs, Hispanic Affairs and the Commission for Women. They offer community based applied policy research; advise the governor, Legislature and departmental leadership on policies affecting communities of color and women; grow leadership from their communities within government; and build success for Asian/Pacific Islander, Black and Hispanic Oregonians and women in Oregon.

Each commission is composed of 11 members, nine of whom are appointed by the governor and confirmed by the Senate to serve four-year terms. The president of the Senate and the speaker of the House each appoint a member to serve a two-year term.

Asian and Pacific Islander Affairs, Commission on
Address: 421 SW Oak St., Suite 770, Portland 97204
Phone: 503-302-9725
Email: oaco.mail@oregon.gov
Web: oregon.gov/ocapia
Statutory Authority: ORS 185.610–185.625
Duties and Responsibilities: The commission focuses on equitable policy advising, advocacy, policy research and leadership development. Their goal is to advise state policy makers on equitable public policy for Asian and Pacific Islander communities and intersectional among communities of color and women statewide. The commission also works to ensure equity focused communication and dissemination of information between state government and Asian and Pacific Islander communities.

Black Affairs, Commission on
Address: 421 SW Oak St., Suite 770, Portland 97204
Phone: 503-302-9725
Web: oregon.gov/ocba
Email: oaco.mail@oregon.gov
Statutory Authority: ORS 185.410–185.430
Duties and Responsibilities: The commission works for the implementation of economic, social, legal and political equity for Oregon's African American and Black populations. The commission is authorized by law to monitor existing programs and legislation designed to meet the needs of the African American and Black community; identify and research concerns and issues affecting the community to recommend actions and programs to the governor and the Legislature; act as a liaison between the community and Oregon's government; encourage African American and Black representation on state boards and commissions; and establish special committees as needed.

Hispanic Affairs, Commission on

Address: 421 SW Oak St., Suite 770, Portland 97204
Phone: 503-302-9725
Email: oaco.mail@oregon.gov
Web: oregon.gov/hispanic
Statutory Authority: ORS 185.310–185.330
Duties and Responsibilities: The commission works for economic, social, legal and political equity for Hispanics in Oregon. They monitor existing programs and legislation to ensure that the needs of Hispanics are met. The commission researches problems and issues and recommends appropriate action, maintains a liaison between the Hispanic community and government entities and encourages Hispanic representation on state boards and commissions.

In addition, the commission focuses on and responds to the wider statewide context of equity and social well-being, identifies and seeks solutions to disparities in services and programs for the ethnically diverse Hispanic/Latino/Indigenous community, and encourages good public policy development. In networking with numerous Hispanic community, civic, cultural/ethnic and professional organizations, OCHA also promotes civic engagement, economic development and ongoing mentoring for the next generation of leaders.

Women, Commission for

Address: 421 SW Oak St., Suite 770, Portland 97204
Phone: 503-302-9725
Email: oaco.mail@oregon.gov
Web: oregon.gov/women
Statutory Authority: ORS 185.510–185.560
Duties and Responsibilities: The Oregon Commission for Women's advocates for women in the community, provides information on women's issues to the governor and Legislature, serves as a link for women and their unique equity focused issues to state agencies and the Legislature.

The Agriculture Building in Salem houses the central offices of the Department of Agriculture. (Oregon State Archives scenic photo)

AGRICULTURE, DEPARTMENT OF

Address: 635 Capitol St. NE, Salem 97301-2532
Phone: 503-986-4550
Fax: 503-986-4750
Email: info@oda.oregon.gov
Web: oregon.gov/oda
Contact: Alexis Taylor, Director
Statutory Authority: ORS Chapter 576
Duties and Responsibilities: The Oregon Department of Agriculture (ODA) works to ensure healthy natural resources, environment and economy for Oregonians now and in the future through inspection and certification, regulation and promotion of agriculture and food.

ODA relies on partnerships with other state and federal agencies, Oregon State University's College of Agricultural Sciences and numerous non-government organizations to help carry out the agency's mission. The 10-member State Board of Agriculture advises ODA on policy issues, develops recommendations on key agricultural issues and provides advocacy of the state's agriculture industry. New responsibilities for the agency include an industrial hemp program and the creation of the Oregon Disaster Assistance Program.

ODA employs about 535 people and is headquartered in Salem. Its laboratory programs are located in Portland at the Food Innovation Center. In addition, many inspectors and other staff members' responsibilities are spread geographically to provide services across the state.

Food Safety and Animal Health Programs

Animal Health Program: 503-986-4680
State Veterinarian: Dr. Ryan Scholz, DVM
Livestock Identification Program (Brands ID): 503-986-4681
Laboratory Services: 503-872-6644
Food Safety Program: 503-986-4720
Email: rusty.rock@oda.oregon.gov
Contact: Rusty Rock, Director
Duties and Responsibilities: This program area provides inspections for all of Oregon's food distribution systems (except restaurants) to ensure food is safe for consumption. It ensures animal feeds meet nutritional and labeling standards to protect and maintain animal health. The program also registers brands and brand inspections to combat the stolen livestock market.

Market Access and Certification Programs

Market Access and Certification Programs: 503-986-4620
Weights and Measures Programs: 503-986-4670

Email: jess.paulson@oda.oregon.gov
Contact: Jess Paulson, Director
Duties and Responsibilities: These programs help Oregon's agricultural producers successfully add value to, sell and ship products to markets by promoting and creating demand for products. They provide consumer protection and facilitate fair competition by ensuring the accuracy and uniformity of Oregon's Commercial Weighing System and the quality of motor fuels sold in Oregon. The programs provides laboratory analysis and technical support to the Department of Agriculture's enforcement programs.

Natural Resources Programs

Phone: 503-986-4635
Email: isaak.stapleton@oda.oregon.gov
Contact: Isaak Stapleton, Director
Duties and Responsibilities: These programs address water quality and natural resource conservation on agricultural lands. They work to protect Oregon's environment and public health by ensuring the proper and legal sale, use and distribution of pesticide products. They assist local soil and water conservation districts as they help landowners properly manage Oregon's natural resources.

Plant Protection and Conservation Programs

Phone: 503-986-4636
Email: chris.benemann@oda.oregon.gov
Contact: Chris Benemann, Interim Director
Duties and Responsibilities: These programs protect Oregon's agricultural industries and natural environment from harmful plant pests, diseases and noxious weeds; enhance the value and marketability of exported nursery stock, Christmas trees, seeds and other agricultural products; register industrial hemp growers and handlers; and further the conservation of threatened and endangered plants.

State Board of Agriculture

Address: 635 Capitol St. NE, Salem 97301-2532
Phone: 503-986-4554
Fax: 503-986-4750
Contact: Karla Valness, Assistant to the Board
Statutory Authority: ORS Chapter 561
Duties and Responsibilities: The 10-member State Board of Agriculture advises ODA on policy, develops recommendations on key agricultural issues and provides advocacy of the state's agriculture industry.

Agricultural Commodity Commissions

Commodity commissions conduct promotional, educational, production and market research projects. The commissions are authorized by ORS chapters 571, 576, 577 and 578 and are funded by assessments on the producers of the commodities. The director of the Department of Agriculture appoints the members of all 23 commissions.

Albacore Commission

Address: PO Box 16338, Portland 97292
Phone/Fax: 971-209-2030
Web: oregonalbacore.org
Contact: Ericka Carlson, Administrator

Alfalfa Seed Commission

Address: PO Box 688, Ontario 97914-0688
Phone: 541-881-1335
Email: ddk@fmtc.com
Contact: Edith Kressly, Administrator

Beef Council

Address: 1827 NE 44th Ave., Suite 315, Portland 97213
Phone: 503-274-2333
Web: orbeef.org
Contact: Will Wise, Executive Director

Blueberry Commission

Address: PO Box 3366, Salem 97302-0366
Phone: 503-364-2944
Web: oregonblueberry.com
Contact: Bryan Ostlund, Administrator

Clover Commission

Web: oregonclover.org
Contact Info: See Blueberry Commission

Dairy Products Commission, dba Oregon Dairy and Nutrition Council

Address: 1353 SW 72nd Ave., Suite 110, Tigard, 97223
Web: odncouncil.org
Contact: Anne Goetze, Executive Director

Dungeness Crab Commission

Address: PO Box 1160, Coos Bay 97420-0301
Phone: 541-267-5810
Web: oregondungeness.org
Contact: Hugh Link, Executive Director

Fine Fescue Commission

Web: oregonfinefescue.org
Contact Info: See Blueberry Commission

Hazelnut Commission

Address: 29100 Town Center Loop W. #200, Wilsonville 97070
Phone: 503-582-8420
Web: oregonhazelnuts.org
Contact: Colleen Nihen, Administrator

Hemp Commission
Address: 635 Capitol St. NE, Salem 97301
Email: hemp@oda.oregon.gov
Phone: 503-986-4652

Hop Commission
Address: PO Box 298, Hubbard 97032
Phone: 503-982-7600
Web: oregonhops.org
Contact: Michelle Palacios, Administrator

Mint Commission
Web: oregonmint.org
Contact Info: See Blueberry Commission

Potato Commission
Address: 1201 NW Naito Pkwy., Suite 154,
Portland 97209
Phone: 503-239-4763
Web: oregonspuds.com
Contact: Gary Roth, Executive Director

Processed Vegetable Commission
Address: PO Box 55401, Portland 97238
Phone: 541-325-6182
Web: opvc.org
Contact: Randi Alexander-Rolison,
Administrator

Raspberry and Blackberry Commission
Address: P.O. Box 56587, Portland 97238
Phone: 503-208-5589
Web: oregon-berries.com
Contact: Darcy Kochis, Administrator

Ryegrass Growers Seed Commission
Web: ryegrass.com
Contact Info: See Blueberry Commission

Salmon Commission
Web: oregonsalmon.org
Contact Info: See Albacore Commission

Sheep Commission
Address: 1270 Chemeketa St. NE, Salem 97301
Phone: 503-364-5462
Web: oregonsheepcommission.com
Contact: Richard Kosesan, Administrator

Strawberry Commission
Address: 1827 NE 44th Ave. Suite 315, Portland
97213
Web: oregon-strawberries.org
Contact: Julie Hoffman, Administrator

Sweet Cherry Commission
Web: osweetcherry.org

Contact Info: See Strawberry Commission

Tall Fescue Commission
Web: oregontallfescue.org
Contact Info: See Blueberry Commission

Trawl Commission
Address: 16289 Hwy. 101 S, Suite C, Brookings
97415
Phone: 541-469-7830
Contact: Yelena Nowak, Executive Director

Wheat Commission
Address: 1200 NW Naito Pkwy., Suite 370,
Portland 97209-2800
Phone: 503-467-2161
Web: owgl.org
Contact: Amanda Hoey, CEO

APPRAISER CERTIFICATION AND LICENSURE BOARD
Address: 200 Hawthorne Ave. SE, Suite C-302,
Salem 97301
Phone: 503-485-2555
Fax: 503-485-2559
Email: chad.koch@aclb.oregon.gov
Web: aclboregon.org
Contact: Chad Koch, Administrator
Statutory Authority: ORS Chapter 674
Duties and Responsibilities: The board regulates
and supervises licensed and certified real estate
appraisers and appraisal management companies.
They ensure real estate appraisals are issued in
writing and conducted in compliance with Oregon
statutes and administrative rules and the National
Uniform Standards of Professional Appraisal
Practice. The board is a semi-independent agency
with six full-time staff members and eight board
members appointed by the governor.

ARCHITECT EXAMINERS, STATE BOARD OF
Address: 205 Liberty St. NE, Suite A, Salem
97301
Phone: 503-763-0662
Email: architectboard@osbae.oregon.gov
Web: osbae.com
Contact: Lisa Howard, Executive Director
Statutory Authority: ORS 671.010–671.220
Duties and Responsibilities: The board regulates
the practice of architecture in Oregon. The agency
assures persons practicing architecture in Oregon
are properly qualified and registered. They determine standards for architect and architectural firm
registration, which consist of a combination of education, examination and experience. The agency
enforces the laws governing the practice of architecture in Oregon by investigating alleged

violations and disciplining those who violate the law. The agency is headquartered in Salem and has seven board members appointed by the governor and five staff.

AVIATION, OREGON DEPARTMENT OF

Address: 3040 25th St. SE, Salem 97302-1125
Phone: 503-378-4880
Fax: 503-373-1688
Email: aviation.mail@odar.oregon.gov
Web: oregon.gov/aviation
Contact: Betty Stansbury, Director
Statutory Authority: ORS 835.100
Duties and Responsibilities: The department works to provide infrastructure, financial resources and expertise to ensure a safe and efficient air transportation system. It registers airports, pilots and aircraft and is responsible for a Statewide Capital Improvement Program in coordination with the Federal Aviation Administration (FAA) and federally funded public use airports around the state. The department is governed by a seven-member board of directors appointed by the governor, and employs 14 staff. The Aviation Board developed the system of airports in Oregon. The board provides policy oversight for the agency and is the modal committee for the Connect Oregon program.

BLIND, COMMISSION FOR THE

Address: 535 SE 12th Ave., Portland 97214
Phone: 971-673-1588
Fax: 503-234-7468
Email: ocb.mail@ocb.oregon.gov
Web: oregon.gov/blind
Contact: Dacia Johnson, Executive Director
Statutory Authority: ORS 346.110–346.570
Duties and Responsibilities: The commission's mission is to empower Oregonians who are blind to fully engage in life. The commission is a consumer-driven organization with a governor-appointed citizen governing body and 66 full-time equivalent staff. Commission members represent consumer organizations, education, ophthalmology/optometry businesses and individual citizens who are blind. The commission operates under its enabling statutes and through the Workforce Innovation and Opportunity Act of 2014.

The commission's major program objectives include helping Oregonians who are blind get and keep jobs; training in alternative skills such as adaptive technology, white cane travel, braille and activities of daily living; helping individuals with vision loss who are unable to work live with high levels of independence and self-sufficiency; and licensing and supporting business owners who

operate food service and vending operations in public buildings and facilities throughout the state.

BUSINESS DEVELOPMENT DEPARTMENT, OREGON

Address: 755 Summer St. NE, Suite 200, Salem 97301-1280
Phone: 503-986-0123; TTY: 1-800-735-2900
Fax: 503-581-5115
Web: oregon.gov/biz
Contact: Sophorn Cheang, Director
Statutory Authority: ORS 285A.070
Duties and Responsibilities: The department, operates as Business Oregon, the state's economic development agency. Business Oregon has primary offices in Salem and Portland, along with staff located in 12 regions across the state. The agency's mission is to invest in Oregon businesses, communities and people to promote a globally competitive, diverse and inclusive economy. Business Oregon is focused on five priorities: innovating Oregon's economy, growing small and middle-market companies, cultivating rural economic stability, advancing economic opportunity for under-represented people, and ensuring an inclusive, transparent and fiscally healthy agency. Core agency functions include rural community development and infrastructure financing; business retention, expansion and recruitment; export promotion and international trade; industry innovation and research and development; entrepreneurship support and small business assistance; and support for arts and cultural organizations.

The overall work of the department is guided by a nine-member commission with additional input and expertise provided by several other advisory bodies and boards.

CHIROPRACTIC EXAMINERS, BOARD OF

Address: 530 Center St. NE, Suite 620, Salem 97301
Phone: 503-378-5816
Fax: 503-362-1260
Email: info@obce.oregon.gov
Web: oregon.gov/obce
Contact: Cassandra C. McLeod-Skinner, J.D., Executive Director
Statutory Authority: ORS Chapter 684
Duties and Responsibilities: The board is responsible for administering the Chiropractic Practice Act, as well as establishing the rules and regulations governing chiropractic medicine in Oregon. The seven-member board is comprised of five licensed chiropractors and two public members appointed by the governor for three-year terms.

The board's mission is to serve the public; regulate the practice of chiropractic medicine; and promote quality, competent and ethical health care. The board's programs include application, examination, continuing education, public information and investigation of complaints. If violations are found, the board issues disciplinary actions and/or rehabilitation plans to meet competency standards.

COLUMBIA RIVER GORGE COMMISSION

Address: PO Box 730, White Salmon WA 98672
Phone: 509-493-3323
Fax: 509-493-2229
Email: info@gorgecommission.com
Web: gorgecommission.org
Contact: Krystyna Wolniakowski, Executive Director
Statutory Authority: ORS 196.150
Duties and Responsibilities: The commission was established by a compact between Oregon and Washington in 1987 in response to the 1986 National Scenic Area Act passed by Congress. The Act established the 292,500 acre Columbia River Gorge National Scenic Area. They work in partnership with the USDA Forest Service, six counties, 13 urban areas and four Columbia River treaty fishing tribes to implement a regional management plan that protects the scenic, natural, cultural and recreational resources of the Columbia River Gorge National Scenic Area and support the area's economy when compatible with resource protections. The commission has 13 members: six appointed by each of the counties, three appointed by the Oregon governor, three appointed by the Washington governor and one representing the U.S. secretary of agriculture. The commission has eight staff specializing in land use planning and resource management.

CONSTRUCTION CONTRACTORS BOARD

Address: 201 High St. SE, Suite 600, PO Box 14140, Salem 97309-5052
Phone: 503-378-4621
Fax: 503-373-2007
Email: ccb.info@ccb.oregon.gov
Web: oregon.gov/ccb
Contact: Chris Huntington, Administrator
Statutory Authority: ORS 701.205
Duties and Responsibilities: The Construction Contractors Board (CCB) serves Oregonians by preventing and resolving construction contracting problems. The agency licenses contractors, investigates complaints against licensees and penalizes unlawful contractors. The CCB educates the public about how to avoid problems on construction projects and helps mediate disputes between homeowners and licensed contractors.

To become licensed, contractors must meet minimum education and experience requirements and pass a test. Some advanced licenses require prior construction experience. Licensed contractors are subject to continuing education requirements.

The CCB employs approximately 60 people. Enforcement officers and dispute mediators are deployed across the state. The board is made up of nine members appointed by the governor and confirmed by the Senate. Members represent different segments of the construction industry, the public and local government.

The Labor and Industries Building in Salem houses the central offices of the Department of Consumer and Business Services. (Oregon State Archives scenic photo)

CONSUMER AND BUSINESS SERVICES, DEPARTMENT OF

Address: 350 Winter St. NE, Salem 97301-3878; Mail: PO Box 14480, Salem 97309-0405
Phone: 503-378-4100
Fax: 503-947-0088
Email: dcbs.info@dcbs.oregon.gov
Web: dcbs.oregon.gov
Contact: Andrew Stolfi, Director
Statutory Authority: ORS Chapter 705
Duties and Responsibilities: The Department of Consumer and Business Services (DCBS) is Oregon's largest business regulatory and consumer protection agency. The department administers state laws and rules to protect consumers and workers in the areas of workers' compensation, occupational safety and health, financial services, insurance and building codes. The department serves as an integrated umbrella agency over most state functions affecting businesses in order to improve efficiency and effectiveness.

DCBS employs about 900 people and is headquartered in Salem. Several of its divisions have offices around the state.

Building Codes Division

Address: 1535 Edgewater St. NW,
PO Box 14470, Salem 97309-0404
Phone: 503-378-4133
Fax: 503-378-2322
Email: bcd.info@dcbs.oregon.gov
Web: oregon.gov/bcd
Contact: Alana Cox, Administrator
Statutory Authority: ORS Chapters 446, 447, 455, 460, 479, 480, 693
Duties and Responsibilities: This division administers a statewide uniform building code. This code helps ensure a minimum level of safety in all areas of the state and a uniform regulatory environment for businesses, the general public and contractors. The division adopts building codes with the advice of seven statutory boards. It certifies inspectors, licenses trade professionals and establishes training and education requirements; provides code and rule interpretation and dispute resolution; enforces license, code and permit requirements to prevent unsafe conditions; and conducts inspections where local entities do not.

Building Codes Advisory Boards

Address: PO Box 14470, Salem 97309-0404
Phone: 503-899-2972
Web: oregon.gov/BCD/boards
Contact: Todd Smith, Policy and Technical Services Manager

Boiler Rules, Board of

Statutory Authority: ORS 480.535, 705.250
Duties and Responsibilities: This board formulates and adopts rules for the safe construction, installation, inspection, operation, maintenance and repair of boilers and pressure vessels. They also review staff enforcement actions. The governor appoints the board's 11 members to four-year terms, subject to Senate confirmation.

Building Codes Structures Board

Statutory Authority: ORS 455.132, 455.144, 705.250
Duties and Responsibilities: The board helps the DCBS director administer the Structural, Prefabricated Structures, Accessibility to People with Physical Disabilities and certain energy programs. The governor appoints the board's nine members to four-year terms, subject to Senate confirmation.

Construction Industry Energy Board

Statutory Authority: ORS 455.492, 705.250
Duties and Responsibilities: The board evaluates proposed state building code standards and administrative rules relating to energy use and efficiency of the electrical, structural, prefabricated structure and low-rise residential specialties. The proposed standards evaluated by the board may include energy conserving technology, construction methods, products and materials. The board has 11 members.

Electrical and Elevator Board

Statutory Authority: ORS 455.138, 455.144, 479.680, 705.250
Duties and Responsibilities: The board helps the DCBS director administer the electrical and elevator programs. It oversees the licensing and enforcement of these programs to ensure people involved are appropriately licensed and the work meets minimum safety standards. The governor appoints the board's 15 members to four-year terms, subject to Senate confirmation.

Mechanical Board

Statutory Authority: ORS 455.140, 705.250
Duties and Responsibilities: The board helps the DCBS director administer the code and associated administrative rules adopted for mechanical devices and equipment. The governor appoints the 10-member board, subject to Senate confirmation.

Plumbing Board, State

Statutory Authority: ORS 693.115, 705.250
Duties and Responsibilities: The board licenses individuals to engage in the trade of a journeyman plumber. The board establishes license, business and supervising plumber registrations, examinations and continuing education fees. The governor appoints the board's seven members, subject to Senate confirmation.

Residential and Manufactured Structures Board

Statutory Authority: ORS 455.135, 705.250
Duties and Responsibilities: The board helps the DCBS director administer the low-rise residential dwelling program. The governor appoints the board's 11 members, subject to Senate confirmation.

Financial Regulation, Division of

Address: 350 Winter St. NE, Salem 97301-3881;
PO Box 14480, Salem 97309-0405
Phone: 503-378-4140
Fax: 503-378-7862
Email: dfr.financialserviceshelp@dcbs.
oregon.gov (financial);
dfr.insurancehelp@dcbs.oregon.gov
(insurance)
Web: dfr.oregon.gov
Contact: T.K. Keen, Administrator
Statutory Authority: ORS Chapters 59, 86A, 97, 446, 645, 646A, 650, 697, 705-708A, 709, 711, 713-717, 723, 725, 725A, 726, 731-735, 737, 741-743, 743A, 743B, 744, 746, 748, 750, 752, 806, 819, 823, 825

Duties and Responsibilities: The division regulates banks and credit unions, check cashing, debt management services, financial and investment advisors, insurance industry, mortgage industry, money transmitters, pawnshops, payday and title lenders, securities and drug price transparency. They investigate consumer complaints; analyze and monitor financial and insurance institution finances; review all insurance policies before they are sold in Oregon; licenses companies and professionals; and register securities and other investments.

Occupational Safety and Health Division, Oregon

Address: 350 Winter St. NE, Salem 97301-3882; PO Box 14480, Salem 97309-0405
Phone: 503-378-3272 (Voice/TTY); Toll-free in Oregon only: 800-922-2689 (Voice/TTY)
Fax: 503-947-7461
Email: admin.web@dcbs.oregon.gov
Web: osha.oregon.gov
Contact: Renee Stapleton, Acting Administrator
Statutory Authority: ORS Chapter 654
Duties and Responsibilities: The division is known as Oregon OSHA. Oregon OSHA is responsible for working with employers and employees to reduce and prevent occupational injuries, illnesses and fatalities and for enforcing Oregon occupational safety and health standards. The division inspects workplaces for occupational safety and health hazards, investigates complaints about safety and health issues on the job and investigates fatal accidents to determine if the Oregon Safe Employment Act has been violated. The division also provides technical, educational and consultative services to help employers and employees implement and improve injury and illness prevention plans.

Workers' Compensation Division

Address: 350 Winter St. NE, Salem 97301-3879; PO Box 14480, Salem 97309-0405
Phone: 503-947-7810
Fax: 503-947-7630
Email: workcomp.questions@dcbs.oregon.gov
Web: wcd.oregon.gov
Contact: Sally Coen, Administrator
Statutory Authority: ORS Chapters 654, 656, 659A
Duties and Responsibilities: The division administers and regulates statutes and rules to ensure employers provide coverage for their workers; provide treatment and benefits to help injured workers return to work as quickly as possible; and resolve disputes as quickly, fairly and with as

little litigation as possible. The division facilitates injured workers' early return-to-work through incentive programs funded through the Workers' Benefit Fund; helps resolve medical, vocational, disability and other disputes; and provides consultation, training and technical services to people and businesses within the system.

Oregon Workers, Ombudsman Office for

Address: 350 Winter St. NE, Salem 97301-3878; PO Box 14480, Salem 97309-0405
Phone: 503-378-3351; Toll-free: 800-927-1271
Email: oow.questions@dcbs.oregon.gov
Web: oregon.gov/dcbs/oow
Contact: Jennifer Flood, Ombuds
Statutory Authority: ORS 656.709
Duties and Responsibilities: The Legislature created this office to serve as an independent advocate for injured workers. They also investigate and attempt to resolve workers' compensation-related complaints, provide information to injured workers to enable them to protect their rights and make recommendations for improving ombudsman services and the workers' compensation system.

Small Business Ombudsman for Workers' Compensation

Address: 350 Winter St. NE, Salem 97301-3878; PO Box 14480, Salem 97309-0405
Phone: 971-283-0997
Email: wcadvocate.dir@dcbs.oregon.gov
Web: oregon.gov/dcbs/sbo
Contact: David Waki, Ombudsman
Statutory Authority: ORS 656.709
Duties and Responsibilities: The ombudsman serves as a workers' compensation resource center, assisting small businesses in the areas of insurance and claims processing. This includes the intervention, investigation and resolution of any workers' compensation-related issue. The office also provides education and information to employers, trade groups, agents and insurers on relevant workers' compensation issues.

Workers' Compensation Management-Labor Advisory Committee

Address: 350 Winter St. NE, Salem 97301-3878; PO Box 14480, Salem 97309-0405
Phone: 503-947-7867
Fax: 503-378-6444
Email: theresa.a.vanwinkle@dcbs.oregon.gov
Web: oregon.gov/dcbs/mlac
Contact: Theresa Van Winkle, Administrator
Statutory Authority: ORS 656.790
Duties and Responsibilities: This committee provides an effective forum for business and labor

to meet, explore and resolve issues involving the workers' compensation system. The committee is charged with reviewing and making recommendations on workers' compensation issues to the DCBS director and the Legislature. Members are appointed by the governor and subject to Senate confirmation. The committee consists of five management and five labor representatives and the DCBS director, who serves as an ex officio member.

Other Groups:

Prescription Drug Affordability Board

Address: 350 Winter St. NE, Salem 97301-3878; PO Box 14480, Salem 97309-0405
Email: pdab@dcbs.oregon.gov
Web: dfr.oregon.gov/pdab
Contact: Ralph Magrish, Executive Director
Statutory Authority: ORS 646A
Duties and Responsibilities: The Legislature created this board to evaluate the cost of prescription drugs and determine whether they present an affordability challenge to consumers and health systems in Oregon. The board informs rulemaking criteria for drugs that including health inequities for communities of color, the number of Oregon residents prescribed the drug, the price in Oregon and other criteria required by law. It also studies the entire prescription drug distribution and payment system in Oregon and elsewhere to lower the list price of prescription drugs and make recommendations to the Legislature.

Workers' Compensation Board

Address: 2601 25th St. SE, Suite 150, Salem 97302-1280
Phone: 503-378-3308, Toll-free: 877-311-8061
Fax: 503-373-1684
Web: oregon.gov/wcb
Contact: Connie Wold, Chair
Statutory Authority: ORS Chapter 656
Duties and Responsibilities: The board conducts contested case hearings and provides mediation for workers' compensation matters, as well as for Oregon OSHA citations and orders. It is the appellate body that reviews administrative law judge workers' compensation orders on appeal, exercises its own motion jurisdiction and reviews claim disposition agreements. The board also hears appeals from Oregon Department of Justice regarding applications for compensation under the Crime Victim Assistance Program and resolves disputes between workers and workers' compensation carriers arising from workers' civil actions against third parties. The five-member board is appointed by the governor for four-year terms, subject to Senate confirmation.

The central Department of Corrections offices are in the Dome Building in Salem. (Oregon State Archives scenic photo)

CORRECTIONS, DEPARTMENT OF

Address: 3723 Fairview Industrial Drive SE, Suite 200, Salem 97302
Phone: 503-945-9090
Web: oregon.gov/doc
Contact: Heidi Steward, Interim Director
Statutory Authority: ORS Chapter 423
Duties and Responsibilities: The department works to promote public safety by holding offenders accountable for their actions and reducing the risk of future criminal behavior. Department of Corrections has custody of about 12,100 adults sentenced to prison for more than a year in 12 state prisons throughout the state. It also oversees community parole and post-prison supervision of about 2,500 individuals in Linn and Douglas Counties. The department is recognized nationally among correctional agencies for providing adults in custody with the cognitive, education and job skills needed to become productive citizens when they transition back to their communities.

Oregon's recidivism rate is about 35% when defined as the total percentage of a release cohort that was convicted of any felony at any time within the specified number of months following release from prison or jail. The recidivism rate is 28.5% when defined as the total percentage of an admission cohort that was convicted of any felony at any time within the specified number of months after beginning probation.

Administrative Services Division

Address: 3723 Fairview Industrial Drive SE, Suite 200, Salem 97302
Phone: 503-779-6054
Contact: Jim Paul, Assistant Director
Duties and Responsibilities: The division supports the daily business of the Department of Corrections. It includes Information Technology, Facility Services and Warehouse Distribution.

Chief Financial Officer, Office of the

Address: 23723 Fairview Industrial Drive SE, Suite 200, Salem 97302
Phone: 503-983-1441
Contact: Jeremiah Stromberg, Acting Chief Financial Officer
Duties and Responsibilities: The office is responsible for determining the resources necessary to support the existing and growing offender populations. The office develops and executes the department's Long-Range Construction Plan to ensure appropriate institutions are in place to house offenders entering the system. Fiscal Services include contracts, purchasing, accounting and Central Trust.

Communications and Government Relations, Office of

Address: 3723 Fairview Industrial Drive SE, Suite 200, Salem 97302
Phone: 503-569-3318
Contact: Jennifer Black, Assistant Director
Duties and Responsibilities: The office is responsible for furthering the department's mission and goals through close collaboration with external and internal stakeholders, both inside and beyond the realm of public safety. This office ensures the department is a transparent governmental organization that members of the public can access at any time. It includes internal and external communications, media relations, legislative and government relations and public record/information coordination.

Community Corrections

Address: 3691 State St., Salem 97301
Phone: 503-983-1441
Contact: Jeramiah Stromberg, Assistant Director
Duties and Responsibilities: The Department of Corrections operates Community Corrections in Linn and Douglas Counties, working in partnership with county-operated community corrections agencies. Activities include supervision, community-based sanctions and services directed at offenders who have committed felony crimes and have been placed under probation by the courts, the Board of Parole and Post-Prison Supervision or the local supervisory authority.

Correctional Services Division

Address: 3723 Fairview Industrial Drive SE, Suite 200, Salem 97302
Phone: 503-930-2415
Contact: Nathaline Frener, Assistant Director
Duties and Responsibilities: The division is dedicated to applying effective corrections programming, services and support. It values comprehensive, collaborative partnerships that support the success of individuals during incarceration

and through their transition from prison to the community.

Its wide-ranging responsibilities include intake to prison, sentence computation and offender records, population management, correctional case management and inmate services. In addition, the division provides patient-centered health services covering medical, mental health, dental and pharmaceutical services.

Inspector General, Office of the

Address: 3723 Fairview Industrial Drive SE, Suite 200, Salem 97302
Phone: 503-602-0089
Contact: Craig Prins, Inspector General
Duties and Responsibilities: The office provides an oversight function on behalf of the director and deputy director of the Department of Corrections. The office was created in 1990 as recommended by an investigative report to the governor. The inspector general has broad responsibility for oversight of suspected, alleged or actual misconduct within the department, reporting to the director or deputy and to other officials as required by law.

Operations Division

Address: 3723 Fairview Industrial Drive SE, Suite 200, Salem 97302
Phone: 503-945-0932
Contact: Rob Persson, Assistant Director
Duties and Responsibilities: Oregon's adult prisons are centrally administered by the assistant director of operations to ensure that Oregon's 12 prisons are safe, civil and productive so that adults in custody (AIC) can pursue the goals specified in their corrections plans. The division's responsibilities encompass prison management, AIC transportation, security threat group (gang) management, emergency preparedness and most inmate work crew activities.

Oregon Corrections Enterprises

Address: 3691 State St., Salem 97301
Phone: 503-428-5500
Web: oce.oregon.gov
Contact: Melanie Doolin, Acting Administrator
Duties and Responsibilities: Oregon Corrections Enterprises (OCE) is semi-independent from the Department of Corrections. By working with the department, state agencies, non-profit agencies and the public, OCE builds partnerships that sustain work opportunities for adults in custody. OCE explores new business opportunities and partnerships while working to reduce recidivism.

State Prisons:

Coffee Creek Correctional Facility

Address: 24499 SW Grahams Ferry Rd., Wilsonville 97070
Phone: 503-570-6400

Contact: Nichole Brown, Superintendent

Minimum and medium-security facility accommodating all of Oregon's female inmates and providing intake services to all male inmates, operational since 2001

Capacity: 1,685

Columbia River Correctional Institution

Address: 9111 NE Sunderland Ave., Portland 97211

Phone: 503-280-6646

Contact: James Hanley, Acting Superintendent

Minimum-security prison, operational since 1990

Capacity: 553

Deer Ridge Correctional Institution

Address: 3920 East Ashwood Rd., Madras 97741

Phone: 541-325-5999

Contact: Chris Randall, Superintendent

Minimum and medium-security prison, operational since 2007

Capacity: Minimum-security, 774 (not currently in operation); Medium-security, 1,228

Eastern Oregon Correctional Institution

Address: 2500 Westgate, Pendleton 97801

Phone: 541-276-0700

Contact: David Pedro, Acting Superintendent

Medium-security prison, operational since 1985

Capacity: 1,659

Oregon State Correctional Institution

Address: 3405 Deer Park Dr. SE, Salem 97310

Phone: 503-373-0125

Contact: Josh Highberger, Superintendent

Medium-security facility, operational since 1959

Capacity: 890

Oregon State Penitentiary

Address: 2605 State St., Salem 97310

Phone: 503-378-2453

Contact: Corey Fhuere, Superintendent

Multi-security penitentiary, operational since 1866

Capacity: 2,194

Powder River Correctional Facility

Address: 3600 13th St., Baker City 97814

Phone: 541-523-6680

Fax: 541-523-6678

Contact: Tom McLay, Superintendent

Minimum-security prison, operational since 1989

Capacity: 286

Santiam Correctional Institution

Address: 4005 Aumsville Hwy. SE, Salem 97317

Phone: 503-378-2144

Fax: 503-378-8235

Contact: Amber Sundquist, Acting Superintendent

Minimum-security prison, operational since 1992

Capacity: 440

Snake River Correctional Institution

Address: 777 Stanton Blvd., Ontario 97914

Phone: 541-881-5000

Contact: Jamie Miller, Superintendent

Multi-security prison, Oregon's largest correctional institution, operational since 1991

Capacity: 3,062

South Fork Forest Camp

Address: 48300 Wilson River Hwy., Tillamook 97141

Phone: 503-842-2811

Contact: James Hanley, Acting Superintendent

Minimum-security work camp, operational since 1951

Capacity: 204

Two Rivers Correctional Institution

Address: 82911 Beach Access Rd., Umatilla 97882

Phone: 541-922-2001

Contact: Erin Reyes, Superintendent

Medium and minimum-security facility, operational since 2000

Capacity: 1,878

Warner Creek Correctional Facility

Address: 20654 Rabbit Hill Rd., Lakeview 97630

Phone: 541-947-8200

Contact: Jeremy Beaumont, Superintendent

Minimum-security facility, operational since 2005

Capacity: 406

CRIMINAL JUSTICE COMMISSION, OREGON

Address: 885 Summer St. NE, Salem 97301

Phone: 503-378-4830

Fax: 503-378-4861

Email: cjc@oregon.gov

Web: oregon.gov/cjc

Contact: Kenneth Sanchagrin, Executive Director

Statutory Authority: ORS 137.651–137.680

Duties and Responsibilities: The commission serves as the policy development forum for state and local criminal justice systems. Twenty-seven staff provide data analysis, planning and grant administration expertise to public safety officials and work with stakeholders to improve Oregon's criminal justice systems. The agency administers the statewide grant programs for specialty courts, illegal marijuana interdiction and prosecution, restorative justice programs and justice reinvestment programs. It administers Oregon's sentencing guidelines, serves as the State Administering Agency for the Byrne Justice Assistance Grant program and other federal public safety grants and houses the Statistical Analysis Center. Nine commissioners direct the staff's work.

DENTISTRY, OREGON BOARD OF

Address: 1500 SW 1st Ave., Suite 770, Portland 97201
Phone: 971-673-3200
Fax: 971-673-3202
Email: information@obd.oregon.gov
Web: oregon.gov/dentistry
Contact: Stephen Prisby, Executive Director
Statutory Authority: ORS Chapter 679, ORS 680.010–680.205, 680.990
Duties and Responsibilities: The board is the oldest licensing board in Oregon, created by an act of the Legislature on February 23, 1887. The mission of the board is to promote quality oral health care and protect all comminities in Oregon by equitably and ethically regulating dental professionals.

The board's goals are to protect the public from unsafe, incompetent or fraudulent practitioners and to encourage licensees to practice safely and competently in the best interests of their patients. The board does this by requiring the competency of applicants through written and clinical examinations, requiring continuing education, investigating complaints and enforcing the provisions of the Dental Practice Act and rules of the board, communicating board policies and other pertinent information on a regular basis, acting as a resource to consumers in determining the adequacy of their dental treatment, and working with other health care boards and associations to develop partnerships to forge a viable health care delivery system.

Early Learning and Care, Department of

Address: 700 Summer St. NE, Suite 350, Salem 97301
Phone: 503-947-1400
Email: early.learning@ode.oregon.gov
Web: oregonearlylearning.com
Contact: Alyssa Chatterjee, Director
Statutory Authority: ORS 326.430
Duties and Responsibilities: This new department will become a stand-alone agency on July 1, 2023, after being a division of Department of Education. It will work to support Oregon's young children and families by focusing on child care, early learning programs, supporting the early childhood

workforce, cross systems integration, policy, research and equity.

EDUCATION, DEPARTMENT OF

Address: 255 Capitol St. NE, Salem 97310-0203
Phone: 503-947-5600
Fax: 503-378-5156
Email: ode.frontdesk@ode.state.or.us
Web: oregon.gov/ode
Contact: Colt Gill, Director
Statutory Authority: ORS 326.111
Duties and Responsibilities: The Oregon Department of Education (ODE) oversees the education of over 582,000 students in Oregon's public kindergarten through grade 12 education system. ODE encompasses early learning, public preschool programs, the state School for the Deaf, regional programs for children with disabilities and education programs in Oregon youth corrections facilities.

While ODE is not in the classroom directly providing services, the agency (along with the State Board of Education) focuses on helping districts achieve both local and statewide goals and priorities through strategies such as developing policies and standards; providing accurate and timely data to inform instruction; training teachers how to use data effectively; administering state and federal grants; and sharing and helping districts implement best practices.

The Public Service Building in Salem houses the central offices of the Department of Education. (Oregon State Archives scenic photo)

State Board of Education

Address: 255 Capitol St. NE, Salem 97310-0203
Phone: 503-947-5600
Fax: 503-378-5156
Email: StateBoard.PublicEmail@ode.state.or.us
Web: oregon.gov/ode/about-us/stateboard
Contact: Guadalupe Martinez Zapata, Chair (Guadalupe.Martinez.Z@ode.oregon.gov); Corey Rosenberg, State Board Administrator
Statutory Authority: ORS 326.011–326.075

Duties and Responsibilities: The board provides leadership and vision for Oregon's public schools and districts by enacting equitable policies and promoting educational practices that lead directly to the educational and life success of every student.

The board sets policies and standards for Oregon's public school districts and educational service districts. All of these agencies have separate governing bodies responsible for transacting business within their jurisdictions. The board is also responsible for adopting administrative rules that the Oregon Department of Education implements.

The board has seven members, appointed by the governor and confirmed by the Senate. Members are appointed to represent Oregon's congressional districts, and two members represent the state at large. One at large appointed member must be engaged in teaching as a licensed teacher. Appointed members serve four-year terms and are limited to two consecutive terms. Board members elect their chair each year. The state treasurer and the secretary of state or their designees also serve on the board as nonvoting, ex officio members. The board holds public meetings at least six times per year.

Fair Dismissal Appeals Board

Address: 255 Capitol St. NE, Salem 97310-0203
Phone: 503-947-5915
Fax: 503-378-5156
Email: Emily.Nazarov@ode.oregon.gov
Web: oregon.gov/ode/educator-resources/
pages/fairdismissalappealsboard.aspx
Contact: Emily Nazarov, Government and Legal Affairs Manager
Statutory Authority: ORS 342.930
Duties and Responsibilities: The Fair Dismissal Appeals Board consists of 24 members appointed by the governor: six public school administrators, six contract teachers, six school board members and six who must have no occupational affiliation with a school district. Each category must be further distributed by size of school district.

The board was created to hear appeals of teacher and administrator dismissals by school districts. Once an appeal is filed, a three-member panel is selected by the board's executive secretary to hear the appeal and render a decision.

Quality Education Commission

Address: 255 Capitol St. NE, Salem 97310-0203
Phone: 503-947-5670
Fax: 503-378-5156
Web: oregon.gov/ode/reports-and-data/
taskcomm
Contact: Cindy Hunt, Chief of Staff
Statutory Authority: ORS 327.497–327.506

Duties and Responsibilities: The commission's role is to identify educational best practices and to estimate the level of funding required to ensure kindergarten through grade 12 public education meets the goals established in statute. To fulfill that charge, the commission researches educational best practices and estimates the costs of implementing them. The model used to estimate educational costs, known as the Quality Education Model, is maintained by the commission with assistance from the Oregon Department of Education.

Educator Advancement Council

Address: 255 Capitol St. NE, Salem 97310
Phone: 503-373-0053
Fax: 503-378-5156
Email: eacinfo@oregonlearning.org
Web: oregon.gov/eac
Contact: Kimberly Matier, Executive Director
Statutory Authority: ORS 342.940, 342.943
Duties and Responsibilities: The Educator Advancement Council (EAC) coordinates a systemic approach to continuous needs assessment, coordinating priorities for services and resources to support Oregon educators. In partnership with state and local education agency partners, professional organizations, and institutions of higher education, the EAC is building capacity to align, coordinate, and integrate educator preparation and professional learning efforts. The goals are for educators to experience a seamless system of support throughout their careers and for students to experience high quality and culturally responsive learning.

Oregon School for the Deaf

Address: 999 Locust St. NE, Salem 97301-5254
Phone: 503-378-3825
Video phone: 503-400-6180
Fax: 503-378-4701
Email: info@osd.k12.or.us
Web: osd.k12.or.us
Contact: Dr. Sharla Jones, Director
Duties and Responsibilities: The Oregon School for the Deaf (OSD) educates Deaf and Hard of Hearing students (K-21) who require services and support not provided through their regular public school. OSD is funded by legislative appropriation and is governed by ODE. In the 2021-2022 school year, 100 students were enrolled at the school at no cost to their families.

Youth Development Council and Youth Development Division

Address: 255 Capitol St. NE, Salem 97310-0203
Phone: 503-378-5148
Email:youth.development.division@state.or.us

Web: oregon.gov/youthdevelopmentdivision
Contact: Brian Detman, Director
Statutory Authority: ORS 417.847, 417.850, 417.852–417.854, 417.855
Duties and Responsibilities: The Youth Development Division (YDD) develops state policy and administers funding for community, tribal and school-based youth development programs, services and initiatives. The Youth Development Council (YDC) is the governing body for the division. They provide strategic guidance, expertise and advocacy for youth through changes in state law and policy. They also direct funding for programs and services that support youth educational success, reengagement in education, career/workforce development and juvenile crime prevention.

The mission of the Youth Development Division and the Youth Development Council is to align systems and invest in communities to ensure equitable and effective services for youth ages six through 24. Throughout Oregon and Tribal nations, the YDD and YDC support educational and career success, disrupt youth crime and violence, and affirm youth strengths and safety.

EMERGENCY MANAGEMENT, DEPARTMENT OF

Address: 3225 State St., Rm. 115, Salem 97301;
Mail: PO Box 14370, Salem 97309-5062
Phone: 503-378-2911
Web: oregon.gov/oem
Contact: Matt Garrett, Interim Director
Statutory Authority: ORS Chapter 401
Duties and Responsibilities: The Oregon Department of Emergency Management (OEM) maintains a statewide emergency response system for emergency and disaster notifications and coordination. OEM provides statewide leadership to prepare for, respond to, recover from and mitigate against emergencies and disasters regardless of cause. OEM provides leadership through its three divisions: The Director's Office, Preparedness and Response and Mitigation and Recovery Services.

OEM supports state agency, local and tribal governments' efforts to reduce disaster risk and manage the consequences of emergencies and disasters through grant funding to local and tribal governments, a network of regional emergency management coordinators, the state's search and rescue program and the state's 9-1-1 Program. The Drought Council, Local Government Emergency Management Advisory Council and the Oregon Seismic Safety Advisory Commission (OSSPAC) are also under OEM's purview.

EMPLOYMENT APPEALS BOARD

Address: 875 Union St. NE, Salem 97311
Phone: 503-378-2077
Fax: 503-378-2129
Contact: Sarah Serres, Chair
Statutory Authority: ORS 657.685–657.690
Duties and Responsibilities: The three-member board is appointed by the governor. They review orders issued by administrative law judges at the Office of Administrative Hearings regarding contested unemployment insurance claims cases. Upon application for review from a party, the board has the authority to affirm, modify, or reverse an order, or remand the case for additional evidence. Final written decisions of the board are subject to review by the Oregon Court of Appeals.

EMPLOYMENT DEPARTMENT

Address: 875 Union St. NE, Salem 97311
Phone: 503-947-1394; Toll-free: 1-800-237-3710
Fax: 503-947-1472
Web: employment.oregon.gov
Contact: David Gerstenfeld, Acting Director
Statutory Authority: ORS 657.601
Duties and Responsibilities: The department supports economic stability for Oregonians by paying unemployment benefits, matching qualified job seekers to businesses, providing quality workforce and economic information to promote informed decision-making and providing paid leave benefits to people working in Oregon. The department employs approximately 1,820 staff and provides services to approximately 152,000 Oregon businesses and over 382,000 individual Oregonians.

Unemployment Insurance Division

Address: 875 Union St. NE, Salem 97311
Phone: 503-947-1330
Fax: 503-947-1668
Contact: Lindsi Leahy, Director
Statutory Authority: ORS 657.601
Duties and Responsibilities: Unemployment insurance benefits replace part of the income lost when workers become unemployed through no fault of their own. The division is responsible for paying benefits to eligible claimants in an accurate and timely manner, deciding eligibility issues, discouraging fraud and collecting taxes to fund the program.

The money used to pay Oregon unemployment insurance benefits comes from Oregon employers' state payroll taxes, which are deposited in a trust fund to pay unemployment insurance benefits to unemployed Oregon workers.

Workforce and Economic Research Division

Address: 875 Union St. NE, Salem 97311
Phone: 503-947-1229
Fax: 503-947-1210
Web: qualityinfo.org
Contact: Bob Uhlenkott, Director
Statutory Authority: ORS 657.601
Duties and Responsibilities: The division's economists, workforce analysts and researchers collect, analyze and disseminate statewide and regional labor market information. They help organizations and businesses apply that information in their day-to-day operations. Analysts provide concise, up-to-date information about the local and state economies and their effects on the workforce. Research staff study the labor force and related topics, supply data and analysis to new and expanding firms and analyze occupational supply and demand, which is gathered through surveys sent to employers.

In addition to offering general information, the division's staff produce special reports and respond to requests. Businesses use labor market information to identify challenges and opportunities to compete and flourish. Economic development planners, educators and training providers, job applicants, legislators and the news media regularly rely on this information to learn about workforce issues that affect Oregonians and Oregon businesses.

Workforce Operations Division

Address: 875 Union St. NE, Salem 97311
Phone: 503-947-1277
Fax: 503-947-1658
Contact: Jim Pfarrer, Director
Statutory Authority: ORS 657.601
Duties and Responsibilities: This division serves employers by recruiting workers with skills matching employers' needs. The department helps job seekers find jobs that match their skills, provides them information about trends in occupations and refers them to appropriate training programs.

The division partners with the Higher Education Coordinating Commission, local workforce development boards, local training providers and the Department of Human Services Self-Sufficiency and Vocational Rehabilitation programs to form the state's workforce system, WorkSource Oregon. The division also oversees programs aimed at assisting certain groups, such as military veterans, migrant seasonal farmworkers and workers adversely affected by foreign trade.

Other Groups:

Employment Department Advisory Council

Address: 875 Union St. NE, Salem 97311
Phone: 503-947-3098
Fax: 503-947-1472
Contact: Rebecca Nance
Statutory Authority: ORS 657.695
Duties and Responsibilities: The council includes volunteer representatives from the public, employers and employees who are appointed by the governor. Council members meet quarterly to assist the Employment Department director in the effective development of policies and programs related to unemployment insurance, employment services and labor market information.

Paid Leave Oregon

Address: 875 Union St. NE, Salem 97311
Contact: Karen Madden Humelbaugh, Director
Statutory Authority: ORS 657B
Duties and Responsibilities: Paid Leave Oregon, formerly known as Paid Family and Medical Leave Insurance, allows employees in Oregon to take paid time off to care for themselves and their families. Leave includes Family Leave to care for a family member with a serious illness or injury; bond with a new child after birth, adoption or foster care placement; Medical Leave during one's own serious health condition; and Safe Leave for survivors of sexual assault, domestic violence, harassment or stalking.

The paid leave program is funded by a trust fund. Both employees and employers contribute to the fund through payroll taxes. By November of each year, the Employment Department will set the contribution rate, which may be up to 1% of an employee's total gross wages.

The Employment Building in Salem houses the central offices of the Employment Department. (Oregon State Archives scenic photo)

EMPLOYMENT RELATIONS BOARD

Address: 1225 Ferry St. SE, Salem 97301
Phone: 503-378-3807
Fax: 503-373-0021
Email: emprel.board@erb.oregon.gov
Web: oregon.gov/erb
Contact: Adam Rhynard, Chair
Statutory Authority: ORS Chapters 240, 663, ORS 243.650–243.795, 662.010–662.455
Duties and Responsibilities: The board resolves labor relations disputes for an estimated 3,000 different employers and 250,000 employees in the public and private sectors under its jurisdiction. The board administers the collective bargaining law that covers public employees of the state of Oregon and its cities, counties, school districts and other local governments; hears and decides appeals from state employees concerning personnel actions; and administers the collective bargaining law that regulates private employers who are not covered by the National Labor Relations Act.

ENERGY, STATE DEPARTMENT OF

Address: 550 Capitol St. NE, Salem 97301
Phone: 503-378-4040; 1-800-221-8035 (Toll-free in Oregon)
Fax: 503-373-7806
Email: askenergy@energy.oregon.gov
Web: oregon.gov/energy
Contact: Janine Benner, Director
Statutory Authority: ORS Chapters 469, 470
Duties and Responsibilities: The Oregon Department of Energy (ODOE) helps Oregonians make informed energy decisions and maintain a resilient and affordable energy system. It advances solutions to shape an equitable clean energy transition, protect the environment and public health, and responsibly balance energy needs and impacts for current and future generations. ODOE serves as a central repository for energy data, information, analysis and as a venue for problem-solving Oregon's energy challenges. The agency also provides energy education and technical assistance, regulation and oversight and energy programs and activities. The agency provides policy expertise to prepare for Oregon's future energy needs and offers technical and financial resources to encourage adoption of and investment in energy efficiency and renewable energy resources.

The agency also staffs the Energy Facility Siting Council, which has jurisdiction over large energy-generating and transmission facilities within the state. This effort brings together project developers, local and regional governments, citizens and others to make sure proposed projects are approved, built, operated and decommissioned consistent with all applicable laws and regulations. ODOE also provides a suite of energy incentive programs that offer grants or rebates for renewable energy, resilience and energy efficiency. The department has about 90 employees.

Energy Facility Siting Council

Address: 550 Capitol St. NE, Salem 97301
Phone: 503-378-4040; Toll-free: 1-800-221-8035
Contact: Marcy Grail, Chair

Global Warming Commission, Oregon

Address: 550 Capitol St. NE, Salem 97301
Phone: 503-378-4040; Toll-free: 1-800-221-8035
Contact: Cathy Macdonald, Chair

Hanford Cleanup Board, Oregon

Address: 550 Capitol St. NE, Salem 97301
Phone: 503-378-4040; Toll-free: 1-800-221-8035
Contact: Jeff Wyatt, Chair

ENGINEERING AND LAND SURVEYING, STATE BOARD OF EXAMINERS FOR

Address: 670 Hawthorne Ave. SE, Suite 220, Salem 97301
Phone: 503-362-2666
Fax: 503-362-5454
Email: osbeels.info@osbeels.oregon.gov
Web: oregon.gov/osbeels
Contact: Jason Barbee, Administrator
Statutory Authority: ORS 672.240
Duties and Responsibilities: The Oregon State Board of Examiners for Engineering and Land Surveying (OSBEELS) regulates the practice of engineering; regulation of the land surveying profession; exercises administrative oversight for Certified Water Right Examiners; regulates the practice of photogrammetric mapping.

The 11-member board and 12 staff ensure registered professional engineers, land surveyors, photogrammetrists and certified water right examiners are qualified in fields in which technical and professional knowledge and skills are required. OSBEELS sets standards of qualification for licensure, ensuring individuals are fully qualified by education, experience and examination to practice in Oregon. The board also reviews relevant laws and rules, revising them expeditiously; enforces regulatory laws and rules by carefully investigating any complaints or information relating to violations; and effectively disseminates information regarding board goals and activities to licensees and the public.

OSBEELS is semi-independent and regulates more than 15,000 licensed professionals.

ENVIRONMENTAL QUALITY, DEPARTMENT OF

Address: 700 NE Multnomah St., Suite 600, Portland 97232
Phone: 503-229-5696; Toll-free (Oregon only): 1-800-452-4011; TTY: 800-735-2900
Fax: 503-229-6124
Web: oregon.gov/deq
Contact: Leah Feldon, Interim Director
Statutory Authority: ORS Chapters 454, 459, 466, 467, 468
Duties and Responsibilities: The Department of Environmental Quality (DEQ) is responsible for protecting and enhancing Oregon's water, air and land quality; managing the proper disposal of solid and hazardous wastes; providing assistance in cleaning up contaminated properties; and enforcing Oregon's environmental laws. Facing increasingly complex environmental problems, DEQ's role has expanded to fight climate change with policies to reduce greenhouse gas emissions, prevent toxic chemical releases and reduce risks from toxins already in the environment. DEQ also provides communities with technical assistance. The agency director has the authority to issue civil penalties for violations of pollution laws and standards. DEQ relies on several citizen advisory committees and government officials to guide its decisions.

DEQ employs approximately 800 scientists, engineers, geologists, toxicologists, inspectors, legal and policy staff, technicians, managers and professional support staff across the state. Their headquarters are located in Portland, with regional offices throughout the state.

Environmental Quality Commission

Address: 700 NE Multnomah St., Suite 600, Portland 97232
Phone: 503-229-5695
Fax: 503-229-6124
Contact: Stephanie Caldera
Duties and Responsibilities: The commission, DEQ's policy and rulemaking board, adopts administrative rules, issues orders and judges appeals of fines or other department actions and hires the DEQ director. Commission members are appointed to four-year terms by the governor.

Air and Water Quality Divisions

Address: 700 NE Multnomah St., Suite 600, Portland 97232

Contact: Ali Mirzakhalili, Air Quality Administrator, 503-229-5041; Jennifer Wigal, Water Quality Administrator, 503-229-5323
Duties and Responsibilities: DEQ's Air and Water Quality Programs work to keep Oregon's air and water clean and clear. Employees monitor air and water quality, and permit and inspect facilities—from major manufacturers to small shops—throughout the state to ensure compliance with environmental regulations. The programs provide valuable data showing long-term trends in Oregon's air and water quality. They also offer real-time conditions through tools such as the Air Quality Index, providing snapshots of air quality conditions across Oregon.

The Water Quality Program ensures the state's waterways are safe for drinking water, fish and wildlife, recreation and irrigation. The program develops and implements water quality standards, regulates sewage treatment systems and industrial dischargers, collects and evaluates water quality data, provides grants and technical assistance to improve water quality and provides loans to communities to upgrade treatment facilities.

The Air Quality Program works to ensure Oregon's air meets the National Ambient Air Quality Standards required by the Federal Clean Air Act. The program monitors and analyzes air quality data, regulates emissions from a variety of sources and conducts vehicle emissions testing in Medford and the Portland metro area.

Land Quality Division

Address: 700 NE Multnomah St., Suite 600, Portland 97232
Phone: 503-229-6411
Contact: Lydia Emer, Administrator
Duties and Responsibilities: The division oversees agency programs in environmental cleanup and site assessment, hazardous and solid waste, spill response, underground storage tanks and materials management. DEQ inventories and assesses sites contaminated with hazardous waste and supervises development and implementation of cleanup strategies. The emergency response program provides DEQ's round-the-clock capability to address releases of hazardous materials and oil to land and water, providing on-scene incident commanders for major cleanups. DEQ oversees Oregon's only hazardous waste landfill, regulates hazardous waste disposal and offers business pollution prevention assistance.

Regional Programs

DEQ operates three regional offices to oversee air, land and water protection throughout the state.

Northwest Region

Address: 700 NE Multnomah St. Suite 600, Portland 97232
Phone: 503-229-5263
Contact: Nina DeConcini, Administrator: 503-229-6721

Western Region

Address: 165 E. 7th Ave. Suite 100, Eugene 97401
Phone: 541-686-7838
Contact: Keith Andersen, Administrator, 541-687-7355

Eastern Region

Address: 475 NE Bellevue Drive, Suite 110, Bend 97701
Phone: 541-388-6146
Contact: Shannon Davis, Administrator, 541-633-2018

FILM AND VIDEO OFFICE, OREGON

Address: 850 SE 3rd Ave., Suite 405, Portland 97214
Phone: 971-254-4020
Email: shoot@oregonfilm.com
Web: oregonfilm.org
Contact: Tim Williams, Executive Director
Statutory Authority: ORS 284.305
Duties and Responsibilities: The office has been helping production companies find, secure and use Oregon locations since 1968. The office's mission is to promote the development of the film, television and multimedia industry in Oregon and to enhance the industry's revenues, profile and reputation. The office administers the state's Oregon Production Investment Fund and Greenlight Oregon Labor Rebate programs that incentivize film, television and multimedia production in Oregon.

FISH AND WILDLIFE, OREGON DEPARTMENT OF

Address: 4034 Fairview Industrial Drive SE, Salem 97302
Phone: 503-947-6000; Toll-free: 1-800-720-6339 (ODFW); Licensing and Controlled Hunts Information: 503-947-6101
Email: odfw.info@state.or.us
Web: odfw.com; myodfw.com
Contact: Curt Melcher, Director
Statutory Authority: ORS 496.080–496.166
Duties and Responsibilities: The Oregon Department of Fish and Wildlife (ODFW) is responsible for sustainably managing fish and wildlife in Oregon. Through its commission, it sets regulations for recreational and commercial fishing, crabbing, clamming and hunting. It also manages species that are not hunted or fished, including state-listed endangered, threatened and sensitive species. ODFW operates more than 30 fish hatcheries raising trout, salmon and steelhead to supplement natural stocks and provide fishing opportunities. It also manages more than 20 wildlife areas providing habitat for fish and wildlife and hunting, fishing, viewing and other outdoor activities. The Oregon State Police play a key role in achieving ODFW's mission through enforcement of fish and wildlife regulations.

ODFW consists of the commission, a commission-appointed director and a statewide staff of approximately 1,000 permanent employees including field staff spread among offices throughout the state.

Fish and Wildlife Commission, Oregon

Address: 4034 Fairview Industrial Dr. SE, Salem 97302-1142
Phone: 503-947-6033
Web: dfw.state.or.us/agency/commission
Contact: Director's Office
Statutory Authority: ORS 496.090
Duties and Responsibilities: The commission consists of seven members appointed by the governor for staggered, four-year terms. One commissioner must be from each congressional district, one from east of the Cascades and one from west of the Cascades.

Commissioners formulate general state programs and policies concerning management and conservation of fish and wildlife resources and establish seasons, methods and bag limits for recreational and commercial take.

Fish Division

Address: 4034 Fairview Industrial Dr. SE, Salem 97302-1142
Phone: 503-947-6201
Fax: 503-947-6200
Web: dfw.state.or.us/fish
Contact: Mike Harrington, Administrator
Statutory Authority: ORS 496.124, 506.142
Duties and Responsibilities: The department is charged by statute to protect and propagate fish in the state. This includes direct responsibility for regulating the harvest, protection and enhancement of fish populations through habitat improvement and the rearing and release of fish into public waters. ODFW maintains hatcheries throughout the state to provide fish for program needs.

Information and Education Division

Address: 4034 Fairview Industrial Dr. SE,
Salem 97302-1142
Phone: 503-947-6002
Fax: 503-947-6009
Contact: Roger Fuhrman, Administrator
Duties and Responsibilities: This division directs and provides all communications and education services for the department. These services include strategic outreach programs, informational campaigns, media and public relations communications, social media, public involvement activities, special events, hunter education programs, aquatic and angler education programs, additional education activities, creation of publications and videos and website management.

Habitat Division

Address: 4034 Fairview Industrial Dr. SE,
Salem 97302-1142
Phone: 503-947-6357
Web: dfw.state.or.us/habitat
Contact: Sarah Reif, Administrator
Statutory Authority: ORS 496.012
Duties and Responsibilities: The division leads proactive, focused, and consistent efforts to protect, restore, and enhance habitat for Oregon's fish and wildlife. The division provides technical assistance to landowners, regulatory agencies, and the public on land and water development actions to ensure fish and wildlife habitat are sustained in a manner consistent with ODFW's mission. The division also provides technical and financial assistance to public and private land managers to restore and enhance fish and wildlife habitats.

Oregon Conservation and Recreation Fund

Address: 4034 Fairview Industrial Dr. SE,
Salem 97302-1142
Phone: 541-961-8421
Web: dfw.state.or.us/conservationstrategy/ocrf
Contact: Charlotte Regula-Whitefield,
Coordinator
Statutory Authority: ORS 496.012, 496.138, 496.146
Duties and Responsibilities: The Legislature created the Oregon Conservation and Recreation Fund as a way for Oregonians to help protect and enhance wildlife species and their habitats. The fund also creates new opportunities for wildlife watching, urban conservation, community science, and other wildlife-associated recreation. The Oregon Conservation and Recreation Advisory Committee advises the Oregon Fish and Wildlife Commission on spending from the Fund.

Wildlife Division

Address: 4034 Fairview Industrial Dr. SE,
Salem 97302-1142
Phone: 503-947-6300
Fax: 503-947-6330
Web: dfw.state.or.us/wildlife
Contact: Bernadette Graham-Hudson,
Administrator
Statutory Authority: ORS 496.124
Duties and Responsibilities: The division has direct responsibility for monitoring the numbers and health of wildlife species, setting population conservation and management objectives, overseeing wildlife habitat restoration and maintenance and regulating harvest of game animals. The Oregon Conservation Strategy is a key part of the division and guides voluntary actions to conserve wildlife on public and private land.

FOREST RESOURCES INSTITUTE, OREGON

Address: 9755 SW Barnes Rd., Suite 210,
Portland 97225
Phone: 971-673-2944
Fax: 971-673-2946
Web: oregonforests.org; knowyourforest.org; learnforests.org; oregonforestlaws.org; oregonforestfacts.org
Contact: Kathy Storm
Statutory Authority: ORS 526.600–526.675
Duties and Responsibilities: The Oregon Forest Resources Institute (OFRI) is statutorily mandated to support and enhance Oregon's forest products industry. OFRI provides forest and forestry education programs for the general public, K-12 teachers and students, and forestland owners. The Institute is governed by a 13-member board and is funded by a portion of the forest products harvest tax. OFRI produces educational media and websites, as well as informational publications and videos. They host forest tours and symposiums covering an array of forest-related topics. OFRI is headquartered in Portland and has a satellite office and demonstration forest at the Oregon Garden in Silverton.

FORESTRY DEPARTMENT, STATE

Address: 2600 State St., Salem 97310
Phone: 503-945-7200
Email: forestry.information@odf.oregon.gov
Web: oregon.gov/odf
Contact: Cal Mukumoto, State Forester
Statutory Authority: ORS Chapters 321, 477, 526, 527, 530, 532
Duties and Responsibilities: Oregon's Department of Forestry (ODF) is committed to ensuring the sustainability of Oregon's forestlands by protecting

them from wildfire, enforcing Oregon's Forest Practices Act and managing state-owned forests. ODF strives to accomplish its mission "to serve the people of Oregon by protecting, managing and promoting stewardship of Oregon's forests to enhance environmental, economic and community sustainability" with oversight from the Oregon Board of Forestry. The department has more than 800 permanent and over 600 seasonal employees, who work out of its Salem headquarters or the 32 field offices throughout Oregon.

The department is organized into three branches: Operational, Administrative and Planning.

Operational

The Fire Protection Division protects just over half of Oregon's 30 million total acres of forestland from wildfire through prevention and suppression activities. This includes all of Oregon's privately-owned forests, state forests and some local and federal government forestlands.

The Forest Resources Division administers Oregon's Forest Practices Act. Enacted in 1971, and modified many times since, the Act regulates stream and water quality protection, timber harvesting, reforestation, road construction and maintenance, and other forest practices on private, non-federal lands. The division is also responsible for supporting partner organizations' efforts to increase the pace, scale and quality of restoration work on federal forestlands through the Federal Forest Restoration program. The division houses the forest health, family forestlands, and urban and community forestry programs.

Through the State Forests Division, the agency manages approximately 745,000 acres of forestland owned by the state, or 3% of the state's forests. State-owned forests are found in the northern Coast and Cascade mountain ranges, in south-central Oregon, and scattered throughout the western part of the state. ODF manages these lands to achieve a balance of social, economic and environmental values. The agency also manages much of the state's Common School Fund forestlands.

This is one of several historic buildings on the campus of the headquarters of the Department of Forestry. (Oregon State Archives scenic photo)

Administrative

The Administrative Branch provides support to the agency in the areas of Human Resources, Public Affairs, Procurement, Budget Management, Fiscal Services, Information Technology, Internal Audits and Safety/Risk Management.

Planning

The Planning Branch provides technical analysis and planning services to the department, as well as other state, federal and local agencies on a wide variety of forestry-related issues.

Board of Forestry, State

Phone: 503-945-7200
Email: boardofforestry@oregon.gov
Contact: Hilary Olivos-Rood, Board Administrator
Statutory Authority: ORS Chapter 526
Duties and Responsibilities: The seven-member citizen board is appointed by the governor and confirmed by the Senate. Its mission is to lead Oregon in implementing policies and programs that promote sustainable management of Oregon's public and private forests. Its responsibilities are to supervise all matters of forest policy, appoint the state forester, adopt rules regulating forest practices and provide general supervision of the state forester's agency-management responsibilities.

No more than three board members may derive a significant portion of their income from the forest products industry. There must be at least one member from each of the state's three major forest regions: northern, southern and eastern. The term of office is four years and no member may serve more than two consecutive full terms. The state forester serves as secretary to the board.

Emergency Fire Cost Committee

Web: oregon.gov/odf/board/pages/efcc.aspx
Contact: Nancy Hirsch, Administrator
Statutory Authority: ORS 477.750–477.775
Duties and Responsibilities: The Oregon Forest Land Protection Fund was established by the Legislature to equalize emergency fire suppression costs among the department's various protection districts. The emergency funding system is designed to operate as an "insurance policy," where all districts pay premiums into the fund so that money will be available to any individual district for fire suppression costs.

Family Forestlands, Committee for

Web: oregon.gov/odf/board/pages/cff.aspx
Email: forestresources.committees @odf.oregon.gov
Statutory Authority: ORS 526.016
Duties and Responsibilities: The committee researches policies impacting family forestland viability, resource protection and forestry benefits.

The committee then makes recommendations to the Board of Forestry and state forester. The 13-member committee includes seven voting and six non-voting members. Voting members include four family forest owners and one representative each from the environmental community, forest products industry and general public. Non-voting ex officio members may include representatives from ODF, Oregon State University, Oregon small forestland groups, forestry-related industry associations and the Oregon Forest Resources Institute.

Forest Trust Land Advisory Committee

Web: oregon.gov/odf/board/pages/ftlac.aspx
Statutory Authority: ORS 526.156
Duties and Responsibilities: The committee is made up of the board of directors of the Council of Forest Trust Land Counties and advises the Board of Forestry and state forester on matters related to state forestlands managed by ODF. The counties that receive revenues from these forestlands are Benton, Clackamas, Clatsop, Columbia, Coos, Douglas, Josephine, Klamath, Lane, Lincoln, Linn, Marion, Polk, Tillamook and Washington.

Regional Forest Practice Committees

Web: oregon.gov/odf/board/pages/rfpc.aspx
Email: forestresources.committees
    @odf.oregon.gov
Statutory Authority: ORS 527.650
Duties and Responsibilities: These three Regional Forest Practice Committees, serve the northwest, southwest and eastern regions of the state. A majority of committee members must be private forest landowners and persons involved with logging or forest operations. The committees advise the Board of Forestry on current forestry issues and forest management approaches.

Smoke Management Advisory Committee

Web: oregon.gov/odf/board/pages/smac.aspx
Duties and Responsibilities: The committee provides advice and assistance to the department's Smoke Management Program. The state forester appoints three members: an industrial forestland owner representative, a non-industrial forestland owner representative and a public representative. A U.S. Forest Service representative and a U.S. Bureau of Land Management representative are also invited to serve as members. Each member serves a two-year term that is renewable after the two-year period.

Committee members gather for public meetings in Salem twice a year to discuss and provide advice to the Smoke Management Program regarding current prescribed burning and smoke intrusion

trends, program fund balance, implementation plan items and other current issues and projects.

State Forests Advisory Committee

Web: oregon.gov/odf/board/pages/sfac.aspx
Duties and Responsibilities: The committee includes interested citizens and representatives of forest industry, environmental and recreation groups. It provides a forum to discuss issues, opportunities and concerns regarding state forestlands and offers advice and guidance to ODF on the implementation of the Northwest Oregon State Forests Management Plan. The plan provides guidance for managing 650,000 acres within the Tillamook, Clatsop and Santiam state forests, and several state-owned forest tracts in Benton, Polk, Lincoln, Clackamas and Lane counties. The plan attempts to take a balanced approach to generating revenue, while prioritizing environmental and social benefits.

GEOLOGIST EXAMINERS, STATE BOARD OF

Address: 707 13th St. SE, Suite 114, Salem 97301
Phone: 503-566-2837
Fax: 503-485-2947
Email: osbge.info@bgelab.oregon.gov
Web: oregon.gov/osbge
Contact: Christine Valentine, Administrator
Statutory Authority: ORS 672.505–672.705
Duties and Responsibilities: The mission of the board is to safeguard the health, welfare and property of Oregonians with respect to geologic practice in Oregon. The board accomplishes this primarily through the registration of geologists. They also review complaints about geologist conduct and practice or unlicensed geologic practice. They also have authority to impose civil penalties, suspend, revoke or not renew registrations or seek other resolutions as appropriate. In addition, the board works to inform the public, government agencies and others about the practice of geology.

The board sets examination, education and experience standards for geologist registration and for a specialty certification in engineering geology, evaluates applications for examination and registration based on these standards and administers national and engineering geology specialty examinations. Geologists licensed in other states or jurisdictions can apply for registration in Oregon but must meet all of the board's standards.

Approximately 956 geologists are registered to practice in Oregon with about 208 also holding certification in engineering geology. The board is composed of four Oregon registered geologists, the state geologist (i.e., the Director of the Oregon Department of Geology and Mineral Industries) and a public member. The board is served by two staff, an executive director and registration specialist.

GEOLOGY AND MINERAL INDUSTRIES, STATE DEPARTMENT OF

Address: 800 NE Oregon St., Suite 965, Portland 97232
Phone: 971-673-1555
Fax: 971-673-1562
Web: oregon.gov/dogami
Contact: Ruarri Day-Stirrat, Director/State Geologist
Statutory Authority: ORS Chapters 516, 517, 520, 522, ORS 455.446, 455.447
Duties and Responsibilities: The department increases understanding of Oregon's geologic resources and hazards through science and stewardship. Established in 1937 as an independent state agency, its early focus on mining and rural economic development has expanded to include helping Oregonians understand and prepare for the natural hazards that accompany the state's geology.

Today, the department provides earth science information and regulation to make Oregon safe and prosperous. The Geological Survey & Services program develops maps, reports and data to help Oregon manage natural resources and prepare for natural hazards such as earthquakes, tsunamis, landslides, floods, volcanoes, coastal erosion and climate change. The Mineral Land Regulation & Reclamation program oversees the state's mineral production and works to minimize impacts of natural resource extraction and to maximize the opportunities for land reclamation. The department has a staff of approximately 35 people.

Department of Geology and Mineral Industries Governing Board

Contact: Scott Ashford, Chair
Duties and Responsibilities: A five-member governing board of citizens, appointed by the governor and confirmed by the Senate, oversees the Department of Geology and Mineral Industries. The board sets policy, oversees general operations and adopts a strategic plan every six years to guide the department's mission and objectives.

GOVERNMENT ETHICS COMMISSION, OREGON

Address: 3218 Pringle Rd. SE, Rm. 220, Salem 97302-1680
Phone: 503-378-5105
Fax: 503-373-1456
Email: mail@ogec.oregon.gov
Web: oregon.gov/ogec
Contact: Ronald A. Bersin, Interim Executive Director
Statutory Authority: ORS 171.725–171.785, 192.660, 192.685, ORS Chapter 244

Duties and Responsibilities: The Oregon Government Ethics Commission (OGEC), is responsible for enforcement of government ethics laws prohibiting public officials from using their office for financial gain and requiring public disclosure of economic conflict of interest. The OGEC also enforces state laws that require lobbyists, and the entities they represent, to register and report their quarterly lobbying expenditures. OGEC also has jurisdiction over the executive session provisions of the public meetings law.

The OGEC is a nine-member citizen commission. It is served by nine staff members who focus on regulation and prevention through education.

HEALTH AUTHORITY, OREGON

Address: 500 Summer St. NE, E20, Salem 97301-1097
Phone: 503-947-2340
Fax: 503-947-5461
Email: oha.directorsoffice@dhsoha.state.or.us;
Web: oregon.gov/oha
Contact: James Schroeder, Interim Director
Statutory Authority: ORS 413.032
Duties and Responsibilities: The Oregon Health Authority (OHA) is responsible for improving the lifelong health of Oregonians, improving quality and access to health services, and containing and lowering health care costs. OHA oversees a system of coordinated care organizations (CCOs) that serve most of the more than 1 million members of the Oregon Health Plan, Oregon's Medicaid program. The 15 CCOs work with partners in all 36 Oregon counties to provide better care at lower cost. OHA is overseen by the nine-member citizen Oregon Health Policy Board and carries out its work through several program areas.

Health Policy Board, Oregon

Address: 500 Summer St. NE, Salem 97301
Phone: 503-947-2340; Toll free 800-375-2863
Fax: 503-947-2341
Email: healthpolicyboard.info@dhsoha. state.or.us
Web: oregon.gov/oha/ohpb
Statutory Authority: ORS 413.032
Duties and Responsibilities: The nine-member board serves as the policy making and oversight body for the Oregon Health Authority. The board is committed to providing access to high quality, affordable health care for all Oregonians and to improving population health.

The board was established by the Legislature in 2009, making the Oregon Health Authority responsible for most state health care services and for reforming the state's health care system.

Executive

Educators Benefit Board, Oregon

Address: 500 Summer St. NE, Dept. 88, Salem 97301-1119
Phone: 888-469-6322
Fax: 503-378-5832
Email: oebb.benefits@dhsoha.state.or.us
Web: oregon.gov/oha/oebb
Contact: Ali Hassoun, Director
Statutory Authority: ORS 243.864
Duties and Responsibilities: The board provides a choice of benefit plans for employees in most of Oregon's kindergarten through grade 12 school districts, education service districts and community colleges, as well as a number of charter schools and local governments.

Equity and Inclusion, Office of

Address: 421 SW Oak St., Suite 750, Portland 97204
Phone: 971-673-1240; 503-890-2944 (Director)
Fax: 971-673-1128
Web: oregon.gov/oha/oei
Contact: Leann Johnson, Director
Email: Leann.R.Johnson@dhsoha.state.or.us
Statutory Authority: ORS 431.137
Duties and Responsibilities: The office works with diverse communities throughout Oregon to eliminate health gaps and disparities by making health care more accessible and ensuring the delivery of care consistent with state and federal civil rights guidelines. It operates a Traditional Health Worker program to help ensure that culturally competent care is delivered by a diverse workforce. The office's Health Care Interpreter program trains and certifies bilingual persons to provide high-quality health care interpretation to Oregon's increasingly diverse populations.

Health Licensing Office (HLO)

Address: 1430 Tandem Ave. NE, Suite180, Salem 97301
Phone: 503-378-8667
Email: hlo.info@dhsoha.state.or.us
Web: oregon.gov/oha/ph/hlo
Contact: Bob Bothwell, Interim Director and Division Manager
Statutory Authority: ORS 676.600–676.992
Duties and Responsibilities: The office works with multiple boards, councils and programs to oversee a variety of health and health-related professions. It protects Oregonians' health and safety by ensuring that these professionals are trained and qualified to practice. The office tests people who apply for professional licenses, inspects facilities, responds to consumer complaints and disciplines practitioners who violate state requirements.

HLO Boards:

Athletic Trainers

Web: oregon.gov/oha/ph/hlo/pages/board-athletic-trainer.aspx
Statutory Authority: ORS 688.701–688.734
Duties and Responsibilities: The board oversees the practice of athletic trainers in Oregon. It has five members appointed by the governor.

Behavior Analysis Regulatory

Web: oregon.gov/oha/ph/hlo/pages/board-behavior-analysis-regulatory.aspx
Statutory Authority: ORS 676.800–676.805
Duties and Responsibilities: The board oversees the licensing of behavior analysts, assistant behavior analysts and the registration of behavior analysis interventionists, all of whom treat individuals with autism spectrum disorder. The board has nine members appointed by the governor and subject to confirmation by the Senate.

Certified Advanced Estheticians

Web: oregon.gov/oha/ph/hlo/pages/board-certified-advanced-estheticians.aspx
Duties and Responsibilities: The board to oversees the safe practice of advanced non-ablative esthetics in Oregon. They have nine members appointed by the governor.

Cosmetology

Web: oregon.gov/oha/ph/hlo/pages/board-cosmetology.aspx
Statutory Authority: ORS 690.005–690.992
Duties and Responsibilities: The board oversees the practice of cosmetologists in Oregon. It has seven members appointed by the governor and subject to confirmation by the Senate.

Denture Technology

Web: oregon.gov/oha/ph/hlo/pages/board-denture-technology.aspx
Statutory Authority: ORS 680.500–680.990
Duties and Responsibilities: The board oversees the practice of denturists in Oregon. It has seven members appointed by the governor and subject to confirmation by the Senate.

Direct Entry Midwifery

Web: oregon.gov/oha/ph/hlo/pages/board-direct-entry-midwifery.aspx
Statutory Authority: ORS 687.405–687.991
Duties and Responsibilities: The board oversees the practice of licensed direct entry midwives in Oregon. It has seven members appointed by the governor and subject to confirmation by the Senate.

Electrologists and Body Art Practitioners

Web: oregon.gov/oha/ph/hlo/pages/board-body-art-practitioners.aspx
Statutory Authority: ORS 690.350–690.992
Duties and Responsibilities: The board oversees the practices of tattoo artists, electrologists and body piercers, including specialty piercers and earlobe-only piercers. It has seven members appointed by the governor and subject to confirmation by the Senate.

Environmental Health Registration

Web: oregon.gov/oha/ph/hlo/pages/board-environmental-health-registration.aspx
Statutory Authority: ORS 700.005–700.995
Duties and Responsibilities: The board oversees the practices of environmental health specialists and waste water specialists in Oregon. It has seven members appointed by the governor.

Hearing Aids, Advisory Council on

Web: oregon.gov/oha/ph/hlo/pages/board-advisory-council-hearing-aids.aspx
Statutory Authority: ORS 694.015–694.991
Duties and Responsibilities: The council oversees the practice of hearing aid specialists in Oregon. It has seven members appointed by the governor and subject to confirmation by the Senate.

Licensed Dietitians

Web: oregon.gov/oha/ph/hlo/pages/board-licensed-dietitians.aspx
Statutory Authority: ORS 691.405
Duties and Responsibilities: The board oversees the practice of dietitians in Oregon. It has seven members appointed by the governor.

The Barbara Roberts Human Services Building in Salem houses the central offices of the Oregon Health Authority. (Oregon State Archives scenic photo)

Long Term Care Administrators

Web: oregon.gov/oha/ph/hlo/pages/board-nursing-home-administrators.aspx
Statutory Authority: ORS 678.800

Duties and Responsibilities: The board oversees the practice of Nursing Home Administrators and Residential Care Facility Administrators in the State of Oregon. It has nine members appointed by the governor and confirmed by the Senate.

Respiratory Therapist and Polysomnographic Technologist Licensing

Web: oregon.gov/oha/ph/hlo/pages/board-rtpt.aspx
Statutory Authority: ORS 688.800–688.995
Duties and Responsibilities: The board oversees the practices of respiratory therapists and polysomnographic technologists in Oregon. It has seven members appointed by the governor and subject to confirmation by the Senate.

Sex Offender Treatment

Web: oregon.gov/oha/ph/hlo/pages/board-sex-offender-treatment.aspx
Statutory Authority: ORS 675.360–675.410
Duties and Responsibilities: The board oversees the practices of clinical and associate sex offender therapists in Oregon. It has seven members appointed by the governor.

Health Policy and Analytics Division

Address: 500 Summer St. NE, E-64, Salem 97301
Phone: 503-378-2978
Fax: 503-945-5872
Web: oregon.gov/oha/hpa/pages/index.aspx
Contact: Ali Hassoun, Interim Director
Duties and Responsibilities: The division collects and analyzes health data from throughout the state and makes reports and recommendations to OHA leaders, the governor and Legislature based on that data. The division also provides support to the Health Policy Board, Medicaid Advisory Committee, Health Care Workforce Committee and others. The chief medical officer supports the work of many programs and committees that are part of the health transformation effort, including the Patient Centered Primary Care Home program, Transformation Center and Health Evidence Review Commission.

Health Systems Division

Address: 500 Summer St. NE, E49, Salem 97301
Phone: 503-945-5772; 800-527-5772
Contact: Margie Stanton, Director
Duties and Responsibilities: The division manages the Oregon Health Plan, Oregon's Medicaid program, which covers more than 1.1 million Oregonians. It also manages the statewide

behavioral health system, working to integrate addiction services and mental health care with the state's physical health system. The division oversees the Children's Wraparound Program, which works with the state's coordinated care organizations to ensure that children with special needs receive integrated care.

Public Employees' Benefit Board

Address: 500 Summer St. NE, E89, Salem 97301
Phone: 503-373-1102
Fax: 503-373-1654
Email: inquiries.pebb@dhsoha.state.or.us
Web: oregon.gov/oha/pebb
Contact: Ali Hassoun, Director
Statutory Authority: ORS 243.125
Duties and Responsibilities: The board designs, contracts and administers benefits for state employees, including medical and dental coverage, life, accident, disability and long-term care insurance and flexible spending accounts. The board also offers health care insurance options for retirees not yet eligible for Medicare.

Public Health Division

Address: 800 NE Oregon St., Suite 930, Portland 97232
Phone: 971-673-1222
Fax: 971-673-1229
Email: health.webmaster@dhsoha.state.or.us
Web: public.health.oregon.gov
Contact: Rachael Banks, Public Health Director
Statutory Authority: ORS Chapters 97, 431–475, 624
Duties and Responsibilities: The division improves lifelong health for Oregonians by promoting health and preventing the leading causes of death, disease and injury in the state. The division assesses the public's health through data collection and uses that information to develop policies and programs that support improved health outcomes. They oversee health promotion and prevention activities, health care facility licensing, environmental health regulation, public health emergency preparedness, epidemiological outbreak investigations and the Oregon State Public Health Laboratory.

The division works with local health departments, tribes, community organizations, health care providers, coordinated care organizations and other partners. The Public Health Advisory Board and other advisory committees provide guidance to the division.

State Hospital, Oregon

Salem Address: 2600 Center St. NE, Salem 97301

Phone: 503-945-2800; Toll free 1-800-544-7078
Junction City Address: 29398 Recovery Way, Junction City 97448
Phone: 541-465-2554; Toll free 1-877-851-7330
Web: oregon.gov/oha/osh
Statutory Authority: ORS 179.321
Contact: Dolly Matteucci, Superintendent
Duties and Responsibilities: The Oregon State Hospital provides in-patient psychiatric care for adults from all over Oregon, with campuses in Salem and Junction City. Their primary goal is to help people recover from their illnesses and return to the community.

HIGHER EDUCATION COORDINATING COMMISSION

Address: 3225 25th St. SE, Salem 97302
Phone: 503-378-5690
Fax: 503-302-3529
Email: info.hecc@hecc.oregon.gov
Web: oregon.gov/highered
Contact: Ben Cannon, Executive Director; Ramona Rodamaker, Deputy Executive Director
Statutory Authority: ORS Chapter 350
Duties and Responsibilities: The Higher Education Coordinating Commission (HECC) is the state commission and agency working to improve equitable access to and success in higher education and workforce training for Oregonians statewide. The HECC coordinates funding and policy for postsecondary education and training and convenes partners across the public and private higher education arena. HECC is a 15-member volunteer commission appointed by the governor. The HECC state agency supports the commission and includes eight offices led by the executive director. Its authorities include advising the Legislature and governor, providing one strategic vision for Oregon higher education planning, funding and policy to meet state goals; authorizing postsecondary programs and degrees; administering key Oregon financial aid programs, collaborating with partners to oversee programs and administer funding to increase employment opportunities, supporting streamlined academic pathways such as transfer pathways; workforce training and support for businesses; and evaluating and reporting the success of higher education efforts.

In addition to the six offices listed below, the HECC has an Office of the Executive Director, responsible for executive leadership, commission administration, communications, legislative affairs, equity leadership, human resources and internal auditing; and an Office of Operations, responsible for support to all HECC offices with budget, procurement, payroll, accounting and information technology.

Academic Policy and Authorization, Office of

Address: 3225 25th St. SE, Salem 97302
Phone: 503-947-5716
Fax: 503-378-8395
Web: oregon.gov/highered/apa
Contact: Veronica Dujon, Director
Statutory Authority: ORS Chapters 340, 345, ORS 348.594–348.615, ORS Chapters 350, 352
Duties and Responsibilities: This office oversees two primary areas: the quality, integrity and diversity of private postsecondary programs in Oregon for the benefit of students and consumers; and public university academic policy coordination, evaluation of public university contributions to State objectives for higher education, mission review and approval, and academic program approval. The private postsecondary units consist of the Office of Degree Authorization (ODA) and the Private Career Schools Licensing Unit (PCS), responsible for policy and regulatory action that affect certain private institutions serving Oregonians. The ODA authorizes degree-granting private institutions, offering academic programs in Oregon or to Oregon students from outside the state. The PCS Licensing Unit licenses private career schools in Oregon. Both units also provide educational leadership, technical assistance, student and consumer protection and serve as conveners of private institutions and partners in Oregon. The office is also the portal entity for distance education offerings in Oregon through the multistate State Authorization Reciprocity Agreement. The public university academic policy unit provides academic coordination related to Oregon's seven public universities, including coordination of policy for transfer initiatives and high school partnerships, student complaints, statewide initiatives and other legislative directives to enhance postsecondary pathways and student success. The office supports the work of the Oregon Transfer Council to build streamlined credit pathways from community colleges to universities.

Community Colleges and Workforce Development, Office of

Address: 3225 25th St. SE, Salem 97302
Phone: 503-979-5162
Fax: 503-378-8434
Email: ccwd.info@hecc.oregon.gov
Web: oregon.gov/highered/ccwd
Contact: Donna Lewelling, Director
Statutory Authority: ORS Chapter 350
Duties and Responsibilities: The office provides coordination, leadership and resources to Oregon's

network of 17 locally-governed community colleges, as well as adult basic skills providers, high school equivalency program providers and other partners. It has responsibility for coordinating community college programs and services, developing biennial budget recommendations for the community college funding and capital projects, allocation of state funding, coordination of the academic approval processes and reporting to the Legislature. The office provides statewide administration of the Adult Education and Family Literacy components of the federally funded Workforce Investment and Opportunity Act; the Carl Perkins Career and Technical Education Act programs; Oregon High School Equivalency General Educational Development (GED®) programs and the work of the Oregon Transfer Council.

Postsecondary Finance and Capital, Office of

Address: 3225 25th St. SE, Salem 97302
Phone: 503-559-9075
Fax: 503-378-8395
Email: info.hecc@hecc.oregon.gov
Web: oregon.gov/highered/pfc
Contact: Jim Pinkard
Statutory Authority: ORS Chapter 350, ORS 350.075
Duties and Responsibilities: This office provides fiscal coordination related to Oregon's public postsecondary institutions, including financial planning, fiscal reporting and analysis, capital bond funding administration, the allocation of state funding to public post-secondary institutions and biennial budget recommendations. The office prepares budget recommendations to the commission for the Public University Support Fund, Public University State Programs, Public University Statewide Public Services and Community College Support Fund, as well as university and community college capital investments.

Research and Data, Office of

Address: 3225 25th St. SE, Salem 97302
Phone: 971-283-4714
Fax: 503-378-8395
Email: info.hecc@hecc.oregon.gov
Web: oregon.gov/highered/rd
Contact: Amy Cox, Director
Statutory Authority: ORS Chapter 350
Duties and Responsibilities: The office collects, analyzes and reports research and data on postsecondary education and training, including data on students and their characteristics, courses, enrollments, academic performance, completion and academic pathways to comply with state and federal reporting requirements and to inform decisions on the postsecondary education enterprise. The office also includes administration of the State Longitudinal Data System, which links data about

students as they move from kindergarten through postsecondary education and employment.

Student Access and Completion, Office of

Address: 3225 25th St. SE, Salem 97302
Phone: 541-687-7400; Toll-free: 1-800-452-8807
Fax: 541-687-7414
Email: osac@hecc.oregon.gov
Web: oregonstudentaid.gov
Contact: Juan Báez-Arévalo, Director
Statutory Authority: ORS 341.522, ORS Chapter 348, ORS Chapter 350, ORS 352.287
Duties and Responsibilities: The Office of Student Access and Completion (OSAC) administers several financial aid programs for students attending college or other postsecondary education and training programs. These include state and federally-funded grants and privately-funded scholarships. In addition, OSAC promotes college access and affordability for Oregonians through ASPIRE, a college and career mentoring program, and statewide community outreach events.

OSAC's largest financial aid programs are the Oregon Opportunity Grant (OOG), the Oregon Promise Grant and the OSAC Scholarship application. The OOG is the state's largest need-based grant program and helps low-income students afford eligible Oregon colleges and universities. Oregon Promise is for recent high school and GED® test graduates to help cover tuition costs at any Oregon community college. The OSAC Scholarship application includes more than 600 scholarships, which students can access through the single application. These scholarships target a variety of student groups and are funded by private donors, foundations and employers. OSAC also administers grant programs supporting specific populations such as foster youth, Oregon tribal students, students raising children and Oregon National Guard members.

Workforce Investments, Office of

Address: 3225 25th St. SE, Salem 97302
Phone: 971-345-1133
Fax: 503-947-1246
Email: info.hecc@hecc.oregon.gov
Web: oregon.gov/highered/owi
Contact: Julia Steinberger, Interim Director
Statutory Authority: ORS Chapters 350, 660
Duties and Responsibilities: The Office of Workforce Investments (OWI) is one of several state entities focused on employment opportunities, skill attainment and work-related training statewide. OWI works in partnership with the Oregon Employment Department, Department of Human Services, Commission for the Blind and others to provide leadership to Oregon's workforce system. It is responsible for convening partnerships, supporting and providing technical assistance to the Workforce and Talent Development Board (WTDB) and local workforce development boards, and implementing the governor's vision and the WTDB strategic plan.

The HECC administrates federally-funded programs authorized by Titles I and II of the U.S. Workforce Innovation and Opportunity Act. This includes Youth, Adult and Dislocated Worker programs and Federal Discretionary grants. The HECC provides program and fiscal oversight as well as policy direction and technical assistance to state and local partners.

The OWI administers and supports Oregon Youth Works including the Oregon Youth Corps, OregonServes, and the STEM Investment Council.

The North Capitol Mall Office Building in Salem houses the central offices of the Housing and Community Services Department. (Oregon State Archives scenic photo)

HOUSING AND COMMUNITY SERVICES DEPARTMENT

Address: 725 Summer St. NE, Suite B, Salem 97301-1266
Phone: 503-986-2000
Email: housinginfo@oregon.gov
Web: oregon.gov/ohcs
Contact: Andrea Bell, Executive
Statutory Authority: ORS 456.555
Duties and Responsibilities: Oregon Housing and Community Services (OHCS) provides resources for Oregonians to reduce poverty and increase access to stable housing. The agency serves Oregonians across the housing continuum, including preventing homelessness, providing housing stability support, financing the building and preservation of affordable housing, and encouraging homeownership.

Housing Stability Council, Oregon

Address: 725 Summer St. NE, Suite B, Salem 97301-1266
Phone: 503-986-2005
Fax: 503-986-2132

Email: housinginfo@oregon.gov
Web: oregon.gov/ohcs/hsc
Contact: Cheyloa Chase, Executive Assistant to the Executive Director
Statutory Authority: ORS 456.567
Duties and Responsibilities: The nine-mmember council is the governing body for OHCS. The council approves affordable housing projects, sets direction on statewide housing policy and serves as an advisory body to the agency. The council also serves as a public body for engagement with stakeholders, housing advocates and the public on affordable housing issues and policy decisions.

Central Services Division

Address: 725 Summer St. NE, Suite B, Salem 97301-1266
Phone: 503-986-2000
Fax: 503-986-2020
Email: housinginfo@oregon.gov
Web: oregon.gov/ohcs
Contact: Caleb Yant, Agency Deputy Director
Statutory Authority: ORS 456.555
Duties and Responsibilities: The division includes the following sections: Human Resources, which delivers personnel services and consultation to agency staff and management; Administrative Services, which manages agency facilities and operations; the Controller, which delivers compliance in all financial areas across the agency in the Finance, Budget and Procurement-Contracts sections; and Information Technology, which manages technology-related interactions and resources for the agency.

The division provides essential services to support the agency's leadership and workforce to achieve the department's mission. Work performed in this division ensures accountability, transparency and stewardship of resources.

Affordable Rental Housing Division

Address: 725 Summer St. NE, Suite B, Salem 97301-1266
Phone: 503-986-2000
Fax: 503-986-2020
Email: housinginfo@oregon.gov
Web: oregon.gov/ohcs
Contact: Natasha Detweiler-Daby, Director
Statutory Authority: ORS 446.525–446.543, 456.515–456.723, 458.210–458.310, 458.600–458.650, 458.655–458.665
Duties and Responsibilities: The division administers federally and state-funded, affordable rental housing resources. The goal is to increase the availability of safe, decent and affordable housing for Oregonians with low incomes. This includes the development of new affordable rental units and the acquisition, rehabilitation and preservation of existing affordable rental units; provision of project-based rent assistance and services to state-funded permanent supportive housing investments; long-term maintenance of affordable rental housing through asset management and compliance; and administration of the HUD portfolio of project-based rent-assisted projects.

Homeownership Division

Address: 725 Summer St. NE, Suite B, Salem 97301-1266
Phone: 503-986-2000
Fax: 503-986-2020
Email: housinginfo@oregon.gov
Web: oregon.gov/ohcs
Contact: Emese Perfecto, Director
Statutory Authority: ORS 456.587, 458.505–458.530, 458.600–458.650
Duties and Responsibilities: The division administers federal and state programs to assist low- to moderate-income Oregonians with homeownership. Across its four sections, the division provides homebuyer and homeowner financial education, down payment assistance, funding for health and safety repairs, mediation for manufactured and marina community members and foreclosure prevention through counseling and mortgage assistance. Additionally, the division facilitates the financing and development of homes for homeownership.

Housing Stabilization Division

Address: 725 Summer St. NE, Suite B, Salem 97301-1266
Phone: 503-986-2000
Fax: 503-986-2020
Email: housinginfo@oregon.gov
Web: oregon.gov/ohcs
Contact: Jill Smith, Director
Statutory Authority: ORS 456.587, 458.505–458.530, 458.600–458.650
Duties and Responsibilities: The division funds community partners across the state. Funding includes shelters, navigation centers, rental assistance, energy bill payment and weatherization assistance. The division also funds anti-poverty programs such as Individual Development Accounts to provide stability and opportunity through wealth-building.

Disaster Recovery and Resilience Division

Address: 725 Summer St. NE, Suite B, Salem 97301-1266
Phone: 503-986-2000
Fax: 503-986-2020
Email: housinginfo@oregon.gov
Web: oregon.gov/ohcs
Contact: Ryan Flynn, Director

Statutory Authority: HB 5006 (2021 session), Sections 278 & 279

Duties and Responsibilities: The division manages state and federal funds to support fire recovery for low-and moderate-income households and communities. Division activities include assistance with intermediate housing (provided through contracts with local agencies, such as community action agencies), support for permanent affordable housing development (both rental and homeownership) and grants for individuals to complete their housing recovery through rebuilding or replacement of lost homes.

Public Affairs Division

Address: 725 Summer St. NE, Suite B, Salem 97301-1266

Phone: 503-986-2000

Fax: 503-986-2020

Email: housinginfo@oregon.gov

Web: oregon.gov/ohcs

Contact: Amy Nehl, Director

Statutory Authority: ORS 456.555

Duties and Responsibilities: The division includes Federal Planning, Community Outreach, Government Relations and Communications. Public Affairs is the primary division that engages with the public, stakeholders, elected officials and the media.

HUMAN SERVICES, DEPARTMENT OF

Address: 500 Summer St. NE, Salem 97301

Phone: 503-945-5944

Fax: 503-581-6198

Email: communications.dhs@odhsoha.oregon.gov

Web: oregon.gov/dhs

Contact: Fariborz Pakseresht, Director

Statutory Authority: ORS 409.010

Duties and Responsibilities: The Oregon Department of Human Services (ODHS) works to help Oregonians in their own communities achieve safety, well-being and independence. The Director's Office is responsible for overall leadership, policy development and administrative oversight of programs, staff, and offices in ODHS. These functions are coordinated with the Office of the Governor, Oregon Legislature, other state and federal agencies, partners and stakeholders.

Key functions include Financial Services, Human Resources, Data and Research, Legislative Relations, Communications, Tribal Relations, Equity and Multicultural Services, Resilience and Emergency Management, Federal Financial Policy, Governor's Advocacy Office, and Internal Audits. The director's office also coordinates operations that support service delivery, including Contracts and Procurement, Facilities Services, Imaging and Records Management Services, Background Checks, Information Support Systems, Business Information Supports, Publications and Creative Services, Payment Accuracy and Recovery and Program Integrity.

Governor's Advocacy Office

Address: 500 Summer St. NE, E17, Salem 97301

Phone: 503-945-6904

Fax: 503-378-6532

Contact: ohso.info@dhsoha.state.or.us

Duties and Responsibilities: The office handles client complaints related to ODHS services. It operates independently in investigations and reports directly to the governor by providing a quarterly report on the status of the complaints. Office staff works closely with field and central office staff, program staff, the Office of the Governor, key stakeholders and the ODHS Director's Office.

Aging and People with Disabilities, Office of

Address: 500 Summer St. NE, E02, Salem 97301

Phone: 503-945-5600

Fax: 503-373-7823; 1-855-673-2372

Contact: Nakeshia Knight-Coyle, Interim Director

Web: adrcforegon.org

Duties and Responsibilities: The Office of Aging and People with Disabilities (APD) provides services to older adults and people with disabilities. This includes opportunities for community living, employment, family support and long-term services.

APD serves about 3,500 older adults who seek to remain in their homes through Oregon Project Independence; more than 35,000 older adults and people with disabilities per month who receive long-term care services paid through Medicaid; about 212,000 people seeking Older Americans Act services; about 180,000 people in need of direct financial support services; and more than 43,000 individuals who receive a Social Security Disability determination. Also, more than 44,000 people live in APD-licensed long-term care facilities. Additionally, individuals in Oregon make about 50,000 calls seeking to report abuse, neglect or request information and referral services from Adult Protective Services.

APD program units include the Aging and Disability Resource Connection (ADRC) of Oregon, a collaborative public-private partnership that streamlines consumer access to the aging and disability service delivery system. The ADRC is free and provides information and assistance that helps people make informed decisions about their care.

Employees from both APD local offices and Area Agencies on Aging throughout Oregon provide direct consumer services and determine eligibility of older adults and people with disabilities for services including Medicaid long-term care.

Deaf and Hard of Hearing Services Program, Oregon

Address: 500 Summer St. NE, E02, Salem 97301
Email: odhhs.info@odhsoha.oregon.gov
Web: oregon.gov/dhs/seniors-disabilities/sppd/pages/odhhs.aspx
Statutory Authority: ORS 410.740

Governor's Commission on Senior Services

Address: 500 Summer St. NE, E02, Salem 97301
Phone: 503-855-8438
Email: gcss.info@odhsoha.oregon.gov
Web: oregon.gov/dhs/seniors-disabilities/advisory/gcss
Contact: Adam Hansen
Statutory Authority: ORS 410.320–410.340

Medicaid Long-Term Care Quality and Reimbursement Advisory Council

Address: 500 Summer St. NE, E02, Salem 97301
Email: council.info@odhsoha.oregon.gov
Web: oregon.gov/dhs/seniors-disabilities/advisory
Contact: Max Brown
Statutory Authority: ORS 410.550–410.555

Oregon Disabilities Commission

Address: 500 Summer St NE, E02, Salem 97301
Phone: 1-800-282-8096
Email: oregondisabilities.commission@odhsoha.oregon.gov
Web: oregon.gov/dhs/seniors-disabilities/advisory/odc
Contacts: Joseph Lowe and Ryan Kibby
Statutory Authority: ORS 185.110–185.200
Duties and Responsibilities: The Oregon Disabilities Commission (ODC) is a 15-member, governor-appointed commission within ODHS. Commission members are broadly representative of major public and private agencies with experience or demonstrated interest in the needs of individuals with disabilities. Most members are people with disabilities. The ODC acts as a coordinating link between and among public and private organizations serving individuals with disabilities.

ODC identifies and hears the concerns of individuals with disabilities and uses the information to prioritize public policy issues; publicizes the needs and concerns of individuals with disabilities related to the full achievement of economic, social, legal and political equity; and educates and advises the ODHS, the governor, Legislature and appropriate state agency administrators about potential improvements.

Child Welfare Division

Address: 500 Summer St. NE, E48, Salem 97301
Phone: 503-945-5600
Fax: 503-373-7032
Web: oregon.gov/dhs/children
Contact: Aprille Flint-Gerner, Interim Director
Duties and Responsibilities: The Child Welfare Division is part of a larger statewide social safety net system that works to support families and communities. This may include providing economic support, enhancing parenting skills, helping people with their housing needs and employment goals, providing health and behavioral services, helping treat alcohol and substance use disorders and ensuring child safety and family well-being.

The division helps families access resources within their natural support networks and the service provider community.

Child Welfare Advisory Committee

Web: oregon.gov/dhs/children/advisory
Statutory Authority: ORS 418.005
Duties and Responsibilities: The 21-member committee counsels the agency on the development and administration of the policies, programs and practices.

Indian Child Welfare Act Advisory Committee

Web: oregon.gov/dhs/children/advisory
Duties and Responsibilities: The committee advises, consults with and makes recommendations to the leadership of the Oregon Department of Human Services on policy, programs, practice and data that impact Indian children. The children are members or eligible for membership in one or more of the nine federally recognized tribes in Oregon. It also includes Indian children who are placed in Oregon, members of or eligible for membership in tribes outside of Oregon and are involved or at risk of involvement in the child welfare system in the state.

Refugee Child Welfare Advisory Committee

Web: oregon.gov/dhs/children/advisory
Statutory Authority: ORS 418.941
Duties and Responsibilities: The 14-member committee assists and advises ODHS in the development and administration policies, programs and practices related to refugee children and families.

Office of Developmental Disabilities Services

Address: 500 Summer St. NE, E09, Salem 97301
Phone: 503-945-5811; Toll-free:1-800-282-8096; TTY: 800-282-8096
Email: odds.info@odhsoha.oregon.gov
Contact: Lilia Teninty, Director
Duties and Responsibilities: The Office of Developmental Disabilities Services (ODDS) supports persons with intellectual and developmental disabilities (I/DD) to live as full participants in their communities.

Individuals eligible for services must have an intellectual disability (IQ of 75 or below) that originates prior to age 18 or a developmental disability that originates prior to age 22. These disabilities must significantly impact a person's ability to function independently. Some persons with I/DD may also have significant medical or behavioral health needs. Most individuals with I/DD meet Medicaid financial eligibility requirements.

Most I/DD program services are administered under the Medicaid State Plan Community First Choice Option. Case management and employment services are available through traditional, home- and community-based service waivers.

Oregon Council on Developmental Disabilities

Address: 2475 SE Ladd Ave., Portland 97214
Phone: 971-304-4191
Email: info@ocdd.org
Contact: Leslie Sutton, Executive Director
Statutory Authority: 42 USC 15001
Duties and Responsibilities: The council's mission is to advance social and policy change so people with developmental disabilities, their families and communities may live, work, play and learn together.

The council is made up of self-advocates, family members and representatives of community organizations that provide services and supports to people with developmental disabilities. Council members also include representatives of state agencies that receive federal funding on behalf of people with developmental disabilities. The governor appoints council members to serve up to two consecutive, four-year terms.

The council ensures people with developmental disabilities and family members are included in legislative and policy discussions about issues that impact their lives. Council members work together to determine goals and objectives in the five-year state plan, allocate funds to state plan activities and annually review the council's progress. The council is supported by full-time staff who are charged with implementing the state plan.

Self-Sufficiency Programs

Address: 500 Summer St. NE, E48, Salem 97301
Phone: 503-945-5600
Fax: 503-373-7032
Contact: Jana McLellan, Interim Director
Duties and Responsibilities: Self-Sufficiency Programs (SSP) provide benefits and services to individuals and families experiencing low or no income. SSP benefits and services are intended to help people find stability and end multi-generational poverty.

The benefits offered through SSP are Employment Related Day Care; Oregon Health Plan; Refugee Program; Supplemental Nutrition Assistance Program (SNAP); SNAP related programs, such as the Employment and Training Program and Able-Bodied Adults without Dependents Program; Temporary Assistance for Domestic Violence Survivors (TA-DVS); Temporary Assistance for Needy Families (TANF); TANF-related programs, such as the Job Opportunity and Basic Skills Program and Family Support and Connections; and Youth Services.

Family Services Review Commission

Address: 500 Summer St. NE, E48, Salem 97301
Email: marc.jolin@multco.us
Contact: Jana McLellan, Self-Sufficiency Programs Interim Director
Statutory Authority: ORS 411.075

Vocational Rehabilitation

Address: 500 Summer St. NE, E87, Salem 97301
Phone: 503-945-5880 or 877-277-5880
Email: keith.s.ozols@dhsoha.state.or.us
Web: oregon.gov/dhs/employment/vr
Contact: Keith Ozols, Director
Statutory Authority: ORS 344.530
Duties and Responsibilities: Vocational Rehabilitation (VR) helps individuals with disabilities get and keep a job that matches their skills, interests and abilities. VR staff work in partnership with the community and businesses to develop employment opportunities and provide individualized services to each individual person for their employment success.

VR's Youth Services programs support youth and young adults with disabilities as they transition to the workplace or postsecondary education. VR also serves businesses to find ready-to-work applicants with a wide range of skills and abilities and to access work incentive programs that can help businesses save money.

State Independent Living Council

Address: 500 Summer St. NE, E87, Salem 97301
Phone: 503-945-6621

Email: brooke.wilson@dhsoha.state.or.us
Web: oregon.gov/dhs/seniors-disabilities/silc
Contact: Brooke Wilson, Executive Director
Statutory Authority: Exec. Order 94-12
Duties and Responsibilities: The council includes people with disabilities and community partners who plan, coordinate and evaluate the design and goals of the Independent Living Program in the Federal Rehabilitation Act. The program services are consumer-directed and designed to help individuals with disabilities achieve personal goals for independence and participate in all aspects of community life.

State Rehabilitation Council

Address: 500 Summer St. NE, E87, Salem 97301
Phone: 971-707-8853 or 877-277-0513
Email: kaire.l.downin@dhsoha.state.or.us
Web: oregon.gov/dhs/employment/vr/src
Contact: Kaire Downin, SRC Coordinator
Statutory Authority: ORS 344.735
Duties and Responsibilities: The Oregon State Rehabilitation Council (SRC) is a group of consumers, advocates and business and community representatives who advise Vocational Rehabilitation (VR) in developing, implementing and reviewing employment services for Oregonians with disabilities.

LAND CONSERVATION AND DEVELOPMENT, DEPARTMENT OF

Address: 635 Capitol St. NE, Suite 150, Salem 97301-2540
Phone: 503-373-0050
Web: oregon.gov/lcd
Contact: Brenda Ortigoza Bateman, Director
Statutory Authority: ORS Chapters 92, 195, 196, 197, 215, 222, 227, 268, 308
Duties and Responsibilities: The Department of Land Conservation and Development (DLCD) assists with implementation of Oregon's statewide land use program in cities and counties all over the state. The program provides tools communities can use to address climate change, housing supply, natural hazards, equity and long-term sustainability. DLCD provides help through technical assistance; partnerships with cities and counties; direct and applied grant assistance; and partnerships with state development agencies (Housing and Community Services, the Department of Transportation and Business Oregon) and natural resource agencies (Agriculture, Forestry, Water Resources, State Lands, Environmental Quality and Fish and Wildlife) as well as Oregonians. The department is guided in policy development by the Land Conservation and Development Commission (LCDC) whose members are appointed by the governor.

Community Services Division

Address: 635 Capitol St. NE, Suite 150, Salem 97301-2540 (Regional Offices in Bend, Eugene, Medford and Portland)
Phone: 503-856-6935
Contact: Gordon Howard, Manager
Duties and Responsibilities: The division administers grant programs for local governments and provides technical land use planning assistance to local government planners and officials, the general public and interest groups. The division reviews local comprehensive plan amendments and provides expertise on a wide range of subjects related to city and county comprehensive plans. Staff in this division include regional representatives serving local governments around the state as well as specialists in urban planning, rural resources and economic development. The division also includes a team of housing planners who help local governments plan for sufficient supply and affordability of housing in Oregon.

Grants Advisory Committee

Address: 635 Capitol St. NE, Suite 150, Salem 97301-2540
Phone: 503-856-6935
Contact: Gordon Howard
Statutory Authority: ORS 197.639
Duties and Responsibilities: The committee is appointed by the Land Conservation and Development Commission. It advises the commission and the department on equitable and appropriate allocation of grants, technical assistance funding and other issues assigned by the commission.

Ocean and Coastal Services Division

Address: 635 Capitol St. NE, Suite 150, Salem 97301-2540 (Offices in Newport, Tillamook and Portland)
Phone: 503-934-0034
Web: oregon.gov/lcd/ocmp
Contact: Patty Snow, Manager
Duties and Responsibilities: The division oversees Oregon's federally designated coastal program providing grants and technical assistance to coastal communities. The division provides assistance related to four statewide coastal planning goals and helps communities adopt local plans that address coastal hazards. It also oversees development of Oregon's Territorial Sea Plan in cooperation with other agencies and conducts federal consistency reviews for federal projects and permits proposed in the Oregon coastal zone. Coastal staff also coordinate Oregon's Climate Change Adaptation Framework with 24 of Oregon's state agencies.

Executive

Planning Services Division

Address: 635 Capitol St. NE, Suite 150, Salem 97301-2540
Phone: 503-798-6419
Contact: Matt Crall, Manager
Duties and Responsibilities: The division oversees specialized planning programs, including the Transportation and Growth Management Program, Floodplain Management and Natural Hazards Planning, Measure 49 Services and Every Mile Counts. Staff in this division coordinate State Recovery Function 1: Community Planning in Oregon's disaster recovery planning.

Other Groups:

Citizen Involvement Advisory Committee

Address: 635 Capitol St. NE, Suite 150, Salem 97301-2540
Phone: 503-383-6648
Contact: Sadie Carney
Statutory Authority: ORS 197.160
Duties and Responsibilities: The committee was established to advise LCDC and local governments on matters pertaining to community engagement in all phases of the land use planning process. It is an advisory body with no explicit or implied authority over any local government or state agency. The committee has up to ten volunteer members who serve four-year terms, including one from each of Oregon's six congressional districts and four who may be chosen at-large.

Local Officials Advisory Committee

Address: 635 Capitol St. NE, Suite 150, Salem 97301-2540
Phone: 503-373-0050
Contact: Esther Johnson
Statutory Authority: ORS 197.165
Duties and Responsibilities: LCDC appoints the committee for the purpose of promoting mutual understanding and cooperation between LCDC, DLCD and local governments in implementing and improving the statewide land use planning system. The committee is comprised of persons serving as city or county elected officials and reflects the geographic diversity of the state.

LAND USE BOARD OF APPEALS

Address: 775 Summer St. NE, Suite 330, Salem 97301-1283
Phone: 503-373-1265
Web: oregon.gov/luba
Email: luba.support@luba.oregon.gov
Statutory Authority: ORS 197.810

Duties and Responsibilities: The Land Use Board of Appeals (LUBA) has exclusive jurisdiction to review appeals of land use decisions made by cities, counties, districts and state agencies. LUBA's decisions are reviewable by appeal to the Court of Appeals. LUBA's secondary mission is to publish its orders and opinions which citizens, decision-makers and participants in land use processes can use to guide future land use decision-making.

LUBA is the first tribunal of its kind in the United States. It is a governor-appointed, three-member board, subject to confirmation by the Oregon Senate, serving four-year terms. Board members must be members of the Oregon State Bar. The board is assisted by two administrative staff and two staff attorneys.

LANDSCAPE ARCHITECT BOARD, STATE

Address: 707 13th St. SE, Suite 114, Salem 97301
Phone: 503-589-0093
Fax: 503-485-2947
Email: oslab.info@bgelab.oregon.gov
Web: oregon.gov/landarch
Contact: Christine Valentine, Administrator
Statutory Authority: ORS 671.310–671.459
Duties and Responsibilities: The board is charged with regulating landscape architecture practice in the state. They review complaints related to registrant practices and unlicensed practices and set examination, education and experience standards for landscape architect licensure. The board includes four Oregon registered landscape architects and three public members. It is served by two staff filling the roles of administrator (executive director) and registration specialist.

Landscape architects licensed in other states or jurisdictions can apply for registration in Oregon but must meet all of the board's standards. Firms that provide landscape architectural services must also be registered. More than 540 landscape architects are registered to practice in Oregon. Approximately 200 firms are registered with the board.

LANDSCAPE CONTRACTORS BOARD, STATE

Address: 2111 Front St. NE, Suite 2-101, Salem 97301
Phone: 503-967-6291
Fax: 503-967-6298
Email: lcb.info@lcb.oregon.gov
Web: oregon.gov/lcb
Contact: Annie von Domitz, Administrator
Statutory Authority: ORS 671.510–671.760
Duties and Responsibilities: The board is a semi-independent agency responsible for regulating land-

scape construction work in Oregon. The agency is overseen by a board of seven individuals, appointed by the governor, who serve a maximum of six years. Five of the seven members are from the landscaping industry and two represent the general public.

The board promotes consumer protection and contractor competency in the Oregon landscape contracting industry through five major program areas: Examinations, Licensing, Enforcement, Claims/Dispute Resolution and Education. The Board employs five staff who administer over 3,000 licensees.

The State Library Building in Salem houses the central offices of the Oregon State Library. (Oregon State Archives scenic photo)

LIBRARY, STATE

Address: 250 Winter St. NE, Salem 97301-3950
Phone: 503-378-4243
Fax: 503-585-8059
Web: oregon.gov/library
Contact: Wendy Cornelisen, State Librarian
Statutory Authority: ORS Chapter 357
Duties and Responsibilities: The library provides information services to state government, library services to Oregonians who are print-disabled, and leadership, grants and other assistance to improve library service for all Oregonians. The State Library of Oregon Library Advisory Board has nine members from across the state appointed by the governor. The library is organized into an operations division and three program divisions.

The Operations Division provides services and support to State Library staff members and volunteers. The division manages the agency finances, provides information technology support, communications support, and recruits, trains and supports volunteers providing services throughout the agency.

The Government Information and Library Services Division provides library services to state employees and to persons on official state business, including research assistance, professional development, training on using library services and

access to both physical and electronic resources. Collections include federal and state government publications and a comprehensive collection of materials about Oregon. The division also provides Oregonians permanent access to state government publications by maintaining a digital state documents repository.

The Library Support and Development Services Division provides leadership and consulting assistance to approximately 1,600 libraries of all types across the state, coordinating statewide library services in partnership with other libraries; providing equal access to information resources for K–12 students through the Oregon School Library Information System; collecting and reporting library statistics; and administering state and federal library grant programs.

The Oregon Talking Book and Braille Library is the Oregon Regional Library for the Library of Congress' National Library Service for the Blind and Print Disabled. as well as the Oregon Center for the Book. Oregonians with a print disability, which includes visual, physical and reading impairments, are eligible for free library services. Braille, audio books, descriptive videos and magazines are available for free through the mail or via download to eligible readers.

LIQUOR AND CANNABIS COMMISSION, OREGON

Address: 9079 SE McLoughlin Blvd., Portland 97222-7355
Phone: 503-872-5000; Toll-free: 1-800-452-6522
Fax: 503-872-5266
Web: oregon.gov/olcc
Contact: Steve Marks, Executive Director
Statutory Authority: ORS Chapters 459A, 471, 472, 473, 475C
Duties and Responsibilities: The Oregon Liquor and Cannabis Commission (OLCC) provides education about and enforcement of liquor and marijuana laws. OLCC places emphasis on addressing alcohol and marijuana sales to minors and visibly intoxicated people.

OLCC manages and distributes distilled spirits; licenses and regulates businesses that sell and serve alcohol; and trains and issues permits for alcohol servers. The agency licenses, regulates, and issues permits for marijuana workers and tracks adult-use cannabis in Oregon's recreational marijuana industry. The OLCC is also responsible for administration and compliance of Oregon's Bottle Bill.

Seven citizen commissioners set policy for the OLCC. The agency also relies on advisory committees, government officials and citizens to guide its decision-making. OLCC employs 347 people, is headquartered in Portland and has four regional and numerous satellite offices throughout the state. Through the sale of distilled spirits and beer and wine privilege fees, OLCC is the third-largest revenue generator for the state, with a 2019–2021 biennium value of over $1.5 billion.

LONG-TERM CARE OMBUDSMAN, OFFICE OF THE

Address: 830 D St. NE, Salem 97301
Phone: 503-378-6533; Toll-free: 1-800-522-2602; TTY: 711
Fax: 503-373-0852
Email: ltco.info@oregon.gov
Web: oregon.gov/ltco
Contact: Fred Steele, Long-Term Care Ombudsman and Director
Statutory Authority: ORS 441.402–441.419
Duties and Responsibilities: The office includes three programs: Long-Term Care Ombudsman, the Residential Facilities Ombudsman and the Oregon Public Guardian. The office works to protect individual rights, promote independence and ensure quality of life for Oregonians living in long-term care and residential facilities and for Oregonians with decisional limitations.

The agency's two Ombudsman programs investigate and resolve complaints on behalf of residents, using a network of trained and certified volunteer ombudsmen. The Oregon Public Guardian program serves as a court-appointed, surrogate decision maker for adults incapable of making decisions about themselves and their affairs, and who have no one else to serve as their guardian or conservator.

LOTTERY, OREGON STATE

Address: PO Box 12649, Salem 97309
Phone: 503-540-1000; TTY: 503-540-1068
Fax: 503-540-1168
Email: lottery.webcenter@state.or.us
Web: oregonlottery.org
Contact: Michael Wells, Interim Director
Statutory Authority: ORS Chapter 461
Duties and Responsibilities: Oregonians created the Oregon Lottery in 1984. The lottery's mission, is to "Operate a lottery with the highest standards of security and integrity to earn maximum profits for the people of Oregon commensurate with the public good." Oregon's lottery is both a public trust and a market-driven business, with about 500 employees.

ORS 461.500 provides that at least 84% of total annual revenues be returned to the public, with at least 50% being returned as prizes and the remainder used for designated public purposes. The remaining 16% of annual revenues are available for the payment of administrative expenses. Lottery administrative expenses are currently at just under 4% of revenue, which makes the agency entirely self-funded.

The Oregon Lottery is the second largest revenue producer for the state, following income tax revenues. Lottery dollars help support public education, economic development, state parks and watershed enhancement, as well as veterans' affairs and Outdoor School. The Oregon Lottery funds problem gambling treatment and awareness. Over the years, Lottery players have been paid over $46 billion in prizes.

MARINE BOARD, STATE

Address: 435 Commercial St. NE, # 400, Salem 97301; Mail: PO Box 14145, Salem 97309-5065
Phone: 503-378-8587
Fax: 503-378-4597
Email: marine.board@state.or.us
Web: oregon.gov/osmb
Contact: Larry Warren, Director
Statutory Authority: ORS Chapter 830
Duties and Responsibilities: The agency is responsible for titling and registering motorboats, registering outfitter/guides, co-managing aquatic invasive species inspection stations throughout the state, licensing charter boats and issuing Waterway Access Permits for non-motorized boats 10 feet long and longer.

The five-member volunteer board adopts boating regulations to promote safety, reduce conflict, preserve traditional boat uses and protect the environment. The agency has 38 staff and four primary program areas: Boating Safety, Policy and Environmental, Registration and Boating Facilities.

The revenue generated helps fund the agency and contracts with county sheriff's offices and the Oregon State Police for statewide marine patrol services. Funding also provides boating facility grants and engineering services to eligible applicants to develop and maintain boat ramps, parking, restrooms and temporary moorage facilities. Additionally, funding supports environmental and educational programs to promote environmental stewardship and boating safety.

MASSAGE THERAPISTS, STATE BOARD OF

Address: 610 Hawthorne Ave. SE, Suite 220 Salem 97301
Phone: 503-365-8657
Fax: 503-385-4465
Email: obmt.info@state.or.us
Web: oregon.gov/obmt
Contact: Robert Ruark, Executive Director
Statutory Authority: ORS 687.011–687.991
Duties and Responsibilities: The mission of the board is to protect the public by regulating and monitoring the practice of massage therapy in

Oregon. The board regulate conduct for massage establishments; issues licenses; refuses, revokes or suspends licenses; and establishes requirements for massage schools.

MEDICAL BOARD, OREGON

Address: 1500 SW 1st Ave., #620, Portland 97201-5847
Phone: 971-673-2700
Fax: 971-673-2670
Email: info@omb.oregon.gov
Web: oregon.gov/omb
Contact: Nicole Krishnaswami, JD, Executive Director
Statutory Authority: ORS Chapter 677
Duties and Responsibilities: The board regulates of the practice of medicine in Oregon. The agency licenses and regulates medical doctors (MD), doctors of osteopathic medicine (DO), doctors of podiatric medicine (DPM), physician assistants (PA) and acupuncturists (LAc).

The 14-member board includes physicians, a physician assistant, and three members of the public. The board sets qualifications for licensure and grants licenses to applicants who meet those requirements. It investigates complaints and disciplines licensees who violate state law (the Medical Practice Act). The board also supports rehabilitation and education for licensees in an effort to promote access to quality care for all Oregonians. The board oversees more than 23,000 licensees and is staffed with 41 employees.

The State Office Building in Portland houses the central offices of the Board of Medical Imaging. (Oregon State Archives scenic photo)

MEDICAL IMAGING, BOARD OF

Address: 800 NE Oregon St., Suite 1160A, Portland 97232
Phone: 971-673-0215
Fax: 971-673-0218
Email: obmi.Info@state.or.us
Web: oregon.gov/obmi

Contact: Stacy Katler. DVM, Executive Director
Statutory Authority: ORS 688.405–688.605, 688.915
Duties and Responsibilities: The board licenses and oversees over 5,700 medical imaging technologists who are qualified to practice radiography, radiation therapy, sonography, nuclear medicine and magnetic resonance imaging (MRI). In addition, the board oversees the educational requirements and issues permits for over 400 limited x-ray machine operators. Members of the board are appointed by the governor and confirmed by the Senate for three-year terms. There are 12 board members, including four physicians, three public members and five medical imaging licensees who represent each of the five medical imaging modalities. The board has four employees.

MENTAL HEALTH REGULATORY AGENCY

Address: 3218 Pringle Rd. SE, Suite 130, Salem 97302-6309
Phone: 503-378-4154
Fax: 503-374-1904
Web: oregon.gov/mhra
Contact: Charles J. Hill, Executive Director
Statutory Authority: ORS 675.160–675.178
Duties and Responsibilities: The agency provides administrative and regulatory oversight to the Board of Psychology and the Board of Licensed Professional Counselors and Therapists. Agency functions include budgeting, recordkeeping, staffing, contracting, procedure and policymaking, and performance and standard setting for the regulated boards. The boards maintain their own separate authority for complaint investigations, regulatory enforcement, establishment and collection of fees, licensing criteria and practice standards.

Counselors and Therapists, Oregon Board of Licensed Professional

Address: 3218 Pringle Rd. SE, Suite 120, Salem 97302-6312
Phone: 503-378-5499
Email: lpct.board@oregon.gov
Web: oregon.gov/oblpct
Contact: Charles J. Hill, Executive Director
Statutory Authority: ORS 675.705–675.835
Duties and Responsibilities: The board protects Oregonians seeking mental health counseling and marriage and family therapy services. They determine if individuals meet initial and continuing education, training and examination standards for licensure and issues new and renewal licenses to those who are qualified. The board also develops policies and standards for professional practice and

enforces disciplinary action against counselors, therapists and interns who engage in misconduct or are incompetent. It issues civil penalties to individuals practicing in Oregon without a license or engaging in misrepresentation. The eight members of the board are appointed by the governor and confirmed by the Senate for three-year terms. Board members may be appointed for up to two terms.

Psychology, Oregon Board of

Address: 3218 Pringle Rd. SE, Suite 130, Salem 97302-6309
Phone: 503-378-4154
Email: psychology.board@oregon.gov
Web: oregon.gov/psychology
Contact: Charles J. Hill, Executive Director
Statutory Authority: ORS 675.010–675.150
Duties and Responsibilities: The board determines if individuals meet appropriate education, training and examination standards for licensure and issues licenses to those who are qualified. They develop policies and standards for professional practice and enforces disciplinary action against psychologists, psychologist associates and residents who engage in misconduct or are incompetent. It also issues civil penalties to individuals practicing in Oregon without a license or engaging in misrepresentation. The nine members of the board are appointed by the governor and confirmed by the Senate for three-year terms. Board members may be appointed for up to two terms.

MILITARY DEPARTMENT, OREGON

Address: 230 Geer Dr. NE, Salem 97301;
Mail: PO Box 14350, Salem 97309-5047
Phone: 971-355-3606
Web: oregon.gov/omd
Statutory Authority: ORS 396.305
Duties and Responsibilities: The Oregon Military Department (OMD) was the first state agency created in Oregon. It administers, equips and trains the Oregon Army and Air National Guard. During peacetime and for natural disasters, the department responds to the governor in support of the citizens of Oregon. During wartime, the Oregon Army and Air National Guard can be federalized in support of national missions as directed by the U.S. president.

Command Group

Address: PO Box 14350, Salem 97309-5047
Phone: 971-355-3602
Email: omd_tag@omd.oregon.gov
Web: oregon.gov/omd/ong/pages/
command-group.aspx
Contact: Major General Michael E. Stencel, Adjutant General

Duties and Responsibilities: The Command Group consists of the Adjutant General Deputy Director; Joint Force Headquarters, including the Assistant Adjutants General for support and operations; and the Land and Air Component Commanders. The group administers all components of the Oregon Military Department/National Guard in cooperation with the governor and Legislature.

Deputy Director, State Affairs

Phone: 971-355-3605
Email: omd_agdd@omd.oregon.gov
Contact: Christopher Shaver, Deputy Director
Duties and Responsibilities: The deputy director functions as liaison to the governor's office, Oregon's senators, representatives, congressional delegates and other governmental agencies. This position provides supervisory oversight of the state division offices within OMD, including the Adjutant General's Comptroller, Installations, Personnel, and Oregon's Youth Challenge Program.

Installations Division

Address: PO Box 14350, Salem 97309-5047
Phone: 971-355-4127
Contact: Todd Farmer, Director
Duties and Responsibilities: The division provides and maintains quality installations to support the missions of the Oregon National Guard and the citizens of Oregon. They provide facilities for localized and statewide emergencies, train and housing soldiers and equipment, and provide environmental support for tactical training and the execution of federal and state missions. The division's rental program allows community groups and private parties to use armories on an as-available basis.

Public Affairs Office

Address: AGPA, PO Box 14350, Salem 97309-5047
Phone: 971-355-3527
Email: omd_agpa@omd.oregon.gov
Contact: Stephen Bomar, Director
Duties and Responsibilities: The office supports the Adjutant General's communication plan and is responsible to support information efforts for all Oregon Army and Air National Guard public, community and media relations including community outreach, social media, print, video and graphic design efforts.

Youth Challenge Program

Address: 23861 Dodds Rd., Bend 97701
Phone: 541-317-9623
Web: oycp.com
Contact: Dan Radabaugh, Director
Duties and Responsibilities: The Oregon National Guard Youth Challenge Program is a statewide accredited, public, alternative high school

that serves 16- to 18-year-old high school dropouts. The program is guided by military principles, structure and discipline and consists of two phases. During the residential phase, cadets (students) live on-site for five months and attend school, where they earn credits to return to high school and earn their GED or high school diploma. The post-residential phase is a mandatory 12-month mentoring period during which cadets work with mentors from their hometowns.

MORTUARY AND CEMETERY BOARD, STATE

Address: 800 NE Oregon St., Suite 430, Portland 97232-2195
Phone: 971-673-1500
Fax: 971-673-1501
Email: mortuary.board@omcb.oregon.gov
Web: oregon.gov/omcb
Contact: Chad Dresselhaus, Executive Director
Statutory Authority: ORS 97.170, 97.931, 692.300, 692.415
Duties and Responsibilities: The board ensures all of Oregon's death care facilities are properly licensed and they regulate the practice of individuals and facilities engaged in the care, preparation, processing, transportation and final disposition of human remains. Death care services are provided by approximately 2,000 licensed practitioners and facilities throughout the state. The board includes 11 members appointed by the governor and confirmed by the Senate. Seven full-time employees provide support and assistance to the board.

The board also provides administration for the Indigent Disposition Program which provides funeral establishments with reimbursement for costs incurred while providing services for the disposition of indigent decedents.

NATUROPATHIC MEDICINE, OREGON BOARD OF

Address: 800 NE Oregon St., Suite 407, Portland 97232
Phone: 971-673-0193
Fax: 971-673-0226
Email: naturopathic.medicine@obnm.oregon.gov
Web: oregon.gov/obnm
Contact: Mary-Beth Baptista, Executive Director
Statutory Authority: ORS Chapter 685
Duties and Responsibilities: The mission of the board is to regulate the practices of naturopathic medicine for the protection of the public. The board licenses over 1,200 naturopathic physicians. The seven-member board includes two public members

and five licensed naturopathic physicians. Three full-time staff support the board's work.

The board administers licensure examinations, conducts background checks, approves educational opportunities for licensees, investigates complaints and issues discipline when appropriate.

NORTHWEST POWER AND CONSERVATION COUNCIL

Address: 851 SW 6th Ave., Portland 97204-1347
Phone: 503-229-5171
Web: nwcouncil.org
Fax: 503-229-5173
Oregon Council Members: Ginny Burdick, Louie Pitt, Jr.
Oregon Staff Contacts: Leann Bleakney, energy policy analyst; Cathy Kellon, fish and wildlife policy analyst
Statutory Authority: ORS 469.805
Duties and Responsibilities: The Northwest Power and Conservation Council is an interstate group with members from Oregon, Washington, Montana and Idaho. Each state has two governor-appointed representatives. The council has two major planning functions: develop a fish and wildlife program to protect, mitigate and enhance fish and wildlife populations affected by the development of the federal Columbia River hydropower system; and develop a 20-year regional power plan. The council updates these plans on a roughly five-year rotation. The council strives to ensure, through public participation, an affordable and reliable energy system while enhancing fish and wildlife in the Columbia River Basin. In addition to the eight council members, there is a staff of approximately 40, located in offices spread throughout the four states.

NURSING, OREGON STATE BOARD OF

Address: 17938 SW Upper Boones Ferry Rd., Portland 97224-7012
Phone: 971-673-0685
Fax: 971-673-0684
Email: oregon.bn.info@osbn.oregon.gov
Web: oregon.gov/osbn
Contact: Ruby R. Jason, MSN, RN, NEA-BC, Executive Director
Statutory Authority: ORS 678.010–678.445
Duties and Responsibilities: The Oregon State Board of Nursing (OSBN) regulates nursing practice and education. It oversees the licensure, certification and compliance of the approximately 100,000 registered nurses, licensed practical

nurses, nursing assistants and advanced practice nurses in Oregon.

The nine OSBN board members are appointed by the governor and include a mix of public members and nursing professionals. They represent a variety of nursing practice settings and geographic locations and serve three-year terms. The OSBN meets monthly and may hold special meetings if necessary. The OSBN employs a staff of about 50 who provide customer service and assist the board in carrying out its mission.

OCCUPATIONAL THERAPY LICENSING BOARD

Address: 800 NE Oregon St., Suite 407, Portland 97232
Phone: 971-673-0198
Fax: 971-673-0226
Email: nancy.schuberg@otlb.oregon.gov
Web: oregon.gov/otlb
Contact: Nancy Schuberg, Executive Director
Statutory Authority: ORS 675.210–675.340
Duties and Responsibilities: The board regulates the practice of occupational therapy. They investigate complaints and take appropriate action; make and enforce laws and rules regarding occupational therapy practice, establish continuing education requirements, process applications and issue licenses and renewals; and collect fees and authorize disbursements of funds. The board includes five volunteer members: two occupational therapists, one occupational therapy assistant and two public members. Each member is appointed by the governor and may serve up to two four-year terms.

OPTOMETRY, OREGON BOARD OF

Address: 1500 Liberty St. SE, Suite 210, Salem 97302
Phone: 971-701-1194 (Exec. Dir); 971-701-1603 (Admin Coor)
Fax: 503-914-5142
Email: shelley.g.sneed@obo.oregon.gov
Web: oregon.gov/obo
Contact: Shelley Sneed, Executive Director
Statutory Authority: ORS Chapter 683
Duties and Responsibilities: The board works to protect Oregonians from the dangers of unqualified and improper practice of optometry. There are five governor-appointed members: four are licensed optometrists and one is a public member. Members serve three-year terms and oversee the agency and its functions. The board is assisted by two full-time staff who help board members enforce the agency's laws and rules. There are currently about 1,200 active and inactive licensed optometrists in Oregon.

Oregonians can submit online complaints to the board for review if they believe an optometrist has breached Oregon law or given an improper standard of care. The board does not handle fee disputes.

PARKS AND RECREATION DEPARTMENT, STATE

Address: 725 Summer St. NE, Suite C, Salem 97301
Phone: 503-986-0707; Campground Reservations: 1-800-452-5687; Parks Information: 1-800-551-6949
Fax: 503-986-0794
Email: Lisa.sumption@oprd.oregon.gov
Web: oregon.gov/oprd; stateparks.oregon.gov
Contact: Lisa Sumption, Director
Statutory Authority: ORS Chapters 97, 358, 390
Duties and Responsibilities: The Oregon Parks and Recreation Department (OPRD) exists to protect and provide outstanding natural, scenic, recreational, cultural and historic places for the enjoyment and education of present and future generations.

OPRD oversees one of the most popular state park systems in the nation—more than 250 properties providing more than 50 million visits a year—and manages other key recreation and heritage programs: Oregon's stunning public ocean shore; scenic waterways and bikeways; the State Historic Preservation Office; archaeological services; historic cemeteries; and all-terrain vehicle safety certifications. OPRD programs serve Oregon communities directly with grants and advice related to outdoor recreation, museums and historic "Main Street" revitalization.

OPRD has about 595 full-time equivalent staff, with a large number of employees being seasonal. The governor-appointed State Parks and Recreation Commission sets OPRD's policy direction.

Historic Preservation Office, State

Address: 725 Summer St. NE, Suite C, Salem 97301
Phone: 503-986-0690
Fax: 503-986-0793
Email: chrissy.curran@oprd.oregon.gov
Web: oregon.gov/oprd/hcd/shpo/pages/index.aspx
Contact: Christine Curran, Heritage Division Director and Deputy State Historic Preservation Officer
Statutory Authority: ORS 358.612
Duties and Responsibilities: The office creates opportunities for individuals, organizations and local governments to be directly involved protect-

ing significant historic and cultural resources. They provide archaeological services, grant programs, planning assistance, tax incentive programs and federal programs such as the National Register of Historic Places. In addition, the Certified Local Government Program and the Oregon Main Street Network collaborate with communities to develop comprehensive revitalization strategies based on a community's unique assets, character and heritage.

The OPRD director is Oregon's designated State Historic Preservation Officer.

Historic Preservation, State Advisory Committee on

Address: 725 Summer St. NE, Suite C, Salem 97301
Phone: 503-602-2468
Fax: 503-986-0793
Email: robert.olguin@oprd.oregon.gov
Web: oregon.gov/oprd/oh/pages/
　Commissions.aspx
Contact: Robert Olguin, robert.olguin
　@oprd.oregon.gov
Statutory Authority: ORS 358.622
Duties and Responsibilities: The committee is a nine-member group that reviews nominations to the National Register of Historic Places. The members are professionally recognized in the fields of history, architecture, archaeology and other related disciplines. The committee conducts three meetings a year at sites around Oregon.

Heritage Commission, Oregon

Address: 725 Summer St. NE, Suite C, Salem 97301
Phone: 503-877-8834
Fax: 503-986-0793
Email: katie.henry@oprd.oregon.gov
Web: oregon.gov/oprd/oh/pages/
　Commissions.aspx
Contact: Katie Henry, Coordinator
Statutory Authority: ORS 358.570
Duties and Responsibilities: The nine-member, governor-appointed commission works as a connector and catalyst for hundreds of organizations and thousands of Oregonians devoted to preserving and interpreting Oregon's heritage resources. Its programs include the Heritage and Museum Grant Programs, technical assistance for heritage organizations and an annual conference. It also gives annual Heritage Excellence Awards and designates Oregon Heritage Traditions, All-Star Communities and Statewide Celebrations.

Historic Cemeteries, Oregon Commission on

Address: 725 Summer St. NE, Suite C, Salem 97301
Phone: 503-986-0685

Fax: 503-986-0793
Email: kuri.gill@oprd.oregon.gov
Web: oregon.gov/oprd/oh/Pages/
　Commissions.aspx
Contact: Kuri Gill, Coordinator
Statutory Authority: ORS 97.772–97.784
Duties and Responsibilities: The commission maintains a list of historic cemeteries and gravesites in Oregon. It works to promote public education on the significance of historic cemeteries and to provide financial and technical assistance for restoring, improving and maintaining their appearance.

Outdoor Recreation, Office of

Address: 725 Summer St. NE, Suite C, Salem 97301
Phone: 503-510-8259
Fax: 503-986-0792
Email: cailin.obrienfeeney@oregon.gov
Web: oregon.gov/orec
Contact: Cailin O'Brien-Feeney
Statutory Authority: ORS 390.233
Duties and Responsibilities: The office pulls support from public, nonprofit and commercial organizations to protect and expand access, promote participation and protect the natural resources upon which outdoor recreation depends. Through policy coordination, research and reporting, and development of common strategies across the public and private sectors, the office works to ensure outdoor recreation delivers personal, community and economic benefits in perpetuity.

PAROLE AND POST-PRISON SUPERVISION, STATE BOARD OF

Address: 1321 Tandem Ave. NE, Salem 97301
Phone: 503-945-9009
Fax: 503-373-7558
Web: oregon.gov/boppps
Contact: Dylan Arthur, Executive Director; Greta Lowry, Board Chair
Statutory Authority: ORS Chapters 144, 163A
Duties and Responsibilities: This five-member board is appointed by the governor to 4-year terms. The governor decides the chair and vice chair for the board. State law requires at least one member be a woman and members can serve a maximum of two terms. Staff consists of an executive director, a supervising executive assistant and 22 support staff. The board works closely with the Department of Corrections and local community corrections agencies to protect the public and reduce the risk of repeat criminal behavior through incarceration and community supervision decisions based on applicable laws, victims' interests, public safety and recognized principles of offender behavioral change.

Executive

The board imposes prison terms and makes release decisions on offenders whose criminal conduct occurred prior to November 1, 1989. It sets conditions of supervision for all offenders being released from prison, imposes sanctions for violations of supervision and determines whether discharge from parole supervision is compatible with public safety. Discharge from supervision for offenders sentenced under sentencing guidelines occurs automatically upon expiration of the statutory period of post-prison supervision.

The board is responsible for assessing and classifying all registered sex offenders in Oregon into a notification level, based on risk to re-offend. This system improves community education and notification of high-risk registered sex offenders in Oregon (Level 3) and introduces opportunities for low-risk offenders (Levels 2 and 1) to be reclassified to a lower notification level and receive relief from registration if they meet statutory requirements.

PATIENT SAFETY COMMISSION, OREGON

Address: PO Box 285, Portland 97207-0285
Phone: 503-928-6158
Fax: 503-224-9150
Email: info@oregonpatientsafety.org
Web: oregonpatientsafety.org
Contact: Valerie Harmon, Executive Director
Statutory Authority: ORS 442.820–442.835, Oregon Laws 2013, Chapter 5
Duties and Responsibilities: The Oregon Patient Safety Commission (OPSC) is a semi-independent state agency supporting healthcare facilities and providers. OPSC's mission is to reduce the risk of patient harm and encourage a culture of patient safety. OPSC fulfills its mission through two programs.

The Patient Safety Reporting Program collects and analyzes information from healthcare facilities about serious patient harm or near misses. It shares the broader lessons learned to support facilities in refining their best practices and preventing future harm.

The Early Discussion and Resolution process helps connect patients (or a family member) who experience harm and their healthcare provider so that they can speak candidly about the harm that occurred, work toward reconciliation and contribute to safeguarding others from similar harm.

OPSC's body of work is independent of any regulatory functions and seeks to advance, support and encourage patient safety in Oregon.

PHARMACY, STATE BOARD OF

Address: 800 NE Oregon St., Suite 150, Portland 97232-2162
Phone: 971-673-0001
Fax: 971-673-0002

Email: pharmacy.board@bop.oregon.gov
Web: oregon.gov/pharmacy
Contact: Joseph Schnabel, Executive Director
Statutory Authority: ORS Chapters 475, 689
Duties and Responsibilities: The nine member board is appointed by the governor with five licensed pharmacists, two public members and two pharmacy technicians. There are 22 staff members led by the executive director. The board is responsible for regulating the practice of pharmacy and the manufacture and distribution of drugs through licensure, registration and compliance. Currently, there are 30,081 licensees, including individuals and drug outlets.

In 2018, the Public Health and Pharmacy Formulary Advisory Committee was established by law. This seven-member committee is appointed by the governor and consists of two physicians, two advanced practice nurses and three pharmacists. The committee recommends protocols and a formulary of drugs and devices to the board that a pharmacist may prescribe and dispense to a patient pursuant to a diagnosis by a qualified health care practitioner.

PHYSICAL THERAPY, OREGON BOARD OF

Address: 800 NE Oregon St., Suite 407, Portland 97232-2187
Phone: 971-673-0200
Fax: 971-673-0226
Web: oregon.gov/pt
Contact: Michelle Sigmund-Gaines, Executive Director
Statutory Authority: ORS 688.160
Duties and Responsibilities: The board regulates the practice of physical therapy in Oregon. They establish and regulate professional standards of practice ensuring physical therapists and physical therapist assistants are properly educated; hold valid/current licenses; practice within their scope of practice and continue to receive ongoing training throughout their careers. The board issues licenses, promulgates rules, monitors continuing competency, investigates complaints, issues civil penalties for violations and may revoke, suspend or impose probation on a licensee or place limits on a licensee's practice.

The board regulates over 6,000 active licensees and is made up of eight volunteer members: five physical therapists, one physical therapist assistant and two public members. Each member is appointed by the governor and confirmed by the Senate to serve a four-year term. A board member may be reappointed to one subsequent term.

The Oregon State Police Office Building in Salem houses the State Police and Fire Marshal. (Oregon State Archives scenic photo)

POLICE, DEPARTMENT OF STATE

Address: 3565 Trelstad Ave. SE, Salem 97317
Phone: 503-378-3720
Fax: 503-378-8282
Email: ask.osp@state.or.us
Web: oregon.gov/osp
Contact: Terri Davie, Superintendent
Statutory Authority: ORS 181A.015
Duties and Responsibilities: The Oregon State Police (OSP) is a multi-disciplined organization charged with protecting the people, wildlife and natural resources in Oregon. The mission of the Oregon State Police is to serve all people with a priority of safeguarding life, property and natural resources by building upon a diverse, professional and trustworthy workforce.

OSP enforces traffic laws on the state's roadways, investigates and solves crimes, conducts post-mortem examinations and forensic analysis and provides background checks and law enforcement data. OSP regulates gaming, the handling of hazardous materials, fire codes, educates the public on fire safety and enforces fish, wildlife and natural resource laws.

Other specialized programs and services include drug investigation, state emergency response coordination, state Fire Marshal Service and Conflagration Act coordination, coordination of federal grants for public safety issues, coordination of Criminal Justice Information Standards, Special Weapons and Tactics (SWAT) and serving as the point of contact to the National Office of Homeland Security. The department employs more than 1,300 sworn and professional staff.

Forensic Science and Pathology Bureau

Address: 3565 Trelstad Ave. SE, Salem 97317
Phone: 503-378-3720
Fax: 503-363-5475
Email: osp.forensics@state.or.us

Web: oregon.gov/osp/programs/forensics
Contact: Major Alex Gardner

Forensic Services Division

Statutory Authority: ORS 181A.150
Duties and Responsibilities: The bureau is a nationally accredited forensic laboratory system serving all state and local law enforcement agencies, medical examiners
and prosecuting attorneys in Oregon. It performs forensic analysis on criminal cases for the defense upon a court order. The bureau is Oregon's only full-service forensic laboratory system. Analysts provide technical assistance and training, evaluate and analyze evidence, interpret results and provide expert testimony related to the full spectrum of physical evidence recovered from crime scenes.

Medical Examiner's Office

Contact: Dr. Sean Hurst, Medical Examiner
Statutory Authority: ORS Chapter 146
Duties and Responsibilities: The office provides direction and support to the state death investigation program. The medical examiner manages all aspects of the state medical examiner program and has responsibility for technical supervision of county offices in each of Oregon's 36 counties.

Gaming and Business Services Bureau

Address: 3565 Trelstad Ave. SE, Salem 97317
Phone: 503-378-3720
Fax: 503-363-5475
Email: ask.osp@state.or.us
Contact: Major Mike Turner

Gaming Enforcement Division

Statutory Authority: ORS 181A.090
Duties and Responsibilities: The division consists of the Lottery Gaming Section and Tribal Gaming Section. Both work to ensure all gaming activities are conducted with fairness, integrity, honesty and security.

Patrol Field Operations Bureau

Address: 3565 Trelstad Ave. SE, Salem 97317
Phone: 503-378-3720
Fax: 503-378-8282
Email: ask.osp@state.or.us
Contact: Major Casey Codding
Duties and Responsibilities: This bureau is responsible for North West Region Operations, South West Region Operations, East Region Operations, Special Weapons and Tactics and Mobile Response Team.

Police Services Bureau

Address: 3565 Trelstad Ave. SE, Salem 97317
Phone: 503-378-3720
Fax: 503-378-8282
Email: ask.osp@state.or.us
Contact: Major Ted Phillips
This bureau is responsible for the following divisions:

Criminal Investigations Division

Web: oregon.gov/osp/programs/pages/cid.aspx
Contact: Captain Ryan Martin
Statutory Authority: ORS 181A.145
Duties and Responsibilities: The division is the statewide investigative resource for the Department of State Police. The division's Major Crimes Section, Drug Enforcement Section and Sex Offender Registration Unit work in conjunction with other state police divisions.

Detectives are strategically located across the state to support local law enforcement with major criminal investigations and to serve on interagency teams. They also provide primary criminal investigative services on state property and at state institutions.

Fish and Wildlife Division

Email: osp.fwd@state.or.us
Web: oregon.gov/osp/programs/fw
Contact: Captain Casey Thomas
Statutory Authority: ORS 181A.015
Duties and Responsibilities: The division enforces works the laws and regulations related to Oregon's fish and wildlife resources and the habitats upon which they depend. Other important services include public safety and enforcement of criminal and traffic laws.

Patrol Services Division

Email: ask.osp@state.or.us
Web: oregon.gov/osp/programs/pages/psd.aspx
Contact: Captain Cord Wood
Statutory Authority: ORS Chapter 181A
Duties and Responsibilities: The division provides a uniform presence and law enforcement services throughout the state. They are primarily responsible for crash and crime reduction and other transportation safety issues. They also respond to emergency calls-for-service on Oregon's state and interstate highways.

Public Safety Services Bureau

Address: 3565 Trelstad Ave. SE, Salem 97317
Phone: 503-378-3720
Fax: 503-378-8282
Email: ask.osp@state.or.us
Web: oregon.gov/osp/programs/cjis
Contact: Commander Rebecca David
Statutory Authority: ORS 181A.280
Duties and Responsibilities: This bureau is responsible for Northern and Southern Command Centers, Bureau Operations – Technology and Computer Services, Central Records Section, Criminal Justice Information Services, Sex Offender Registration and School Safety Tip Line.

The systems provide information-sharing services for security background checks and for assisting law enforcement and criminal justice agencies in their investigations. The unit also includes the Oregon State Athletic Commission charged with protecting the public and participants involved in ring sports.

State Fire Marshal, Office of

Address: 3565 Trelstad Ave. SE, Salem 97317
Phone: 503-378-3473
Fax: 503-373-1825
Email: oregon.sfm@state.or.us
Web: oregon.gov/osp/programs/sfm
Contact: Mariana Ruiz-Temple, State Fire Marshal
Statutory Authority: ORS 476.020
Duties and Responsibilities: This office is responsible for Fire and Life Safety Education, Emergency Response Services, Regulatory Services Unit, Fire & Life Safety Services and Deputy Fire Marshals. The office works to protect citizens, their property and the environment from fire and hazardous materials.

Workforce Development and Support Bureau

Address: 3565 Trelstad Ave. SE, Salem 97317
Phone: 503-378-3720
Fax: 503-378-8282
Email: ask.osp@state.or.us
Contact: Major Andy Heider
Duties and Responsibilities: This bureau is responsible for Professional Standards, Agency Services, Training and Recruitment and Health, Wellness and Resiliency.

PSYCHIATRIC SECURITY REVIEW BOARD

Address: 610 SW Alder St., Suite 420, Portland 97204
Phone: 503-229-5596
Fax: 503-224-0215
Email: psrb@psrb.oregon.gov
Web: oregon.gov/prb
Contact: Alison Bort, J.D., Ph.D., Executive Director
Statutory Authority: ORS 161.327, Chapter 163A, 426.701, 426.702, 419C.530
Duties and Responsibilities: The Psychiatric Security Review Board supervises individuals who successfully asserted the insanity defense (Guilty

Except for Insanity or GEI) to a criminal charge. The board also supervises youth who successfully assert the insanity defense (Responsible Except for Insanity or REI) and certain civil commitments. It has been designated by the Legislature as the "relief" authority for two different populations: GEI sex offenders who request relief from sex offender registration and those who are barred from possessing a firearm due to a mental health determination (e.g. civil commitment, competency, GEI) who request restoration of firearm rights.

The board includes adult and juvenile panels. Each consists of five members, appointed by the governor and confirmed by the Senate for four-year terms. The adult panel is made up of of a psychiatrist and a psychologist experienced in the criminal justice system, an experienced parole and probation officer, an attorney experienced in criminal trial practice and a member of the general public. The juvenile panel has a child psychiatrist, child psychologist, parole and probation officer experienced in juvenile criminal justice, an attorney experienced in juvenile criminal trial practice and a member of the general public. The agency employs 12 staff.

PUBLIC EMPLOYEES RETIREMENT SYSTEM

Address: 11410 SW 68th Pkwy., Tigard 97223; PO Box 23700, Tigard 97281-3700
Phone: 888-320-7377; TTY: 503-603-7766
Fax: 503-598-0561
Web: oregon.gov/pers
Contact: Kevin Olineck, Director
Statutory Authority: ORS 237.350–237.980, 238.005–238.750, 238A.005–238A.475, 243.401–243.507
Duties and Responsibilities: The Public Employees Retirement System (PERS) administers retirement benefits for Oregon's public sector workers (state, local government and school district employees). PERS serves more than 228,000 active/inactive members, 156,000 benefit recipients, and 906 employers. The system pays approximately $4.86 billion in benefits annually; about $4.08 billion is paid to Oregon residents. Those in-state payments support an estimated 36,914 jobs in Oregon. Investment income provided 74.2% of total PERS revenue since 1970, with member contributions providing 4.3%, and employer contributions providing 21.5%. Nearly 30% of PERS members are currently eligible to retire.

Public Employees Retirement Board
Address: PO Box 23700, Tigard 97281-3700
Phone: 888-320-7377
Contact: Sadhana Shenoy, Chair
Statutory Authority: ORS 238.630

Oregon Savings Growth Plan Advisory Committee
Address: 800 Summer St. NE, Salem 97310
Phone: 888-320-7377
Web: oregon.gov/pers/osgp
Contact: Colin Benson, Chair

PUBLIC RECORDS ADVOCATE, OFFICE OF THE
Address: 2850 SW Cedar Hills Blvd, #1121, Beaverton 97005
Phone: 503-871-9036
Email: todd.albert@pra.oregon.gov
Web: oregon.gov/pra
Contact: Todd Albert, Public Records Advocate
Statutory Authority: ORS 192.461-477
Duties and Responsibilities: The Public Records Advocate is appointed by the Public Records Advisory Council. They provide advice, policy development and facilitated dispute resolution services at the request of government bodies or public records requesters regarding the Oregon public records law, provides public employee and public trainings on requirements and best practices. They serve as Executive Director and voting member of the Public Records Advisory Council.

Public Records Advisory Council
Address: 2850 SW Cedar Hills Blvd, #1121, Beaverton 97005
Phone: 503-871-9036
Contact: Todd Albert, Public Records Advocate
Statutory Authority: ORS 192.481-483
Duties and Responsibilities: The Public Records Advisory Council (PRAC) are bipartisan public records experts representing state and local governments, the media, the public and public sector workforce. The PRAC meets at least once every six months and at other times and places specified by the call of the chair or a majority of the members.

The PRAC selects and appoints the Public Records Advocate and surveys state agency, other jurisdictions and public body practices and procedures for receiving public records requests. The committee identifies the existence of records responsive to requests, gathers and discloses responsive records, determines fee estimates and imposes or waives fees. They are also responsible for determining and applying exemptions from required disclosure, identifying inefficiencies and inconsistencies in application of the public records law and making recommendations on changes in law, policy or practice related to public records and transparency in government. The committee makes recommendations on the role of the Public Records Advocate as facilitator in disputes between custodians of public records and public record requesters. They report to the governor and Legislature by December 1 of each even-numbered year the findings of the council, including recommendations for legislation.

PUBLIC SAFETY STANDARDS AND TRAINING, DEPARTMENT OF

Address: 4190 Aumsville Hwy. SE, Salem 97317
Phone: 503-378-2100
Fax: 503-378-4600
Web: oregon.gov/dpsst
Contact: Brian Henson, Acting Director
Statutory Authority: ORS 181A.355–181A.995, 206.010–206.015, 243.950–243.974, 703.010–703.325
Duties and Responsibilities: The mission of the Department of Public Safety Standards and Training (DPSST) is to cultivate excellence in public safety by developing and delivering training and upholding established professional standards. The DPSST certifies/licenses police officers, corrections officers, parole and probation officers, regulatory specialists (OLCC), telecommunicators (9-1-1), emergency medical dispatchers, criminal justice instructors, private security providers, private investigators, fire service professionals and polygraph examiners in the State of Oregon. The agency determines candidates' eligibility to run for the office of Sheriff, authorizing federal officers to make arrests pursuant to ORS 133.245 and provides staffing for the Public Safety Memorial Fund and Governor's Commission for the Law Enforcement Medal of Honor. The DPSST works with public and private safety agencies around the state to provide basic, leadership and specialized training at the 237-acre Oregon Public Safety Academy in Salem and regionally throughout the state.

DPSST is governed by a 26-member board and six discipline-specific policy committees. They serve more than 43,000 public safety constituents across the state. DPSST employs 160 full-time staff and approximately 400 part-time employees and agency-loaned instructors. They also provide staff for the board and policy committees and work with various board advisory committees and workgroups

DPSST's campus is home to the Fallen Law Enforcement Officers Memorial and the Fallen Firefighters Memorial. Memorial ceremonies for each are hosted annually to honor the officers and firefighters who have been killed in the line of duty.

Public Safety Standards and Training, Board on

Address: 4190 Aumsville Hwy. SE, Salem 97317
Phone: 503-378-2100

Web: oregon.gov/dpsst/bd
Contact: Darren Bucich, Chair; DaNeshia Barrett, Vice Chair
Statutory Authority: ORS 181A.360
Duties and Responsibilities: DPSST's overall mission is guided by this board and five discipline-specific public safety policy committees. Membership of the board is outlined in statute and provides a comprehensive representation of the constituent base.

The board and committees set standards for employment, training and certification or licensure of public safety professionals, fire service professionals, private security professionals, private investigators and polygraph examiners. Quarterlyboard and committee meetings review standards and curriculum, administrative rule changes, requests for waivers of the standards and cases addressing the denial or revocation of certification or licensure. The board and committees assist DPSST to set agency goals for the future through guidance and input regarding policy direction and strategic planning.

PUBLIC UTILITY COMMISSION

Address: PO Box 1088, 201 High St. SE, #100, Salem 97308-1088
Phone: 503-378-6600
Fax: 503-378-5743
Email: puc.consumer@state.or.us
Web: oregon.gov/puc
Contact: Michael Grant, Executive Director
Statutory Authority: ORS Chapters 756, 757, 758, 759, 772
Duties and Responsibilities: The Oregon Public Utility Commission (PUC) regulates investor-owned electric, natural gas, telephone utilities and select water companies. The PUC's mission is to ensure Oregonians have access to safe, reliable and fairly priced utility services.

The rules governing PUC proceedings and the regulatory process are set forth in Oregon Administrative Rules Chapter 860, while the PUC's Internal Operating Guidelines inform the public of its decision-making process and describes the responsibilities of the PUC. Decisions are made by the three governor-appointed commissioners during regularly scheduled public meetings.

The PUC's Residential Service Protection Fund includes the following programs: Oregon Telecommunications Relay Service allowing Oregonians who are deaf, hard of hearing, DeafBlind or have a speech disability to make and receive calls through specially trained operators; Oregon Telephone Assistance Program providing a monthly discount on phone or high-speed internet service for those eligible; Telecommunication Devices

Access Program loans providing specialized telecommunications equipment to Oregonians with a disability in hearing, vision, speech, mobility or cognition; Emergency Medical Certificates assisting Oregonians with a lenient payment arrangement if they are under a doctor's care and have medical equipment needing utility service.

Maritime Pilots, Oregon Board of

Address: 800 NE Oregon St., Portland 97232
Phone: 971-673-1530
Fax: 971-673-1531
Web: oregon.gov/puc/bmp
Contact: Tom Griffitts, Executive Director; Susan Johnson, Administrator
Statutory Authority: ORS Chapters 670, 776
Duties and Responsibilities: This board is part of the PUC for budget and administrative purposes. They protect public health, safety and welfare by ensuring only highly qualified and carefully trained persons are licensed to pilot vessels.

RACING COMMISSION, OREGON

Address: 800 NE Oregon St., Suite 310, Portland 97232
Phone: 971-673-0207
Fax: 971-673-0213
Email: connie.winn@orc.oregon.gov
Web: oregon.gov/racing
Contact: Connie Winn, Executive Director
Statutory Authority: ORS 462.210
Duties and Responsibilities: The commission regulates the pari-mutuel industry in Oregon, including horse racing, on- and off-track wagering for the good of the horses, those who work with the horses, the bettors, the licensees and the citizenry. The commission also regulates multi-jurisdictional account wagering hubs licensed in Oregon. By statute, 25% of the fees on wagering through these hubs goes to the state General Fund; the remaining 75% is used to support racing industry activities such as a commercial race meet in Grants Pass and the summer race meets in communities throughout the state.

The commission's five-member governing board is appointed by the governor and confirmed by the Senate. Terms are four years.

REAL ESTATE AGENCY

Address: 530 Center St. NE, Suite 100, Salem 97301
Phone: 503-378-4170
Fax: 503-378-2491
Email: orea.info@rea.oregon.gov
Web: oregon.gov/rea
Contact: Steve Strode, Commissioner

Statutory Authority: ORS 696.375
Duties and Responsibilities: The agency is responsible for licensing, registering and regulating real estate brokers, principal real estate brokers, property managers, escrow agents, real estate marketing organizations and membership campgrounds. It also regulates aspects of condominium filings, timeshare filings and manufactured dwelling subdivisions. The agency is managed by a real estate commissioner appointed by the governor. The commissioner is advised by the nine-person Real Estate Board. The agency serves over 28,000 licensees and registrants.

Real Estate Board

Address: 530 Center St. NE, Suite 100, Salem 97301
Phone: 503-378-4170
Fax: 503-378-2491
Email: orea.board@rea.oregon.gov
Web: oregon.gov/rea/about_us/pages/real_estate_board.aspx
Contact: Anna Higley, Deputy Commissioner
Statutory Authority: ORS 696.405
Duties and Responsibilities: The board consists of seven industry and two public members appointed by the governor. It meets at least six times a year. The board advises the real estate commissioner and the governor's office on real estate industry matters. It is also responsible for reviewing experience waiver requests and continuing education provider qualification petitions for approval.

REVENUE, DEPARTMENT OF

Address: 955 Center St. NE, Salem 97301-2555
Phone: 503-378-4988; Toll-free 800-356-4222; TTY: 800-886-7204
Fax: 503-945-8738
Email: questions.dor@oregon.gov
Web: oregon.gov/dor
Contact: Betsy Imholt, Director
Statutory Authority: ORS 305.025

The Revenue Building in Salem houses the central offices of the Department of Revenue. (Oregon State Archives scenic photo)

Duties and Responsibilities: The Oregon Department of Revenue collects the revenue that Oregon counts on. The agency has about 1,000 employees. Each biennium, more than 95% of Oregon's General Fund is attributable to the work done by the department. The department administers 65 revenue streams, including Oregon's Personal Income Tax, Corporation Excise Tax, Marijuana Retail Tax, Corporate Activity Tax, and cigarette and other tobacco tax programs.

The agency also supervises the state's property tax system and supports county property tax administration, appraises large industrial and centrally assessed properties, administers tax programs for other state agencies and local governments, including the State Transient Lodging Tax, vehicle privilege and use taxes, local marijuana taxes, and transit district taxes, and serves as the primary collections agency for executive branch agencies and state boards and commissions.

The department is headquartered in Salem, with regional offices throughout the state.

SOCIAL WORKERS, STATE BOARD OF LICENSED

Address: 3218 Pringle Rd. SE, Suite 240, Salem 97302-6310
Phone: 503-378-5735
Fax: 888-252-1046
Email: randy.harnisch@blsw.oregon.gov
Web: oregon.gov/blsw
Contact: Randy Harnisch, Executive Director
Statutory Authority: ORS 675.510–675.600
Duties and Responsibilities: Social workers in Oregon are licensed mental health professionals who work in a variety of settings from schools and social service agencies to hospitals and hospice facilities. The board was created to ensure social workers have the education and skills to do the job safely, effectively and efficiently. There are over 7,500 licensed social workers in Oregon.

The board has seven members, four who are social workers and three who represent the public. The board's office in Salem has seven staff members. Board meetings are held monthly and are open to the public.

The board offers four license types: Registered Baccalaureate Social Worker (RBSW), Licensed Master's Social Worker (LMSW), Clinical Social Work Associate (CSWA) and Licensed Clinical Social Worker (LCSW).

SPEECH-LANGUAGE PATHOLOGY AND AUDIOLOGY, STATE BOARD OF EXAMINERS FOR

Address: 800 NE Oregon St., Suite 407, Portland 97232-2162
Phone: 971-673-0220; TDD: 503-731-4031
Fax: 971-673-0226
Email: speechaud.board@bspa.oregon.gov
Web: oregon.gov/bspa
Contact: Erin K. Haag, Executive Director
Statutory Authority: ORS 681.205–681.505
Duties and Responsibilities: The board licenses and regulates the performance of approximately 3,500 audiologists, speech-language pathologists, and speech-language pathology assistants in Oregon. The office is staffed by three full-time equivalent employees and is overseen by the board of two audiologists, two speech-language pathologists, one otolaryngologist, two public members and a speech-language pathology assistant.

STATE FAIR COUNCIL

Address: 2330 17th St. NE, Salem 97301
Phone: 971-701-6573
Fax: 503-947-3206
Web: oregonstatefaircouncil.org
Contact: Kim Grewe-Powell, CEO
Statutory Authority: ORS 565.456
Duties and Responsibilities: The council oversees the Oregon State Fair and Exposition Center. Their mission is to showcase Oregon products and people; educate and communicate to Oregonians about key industries with emphasis on agriculture, forestry, technology and manufacturing; and to create an event that celebrates all of Oregon and Oregonians in an atmosphere of responsible community involvement and citizenship. The exposition center hosts the annual state fair at the end of August through Labor Day and provides a venue for meetings, concerts, trade shows and other events the rest of the year from its location in Salem.

STATE LANDS, DEPARTMENT OF

Address: 775 Summer St. NE, Suite 100, Salem 97301-1279
Phone: 503-986-5200
Fax: 503-378-4844
Email: dsl@dsl.oregon.gov
Web: oregon.gov/dsl
Contact: Vicki Walker, Director
Statutory Authority: ORS Chapter 273

Duties and Responsibilities: When Congress admitted Oregon to the Union in 1859, they granted nearly 3.4 million acres of the new state's land "for the use of schools." The State Land Board was established by the Oregon Constitution to oversee those school lands. School lands generate revenue for the Common School Fund, today a $2.2-billion fund that distributes millions of dollars to Oregon's K–12 public schools every year.

The State Land Board includes the governor, secretary of state and state treasurer.

The Department of State Lands' (DSL) manages land to benefit education. The Real Property Program manages Oregon's remaining 775,000 acres of school lands and assets to generate revenue for the Common School Fund, carrying on the department's historic responsibilities in the present day.

DSL also protects waters and wetlands. The Aquatic Resource Management Program oversees the state's removal-fill law, the federal North American Wetlands Conservation Act and use of Oregon's public waterways.

The DSL team includes just over 100 people, with offices in Salem and Bend.

South Slough National Estuarine Research Reserve

Address: PO Box 5417, 61907 Seven Devils Rd., Charleston 97420
Phone: 541-888-5558
Fax: 541-888-5559
Web: oregon.gov/dsl/ss
Contact: Bree Yednock, Manager
Statutory Authority: ORS 273.554
Duties and Responsibilities: South Slough Reserve is a 5,900-acre protected area located on the South Slough inlet of the Coos Estuary in Charleston, near Coos Bay. The reserve is managed in partnership with the Department of State Lands and the National Oceanic and Atmospheric Administration. The reserve's mission is to improve the understanding and management of estuaries and coastal watersheds in the Pacific Northwest. South Slough Reserve was the first of 29 estuarine reserves nationwide and is the only program of its kind in Oregon.

The reserve has two core areas of service: education and science. Education staff provide classes and training for a wide variety of Oregonians, including schoolchildren, science teachers, local decision-makers and professionals involved in managing estuaries and coastal watersheds. The reserve's interpretive center offers informative displays and a system of hiking and water trails. Scientists provide research data for national and regional organizations.

The reserve is guided by an eight-member, governor-appointed management commission chaired by the director of DSL. There 17 full-time staff who hosts numerous student researchers and interns on an annual basis. The Friends of South Slough, an all-volunteer nonprofit group, assists the reserve with educational and research activities and obtains grants and other funding to promote and support the reserve's programs.

TAX PRACTITIONERS, STATE BOARD OF

Address: 3218 Pringle Rd. SE, Suite 250, Salem 97302-6308
Phone: 503-378-4034
Fax: 503-585-5797
Email: tax.bd@oregon.gov
Web: oregon.gov/obtp
Contact: Laura Kardokus, Executive Director; Maime Carter, Chair
Statutory Authority: ORS 673.605–673.740
Duties and Responsibilities: The board licenses and regulates roughly 3,200 individual tax practitioners and more than 1,200 tax preparation businesses. They have seven volunteer members who serve staggered three-year terms. Six members are licensed tax consultants, and the seventh member represents the general public. Two full-time staff administer day-to-day operations.

TEACHER STANDARDS AND PRACTICES COMMISSION

Address: 250 Division St. NE, Salem 97301-1012
Fax: 503-378-4448
Email: contact.tspc@tspc.oregon.gov
Web: oregon.gov/tspc
Contact: Dr. Anthony Rosilez, Executive Director
Statutory Authority: ORS 342.350
Duties and Responsibilities: The commission advises the State Board of Education on licensure, education and performance of teachers and other matters on which the board requested assistance. They have full responsibility for educator licensure, educator licensure preparation programs and maintenance of professional standards of conduct to the commission. The commission processes approximately 20,000 licensure applications a year.

The commission members are appointed to three-year terms by the governor and confirmed by the Senate.

Executive

TOURISM COMMISSION, OREGON

Address: 319 SW Washington St., Suite 700, Portland 97204
Phone: 971-717-6205
Fax: 971-717-6215
Email: info@traveloregon.com
Web: traveloregon.com;
  industry.traveloregon.com
Contact: Todd Davidson, CEO
Statutory Authority: ORS 284.101–284.146
Duties and Responsibilities: The commission does business as Travel Oregon and is charged with strengthening tourism throughout the state. They provide information, resources and trip-planning tools that inspire travel and consistently convey the exceptional qualities of Oregon.

Travel Oregon is semi-independent and led by a nine-member governor-appointed board. They employ 47 staff members responsible for the stewardship of the state as a travel destination for domestic and international visitors. Functions include advertising campaigns, publications, destination development, community enrichment initiatives and managing the state's Welcome Centers. Travel Oregon works with local communities, industry partners, government agencies and private businesses to implement its 10-year strategic vision.

The agency ensures broad economic impact throughout the state by partnering with Oregon's Regional Destination Management organizations in the state's seven tourism regions.

TRANSPORTATION COMMISSION, OREGON

Address: MS 11, 355 Capitol St. NE, Salem 97301-3871
Phone: 503-986-3450
Fax: 503-986-3432

The Transportation Building in Salem houses the central offices of the Department of Transportation. (Oregon State Archives scenic photo)

Web: oregon.gov/odot/get-involved/pages/otc_main.aspx
Contact: Bob Van Brocklin, Chair
Statutory Authority: ORS 184.615–184.620
Duties and Responsibilities: The commission establishes statewide transportation policy and provides direction and oversight to the Oregon Department of Transportation. The commission has five volunteer members appointed by the governor and confirmed by the Senate. Members serve a four-year term and may be reappointed. No more than three members may belong to the same political party, and at least one member must reside east of the Cascade mountain range.

Transportation, Department of

Address: 355 Capitol St. NE, Salem 97301
Phone: 503-986-3200; 1-888-ask-odot (275-6368) for questions and concerns
Fax: 503-986-3432
Web: oregon.gov/odot
Contact: Kristopher Strickler, Director
Statutory Authority: ORS 184.615
Duties and Responsibilities: The Oregon Department of Transportation (ODOT) operates under the Oregon Transportation Commission, executing statewide transportation policy and serving as a statewide leader on transportation issues. ODOT builds and maintains Oregon's robust multimodal transportation network. The agency is organized under four assistant directors and a chief administrative officer who manage Government and External Relations; Operations; Revenue, Finance and Compliance; Social Equity; and Support Services.

Government and External Relations

Address: MS 11, 355 Capitol St. NE, Salem 97301-3871
Phone: 503-986-2840
Fax: 503-986-3432
Contact: Lindsay Baker, Assistant Director
Duties and Responsibilities: The office includes the Government Relations team, Communications team, Public Records and Rulemaking team and ODOT's single-point constituent service and ombudsman office: AskODOT. The office collaborates with internal and external stakeholders, Tribal governments, local and federal government partners, news media and communities and businesses across the state to advance ODOT's priorities and ensure Oregon's transportation system serves all Oregonians.

Operations

Address: MS 11, 355 Capitol St. NE, Salem 97301-3871
Phone: 503-986-3939

Fax: 503-986-3432
Contact: Cooper Brown, Assistant Director

Delivery and Operations Division

Address: 4040 Fairview Industrial Dr. SE, Salem 97302-1142
Phone: 503-986-2840
Fax: 503-986-3150
Contact: McGregor (Mac) Lynde, Administrator
Duties and Responsibilities: The division is responsible for the design, maintenance, operation and construction of Oregon's roughly 8,000 miles of state highways. Their activities include identifying highway needs; maintaining state highway routes; building multimodal capacity on facilities; acquiring rights of way; designing highways, bridges and related structures; evaluating environmental impacts of proposed projects; and conducting traffic studies.

Policy, Data and Analysis Division

Address: 555 13th St. NE, Suite 2, Salem 97301-4178
Phone: 503-986-3421
Fax: 503-986-4173
Web: oregon.gov/odot/planning
Contact: Amanda Pietz, Administrator
Duties and Responsibilities: The division produces statewide transportation plans and policies; assists local governments in planning; collects and analyzes data to support strategic investment decisions; oversees transportation research; manages mulitmodal grant programs; and leads ODOT's efforts to address climate change through transportation policy and investments. The division also develops the Statewide Transportation Improvement Program, which is the state's four-year transportation capital improvement program.

Public Transportation Division

Address: 555 13th St. NE, Suite 3, Salem 97301-4179
Phone: 503-986-3412
Fax: 503-986-3183
Web: oregon.gov/odot/rptd
Contact: Karyn Criswell, Administrator
Duties and Responsibilities: The division provides statewide leadership to encourage multimodal collaboration and build Oregon's statewide public transportation network. The division supports intercity passenger bus and rail service and provides grants to local and regional governments and non-profit organizations for transportation services. Programs include Transit, Intercity Passenger Rail and Bus and Rail and Transit Safety.

Urban Mobility Office

Address: 123 NW Flanders St., Portland 97209
Phone: 503-731-3170

Web: oregon.gov/odot/umo
Contact: Brendan Finn, Director
Duties and Responsibilities: The office is charged with advancing ODOT's mission to comprehensively address the most pressing transportation challenges in the Portland region. The office executes ODOT's Urban Mobility Strategy, a Portland area program to manage traffic with tolling, reduce highway bottlenecks and make strategic multimodal transportation investments.

Revenue, Finance and Compliance

Address: MS 11, 355 Capitol St., NE, Salem 97301
Phone: 503-986-3452
Fax: 503-986-3432
Contact: Travis Brouwer, Assistant Director

Budget and Finance Office

Address: MS 11, 355 Capitol St. NE, Salem 97301-3871
Phone: 503-986-3049
Contact: Daniel Porter, Manager
Duties and Responsibilities: The office leads the agency's budget development and execution processes. They provids reliable, accessible and credible information to partners, stakeholders and the public on ODOT's funds and its role as a steward of public funds.

Commerce and Compliance Division

Address: 3930 Fairview Industrial Dr. SE, Salem 97302-6351
Phone: 503-378-5849
Fax: 503-373-1940
Web: oregontruckingonline.com
Contact: Amy Ramsdell, Administrator
Duties and Responsibilities: The Commerce and Compliance Division (CCD) ensures the safety of commercial trucks and buses and collects fees for their use of the roads. The division collects weight-mile tax and truck registration fees from trucking companies an enforcement program to ensure trucks follow size and weight requirements. CCD enforces commercial vehicle laws, including regulations on driver hours of service. They also oversee Oregon rail operations to ensure the structural safety of railroad cars, equipment, track, crossings and signals. Other duties include ensuring a safe environment for railroad employees and monitoring the safety compliance of light rail, streetcar and trolley service providers.

Driver and Motor Vehicle Division

Address: 1905 Lana Ave. NE, Salem 97314
Phone: 503-945-5000;
  Toll-free (Portland): 503-299-9999
Fax: 503-945-0893

Web: oregon.gov/odot/dmv
Contact: Amy Joyce, Administrator
Duties and Responsibilities: The Driver and Motor Vehicle Division (DMV) protects financial and ownership interests in vehicles, provides driver licenses and identification cards for Oregon residents and collects revenues for Oregon's statewide multimodal transportation system. There are currently more than 3.1 million licensed drivers and more than 4.5 million registered vehicles in Oregon. DMV regulates and inspects about 3,500 vehicle- and driver-related businesses, such as auto dealers and dismantlers. Additionally, the division is home to statewide transportation safety programs. These programs conduct campaigns focused on increasing safe driving behaviors such as using safety belts and child safety seats, and reducing dangerous driving behaviors such as impaired driving, speeding and distracted driving. The Safety team partners with law enforcement, safety advocates and others to promote transportation safety. Headquartered in Salem, DMV has 60 field offices throughout the state.

Social Equity

Address: MS 11, 355 Capitol St. NE, Salem 97301-3871
Phone: 503-986-4353
Fax: 503-986-3432
Web: oregon.gov/odot/equity
Contact: Erika McCalpine, Assistant Director
Duties and Responsibilities: The office, which includes the Office of Civil Rights, works to institutionalize equity, diversity and inclusion practices in ODOT's programs, policies, performance and priorities.

Support Services Division

Address: 355 Capitol St. NE, Salem 97301
Phone: 503-986-5801
Contact: Carolyn Sullivan, Chief Administrative Officer
Duties and Responsibilities: The Support Services Division (SSD) includes the Office of Employee Safety, Human Resources, Procurement Office, Information Systems, Facilities Services and Data Solutions. These branches provide administrative, operational and managerial services for all ODOT divisions, the Oregon Transportation Commission and other stakeholders.

ODOT Advisory Groups

Web: oregon.gov/odot/get-involved/pages/advisory-committees.aspx
Duties and Responsibilities: ODOT values community and public engagement to ensure its work meets the needs of communities, businesses and individuals across the state. ODOT's programs, projects and initiatives often collaborate with advisory groups to gather feedback, build consensus and reach communities through trusted partners.

TRAVEL INFORMATION COUNCIL

Address: 1500 Liberty St. SE, Suite 150, Salem 97302
Phone: 503-378-4508
Fax: 503-378-6282
Web: oregontic.com
Contact: Elizabeth Boxall, Executive Director
Statutory Authority: ORS 377.835–377.845
Duties and Responsibilities: The Oregon Travel Information Council (OTIC) is a semi-independent state agency. OTIC's programs help travelers navigate to essential services, attractions and points of historic interest. The agency is responsible for the operation of 39 highway safety rest areas around the state under interagency agreements with the Oregon Department of Transportation and Oregon Parks and Recreation Department. OTIC administers the statewide "Blue Logo" Sign Program and information centers that identify gas, food, lodging and attractions on highways throughout Oregon. They lead the Oregon Heritage Tree and Oregon Historical Marker programs.

The nine-member governing council has eight volunteers appointed by the governor and one member of the Oregon Transportation Commission, to guide the work of the agency. Members are selected for their knowledge of, experience with or interest in economic development, travel within Oregon, recreational opportunities in Oregon and Oregon's history and natural history.

VETERANS' AFFAIRS, DEPARTMENT OF

Address: 700 Summer St. NE, Salem 97301-1285
Phone: 503-373-2000; Toll-free: 1-800-828-8801; TTY: 503-373-2217
Fax: 503-373-2362
Web: oregon.gov/odva
Contact: Kelly Fitzpatrick, Director
Statutory Authority: ORS Chapters 406, 407, 408
Duties and Responsibilities: The Oregon Department of Veterans' Affairs (ODVA) provides direct access to earned benefits and services to nearly 300,000 Oregon veterans and their families. ODVA conducts advocacy for traditonally underserved-veteran communities. They build partnerships with organizations to provide veteran-specific services for sustainable and supportive housing, access to health and behavioral health services and services to assist veterans in completing their educational goals. ODVA has three major program areas: aging veteran services, the veteran home loan program and statewide veteran services, plus core

operations to support and enhance the effectiveness and efficiency of each division.

Aging Veteran Services Division

Address: 700 Summer St. NE, Salem 97301-1285
Phone: 503-373-2028
Fax: 503-373-2391
Contact: Ana Potter
Duties and Responsibilities: ODVA's Aging Veteran Services Division includes its Conservatorship and Representative Payee Programs, which help veterans, survivors and dependents who are legally designated "protected persons" to preserve and manage their estates and veterans benefits. They provide income and assets for shelter, medical, personal and other needs. The division operates two Oregon Veterans' Homes located in Lebanon and The Dalles where skilled nursing, rehabilitative care and Alzheimer's disease care are provided for veterans, spouses and Gold Star parents (parents whose children died while serving in the U.S. Armed Forces). They also train and coordinate volunteers who aid and provide benefit referrals to aging veterans.

The Veterans' Building in Salem houses the central offices of the Department of Veterans' Affairs. (Oregon State Archives scenic photo)

Home Loan Program

Address: 700 Summer St. NE, Salem 97301-1285
Phone: 503-373-2051;
  Toll-free: 1-800-828-8801; 1-888-673-8387 (within Oregon)
Fax: 503-373-2393
Contact: Cody Cox
Duties and Responsibilities: The Oregon Veteran (ORVET) Home Loan Program is designed to provide eligible veterans with home loans at the lowest possible interest rates.

Statewide Veteran Services Division

Address: 700 Summer St. NE, Salem 97301-1285
Phone: 503-373-2249
Contact: Sheronne Blasi

Duties and Responsibilities: The division is responsible for training Veteran Service Officers in the state of Oregon who provide free benefits counseling and claims services to veterans, survivors and dependents. The division serves the State Approving Agency and is responsible for the review, evaluation, approval and oversight of schools and training facilities to ensure state and federal quality criteria are met for veterans using their G.I. Bill® benefits. The division also includes Veteran Service Officers who provide services to underserved groups within Oregon's increasingly diverse veteran population, including women, tribal, incarcerated, LGBTQ and veterans currently enrolled in programs of higher education. Additionally, the division oversees the administration of several grant programs, including medical transportation for highly rural veterans, Campus Veteran Resource Programs and various Veteran Services Grants to assist homeless veterans, aid tribal veterans and providing legal services for veterans.

Advisory Committee to the Director of Veterans' Affairs

Address: 700 Summer St. NE, Salem 97301-1285
Phone: 503-373-2383
Contact: James Gardner, Chair
Statutory Authority: ORS 406.210
Duties and Responsibilities: The committee consists of nine veterans appointed by the governor who advise the director and staff of the ODVA on a wide variety of matters. The committee members act as advocates for veterans' issues and represent veterans' concerns across Oregon.

VETERINARY MEDICAL EXAMINING BOARD

Address: 800 NE Oregon St., Suite 407, Portland 97232
Phone: 971-673-0224
Fax: 971-673-0226
Email: ovmeb.info@state.or.us
Web: oregon.gov/ovmeb
Contact: Cassandra C. McLeod-Skinner, Interim Executive Director
Statutory Authority: ORS 686.210
Duties and Responsibilities: The board regulates the practice of veterinary medicine in Oregon. They make and enforce rules for competency, health and safety standards for practitioners and facilities. They also license and investigate complaints against veterinarians, Certified Veterinary Technicians, euthanasia technicians and veterinary facilities to ensure compliance the Veterinary Practice Act. Facilities are regularly inspected for compliance with health, sanitation and drug safety

requirements. Board members include five veteri-narians, two members of the public and one Certified Veterinary Technician.

WATER RESOURCES DEPARTMENT

Address: 725 Summer St. NE, Suite A, Salem 97301
Phone: 503-986-0900
Fax: 503-986-0904
Web: oregon.gov/owrd
Contact: Doug Woodcock, Acting Director
Statutory Authority: ORS Chapters 536, 537, 538, 540, 541, 542, 543, 543A, 555
Duties and Responsibilities: The Oregon Water Resources Department (OWRD) is charged with administering the laws governing the management and distribution of Oregon's surface and ground-water resources. OWRD protects existing water rights, processes water right transactions, facilitates voluntary streamflow restoration, increases under-standing of demands on the state's water resources, provides accurate and accessible water resource data and facilitates water supply solutions. The department also protects public health and safety through its dam safety and well construction programs.

Department headquarters and the Northwest Regional office are located in Salem. The depart-ment also has four other regional offices and 15 small field offices throughout Oregon.

Water Resources Commission

Address: 725 Summer St. NE, Suite A, Salem 97301
Phone: 503-986-0876
Contact: Nirvana Cook, Commission Assistant
Statutory Authority: ORS 536.022
Duties and Responsibilities: The seven-member commission oversees department activities and sets policy consistent with state law.

Director's Office

Address: 725 Summer St. NE, Suite A, Salem 97301
Phone: 503-986-0876
Contact: Doug Woodcock, Acting Director
Duties and Responsibilities: The office develops and supervises policies and programs to ensure that water management practices follow Oregon Water Law. They oversee implementation of the State's Integrated Water Resources Strategy and serve as the principal contact with the Legislature, tribes, stakeholder groups and the Western States Water Council. The Planning, Collaboration and Invest-ments Section administers grant and loan programs and provides funding and technical assistance to

help individuals and communities meet their water needs.

Field Services Division

Address: 725 Summer St. NE, Suite A, Salem 97301
Phone: 971-283-6010
Contact: Ivan Gall, Administrator
Duties and Responsibilities: The division enforces the state's water laws and implements the Water Resources Commission's policies in the field. They have sole responsibility for regulating water use based upon the water rights of record. Staff inspect wells for groundwater resource protection and dams for public safety. The division collects streamflow and groundwater data for use by staff and the public.

Water Right Services Division

Address: 725 Summer St. NE, Suite A, Salem 97301
Phone: 503-871-7292
Contact: Dwight French, Administrator
Duties and Responsibilities: The division is responsible for processing water right permits to meet a variety of needs, including agriculture, drinking water, fish, wildlife, recreation and indus-try. Additionally, the division processes transactions that allow water right holders to change how their existing water rights are used, including changes involving the transfer or lease of water instream. The division also adjudicates water right claims that predate the 1909 water code as well as federal and tribal rights.

Technical Services Division

Phone: 971-375-7322
Contact: Annette Liebe, Administrator
Duties and Responsibilities: The division includes groundwater and surface water scientists responsi-ble for understanding the surface and groundwater resources of the state. The division also oversees the safety of dams, develops databases to share water resources information, licenses well drillers, enforces well construction standards and conducts enforcement proceedings for the department.

Groundwater Advisory Committee

Address: 725 Summer St. NE, Suite A, Salem 97301
Phone: 503-302-9728
Contact: Justin Iverson, Department Liaison
Statutory Authority: ORS 536.090
Duties and Responsibilities: The committee's nine members, appointed by the Water Resources Com-mission, advise the commission and OWRD on rules, legislation, groundwater public policy and the licensing of well constructors. The committee also reviews proposed expenditures of revenues

generated from start card fees associated with constructing wells.

Klamath River Basin Compact Commission

Address: 6600 Washburn Way, Klamath Falls 97603
Phone: 541-973-4431
Contact: Vacant, federal government representative; Tom Byler, Oregon representative; Curtis Anderson, California representative
Statutory Authority: 542.610
Duties and Responsibilities: Members of the commission facilitate inter-governmental cooperation in the development and proper use of the water resources of the Klamath River Basin.

WATERSHED ENHANCEMENT BOARD, OREGON

Address: 775 Summer St. NE, Suite 360, Salem 97301-1290
Phone: 971-345-7001
Fax: 503-986-0199
Email: april.mack@oweb.oregon.gov
Web: oregon.gov/oweb
Contact: Lisa Charpilloz Hansen, Executive Director
Statutory Authority: ORS Chapter 541
Duties and Responsibilities: The Oregon Watershed Enhancement Board (OWEB) provides grants to help Oregonians take care of local streams, rivers, wetlands and natural areas; protect farm and ranch lands; and support landscape recovery from drought and fire. Community members and landowners use scientific criteria to jointly make decisions for conservation and improvement of rivers, natural habitats and landscapes in the places where they live. OWEB grants are funded from the Oregon Lottery, federal dollars, general funds and salmon license plate revenue. The agency, which was created in 1999, is led by an 18-member citizen board drawn from the public at large, tribes and federal and state natural resource agency boards and commissions. Headquartered in Salem, OWEB has approximately 46 staff, including six regional field representatives located in offices around the state.

WINE BOARD, OREGON

Address: 5331 S Macadam Ave., Suite 258, PMB121, Portland 97239
Phone: 503-967-8978
Email: info@oregonwine.org
Web: oregonwine.org; industry.oregonwine.org
Contact: Tom Danowski, President and CEO
Statutory Authority: ORS 576.753
Duties and Responsibilities: The board consists of nine volunteer members appointed by the governor for a term of three years. The board and staff work on behalf of all Oregon wineries and independent growers throughout the state's diverse winegrowing regions, managing marketing, research and education initiatives that support and advance the Oregon wine and wine grape industry.

YOUTH AUTHORITY, OREGON

Address: 530 Center St. NE, Suite 500, Salem 97301-3777
Phone: 503-373-7205
Fax: 503-373-7622
Email: info@oya.oregon.gov
Web: oregon.gov/oya
Contact: Joseph O'Leary, Director
Statutory Authority: ORS Chapters 419A, 419C, 420, 420A
Duties and Responsibilities: The Oregon Youth Authority (OYA) protects the public and reduces crime by holding youth accountable for their behavior and providing opportunities for reformation in safe environments.

OYA provides treatment, education and job training services to youths aged 12 to 25. OYA is responsible for youth who commit offenses between the ages of 12 and 18 and have been committed to OYA by county juvenile courts.OYA is also responsible for physical custody over youths sentenced as adults to the legal custody of the Oregon Department of Corrections.

OYA employs approximately 1,000 people throughout Oregon with central offices in Salem; provides probation and parole services in all 36 counties in Oregon; operates nine close-custody facilities; and contracts with a range of residential treatment providers and foster parents to ensure youth receive the most appropriate combination of placement, treatment and other services needed to leave OYA's custody ready to lead productive, crime-free lives.

Executive

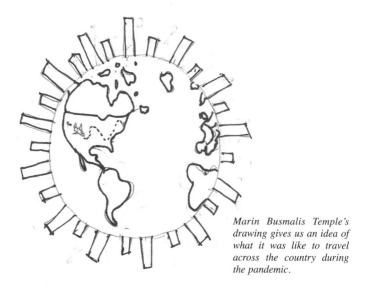

Marin Busmalis Temple's drawing gives us an idea of what it was like to travel across the country during the pandemic.

STUDENT ESSAY CONTEST WINNER

Traveling in Covid

Marin Busmalis Temple
Amy York's 8th Grade Class
Mitchell Middle School, Mitchell

It all started on March 15, but the day before was 3/14/20 also known as pi day. I like to compete in reciting pi. I got the school record again with 151 digits. Then we got the call that changed everything. Not seeing friends online, stores closed. I was in 6th grade after the school year. We were lucky that we could go back to school but with masks. November 27, 2020 my mom got bad news that she has a kind of cancer called Myelodysplastic Syndrome. Because of this my mom will had to go to Boston for treatment.

Traveling in Covid is hard. KN95 masks, tests lots of tests, face shield you name it. After about ten hours of traveling I was in a very different place. Boston was really cautious unlike Central Oregon. Being in Boston I felt like I wasn't being judged the way I felt when I was in Oregon. There was an unexpected delay with my mom's transplant, I was stuck in Boston for three months because of that. I did online school while everybody was together. That was really I hard I remember. When I came back from Boston it was the same how I left it being judged and feeling left out. The rest of 6th and 7th I started getting tired of masks and testing. This year I am still traveling but not as safe as I was before.

Judicial

Oregon's judicial branch of government helps individuals, businesses and government groups resolve disputes, protect their rights and enforce their legal duties. Oregon judges review cases for compliance with federal, state and local laws. This section describes the judicial system and introduces Oregon's judges.

OREGON SUPREME COURT

Address: Supreme Court Bldg., 1163 State St., Salem 97301-2563
Records and Case Information: 503-986-5555; Oregon Relay 711
Fax: 503-986-5560

The Supreme Court of Oregon has seven justices elected by nonpartisan, statewide ballot to serve six-year terms. Justices elected to the Supreme Court must be United States citizens, members of the Oregon State Bar and residents of Oregon for at least three years. The court has its offices and courtroom in the Supreme Court Building, one block east of the State Capitol in Salem. The members of the court elect one of their number to serve as chief justice for a six-year term.

Powers and Authority

The Supreme Court was created, and its role largely defined, by Article VII of the Oregon Constitution, as amended. It is primarily a court of review in that it reviews, in selected cases, the decisions of the Court of Appeals. The Supreme Court usually selects cases with significant legal issues calling for interpretation of laws or legal principles affecting many citizens and institutions of society. When the Supreme Court decides not to review a Court of Appeals case, the Court of Appeals' decision becomes final. In addition to its discretionary review function, the Supreme Court hears direct appeals in death penalty, lawyer and judicial discipline and Oregon Tax Court cases. It may accept original jurisdiction in mandamus, quo warranto and habeas corpus proceedings. It also reviews ballot measure titles, prison siting disputes, reapportionment of legislative districts and legal questions on Oregon law referred by federal courts.

Administrative Authority

The chief justice is the administrative head of the Judicial Department and exercises administrative authority over the appellate, circuit and tax courts. The chief justice makes rules and issues orders to carry out necessary duties and requires appropriate reports from judges and other officers and employees of the courts. As head of the Judicial Department, the chief justice appoints the chief judge of the Court of Appeals and the presiding judges of all state trial courts from the judges elected to those courts. The chief justice adopts certain rules and regulations respecting procedures for state courts. The chief justice also supervises a statewide plan for budgeting, accounting and fiscal management of the judicial department.

The chief justice and the Supreme Court have the authority to appoint lawyers, elected judges and retired judges to serve in temporary judicial assignments.

Admission and Discipline of Lawyers and Judges

The Supreme Court admits lawyers to practice law in Oregon and has the power to reprimand, suspend or disbar lawyers whose actions have been investigated and prosecuted by the Oregon State Bar. In admitting lawyers, the Supreme Court acts on the recommendation of the Board of Bar Examiners, which conducts examinations for lawyer applicants each February and July and screens applicants for character and fitness to practice law. The Supreme Court appoints at least 14 members to the Board of Bar Examiners. The board includes two public members who are not lawyers. The Supreme Court also has the power to censure, suspend or remove judges after investigation and recommendation by the Commission on Judicial Fitness and Disability.

Oregon Court of Appeals

Address: Supreme Court Bldg., 1163 State St., Salem 97301-2563
Records and Case Information: 503-986-5555; Oregon Relay 771
Fax: 503-986-5865

Created in 1969 as a five-judge court, the Court of Appeals was expanded to six judges in 1973, ten judges in 1977 and 13 judges in 2012. The judges, are elected on a statewide, nonpartisan basis for six-year terms, must be United States citizens, members of the Oregon State Bar and qualified electors of their county of residence. The chief justice of the Supreme Court appoints a chief judge from among the judges of the Court of Appeals.

Court of Appeals judges have their offices in the Justice Building in Salem and usually hear cases in the courtroom of the Supreme Court Building. The court ordinarily sits in panels of three judges. The Supreme Court has authority to appoint a Supreme Court justice, a circuit court judge or an Oregon Tax Court judge to serve as a judge pro tempore of the Court of Appeals. In 1995, the Court of Appeals established an Appellate Settlement Conference Program for mediation of cases in that court.

Jurisdiction

The Court of Appeals has jurisdiction to review appeals of most civil and criminal cases and most state administrative agency actions. The exceptions are appeals in death penalty, lawyer and judicial disciplinary, and Oregon Tax Court cases, which go directly to the Oregon Supreme Court.

Reviews and Decisions

A party aggrieved by a decision of the Court of Appeals may petition the Supreme Court for review within 35 days after the Court of Appeals issues its decision. The Supreme Court determines whether to review the case. The Supreme Court allows a petition for review whenever at least one fewer than a majority of the participating judges vote to allow it.

Oregon Tax Court

Address: Robertson Bldg., 1241 State St., 4th Floor, Salem 97301-2563
Phone: 503-986-5645; TTY: 503-986-5651
Fax: 503-986-5507

The Oregon Tax Court has exclusive, statewide jurisdiction in all questions of law or fact arising under state tax laws, including income taxes, corporate excise taxes, property taxes, timber taxes, cigarette taxes, local budget law and property tax limitations.

The Oregon Tax Court consists of the Magistrate Division and the Regular Division.

Trials in the Magistrate Division are informal proceedings. Statutory rules of evidence do not apply, and the trials are not reported. The proceedings may be conducted by telephone or in person. A taxpayer may be represented by a lawyer, public accountant, real estate broker or appraiser. All decisions of the magistrates may be appealed to the Regular Division of the Oregon Tax Court.

The judge of the Oregon Tax Court presides over trials in the Regular Division. The Regular Division is comparable to a circuit court and exercises equivalent powers. All trials are reported and only before the judge. The parties may either represent themselves or be represented by an attorney. Appeals from the judge's decision are made directly to the Oregon Supreme Court.

The judge serves a six-year term and is elected on the nonpartisan, statewide judicial ballot.

Circuit Courts

Each county has a circuit court, which is a state trial court of general jurisdiction. However, except for cases involving the termination of parental rights, Gilliam, Sherman and Wheeler Counties also have "county courts," which exercise jurisdiction in juvenile cases. In addition, Gilliam, Grant, Harney, Malheur, Sherman and Wheeler Counties' county courts exercise jurisdiction in probate, adoption, guardianship and conservatorship cases.

Circuit court judges are elected on a nonpartisan ballot for six year terms. They must be citizens of the United States, members of the Oregon State Bar, residents of Oregon for at least three years and residents of their judicial district for at least one year, except Multnomah County judges who may reside within ten miles of the county. There are 179 circuit judges serving 36 counties. The circuit judges are grouped in 27 geographical areas called judicial districts. Of the 179, Multnomah County District has 38 circuit judges; Lane, Marion and Washington, 15; Clackamas, 11; Jackson, 10; Deschutes, 9; Coos/Curry, 6; Douglas, Josephine, Klamath, Linn and Umatilla/Morrow districts have 5; Yamhill and Hood River/Wasco/Sherman/Wheeler/Gilliam districts have 4; Benton, Clatsop, Columbia, Lincoln, Polk and Crook/Jefferson districts have 3; Malheur, Tillamook, Union/Wallowa districts have 2 and Baker, Lake, Grant/Harney districts have 1.

To expedite judicial business, the chief justice of the Supreme Court may assign any circuit judge to sit in any judicial district in the state.

Senior Judges

Under Oregon law, a judge who retires from the circuit court, Oregon Tax Court, Court of Appeals or Supreme Court, except a judge retired under the provisions of ORS 1.310, may be designated a

continued on page 85

Supreme Court

Flynn, Meagan A.
Chief Justice
Position 3
Served since 2017
Term expires 1/2025

Bushong, Stephen K.
Associate Justice
Position 1
Served since 2023
Term expires 1/2025

Duncan, Rebecca A.
Associate Justice
Position 2
Served since 2017
Term expires 1/2025

Garrett, Christopher L.
Associate Justice
Position 4
Served since 2019
Term expires 1/2027

Nelson, Adrienne C.
Associate Justice
Position 5
Served since 2018
Term expires 1/2025

DeHoog, Roger
Associate Justice
Position 6
Served since 2022
Term expires 1/2029

James, Bronson D.
Associate Justice
Position 7
Served since 2023
Term expires 1/2025

Judicial

Court of Appeals

Lagesen, Erin C.
Chief Judge
Position 12
Served since 2013
Term expires 1/2027

Aoyagi, Robyn R.
Associate Judge
Position 4
Served since 2017
Term expires 1/2025

Egan, James C.
Associate Judge
Position 6
Served since 2013
Term expires 1/2025

Hellman, Kristina S.
Associate Judge
Position 10
Served since 2022
Term expires 1/2029

Jacquot, Megan L.
Associate Judge
Position 2
Served since 2023
Term expires 1/2025

Joyce, Anna M.
Associate Judge
Position 11
Served since 2022
Term expires 1/2029

Kamins, Jacqueline S.
Associate Judge
Position 9
Served since 2020
Term expires 1/2027

Mooney, Josephine H.
Associate Judge
Position 1
Served since 2019
Term expires 1/2027

Ortega, Darleen
Associate Judge
Position 3
Served since 2003
Term expires 1/2029

Pagán, Ramón A.
Associate Judge
Position 8
Served since 2022
Term expires 1/2029

Powers, Steven R.
Associate Judge
Position 7
Served since 2017
Term expires 1/2025

Shorr, Scott A.
Associate Judge
Position 5
Served since 2016
Term expires 1/2029

Tookey, Douglas L.
Associate Judge
Position 13
Served since 2013
Term expires 1/2027

Oregon
Tax
Court

Manicke, Robert T.
Tax Judge
Served since 2018
Term expires 1/2025

continued from page 82

senior judge of the state by the Supreme Court and is eligible for temporary assignment by the Supreme Court to any state court at or below the level in which he or she last served as a full-time judge. The current roster of senior judges is as follows:

Supreme Court: Richard C. Baldwin, Thomas A. Balmer, David V. Brewer, Wallace P. Carson, Jr., Paul J. De Muniz, Robert D. Durham, W. Michael Gillette, Rives Kistler, Jack L. Landau, Susan M. Leeson, Virginia L. Linder, Lynn R. Nakamoto, Edwin J. Peterson, George VanHoomissen, Martha L. Walters

Court of Appeals or Oregon Tax Court: Rex E. Armstrong, Henry Breithaupt, Carl N. Byers, Mary J. Deits, Joel S. DeVore, Walter I. Edmonds, Jr., Erika L. Hadlock, Rick T. Haselton, William L. Richardson, Timothy J. Sercombe

Circuit courts: Pamela Abernethy, Ted Abram, A. Michael Adler, Daniel Ahern, Marshall Amiton, G.

Philip Arnold, Fred Avera, Raymond Bagley, Glen Baisinger, Richard Barron, Gregory L. Baxter, Frank L. Bearden, Mary Ann Bearden, William Beckett, Douglas G. Beckman, Linda Bergman, Eric J. Bergstrom, Jack A. Billings, Carol Bispham, Alan C. Bonebrake, Alta Brady, Thomas O. Branford, Paula Brownhill, William D. Bunch, Frances E. Burge, Claudia M. Burton, Nancy W. Campbell, Cynthia Carlson, Joseph Ceniceros, Suzanne B. Chanti, Ronald E. Cinniger, Rita Cobb, John L. Collins, Allan H. Coon, Charles D. Carlson, Patricia Crain, William D. Cramer, Jr., Kathleen M. Dailey, Deanne Darling, David E. Delsman, Don A. Dickey, Henry R. Dickinson, Jr., Hugh C. Downer, Jr., Greg Foote, Stephen P. Forte, Kimberly Frankel, Julie Franz, James. L. Fun, Jr., Randolph Garrison, David Gernant, Michael J. Gillespie, James Goode, Dennis Graves, Ted E. Grove, Joe Guimond, David Hantke, Daniel L. Harris, Wayne R. Harris, Barbara Haslinger, Eveleen Henry, Robert D. Herndon, Janet S. Holcomb, Lauren S. Holland, William Horner, Robert J. Huckleberry,

Jeremy B. Hodson, Don Hull, Thomas M. Hull, Mary M. James, Nely L. Johnson, Edward Jones, Donald Kalberer, Henry Kantor, Mitchell Karaman, John V. Kelly, Rick Knapp, Karla J. Knieps, Frank D. Knight, Dale R. Koch, Thomas W. Kohl, Thomas Kolberg, Paula J. Kurshner, Jerome LaBarre, Kristena LaMar, Darryl Larson, Terry A. Leggert, Kip Leonard, Donald Letourneau, William O. Lewis, Paul Lipscomb, Angel Lopez, Jon B. Lund, Charles E. Luukinen, William S. Mackay, William A. Marshall, Cindee S. Maytas, Jean Maurer, Steven Maurer, Robert McConville, John A. McCormick, Rick J. McCormick, Maureen McKnight, Keith Meisenheimer, Lorenzo A. Mejia, Maurice Merten, Richard Mickelson, Eve Miller, Robert Millikan, Douglas Mitchell, Robert J. Morgan, Thomas Moultrie, Rudy Murgo, Gayle Nachtigal, George W. Neilson, Philip L. Nelson, Michael Newman, Robert F. Nichols, Jr., DeAnn Novotny, Joseph V. Ochoa, Loyd O'Neal, Rebecca Orf, Roxanne Osborne, Ronald J. Pahl, Cheryl A. Pellegrini, Dale W. Penn, J. Burdette Pratt, Steven Price, William G. Purdy, Keith R. Raines, Richard Rambo, Karsten Rasmussen, Robert Redding, Steven B. Reed, Garry L. Reynolds, Jamese Rhoades, Leslie M. Roberts, Rick W. Roll, Ilisa Rooke-Ley, Don H. Sanders, Mark S. Schiveley, Joan G. Seitz, Robert Selander, Gregory F. Silver, Lane W. Simpson, Berkeley Smith, Bernard L. Smith, Janet L. Stauffer, Diana Stuart, Michael C. Sullivan, Patricia A. Sullivan, Ronald D. Thom, Gary S. Thompson, Kirsten E. Thompson, Carroll Tichenor, Stephen Tiktin, Susan M. Tripp, Suzanne Upton, Eric Valentine, Douglas V. Van Dyk, Pierre Van Rysselberghe, Lyle Velure, Kenneth R. Walker, Elizabeth Welch, C. Gregory West, Russell West, Raymond B. White, Gary Williams, Janice R. Wilson, John Wilson, John Wittmayer, Cameron F. Wogan, Merri Souther Wyatt, Jan Wyers, Frank J. Yraguen

District courts:* Richard J. Courson, Robert L. Gilliland, Charles H. Reeves

*Effective January 15, 1998, all district courts were abolished, and the powers, functions and judges of the district courts were transferred to the circuit courts.

JUDICIAL CONFERENCE

The Oregon Judicial Conference, created under ORS 1.810, is composed of all judges of the Supreme Court, Court of Appeals, Tax Court, circuit courts and all senior judges certified under ORS 1.300. The chief justice of the Supreme Court is chair of the conference, and the state court administrator acts as executive secretary. Under ORS 1.820, the conference may make a continuous survey and study of the organization, jurisdiction, procedure, practice and methods of administration and operation of the various courts within the state.

The Judicial Conference meets annually to conduct business, attend educational seminars, issue committee reports and adopt resolutions, if any.

OFFICE OF THE STATE COURT ADMINISTRATOR

Source: Nancy J. Cozine, Administrator
Address: 510 Justice Bldg. Mail: Supreme Court Bldg., 1163 State St., Salem 97301-2563
Phone: 503-986-5500; Oregon Relay 711
Web: courts.oregon.gov/about/Pages/osca.aspx

The state court administrator position was created in 1971 to assist the chief justice in exercising administrative authority over the state courts. In 1983, with unification and state funding of the trial and appellate courts, the duties of the position expanded to include human resources, accounting, budget preparation, revenue, management of the legislative program, state court property inventory and procurement, internal audit, maintenance of a statewide automated info system, continuing education programs for judges and staff, public information and long-range planning for future court needs. (*See ORS 8.110 and 8.125*)

In addition, the state court administrator oversees staff responsible for managing records of all cases filed with the Supreme Court, Court of Appeals and Oregon Tax Court; publishes the opinions of the Supreme Court, Court of Appeals and Oregon Tax Court; oversees the State Law Library; and oversees the Office of the State Court Administrator, State Court Security, State Court Interpreter, Certified Shorthand Reporters and State Citizen Review Board programs. Under ORS 30.273, the state court administrator also calculates and posts the annual adjustment to the liability limitations under the Oregon Tort Claims Act.

Cases Filed in Oregon Courts 2016–2021

	2016	2017	2018	2019	2020	2021
Oregon Supreme Court	820	944	848	893	874	919
Oregon Court of Appeals	2,817	2,768	3,063	3,340	2,112	2,484
Oregon Tax Court, Regular	22	24	38	36	20	18
Oregon Tax Court, Magistrate	410	396	409	360	404	410
Circuit Courts	480,818	519,956	510,632	483,397	456,613	493,899

Circuit Court

(P) = Presiding Judge

Abar, Donald D.
District 3, Position 11

**Adkisson, Marci W.
(P)**
District 13, Position 3

**Alarcón, Jacqueline
L.**
District 4, Position 3

Albrecht, Cheryl A.
District 4, Position 31

Alexander, Steffan K.
District 4, Position 26

Allen, Beth A.
District 4, Position 34

Ambrosini, George W.
District 16, Position 5

Armstrong, Sean E.
District 3, Position 7

Ashby, Wells B. (P)
District 11, Position 6

Bachart, Sheryl (P)
District 17, Position 1

Baggio, Amy M.
District 4, Position 38

Bagley, Beth M.
District 11, Position 2

Bailey, D. Charles
District 20, Position 6

Bain, Robert S. (P)
District 14, Position 3

Barnack, Timothy
District 1, Position 6

Bassi, Michelle P.
District 2, Position 2

Beaman, Cynthia L.
District 15, Position 6

Benjamin, Amanda R.
District 17, Position 3

Bennett, J. Channing
District 3, Position 1

Bloom, Benjamin M. (P)
District 1, Position 7

Bottomly, Leslie G.
District 4, Position 6

Brauer, Christopher R.
District 6, Position 5

Brown, Adrian L.
District 4, Position 12

Broyles, Audrey J.
District 3, Position 9

Buchér, Erik M.
District 20, Position 3

Buckley, Marcia L.
District 17, Position 2

Bureta, Jodie A.
District 3, Position 4

Butterfield, Eric C.
District 20, Position 4

Callahan, Cathleen B.
District 19, Position 1

Campbell, Monte S.
District 12, Position 2

Photo
Not
Submitted

Cascagnette, Bradley A.
District 2, Position 3

Caso, Rafael A.
District 12, Position 1

Chapman, Jennifer K.
District 25, Position 2

Charter, Josepth M.
District 1, Position 8

Clarke, Michael T. (P)
District 19, Position 3

Collins Jr., Robert W.
District 6, Position 1

Combs, Andrew E.
District 15, Position 2

Conover, R. Curtis
District 2, Position 12

Cromwell, Laura A.
District 1, Position 4

Crutchley, Raymond D.
District 11, Position 1

Dahlin, Eric L.
District 4, Position 24

Demarest, Joan E.
District 21, Position 3

Donohue, Matthew J.
District 21, Position 2

Easterday, Cynthia L.
District 25, Position 3

Judicial

Edmonds, James C.
District 3, Position 6

Emerson, Alison M.
District 11, Position 7

Erwin, Andrew R.
District 20, Position 7

Fennerty, Erin A.
District 2, Position 9

Flint, Bethany P.
District 11, Position 3

Francesconi, Bryan
District 4, Position 20

Galli, Matthew G.
District 14, Position 5

Garcia, Oscar
District 20, Position 9

Gardiner, Jennifer K.
District 3, Position 3

Gates, Maurisa R.
District 4, Position 25

Gerking, Timothy C.
District 1, Position 5

Geyer, Courtland
District 3, Position 12

Ghandour, Rima I.
District 4, Position 21

Grace, Beatrice N.
District 2, Position 11

Greenlick, Michael A.
District 4, Position 19

Guptill, Rebecca D.
District 20, Position 2

Hart, Thomas M.
District 3, Position 13

Hedlund, Stephen R.
District 13, Position 5

Henry, Patrick W.
District 4, Position 35

Herriott, Alycia M.
District 11, Position 9

Hill, Daniel J. (P)
District 6, Position 3

Hill, Jonathan R. (P)
District 27, Position 1

Hill, Norman R. (P)
District 12, Position 3

**Hillman, Annette C.
(P)**
District 22, Position 1

Hoddle, Steve H.
District 16, Position 2

Holmes Hehn, Amy
District 4, Position 14

Hoppe, David G.
District 1, Position 2

Howe, Celia A.
District 4, Position 8

Hung, Lung S. (P)
District 9, Position 2

Janney, Andrea M.
District 13, Position 1

**Johnson, Kathleen E.
(P)**
District 16, Position 3

Johnson, Robert B.
District 16, Position 4

Judicial

Jones, Jeffrey S.
District 5, Position 1

Kane, Brendan J.
District 23, Position 4

Kapoor, Amit
District 2, Position 6

Karabeika, Heather L.
District 5, Position 8

Kaufman Noble, Cynthia
District 25, Position 1

Keppinger, Denise E.
District 19, Position 2

Kersey, Alycia E.
District 13, Position 2

Kittson-MaQatish, Rachel
District 23, Position 3

Kochlacs, Charles G.
District 1, Position 10

Kritzer, Kelly N.
District 13, Position 4

Landis, Erin K.
District 9, Position 1

Lavin, Andrew M.
District 4, Position 7

Leith, David E.
District 3, Position 8

Lemarr, Kelly D.
District 20, Position 5

Lieuallen, Jon S.
District 6, Position 2

Lininger, Ann M.
District 5, Position 2

Long, Morgan W.
District 4, Position 13

Love, Valeri L.
District 2, Position 8

Loy, Michael S.
District 4, Position 33

Lucero, Angela F.
District 4, Position 11

Margolis, Jesse
District 15, Position 3

Markiewicz, Jeremy A.
District 1, Position 1

Marshall, Christopher J.
District 4, Position 5

Matarazzo, Judith H. (P)
District 4, Position 28

McAlpin, Jay A. (P)
District 2, Position 7

McGlaughlin, Sarah E.
District 14, Position 4

McGuire, Patricia L.
District 4, Position 27

McHill, Thomas A. (P)
District 23, Position 5

McIntosh, Dawn M. (P)
District 18, Position 2

McIntyre, Karrie K.
District 2, Position 13

McIver, Michelle A.
District 11, Position 8

Menchaca, Ricardo J.
District 20, Position 8

Miller, Walter R., Jr.
District 11, Position 5

Moawad, Heidi H.
District 4, Position 36

Morgan, Stephen W.
District 2, Position 5

Norby, Susie L.
District 5, Position 11

Oden-Orr, Melvin
District 4, Position 23

Olson, John A.
District 7, Position 1

Orr, David J.
District 1, Position 9

Ostrye, Karen (P)
District 7, Position 3

Partridge, Lindsay R.
District 3, Position 10

Perez, Manuel D.
District 3, Position 15

Peterson, Beau V.
District 18, Position 1

Plank, Jenna R.
District 4, Position 37

Powers, Thomas B. (P)
District 10, Position 1

Prall, Tracy A. (P)
District 3, Position 2

Proctor, Kathleen J. (P)
District 20, Position 15

Pruess, Brett A.
District 15, Position 5

Queen, Amy M.
District 3, Position 14

Ramras, Christopher A.
District 4, Position 15

Raschio, Robert S. (P)
District 24, Position 1

Rastetter, Thomas J.
District 5, Position 10

Ravassipour, Kelly W.
District 1, Position 3

Rees, David F.
District 4, Position 9

Rigmaiden, Clara L.
District 2, Position 15

Rini, Michele C.
District 20, Position 13

Roberts, Beth L.
District 20, Position 12

Russell, Shelley D.
District 4, Position 4

Ryan, Thomas M.
District 4, Position 18

Shirtcliff, Matthew B. (P)
District 8, Position 1

Shugar, Kamala H.
District 2, Position 10

Simmons, Ann Marie G.
District 16, Position 1

Sims, Theodore E.
District 20, Position 1

Sinlapasai, Chanpone P.
District 4, Position 22

Skye, Kelly
District 4, Position 17

Souede, Benjamin N.
District 4, Position 30

Steele, Kathie F.
District 5, Position 6

Stein, Keith B.
District 23, Position 2

Stone, Martin E. (P)
District 15, Position 1

Summer, Miranda S.
District 20, Position 14

Svetkey, Susan M.
District 4, Position 16

Sykora, Alycia N.
District 11, Position 4

Temple, Eva J.
District 6, Position 4

Thompson, Brandon M.
District 20, Position 10

Thueson, Brandon S.
District 14, Position 1

Torres, Xiomara Y.
District 4, Position 32

Trevino, Mari G.
District 27, Position 2

Troy II, Francis G.
District 4, Position 1

**Van Rysselberghe,
Todd L.**
District 5, Position 7

**Vandenberg, David M.
(P)**
District 26, Position 1

Velure, Debra E.
District 2, Position 1

Villa-Smith, Kathryn L.
District 4, Position 29

Vitolins, Daina A.
District 22, Position 3

Vogt, Debra K.
District 2, Position 14

Von Ter Stegge, Katharine
District 4, Position 10

Waller, Nan G.
District 4, Position 2

Watkins, Ulanda L.
District 5, Position 9

Photo Not Submitted

Weatherford, Marion T.
District 7, Position 2

Weber, Katherine E.
District 5, Position 5

Weston, Cody M.
District 5, Position 4

Wetzel, Michael (P)
District 5, Position 3

Whiting, Wade L.
District 22, Position 2

Wiles, Ladd J (P).
District 25, Position 4

Williams, Locke A. (P)
District 21, Position 1

Williams, Wes
District 10, Position 2

Photo Not Submitted

Wintermute, Kirk
District 18, Position 3

Judicial

Judicial

Wipper, Janelle F.
District 20, Position 11

Wolf, John A.
District 7, Position 4

Wolke, Pat
District 14, Position 2

Wren, Daniel J.
District 3, Position 5

Wynhausen, Michael B.
District 23, Position 1

Zennaché, Charles
District 2, Position 4

Photo Not Submitted

VACANT
District 15, Position 4

CIRCUIT COURT JUDGES BY DISTRICT

District 1—Jackson

Jackson County Justice Bldg., Medford 97501

Barnack, Timothy
Pos. 6, Exp. 1-4-27, 541-776-7171 x71158

Bloom, Benjamin M. (presiding judge)
Pos. 7, Exp. 1-6-25, 541-776-7171 x71160

Charter, Joseph M.
Pos. 8, Exp. 1-4-27, 541-776-7171 x71520

Cromwell, Laura A.
Pos. 4, Exp. 1-6-25, 541-776-7171 x71113

Gerking, Timothy C.
Pos. 5, Exp. 1-6-25, 541-776-7171 x71103

Hoppe, David G.
Pos. 2, Exp. 1-4-27, 541-776-7171 x71651

Kochlacs, Charles G.
Pos. 10, Exp. 1-4-27, 541-776-7171 x71166

Markiewicz, Jeremy A.
Pos. 1, Exp. 1-4-27, 541-776-7171 x71154

Orr, David J.
Pos. 9, Exp. 1-6-25, 541-776-7171 x71123

Ravassipour, Kelly W.
Pos. 3, Exp. 1-4-27, 541-776-7171 x71122

District 2—Lane

Lane County Courthouse, Eugene 97401

Bassi, Michelle P.
Pos. 2, Exp. 1-1-29, 541-682-4257

Cascagnette, Bradley A.
Pos. 3, Exp. 1-4-27, 541-682-4256

Conover, R. Curtis
Pos. 12, Exp. 1-6-25, 541-682-6289

Fennerty, Erin A.
Pos. 9, Exp. 1-1-29, 541-682-4254

Grace, Beatrice N.
Pos. 11, Exp. 1-1-29, 541-682-4415

Kapoor, Amit
Pos. 6, Exp. 1-2-27, 541-682-4258

Love, Valeri L.
Pos. 8, Exp. 1-6-25, 541-682-4250

McAlpin, Jay A. (presiding judge)
Pos. 7, Exp. 1-6-25, 541-682-4240

McIntyre, Karrie K.
Pos. 13, Exp. 1-1-29, 541-682-4218

Morgan, Stephen W.
Pos. 5, Exp. 1-2-25, 541-682-4300

Rigmaiden, Clara L.
Pos. 15, Exp. 1-4-27, 541-682-4753

Shugar, Kamala H.
Pos. 10, Exp. 1-6-27, 541-682-3601

Velure, Debra E.
Pos. 1, Exp. 1-6-25, 541-682-4253

Vogt, Debra K.
Pos. 14, Exp. 1-6-25, 541-682-4027

Zennaché, Charles
Pos. 4, Exp. 1-4-27, 541-682-4259

District 3—Marion
Marion County Courthouse, Salem 97309-0869

Abar, Donald D.
Pos. 11, Exp. 1-6-25, 503-588-8485

Armstrong, Sean E.
Pos. 7, Exp. 1-1-29, 503-585-4939

Bennett, J. Channing
Pos. 1, Exp. 1-1-29, 503-588-7950

Broyles, Audrey J.
Pos. 9, Exp. 1-1-29, 503-588-5492

Bureta, Jodie A.
Pos. 4, Exp. 1-2-27, 503-588-8485

Edmonds, James C.
Pos. 6, Exp. 1-1-29, 503-373-4303 x8526

Gardiner, Jennifer K.
Pos. 3, Exp. 1-1-29, 503-584-7783

Geyer, Courtland
Pos. 12, Exp. 1-6-25, 503-373-4445

Hart, Thomas M.
Pos. 13, Exp. 1-1-29, 503-584-7749

Leith, David E.
Pos. 8, Exp. 1-6-25, 503-588-5160

Partridge, Lindsay R.
Pos. 10, Exp. 1-6-25, 503-588-5028

Perez, Manuel D.
Pos. 15, Exp. 1-4-27, 503-588-5735

Prall, Tracy A. (presiding judge)
Pos. 2, Exp. 1-4-27, 503-588-5030

Queen, Amy M.
Pos. 14, Exp. 1-1-29, 503-804-6591

Wren, Daniel J.
Pos. 5, Exp. 1-6-25, 503-588-8485

District 4—Multnomah
Multnomah County Courthouse, Portland 97204

Alarcón, Jaqueline L.
Pos. 3, Exp. 1-1-29, 971-274-0624

Albrecht, Cheryl A.
Pos. 31, Exp. 1-6-25, 971-274-0680

Alexander, Steffan K.
Pos. 26, Exp. 1-1-29, 971-274-0670

Allen, Beth A.
Pos. 34, Exp. 1-4-27, 971-274-0686

Baggio, Amy M.
Pos. 38, Exp. 1-4-27, 971-274-0694

Bottomly, Leslie G.
Pos. 6, Exp. 1-1-29, 971-274-0630

Brown, Adrian L.
Pos. 12, Exp. 1-4-27, 971-274-0642

Dahlin, Eric L.
Pos. 24, Exp. 1-1-29, 971-274-0666

Francesconi, Bryan
Pos. 20, Exp. 1--29, 971-274-0698

Ghandour, Rima I.
Pos. 21, Exp. 1-4-27, 971-274-0674

Gates, Maurisa R.
Pos. 25, Exp. 1-1-29, 971-274-0668

Greenlick, Michael A.
Pos. 19, Exp. 1-4-27, 971-274-0656

Henry, Patrick W.
Pos. 35, Exp. 1-1-28, 971-274-0688

Holmes Hehn, Amy
Pos. 14, Exp. 1-4-27, 971-274-0646

Howes, Celia A.
Pos. 8, Exp. 1-1-29, 971-274-0634

Lavin, Andrew M.
Pos. 7, Exp. 1-6-25, 971-274-0632

Long, Morgan W.
Pos. 13, Exp. 1-4-27 971-274-0644

Loy, Michael S.
Pos. 33, Exp. 1-4-27, 971-274-0684

Lucero, Angela F.
Pos. 11, Exp. 1-4-27, 971-274-0640

Marshall, Christopher J.
Pos. 5, Exp. 1-4-27, 971-274-0628

Matarazzo, Judith H. (presiding judge)
Pos. 28, Exp. 1-6-25, 971-274-0660

McGuire, Patricia L.
Pos. 27, Exp. 1-6-25, 971-274-0672

Moawad, Heidi H.
Pos. 36, Exp. 1-4-27, 971-274-0690

Oden-Orr, Melvin
Pos. 23, Exp. 1-6-25, 971-274-0664

Plank, Jenna R.
Pos. 37, Exp. 1-1-29, 971-274-0692

Ramras, Christopher A.
Pos. 15, Exp. 1-6-25, 971-274-0648

Rees, David F.
Pos. 9, Exp. 1-1-29, 971-274-0636

Russell, Shelley D.
Pos. 4, Exp. 1-6-25, 971-274-0626

Ryan, Thomas M.
Pos. 18, Exp. 1-4-27, 971-274-0654

Sinlapasai, Chanpone P.
Pos. 22, Exp. 1-1-29, 971-274-0662

Skye, Kelly
Pos. 17, Exp. 1-1-29, 971-274-0652

Souede, Benjamin N.
Pos. 30, Exp. 1-6-25, 971-274-0678

Svetkey, Susan M.
Pos. 16, Exp. 1-6-25, 971-274-0650

Torres, Xiomara Y.
Pos. 32, Exp. 1-6-25, 971-274-0682

Troy II, Francis G.
Pos. 1, Exp. 1-4-27, 971-274-0620

Villa-Smith, Kathryn L.
Pos. 29, Exp. 1-6-25, 971-274-0676

Von Ter Stegge, Katharine
Pos. 10, Exp. 1-6-25, 971-274-0638

Waller, Nan G.
Pos. 2, Exp. 1-4-27, 971-274-0622

District 5—Clackamas

Clackamas County Courthouse, Oregon City 97045

Jones, Jeffrey S.
Pos. 1, Exp. 1-6-25, 503-655-8687

Karabeika, Heather L.
Pos. 8, Exp. 1-4-27, 503-722-2732

Lininger, Ann M.
Pos. 2, Exp. 1-6-25, 503-655-2841

Norby, Susie L.
Pos. 11, Exp. 1-6-25, 503-650-8902

Rastetter, Thomas J.
Pos. 10, Exp. 1-1-29, 503-655-8432

Steele, Kathie F.
Pos. 6, Exp. 1-4-27, 503-655-8678

Van Rysselberghe, Todd L.
Pos. 7, Exp. 1-6-25, 503-655-8644

Watkins, Ulanda L.
Pos. 9, Exp. 1-5-25, 503-655-8686

Weber, Katherine E.
Pos. 5, Exp. 1-1-29, 503-655-8233

Weston, Cody M.
Pos. 4, Exp. 1-1-29, 503-655-8688

Wetzel, Michael (presiding judge)
Pos. 3, Exp. 1-6-25, 503-655-8685

District 6—Morrow, Umatilla

Umatilla County Courthouse, Pendleton 97801

Brauer, Christopher R.
Pos. 5, Exp. 1-6-25, 541-278-0341 x222

Collins Jr., Robert W.
Pos. 1, Exp. 1-6-25, 541-278-0341 x232

Lieuallen, Jon S.
Pos. 2, Exp. 1-9-29, 541-278-0341 x225

Stafford Hansell Gov't Center, Hermiston 97838

Hill, Daniel J. (presiding judge)
Pos. 3, Exp. 1-9-29, 541-667-3034

Temple, Eva J.
Pos. 4, Exp. 1-6-25, 541-667-3031

District 7—Gilliam, Hood River, Sherman, Wasco, Wheeler

Hood River Co. Courthouse, Hood River 97031

Olson, John A.
Pos. 1, Exp. 1-6-25, 541-386-3535 x70900

Ostrye, Karen (presiding judge)
Pos. 3, Exp. 1-4-27, 541-386-3535 x70904

Wasco County Courthouse, The Dalles 97058

Weatherford, Marion T.
Pos. 2, Exp. 1-9-29, 541-506-2700 x70899

Wolf, John A.
Pos. 4, Exp. 1-9-29, 541-506-2700 x70908

District 8—Baker

Baker County Courthouse, Baker City 97814

Shirtcliff, Matthew B. (presiding judge)
Pos. 1, Exp. 1-4-27, 541-523-6303

District 9—Malheur

Malheur County Courthouse, Vale 97918

Hung, Lung S. (presiding judge)
Pos. 2, Exp. 1-6-25, 541-473-5194

Landis, Erin K.
Pos. 1, Exp. 1-9-25, 541-473-5718

District 10—Union, Wallowa

Union County Courthouse, La Grande 97850
Wallowa County Courthouse, Enterprise 97828

Powers, Thomas B. (presiding judge)
Pos. 1, Exp. 1-6-25, 541-962-9500 x3,2

Williams, Wes
Pos. 2, Exp. 1-6-25, 541-962-9500 x3,2

District 11—Deschutes

Deschutes County Courthouse, Bend 97701

Ashby, Wells B. (presiding judge)
Pos. 6, Exp. 1-1-29, 541-388-5300 x2520

Bagley, Beth M.
Pos. 2, Exp. 1-6-25, 541-388-5300 x2410

Crutchley, Raymond D.
Pos. 1, Exp. 1-6-25, 541-388-5300 x2450

Emerson, Alison M.
Pos. 7, Exp. 1-4-27, 541-388-5300 x2580

Flint, Bethany P.
Pos. 3, Exp. 1-1-29, 541-388-5300 x2370

Herriott, Alycia M.
Pos. 9, Exp. 1-1-29, 541-388-5300

McIver, Michelle A.
Pos. 8, Exp. 1-1-29, 541-388-5300

Miller, Walter R., Jr.
Pos. 5, Exp. 1-4-27, 541-388-5300 x2550

Sykora, Alycia N.
Pos. 4, Exp. 1-4-27, 541-388-5300 x2490

District 12—Polk

Polk County Courthouse, Dallas 97338

Campbell, Monte S.
Pos. 2, Exp. 1-1-29, 503-623-9245

Caso, Rafael A.
Pos. 1, Exp. 1-6-25, 503-831-1776

Hill, Norman R. (presiding judge)
Pos. 3, Exp. 1-6-25, 503-623-5235

District 13—Klamath

Klamath Co. Courthouse, Klamath Falls 97601

Adkisson, Marci W. (presiding judge)
Pos. 3, Exp. 1-1-29, 541-883-5503 x251

Hedlund, Stephen R.
Pos. 5, Exp. 1-2-23, 541-883-5503 x255

Janney, Andrea M.
Pos. 1, Exp. 1-1-29, 541-883-5503 x247

Kersey, Alycia E.
Pos. 2, Exp. 1-4-27, 541-883-5503 x257

Kritzer, Kelly N.
Pos. 4, Exp. 1-1-29, 541-883-5503 x244

District 14—Josephine

Josephine County Courthouse, Grants Pass 97526

Bain, Robert S. (presiding judge)
Pos. 3, Exp. 1-6-25, 541-476-2309 x4541

Galli, Matthew G.
Pos. 5, Exp. 1-6-25, 541-476-2309 x4525

McGlaughlin, Sarah E.
Pos. 4, Exp. 1-4-27, 541-476-2309 x4539

Thueson, Brandon S.
Pos. 1, Exp. 1-4-27, 541-476-2309 x4543

Wolke, Pat
Pos. 2, Exp. 1-6-25, 541-476-2309 x7916

District 15—Coos, Curry

Coos County Courthouse, Coquille 97423

Beaman, Cynthia L.
Pos. 6, Exp. 1-4-27, 541-373-6894 x70018
29821 Ellensburg Ave., Gold Beach 97444

Combs, Andrew E.
Pos. 2, Exp. 1-6-25, 541-396-8372 x10024

VACANT
Pos. 4

Margolis, Jesse
Pos. 3, Exp. 1-6-25, 541-373-6894 x70038
29821 Ellensburg Ave., Gold Beach 97444

Pruess, Brett A.
Pos. 5, Exp. 1-6-25, 541-396-8372 x70020

Stone, Martin E. (presiding judge)
Pos. 1, Exp. 1-1-29, 541-396-8372 x70012

District 16—Douglas

Douglas County Justice Bldg., Roseburg 97470

Ambrosini, George W.
Pos. 5, Exp. 1-6-25, 541-957-2422

Hoddle, Steve H.
Pos. 2, Exp. 1-1-29, 541-957-2436 x70974

Johnson, Kathleen E. (presiding judge)
Pos. 3, Exp. 1-1-29, 541-957-2433

Johnson, Robert B.
Pos. 4, Exp. 1-1-29, 541-957-2420 x2433

Simmons, Ann Marie G.
Pos. 1, Exp. 1-4-27, 541-957-2430

District 17—Lincoln

Lincoln County Courthouse, Newport 97365

Bachart, Sheryl (presiding judge)
Pos. 1, Exp. 1-4-27, 541-574-8803

Benjamin, Amanda R.
Pos. 3, Exp. 1-1-29, 541-265-4256

Buckley, Marcia L.
Pos. 2, Exp. 1-4-27, 541-574-8812

District 18—Clatsop

Clatsop County Courthouse, Astoria 97103

McIntosh, Dawn M. (presiding judge)
Pos. 2, Exp. 1-1-29, 503-325-8555 x70130

Peterson, Beau V.
Pos. 1, Exp. 1-4-27, 503-325-8555 x70138

Wintermute, Kirk
Pos. 3, Exp. 1-1-29, 503-325-8555 x70096

District 19—Columbia

Columbia County Courthouse, St. Helens 97051

Callahan, Cathleen B.
Pos. 1, Exp. 1-4-27; 503-397-2327 x302

Clarke, Michael T. (presiding judge)
Pos. 3, Exp. 1-4-27, 503-397-2327 x322

Keppinger, Denise E.
Pos. 2, Exp. 1-1-29, 503-397-2327 x70115

District 20—Washington

Washington County Courthouse, Hillsboro 97124

Bailey, D. Charles
Pos. 6, Exp. 1-6-25, 503-846-8888 x70595

Buchér, Erik M.
Pos. 3, Exp. 1-6-25, 503-846-8888 x70597

Butterfield, Eric E.
Pos. 4, Exp. 1-1-29, 503-846-8888 x70571

Erwin, Andrew R.
Pos. 7, Exp. 1-4-27, 503-846-8888 x70581

Garcia, Oscar
Pos. 9, Exp. 1-6-25, 503-846-8888 x70604

Guptill, Rebecca D.
Pos. 2, Exp. 1-4-27, 503-846-8888 x70579

Lemarr, Kelly D.
Pos. 5, Exp. 1-4-27, 503-846-8888 x70630

Menchaca, Ricardo J.
Pos. 8, Exp. 1-4-27, 503-846-8888 x70588

Proctor, Kathleen J. (presiding judge)
Pos. 15, Exp. 1-6-25, 503-846-8888 x70583

Judicial

Rini, Michele C.
Pos. 13, Exp. 1-1-29, 503-846-8888 x70580

Roberts, Beth L.
Pos. 12, Exp. 1-4-27, 503-846-8888 x70626

Sims, Theodore E.
Pos. 1, Exp. 1-1-29, 503-846-8888 x70681

Summer, Miranda S.
Pos. 14, Exp. 1-1-29, 503-846-8888 x70622

Thompson, Brandon M.
Pos. 10, Exp. 1-4-27, 503-846-8888 x70585

Wipper, Janelle F.
Pos. 11, Exp. 1-6-25, 503-846-8888 x70620

District 21—Benton

Benton County Courthouse, Corvallis 97330

Demarest, Joan E.
Pos. 3, Exp. 1-4-27, 541-243-7802

Donohue, Matthew J.
Pos. 2, Exp. 1-4-27, 541-243-7805

Williams, Locke A. (presiding judge)
Pos. 1, Exp. 1-4-27, 541-243-7822

District 22—Crook, Jefferson

Jefferson Co. Circuit Court, 129 SW E St., Suite 101, Madras 97741
Crook County Courthouse, Prineville 97754

Hillman, Annette C. (presiding judge)
Pos. 1, Exp. 1-6-25, 541-475-3317;
541-447-6541

Vitolins, Daina A.
Pos. 3, Exp. 1-6-25, 541-475-3317;
541-447-6541

Whiting, Wade L.
Pos. 2, Exp. 1-1-29, 541-475-3317;
541-447-6541

District 23—Linn

Linn County Courthouse, Albany 97321

Kane, Brendan J.
Pos. 4, Exp. 1-4-27, 541-967-3848

Kittson-MaQatish, Rachel
Pos. 3, Exp. 1-6-25, 541-812-8766

McHill, Thomas A. (presiding judge)
Pos. 5, Exp. 1-1-29, 541-812-8765

Stein, Keith B.
Pos. 2, Exp. 1-2-29, 541-812-8769

Wynhausen, Michael B.
Pos. 1, Exp. 1-6-25, 541-812-8767

District 24—Grant, Harney

Grant County Courthouse, Canyon City 97820
Harney County Courthouse, Burns 97720

Raschio, Robert S. (presiding judge)
Pos. 1, Exp. 1-4-27, 541-573-5207;
541-575-1438

District 25—Yamhill

Yamhill County Courthouse, McMinnville 97128

Chapman, Jennifer K.
Pos. 2, Exp. 1-6-25, 503-434-7485

Easterday, Cynthia L.
Pos. 3, Exp. 1-1-29, 503-434-7486

Kaufman Noble, Cynthia
Pos. 1, Exp. 1-1-29, 503-434-7485

Wiles, Ladd J. (presiding judge)
Pos. 4, Exp. 1-4-27, 503-434-3054

District 26—Lake

Lake County Courthouse, Lakeview 97630

Vandenberg, David M. (presiding judge)
Pos. 1, Exp. 1-4-27, 541-947-6051

District 27—Tillamook

Tillamook County Courthouse, Tillamook 97141

Hill, Jonathan R. (presiding judge)
Pos. 1, Exp. 1-1-29, 503-842-2598 x2113

Trevino, Mari G.
Pos. 2, Exp. 1-4-27, 503-842-2598 x2114

Circuit Judges Association:

President—Hon. Benjamin Souede
President Elect—Hon. Beth M. Bagley
Secretary—Hon. Matthew G. Galli
Treasurer— Hon. Robert S. Raschio
Immediate Past President—Hon. Rafael A. Caso

STATE OF OREGON LAW LIBRARY

Source: Cathryn Bowie, State Law Librarian
Address: 1163 State St., Supreme Court Bldg., Salem 97301-2563

Phone: 503-986-5640
Web: soll.libguides.com/index

The State of Oregon Law Library (SOLL) traces its origins to the organization of the territorial government of Oregon. The Territorial Act of 1848 provided for the establishment of a library "to be kept at the seat of government." An 1851 act provided for the appointment of a librarian and defined the librarian's duties. The library served a broad constituency from its beginnings: "Members of the legislature, and its clerks and officers; Judges of the Supreme and District Courts, and their clerks; Attorney-general and marshal of the Territory; attorneys-at-law, secretary of the Territory; and all other persons, shall have access to the library, and the privileges allowed by law." This inclusive policy was continued with statehood in 1859. Charge and control of the library was transferred to the Supreme Court in 1913.

Today, the library operates under the administrative authority of the office of the state court administrator. Its mission is to provide the comprehensive legal resources that the executive, legislative and judicial branches of state government require to serve the public effectively, and to afford all Oregonians access to legal information.

The library is the largest collection of legal information resources in state government, including the primary law of all U.S. jurisdictions and secondary material in virtually all areas of law.

Related Organizations

BOARD OF BAR EXAMINERS

Source: Troy Wood, Regulatory Counsel
Address: 16037 SW Upper Boones Ferry Rd., PO Box 231935, Tigard 97281-1935
Phone: 503-620-0222
Web: osbar.org/admissions
Stephanie J. Tuttle, Chair, 2023; Dr. Anthony J Rosilez, Vice-Chair, 2023; Hon. Jacqueline Alarcón Member, 2025; Dr. David Corey, Public Member, 2023; Christy Doornink, Member, 2023; Richard Kolbell, Ph.D., Public Member, 2023; Angela Franco Lucero, Member, 2024; Kendra Matthews, Member, 2025; Cassandra C. McLeod-Skinner, Member, 2023; Joanna Perinni-Abbott, Member, 2025; Hon. Kelly Skye, Member, 2023; Michael Slauson, Member, 2024; Adrian Tobin Smith, Member, 2024; Glen Ujifusa, Member, 2025

The Board of Bar Examiners, established in 1913, acts for the Supreme Court in evaluating an applicant's qualifications to practice law in Oregon. The Board determines an applicant's qualifications for admission to the Bar by administering and grading the Oregon bar examination twice a year. They also investigate and evaluate the character and fitness of each applicant.

OREGON STATE BAR

Source: Helen Hierschbiel, Chief Executive Officer
Address: 16037 SW Upper Boones Ferry Rd., PO Box 231935, Tigard 97281-1935
Phone: 503-620-0222; Toll-free: 1-800-452-8260
Fax: 503-684-1366

Web: osbar.org
Board of Governors: Lee Ann Donaldson, President, Portland, 2023; Christopher Cauble, Grants Pass, 2024; Gabriel Chase, Portland, 2024; Candace Clark, St. Helens, 2025; Stephanie Engelsman, Portland, 2025; Kellie Furr, Portland, 2026; Tomas Hernandez, Albany, 2026; Joseph Hesbrook, Bend, 2026; Ryan Hunt, Salem, 2023; Elizabeth Inayoshi, Hillsboro, 2026; Myah Kehoe, Portland, 2025; John Marandas, Lake Oswego, 2026; Matt McKean, Hillsboro, 2024; Rob Milesnick, Vancouver, 2023; Curtis Peterson, Portland, 2024; Joseph Piucci, Portland, 2023; David Rosen, Bend, 2024; Apolinar Montero-Sánchez, Eugene, 2025; David Wade, Eugene, 2025; Tasha Winkler, Portland, 2023

Established in 1935, the Oregon State Bar is a public corporation and instrumentality of the Oregon Judicial Department that serves the public by regulating lawyers and improving access to justice and the delivery of legal services. The state bar oversees the admission and discipline of Oregon's lawyers. It also operates a lawyer referral service program, conducts continuing legal education programs, publishes legal and public service material, sponsors a legislative program to improve the laws and judicial system of Oregon, provides malpractice coverage for lawyers in private practice, distributes state funds allocated to legal service programs and monitors the programs for adherence to adopted standards.

COUNCIL ON COURT PROCEDURES

Source: Mark A. Peterson, Executive Director
Address: c/o Lewis & Clark Law School, 10101 SW Terwilliger Blvd., Portland 97219
Phone: 503-768-6505
Web: counciloncourtprocedures.org

Oregon's civil trial procedures were once found in laws passed by the Legislature and scattered among the Oregon Revised Statutes (ORS), until the Council on Court Procedures was established by the Legislature in 1977 (ORS 1.725 to 1.760).

The Council codified Oregon's requirements governing pleading, practice and procedure in all civil proceedings in the circuit courts of the state — the Oregon Rules of Civil Procedure (ORCP) as the product of the Council, is charged with the responsibility for maintaining the ORCP by promulgating amendments in odd-numbered years each biennium. The Council's promulgations amend the ORCP unless the Legislature by statute repeals, amends, or supplements a rule or a promulgation. See the Council's website and the above-referenced statutes for more detailed information.

Members with term-expiration dates:
Hon. Christopher L. Garrett, Oregon Supreme Court, 2025; Hon. Scott Shorr, Oregon Court of Appeals, 2025; Hon. Benjamin M. Bloom, Jackson County Circuit Court, 2025; Hon. Jonathan R. Hill, Tillamook County Circuit Court, 2025; Hon. Norman R. Hill, Polk County Circuit Court, 2025; Hon. David Euan Leith, Marion County Circuit Court, 2023; Hon. Thomas McHill, Linn County Circuit Court 2023; Hon. Susie L. Norby, Clackamas County Circuit Court, 2025; Hon. Melvin Oden-Orr, Multnomah County Circuit Court, 2025; Hon. D. Charles Bailey, Washington County Circut Court, 2025; Kelly L. Andersen, Medford, 2025 (Vice Chair); Troy S. Bundy, Portland, 2023; Kenneth Crowley, Salem, 2023 (Chair); Nadia Dahab, Portland, 2025; Barry Goehler, Lake Oswego, 2023; Meredith Holley, Eugene, 2025; Drake A. Hood, Hillsboro, 2023; Derek Larwick, Eugene, 2025; Scott O'Donnell, Portland, 2025; Tina Stupasky, Eugene, 2023; Stephen J. Vorhees, Portland, 2025; Jeffrey Young, Portland, 2023; Margurite Weeks, Public Member, Portland, 2025 (Treasurer)

COMMISSION ON JUDICIAL FITNESS AND DISABILITY

Source: Rachel L. Mortimer, Executive Director
Address: PO Box 90398, Portland 97290
Phone: 503-626-6776
Fax: 503-626-6787
Web: courts.oregon.gov/programs/cjfd/Pages/default.aspx

Chair Hon. Steven R. Powers, 2026; Hon. Cheryl Albrecht, 2025; Hon. Monte S. Campbell, 2025; Karyn L. Goodfriend, Public Member, 2024; Roland Herrera, Public Member, 2024; Melanie Kebler, Attorney, 2023; Wilson Kenney, PhD, Public Member, 2023; Judith Parker, Attorney, 2023; Jeffrey Wallace, Public Member, 2024

Commission members are volunteers serving four-year terms. Three are judges appointed by the Supreme Court, three are lawyers appointed by the Oregon State Bar and three are citizens appointed by the governor and confirmed by the senate.

Pursuant to ORS 1.410 to 1.480, the Oregon Constitution and the Rules of Judicial Conduct, the commission investigates complaints regarding Oregon judges. If the commission believes there is substantial evidence of misconduct, a public hearing is held. The commission makes recommendations regarding disciplinary actions to the Supreme Court. A judge may be censured, suspended or removed from office by the Supreme Court. The commission cannot change the decision of a judge and does not have jurisdiction over arbitrators, mediators or municipal court judges.

COUNTY COURTS

At one time county courts existed in all 36 Oregon counties. The title "county judge" is retained in some counties as the title of the chair of the board of county commissioners. There is no requirement that county judges be members of the bar.

Where a county judge's judicial function still exists, it is limited to juvenile and probate matters. These only occupy a portion of the judge's time, which is primarily devoted to nonjudicial administrative responsibilities as a member of the county board.

Today, only six counties, all east of the Cascades, have county judges who retain any judicial authority. Gilliam, Sherman and Wheeler have juvenile and probate jurisdiction, while Grant, Harney and Malheur have probate jurisdiction.

MUNICIPAL COURT

Oregon Municipal Judges Association

Source: Hon. Juliet Britton
Address: OMJA, PO Box 1472, Beaverton 97075
Email: oregonmunijudgesassociation@gmail.com
Web: omjaonline.com

The Oregon Municipal Judges Association (OMJA) participates in arranging continuing educational training sessions for municipal judges. It maintains a listserv system for judges to gain access to other municipal court judges and justices of the peace, whose two associations trade off on annual conferences in Oregon. OMJA coordinates with the Oregon Department of Transportation, which has its own annual conference for judges.

Many incorporated cities in Oregon have a municipal court as authorized by charter and state law. Municipal courts have concurrent jurisdiction with circuit and justice courts over all violations and misdemeanors committed or triable in the city in which the court is located. They do not have jurisdiction over felonies. Municipal courts primarily hear traffic violations and crimes; violations of municipal codes and ordinances, including animal, high grass and trash nuisances; vehicle impoundments and forfeitures; and parking and pedestrian violations. They also hear certain minor tobacco, liquor and drug violations.

Municipal courts may be a court of record, although most are not. Municipal court procedures are controlled to a large extent by state law.

A municipal judge need not be an attorney, although most are. Municipal judges are usually appointed by, and serve at the pleasure of, the city council. A few Oregon cities have elected judges. Qualifications for office are determined by the city council or charter. A municipal judge may perform weddings anywhere within the state of Oregon.

JUSTICE COURTS

Source: Damian Idiart, Justice of the Peace
Address: 4173 Hamrick Rd., Central Point 97502
Phone: 541-774-1286
Web: jacksoncountyor.org/departments/justice court/home

Justice court is held by a justice of the peace within the district for which he or she is elected. The county commissioners have power to establish justice court district boundaries. The justice of the peace is a remnant of territorial days when each precinct of the state was entitled to a justice court. Thirty-two justice courts currently administer justice in 21 counties.

Justice courts have jurisdiction within their county, concurrent with the circuit court, in all criminal prosecutions, except felony trials. Actions at law in justice courts are conducted using the mode of proceeding and rules of evidence similar to those used in the circuit courts, except where otherwise specifically provided.

Justice courts have jurisdiction over traffic, boating, wildlife and other violations occurring in their county. Justices of the peace also perform weddings at no charge if performed at their offices during regular business hours.

The justice court has small claims civil jurisdiction where the money or damages claimed do not exceed $7,500, except in actions involving title to real property, false imprisonment, libel, slander or malicious prosecution.

A justice of the peace must be a citizen of the United States, a resident of Oregon for three years, and a resident of the justice court district for one year prior to becoming a nonpartisan candidate for election to that office. They are elected to six-year terms. The names of the Oregon justices of the peace are listed by county in the Local Governments section.

OFFICE OF PUBLIC DEFENSE SERVICES

Source: Per Ramfjord, Chair
Address: 198 Commercial Street SE, Suite 200, Salem 97301
Phone: 503-378-3349
Fax: 503-378-2163
Web: oregon.gov/opds

The Public Defense Services Commission (PDSC) is an independent agency in the judicial branch. Its primary responsibility is securing public defense counsel and required legal services for eligible individuals in Oregon's circuit and appellate courts. The agency was created by SB 145 (2001).

The chief justice of the Oregon Supreme Court appoints nine commissioners to four-year terms. The commission's function is to provide oversight over the Office of Public Defense Services (OPDS). Its charge is to establish "a public defense system that ensures the provision of public defense consistent with the Oregon Constitution, the United States Constitution and Oregon and national standards of justice." To carry out this charge, the commission appoints an executive director to lead OPDS.

OPDS has 113 positions over five divisions: Executive, Administrative Services, Trial, Appellate, and Compliance, Audit and Performance (CAP). The Executive Division contains the agency's core leadership team. The Administrative Services Division includes Budget and Finance, Human Resources and Information Technology. The Trial Division relies upon contracts and hourly fee agreements to ensure eligible individuals receive legal services in Oregon's circuit courts. The Appellate Division employs attorneys to provide legal representation to eligible individuals in Oregon's appellate courts. The CAP Division both monitors and reports on agency performance.

The majority of the agency's budget is distributed to external attorney and non-attorneys who provide public defense services pursuant to contract and fee agreements.

STUDENT ESSAY CONTEST WINNER

Oregon Blue Book Covid-19 Essay

Anileh Chen
Mr. Germer's 5th Grade Class
Hope Chinese Charter School, Beaverton

This drawing by Anileh Chen shows a lighthouse of hope.

Covid-19 marked an epoch in my life. It was a whirlwind; mixing feelings. I said goodbye to Ms Dennis for Spring Break, and it was like Spring Break never ended. We had changed from rarely using computers to relying on them for everything concerning our learning. Sometimes I missed lessons because the computer wasn't working. Often I'd stay up late trying to type out essays. School had clearly changed along with the rest of the world. Even two years later, I couldn't go to school without hearing "Covid-19" thrice a week. To add on, we had to wear masks each day, which was rather unpleasant.

Change is contrary and often confusing. It's like the wind, quickly turning course. Yet sometimes change is good, like a new friend who becomes such an important part of your life that you wonder how you'd lived with out her. My family was able to have more R.V. trips or "Great Explorations". Not only that, as people became less interactive, we'd find welcoming silence replacing the crowds. Another bright side was that my sisters could watch my Zoom lessons, so they'd be prepared for Second Grade.

Covid-19 was a hard change, so desperately hard that some people still aren't adjusted to it. It came thundering down on us, taking us by suprise. Despite this, I believe we need not be discouraged. Nowhere in the world is without love and joy, even in difficult times. We should understand this pandemic not merely as another obstacle on our path but a reminder to be grateful for our blessings. I have learned to always hold on to hope. Hope is the joy of sailors reaching a lighthouse full of guidance. Through the darkness Coronavirus brings, hope is light for the world. We surely need it for ours.

Legislative

Oregon's Provisional Legislature first met formally in 1845 in Oregon City. They were a unicameral body that operated on an uncertain schedule. The present bicameral system—two houses with senators and representatives—was adopted in 1859 upon statehood. Today's legislators meet annually in Salem and deal with complex matters, by passing bills and appropriating funding. This section introduces the members of the Legislature and describes how the Legislature is organized.

OREGON'S LEGISLATIVE ASSEMBLY

Source: Legislative Administration
Address: 900 Court St. NE, Rm. 140-A, Salem 97301
Phone: 503-986-1848
Web: oregonlegislature.gov

President of the Senate

Rob Wagner, Senate President
Address: 900 Court St. NE, Rm. S-201, Salem 97301
Phone: 503-986-1600

The Senate president is elected by members of the Senate to select committee chairs and membership, preside over its daily sessions and coordinate its administrative operations. Subject to the rules of the Senate, the president refers measures to committees, directs Senate personnel and mediates questions on internal operations.

The Senate president's staff assists in carrying out official duties, helps coordinate Senate operations and provides a variety of public information services. In cooperation with the speaker of the House, the president coordinates and supervises the work product of the legislative branch of Oregon state government and represents that branch in contacts with the executive and judicial branches. The president's office works closely with all political parties to ensure that session goals are met.

Secretary of the Senate

Lori Brocker, Secretary of the Senate
Address: 900 Court St. NE, Rm. 233, Salem 97301
Phone: 503-986-1851

The secretary of the Senate is an elected officer of the state Senate. The secretary is responsible for and supervises Senate employees engaged in keeping measures, papers and records of proceedings and actions of the Senate. The secretary supervises preparation of the daily agenda, all measures, histories, journals and related publications and is in charge of publication of documents related to the Senate. In addition, the secretary has custody of all measures, official papers and records of the Senate, except when released to authorized persons

by signed receipt. The secretary also serves as parliamentary consultant to the Senate, advises officers of the Senate on parliamentary procedure and manages the Honorary Page program.

During the interim, the secretary receives messages from the governor announcing executive appointments requiring Senate confirmation, prepares the agenda for the convening of the Senate and supervises publication of the official record of proceedings.

Speaker of the House of Representatives

Dan Rayfield, Speaker of the House
Address: 900 Court St. NE, Rm. 271, Salem 97301
Phone: 503-986-1200

The speaker of the House is elected by House members to preside over the deliberations of the House, preserve order and decorum and decide questions of order. The speaker appoints chairs and members to each committee and refers measures to appropriate committees in accordance with provisions of the rules of the House.

The House speaker's staff coordinates operations of the speaker's office, assists the presiding officer in performing official duties, provides research and policy support in issue areas, provides information to the news media and assists legislators in solving constituent problems. In conjunction with the Senate president's office, the speaker's office coordinates and supervises operations of the legislative branch of government, joint statutory committees, joint interim committees and task forces.

Chief Clerk of the House of Representatives

Timothy G. Sekerak, Chief Clerk
Address: Oregon State Capitol Building, Salem 97301
Phone: 503-986-1870

The chief clerk, elected by members of the House of Representatives, supervises and keeps a correct journal, and is the official custodian of all other records of House proceedings. The chief clerk notifies the Senate of all acts of the House, certifies and transmits all bills, resolutions and papers requiring Senate concurrence immediately upon their passage or adoption and secures proper authentication of bills that have passed both houses and transmits them to the governor.

The chief clerk prepares the agenda, coordinates details for the organization of the House and acts as parliamentarian as directed by House rules. In addition, at the end of the legislative session, the chief clerk supervises and authenticates the revision and printing of the *House Journal* and prepares all legislative records that are to be permanently filed with the state archivist.

Caucus Offices

Kate Lieber (D), Senate Majority Leader
Address: 900 Court St. NE, Rm. S-223, Salem 97301
Phone: 503-986-1714

Tim Knopp (R), Senate Republican Leader
Address: 900 Court St. NE, Rm. S-323, Salem 97301
Phone: 503-986-1950

Julie Fahey (D), House Majority Leader
Address: 900 Court St. NE, Rm. H-295, Salem 97301
Phone: 503-986-1900

Vikki Breese-Iverson (R), House Republican Leader
Address: 900 Court St. NE, Rm. H-395, Salem 97301
Phone: 503-986-1400

Caucus offices provide many services to their members during session and interim periods. Each office is directed by a leader chosen by the respective political party. The operations of the four offices are not identical, but typical services include conducting research, writing speeches and press releases, providing public information services, serving as liaison to state and federal agencies to help solve constituent problems, organizing caucus activities and circulating information about legislative business among caucus members during both session and interim periods.

Organization

Oregon's Legislative Assembly is composed of two chambers, House of Representatives and Senate. The Senate consists of 30 members elected to four-year terms. Half of the Senate seats are up for election every two years. The House consists of 60 representatives elected to two-year terms. Except in cases of persons selected to fill vacancies, legislators are elected in even-numbered years from single-member districts. Election by single-member district means that each Oregonian is represented by one senator and one representative. To qualify for a seat in the Legislature, one must be at least 21 years of age, a U.S. citizen and reside in the legislative district for at least one year prior to election. Each chamber elects presiding officers to oversee daily sessions and operations and perform other duties set by rule, custom and law. These officers are known as the president of the Senate and speaker of the House.

Functions

The Legislature enacts new laws and revises existing ones, makes decisions that keep the state in good economic and environmental condition and provides a forum for discussion of public issues.

The Legislature reviews and revises the governor's proposed budget and passes tax laws to provide needed revenue. The Oregon Constitution requires that the state must not spend money in excess of revenue.

The Legislature also influences executive and judicial branch decisions, enacting laws and adopting the budget and establishing state policy that directs all state agency activity and impacts the courts. The Senate confirms gubernatorial appointments to certain offices. Legislative Counsel Committee reviews state agency administrative rules to ensure that legislative intent is followed.

Legislative Process

During the 2021 Regular Session, 714 of 2,519 introduced bills became law. During the 2022 Regular Session, 127 of 275 introduced bills became law.

Most of the discussion and revision of bills and other measures are done in committees. The process begins when a measure is introduced and referred to a committee. The committee may hear testimony on the measure, frequently from members of the public, and may amend the measure and send it to the floor of its respective chamber for debate. The committee can also table the measure and end its consideration. Unlike many

Senate and House District Numbers

Senate	House Dist.	Senate	House Dist.	Senate	House Dist.	Senate	House Dist.
1	1 and 2	9	17 and 18	17	33 and 34	25	49 and 50
2	3 and 4	10	19 and 20	18	35 and 36	26	51 and 52
3	5 and 6	11	21 and 22	19	37 and 38	27	53 and 54
4	7 and 8	12	23 and 24	20	39 and 40	28	55 and 56
5	9 and 10	13	25 and 26	21	41 and 42	29	57 and 58
6	11 and 12	14	27 and 28	22	43 and 44	30	59 and 60
7	13 and 14	15	29 and 30	23	45 and 46		
8	15 and 16	16	31 and 32	24	47 and 48		

state legislatures, Oregon does not amend measures during floor debate.

After a measure has been considered by a committee and passed by the chamber in which it was introduced, it is sent to the other chamber where a similar procedure is followed.

If both chambers pass a bill in identical form, including any amendments approved by the other chamber, it is enrolled (printed in final form) for the signatures of the presiding officers and governor. The governor may sign the bill, veto it or let it become law without signature. The governor may

Chronology of Regular Legislative Sessions in Oregon

Leg. Assembly	Year	Dates	Length in Days	Leg. Assembly	Year	Dates	Length in Days
1	1860	Sept. 10–Oct. 19	40	49	1957	Jan. 14–May 21	128
2	1862	Sept. 8–Oct. 17	40	50	1959	Jan. 12–May 6	115
3	1864	Sept. 12–Oct. 22	41	51	1961	Jan. 9–May 10	122
4	1866	Sept. 10–Oct. 20	41	52	1963	Jan. 14–June 3	141
5	1868	Sept. 14–Oct. 28	44	53	1965	Jan. 11–May 14	124
6	1870	Sept. 12–Oct. 20	39	54	1967	Jan. 9–June 14	157
7	1872	Sept. 9–Oct. 23	45	55	1969	Jan. 13–May 23	131
8	1874	Sept. 14–Oct. 21	38	56	1971	Jan. 11–June 10	151
9	1876	Sept. 11–Oct. 20	40	57	1973	Jan. 8–July 6	180
10	1878	Sept. 9–Oct. 18	40	58	1975	Jan. 13–June 14	153
11	1880	Sept. 13–Oct. 23	41	59	1977	Jan. 10–July 5	177
12	1882	Sept. 11–Oct. 19	39	60	1979	Jan. 8–July 4	178
13	1885	Jan. 12–Feb. 21	40	61	1981	Jan. 12–August 2	203
14	1887	Jan. 10–Feb. 18	39	62	1983	Jan. 10–July 16	188
15	1889	Jan. 14–Feb. 22	39	63	1985	Jan. 14–June 21	159
16	1891	Jan. 12–Feb. 20	39	64	1987	Jan. 12–June 28	168
17	1893	Jan. 9–Feb. 17	39	65	1989	Jan. 9–July 4	177
18	1895	Jan. 14–Feb. 23	40	66	1991	Jan. 14–July 1	168
19	1897	Jan. 11–March 2	*	67	1993	Jan. 11–August 5	207
20	1899	Jan. 9–Feb. 18	40	68	1995	Jan. 9–June 10	153
21	1901	Jan. 14–March 4	50	69	1997	Jan. 13–July 5	174
22	1903	Jan. 12–Feb. 20	39	70	1999	Jan. 11–July 24	195
23	1905	Jan. 9–Feb. 17	40	71	2001	Jan. 8–July 7	181
24	1907	Jan. 14–Feb. 23	41	72	2003	Jan. 13–August 27	227
25	1909	Jan. 11–Feb. 20	41	73	2005	Jan. 10–August 5	208
26	1911	Jan. 9–Feb. 18	41	74	2007	Jan. 8–June 28	171
27	1913	Jan. 13–March 5	51	75	2009	Jan. 12–June 29	169
28	1915	Jan. 11–Feb. 20	41	76	2011	Feb. 1–June 30	150
29	1917	Jan. 8–Feb. 19	43	76	2012	Feb. 1–March 5	34
30	1919	Jan. 13–Feb. 27	46	77	2013	Feb. 4–July 8	155
31	1921	Jan. 10–Feb. 23	45	77	2014	Feb. 3–March 7	33
32	1923	Jan. 8–Feb. 22	46	78	2015	Feb. 2–July 6	155
33	1925	Jan. 12–Feb. 26	46	78	2016	Feb. 1–March 3	32
34	1927	Jan. 10–Feb. 25	47	79	2017	Feb. 1–July 7	157
35	1929	Jan. 14–March 5	50	79	2018	Feb. 5–March 3	27
36	1931	Jan. 12–March 6	54	80	2019	Jan. 22–June 30	160
37	1933	Jan. 9–March 9	60	80	2020	Feb. 3–March 8	35
38	1935	Jan. 14–March 13	59	81	2021	Jan. 19–June 26	159
39	1937	Jan. 11–March 8	57	81	2022	Feb. 1 — March 4	32
40	1939	Jan. 9–March 15	66				
41	1941	Jan. 13–March 15	62				
42	1943	Jan. 11–March 10	59				
43	1945	Jan. 8–March 17	69				
44	1947	Jan. 13–April 5	83				
45	1949	Jan. 10–April 16	97				
46	1951	Jan. 8–May 3	116				
47	1953	Jan. 12–April 21	100				
48	1955	Jan. 10–May 4	115				

The House of Representatives never formally convened because its members failed to reach agreement on organization.

Legislative

also veto line items of appropriation bills, but may not veto an act referred for a vote of the people or an act initiated by the people.

The Oregon Constitution and state law require that deliberations of the Legislative Assembly and its committees be open to the public. The law also requires public notice of meetings and maintenance of public meeting records. These practices ensure that the legislative process is open to public scrutiny.

Effective Date of Laws

The regular effective date of a measure is January 1 of the year following passage of the measure. Some measures may contain a provision, such as an emergency clause, that specifies an earlier effective date.

The Oregon Constitution prohibits tax measures from having an emergency clause. This ensures that the people have the right to refer a tax measure for a vote by petition before it goes into effect.

Session Schedule

Since 2011, the Legislature convenes each February at the State Capitol in Salem. Sessions may not exceed 160 days in odd-numbered years and 35 days in even-numbered years. Five-day extensions are allowed by a two-thirds vote in both houses. In addition, the Legislature may hold an organizational session to swear in newly elected officials, elect legislative leaders, adopt rules, organize and appoint committees and begin introducing bills.

Special sessions to deal with emergencies may be called by the governor or by a majority of each chamber. For example, the Legislative Assembly called itself into a special session in 2002, 2006, 2008 and 2010, and Governor Kate Brown called for three special sessions in 2020 to deal with the COVID-19 pandemic.

Contacting a Legislator and Obtaining Legislative Information

During session, the following numbers are available to obtain legislative information:
• Outside Salem: 1-800-332-2313
• Within Salem: 503-986-1388
During the interim, individual legislators may be reached by calling the telephone numbers listed on pages 119–121 and 125–130. Legislative information may be obtained by calling Legislative Administration at 503-986-1848.

Session Interim

After adjournment of regular or special sessions, the work of the Legislature continues. Legislators study issues likely to be important during future sessions, become acquainted with new issues, prepare drafts of legislation and exercise legislative oversight.

Convening of the Senate to Act on Executive Appointments

The Legislative Assembly may require that appointments to state public office made by the governor, be subject to Senate confirmation.

During the legislative session, the Senate president refers executive appointments to a standing or special committee to review the background and qualifications of appointees, ensuring that statutory requirements are met. Appointees may be asked to come before the committee for personal interviews. The committee submits its recommendations to the full Senate for confirmation votes.

During the interim, the secretary of the Senate receives the governor's announcements of executive appointments requiring Senate confirmation. Generally, gubernatorial appointments made during a regular or special session of the Legislature are acted upon by the Senate prior to adjourning *sine die* or final adjournment.

History

Oregon's Provisional Legislature initially met formally in Oregon City, December 2 to December 19, 1845. An earlier pre-provisional committee met in August of 1845 after the formal ratification of Oregon's Organic Articles and Laws of 1843 and the inauguration of George Abernethy as governor. The first Provisional Legislature, a unicameral body with autonomous powers, conducted its sessions in a rather casual manner and frequently suspended its rules to take care of unexpected situations. It met at least annually until February 1849, five months before the first Territorial Legislature met during July 16 to July 24, 1849, also in Oregon City.

The Territorial Legislature was bicameral. It had an upper council of nine members and a lower house of 18 members elected from the eight existing counties that had regular annual meetings. Unlike the Provisional Legislature, its actions were subject to review in Washington, D.C. At the time of statehood and adoption of the constitution in 1859, the present bicameral system was adopted. The Legislature then met in the fall of even-numbered years until 1885 when the sessions were moved to the early winter months of odd-numbered years to accommodate members who farmed.

In 2010, voters approved a Legislative referral requiring the Legislature to meet annually.

Statistical Summary of the Eighty-First Legislative Assembly

Source: Legislative Counsel

Senate Total Membership	30
Democrats	18
Republicans	10
Independents:	2
President: Peter Courtney (D), Salem	

House Total Membership			60
Democrats			37
Republicans			23

Speakers: Tina Kotek (D), Portland (2021 sessions); Dan Rayfield (D), Corvallis, (2022 sessions)

2021 Regular Session

Session Length		159 Calendar Days
Convened		January 19, 2021
Adjourned		June 26, 2021

Bills Introduced		2,390
Other Measures		129
Total		2,519

Bills	House	Senate	Total
Introduced	1,465	925	2,390
Passed Both Houses	381	302	683
Vetoed	1+*	2+**	3+**
Became Law	380	300	680
Unsigned by Governor	0	0	0

*HB 2646; HB 5514, section 5
** SB 574 and SB 721

Resolutions and Memorials			
Introduced	66	63	129
Adopted	16	18	34

2022 Regular Session

Session Length		32 Calendar Days
Convened		February 1, 2022
Adjourned		March 4, 2022

Bills Introduced		254
Other Measures		21
Total		275

Bills	House	Senate	Total
Introduced	160	94	254
Passed Both Houses	70	49	119
Vetoed	0	0	0
Became Law	70	49	119
Unsigned by Governor	0	0	0

Resolutions and Memorials			
Introduced	12	9	21
Adopted	3	5	8

STATUTORY COMMITTEES AND INTERIM OFFICES

Source: Legislative Administration
Address: 900 Court St. NE, Rm. 140-A, Salem 97301
Phone: 503-986-1848
Web: oregonlegislature.gov/la

Legislative Administration Committee

Brett Hanes, Interim Legislative Administrator

The Legislative Administration Committee provides services to the Legislative Assembly, its

Special Legislative Sessions

Year	Date	Length in Days
1860	Oct. 1–Oct. 2	2
1865	Dec. 5–Dec. 18	14
1885	Nov. 11–Nov. 24	14
1898	Sept. 26–Oct. 15	20
1903	Dec. 21–Dec. 23	3
1909	Mar. 15–Mar. 16	2
1920	Jan. 12–Jan. 17	6
1921	Dec. 19–Dec. 24	6
1933	Jan. 3–Jan. 7	5
1933	Nov. 20–Dec. 9	20
1935	Oct. 21–Nov. 9	20
1957	Oct. 28–Nov. 15	19
1963	Nov. 11–Dec. 2	13[1]
1965	May 21–May 25	5
1967	Oct. 30–Nov. 21	23
1971	Nov. 16–Nov. 22	7
1974	Jan. 24–Feb. 24	15
1975	Sept. 16–Sept. 16	1
1978	Sept. 5–Sept. 9	5[2]
1980	Aug. 4–Aug. 8	5
1981	Oct. 24–Oct. 24	1
1982	Jan. 18–Mar. 1	43
1982	June 14–June 14	1
1982	Sept. 3–Sept. 3	1
1983	Sept. 14–Oct. 4	21
1984	July 30–July 30	1
1990	May 7–May 7	1
1992	July 1–July 3	3
1995	July 28–Aug. 4	8
1996	Feb. 1–Feb. 2	2
2002	Feb. 8–Feb. 11	4
2002	Feb. 25–Mar. 2	6
2002	June 12–June 30	19
2002	Aug. 16–Aug. 20	5
2002	Sept. 1–Sept. 18	18
2006	April 20–April 20	1
2008	Feb. 4–Feb. 22	19
2010	Feb. 1–Feb. 25	25
2012	Dec. 14–Dec. 14	1
2013	Sept. 30–Oct. 2	3
2018	May 21–May 21	1
2020	June 24–June 26	3
2020	Aug. 10–Aug. 10	1
2020	Dec. 21–Dec. 21	1
2021	Sept. 20—Sept. 27	8
2021	Dec. 13—Dec. 13	1

[1]Nine-day recess, Nov. 22 to Dec. 2, due to death of President Kennedy.

[2]Does not include recess from Jan. 24 to Feb. 11.

Legislative

support staff and the public. The committee, authorized by ORS 173.710, includes the president of the Senate, speaker of the House, members of the Senate appointed by the president and members of the House appointed by the speaker. The committee appoints its executive officer. The administrator's office coordinates and oversees the operation of the following administrative units:

Facility Services

Address: Room 49
Phone: 503-986-1360
Facility Services manages the infrastructure of the State Capitol Building, including maintenance, capital improvement projects, centralized purchasing, mail handling and distribution of legislative publications.

Visitor Services

Address: Capitol Kiosk and Room 148
Phone: 503-986-1388
Web: oregonlegislature.gov/capitol historygateway/ Pages/Visit-the-Capitol.aspx
Visitor Services provides guided tours and information on the legislative process and Capitol history. It also operates the Capitol Gift Shop.

Employee Services

Address: Room 140-B
Phone: 503-986-1373

Financial Services

Address: Room 140-C
Phone: 503-986-1695

Information Services

Address: Room 40
Phone: 503-986-1914

Legislative Media

Address: Room 35
Phone: 503-986-1195

Legislative Counsel Committee and Office of Legislative Counsel

Dexter Johnson, Legislative Counsel
Address: 900 Court St. NE, Rm. S-101, Salem 97301
Phone: 503-986-1243
Fax: 503-373-1043
Web: oregonlegislature.gov/lc
The Legislative Counsel Committee, established by ORS 173.111, consists of the president of the Senate, senators appointed by the president, the speaker of the House of Representatives and representatives appointed by the speaker. The legislative counsel, selected by the committee, serves as executive officer.

The office drafts legislative measures for legislators, legislative committees, state agencies and statewide elected officials. The office provides legal opinions and other legal services to legislators, legislative committees and legislative staff. During legislative sessions, the office drafts amendments to measures and publishes the introduced, engrossed and enrolled measures.

The Office of the Legislative Counsel publishes *Oregon Laws*, the official compilation of that session's laws. The office also compiles and publishes *Oregon Revised Statutes* (ORS), the official codification of Oregon's statute laws, every two years. Each edition of ORS incorporates the new statutory provisions and amendments to statutory provisions passed by the Legislative Assembly or approved by the voters in the preceding two years. The ORS set includes a supplement of laws enacted during the even-year regular legislative session. The office also incorporates any new sections or amendments into its annual printing of the *Constitution of Oregon*.

Pursuant to ORS 183.710 to 183.725, the Office of the Legislative Counsel reviews all administrative rules adopted by state agencies to monitor whether an agency's rules are consistent with the agency's constitutional and statutory authority.

Oregon Law Commission

P.K. Runkles-Pearson, Chair
Sandy Weintraub, Executive Director
Address: University of Oregon School of Law, 1515 Agate St., Eugene 97403
Phone: 541-346-0042
Web: law-olc.uoregon.edu/
The Oregon Law Commission was established in 1997 by ORS 173.315 to 173.357. It is the state's official law reform body. The commission and its work groups help to reform, correct and revise Oregon law based on suggestions for revision and its own review of Oregon's laws.

The commission consists of 15 commissioners: two appointed by the president of the Senate (one of whom must be a senator), two appointed by the speaker of the House of Representatives (one of whom must be a representative), the deans (or an appointee) from each of Oregon's three law schools, three appointed by the Oregon State Bar, the attorney general, the chief justice of the Supreme Court, the chief judge of the Court of Appeals, a circuit court judge and one appointed by the governor.

The commission submits a biennial report to the Legislative Assembly.

Legislative Equity Office

VACANT, Director
Address: 900 Court St. NE, Rm. 62, Salem 97301
Phone: 503-986-1625
Web: oregonlegislature.gov/leo
The Legislative Equity Office is authorized by 2019 HCR 20, is a permanent, non-partisan office to prevent and respond to conduct at the Oregon State Capitol that is intimidating, hostile, offensive or retaliatory in nature.

Legislative Fiscal Office

Amanda Beitel, Legislative Fiscal Officer
Address: 900 Court St. NE, Rm. H-178, Salem 97301
Phone: 503-986-1828
Web: oregonlegislature.gov/lfo

The Legislative Fiscal Office is a permanent, nonpartisan legislative agency created in 1959, pursuant to ORS 173.410 to 173.450, to serve legislators and committees on matters related to the state's fiscal affairs. The office provides research, analysis, evaluation and recommendations concerning state expenditures, budget issues, agency organization, program administration, audit findings and state information technology projects. It also provides fiscal impact assessments of proposed legislation and provides staff assistance to the Joint Legislative Committee on Information Management and Technology and the Joint Legislative Audit Committee. The office staffs the the Emergency Board and the Joint Committee on Ways and Means and any appointed budget committees during sessions.

Emergency Board

The Emergency Board, authorized by Article III, section 3, of the Oregon Constitution and by ORS 291.324, consists of the president of the Senate, the speaker of the House of Representatives, the co-chairs of the Joint Committee on Ways and Means and eight Senate and eight House members, totaling 20 members. Between sessions, the Emergency Board may allocate to state agencies, out of emergency funds appropriated to the board, additional monies to carry on activities required by law for which appropriations were not made. The board may authorize an agency to spend over the budgeted amount by accessing funds that are dedicated or continuously appropriated for the agency, approve a new budget for a new agency task and authorize transfers of funds between an agency's expenditure classifications.

Joint Committee on Ways and Means

The Joint Committee on Ways and Means, created under ORS 171.555, is the legislative appropriations committee that determines state budget policy. Staffed by the Legislative Fiscal Office and made up of both Senate and House members appointed by the president of the Senate and the speaker of the House, the committee works to determine state budget priorities. This joint appropriation process structure, employed in Oregon and a few other states, is especially effective in resolving budgetary differences.

Legislative Policy and Research Office

Misty Mason Freeman PhD., Director
Address: 900 Court St. NE, Rm. 453, Salem 97301
Phone: 503-986-1813
Web: oregonlegislature.gov/lpro

The Legislative Policy and Research Office (LPRO), established in 2016, provides professional and nonpartisan staffing, analysis and research that supports and informs the policy-making process. LPRO staff administer committee meetings, analyze legislative measures, provide policy research for legislators, support legislative task forces and work groups and produce committee meeting records. Staff also serve as a resource and additional communications link for legislators, legislative personnel, state agencies, the public and other participants in the legislative process.

The LPRO Director is selected by the Legislative Policy and Research Committee and is responsible for managing the office and its employees to execute the duties outlined in ORS 173.635.

Legislative Revenue Office

Christopher Allanach, Legislative Revenue Officer
Address: 900 Court St. NE, Rm. 160, Salem 97301
Phone: 503-986-1266
Web: oregonlegislature.gov/lro

Pursuant to ORS 173.810 to 173.850, the Legislative Revenue Office, established by the 1975 Legislature, provides nonpartisan analysis of tax and school finance issues.

The legislative revenue officer is appointed by, and responsible to, the House and Senate committees that deal with revenue and school finance.

The office staffs the House and Senate Revenue Committees, writes revenue impact statements for proposed legislation and researches tax and other revenue related issues.

Legislative Commission on Indian Services

Patrick Flanagan, Executive Director
Address: 900 Court St. NE, Rm. 167, Salem 97301
Phone: 503-986-1067
Web: oregonlegislature.gov/cis

The Legislative Commission on Indian Services consists of 14 members. Thirteen members are appointed by legislative leadership to two-year terms: one member from each of Oregon's nine federally-recognized tribal governments, two state senators and two state representatives. The commission may appoint one additional non-voting member from an area in which non-reservation Indians reside and who is associated with an Urban Indian Health Program under Title V of the federal Indian Health Care Improvement Act.

The commission works to improve services to American Indians in the state and to promote communication and relations between the State of Oregon and the nine federally-recognized tribes in Oregon.

Senate Districts

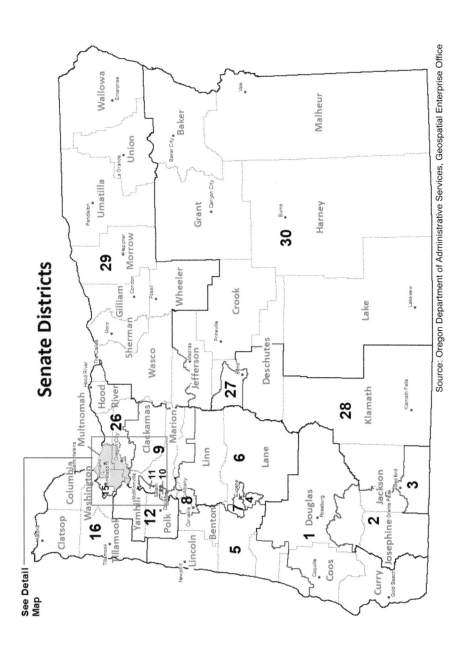

Source: Oregon Department of Administrative Services, Geospatial Enterprise Office

House Districts

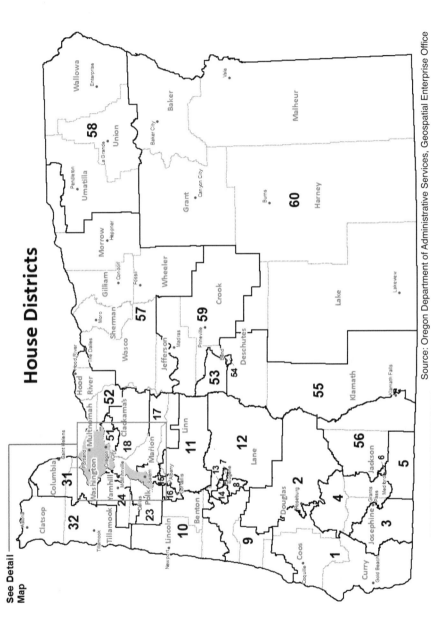

Legislative

Metro Area Detail Maps

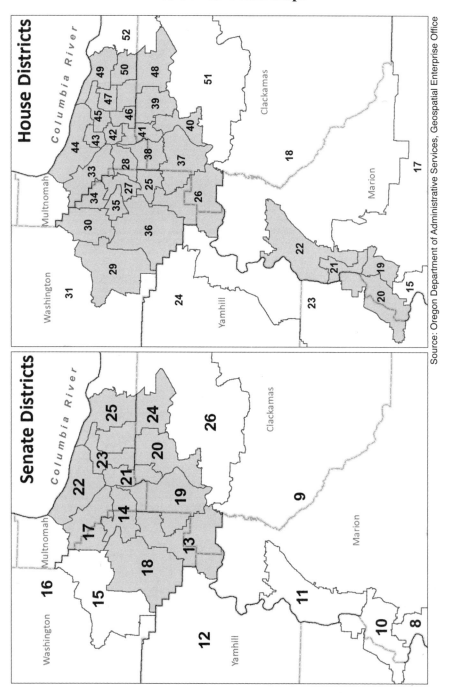

Source: Oregon Department of Administrative Services, Geospatial Enterprise Office

President of the Senate

Senator Wagner was appointed to the Oregon Senate in 2018, elected to a full term later that year and reelected in 2022. He grew up in his Senate District and graduated from Lake Oswego High School. A sense of dedication to public service was instilled in him at a young age by his parents.

Senator Wagner received his bachelor's degree from Portland State University and earned a master's degree in public policy from The George Washington University. His introduction to the Oregon Legislature came early, serving as a legislative aide in the Oregon House of Representatives in the late 1990s. His passion for education led him to a position with American Federation of Teachers - Oregon, where he spent a decade advocating for Oregon's teachers, faculty, health care workers and academic support professionals. He served as Associate Vice President at Portland Community College, where his duties included overseeing community outreach and working to secure student scholarship funding.

Rob Wagner

Senator Wagner and his wife, Laurie, share four wonderful children. An avid and lifelong hiker, one of Senator Wagner's favorite views is from the summit of South Sister in the Central Cascades. He also enjoys singing, and playing piano and guitar.

Anderson, Dick
R—District 5

Blouin, Sara Gelser
D—District 8

Bonham, Daniel
R—District 26

Boquist, Brian
I—District 12

Campos, Wlnsvey E.
D—District 18

Dembrow, Michael.
D—District 23

Findley, Lynn
R—District 30

Frederick, Lew
D—District 22

Girod, Fred
R—District 9

Golden, Jeff
D—District 3

Gorsek, Chris
D—District 25

Hansell, Bill
R—District 29

Legislative

Hayden, Cedric
R—District 6

Jama, Kayse
D—District 24

Knopp, Tim
R—District 27

Lieber, Kate
D—District 14

Linthicum, Dennis
R—District 28

Manning Jr., James
D—District 7

Meek, Mark
D—District 20

Patterson, Deb
D—District 10

Prozanski, Floyd
D—District 4

Robinson, Art
R—District 2

Smith, David Brock
R—District 1

Sollman, Janeen
D—District 15

Steiner, Elizabeth
D—District 17

Taylor, Kathleen
D—District 21

Thatcher, Kim
R—District 11

Wagner, Rob
D—District 19

Weber, Suzanne
R—District 16

Woods, Aaron
D—District 13

State Senators by District

District/Counties	Name/Address/Phone	Occupation/Yr. Elected*	Birthplace/Year
1. Curry and portions of Coos and Douglas	David Brock Smith (R) 900 Court St. NE, S-316 Salem 97301 541-673-1701	Small Business 2023 (2017/2019/2021/2023)	California 1976
2. Josephine and portions of Douglas and Jackson	Art Robinson (R) 900 Court St. NE, S-309 Salem 97301 503-986-1702	Scientist 2021	Illinois 1942
3. Portion of Jackson	Jeff Golden (D) 900 Court St., NE, S-421 Salem 97301 503-986-1703	Public Television Producer/Journalist 2019/2023	California 1950
4. Portion of Lane	Floyd Prozanski (D) PO Box 11511 Eugene 97440 541-342-2447	Attorney 2005/2009/2015/2019/ 2023 (1995–2003)	Texas 1954
5. Lincoln and portions of Benton, Coos, Douglas and Lane	Dick Anderson (R) PO Box 263 Lincoln City 97367 503-986-1705	Real Estate Finance 2021	Ohio 1950
6. Portions of Lane, Linn and Marion	Cedric Hayden (R) 900 Court St NE S-315 Salem 97301 503-986-1706	Dental Surgeon/Rancher 2023 (2015–2021)	Oregon 1968
7. Portion of Lane	James I. Manning, Jr. (D) 900 Court St. NE, S-209 Salem 97301 503-986-1707	U.S. Army, retired 2017/2021/2023	Missouri 1953
8. Portions of Benton and Linn	Sara Gelser Blouin (D) 900 Court St. NE, S-211 Salem 97301 503-986-1708	Educator/Civil Servant 2015/2019/2023 (2007–2015)	Nevada 1973
9. Portions of Clackamas, Linn and Marion	Fred Girod (R) 101 Fern Ridge Rd. SE Stayton 97383 503-769-4321	Dentist 2008/2009/2013/2017/ 2021 (1993–2007)	Oregon 1951
10. Portions of Marion and Polk	Deb Patterson (D) 900 Court St. NE, S-411 Salem 97301 503-986-1710	Ordained Clergy 2021/2023	Alberta, Canada 1958
11. Portion of Marion	Kim Thatcher (R) 900 Court St. NE, S-307 Salem 97301 503-986-1711	Small Business Owner 2015/2019/2023 (2005-2013)	Idaho 1964
12. Portions of Polk and Yamhill	Brian Boquist (I) 900 Court St. NE, S-311 Salem 97301 503-986-1712	Businessman/Rancher 2009/2013/2017/2021 (2005/2007)	Oregon 1958

Senate terms are four years, and House terms (in parentheses) are two years, unless appointed mid-term.

District/Counties	Name/Address/Phone	Occupation/Yr. Elected*	Birthplace/Year
13. Portions of Clackamas, Washington and Yamhill	Aaron Woods (D) 900 Court St. NE, S-425 Salem 97301 503-986-1713	Clackamas Community College Board 2022	Illinois 1949
14. Portions of Multnomah-Washington	Kate Lieber (D) 900 Court St. NE, S-223 Salem 97301 503-986-1714	Attorney 2021	Indiana 1966
15. Portion of Washington	Janeen Sollman (D) 900 Court St. NE, S-207 Salem 97301 503-986-1715	Customer Service Specialist 2022/2023 (2017/2019/2021)	Philippines 1969
16. Clatsop, Columbia, Tillamook and portions of Multnomah, and Washington	Suzanne Weber (R) 900 Court St NE S-405 Salem, 97301 503-986-1716	Retired Teacher 2023 (2021)	Minnesota 1946
17. Portions of Multnomah and Washington	Elizabeth Steiner (D) 3879 SW Hall Blvd. Beaverton 97005 503-277-2467	OHSU Associate Professor of Family Medicine 2011/2015/2019/2023	New York 1963
18. Portion of Washington	Wlnsvey E. Campos (D) 900 Court St NE. S-215 Salem, 97301 503-986-1718	Strategic Initiatives Manager 2023 (2022)	California 1995
19. Portions of Clackamas, Multnomah and Washington	Rob Wagner (D) 900 Court St. NE, S-201 Salem 97301 503-986-1719	Legislator/Communications Consultant 2019/2023	California 1973
20. Portion of Clackamas	Mark Meek (D) 900 Court St. NE, S-417 Salem 97301 503-986-1720	Small Business Owner 2023 (2017-2021)	California 1964
21. Portions of Clackamas and Multnomah	Kathleen Taylor (D) 900 Court St. NE, S-205 Salem 97301 503-986-1721	Management Auditor 2017/2021	Wisconsin 1966
22. Portion of Multnomah	Lew Frederick (D) 900 Court St. NE, S-419 Salem 97301 503-231-2564	Communications Consultant 2017/2021 (2009–2015)	Washington 1951
23. Portion of Multnomah	Michael E. Dembrow (D) 900 Court St. NE, S-407 Salem 97301 503-986-1723	College Teacher 2013/2015/2017/2021 (2009/2011/2013)	Connecticut 1951
24. Portions of Clackamas and Multnomah	Kayse M. Jama (D) 900 Court St. NE, S-409 Salem 97301 503-986-1724	Legislator 2021/2023	Somalia 1974
25. Portion of Multnomah	Chris Gorsek (D) 900 Court St. NE, S-403 Salem 97301 503-986-1725	Teacher 2021 (2013/2015/2017/2019)	Oregon 1958

District/Counties	Name/Address/Phone	Occupation/Yr. Elected*	Birthplace/Year
26. Hood River and portions of Clackamas, Multnomah and Wasco	Daniel Bonham (R) 900 Court St. NE, S-423 Salem 97301 503-986-1726	Small Business Owner 2023 (2017-2021)	California 1977
27. Portion of Deschutes	Tim Knopp (R) 900 Court St. NE, S-323 Salem 97301 503-986-1727	Exec. Vice President Non-Profit Trade Assoc. 2013/2017/2021	Oregon 1965
28. Klamath and portions of Deschutes and Jackson	Dennis Linthicum (R) 900 Court St. NE, S-305 Salem 97301 503-986-1728	Software and Applications Developer 2017/2021	California 1956
29. Gilliam, Morrow, Sherman, Umatilla, Union Wallowa ,Wheeler; portions of Jefferson and Wasco	Bill Hansell (R) 900 Court St. NE, S-415 Salem 97301 503-986-1729	Former County Commissioner 2013/2017/2021	Washington 1945
30. Baker, Crook, Grant, Harney, Lake and Malheur; portions of Deschutes and Jefferson	Lynn P. Findley (R) 900 Court St. NE, S-301 Salem 97301 503-986-1730	Retired Bureau of Land Mgmt, City Manager 2021 (2018/2019)	Oregon 1952

Senate terms are four years, and House terms (in parentheses) are two years, unless appointed mid-term.

MEMBERS OF THE OREGON HOUSE OF REPRESENTATIVES

Speaker of the House

From the time he started gathering signatures as a teenager to put campaign finance reform on the ballot, Dan Rayfield has made efforts to bring people together and help them create opportunities for a better future. Born in California, Rayfield graduated from Tigard High School, Western Oregon University and the Willamette University College of Law. His work as an attorney primarily involves fighting for individuals with consumer and civil rights cases against large corporations, insurance companies and others.

Rayfield was first elected to the Legislature in 2014 to represent House District 16. The Corvallis resident served as co-chair of the Joint Committee on Ways and Means, the state's lead budget writing committee, from 2019-2022 and his careful budget management has helped stabilize the state's once unreliable revenue system. Oregon has built record reserves to protect essential social services during his tenure

Dan Rayfield

as budget chair and is among the best-prepared states for a future economic downturn.

In 2022, Rayfield was elected as Speaker of the Oregon House. In his first session serving in the role, he guided critical investments to support housing development, prevent homelessness, support small businesses, working families and stronger schools. This included more support for continuing summer education opportunities; increasing and enhancing behavioral health services; a dedicated climate budget to address drought, extreme weather and infrastructure needs; and a bipartisan infrastructure package for rural Oregon.

Andersen, Tom
D—District 19

Boshart Davis, Shelly
R—District 15

Bowman, Ben
D—District 25

Breese-Iverson, Vikki
R—District 59

Bynum, Janelle
D—District 39

Cate, Jami
R—District 11

Chaichi, Farrah
D—District 35

Conrad, Charlie
R—District 12

Cramer, Tracy
R—District 22

Dexter, Maxine
D—District 33

Diehl, Ed
R—District 17

Elmer, Lucetta
R—District 24

Evans, Paul
D—District 20

Fahey, Julie
D—District 14

Gamba, Mark
D—District 41

Gomberg, David
D—District 10

Goodwin, Christine
R—District 4

Grayber, Dacia
D—District 28

Hartman, Annessa
D—District 40

Helfrich, Jeffrey
R—District 52

Helm, Ken
D—District 27

Hieb, James
R—District 51

Holvey, Paul
D—District 8

Hudson, Zachary
D—District 49

Javadi, Cyrus
R—District 32

Kropf, Jason
D—District 54

Levy, Bobby
R—District 58

Levy, Emerson
D—District 53

Lewis, Rick
R—District 18

Lively, John
D—District 7

Mannix, Kevin
R—District 21

Marsh, Pam
D—District 5

Legislative

McIntire, Emily
R—District 56

McLain, Susan
D—District 29

Morgan, Lily
R—District 3

Nathanson, Nancy
D—District 13

Nelson, Travis
D—District 44

Neron, Courtney
D—District 26

Nguyen, Daniel
D—District 38

Nguyen, Hoa
D—District 48

Nosse, Rob
D—District 42

Osborne, Virgle
R—District 2

Owens, Mark
R—District 60

Pham, Hai
D—District 36

Pham, Khanh
D—District 46

Rayfield, Dan
D—District 16

Reschke, E. Werner
R—District 55

Reynolds, Lisa
D—District 34

Ruiz, Ricki
D—District 50

Sanchez, Tawna
D—District 43

Scharf, Anna
R—District 23

Smith, Greg
R—District 57

Sosa, Nathan
D—District 30

Stout, Brian
R—District 31

Tran, Thuy
D—District 45

Valderrama, Andrea
D—District 47

Wallan, Kim
R—District 6

Walters, Jules
D—District 37

**Wright, Gerald D.
"Boomer"**
R—District 9

VACANT
R—District 1

State Representatives by District

District/Counties	Name/Address/Phone	Occupation/Yr. Elected*	Birthplace/Year

*House terms are two years, unless appointed mid-term.

District/Counties	Name/Address/Phone	Occupation/Yr. Elected*	Birthplace/Year
1. Curry and portions of Coos and Douglas	VACANT (R) 900 Court St. NE, H-376 Salem 97301 503-986-1401		
2. Portion of Douglas	Virgle Osborne (R) 900 Court St. NE, H-375 Salem 97301 503-986-1402	Business Owner 2023	Oregon 1968

District/Counties	Name/Address/Phone	Occupation/Yr. Elected*	Birthplace/Year

House terms are two years, unless appointed mid-term.

District/Counties	Name/Address/Phone	Occupation/Yr. Elected*	Birthplace/Year
3. Portion of Josephine	Lily Morgan (R) 900 Court St. NE, H-390 Salem 97301 503-986-1403	Parole/Probation Officer 2021/2023	Oregon 1975
4. Portions of Douglas, Jackson and Josephine	Christine Goodwin (R) 900 Court St. NE, H-386 Salem 97301 503-986-1404	Small Business Owner 2022/2023	Oregon 1953
5. Portion of Jackson	Pam Marsh (D) 900 Court St. NE, H-474 Salem 97301 503-986-1405	Small Business Owner 2017/2019/2021/2023	Missouri 1954
6. Portion of Jackson	Kim Wallan (R) 900 Court St. NE, H-388 Salem 97301 503-986-1406	Lawyer 2019/2021/2023	Oregon 1961
7. Portion of Lane	John Lively (D) 900 Court St NE H-481 Salem, 97301 503-986-1407	Account Manager 2013/2015/2017/2019/ 2021/2023	Oregon 1946
8. Portion of Lane	Paul Holvey (D) PO Box 51048 Eugene 97405 541-344-5636	Carpenters' Union Rep. 2005/2007/2009/2011/ 2013/2015/2017/2019/ 2021/2023	Oregon 1954
9. Portions of Coos, Douglas and Lane	Gerald D. "Boomer" Wright (R) 900 Court St. NE, H-372 Salem 97301 503-986-1409	Retired Educator 2021/2023	California 1948
10. Lincoln, portions of Benton and Lane	David Gomberg (D) 900 Court St. NE, H-480 Salem 97301 503-986-1410	Small Business Owner 2013/2015/2017/2019/ 2021/2023	Oregon 1953
11. Portions of Linn and Marion	Jami Cate (R) 900 Court St NE, H-381 Salem, 97301 503-986-1411	Farmer 2021/2023	Oregon 1987
12. Portion of Lane	Charlie Conrad (R) 900 Court St. NE, H-483 Salem 97301 503-986-1412	Operations Supervisor 2023	Oregon 1972
13. Portion of Lane	Nancy Nathanson (D) PO Box 41895 Eugene 97404 541-343-2206	Library Program Manager 2007/2009/2011/2013/ 2015/2017/2019/2021/ 2023	Texas 1951
14. Portion of Lane	Julie Fahey (D) 900 Court St. NE, H-295 Salem 97301 503-986-1414	Business Consultant 2017/2019/202/20231	Illinois 1978

District/Counties	Name/Address/Phone	Occupation/Yr. Elected*	Birthplace/Year
15. Portions of Benton, Linn and Marion	Shelly Boshart Davis (R) 900 Court St. NE, H-389 Salem 97301 503-986-1415	Small Business Owner 2019/2021/2023	Oregon 1980
16. Portion of Benton	Dan Rayfield (D) 900 Court St. NE, H-271 Salem 97301 503-986-1416	Attorney 2015/2017/2019/2021/ 2023	California 1979
17. Portions of Linn and Marion	Ed Diehl (R) 900 Court St. NE, H-378 Salem 97301 503-986-1417	Control System Integrator 2023	Montana 1964
18. Portions of Clackamas and Marion	Rick Lewis (R) 900 Court St. NE, H-382 Salem 97301 503-986-1418	Retired Law Enforcement 2017/2019/2021/2023	Wyoming 1950
19. Portion of Marion	Tom Andersen (D) 900 Court St. NE, H-479 Salem 97301 503-986-1419	Attorney 2023	Illinois 1951
20. Portions of Marion and Polk	Paul Evans (D) 900 Court St. NE, H-471 Salem 97301 503-986-1420	Educator, Small Business Owner 2015/2017/2019/2021/ 2023	Oregon 1970
21. Portion of Marion	Kevin Mannix (R) 900 Court St. NE, H-384 Salem 97301 503-986-1421	Attorney 2023	New York 1949
22. Portion of Marion	Tracy Cramer (R) 900 Court St. NE, H-476 Salem 97301 503-986-1422	Business Owner 2023	Oregon 1989
23. Portions of Polk and Yamhill	Anna Scharf (R) 900 Court St. NE, H-387 Salem 97301 503-986-1423	Farmer 2021/2023	Oregon 1969
24. Portions of Polk and Yamhill	Lucetta Elmer (R) 900 Court St. NE, H-374 Salem 97301 503-986-1424	Business Owner 2023	Oregon 1970
25. Portion of Washington	Ben Bowman (D) 900 Court St. NE, H-484 Salem 97301 503-986-1425	School District Administrator 2023	Oregon 1992
26. Portions of Clackamas, Washington and Yamhill	Courtney Neron (D) 900 Court St. NE, H-281 Salem 97301 503-986-1426	Teacher 2019/2021/2023	California 1979
27. Portion of Washington	Ken Helm (D) 900 Court St. NE, H-490 Salem 97301 503-986-1427	Attorney 2015/2017/2019/2021/ 2023	California 1965

Legislative

District/Counties	Name/Address/Phone	Occupation/Yr. Elected*	Birthplace/Year
28. Portions of Multnomah and Washington	Dacia Grayber (D) 900 Court St. NE, H-492 Salem 97301 503-986-1428	Firefighter 2021/2023	New York 1975
29. Portion of Washington	Susan McLain (D) 900 Court St. NE, H-493 Salem 97301 503-986-1429	Retired Teacher 2015/2017/2019/2021/ 2023	Oregon 1949
30. Portion of Washington	Nathan Sosa (D) 900 Court St. NE, H-280 Salem 97301 503-986-1430	Attorney 2022/2023	California 1983
31. Portions of Columbia, Multnomah and Washington	Brian Stout (R) 900 Court St. NE, H-380 Salem 97301 503-986-1431	Self Employed 2023	Texas 1967
32. Clatsop, Tillamook and portions of Columbia	Cyrus Javadi (R) 900 Court St. NE, H-373 Salem, 97301 503-986-1432	Dentist 2023	Utah 1977
33. Portions of Multnomah and Washington	Maxine E. Dexter (D) 900 Court St. NE, H-283 Salem 97301 503-986-1433	Physician 2021/2023	Washington 1972
34. Portion of Multnomah and Washington	Lisa Reynolds (D) 900 Court St. NE, H-485 Salem 97301 503-986-1434	Physician 2021/2023	Illinois 1964
35. Portion of Washington	Farrah Chaichi (D) 900 Court St. NE, H-478 Salem 97301 503-986-1435	Intake & Conflicts Specialist 2023	Oregon 1985
36. Portion of Washington	Hai Pham (D) 900 Court St. NE, H-282 Salem 97301 503-986-1436	Pediatric Dentist 2023	Malaysia 1979
37. Portions of Clackamas and Washington	Jules Walters (D) 900 Court St. NE, H-489 Salem 97301 503-986-1437	Communications Consultant 2023	Maryland 1970
38. Portions of Clackamas and Multnomah	Daniel Nguyen (D) 900 Court St. NE, H-488 Salem 97301 503-986-1438	Small Business Owner 2023	Washington 1978
39. Portion of Clackamas	Janelle Bynum (D) 900 Court St. NE, H-276 503-986-1439	Restaurant Owner 2017/2019/2021/2023	District of Columbia 1975
40. Portion of Clackamas	Annessa Hartman (D) 900 Court St. NE, H-487 Salem 97301 503-490-6243	Non-Profit 2023	Arkansas 1988

District/Counties	Name/Address/Phone	Occupation/Yr. Elected*	Birthplace/Year
41. Portions of Clackamas and Multnomah	Mark Gamba (D) 900 Court St. NE, H-477 Salem 97301 503-986-1441	Photographer 2023	Colorado 1959
42. Portion of Multnomah	Rob Nosse (D) 900 Court St. NE, H-472 Salem 97301 503-986-1442	Labor Representative 2015/2017/2019/2021/ 2023	Ohio 1967
43. Portion of Multnomah	Tawna Sanchez (D) 900 Court St. NE, H-273 Salem 97301 503-986-1443	Family Services Director 2017/2019/2021/2023	Oregon 1961
44. Portion of Multnomah	Travis E. Nelson (D) 8105 N. Brandon Ave Portland 97217 503-986-1444	Nurse 2022/2023	Louisiana 1978
45. Portion of Multnomah	Thuy Tran (D) 900 Court St. NE, H-285 Salem 97301 503-986-1445	Physician 2023	Vietnam 1966
46. Portion of Multnomah	Khanh Pham (D) 900 Court St. NE, H-274 Salem 97301 503-986-1446	Community Organizer 2021/2023	Califonia 1987
47. Portion of Multnomah	Andrea Valderrama (D) 900 Court St. NE, H-286 Salem 97301 503-986-1447	Policy Director 2021/2023	California 1989
48. Portions of Clackamas and Multnomah	Hoa Nguyen (D) 900 Court St. NE, H-473 Salem 97301 503-986-1448	Student 2023	Louisiana 1983
49. Portion of Multnomah	Zachary Hudson (D) 900 Court St. NE, H-284 Salem 97301 503-378-1449	Teacher 2021/2023	Oregon 1979
50. Portion of Multnomah	Ricki Ruiz (D) PO Box 171 Gresham 97030 503-986-1450	Community Coordinator 2021/2023	Oregon 1994
51. Portion of Clackamas	James Hieb (R) 900 Court St. NE, H-377 Salem 97301 503-986-1451	Teacher/Small Business Owner 2022/2023	Oregon 1985
52. Hood River, portions of Clackamas, Multnomah and Wasco	Jeffrey Helfrich (R) 900 Court St. NE, H-371 Salem 97301 503-986-1452	Police Officer, retired 2023	Colorado 1968
53. Portion of Deschutes	Emerson Levy (D) 900 Court St. NE, H-486 Salem 97301 503-986-1453	Attorney 2023	Oklahoma 1984

Legislative

District/Counties	Name/Address/Phone	Occupation/Yr. Elected*	Birthplace/Year
54. Portion of Deschutes	Jason Kropf (D) 900 Court St. NE, H-491 Salem 97301 503-986-1454	Attorney 2021/2023	Washington 1970
55. Portions of Deschutes and Klamath	E. Werner Reschke (R) 900 Court St. NE, H-383 Salem 97301 541-233-4411	Online Marketing/Web Development 2017/2019/2021/2023	California 1965
56. Portions of Jackson and Klamath	Emily McIntire (R) 900 Court St. NE, H-379 Salem 97301 503-986-1456	Business Owner 2023	Oregon 1981
57. Gilliam, Morrow, Sherman, Wheeler, portions of Clackamas, Jefferson, Marion and Wasco	Greg Smith (R) PO Box 215 Heppner 97836 541-676-5154	Small Business Owner 2001/2003/2005/2007/ 2009/2011/2013/2015/ 2017/2019/2021/2023	Oregon 1968
58. Union, Wallowa and portion of Umatilla	Bobby Levy (R) PO Box 69 Echo 97826 503-986-1458	Farmer, Small Business Owner 2021/2023	Oregon 1953
59. Crook, portions of Deschutes and Jefferson	Vikki Breese-Iverson (R) 900 Court St. NE, H-395 Salem 97310 503-986-1459	Realtor 2019/2021/2023	Oregon 1974
60. Baker, Grant, Harney, Lake, Malheur and a portion of Deschutes	Mark Owens (R) 258 S Oregon St Ontario 97914 541-889-8866	Farmer 2021/2023	California 1970

House terms are two years, unless appointed mid-term.

State and Local Government Finance

Government finance—where government gets its money and how it spends it—affects all Oregonians. The connections between state and local government revenues and state and local government services are important. This section describes revenue sources and distribution.

Source: Department of Administrative Services, Chief Financial Office

State Government

Oregon operates under a biennial budget. Budgets begin July 1 of odd-numbered years and continue for two years. Oregon law requires all state and local governments to balance their budgets. How does the state government's budget work? The state receives money from a variety of sources which are grouped into funds. These funds are known as the General Fund, Lottery Fund, Other Funds and Federal Funds.

The total Legislatively Adopted Budget (LAB) for the 2021–2023 biennium is $112.8 billion total funds. This represents a 0.2% increase over the 2019–2021 LAB of $112.5 billion. The total adopted budget for 2021–2023 includes $26.8 billion in combined General Funds and Lottery Funds, $48.6 billion Other Funds, and $37.4 billion Federal Funds.

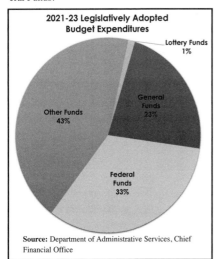

2021-23 Legislatively Adopted Budget Expenditures

Lottery Funds 1%
General Funds 23%
Other Funds 43%
Federal Funds 33%

Source: Department of Administrative Services, Chief Financial Office

General Fund

The General Fund is largely made up of personal and corporate income taxes collected by the Oregon Department of Revenue. The personal income tax makes up the largest share of General Fund revenue. It accounts for 86% of projected revenue for the 2023–2025 biennium. Other sources make up the remainder. The largest of these other revenue sources are corporate income tax, cigarette tax, estate tax and the liquor apportionment transfer. The 2021–2023 LAB included approximately $25.5 billion in General Fund expenditures — a 22.5% share of the total budget. General Fund appropriation increased by $3 billion (or 13.3%) in the adopted budget over the 2019–2021 approved level. As of the June 2022 revenue forecast, the gross General Fund revenues for the 2021–2023 biennium are expected to reach $27.1 billion. This represents an increase of $2.3 billion from the March 2022 forecast, and an increase of $3.9 billion relative to the Close of Session forecast.

General Fund appropriations provide funding to agencies that do not generate revenues, receive federal funds or generate sufficient other funds to support their approved programs. Agencies do not actually receive money from the General Fund. Instead, they expend against an appropriation from the General Fund that is established for general government purposes up to the amount approved in their budget bill. General Fund monies are a scarce resource that can be used for any public purpose; therefore, allocations of monies are competitive and require fiscal oversight.

In 1990, voters approved Ballot Measure 5. This reduced local property tax rates, which reduced local revenue and, in turn, shifted much of the responsibility for funding public schools to the state's General Fund. The 2021–2023 LAB had $8.6 billion, or 32%, of the General and Lottery Funds allocated for spending on kindergarten through twelfth grade education.

Government Finance

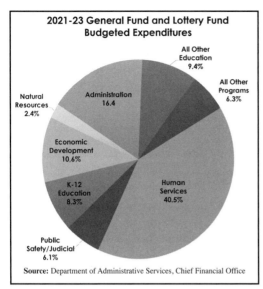

2021-23 General Fund and Lottery Fund Budgeted Expenditures

- All Other Education 9.4%
- All Other Programs 6.3%
- Natural Resources 2.4%
- Administration 16.4
- Economic Development 10.6%
- K-12 Education 8.3%
- Human Services 40.5%
- Public Safety/Judicial 6.1%

Source: Department of Administrative Services, Chief Financial Office

Lottery Fund

The Lottery Fund derives from the sale of lottery game tickets and from Video Lottery. After prizes and lottery expenses are paid, revenue flows to the Economic Development Fund. A portion of the Lottery Fund is constitutionally dedicated to be spent in specific ways. The remainder is distributed at the discretion of the Legislature for economic development.

The 2021–2023 LAB included $1.4 billion of expenditures from the Lottery Fund, which is 1.2% of the total budget. The Lottery Fund distributes certain portions through three constitutionally dedicated transfers. These dedicated transfers are to the Education Stability Fund (18% of net lottery proceeds), Parks and Natural Resources Fund (15% of net lottery proceeds) and Veterans' Services Fund (1.5% of net lottery proceeds). Sports Betting proceeds are transferred to the Employer Incentive Fund. The remainder is distributed to the State School Fund and other projects. Overall, approximately 52% of the Lottery Fund is distributed to education.

Other Funds

Other Funds revenue generally refers to monies collected by agencies in return for services. Legislative actions may allow an agency to levy taxes, provide services for a fee, license individuals or otherwise earn revenues to pay for programs. The 2021–2023 LAB included $48.6 billion in Other Funds, which is 43.1% of the total funds. This represents an increase of $845.6 million (or 1.8%) over the 2019–2021 LAB. Other Funds are often separate and distinct from monies collected for general government purposes (General Fund), and they may be based on statutory language, federal mandate, legal requirements or for specific business reasons. Some funds are "dedicated"— the income and disbursements are limited by the state's constitution or by another law (for example, the Highway Fund). Since Other Funds are typically for a specific program, competition for these monies is limited.

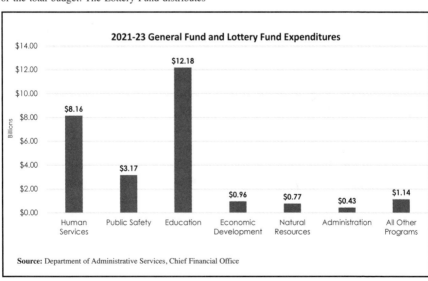

2021-23 General Fund and Lottery Fund Expenditures

	Human Services	Public Safety	Education	Economic Development	Natural Resources	Administration	All Other Programs
Billions	$8.16	$3.17	$12.18	$0.96	$0.77	$0.43	$1.14

Source: Department of Administrative Services, Chief Financial Office

Federal Funds

Federal Funds are monies received from the federal government through entitlement programs, grants and aid awarded to various state agencies. The 2021–2023 LAB included $37.4 billion in Federal Funds, a decrease of $3.7 billion from the 2019–2021 legislatively approved Federal Funds level. This decrease is primarily attributable to the scheduled phase out of major investments of pandemic-related assistance that were approved in 2020 and early 2021. Federal Funds Nonlimited can include payments made directly to beneficiaries of federally funded unemployment insurance benefits, rental assistance payments and supplemental nutrition assistance.

State Budget Process

Oregon state agencies develop biennial budgets according to instructions provided by the Department of Administrative Services Chief Financial Office. This budget development process begins in even-numbered years, well before the Legislative Assembly convenes in January of odd-numbered years. Agencies are required to prepare and submit their budget requests to the Chief Financial Office. These budget requests consist of narrative descriptions of agency programs, completed budgetary forms and reports from the Oregon Budget Information and Tracking System (ORBITS). An agency budget request serves as a conduit to the governor and the Legislature that identifies the agency's needs and priorities.

Agencies begin by building a Current Service Level (CSL) budget, which is the amount of money needed in the upcoming biennium to continue existing authorized programs into the next biennium. An agency may request additions to their CSL budget through policy option packages, which describe the purpose and the amount needed. Agencies also must identify program reductions and key performance measure targets. For their 2023–2025 budget requests, agencies began in March 2022 and submitted their completed requests by September 2022. An agency's budget provides an outline of what an agency does, what it costs and how many people are involved.

After analysis by the Governor's Office and the Chief Financial Office, the governor aligns their priorities with the agencies' requests, resulting in the Governor's Recommended Budget. The governor has a legal obligation to submit a balanced budget for the entire state government; therefore, the Governor's Recommended Budget includes the proposed budgets for the Legislative Assembly and the Judicial Department. However, because of separation of power principles, the governor's budget recommendations are advisory only for the other two branches. The governor presents the Governor's Recommended Budget to the Legislative Assembly when it convenes in January of odd-numbered years.

When the Legislative Assembly is in session, a subcommittee of the Joint Committee on Ways and Means considers each agency's budget. At the budget hearings, an agency presents its budget request and answers questions asked by members of the committee. Staff members from the Legislative Fiscal Office and the Chief Financial Office are also present at the budget hearings. Members of the public may attend the hearings and request an opportunity to testify. At the end of an agency's budget hearings, the agency's budget goes to the full Joint Committee on Ways and Means for a vote and then on to the full House and Senate for a vote. The agency's budget may be amended at any point in this process, although changes typically occur during the subcommittee hearings. After passage by both chambers, an agency's budget becomes its LAB for the biennium, and it goes into effect July 1 of odd-numbered years. If the Legislature makes changes to the adopted budget in legislative sessions or through the Emergency Board, it becomes known as the Legislatively Approved Budget.

Kicker Provision

The Oregon Constitution requires the governor to provide an estimate of biennial General Fund revenues. In 1979, the Legislature placed a condition on those revenue estimates that required excess funds to be "kicked back" to taxpayers if actual revenues exceeded estimated revenues by 2% or more of the close-of-session estimate.

For revenues from corporate income and excise taxes, the provision had required that the excess be returned to taxpayers who paid corporate income and excise taxes. However, this provision was amended in November 2012 by the citizen initiative process. Ballot Measure 85 requires that this excess be retained in the General Fund to provide additional funding for public education of kindergarten through twelfth grade. This measure is applicable to biennial estimates on or after July 1, 2013.

For General Fund revenues from all other sources where the actual revenues exceed the estimated revenues by 2% or more, the excess is "kicked back" to taxpayers who paid personal income tax. Ballot Measure 85 did not affect this provision. These taxpayers receive the refund as a tax credit in the following year's tax return. The refund is an identical proportion of each taxpayer's personal income tax liability for the prior year. Following the 2019–2021 biennium, the personal income tax kicker reached a new high dollar amount of $1.9 billion. The corporate kicker also set a new high at $847 million.

Government Finance

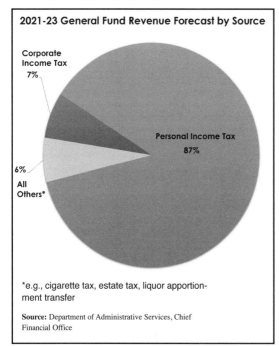

2021-23 General Fund Revenue Forecast by Source

Corporate Income Tax 7%

Personal Income Tax 87%

6% All Others*

*e.g., cigarette tax, estate tax, liquor apportionment transfer

Source: Department of Administrative Services, Chief Financial Office

Rainy Day Fund and Education Stability Fund

Established in 2007, the Oregon Rainy Day Fund is essentially a savings account for state government. Withdrawals can be made, after a three-fifths vote of approval by the Legislature, if there is a decline in the General Fund for the current or subsequent biennium budgets, there is a prolonged employment decline or the governor declares an emergency.

The Education Stability Fund (ESF) was created through a constitutional amendment approved by voters in 2002. The ESF receives 18% of net lottery proceeds deposited on a quarterly basis. The ESF has similar requirements as the Rainy Day Fund. During the 2019–2021 biennium, $400 million was withdrawn from the ESF to balance the budget.

The 2021–2023 ending balance for the Rainy Day Fund is projected to be $1.3 billion. The 2021–2023 ending balance for the Education Stability Fund is projected to be $703.1 million.

State Spending Limit

The state spending limit was first enacted by the 1979 Legislative Assembly. It limited the growth of General Fund appropriations to the growth of personal income in Oregon. The 2001 Legislative Assembly replaced this spending limit with one tying appropriations for a biennium to personal income for that biennium. The appropriations subject to this limit may not exceed 8% of projected personal income for the same biennium. The limit may be exceeded if the governor declares an emergency and three-fifths of the members of both chambers vote to exceed it.

Local Government

Local government in Oregon is predominantly financed by the property tax, although there are other local taxes, such as hotel/motel taxes, transit taxes and, in Multnomah County, a business income tax.

Most local governments must prepare and adopt an annual budget. This includes schools, counties, cities, ports, rural fire protection districts, water districts, urban renewal agencies and special districts. Oregon's Local Budget Law establishes standard budget procedures and requires citizen participation in budget preparation and public disclosure of the budget before it is formally adopted. A budget officer must be appointed and a budget committee formed. The budget officer prepares a draft budget, and the budget committee reviews and revises it before it is approved. Notices are then published, copies of the budget are made available for public review, and at least two opportunities for public comment are provided.

Local government budgets are usually for a fiscal year beginning July 1 and ending June 30. However, local governments have the option of creating a two-year biennial budget like the state. The governing body must enact a resolution or an ordinance to formally adopt the budget, make appropriations, and levy and categorize any tax. This must be done no later than June 30. Budget revenues are divided into ensuing year property tax and non-property tax revenues.

The Oregon Constitution allows a local government to levy annually the amount that would be raised by its permanent rate limit without further authorization from the voters. When a local government has to increase the permanent rate limit, or when the rate limit does not provide enough revenue to meet estimated expenditures, the government may request a local option levy from the voters. Approval requires a "double majority." This means that at least 50% of registered voters must vote, and a majority of those who vote must approve the levy, unless the measure is submitted during an election held in any May or November, which are exempt from the "double majority" approval requirement.

Taxes

Personal income tax and corporate excise tax are the most significant components of the state General Fund, and property tax is the most significant local tax in Oregon. The Corporate Activity Tax (CAT) provides additional education funding. Oregon does not have a state sales tax.

Personal Income Tax

Oregon residents and nonresidents who earn income in Oregon pay personal income tax. As part of the 2019 legislation that created the Corporate Activity Tax effective beginning in tax year 2020, the Legislature reduced Oregon's first three income tax brackets from 5%, 7% and 9%, to 4.75%, 6.75% and 8.75% respectively. After deductions and credits, the average effective tax rate is about 6.4% of adjusted gross income. Since 1993, the income tax brackets have been indexed to changes in the Consumer Price Index. The current standard deduction is $4,840 on joint returns, $2,420 on single and married filing separate returns, and $3,895 for a head of household return. Blind or elderly taxpayers and persons over the age of 65, will receive an additional $1,200 standard deduction on a single return and an additional $1,000 per eligible person on a joint return.

The personal income tax is the largest source of state tax revenue and is projected to make up 86% of the total General Fund revenues in the 2021–2023 biennium. In January 2010, Oregon voters approved Ballot Measure 66, which made two permanent changes to personal income tax calculations. First, it established a new tax bracket for adjusted gross income above $125,000 (single filers) and $250,000 (joint filers) and second, phased out the federal tax subtraction for those same filers.

Business Taxes

The corporate excise and income tax is the second largest source of state tax revenue for the General Fund. Corporations that do, or are authorized to do, business in Oregon pay an excise tax. Corporations not doing, or that are not authorized to do, business in Oregon, but have income from an Oregon source, pay income tax. The tax rate is 6.6% on Oregon taxable income of $1 million or less and 7.6% on Oregon taxable income above $1 million. There is a minimum excise tax of $150 for S corporations and one between $150 and $100,000 for C corporations, based on Oregon sales.

During the 2019 Legislative Session, the Legislature passed HB 3427, referred to as the Student Success Act, which created a Corporate Activity Tax (CAT) dedicated to education funding. The CAT is imposed on all business types, including partnerships and sole proprietorships, and is based on a business's Oregon commercial activity. The

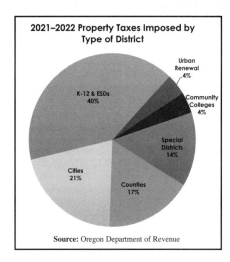

2021–2022 Property Taxes Imposed by Type of District

- Urban Renewal 4%
- K-12 & ESDs 40%
- Community Colleges 4%
- Special Districts 14%
- Cities 21%
- Counties 17%

Source: Oregon Department of Revenue

tax is $250 plus .057% of taxable commercial activity greater than $1 million. Taxpayers are allowed a subtraction equal to 35% of the greater of cost inputs or labor costs. General contractors who incur labor costs for single-family residential construction located in Oregon qualify for an exclusion equal to 15% of the labor costs paid to subcontractors. Some items, such as the wholesale and retail sale of groceries and motor fuel, are exempt from the tax. CAT revenue is forecasted to be $2.44 billion for the 2021–2023 biennium.

Property Tax

Property tax rates differ across Oregon. The rate depends on the tax rate approved by local voters and the limits established by the Oregon Constitution. Most properties are taxed by a number of districts, such as a city, county, school district, community college, fire district or port. The total tax rate on any particular property is calculated by adding all the local taxing district rates in the area. The total tax rate is then multiplied by the assessed value of the property. The county assessor verifies the tax rates and levies submitted by each local taxing district on an annual basis. The county tax collector collects the taxes and distributes the funds to the local districts.

Taxable property includes real property, mobile homes and some tangible personal property used by business. The state and each county assessor determine the value of property in each county. Measure 5, which was passed by the voters in November 1990, restricted non-school taxes on any property to $10 per $1,000 of real market value. It restricted school taxes on any property to $5 per $1,000 of real market value.

Measure 50 was passed by the voters in May 1997. Measure 50 added another limit to the Measure 5 limits. Now, each property has a real market value and an assessed value. Each taxing district has a fixed, permanent tax rate for operations which they may not increase. Districts may not increase this rate. Voters can approve local option levies for up to five years for operations and up to 10 years or the useful life of capital projects, whichever is less. Voters can also approve bond levies, which are used exclusively to repay a bond used to fund capital projects. Local option levies require a "double majority" for approval. Measure 50 established the 1997–1998 maximum assessed value as 90% of a property's 1995–1996 real market value. In subsequent tax years, the assessed value is limited to 3% annual growth until it reaches real market value. The assessed value can never exceed real market value. New property is assessed at the average county ratio of assessed to real market value of existing property of the same class. For 2021–2022, the total assessed value of all property in the state was about 58% of real market value.

Resources

Department of Administrative Services - Chief Financial Office
oregon.gov/DAS/financial/
The Chief Financial Office publishes the "Budget Process Overview" and Governor's Recommended Budget.

Department of Administrative Services, Office of Economic Analysis
oregon.gov/das/oea
The Office of Economic Analysis publishes Economic and Revenue Forecasts and related demographic data.

Department of Revenue
oregon.gov/dor
The Department of Revenue publishes information about taxes in Oregon.

Legislative Fiscal Office
oregonlegislature.gov/lfo
The Legislative Fiscal Office publishes detailed analyses of the *Legislatively Adopted Budget* and the *Governor's Recommended Budget*.

Legislative Revenue Office
oregonlegislature.gov/lro
The Legislative Revenue Office publishes reports on revenue-related issues including *Oregon Public Finance: Basic Facts*, which serves as an introduction to how Oregon government is financed.

Education

As Oregon's population grows and our economy evolves, the strength of our educational institutions is an important public policy issue. This section describes public education in Oregon and also lists independent colleges and universities.

PUBLIC EDUCATION IN OREGON

Oregon has 197 public school districts, operating a total of 1,274 public schools. For the school year 2020–2021, the teaching staff working in Oregon's public schools numbered the equivalent of 30,284 full-time positions. The median class size in Oregon is 18.

Public schools enrolled 571,018 students from kindergarten through grade 12 (K–12), of which:

39.6% of students were students of color (national average: 54.3%);

14.2% of students were in Special Education (national average: 11.5%);

3.7% of Oregon students were experiencing houselessness, down from 3.9% in 2018–2019 (national average 2.5%); and

almost 10% of students were English Language Learners (national average: 10.4%).

Oregon's combined state and local share of the K–12 education budget was $7.4 billion for the year ending June 30, 2021.

Sources:
Oregon Department of Education, Oregon Statewide Report Card, 2020–2021;

U.S. Department of Education, National Center for Education Statistics, 2020–2021. The exception is for English Language Learners, where the latest data are for 2019–2020

National Center for Homeless Education, Student Homeless in America: PreK-12th grade; school years 2017–2018 to 2019–2020, where the latest data are for 2019–2020

Chief Education Office

The office was created in 2015 for the purpose of building a seamless system of education from birth to college and career. The office directs and coordinates multi-agency planning and stakeholder convening to eliminate barriers impeding student success and works to increase educational equity and opportunity for all students and education settings.

The office is focused on ensuring every student in the state graduates from high school, and Oregon reaches its "40-40-20" goal of 40% of students completing a two-year degree, 40% completing a four-year degree and 20% graduating from high school career ready. These goals reflect a shared commitment by the state and education groups to create the conditions for students to pursue an education and career path meaningful to them. A target date of 2025 has been set for reaching the "40-40-20" goal.

State Board of Education

The board sets educational policies and standards for Oregon's public school districts and educational service districts, providing leadership and vision by enacting equitable policies and promoting educational practices that help students achieve success in school and life.

The board has seven members appointed to four-year terms by the governor. Board members are:

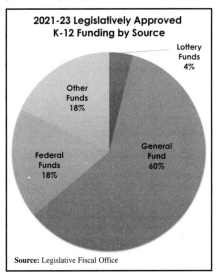

2021-23 Legislatively Approved K-12 Funding by Source

Lottery Funds 4%

Other Funds 18%

Federal Funds 18%

General Fund 60%

Source: Legislative Fiscal Office

Guadalupe Martinez Zapata, Chair (2024); Jennifer Scurlock, Vice-Chair (2024); Kimberly Howard Wade (2024); Jerome Colonna (2022); George Russell (2024); and Bridgett Wheeler (2024). One seat is vacant.

Department of Education

The governor acts as the superintendent of schools. The governor has authority to appoint a deputy superintendent of public instruction to run the Oregon Department of Education (ODE).

ODE oversees Oregon's public K–12 education system and encompasses the Youth Development Division, Oregon School for the Deaf and other programs.

For more information, see ODE's entry in the Executive section, pp. 37–39.

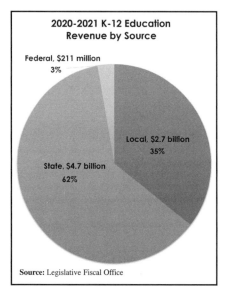

2020-2021 K-12 Education Revenue by Source

Federal, $211 million
3%

Local, $2.7 billion
35%

State, $4.7 billion
62%

Source: Legislative Fiscal Office

Education Funding

Money to support public education in grades K–12 comes from state income taxes, the lottery fund, local revenues primarily consisting of property taxes, and federal funds. Historically, the largest source of funding had been local property taxes, but this changed dramatically in 1990 when voters passed Measure 5, which lowered the amount of property taxes dedicated to schools. By the 1995–1996 school year, local property taxes for education were limited to $5 per every $1,000 of a property's assessed real market value. In 1997, voters passed Measure 50, which further limited local property taxes for schools by placing restrictions on assessed valuation of property and property tax rates. The effect of these measures was to shift the bulk of public school funding from local property taxes to Oregon's General Fund, which comes from state income taxes.

Oregon uses a formula to provide financial equity among school districts. Each school district receives (in combined state and local funds) an allocation per student, plus an additional amount for each student enrolled in more costly programs such as Special Education or English Language Learners.

The 2021–2023 legislatively adopted General Fund and Lottery Funds budget for the Education program area is $12.624 billion. This was an increase of $1.1 billion (or 9.9%) from the 2019–2021 legislatively approved budget.

HIGHER EDUCATION IN OREGON

Prospective students and families in Oregon can choose from a wide variety of postsecondary education options to earn degrees, certificates and training to build their futures and achieve their career goals. Oregon's higher education system enrolls hundreds of thousands of students in seven public universities, 17 community colleges, the Oregon Health & Science University, 42 private colleges and universities and many private career and trade schools.

Higher Education Coordinating Commission

Ben Cannon, Executive Director
Address: 3225 25th St. SE, Salem 97302
Phone: 503-378-5690
Email: info.HECC@state.or.us
Web: oregon.gov/highered

For information about the HECC's duties and responsibilities, see entry in the Executive section, pp. 52–54.

Community Colleges

Oregonians are served by 17 community colleges with campuses and centers throughout the state, providing open access to advance their education and training. Providing certificates, two-year degrees and training programs, Oregon's community colleges prepare students with degrees and coursework to transfer to a four-year university and deliver customized workforce training programs designed to meet local labor market demand. The colleges are governed by locally-elected boards.

In 2019–2020, Oregon's community colleges awarded Associates Degrees to 10,102 individuals and Certificates and Oregon Transfer Modules (OTMs) to 3,296 individuals.

Blue Mountain Community College
J. Mark Browning, President
Address: 2411 NW Carden Ave., PO Box 100, Pendleton 97801-1000

Phone: 541-276-1260
Web: bluecc.edu
Fall 2021 Enrollment: 876
Fall 2021 Tuition: $6,460

Central Oregon Community College
Dr. Laurie Chesley, President
Address: 2600 NW College Way, Bend 97703
Phone: 541-383-7700
Web: cocc.edu
Fall 2021 Enrollment: 5,925
Fall 2021 Tuition: $5,659

Chemeketa Community College
Dr. Jessica Howard, President, Salem
Jim Eustrom, President, Yamhill
Address: 4000 Lancaster Dr. NE, PO Box 14007,
Salem 97309-7070
Phone: 503-399-5000
Web: chemeketa.edu
Fall 2021 Enrollment: 9,460
Fall 2021 Tuition: $5,850

Clackamas Community College
Dr. Tim Cook, President
Address: 19600 S Molalla Ave., Oregon City
97045-7998
Phone: 503-594-6000
Web: clackamas.edu
Fall 2021 Enrollment: 17,638
Fall 2021 Tuition: $5,625

Clatsop Community College
Chris Breitmeyer, President

Address: 1651 Lexington Ave., Astoria 97103
Phone: 503-338-2411
Web: clatsopcc.edu
Fall 2021 Enrollment: 815
Fall 2021 Tuition: $4,800

Columbia Gorge Community College
Dr. Marta Yera Cronin, President
Address: 400 E Scenic Dr., The Dalles 97058-
3434
Phone: 541-506-6000
Web: cgcc.edu
Fall 2021 Enrollment: 884
Fall 2021 Tuition: $5,940

Klamath Community College
Roberto Gutierrez, President
Address: 7390 S 6th St., Klamath Falls 97603-
7121
Phone: 541-882-3521
Web: klamathcc.edu
Fall 2021 Enrollment: 1,766
Fall 2021 Tuition: $5,604

Lane Community College
Margaret Hamilton, President
Address: 4000 E 30th Ave., Eugene 97405-0640
Phone: 541-463-3000
Web: lanecc.edu
Fall 2021 Enrollment: 6,968
Fall 2021 Tuition: $6,539

Linn-Benton Community College
Dr. Lisa Avery, President

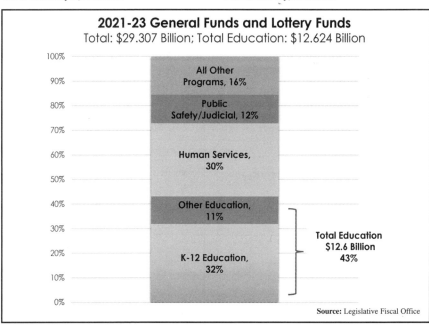

2021-23 General Funds and Lottery Funds
Total: $29.307 Billion; Total Education: $12.624 Billion

- All Other Programs, 16%
- Public Safety/Judicial, 12%
- Human Services, 30%
- Other Education, 11%
- K-12 Education, 32%

Total Education $12.6 Billion 43%

Source: Legislative Fiscal Office

Address: 6500 Pacific Blvd. SW, Albany 97321
Phone: 541-917-4999
Web: linnbenton.edu
Fall 2021 Enrollment: 5,911
Fall 2021 Tuition: $6,102

Mount Hood Community College
Dr. Lisa Skari, President
Address: 26000 SE Stark St., Gresham 97030-3300
Phone: 503-491-6422
Web: mhcc.edu
Fall 2021 Enrollment: 9,582
Fall 2021 Tuition: $4,248

Oregon Coast Community College
Dr. Birgitte Ryslinge, President
Address: 400 SE College Way, Newport 97366
Phone: 541-867-8501
Web: oregoncoast.edu
Fall 2021 Enrollment: 1,110
Fall 2021 Tuition: $6,435

Portland Community College
Dr. Adrien Bennings, President
Address: PO Box 19000, Portland 97219-0990
Phone: 971-722-4365
Web: pcc.edu
Fall 2021 Enrollment: 26,594
Fall 2021 Tuition: $5,996

Rogue Community College
Randy Weber, Ed.D., President
Address: 3345 Redwood Hwy., Grants Pass 97527-9291
Phone: 541-956-7500
Web: roguecc.edu
Fall 2021 Enrollment: 6,837
Fall 2021 Tuition: $6,480

Southwestern Oregon Community College
Dr. Patty M. Scott, President
Address: 1988 Newmark Ave., Coos Bay 97420
Phone: 541-888-2525
Web: socc.edu
Fall 2021 Enrollment: 1,871
Fall 2021 Tuition: $6,270

Tillamook Bay Community College
Ross Tomlin, President
Address: 4301 Third St., Tillamook 97141
Phone: 503-842-8222
Web: tillamookbaycc.edu
Fall 2021 Enrollment: 1,293
Fall 2021 Tuition: $4,680

Treasure Valley Community College
Dana Young, President
Address: 650 College Blvd., Ontario 97914-3498
Phone: 541-881-8822
Web: tvcc.cc

Fall 2021 Enrollment: 1,813
Fall 2021 Tuition: $5,895

Umpqua Community College
Rachel Pokrandt, President
Address: 1140 Umpqua College Rd., Roseburg 97470
Phone: 541-440-4600
Web: umpqua.edu
Fall 2021 Enrollment: 3,053
Fall 2021 Tuition: $4,056

Community college tuition figures are based on annualized in-district resident status. Enrollment numbers are based on fall, fourth-week headcount enrollment.

Public Universities

Oregon's public universities serve as educational, scholarly and research centers preparing students to succeed in the workforce and serve the needs of Oregon students and communities. Providing education at the baccalaureate level and beyond, the seven Oregon public universities include Eastern Oregon University (EOU), La Grande; Oregon Institute of Technology (OIT), Klamath Falls and Wilsonville; Oregon State University (OSU), Corvallis and Bend; Portland State University (PSU), Portland; Southern Oregon University (SOU), Ashland; University of Oregon (UO), Eugene; and Western Oregon University (WOU), Monmouth.

In 2020–2021, the seven public universities collectively awarded degrees and certificates across the state to 23,655 individuals. 17,313 people were awarded bachelor's degrees and 5,207 were awarded advanced degrees and graduate certificates. The universities offer bachelor degrees in hundreds of majors and minors, certificate programs, professional programs, graduate programs, as well as research, scholarship, innovation and public service that directly serve Oregon's communities and industries and the needs of national and international constituents.

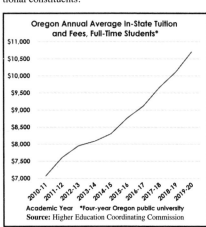

Oregon Annual Average In-State Tuition and Fees, Full-Time Students*

$11,000
$10,500
$10,000
$9,500
$9,000
$8,500
$8,000
$7,500
$7,000

Academic Year   *Four-year Oregon public university
Source: Higher Education Coordinating Commission

Eastern Oregon University
Lara Moore and Richard Chaves, Co-Interim Presidents
Address: One University Blvd., La Grande 97850-2899
Phone: 541-962-3512; Toll-free: 1-800-452-8639
Web: eou.edu
Board of Trustees: eou.edu/governance
Fall 2021 Enrollment: 2,825
Fall 2022 Tuition and Fees: $9,696

Oregon Institute of Technology
Dr. Nagi Naganathan, President
Address: 3201 Campus Dr., Klamath Falls 97601-8801
Phone: 541-885-1000
Web: oit.edu
Board of Trustees: oit.edu/trustees
Fall 2021 Enrollment: 4,910
Fall 2021 Tuition and Fees: $11,622

Oregon State University
Dr. Jayati Murthy, President
Address: 634 Kerr Administration Building, Corvallis 97331-2128
Phone: 541-737-4133
Web: oregonstate.edu; osucascades.edu
Board of Trustees:
leadership.oregonstate.edu/trustees
Fall 2021 Enrollment: Corvallis campus, 33,193; OSU-Cascades Bend campus, 915
2019–2020 Tuition and Fees: Corvallis campus, $12,683; OSU-Cascades Bend campus, $11,667

Portland State University
Dr. Stephen Percy, President
Address: PO Box 751, Portland 97207-0751
Phone: 503-725-4419; Toll-free: 1-800-547-8887
Web: pdx.edu
Board of Trustees: pdx.edu/board
Fall 2021 Enrollment: 23,177
2021 Tuition and Fees: $10,386

Southern Oregon University
Dr. Linda Schott, President
Address: 1250 Siskiyou Blvd., Ashland 97520
Phone: 541-552-7672
Web: sou.edu
Board of Trustees: governance.sou.edu
Fall 2021 Enrollment: 5,056
2020-21 Tuition and Fees: $11,166

University of Oregon
Patrick Phillips, Interim President
Address: 110 Johnson Hall, Eugene 97403
Phone: 541-346-3036
Web: uoregon.edu
Board of Trustees: trustees.uoregon.edu
Fall 2021 Enrollment: 22,298
2020–2021 Tuition and Fees: $14,421

Western Oregon University
Dr. Rex Fuller, President
Address: 345 N Monmouth Ave., Monmouth 97361
Phone: 503-838-8888
Web: wou.edu
Board of Trustees: wou.edu/board
Fall 2021 Enrollment: 4,029
2019–2020 Tuition and Fees: $10,269

Tuition and fee figures are based on 15 credit hours per term for undergraduate resident students. Certain programs are assessed at different rates than noted. Enrollment numbers are fall, fourth-week enrollment.

OREGON HEALTH & SCIENCE UNIVERSITY
Danny Jacobs, MD, President
Address: 3181 SW Sam Jackson Park Rd., Portland 97239-3098
Web: ohsu.edu/
Board of Directors: ohsu.edu/about/board-directors

The Oregon Health & Science University (OHSU) includes Oregon's only academic health center and has schools of medicine, dentistry, nursing, public health (in partnership with PSU) and other health care professional programs. OHSU has been organized as a public corporation since 1995 and is governed by a board of directors, appointed by the governor and confirmed by the Senate. The state continues to support OHSU programs through grants and general funds that totaled $79.2 million in the 2019–2021 biennium.

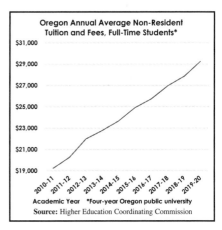

Oregon Annual Average Non-Resident Tuition and Fees, Full-Time Students*
Source: Higher Education Coordinating Commission

WESTERN INTERSTATE COMMISSION FOR HIGHER EDUCATION
Address: PO Box 3175, Eugene 97403
Phone: 541-346-5729
Web: wiche.edu

Education

The Western Interstate Commission for Higher Education (WICHE) is a regional organization created by the Western Regional Education Compact, adopted in the 1950s. WICHE facilitates resource sharing among the higher education systems of the West. Fifteen states, including Oregon, are members of WICHE, which is governed by three governor-appointed commissioners from each state. Under terms of the compact, each state commits to support WICHE's basic operations through annual dues established by the full commission. Oregon's three commissioners are Ben Cannon, Salem; Camille Preus, Pendleton; and Hilda Rosselli, Salem.

PRIVATE AND INDEPENDENT COLLEGES AND UNIVERSITIES

Oregon is home to many private colleges, universities and career schools providing a wide range of college and career training opportunities to Oregonians.

Northwest Commission on Colleges and Universities

Web: nwccu.org

The Northwest Commission on Colleges and Universities (NWCCU) recognizes higher education institutions for performance, integrity and quality to merit the confidence of the educational community and the public. The commission's accreditation of postsecondary institutions is a voluntary, non-governmental, self-regulatory process of quality assurance and institutional improvement.

Accreditation or preaccreditation by NWCCU also qualifies institutions and enrolled students for access to Title IV federal funds to support teaching, research and student financial aid.

Unless otherwise noted, the independent, non-profit higher education institutions listed below are accredited by NWCCU and have independent or exempt status from ongoing regulatory oversight by Oregon's Office of Degree Authorization.

Bushnell University, Eugene
Dr. Joseph Womack, President
Phone: 541-684-7201
Web: bushnell.edu

Corban University, Salem
Dr. Sheldon Nord, President
Phone: 503-581-8600
Web: corban.edu

Embry-Riddle Aeronautical University, Portland
Jennifer Stevens, Campus Director
Phone: 503-288-8690

Web: worldwide.erau.edu/locations/portland
(Accredited by the Southern Association of Colleges and Schools, Commission on Colleges)

George Fox University, Newberg
Dr. Robin E. Baker, President
Phone: 503-538-8383
Web: georgefox.edu

Lewis & Clark College, Portland
Dr. Robin Holmes-Sullivan, President
Phone: 503-768-7000
Web: lclark.edu

Linfield University, McMinnville
Dr. Miles K. Davis, President
Phone: 503-883-2200
Web: linfield.edu

Pioneer Hall on the campus of Linfield College in McMinnville. (Oregon State Archives scenic photo)

Mount Angel Seminary, Saint Benedict
Joseph Betschart, President
Phone: 503-845-3951
Web: mountangelabbey.org/seminary

Multnomah University, Portland
Rev. Dr. Eric Anthony Joseph, President
Phone: 503-255-0332
Web: multnomah.edu

National University of Natural Medicine, Portland
Melanie Henriksen,ND,LAc,CNM, President/CEO
Phone: 503-552-1555
Web: nunm.edu

Northwest University, Salem
Dr. Joseph Castleberry, President
Phone: 503-304-0092
Web: oregon.northwestu.edu

Pacific University, Forest Grove
Dr. Jenny Coyle, President
Phone: 503-352-6151
Web: pacificu.edu

Reed College, Portland
Dr. Audrey Bilger, President
Phone: 503-771-1112
Web: reed.edu

Eliot Hall on the campus of Reed College in southeast Portland. (Oregon State Archives scenic photo)

University of Portland, Portland
Dr. Robert D. Kelly, President
Phone: 503-943-8000
Web: up.edu

University of Western States, Portland
Joseph Brimhall, President
Phone: 503-256-3180
Web: uws.edu

Walla Walla University School of Nursing, Portland
John McVay, President
Phone: 800-541-8900
Web: wallawalla.edu

Warner Pacific University, Portland
Dr. Brian L. Johnson, President
Phone: 503-517-1020
Web: warnerpacific.edu

Western Seminary, Portland
Chuck Conniry, PhD, President
Phone: 503-517-1800
Web: westernseminary.edu

Western University of Health Sciences, Lebanon
Dr. Robin Farias-Eisner, MD, PhD, MBA, FACOG, President
Phone: 541-259-0200
Web: westernu.edu/
(Accredited by the Western Association of Schools and Colleges)

Willamette University, Salem
Stephen E. Thorsett, PhD, President
Phone: 503-370-6209
Web: willamette.edu

Willamette University Pacific Northwest College of Art, Portland
Dr. David Ellis, Interim President
Phone: 503-226-4391
Web: pnca.willamette.edu

Egtvedt Hall on the campus of Warner Pacific University in southeast Portland. (Oregon State Archives scenic photo)

STUDENT ESSAY CONTEST WINNER
The time of lost smiles

Keina Ga
Ms. Hellman's 8th Grade Class
ACCESS Academy, Portland

In the efforts to manage Covid, we masked up and hid a lot of our faces. As we avoided Covid, we avoided each other. Where did the smiles go? Back then, school was fun. We received unconditional smiles from friends, as well as the occasional grins from strangers in the hallway. Now, people have to hide it. No more bright toothy beams. Because of Covid, school became gloomy. Smiles were lost.

A smile is a chain reaction. Like how Covid infects people, passing from host to host, a smile infects people with happiness, passing from person to person. Anyone who receives it, is bound to give back. So much of our joy derived from day-to-day smiles. Without them, I became heavy from drudgery and lost the bounce in my step.

One day, I felt my friend smile. I was heartened. *But how could I understand that she was smiling if her face was covered up by her mask?* Later in the day, I somehow sensed another smile. It made me realize that even as Covid changed our lives, happiness could never really be hidden. Even if we are unable to smile with our mouths, we still had our eyes. We can all learn to smile better with our eyes, passing on kindness and still feel connected to each other. Covid, recalled differently, as the time of seeking eyes.

Arts, History and Sciences

Through the organizations described in this section, we are fortunate to have many opportunities to gain greater understanding and appreciation for the arts and culture, history and heritage, Earth sciences and technology of Oregon.

ARTS AND CULTURE IN OREGON

Oregon Arts Commission
Brian Rogers, Executive Director
Address: 775 Summer St. NE, Suite 200, Salem 97301-1280
Phone: 503-986-0082
Web: oregonartscommission.org
The Oregon Arts Commission enhances all Oregonian's quality of life through the arts by stimulating creativity, leadership and economic vitality.

The commission provides leadership, funding and arts programs through its grants, special initiatives and services. The commission works to improve access to the arts all around the state, and supports the Oregon Folklife Network.

Oregon Cultural Trust
Brian Rogers, Executive Director
Address: 775 Summer St. NE, Suite 200, Salem 97301-1280
Phone: 503-986-0088
Web: culturaltrust.org
Founded in 2001, the Oregon Cultural Trust leads Oregon in cultivating, growing and valuing culture as an integral part of communities. Working with the Oregon Arts Commission, the Oregon Heritage Commission, the Oregon Historical Society, Oregon Humanities and the State Historic Preservation Office, the Cultural Trust inspires Oregonians to invest in a permanent fund that provides grants to cultural organizations. It is governed by a 13-member board of directors. Eleven voting members are appointed by the governor, and the president of the Senate and speaker of the House of Representatives each appoint a member of the Legislature as non-voting, advisory members.

Oregon Humanities
Adam Davis, Executive Director
Address: 610 SW Alder St. Ste. 111, Portland 97205
Phone: 503-241-0543; Toll-free: 1-800-735-0543
Web: oregonhumanities.org

Oregon Humanities, formerly the Oregon Council for the Humanities, was established in 1971 as an independent, nonprofit affiliate of the National Endowment for the Humanities. It is one of five statewide partners of the Oregon Cultural Trust — programs that support an Oregon that invites diverse perspectives, explores challenging questions and strives for just communities.

Oregon Arts Organizations

All Classical Public Media, Inc.
Suzanne Nance, President & CEO
Address: 211 SE Caruthers St. Ste. 200, Portland 97214
Phone: 503-943-5828, 1-800-306-5277
Web: allclassical.org

Alberta Rose Theatre
Address: 3000 NE Alberta St.,Portland 97211
Phone: 503-719-6055
Web: albertarosetheatre.com

Artist Repertory Theatre
Jeanette Harrison, Artistic Director; J.S. May, Executive Director
Address: 128 NW 11th Ave, Portland 97209
Phone: 503-241-9807
Web: artistsrep.com

Broadway Rose Theatre Company
Dan Murphy, Managing Director
Address: 12580 SW Grant Ave., Tigard 97223
Phone: 503-620-5262
Web: broadwayrose.org

Chamber Music Northwest
Peter Bilotta, Executive Director
Address: 1201 SW 12th Ave, Suite 420, Portland 97205
Phone: 503-223-3202
Web: cmnw.org

The Children's Museum of Southern Oregon
Eric Dames, Board President
Address: 413 W Main St, Medford 97501

Phone: 541-772-9922
Web: tcmso.org

Eugene Ballet Company

Toni Pimble, Artistic Director; Josh Neckels, Executive Director
Address: 174 East 16th Ave., Eugene 97401
Phone: 541-485-3992
Web: eugeneballet.org

Eugene Symphony

Scott Freck, Executive Director
Address: 115 West 8th Ave., Ste 115, Eugene 97401
Phone: 541-687-9487
Web: eugenesymphony.org

Hallie Ford Museum of Art

John Olbrantz, Director
Address: 700 State St., Salem 97310
Phone: 503-370-6855
Web: willamette.edu/arts/hfma/

High Desert Museum

Dr. Dana Whitelaw, Executive Director
Address: 59800 S Hwy 97, Bend 97702
Phone: 541-382-4754
Web: highdesertmuseum.org

Hult Center for the Performing Arts

Address: One Eugene Center, Eugene 97401
Phone: 541-682-5000
Web: hultcenter.org

John G. Shedd Institute for the Arts

Jim Ralph, Executive Director
Address: 868 High St., Eugene 97401
Phone: 541-434-7000
Web: theshedd.org

Jordan Schnitzer Museum of Art

John Weber, Executive Director
Address: 1430 Johnson Ln., Eugene 97403
Phone: 541-346-3027
Web: jsma.uoregon.edu

Lane Arts Council

Stacey Ray, Executive Director
Address: 174 East 16th Ave., Ste. 125 Eugene 97401
Phone: 541-485-2278
Web: lanearts.org

Literary Arts

Andrew Proctor, Executive Director
Address: 925 SW Washington St, Portland 97205
Phone: 503-227-2583
Web: literary-arts.org

Newport Symphony Orchestra

Lisa Lipton, Executive Director
Address: PO Box 1617, Newport 97365
Phone: 458-868-9155
Web: newportsymphony.org

Northwest Professional Dance Project

Scott Lewis, Executive Director
Address: 211 NE 10th Ave, Portland 97232
Phone: 503-421-7434
Web: nwdanceproject.org

Oregon Bach Festival

James Boyd, Director of Programming & Administration; Sandy Cummings, Director of Finance & Operations
Address: 1257 University of Oregon, Eugene 97403
Phone: 541-346-5666
Web: oregonbachfestival.org

Oregon Ballet Theatre

Thomas Bruner, Executive Director
Address: 720 S Bancroft St., Portland 97239
Phone: 503-222-5538
Web: obt.org

Oregon Children's Theatre Company

Lucas Welsh, Director of Finance & Administration
Address: 1111 SW Broadway, Portland 97205
Phone: 503-228-9571
Web: octc.org

Oregon Shakespeare Festival

Nataki Garrett, Artistic Director; David Schmitz, Executive Director
Address: 15 S Pioneer St., PO Box 158, Ashland 97520
Phone: 1-800-219-8161
Web: osfashland.org

Oregon Symphony Association

Scott Showalter, President and CEO
Address: 921 SW Washington St., Portland 97205
Phone: 503-228-4294; Toll Free: 1-800-228-7343
Web: orsymphony.org

Patricia Reser Center for the Arts

Chris Ayzoukian, Executive Director
Address: 12625 SW Crescent St., Beaverton 97005
Phone: 971-501-7762
Web: thereser.org

Portland Art Museum

Brian Ferriso, Executive Director
Address: 1219 SW Park Ave., Portland 97205
Phone: 503-226-2811
Web: portlandartmuseum.org

Portland Baroque Orchestra
Dave Pearson, Interim Executive Director
Address: 610 SW Broadway, Ste 605, Portland 97205
Phone: 503-222-6000
Web: pbo.org

Portland Center Stage
Liam Kass-Lentz, Interim Managing Director
Address: 128 NW 11th Ave, Portland 97209
Phone: 503-445-3700
Web: pcs.org

Portland Institute For Contemporary Art
Victoria Frey, Executive Director
Address: 15 NE Hancock St., Portland 97212
Phone: 503-242-1419
Web: pica.org

Portland Opera
Sue Dixon, General Director
Address: 211 SE Caruthers St., Portland 97214
Phone: 503-241-1407
Web: portlandopera.org

Portland Playhouse
Brian Weaver, Artistic Director
Address: 602 NE Prescott St., Portland 97211
Phone: 503-488-5822
Web: portlandplayhouse.org

Portland Youth Philharmonic
David Hattner, Musical Director; Noreen Murdock, Executive Director
Address: 9320 SW Barbur Blvd,. Ste 140, Portland 97219
Phone: 503-223-5959
Web: portlandyouthphil.org

Regional Arts and Culture Council
Della Rae and Carol Tatch, Co-Executive Directors
Address: 411 NW Park Ave., Ste 101, Portland 97209
Phone: 503-823-5111
Web: racc.org

Rogue Valley Symphony
Joelle Graves, Executive Director
Address: 33 N First St., Ste 1, Ashland 97520
Phone: 541-708-6400
Web: rvsymphony.org

Salem Art Association
Matthew Boulay, Executive Director
Address: 600 Mission St. SE, Salem 97302
Phone: 503-581-2228
Web: salemart.org

Sisters Folk Festival
Crista Munro, Executive Director
Address: PO Box 3500 PMB 304, Sisters 97759
Phone: 541-549-4979
Web: sistersfolkfestival.org

Tower Theatre Foundation
Ray Solley, Executive Director
Address: PO Box 1378, Bend 97709
Phone: 541-317-0700
Web: towertheatre.org

Waterfront Blues Festival
Christina Fuller, Festival Director; Tyler Fuller, Director of Operations
Address: 312 S. Moody Ave,. Ste 150, Portland 97239
Email: info@waterfrontbluesfest.com
Web: waterfrontbluesfest.com

Young Audiences of Oregon
Lauren Jost, Executive Director
Address: 1220 SW Morrison, Ste 1000, Portland 97205
Phone: 503-225-5900
Web: ya-or.org

OREGON HISTORY ORGANIZATIONS

Oregon's Statewide History, Heritage and Cultural Organizations

State Archives
see Executive Section, page 13

Gay & Lesbian Archives of the Pacific Northwest
Address: PO Box 3646, Portland 97208
Email: info@glapn.org
Web: glapn.org

Genealogical Forum of Oregon
Address: 2505 SE 11th Ave., Suite B18, Portland 97202
Phone: 503-963-1932
Web: gfo.org

Japanese American Museum of Oregon
Address: 411 NW Flanders St., Portland 97209
Phone: 503-224-1458
Web: jamo.org

National Historic Oregon Trail Interpretive Center
Sarah Sherman, Project Manager
Address: 22267 OR Hwy. 86, Baker City 97814
Phone: 541-523-1843
Web: oregontrail.blm.gov

Nordic Northwest
Jodi Lippert, Executive Director
Address: 8800 SW Oleson Rd., Portland 97223
Phone: 503-977-0275
Web: nordicnorthwest.org

Oregon Black Pioneers
Zachary Stocks, Executive Director
Address: 117 Commercial St. NE., Suite 210, Salem 97301
Phone: 503-540-4063
Web: oregonblackpioneers.org

Oregon Geographic Names Board
Bruce J. Fisher, Board President
Address: 1200 SW Park Ave., Portland 97205
Phone: 503-319-1714
Web: ohs.org/about-us/affiliates-and-partners/oregon-geographic-names-board

Oregon Heritage Commission, State Historic Preservation Office, Oregon Commission on Historic Cemeteries
see Executive Section, pages 66–67

Oregon Historical Society
Kerry Tymchuk, Executive Director
Address: 1200 SW Park Ave., Portland 97205
Phone: 503-222-1741; TDD: 503-306-5194
Web: ohs.org

Visitors view an exhibit at the Oregon Historical Society in Portland. (Oregon State Archives scenic photo)

Oregon Health & Sciences University Historical Collections & Archives
Maria Cunningham, Director of Special Collections
Address: 3181 SW Sam Jackson Park Rd., Portland 97239
Phone: 503-494-5587
Web: ohsu.edu/historical-collections-archives

Oregon Jewish Museum and Center for Holocaust Education
Judy Margles, Executive Director
Address: 724 NW Davis St. Portland 97209
Phone: 503-226-3600
Web: ojmche.org

Oregon Rail Heritage Foundation
Renee Deveraux, Executive Director
Address: 2250 SE Water Ave., Portland 97214
Phone: 503-233-1156
Web: orhf.org

Oregon State Hospital Museum of Mental Health
Address: 2600 Center St. NE, Salem 97301
Phone: 971-599-1674
Web: oshmuseum.org

Portland Japanese Garden
Stephen D. Bloom, Chief Executive Officer
Address: 611 SW Kingston Ave, Portland 97205
Phone: 503-223-1321
Web: japanesegarden.org

Restore Oregon
Nicole Possert, Executive Director
Address: 1327 SE Tacoma St. #114, Portland 97202
Phone: 503-243-1923
Web: restoreoregon.org

Western Antique Aeroplane & Automobile Museum
Stephanie Hatch, Museum Director
Address: 1600 Air Museum Rd., Hood River 97301
Phone: 541-308-1600
Web: waaamuseum.org

See also Oregon Museums Association
Address: PO Box 8604, Portland 97207
Email: connect@oregonmuseums.org
Web: oregonmuseums.org

Tribal Historical Cultural and Heritage Organizations

Chachalu Museum and Cultural Center
Address: 8270 Grand Ronde Road, Grand Ronde, 97347
Phone: 503 879-2226
Web: granderonde.org/history-culture/culture/chachalue-museum-and-cultural-center/

Kaku-Ixt Mana Ina Haws
Luhui Whitebear, Center Director
Address: 311 SW 26th St., Corvallis 97331
Phone: 541-737-2738
Web: dce.oregonstate.edu/inahaws

The Museum at Warm Springs
Address: 2189 Hwy 26, Warm Springs 97761
Phone: 541-553-3331
Web: warmsprings-nsn.gov/program/the-museum-at-warm-springs

Tamástslikt Cultural Institute
Roberta Conner, Director
Address: 47106 Wildhorse Blvd., Pendleton 97801
Phone: 541-429-7700
Web: tamastslikt.org

The Benton County Historical Museum in Philomath. (Oregon State Archives scenic photo)

Regional Historical Societies and Heritage Organizations

Aurora Colony Historical Society
Old Aurora Colony Museum
Address: 15018 Second St., NE, PO Box 202, Aurora 97002
Phone: 503-678-5754
Web: auroracolony.org

Baker Heritage Museum
Address: 2480 Grove St., Baker City 97814-2719
Phone: 541-523-9308
Web: bakerheritagemuseum.com

Benton County Historical Society & Museum
Address: 1101 Main St., Philomath 97370
Phone: 541-929-6230
Web: bentoncountymuseum.org

Cannon Beach History Center and Museum
Address: 1387 S Spruce St., Cannon Beach 97110
Phone: 503-436-9301
Web: cbhistory.org

Centro Cultural del Condado de Washington
Address: 1110 North Adair St., Cornelius 97113
Phone: 503-359-0446
Web: centrocultural.org

Clackamas County Historical Society and Museum of the Oregon Territory
Address: 211 Tumwater Dr., PO Box 2211, Oregon City 97045
Phone: 503-655-5574
Web: clackamashistory.org

Clatsop County Historical Society
Address: 714 Exchange St., PO Box 88, Astoria 97103
Phone: 503-325-2203
Web: astoriamuseums.org

Columbia River Maritime Museum
Address: 1792 Marine Dr., Astoria 97103
Phone: 503-325-2323
Web: crmm.org

Corvallis Museum
Address: 411 SW 2nd St., Corvallis 97333
Phone: 541-929-6230
Web: bentoncountymuseum.org/index.php/visit/corvallis-museum-visitor-info

Coos History Museum & Maritime Collection
Address: 1210 N Front St., Coos Bay 97420
Phone: 541-756-6320
Web: cooshistory.org

Cottage Grove Genealogical Society
Address: PO Box 388, Cottage Grove 97424
Phone: 541-942-9570
Web: cggeneaolgy.org

Cottage Grove Historical Society
Address: PO Box 142, Cottage Grove 97424

Phone: 541-942-5022
Web: cghistory.org

Crook County Historical Society and Bowman Museum
Address: 246 N Main St., Prineville 97754
Phone: 541-447-3715
Web: crookcountyhistorycenter.org

Curry Historical Society and Museum
Address: 29419 S Ellensberg Ave., PO Box 1598, Gold Beach 97444
Phone: 541-247-9396
Web: curryhistory.com

Deschutes County Historical Society and Museum
Address: 129 NW Idaho Ave., Bend 97703
Phone: 541-389-1813
Web: deschuteshistory.org

Douglas County Museum and Umpqua River Lighthouse Museum
Address: 123 Museum Dr., Roseburg 97471; 1020 Lighthouse Rd., Winchester Bay 97467
Phone: 541-957-7007; 541-271-4631
Web: umpquavalleymuseums.org

Five Oaks Museum
Address: 17677 NW Springville Rd., Portland 97229, PO Box 3790, Hillsboro 97123
Phone: 503-645-5353
Web: fiveoaksmuseum.org

Four Rivers Cultural Center and Museum
Address: 676 SW Fifth Ave., Ontario 97914
Phone: 541-889-8191
Web: 4rcc.com

Gilliam County Historical Museum
Address: 505 N Washington, PO Box 377, Condon 97823
Phone: 541-384-4233
Web: co.gilliam.or.us/recreation/museums

Grant County Historical Museum
Address: 101 S Canyon City Blvd., Hwy 395, PO Box 464, Canyon City 97820
Phone: 541-575-0362
Web: grantcountyhistoricalmuseum.org

Gresham Historical Society
Address: 410 N Main Ave., P.O. Box 65, Gresham 97030
Phone: 503-661-0347
Web: greshamhistorical.org

Independence Heritage Museum
Address: 281 S 2nd Street, P.O. Box 7, Independence 97351

Phone: 503-838-4989
Web: orheritage.org

Harney County Historical Society
Address: 18 W D St., PO Box 388, Burns 97720
Phone: 541-573-5618
Web: hchistoricalsociety.com

The History Museum of Hood River County
Address: 300 E Port Marina Dr., PO Box 781, Hood River 97031
Phone: 541-386-6772
Web: hoodriverhistorymuseum.org

Josephine County Historical Society
Address: 512 SW Fifth St., Grants Pass 97526
Phone: 541-479-7827
Web: jocohistorical.org

Lake County Museum and Schminck Memorial Museum
Address: 118 S E St., PO Box 1222 Lakeview 97630;
Phone: 541-947-2220
Web: lakecountyor.org/links/museum.php

Lane County Historical Society and Museum
Address: 740 W 13th Ave., Eugene 97402
Phone: 541-682-4242
Web: lchm.org

Lincoln County Historical Society
Address: 545 SW Ninth St., Newport 97365
Phone: 541-265-7509
Web: oregoncoasthistory.org

Linn County Historical Museum
Address: 101 Park Ave., PO Box 607, Brownsville 97327
Phone: 541-466-3390
Web: linnparks.com/museums/

Malheur Country Historical Society
Address: PO Box 691, Ontario 97914
Email: malheurcountryhist@gmail.com
Web: sites.google.com/site/malheurcountryhistorical

Morrow County Museum and Historical Society
Address: 444 N Main St, Heppner 97836
Phone: 541-676-5524; 541-676-5536
Web: morrowcountymuseum.com

North Lincoln County Historical Museum
Address: 4907 SW Hwy. 101, Lincoln City 97367
Phone: 541-996-6614
Web: northlincolncountyhistoricalmuseum.org

Oaks Park Association
Address: 7805 SE Oaks Park Way, Portland 97202
Phone: 541-233-5777
Web: oakspark.com

Pacific Maritime Heritage Center
Address: 333 SE Bay Blvd, Newport 97365
Phone: 503-265-7509
Web: oregoncoasthistory.org/museums-exhibits/maritime-center

Pittock Mansion Society
Address: 3229 NW Pittock Dr, Portland 97210
Phone: 503-823-3623
Web: pittockmansion.org

Polk County Historical Society
Address: 560 S Pacific Hwy., Rickreall 97371, PO Box 67, Monmouth 97361
Phone: 503-623-6251
Web: polkcountyhistoricalsociety.org

Portland Rose Festival Foundation
Address: 1020 SW Naito Parkway, Portland 97204
Phone: 503-227-2681
Web: rosefestival.org

Rogue Valley Genealogical Society & Library
Address: 3405 S Pacific Hwy., Medford 97501
Phone: 541-512-2340
Web: rvgslibrary.org

Sandy Historical Society
Address: 39345 Pioneer Blvd, Sandy 97055
Phone: 503-668-3378
Web: sandyhistory.com

Santiam Historical Society
Address: PO Box 326, Stayton 97383
Phone: 503-769-1406
Email: santiamhistoricalsociety@gmail.com

Seaside Museum and Historical Society
Address: 570 Necanicum Drive, Seaside 97138
Phone: 503-738-7065
Web: seasideoregonmuseum.com

Sherman County Historical Society and Museum
Address: 200 Dewey St., PO Box 173, Moro 97039
Phone: 541-565-3232
Web: shermanmuseum.org

Silverton Country Historical Society
Address: 428 South Water St., Silverton 97381
Phone: 503-873-7070
Web: silvertonmuseum.org

Southern Oregon Historical Society
Address: 106 N Central Ave., Medford 97501
Phone: 541-622-2025 x200
Web: sohs.org

St. Paul Rodeo Association
Address: PO Box 175, St Paul 97137
Phone: 1-800-237-5920
Web: stpaulrodeo.com

Talent Historical Society
Address: PO Box 582, Talent 97540
Phone: 541-512-8838
Web: talenthistory.org

Tillamook County Pioneer Museum
Address: 2106 Second St., Tillamook 97141
Phone: 503-842-4553
Web: tcpm.org

Troutdale Historical Society
Address: 732 E Historic Columbia River Hwy., Troutdale 97060
Phone: 503-661-2164
Web: troutdalehistory.org

Umatilla County Historical Society and Heritage Station Museum
Address: 108 SW Frazer Ave., PO Box 253, Pendleton 97801
Phone: 541-276-0012
Web: heritagestationmuseum.org

Union County Museum
Address: 333 South Main St., Union 97883
Phone: 541-562-6003
Web: ucmuseumoregon.com

Wasco County Museum
Address: 5000 Discovery Dr., The Dalles 97058
Phone: 541-296-8600
Web: gorgediscovery.org

Willamette Heritage Center
Address: 1313 Mill St. SE, Suite 200, Salem 97301
Phone: 503-585-7012
Web: willametteheritage.org

Yaquina Pacific Railroad Historical Society
Address: 100 NW A St., Toledo 97391
Phone: 541-336-5256
Web: yaquinapacificrr.org

Yamhill County Historical Society
Address: 11275 SW Durham Lane, McMinnville 97128
Phone: 503-472-2842
Web: yamhillcountyhistory.org

EARTH SCIENCES AND TECHNOLOGY

Oregon's Major Industry, Science and Technology Organizations

Columbia Gorge Discovery Center
Carolyn Purcell, Executive Director
Address: 5000 Discovery Dr., The Dalles 97058
Phone: 541-296-8600
Web: gorgediscovery.org

Eugene Science Center
Tim Scott, Executive Director
Address: 2300 Leo Harris Parkway, Eugene 97401
Phone: 541-682-7888
Web: eugenesciencecenter.org

Evergreen Aviation & Space Museum
Tyson Weinert, President and CEO
Address: 500 NE Captain Michael King Smith Wy., McMinnville 97128
Phone: 503-434-4180
Web: evergreenmuseum.org

Malheur Field Station
Rose Garacci, Station Manager
Address: 34848 Sodhouse Ln., Princeton 97721
Phone: 541-493-2629
Web: malheurfieldstation.org

Oregon Coast Aquarium
Carrie E. Lewis, President and CEO;
Signe Grimstad, Board Chair
Address: 2820 SE Ferry Slip Rd., Newport 97365
Phone: 541-867-3474
Web: aquarium.org

Oregon Museum of Science and Industry (OMSI)
Erin Graham, President and CEO;
Alistair Firmin, Board Chair
Address: 1945 SE Water Ave., Portland 97214-3354
Phone: 503-797-4000
Web: omsi.edu

Oregon State University Hatfield Marine Science Center
Bob Cowen, Director
Address: 2030 SE Marine Science Dr., Newport 97365
Phone: 541-867-0100
Web: hmsc.oregonstate.edu

Oregon Zoo
Heidi Rahn, Director
Address: 4001 SW Canyon Rd., Portland 97221
Phone: 503-220-2540
Web: oregonzoo.org

Rice Museum of Rocks and Minerals
Aurore Giguet, Executive Director
Address: 26385 NW Groveland Drive, Hillsboro 97124
Phone: 503-647-2418
Web: ricenorthwestmuseum.org

ScienceWorks Hands-On Museum
Aaron Moffatt, Interim Executive Director
Address: 1500 E Main St., Ashland 97520
Phone: 541-482-6767
Web: scienceworksmuseum.org

University of Oregon Museum of Natural and Cultural History
Jon Erlandson, Executive Director
Address: 1680 E 15th Ave., Eugene 97403-1224
Phone: 541-346-3024
Web: mnch.uoregon.edu

World Forestry Center
Joseph Furia, Executive Director
Address: 4033 SW Canyon Rd., Portland 97221
Phone: 503-228-1367
Web: worldforestry.org

My Life After Covid

Bairon Lai
Katie Luken's 3rd Grade Class
Flex Online School, Beaverton

Barion Lai's drawing shows the apple tree planted at Bethany Elementary School (Bairon's home school) during Covid-19. It also shows messages written on rocks and placed under the tree to cheer up the community. Bairon's self portrait is at bottom left, next to a laptop computer.

Arts, History and Sciences

I opened my eyes. "Is it another normal day?" I thought. When I looked out the window, I started to remember the day, March 22, 2020 when the principal announced the Covid-19 outbreak. We couldn't go to school in person, but we could learn online. The change affected my school life, and made me learn how to protect myself more.

In the beginning of the virtual learning, I was actually very happy. However, soon the happiness went all the way to dissapointment because I could not have the same ongoing life. I missed sharing ideas during circle time with my friends and teachers, eating in the cafeteria, reading books in the library, and hanging out with my friends in recess. I missed hearing all the chit-chatting sounds, giggling sounds, munching sounds, and pages flipping sound. All those images of boring normal life were in my head, but, suddenly, were snapped off by a lound **bang**! Covid-19, the abstract foe, swarmed around my head, covering all the happy images of my happy school life.

Covid-19 is a contaigious virus. However I am strong and not letting the virus terminate me. I learned to protect myself. For example, I need to wash my hands before eating something. I also keep social distance with other people. Wearing masks is an important way to protect myself and others. Finally, I get a Covid-19 vaccine. These are strategies to stay safe from Covid-19.

Covid-19 doesn't just change my life, but also the people around the world. There is a good saying that goes, "Every cloud has a silver lining." We should be cherishing our everyday lives and finding ways to prevent the virus, so we will prosper and not be ruined by this dangerous enemy.

Covid-19 in School and Summer

Chazlyn Hale
Amy York's 8th Grade Class
Mitchell Middle School, Mitchell

Covid-19 started back when I was in 5th grade during our Spring Break. At first we thought it was just going to be a longer Spring Break, but we were all wrong about that. After a week or two we got our computers to use at our homes. We started to use them everyday for school work. At first, it was a little hard, because it was all online. That summer everything was shut down.

When I got into 6th grade it got way easier to work on the computer because we all had the time to work and figure out how they worked fully and what to do on them. Halfway through the year we went into a hybrid school system where we switched with a "B" group. When you got to school you had to have a mask on whether you rode the bus or not.

During the summer most things were closed and you culd not do a lot but some states had almost everything open. Texas was one of the places that I got to go to and it had everything open to the public. We went to a lot of things that a lot of people recommend you do in Texas.

Seventh grade was a bit harder because I changes schools. I used to go to Crook County Middle School. I now go to Mitchell. Mitchell is small so everyone knows everyone so it was a lot easier to spread Covid there. When it hit Spring Break of 2021 we were finally free from the masks and we did not have to wear them any more. I finally felt free from the mask and everyone in the school did too.

This drawing by Chazlyn Hale shows businesses shut down and online learning during the Covid-19 pandemic.

Economy

Historically, Oregon's economy was based on natural resources. Today, the economy is a mix of high-tech manufacturing and services and the agricultural and forestry sectors. Oregon's economy continues to evolve following the Covid-19 pandemic.

OREGON'S ECONOMY

Source: Employment Department, Workforce and Economic Research Division

Employment

In spring 2020, the pandemic recession brought unparalleled job losses to Oregon. One out of seven jobs were lost in two months' time. Unemployment hit a record high rate of 13.3% in April 2020. Oregon had never seen job losses at that scale and speed.

Two years after employment hit its recessionary bottom, Oregon experienced a remarkable rebound. Oregon employers added 123,500 jobs back by the end of 2020, and another 98,500 in calendar year 2021. Strong job gains continued into the early months of 2022. By April 2022, we had regained about nine out of 10 jobs that were lost in the pandemic recession. Prior to the pandemic recession, it took nearly six years (69 months) to add as many jobs (248,000) as in the two years since April 2020.

While all sectors initially experienced job losses, the pandemic recession hit service-providing industries the hardest, including leisure and hospitality, education and other services. The jobs recovery since spring 2020 has been uneven too. Widespread gains across several sectors pushed employment to new highs in many areas of Oregon's economy. Meanwhile, other sectors lag behind, struggling to add back jobs.

By spring 2022, several sectors recovered their recession losses and expanded to new highs. For a variety of reasons, these sectors experienced smaller job losses than the overall economy and bounced back faster during the recovery. They included construction; wholesale trade; real estate and rental and leasing; the information sector; professional and technical services; and transportation, warehousing and utilities.

The sectors leading recovery have homes and residences as a common thread: greater likelihood to be working from them, building them, or making deliveries to them. In addition to all this, eco-nomic recovery from the pandemic recession has also been marked by strong demand and rapidly rising prices for homes themselves. Amid these dynamics, the real estate and rental and leasing industry reached new employment highs in spring 2022.

The hard-hit service sectors in the pandemic recession are also among those lagging in recovery. Leisure and hospitality lost 112,100 jobs in spring 2020, more than half (52%) of the sector's total employment. Oregon's hotels, restaurants, bars, and entertainment places added back 92,300 jobs by April 2022, and regained 82% of recession job losses. Yet leisure and hospitality remained 19,800 jobs below its pre-recession employment level. That was the largest job recovery deficit of any sector.

The education services sector in Oregon has also lagged in its jobs recovery. One part of that could be timing. Most schools were shuttered—either partially or fully—from at least spring 2020 through late summer 2021. That effectively made education the last sector to fully re-open in Oregon.

Public K–12, community colleges and public universities make up about half of all jobs in Oregon's local government sector. During summer 2021, job gains rose sharply as enrichment programs picked up, and education institutions made fewer seasonal summer layoffs. The summer gains were not sustained. Public education fell short of typical hiring levels as the 2021–2022 academic year got underway, and employment levels changed little into 2022.

Private education services includes both privately owned K–12 and higher education institutions. They lost 8,100 jobs (-22%) in the pandemic recession. By April 2022, they regained 5,700 (or 70%) of those losses.

Labor Force

Although uneven across sectors, more Oregonians moving into jobs during the relatively rapid overall jobs recovery has resulted in dramatic improvements in the state's unemployment rate. Two years after reaching an all-time high of 13.3%,

Oregon's unemployment rate has improved by nearly 10 percentage points and near our all-time record low again.

What's more, the unemployment rate improved as the labor force grew to new highs, and participation rose. Oregon's labor force has recovered from the pandemic recession and hit new record highs in early 2022. Labor force participation also shows strong trends. The share of Oregonians ages 16 or older either working, or unemployed and actively seeking a job (and available and able to take one if offered), is at its highest rate in a decade.

Job Openings

The relatively fast jobs recovery, low unemployment and more workers forging self-employment or other paths have all made it more difficult for employers seeking to hire. That was also the case when unemployment was low in 2019, before the pandemic. Employers' difficulty finding enough workers has been exacerbated during this economic recovery by the record high number of job openings. These job openings—and resulting worker shortages—have been widespread across Oregon's economy. Ten of 14 broad sectors hit record levels of vacancies at some point since spring 2021.

The low-unemployment and high-competition environment has also created record difficulty for employers to fill their job vacancies. At least seven out of 10 job openings have been hard for private employers to fill for more than a year. Given the high number of job vacancies and relatively low available workforce, it's not surprising that employers cited a lack of applicants as the primary challenge for nearly half (47%) of all hard-to-fill job openings in 2021.

Oregon's Top Ten Private Sector Industries by Employment in 2021:

1. Food services and drinking places (134,000)
2. Ambulatory health care services (94,300)
3. Administrative and support services (92,900)
4. Specialty trade contractors (69,000)
5. Social assistance (65,200)
6. Hospitals (58,400)
7. Nursing & residential care facilities (49,600)
8. Food and beverage stores (45,900)
9. Real estate (42,300)
10. General merchandise stores (41,200)

Wages

Oregon implemented a new three-tier minimum wage on July 1, 2020, and the tiers vary by geography. From July 1, 2022 through June 30, 2023 the highest wage is $14.75 per hour within the Portland urban growth boundary, a standard rate of $13.50 per hour in other areas of the state, and a rate of $12.50 per hour in designated nonurban counties mostly in eastern and southwestern Oregon. Starting in 2023, Oregon's minimum wage will be adjusted annually according to the increase in the U.S. Consumer Price Index.

Although Oregon's minimum wage is higher than most other states, private-sector workers in Oregon tend to work slightly fewer hours per week and their average wage earnings are below the national level. Workers in Oregon earned an average of $1,017 weekly in 2021, which is below the national average of $1,062 per week.

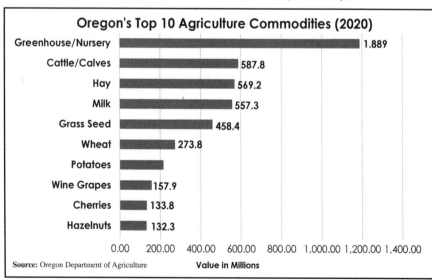

Oregon's Top 10 Agriculture Commodities (2020)

Commodity	Value in Millions
Greenhouse/Nursery	1.889
Cattle/Calves	587.8
Hay	569.2
Milk	557.3
Grass Seed	458.4
Wheat	273.8
Potatoes	
Wine Grapes	157.9
Cherries	133.8
Hazelnuts	132.3

Source: Oregon Department of Agriculture

Oregon workers (excluding self-employed and most agricultural workers) earned an annual average of $64,018 in 2021, although wages vary widely by industry and occupation. The average annual pay in the information industry was $113,955, the most of any broad sector. This was followed by professional and business services ($88,684), financial activities ($86,091), federal government ($85,961), and manufacturing ($78,432). The lowest average wage was in leisure and hospitality, where pay averaged $27,054 per year.

Of course, the average wage for an industry does not reveal how many low- or high-wage jobs are in an industry. Nearly one-fifth of Oregon's jobs paid an average wage of less than $15 per hour in 2021 and about one-quarter were between $15 and $20 per hour. The remaining 55% of jobs paid at least $20 per hour.

Income

Per capita personal income, a broader measure than just wages of the income Oregonians receive from all sources, was $56,311 per person in 2020. In addition to wages, personal income includes proprietors' income; income from dividends, interest, and rent; and transfer receipts.

The national per capita personal income reached $59,147 in 2020. Oregon's per capita personal income was 95% of the nation's and ranked 23rd among the states and Washington, D.C. Oregon's real per capita personal income, adjusted for inflation, grew 15.8% from 2020. That was the sixth fastest income growth among the states and Washington, D.C. and faster than the national inflation-adjusted growth rate of 11.6%.

Despite lower average incomes than the nation as a whole, Oregon's poverty rate is about the same as the nation. According to the U.S. Census Bureau, an average of 12.4% of Oregon residents lived in families with incomes below the poverty threshold from 2016 through 2020. The U.S. poverty rate was 12.8%. Oregon ranked 26th among the states with the lowest percentage of people living in poverty.

Revenue and Taxes

Oregon's state and local governments receive revenue from numerous sources including federal transfer payments; tuition, hospital and other charges; Lottery revenue; and taxes. Of all these sources, half of total state revenue is from taxation. Personal income tax and corporate excise tax are the most significant components of the state General Fund, and property tax is the most significant local tax in Oregon. These three taxes represent about 80% of all state and local taxes. Oregon does not have a general state sales tax.

The personal income tax is the largest source of state tax revenue, expected to account for 86% of the state's General Fund for the 2021–2023 biennium. Oregon's taxable income is closely connected to federal taxable income. The state personal income tax rates range from 4.75% to 9.9% of taxable income. For tax year 2020, Oregon residents filed about 2.02 million Oregon personal income tax returns, representing about 2.74 million taxpayers, which includes spouses. Those taxpayers paid a final tax after adjustments, deductions and credits on average equal to about 6% to 7% of their total income. The top 10% of taxpayers in income paid roughly half of Oregon's personal income tax, while the bottom half of taxpayers in income paid 9% of the total income tax.

The corporate excise and income tax is the second largest source of state tax revenue. The corporate tax rates are 6.6% and 7.6% of taxable business income. For tax year 2019, about 1% of corporate taxpayers accounted for 56% of income and excise tax revenue from C corporations (standard corporations). The minimum corporate excise tax ranges from $150 to $100,000, depending on the corporation's Oregon sales. Close to 68% of all C corporations paid the minimum tax for tax year 2019, but minimum taxpayers accounted for less than 7% of the total tax paid by C corporations in 2019.

Local governments in Oregon began taxing property before statehood, but the current system is mainly the product of two statewide ballot measures passed in the 1990s, Measures 5 and 50. In Oregon's property tax system, each taxing district is limited to a fixed permanent tax rate, but voters can temporarily increase rates through local options levies or to repay bonds used to fund capital projects. Individual properties have a taxable assessed value equal to, or less than, the real market value. The taxable assessed value generally cannot increase by more than 3% per year, and it cannot exceed the real market value. Taxes for an individual property are calculated by applying the tax rates of the local districts to the taxable assessed value of each property and are generally limited to no more than $5 per $1,000 of real market value for education districts and $10 per $1,000 of real market value for all other taxing districts. Levies to repay bonds are outside of this limit.

Additional Information

Department of Agriculture: oregon.gov/oda
Bureau of Labor and Industries – Minimum Wage: oregon.gov/boli/whd/omw/pages/minimum-wage-rate-summary.aspx
Employment Department – Labor Market Information: QualityInfo.org
Oregon's Department of Forestry: oregon.gov/odf
Department of Revenue: oregon.gov/dor
U.S. Department of Labor, Bureau of Labor Statistics: bls.gov/home.htm

STUDENT ESSAY CONTEST WINNER

The effects of COVID-19

Saffron Theresa Estrada
Aaron Franklin's 5th Grade Class
Awbrey Park Elementary School, Eugene

Saffron Theresa Estrada's drawing shows an animated earth masked up during the pandemic.

COVID-19 has been part of our daily basis for about 2 and a half years. It has affected our daily lives and has caused strong emotions to a lot of people.

I would like to tell you about my experience with the pandemic of COVID-19.

COVID-19 has affected me and my family in many ways and still is. I remember a normal day of third grade. It was a Friday and we were living a normal happy mask-free life.

That weekend there was a lot of news about Covid possibly entering our state. Well it was true, the next week of school was cancelled due to staff members catching COVID.

We had to proceed with school online. It was confusing and hard to learn so far apart from friends and teachers. I finished the year and so I became a fourth grader after summer.

In fourth grade we still had to learn online. It became "The new normal". During that year I was on the computer more than 7 hours a day.

That summer I ended up needing glasses. Apparently the online school and being on the computer all day made me nearsighted.

Covid-19 affected me and other people so much. Such as wearing a mask, or online school, and even social distancing.

Covid has taught me to "Be careful". You never know who has a sickness or not. I'm sure the COVID-19 pandemic will be a big part of our history.

It will also frighten some people about who's got it and who doesn't. No matter what the witnesses will always have a memory of how covid affected the world.

Media Directories

Oregon's long tradition of open government and citizen involvement depends in part on its citizens receiving accurate and timely information. This section lists Oregon's newspapers and selected periodicals.

NEWSPAPERS PUBLISHED IN OREGON

The following newspapers are published at least once a week. See "Selected Periodicals" following this section for other magazines and journals.

Key: (P) = Publisher, (Pr) = President; (E) = Editor, (GM) = General Manager

Albany
Albany Democrat-Herald
Mon–Sun a.m.; David Cuddihy (Pr); Penny Rosenberg (E); Estab. 1865
PO Box 130, Albany 97321; 541-926-2211
Web: democratherald.com

Astoria
The Daily Astorian
Mon–Fri a.m.; Kari Borgen (P); Derrick DePledge (E); Estab. 1873
949 Exchange St, Astoria 97103; 503-325-3211; 800-781-3211
Web: dailyastorian.com

Baker City
Baker City Herald
Mon, Wed, Fri p.m.; Karrine Brogiotto (P); Jason Jacoby (E); Estab. 1870
PO Box 807, Baker City 97814; 541-523-3673
Web: bakercityherald.com

Bandon
Bandon Western World
Wed; David Thornberry (P); David Rupkalvis (E) Estab. 1912
172 Anderon Ave; Coos Bay, 97420; 541-266-6047
Web: theworldlink.com/community/bandon

Beaverton
Beaverton Valley Times
Thur; Nikki DeBuse (P); Mark Miller (E); Estab. 1921
PO Box 22109, Portland 97269; 503-684-0360
Web: beavertonvalleytimes.com

Bend
The Bulletin
Mon–Sun a.m.; Heidi Wright (P); Gerry O'Brien (E); Estab. 1903
PO Box 6020, Bend 97708-6020; 541-382-1811
Web: bendbulletin.com

The Source Weekly
Wed; Aaron Switzert (P); Nicole Vulcan (E); Estab. 1997
704 NW Georgia Ave, Bend 97703; 541-383-0800
Web: bendsource.com

Brookings
Curry Coastal Pilot
Wed, Sat; David Thornberry (P); David Rupkalvis (E); Estab. 1946
PO Box 700, Brookings 97415; 541-813-1717; Fax: 541-813-1931
Web: currypilot.com

Brownsville
The Times
Wed; Vance and Holly Parrish (P); Vance Parrish (E); Estab. 1888
PO Box 278, Brownsville 97327; 541-466-5311
Web: thebrownsvilletimes.com

Burns
Burns Times-Herald
Wed; Randy Fulton (P); Randy Parks (E); Estab. 1887
355 N. Broadway Ave., Burns 97720; 541-573-2022; Fax: 541-573-3915
Web: btimesherald.com

Canby
Canby Herald
Wed; John Baker (E); Sandy Storey (GM); Estab. 1906
911 SW 4th Ave., Canby 97013; 503-266-6831; Fax: 503-266-6836
Web: canbyherald.com

Cave Junction
Illinois Valley News
Wed; Dan Mancuso (P); Laura Mancuso (E); Estab. 1937
PO Box 1370, Cave Junction 97523; 541-592-2541

Clackamas
Clackamas Review
Wed; Aaron Breniman (P); Raymond Rendleman (E); Estab. 1891
6605 SE Lake Rd, Portland 97222; Phone: 971-204-7742
Web: clackamasreview.com

Clatskanie
The Chief
Wed; Jeremy Ruark (P)(E); Estab. 1891
1805 Columbia Blvd, St Helens 97051; Phone: 503-397-0116; Fax: 503-397-4093
Web: thechiefnews.com

Condon
The Times-Journal
Thur; Stephen and Renee Allen (P)(E); Estab. 1886
PO Box 746, Condon 97823; 541-384-2421
Web: timesjournal1886.com

The Hotel Condon in downtown Condon. (Oregon State Archives scenic photo)

Coos Bay
The World
Mon–Thur, Sat; David Thornberry (P); David Rupkalvis (E); Estab. 1878
172 Anderson Ave., Coos Bay 97420; 541-266-6047
Web: theworldlink.com

Corvallis
Corvallis Gazette-Times
Mon–Sun a.m.; David Cuddihy (Pr); Penny Rosenberg (E); Estab. 1862
PO Box 130, Albany 97321; 541-926-2211
Web: gazettetimes.com

Cottage Grove
Cottage Grove Sentinel
Wed; Jenna Bartlett (P); Sarah Glass (E); Estab. 1889
1498 E. Main St. Ste 104, Cottage Grove 97424; 541-942-3325
Web: cgsentinel.com

Creswell
The Creswell Chronicle
Thur; Noel Nash (P); Erin Tierney (E); Estab. 1909
655 A St. Ste. E, Springfield 97477; 541-515-6233
Web: chronicle1909.com

Dallas
Polk County Itemizer-Observer
Wed; Scott Olson (P); David Hayes (E); Estab. 1875
147 SE Court St. PO Box 108, Dallas 97338; 503-623-2373
Web: polkio.com

Enterprise
Wallowa County Chieftain
Wed; Karrine Brogoitti (GM); Jeff Budlong (E); Estab. 1884
209 NW First St., Enterprise 97828; 800-781-3214; Fax: 541-426-3921
Web: wallowa.com

Estacada
Estacada News
Thur; Mark Garber (Pr); Steve Brown (P)(E); Estab. 1904
PO Box 549 Estacada 97023; 503-630-3241
Web: estacadanews.com

Eugene
Eugene Weekly
Thur; Camilla Mortensen (E); Estab. 1982
1251 Lincoln St., Eugene 97401; 541-484-0519
Web: eugeneweekly.com

The Register-Guard
Mon–Sun a.m.; Michelle Maxwell (E); Estab. 1862
3500 Chad Dr., Suite 600, Eugene 97408; (800) 377-7428
Web: registerguard.com

Florence
Siuslaw News
Wed & Sat; Jenna Bartlett (P); Chantelle Meyer (E); Estab. 1890
148 Maple St., Florence 97439; 541-997-3441
Web: thesiuslawnews.com

Forest Grove
News-Times

Wed; Nikki DeBuse (P); Mark Miller (E); Estab. 1886

2004 Main St., Suite 309; Forest Grove 97116; 503-357-3181

Web: forestgrovenewstimes

Gold Beach

Curry County Reporter
Wed; Matt Hall (P); Matt Smith (E); Estab. 1914

PO Box 5, Port Orford 97465; 541-332-6397
Web: currycountyreporter.com

Grants Pass

Grants Pass Daily Courier
Tue–Fri, Sun; Travis Moore (P); Scott Stoddard (E); Estab. 1885

PO Box 1468, Grants Pass 97526; 541-474-3700

Web: thedailycourier.com

Gresham

Outlook
Tue, Fri; Mark Garber (Pr); Steve Brown (P) (E); Estab. 1911

PO Box 747, Gresham 97030; 503-665-2181; Fax: 503-665-2181

Web: theoutlookonline.com

Heppner

Heppner Gazette-Times
Wed; David Sykes (P); Bobbi Gordon (E); Estab. 1883

PO Box 337, Heppner 97836; 541-676-9228; Fax: 541-676-9211

Web: heppner.net

Hermiston

Hermiston Herald
Wed; Andrew Cutler (P); Erick Peterson (E); Estab. 1906

333 E. Main St., Hermiston 97838; 541-567-6457

Web: hermistonherald.com

Hillsboro

Hillsboro News Times
Nikki DeBuse (P); Mark Miller (E); Estab. 1886

2004 Main St. Ste. 309 Forest Grove, OR 97116; 503-357-3181

Web: hillsboronewstimes.com

Hood River/The Dalles

Columbia Gorge News
Wed & Sat; Chelsea Marr (P); Mark Gibson (E); Estab. 2020

PO Box 390, Hood River 97031; 541-386-1234
Web: columbiagorgenews.com

John Day

Blue Mountain Eagle

Wed; Kari Borgen (P); Sean Hart (E); Estab. 1898

195 N. Canyon Blvd., John Day 97845; 800-781-3214; Fax: 541-575-1244

Web: bluemountaineagle.com

Keizer

Keizertimes
Fri; Lyndon Zaitz (P); Charles Glenn (E); Estab. 1979

142 Chemawa Rd. N. Keizer 97303; 503-390-1051; Fax: 503-390-8023

Web: keizertimes.com

The Wasco County Courthouse in The Dalles. (Oregon State Archives scenic photo)

Klamath Falls

Herald and News
Tue, Wed, Fri & Sun a.m.; Mark Dobie (P); Joe Hudon (GM); Estab. 1906

PO Box 788, Klamath Falls 97601; 800-275-0982; Fax: 541-883-4007

Web: heraldandnews.com

La Grande

The Observer
Mon, Wed, Fri; Karrine Brogoitti (P); Andrew Cutler (E); Estab. 1896

911 Jefferson Ave., La Grande 97850; 541-963-3161

Web: lagrandeobserver.com

Lake Oswego

Lake Oswego Review
Thur; J. Brian Monihan (P); Patrick Malee (E); Estab. 1920

PO Box 548, Lake Oswego 97034; 503-635-8811

Web: lakeoswegoreview.com

Lakeview

Lake County Examiner
Wed; Mark Dobie (Pr); Danielle Jester (GM); Estab. 1880

Media Directories

739 N. Second St., Lakeview 97630; 541-947-3378; Fax: 541-947-4359
Web: lakecountyexam.com

Lebanon
Lebanon Local
Daily; Scott Swanson (P); Estab. 1887
1313 Main St., Sweet Home, 97386; 541-367-2136
Web: lebanonlocalnews.com

Lincoln City
The News Guard
Wed; David Thornberry (P); Hilary Dorsey (E); Estab. 1927
1818 N.E. 21st St., Lincoln City 97367; 541-994-2178
Web: thenewsguard.com

Madras
The Madras Pioneer
Wed; Tony Ahern (P); Pat Kruis (E); Estab. 1904
345 SE Fifth St., Madras 97741; 541-475-2275; Fax: 541-475-3710
Web: madraspioneer.com

McKenzie Bridge
McKenzie River Reflections
Thur; Ken Engelman (P)(E); Estab. 1978
59059 Old McKenzie Hwy., McKenzie Bridge 97413; 541-822-3358; Fax: 541-663-4550
Web: mckenzieriverreflectionsnewspaper.com

McMinnville
News-Register
Tue, Fri; Jeb Bladine (P); Ossie Bladine (E); Estab. 1866
PO Box 727, McMinnville 97128; 503-472-5114; 800-472-1198
Web: newsregister.com

Milton-Freewater
Valley Herald
Fri; Sherrie Widmer (P)(E); Estab. 2001
PO Box 664, Milton-Freewater 97862; 541-938-6688

Molalla
Molalla Pioneer
Wed; Sandy Storey (GM); John Baker (E); Estab. 1913
911 SW Fourth Ave., Canby 97013; 503-263-7511
Web: molallapioneer.com

Myrtle Point
Myrtle Point Herald
Wed; Matt Hall (P); Matt Smith (E); Estab. 1889
PO Box 5, Port Orford 97465; 541-332-6397

Newberg
The Newberg Graphic
Wed; Allen Herriges (P); Gary Allen (E); Estab. 1888
1505 Portland Rd., Suite 210, Newberg 97132; 503-538-2181; Fax: 503-538-1632
Web: newberggraphic.com

Newport
News-Times
Wed, Fri; Jeremy Burke (P); Steve Card (E); Estab. 1882
831 NE Avery St., Newport 97365; 541-265-8571; Fax: 541-265-3862
Web: newportnewstimes.com

Ontario
The Argus Observer
Tue–Fri p.m., Sun a.m.; Brad Bailey (P); Leslie Thompson (E); Estab. 1897
1160 SW 4th St., Ontario 97914; 541-889-5387; Fax: 541-889-3347
Web: argusobserver.com

Oregon City
Oregon City News
Wed; Aaron Breniman (P); (E) Raymond Rendleman;
6605 SE Lake Rd., Portland 97222; (971) 204-7742
Web: oregoncitynewsonline.com

Pendleton
East Oregonian
Tue–Sat; Andrew Cutler (P)(E); Estab. 1875
211 SE Byers Ave., Pendleton 97801; 800-522-0255
Web: eastoregonian.com

Port Orford
Port Orford News
Wed; Matt Hall (P); Matt Smith (E); Estab. 1958
PO Box 5, Port Orford 97465; 541-332-6397
Web: portorfordnews.net

Portland
Daily Journal of Commerce
Mon, Wed, Fri; Nick Bjork (P); Joe Yovino (E); Estab. 1872
11 NE Martin Luther King Jr. Blvd. Ste 201, Portland 97232; 503-226-1311
Web: djcoregon.com

Portland Tribune
Tue, Thur; Mark Garber (Pr)(P); Vance W. Tong (E); Estab. 2001
6605 SE Lake Rd., Portland 97222-2161; 503-226-6397
Web: pamplinmedia.com

The Asian Reporter
  Bi-monthly (1st and 3rd Mon); Jaime Lim (P); Estab. 1991
  922 N. Killingsworth St., Portland 97217; 503-283-4440; Fax: 503 283-4445
  Web: asianreporter.com

A statue by Greg Congleton in Prineville. (Oregon State Archives scenic photo)

The Bee
  Brian Monihan (P); Eric Norberg (E); Estab. 1906
  1837 SE Harold St, Portland 97217; 503-232-2326
  Web: thebeenews.com

The Oregonian
  Mon–Sun digital (Wed, Fri, Sat, Sun print a.m.); John Maher (Pr.); Therese Bottomly (E); Estab. 1850
  1500 SW First Ave., Portland 97201; 503-221-8327
  Web: oregonlive.com

The Skanner
  Bernie Foster (P); Bobbie Foster (E); Estab. 1975
  415 N. Killingsworth St., Portland 97217; 503-285-5555; Fax: 503-285-2900
  Web: theskanner.com

Willamette Week
  Wed; Mark Zusman (P)(E); Estab. 1974
  PO Box 10770, Portland 97296; 503-243-2122
  Web: wweek.com

Prineville
Central Oregonian
  Tue, Fri; Tony Ahern (P); Angie Bernard (E); Estab. 1881
  558 N. Main St., Prineville 97754; 541-447-6205
  Web: centraloregonian.com

Redmond
The Redmond Spokesman
  Heidi Wright (P); Tim Trainor (E); Estab. 1910

PO Box 6020, Bend 97708; 541-548-2184
  Web: redmondspokesman.com

Rogue River
Rogue River Press
  Wed; Teresa Pearson (P)(E); Estab. 1915
  PO Box 1485, Rogue River 97537; 541-582-1707
  Web: rogueriverpress.com

Roseburg
The News-Review
  Tue–Sun a.m.; Patrick A Markham (P); Tiffany Coleman (E); Estab. 1867
  345 NE Winchester St., Roseburg 97470; 541-672-3321
  Web: nrtoday.com

St. Helens
The Chronicle
  Wed; Jeremy Ruark (P)(E); Estab. 1881
  PO Box 1153, St. Helens 97051; 503-397-0116
  Web: thechronicleonline.com

Salem
Capital Press
  Fri; Joe Beach (P)(E); Estab. 1928
  PO Box 2048, Salem 97308; 800-882-6789
  Web: capitalpress.com

Oregon Capital Chronicle
  Lynne Terry (E); Estab. 2021; Email: lterry@oregoncapitalchronicle.com;
  Web: oregoncapitalchronicle.com

Statesman Journal
  Mon–Sun a.m.; Cherrill Crosby (E); Estab. 1851
  340 Vista Ave SE, Suite 200, Salem 97302; 800-452-2511
  Web: statesmanjournal.com

Sandy
Sandy Post
  Wed; J. Mark Garber (Pr.); Steve Brown (P)(E); Estab. 1937
  PO Box 68, Sandy 97055; 503-665-2181; Fax: 503-665-2187
  Web: sandypost.com

Scappoose
Columbia County Spotlight
  Fri a.m.; Nikki DeBuse (P); Mark Miller (E); Estab. 1961
  52490 SE Second St., Suite 140, Scappoose 97056; 503-543-6387; Fax: 503-543-6380
  Web: columbiacountyspotlight.com

Seaside
Seaside Signal
  Every other Fri; Kari Borgen (P); RJ Marx (E); Estab. 1905
  949 Exchange St, Astoria 97103; 503-738 5561
  Web: seasidesignal.com

Media Directories

Sherwood

Sherwood Gazette
Thur; Nikki DeBuse (P); Mark Miller (E);
Estab. 1958
6605 SE Lake Road, Portland 97222
Web: sherwoodgazette.com

Sisters

The Nugget Newspaper
Jim Cornelius (E); Estab. 1978
PO Box 698, Sisters 97559; 541-549-9941
Web: nuggetnews.com

Sweet Home

The New Era
Wed; Scott Swanson (P)(E); Estab. 1929
1313 Main St, Sweet Home 97386; 541-367-2135
Web: sweethomenews.com

Tigard/Tualatin/Sherwood

The Times
Thur; Nikki DeBuse (P); Mark Miller (E);
Estab. 1958
6605 SE Lake Road, Portland 97222
Web: valleytimes.news

Tillamook

Headlight Herald
Wed; Joe Warren (P)(E); Estab. 1888
1906 Second St., Tillamook 97141; 503-842-7535; Fax: 503-842-8842
Web: tillamookheadlightherald.com

Vale

Malheur Enterprise
Wed; Les Zaitz (P)(E); Estab. 1909
PO Box 310, Vale 97918; 541-473-3377
Web: malheurenterprise.com

Warrenton

The Columbia Press
Fri; Cindy Yingst (P)(E); Estab. 1922
5 N. Hwy. 101, Suite 500, Warrenton 97146;
503-861-3331; Fax: 503-861-7039

West Linn

West Linn Tidings
Thur; J. Brian Monihan (P); Patrick Malee (E);
Estab. 1981
PO Box 548, Lake Oswego 97034;
503-635-8811
Web: westlinntidings.com

Wilsonville

Wilsonville Spokesman
Wed; J. Brian Monihan (P); Patrick Malee (E);
Estab. 1985
PO Box 548, Lake Oswego 97034;
503-635-8811
Web: wilsonvillespokesman.com

Woodburn

Woodburn Independent
Wed; Allen Herriges (P); Justin Much (E);
Estab. 1888
1585 N Pacific Hwy., Suite H, Woodburn
97071; 503-981-3441
Web: woodburnindependent.com

Oregon Newspaper Publishers Association

Executive Director: Laurie Hieb
Address: 400 Second St., Suite 100, Lake
Oswego 97034
Phone: 503-624-6397
Fax: 503-639-9009
Web: orenews.com

SELECTED PERIODICALS PUBLISHED IN OREGON

The State Library has compiled a representative sample of the many periodicals published in Oregon. The first year of each periodical's publication follows its title and publication schedule.

Key: A = Annual; BM = Bi-monthly; BW = Bi-weekly; IRR=irregular schedule; M = Monthly; SA = Semi-annual; SM = Semi-monthly; W = Weekly

1859: Oregon's magazine (BM) 2009: Statehood Media, 70 SW Century Dr., Suite 100-218, Bend 97702; 541-728-2764;

Web: 1859oregonmagazine.com

Ada: A Journal of Gender, New Media and Technology (IRR) 2012: University of Oregon Libraries, Eugene 97403; editor@adanewmedia.org

Web: adanewmedia.org

Animal Law Review (SA) 1995: Lewis & Clark Law School, 10015 SW Terwilliger Blvd., Portland 97219; 503-768-6600;

Web: law.lclark.edu/law_reviews/animal_law_review

Backwoods Home Magazine (Q) 1989: PO Box 308, Philomath 97370; 541-250-5134;

Web: backwoodshome.com

Calyx (SA) 1976: 216 SW Madison, Suite 7 Corvallis 97333; 541-753-9384;

Web: calyxpress.org

Digger (M) 1988: Oregon Association of Nurseries, 29751 SW Town Center Loop W. Wilsonville 97070; 503-582-2008; 888-283-7219; Fax: 503-682-5727;

Web: diggermagazine.com

Environmental Law (Q) 1970: Lewis & Clark Law School, 10011 SW Terwilliger Blvd., Portland 97219; 503-768-6700; Fax: 503-768-6783;

Web: law.lclark.edu/law_reviews/environmental_law

Ethos (IRR) 2009: Emerald Media Group, Eugene 97403; editor@ethosmagonline.com;

Web: dailyemerald.com/ethos

Eugene Magazine (Q) 2006: Olive Tree, LLC, 1255 Railroad Blvd., Eugene 97402; 541-686-6608;

Web: eugenemagazine.com

HIPFiSHmonthly (M) 1997: 1017 Marine Drive, Astoria 97103; 503-338-4878;

Web: hipfishmonthly.com

Journal of Environmental Law and Litigation (SA) 1985: 138 Knight Law Center, 1221 University of Oregon, Eugene 97403; 541-346-1559;

Web: law.uoregon.edu/explore/JELL

Konturen (IRR) 2008: Department of German and Scandinavian, 1250 University of Oregon, Eugene 97403;

Web: journals.oregondigital.org/index.php/konturen/index

El Latino de Hoy: Semanario Latinoamericano de Oregon (W) 1991: 2318 SW 18th Ave., Portland 97201; 503-493-1106; Fax: 503-753-1183;

Web: ellatinodehoy.com

Metroscape (SA) 1995: Institute of Portland Metropolitan Studies, Portland State University, 1825 SW Broadway, Portland 97201; 503-725-3000;

Web: pdx.edu/metropolitan-studies/metroscape

Midwifery Today (Q) 1987: PO Box 2672, Eugene 97402; 541-344-7438;

Web: midwiferytoday.com/magazine

Northwest Labor Press (SM) 1987: PO Box 13150, Portland 97213; 503-288-3311;

Web: nwlaborpress.org

Noticias Latinas! Latin News! (BW) 1995: Latin Media Northwest, 16239 SE McLoughlin Blvd., Suite 209, Milwaukie 97267; 503-227-7780; Fax: 503-227-7790;

Web: latinmedianw.com

OLA Quarterly (Q) 1995: Oregon Library Association, PO Box 3067, La Grande 97850; 541-962-5824;

Web: journals3.library.oregonstate.edu/olaq

Oregon Birds (SA) 1977: Oregon Birding Association, PO Box 675, Lincoln City 97367-0675;

Web: oregonbirding.org/oregon-birds

Oregon Business Magazine (M) 1981: MIF Publications, Inc., 12570 SW 69th Ave. Ste 102 Portland 97223; 503-445-8811;

Web: oregonbusiness.com

Oregon Grange Bulletin (BM) 1990: Oregon State Grange, 643 Union St. NE, Salem 97301; 503-316-0106; Fax: 503-316-0109;

Web: orgrange.org/the-oregon-state-grange/oregon-state-grange-bulletin

Oregon Historical Quarterly (Q) 1900: Oregon Historical Society, 1200 SW Park Ave., Portland 97205; 503-222-1741;

Web: ohs.org/oregon-historical-quarterly

Media Directories

Oregon Home (Q) 1997: MediAmerica, 12750 SW 69th Ave Ste 102,, Portland 97223; 503-445-8811;

Web: oregonhomemagazine.com

Oregon Humanities (Q) 1983: Oregon Humanities, 610 SW Alder St. Ste 1111, Portland 97205; 503-241-0543; 800-735-0543; Fax: 503-241-0024;

Web: oregonhumanities.org/rll/magazine/

Oregon Hunter (BM) 1983: Oregon Hunters Association, PO Box 1706, Medford 97501; 541-772-7313; Fax: 541-772-0964;

Web: oregonhunters.org/publications

Oregon Law Review (SA) 1921: University of Oregon, 1221 University of Oregon, Eugene 97403-1221; 541-346-1559;

Web: law.uoregon.edu/explore/OLR

Oregon Small Farm News (Q) 2007: OSU College of Agricultural Sciences, 403 Strand Agriculture Hall, Corvallis, 97331; 541-713-5009

Web: smallfarms.oregonstate.edu/smallfarms /oregon-small-farm-news

Oregon Wheat (BM) 1962: Oregon Wheat Growers League, 115 SE 8th St., Pendleton 97801-2319; 541-276-7330;

Web: owgl.org

Peaceworker (M) 2003: 1850 Saginaw St. S, Salem 97302; 503-428-4280;

Web: peaceworker.org

Portland Monthly (M) 2003: SagaCity Media, 921 SW Washington St., Suite 750, Portland 97205; 503-222-5144; Fax: 503-227-8777;

Web: pdxmonthly.com

Progress (SA) 1953: College of Agricultural Sciences Communications Team, Strand Agriculture Hall, Suite 200, Corvallis 97331; 541-737-9180;

Web: progress.oregonstate.edu

Random Lengths (W) 1944: 450 Country Club Road Suite 315, Eugene 97401; 708-329 2641;

Web: randomlengths.com

Resource Recycling (M) 1982: Resource Recycling, PO Box 42270, Portland 97242-0270; 503-233-1305;

Web: resource-recycling.com

Rubberstampmadness (Q) 1980: RSM Enterprises, Inc., PO Box 610, Corvallis 97339-0610; 541-752-0075; 877-782-6762;

Web: rsmadness.com

Ruralite (M) 1953: Pioneer Utility Resources, 5625 NE Elam Young Pkwy. Ste 100, Hillsboro 97124; 503-357-2105;

Web: ruralite.com

Skipping Stones (SA) 166 W. 12th Avenue, Eugene 97401; 541-342-4956;

Web: skippingstones.org/wp

Small Farmers Journal (Q) 1976: PO Box 1627, Sisters 97759-1627; 541-549-2064; 800-876-2893;

Web: smallfarmersjournal.com

Take Root (SA) 2011: Duhn & Associates, PO Box 636, Junction City 97448-0636; 541-952-0300;

Web: takerootmagazine.com/index.html

The Timberline Review (A) 2015: Willamette Writers, 5331 SW Macadam Ave., Suite 258, PMB 215, Portland 97239;

Web: timberlinereview.com/

We'Moon (A) 1981: Mother Tongue Ink, PO Box 187, Wolf Creek 97497; 541-956-6052;

Web: wemoon.ws

Willamette Journal of International Law and Dispute Resolution (A) 1997: Willamette University College of Law, 245 Winter St. SE, Salem 97301; 503-370-6632;

Web: willamette.edu/law/resources/ journals/wjildr/

Willamette Law Review (Q) 1978: Willamette University College of Law, 245 Winter St. SE, Salem 97301; 503-370-6186; Fax: 503-375-3158;

Web: willamette.edu/law/resources/journals /review/index.html

National, International and Tribal

The citizens of the United States, through our federal government, own more than half the land in Oregon. Oregon's position on the Pacific Rim has resulted in strong ties between Oregon and other nations. Oregon has nine federally recognized tribes, who have distinct relationships with state government. This section contains information about the federal government, representatives of other nations, and tribes in Oregon.

U.S. SENATORS

Jeff Merkley

Democrat. Born in Myrtle Creek, October 24, 1956. Stanford University, B.A., 1979; master's degree in Public Policy from Woodrow Wilson School at Princeton University, 1982. He was Executive Director of Portland Habitat for Humanity before serving as President of the World Affairs Council of Oregon for seven years. He and his wife Mary have two children.

Elected to the Oregon House of Representatives, 1999; became speaker of the House in 2007. Elected to the U.S. Senate, 2008; reelected 2014 and 2020.

Committee member: Appropriations, Chair—Subcommittee on Interior & Environment; Environment & Public Works, Chair—Subcommittee on Chemical Safety, Waste Management & Environmental Justice; Budget; Foreign Relations; Rules & Administration. Term expires 2027.

Washington, D.C., Office: 531 Hart Senate Office Bldg., Washington, D.C. 20510; 202-224-3753; Fax: 202-228-3997; Web/email: merkley.senate.gov

District Offices: Baker City: 1705 Main St, Suite 504, Baker City 97814; 541-278-1129
Bend: 1705131 NW Hawthorne Ave, Suite 208, Bend 97701; 541-318-1298
Eugene: 405 E Eighth Ave., Suite 2010, Eugene 97401; 541-465-6750
Medford: 10 S Bartlett St., Suite 201, Medford 97501; 541-608-9102
Portland: One World Trade Center, 121 SW Salmon St., Suite 1400, Portland 97204; 503-326-3386
Salem: 500 Liberty St. SE, Suite 320, Salem 97301; 503-362-8102

Ron Wyden

Democrat. Born in Wichita, Kansas, May 3, 1949. Stanford University, A.B. in Political Science, 1971; University of Oregon School of Law, J.D., 1974. Co-director, Oregon Gray Panthers, 1974–1980; director, Oregon Legal Services for the Elderly, 1977–1979; public member, Oregon Board of Examiners of Nursing Home Administrators, 1978–1979.

Elected to the U.S. House of Representatives, 1980; reelected 1982, 1984, 1986, 1988, 1990, 1992 and 1994. Elected to the U.S. Senate, 1996; reelected 1998, 2004, 2010, 2016 and 2022

Chairman of Finance Committee; Vice Chair, Joint Committee on Taxation; Committee member: Budget; Energy and Natural Resources; Select Committee on Intelligence; Term expires 2029.

Washington, D.C., Office: 221 Dirksen Senate Office Bldg., Washington, D.C. 20510-3703; 202-224-5244; Fax: 202-228-2717; Web/email: wyden.senate.gov

District Offices: Bend: Jamison Bldg., 131 NW Hawthorne Ave., Suite 107, Bend 97701; 541-330-9142; Fax: 541-330-6266
Eugene: Wayne Morse Federal Courthouse, 405 E Eighth Ave., Suite 2020, Eugene 97401; 541-431-0229; Fax: 541-431-0610
La Grande: SAC Annex Bldg., 105 Fir St., Suite 201, La Grande 97850; 541-962-7691; Fax: 541-963-0885
Medford: The Federal Courthouse, 310 W Sixth St., Rm. 118, Medford 97501; 541-858-5122; Fax: 541-858-5126
Portland: 911 NE 11th Ave., Suite 630, Portland 97232; 503-326-7525; Fax: 503-326-7528
Salem: 707 13th St. SE, Suite 285, Salem 97301; 503-589-4555; Fax: 503-589-4749

Suzanne Bonamici—First District

Counties: Clatsop, Columbia, Tillamook and large portions of Washington, and Multnomah

Democrat. Born in Detroit, Michigan, October 14, 1954. University of Oregon, B.A., 1980; University of Oregon School of Law, J.D., 1983. Before going into private practice in Portland, she was a consumer protection attorney for the Federal Trade Commission in Washington, D.C. She and her husband Michael Simon have two children.

Elected to the Oregon House of Representatives, 2006. Appointed to the Oregon State Senate, 2008; elected 2008; reelected 2010. Elected to the U.S. House of Representatives, 2012; reelected 2014, 2016, 2018, 2020 and 2022.

Committee member: Education and Labor; and Science, Space and Technology. Term expires 2025.

Washington, D.C., Office: 2231 Rayburn House Office Bldg., Washington, D.C. 20515; 202-225-0855; Web and email: bonamici.house.gov

District Office: 12725 SW Millikan Way, Suite 220, Beaverton 97005; 503-469-6010; Toll-free: 800-422-4003

Cliff Bentz—Second District

Counties: Baker, Crook, Deschutes, Gilliam, Grant, Harney, Hood River, Jackson, Jefferson, Grants Pass area of Josephine, Klamath, Lake, Malheur, Morrow, Sherman, Umatilla, Union, Wallowa, Wasco and Wheeler

Republican. Born January 12, 1952, in Salem, Oregon. Eastern Oregon State College, B.S., 1974; Lewis & Clark Law School, J.D., 1977. Attorney and farmer. Served in the Oregon Legislature. He and his wife Lindsay, a veterinarian, live in Ontario and have two children.

Served in the Oregon House of Representatives, 2008–2018; Served in the Oregon Senate, 2018–2019.

Elected to the U.S. House of Representatives, 2020 and 2022

Committee memberships not yet assigned at press time. Term expires 2025.

Washington, D.C., Office: 1239 Longworth House Office Bldg., Washington, D.C. 20515; 202-225-6730; Web and email: bentz.house.gov

District Offices: Medford: 14 N Central Ave., Suite 112, Medford 97501; 541-776-4646;

Earl Blumenauer—Third District

Counties: East Multnomah, Hood River and North Clackamas Counties

Democrat. Born in Portland, August 16, 1948. Attended Lewis & Clark College and Law School and Harvard University's Kennedy School of Government. Received B.A. degree, political science, 1970; law degree, 1976.

Elected to Oregon House of Representatives, 1972; reelected 1974 and 1976. Elected to Multnomah County Board of Commissioners, 1978; reelected 1982. Elected to Portland City Council, 1986; reelected 1990 and 1994.

Elected to Congress, 1996; reelected 1998, 2000, 2002, 2004, 2006, 2008, 2010, 2012, 2014, 2016, 2018, 2020 and 2022.

Committee member: Ways and Means, and its Subcommittees on Health and Trade. Term expires 2025.

Washington, D.C., Office: 1111 Longworth House Office Bldg., Washington, D.C. 20515; 202-225-4811; Web and email: blumenauer.house.gov

District Office: 911 NE 11th Ave., Suite 200, Portland 97232; 503-231-2300

Val Hoyle—Fourth District

Counties: Lincoln, Coos, Curry, Benton, Lane and parts of Linn and Douglas

Democrat. Born in Fairfield, California (Travis Air Force Base), February 14, 1964. Emmanuel College, B.A., She spent 25 years working in the bicycle industry in domestic and international sales. She served on the Federal Export Council of Oregon from 2003–2009 and was Chairwoman from 2006–2009. Lane County resident for over 20 years. She and her husband Stephen have two grown children and live in Springfield.

Appointed to the Oregon House of Representatives, 2009, reelected 2010, 2012, 2014. Elected as Oregon's Labor Commissioner in 2018. Committee member: Committee memberships not yet assigned at press time. Elected to the U.S. House of Representatives, 2022. Term expires 2025.

Washington, D.C., Office: Web and email: hoyle.house.gov
District Offices: Eugene: 940 Willamette St, Ste 520 Eugene, OR 97401

Lori Chavez DeRemer—Fifth District

Counties: Linn, Deschutes and parts of Marion

Republican. Born in San Jose, California, April 7, 1968. California State University, Fresno, B.S., 1990. Owner, Anesthesia Associates Northwest and Evolve Health. Married to husband Shawn DeRemer. She has twin daughters.

Elected to Happy Valley City Council 2004; served through 2010; Elected Mayor of Happy Valley, 2010, served until 2018. Elected to the U.S. House of Representatives, 2022.

Committee member: Committee memberships not yet assigned at press time. Term expires 2025.

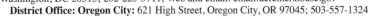

Washington, D.C., Office: 1722 Longworth House Office Building, Washington, DC 20515; 202-225-5711; Web and email: email:deremer.house.gov
District Office: Oregon City: 621 High Street, Oregon City, OR 97045; 503-557-1324

Andrea Salinas—Sixth District

Counties: Polk and Yamhill; parts of Clackamas, Marion and Washington

Democrat. Born in San Mateo, California, December 6, 1969. University of California, Berkley; BA, 1994. Served as a Congressional Aide for three members of Congress. Worked as an advocate for labor unions, environmental groups and reproductive rights organizations. Adrea and her husband Chris have one daughter, Amelia.

Appointed to the Oregon House of Representatives, 2017; reelected in 2018 and 2020. Elected to the U.S. House of Representatives, 2022. Term Expires 2025. Committees unknown at pres time. Committee member: Committee memberships not yet assigned at press time. Term expires 2025.

Washington, D.C., Office: 109 Cannon House Office Building, Washington, D.C. 20515; Phone: (202) 225-5643;Web and email:salinas.house.gov
District Office: 530 Center Street NE, Salem, 97301; Phone: 503-385-0906

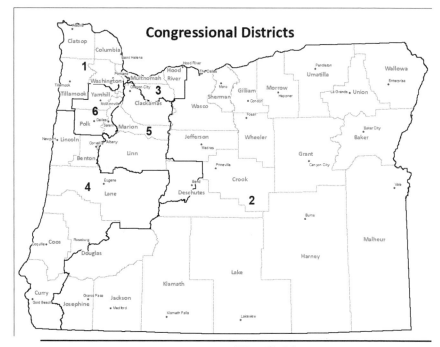

Congressional Districts

U.S. GOVERNMENT OFFICIALS

President of the United States

Joseph R. Biden
Address: The White House, 1600 Pennsylvania Ave., Washington, D.C. 20500
Phone: 202-456-1414
Web: whitehouse.gov
Occupational Background: Attorney; U.S. Senator; Vice President. **Educational Background:** University of Delaware, bachelor's degree, 1965; Syracuse University, law degree, 1968. **Governmental Experience:** U.S. Senate since 1972; U.S. Senate Committee member: Foreign Relations since 1975, Chair 2001–2003, and 2007–2008; Judiciary Chair, 1987–1995; Vice President of the United States, 2009–2017

Vice President of the United States

Kamala Harris
Occupational Background: Attorney; Author; U.S. Senator. **Educational Background:** Howard University, bachelor's degree; 1986; University of California, Hastings, law degree, 1989. **Governmental Experience:** California Attorney General, 2011–2017; U.S. Senate, 2017–2021; U.S. Senate Committee member; Budget; Homeland Security and Governmental Affairs; Intelligence; Judiciary

The Cabinet:

Chief of Staff
Ron Klain
Address: The White House, 1600 Pennsylvania Ave., Washington, D.C. 20500
Phone: 202-456-1414
Web: whitehouse.gov

Council of Economic Advisors
Cecilia Rouse, Chair
Address: 1800 G Street NW, Washington, D.C. 20502
Phone: 202-395-5084
Web: whitehouse.gov/cea

Enviornmental Protection Agency
Michael S. Regan, Administrator
Address: 1200 Pennsylvania Ave. NW, Washington, D.C. 20460
Phone: 202-564-4700
Web: epa.gov

Department of Agriculture
Tom Vilsack, Secretary
Address: 1400 Independence Ave. SW, Washington, D.C. 20250
Phone: 202-720-2791
Web: usda.gov

Department of Commerce
Gina Raimondo, Secretary
Address: 1401 Constitution Ave. NW, Washington, D.C. 20230
Phone: 202-482-2000

Web: commerce.gov

Department of Defense
Lloyd Austin, Secretary
Address: 1400 Defense Pentagon, Washington, D.C. 20301-1400
Phone: 703-571-3343
Web: defense.gov

Department of Education
Miguel Cardona, Secretary
Address: 400 Maryland Ave SW, Washington, D.C. 20202
Phone: 800-872-5327
Web: ed.gov

Department of Energy
Jennier Granholm, Secretary
Address: 1000 Independence Ave. SW, Washington, D.C. 20585
Phone: 202-586-5000
Web: energy.gov

Department of Health and Human Services
Xavier Becerra, Secretary
Address: 200 Independence Ave. SW, Washington, D.C. 20201
Phone: 1-877-696-6775
Web: hhs.gov

Department of Homeland Security
Alejandro Mayorkas, Secretary
Address: 2707 Martin Luther King Jr. Ave. SE, Washington, D.C. 20250
Phone: 202-282-8000
Web: dhs.gov

Department of Housing and Urban Development
Marcia Fudge, Secretary
Address: 451 7th Street SW, Washington, D.C. 20410
Phone: 202-708-1112
Web: hud.gov

Department of the Interior
Deb Haaland, Secretary
Address: 1849 C Street NW, Washington D.C. 20240
Phone: 202-208-3100
Web: doi.gov

Department of Justice
Merrick Garland, Attorney General
Address: 950 Pennsylvania Ave. NW, Washington, D.C. 20250
Phone: 202-647-6575
Web: justice.gov

Department of Labor
Marty Walsh, Secretary
Address: 200 Constitution Ave. NW, Washington, D.C. 20210

Phone: 1-866-487-2365
Web: dol.gov

Department of State
Antony Blinken, Secretary
Address: 2201 S Street NW, Washington, D.C. 20250
Phone: 202-647-6575
Web: state.gov

Department of Transportation
Pete Buttigieg, Secretary
Address: 1200 New Jersey Ave. SE,
Phone: 202-366-4000
Web: transportation.gov

Department of the Treasury
Janet Yellin, Secretary
Address: 1500 Pennsylvania Ave. NW, Washington, D.C. 20220
Phone: 202-622-2000
Web: treasury.gov

Department of Veteran's Affairs
Denis McDonough, Secretary
Address: 810 Vermont Ave. NW, Washington, D.C. 20420
Phone: 1-800-827-1000
Web: va.gov

Director of National Intelligence, Office of the
Avril Haines, Director
Address: 1201 New York Ave. NW, Washington, D.C. 20005
Phone: 202-482-9300
Web: dni.gov

Management and Budget, Office of
Shalanda Young, Director
Address: 725 17th Street NW, Washington, D.C. 20503
Phone: 202-456-4444
Web: whitehouse.gov/omb

Science and Technology Policy, Office of
Arati Prabhakar, Director
Address: 1650 Pennsylvania Ave. NW, Washington, D.C. 20504
Phone: 202-456-4444
Web: dni.gov

Small Business Administration
Isabel Guzman, Administrator
Address: 409 3rd Street SW, Washington, D.C. 20416
Phone: 1-800-827-5722
Web: sba.gov

United States Ambassador to the United Nations
Linda Thomas-Greenfield, Ambassador

Address: 799 United Nations Plaza, New York, NY 10017

Phone: 212-415-4062

Web: usun.mission.gov

U.S. Trade Representative, Office of the

Katherine Tai, U.S. Trade Representative

Address: 600 17th St NW, Washington, D.C. 20508

Phone: 202-395-2870

Web: ustr.gov

U.S. GOVERNMENT IN OREGON

For information about U.S. Government, contact the Federal Government Information Line at 1-800-FED-INFO (1-800-333-4636), or go to: http://www.loc.gov/rr/news/fedgov.html

U.S. DISTRICT COURTS

https://ord.uscourts.gov/index.php/211-divisions

Main Office:

U.S. Courthouse

Address: 1000 SW Third Ave., Suite 740, Portland 97204; 503-326-8000

Eugene Divisional Office:

Wayne L. Morse U.S. Courthouse

Address: 405 E Eighth Ave., Suite 2100, Eugene 97401; 541-431-4100

Medford Divisional Office:

James A. Redden U.S. Courthouse

Address: 310 W Sixth St., Room 201, Medford 97501; 541-608-8777

Pendleton Divisional Office:

John F. Kilkenny U.S. Courthouse

Address: 104 SW Dorian Ave., Pendleton 97801; 541-278-4053

MAJOR POLITICAL PARTIES

Democratic National Committee

Address: 430 S Capitol St. SE, Washington, D.C. 20003

Phone: 202-863-8000

Web: democrats.org

Democratic State Central Committee of Oregon

Address: 232 NE Ninth Ave., Portland 97232-2915

Phone: 503-224-8200

Web: dpo.org

Republican National Committee

Address: 310 First St. SE, Washington, D.C. 20003

Phone: 202-863-8500

Web: gop.com

Republican State Central Committee of Oregon

Address: 25375 SW Parkway Ave., #200, Wilsonville 97070

Phone: 503-595-8881

Web: oregon.gop

NATIVE PEOPLES OF OREGON

Source: Legislative Commission on Indian Services
Contact: Patrick Flanagan, Executive Officer
Address: 900 Court St. NE, Rm. 167, Salem 97301
Phone: 503-986-1067
Web: oregonlegislature.gov/cis

Oregon's total "American Indian" population, according to the 2020 U.S. Census, included 185,723 people as "American Indian or Alaskan Native." Oregon's "American Indians" live in all 36 counties and are about 4% of Oregon's total population. In addition to members of the nine federally recognized tribes in Oregon, there are a significant number of enrolled members of other tribes based outside of Oregon who also reside within our state. Members of Oregon's nine federally recognized tribes speak of being in this area from time immemorial. Village sites and traditional ways are known to date back many thousands of years.

Tribal governments are separate and unique sovereign nations with powers to protect the health, safety and welfare of their enrolled members and to govern their lands. This tribal sovereignty predates the existence of the U.S. government and the State of Oregon. The members residing in Oregon are citizens of their tribes, citizens of Oregon, and since 1924, citizens of the United States of America.

The U.S. Department of the Interior, Bureau of Indian Affairs, oversees tribal interests and administers the federal government's trust obligations. At times, the federal government has been supportive of tribal self-determination, and in other periods, has adopted policies and passed legislation having a negative impact on the ability of tribes to govern as sovereigns. "Termination," one such policy in the 1950s, was an attempt to sever federal trusteeship and support for tribal sovereignty. Of the 109 tribes and bands terminated nationwide, 62 were in Oregon. In 1975, the federal government recognized the failure of its termination policy and passed the Indian Self-Determination and Education Assistance Act, and later, the Tribal Self-Governance Act.

Several tribes began the process to restore their status as sovereign nations. In 1977, The Confederated Tribes of Siletz was the second tribe in the nation to achieve restoration. Following Siletz was the Cow Creek Band of the Umpqua Tribe of Indians in 1982, the Confederated Tribes of Grand Ronde in 1983, the Confederated Tribes of Coos, Lower Umpqua and Siuslaw in 1984, the Klamath Tribes in 1986 and the Coquille Indian Tribe in 1989. Another three federally recognized tribal governments exist in Oregon: The Confederated Tribes of Warm Springs (Treaty of 1855), the Confederated Tribes of Umatilla (Treaty of 1855) and the Burns Paiute Tribe (1972 Executive Order). Fort McDermitt Paiute Shoshone Tribe is a federally recognized tribe with reservation lands straddling Oregon and Nevada, but the tribe's population center is in Nevada. Celilo Village is a federally recognized tribal entity near The Dalles, jointly administered by the Confederated Tribes of Warm Springs, the Confederated Tribes of Umatilla, and the Yakama Indian Nation (Washington).

All Oregon tribal governments have reservation or trust lands created by treaties, statutes or executive branch actions. Tribal governments have regulatory authority over these lands, unless that authority has been removed by Congress. Nearly 904,000 acres, or at least 1.6 percent of land within Oregon's boundaries, are held in trust by the federal government or are designated reservation lands. Tribal governments have the authority to decide their own membership qualifications and have a right to exclude individuals from their reservations. Just as Oregon does not collect tax on federal lands nor tax federal or local governments or non-profit corporations, Oregon does not tax tribal governments, but all tribal members as individual citizens pay federal taxes and most pay state taxes, with the exception of those who live and work on a reservation or earn money on reservation or trust lands or from trust resources.

Public Law 280 gave the state certain civil and criminal jurisdiction over tribes with the exception of the Confederated Tribes of Warm Springs, the Confederated Tribes of Umatilla and the Burns Paiute Tribe, which are "non Public Law 280" tribes. Notwithstanding Public Law 280, all Oregon tribes have the authority to elect their own governments and adopt laws and ordinances. Oregon tribal governments have their own departments dealing with governmental services, including law enforcement and tribal court systems. In addition, each tribal government operates programs in the areas of natural resources, cultural resources, education, health and human services, public safety, housing, economic development and other areas to serve their members. Oregon maintains a government-to-government relationship with the tribal governments as directed in ORS 182.162 to 182.168.

Passage of the National Indian Gaming Regulatory Act in 1988 created the opportunity to build gaming centers on reservation and trust lands. Besides providing employment opportunities for tribal members and citizens of surrounding communities, revenues from these tribal enterprises fund health clinics, education, scholarships, housing and other services. Gaming and other enterprises have made these tribal governments some of the largest employers in their counties—generating employment for tax-paying employees, benefiting local communities and the entire state. All Oregon tribal governments are striving to diversify their revenue streams and are actively pursuing other avenues of generating revenue.

Most Oregon tribes are "confederations" of three or more tribes and bands. Each tribe's area of interest may extend far beyond its tribal governmental center or reservation location.

Burns Paiute Tribe

Address: 100 Pasigo St., Burns 97720
Phone: 541-573-2088
Email: Beverly.Beers@burnspaiute-nsn.gov
Web: burnspaiute-nsn.gov
Restoration: by Executive Order, October 13, 1972
Number of
Members: 420
Land Base Acreage:
13,736 acres
Number of people
employed by the
Tribe: 54

Economy: Burns Paiute Tribe Old Camp RV Park, Burns Paiute Foundation

Points of Interest: Steens Mountain recreational area; Malheur National Wildlife Refuge; Reservation Day Powwow occurs two days each fall about October 13; annual Mother's Day Powwow

History and Culture: The Burns Paiute Reservation is located north of Burns in Harney County. Today's tribal members are primarily the descendants of the "Wadatika" band of Paiutes of central and southern Oregon. The Wadatika, named for the wada seeds collected near Malheur Lake shores, lived on seeds, berries, roots and vegetation they gathered and wild animals they hunted. Their territory included the area from the Cascade Mountains to Boise, Idaho, and the Blue Mountains to Steens Mountain. Paiute legends say that the Paiutes have lived in this area since before the Cascade Mountains were formed, coming from the south as part of a migration through the Great Basin. People of the Burns Paiute Tribe were basket makers who used fibers of willow, sagebrush, tule plant and Indian hemp to weave baskets, sandals, fishing nets and traps. Archeologists have found clothing made from animal and bird hides and sandals made from sagebrush fibers believed to be close to 10,000 years old. The tribe continues to hunt, gather food and do beadwork and drum-making in traditional ways.

Tribal Court: Tribal Judge Christie Timko; Associate Judge Patricia Davis, 100 Pasigo St., Burns 97720; 541-573-2793

Tribal Council: Chairperson Diane Teeman, Vice-Chair Gabe First Raised, Secretary-Treasurer Brenda Sam, Sergeant at Arms Rachel Hofman, Members at Large: Eric Hawley, Charisse Soucie and Margarita Zacarias

Confederated Tribes of Coos, Lower Umpqua and Siuslaw Indians (CTCLUSI)

Address: 1245 Fulton Ave., Coos Bay 97420
Phone: 541-888-9577, 888-280-0726
Email: lwander@ctclusi.org
Web: ctclusi.org
Restoration Date: October 17, 1984
Number of Members: 1,314
Land Base Acreage: 15,313 acres of the 1.9 million acres of ancestral lands
Number of people employed by the Tribes: 562

Economy: Three Rivers Casino & Hotel, Three Rivers Casino-Coos Bay, Ocean Dunes Golf Course, Restorative Economy

Points of Interest: Three Rivers Casino-Coos Bay; Ocean Dunes Golf Course; Tribal Hall in Coos Bay; Laqauwiiyatas Gallery. The Tribe's Ancestral lands covers the Siuslaw Watershed, the Lower Umpqua Watershed and the Coos Watershed. Within this large area of lands and waters the tribes hold traditional activities, ceremonies, most of which are only open to Tribal Citizens but much of these lands and waters are open to visitors.

History and Culture: The people of the miluk (Coos), hanis, (Coos), quuiich (Lower Umpqua) and sha'yuushtl'a (Siuslaw) Tribes have lived on the central to southern Oregon coast and inland along the rivers they belonged to, since time immemorial. These rivers today are called the Siuslaw River, the Umpqua River and the Coos River, which take their linguistic heritage from the tribes. The tribes' ancestors worked to manage and steward the lands in a way that provided sustainable resources for future generations; they practiced a culture of abundance. This way of living was severely disrupted due to the exposure of European diseases, the removal of the people from their lands for

Euro-American settlement, the boarding school era and the Western Oregon Termination Act of 1954. Despite all of this, the peoples' resiliency and hard work ethic regained them Federal Recognition as a sovereign nation in 1984. Since this time, CTCLUSI has rebuilt its culture of abundance by once again practicing the culture of their lands and waters: actively gathering and propagating first foods, weaving, carving and canoeing. They utilize the lessons from their ancestors, their elders and their culture to work with federal, tribal, state and local partners on restoration efforts within their ancestral lands and waters to bring back the abundance that was once here for everyone.

Tribal Court: Tribal Judge J. D. Williams, 1245 Fulton Ave., Coos Bay 97420; 541-888-9577

Tribal Council: Chief Doc Slyter (2030), Chair Brad Kneaper (2026), Vice-Chair Julie Siestreem (2023), Doug Barrett (2026), Enna Helms (2023), Teresa Spangler (2026) and Iliana Montiel (2023)

Coquille Indian Tribe

Address: 3050 Tremont St., North Bend 97459
Phone: 541-756-0904
Email: kwen@coquilletribe.org
Web: coquilletribe.org
Restoration Date: June 28, 1989
Number of Members: 1,171
Land Base Acreage: approximately 10,290 acres
Number of people employed by the Tribe: 820

Economy: The tribe contributes to the economy of Coos, Curry, Douglas, Jackson and Lane counties through its timber operations; the Mill Casino-Hotel and RV Park on Coos Bay; the Ko-Kwel Wellness Centers in Coos Bay and Eugene; a hotel, golf course and bowling center in Medford; and diverse enterprises operating nationwide under the Tribal One banner. The tribe is Coos County's second-largest employer.

Points of Interest: Oregon's South Coast area features charter fishing, crabbing, world-class golf, mountain biking, dune riding, kayaking, storm watching, beachcombing, tide pooling, and the famous gardens and holiday lights at Shore Acres State Park

History and Culture: More than 1 million acres of ancestral homelands in southwest Oregon were ceded to the U.S. government in the 1850s. The U.S. Senate never ratified the treaties, and a promise of reservation land never materialized. The federal government declared the tribe "terminated" in 1954, but the tribe regained federal recognition in 1989 after a determined struggle. Since its restoration, the Coquille Tribe has sought self-sufficiency for itself and its members, emphasizing education, health care, housing and elder services. Cultural preservation efforts include teaching oral histories, traditions and ancestral languages to members of the tribe. Congress restored 5,410 acres of forest land to the tribe in 1996, and the tribe has nearly doubled that acreage through strategic purchases. Today it manages its forests under certification standards of the Forest Stewardship Council. In 2022 the tribe entered an agreement with the state for cooperative management of fish and wildlife in the tribe's five-county service area.

Tribal Court: Chief Judge Melissa Cribbins, 3050 Tremont St., North Bend 97459; 541-756-0904

Tribal Council: Chair Brenda Meade (2024), Vice Chair Jon Ivy (2023), Chief Jason Younker (2025), Secretary-Treasurer Jackie Chambers (2024), Representatives Laurabeth Barton (2024), Don Garrett (2023) and Jen Procter Andrews (2025)

Cow Creek Band of Umpqua Tribe of Indians

Address: 2371 NE Stephens St., Suite 100, Roseburg 97470
Phone: 541-672-9405, 800-929-8229
Email: dfields@cowcreek.com
Web: cowcreek-nsn.gov
Treaty Date: September 19, 1853
Restoration Date: December 29, 1982
Number of Members: 1,760
Land Base Acreage: 1,840 acres (in trust)
Number of people employed by the Tribe: 1,100

Economy: The tribe was restored without reservation land in 1982. All land held by the tribe has been by purchase. The Seven Feathers Casino Resort in Canyonville, including hotels, restaurants and entertainment venues, is the tribe's main income source. Other businesses, such as the K-BAR cattle ranch in Rogue River, have been acquired in their economic diversification program. Since recognition, the tribe has developed housing, education and social services programs, business corporations, a utility cooperative, charitable foundation and tribal court system. The tribe is one of the largest employers in Douglas County.

Points of Interest: Oregon's Interstate-5 passes through Canyonville, the Seven Feathers Resort and the heart of Cow Creek's homeland. The area includes the Umpqua River, the Cascade Mountains, the Pacific Ocean and dunes and a growing wine industry.

History and Culture: The Cow Creeks lived between the Cascade and Coast Ranges in southwestern Oregon, along the South Umpqua River. They hunted deer and elk and fished silver salmon and steelhead as far north as the Columbia River, east to Crater Lake, and south to the Klamath Marsh. Except for the purpose of the Termination Act in 1954, which called for the immediate termination of federal relations with more than 60 tribes in western Oregon, the Cow Creek's Treaty of 1853 was ignored by the U.S. government for over 128 years until federal recognition in 1982.

Tribal Court: Tribal Judge Ronald Yockim, 2371 NE Stephens St., Suite 100, Roseburg 97470; 541-672-9405

Tribal Council: Chairman Carla Keene, Vice-Chair Gary Jackson, Secretary Yvonne Dumont-McCafferty, Treasurer Robert VanNorman, Members: Jessica Bochart-Leusch, Dan Courtney, Tom Cox, Royce Deardorff, Gerald Rainville, Susie Steward and Luann Urban

Confederated Tribes of The Grand Ronde

Address: 9615 Grand Ronde Rd., Grand Ronde 97347
Phone: 503-879-5211, 1-800-422-0232
Email: info@grandronde.org
Web: grandronde.org
Restoration Date: November 22, 1983
Number of Members: 5,623
Land Base Acreage: about 16, 967 acres
Number of people employed by the Tribes: 1,646

Economy: Spirit Mountain Casino, over 10,000 acres of forest lands and wildfire fighting crew

Points of Interest: Spirit Mountain Casino is one of Oregon's top attractions, and the Tribe dedicates 6% of the profits to its Spirit Mountain Community Fund, which supports charitable organizations in an 11-county area of western Oregon. The fund has given more than $89 million to area charities since 1997. The West Valley Veterans' Memorial, four granite pillars representing the four branches of the armed services, holds the names of tribal members and area veterans who fought and served their country. The tribe hosts a Veterans' Powwow each July and a Competition Powwow on the third weekend of August. Fort Yamhill Heritage Area nearby tells the story of the relocation, transition and sadness for Grand Ronde's people when they were forced from their ancestral homelands, which extended from the banks of the Columbia River to the

Oregon–California border, on to the Grand Ronde Reservation under military guard.

History and Culture: The tribes include Athabaskan-speaking Chasta from Rogue River and Upper Umpqua from southern Oregon. Molalla tribes are from the western Cascade Mountains, Kalapuya Tribes are from the Willamette Valley, and Chinookan-speaking Tumwater, Clackamas, Watlala and Multnomah are from the lower Willamette and Columbia Rivers. Chinuk Wawa became the tribes' common language. Traditional basket making and weaving, skills still practiced today, were important tribal utility and cultural skills.

Tribal Council 2022: Chairwoman Cheryle A. Kennedy, Vice-Chairman Chris Mercier, Secretary Michael Langley; Lisa Leno, Jon George, Kathleen George, Brenda Tuomi, Denise Harvey and Michael Cherry

Klamath Tribes
Address: PO Box 436, 501 Chiloquin Blvd., Chiloquin 97624
Phone: 541-783-2219, 800-524-9787
Email: taylor.tupper@klamathtribes.com
Web: klamathtribes.org
Restoration Date: August 27, 1986
Number of Members: 5,200
Land Base Acreage: no reservation land
Number of people employed by the Tribes: Over 350

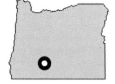

Economy: Kla-Mo-Ya Casino, Crater Lake truck stop, travel center and hotel, wellness center

Points of Interest: Kla-Mo-Ya Casino, Crater Lake National Park, Lava Beds National Monument and Tulelake History Museum. Named by *Sunset Magazine* as one of the nation's five best birding hotspots, the Klamath Basin in the Pacific Flyway is a migratory flyway for more than 350 species of birds, including Bald Eagles, Clarke's Grebes and Black Terns.

History and Culture: Traditionally, every March, the c'waam (Lost River Suckerfish) swims up the Sprague River to spawn. A certain snowfall at this time of year heralds the c'waam's return, and the evening sky reveals the fish constellation (three stars in line making "Orion's Belt") on the southwestern horizon. Klamath traditions state that watchmen, or swaso.llalalYampgis, monitored the riverbanks to see exactly when the fish would return. The head "shaman" would then give thanks for their return. Tribal elders continue this ceremony to ensure the survival of a species, tribal traditions, and mankind. The celebration includes traditional dancing, drumming, feasting and releasing of a

pair of c'waam into the river. Other annual events include the Restoration Celebration held the fourth weekend in August and the New Year's Eve Sobriety Powwow.

The Klamath Tribes, the Klamath, Modoc and Yahooskin Paiute people, have lived in the Klamath Basin from time beyond memory. Legends and oral history tell about when the world and the animals were created, when the animals and gmok'am'c, the Creator, sat together and discussed the creation of man. According to tribal sayings, if stability defines success, their presence here has been, and always will be, essential to the economic well-being of their homeland.

Tribal Court: Tribal Judge Patricia Davis Gibson 118 W. Chocktoot St., PO Box 1260, Chiloquin 97624; 541-783-3020

Tribal Council: Chairman Clayton Dumount, Jr, Vice-Chair Gail Hatcher, Secretary Roberta Frost, Treasurer Brandi Hatcher, council members Leslie Anderson, Natalie Ball, Ellsworth Lang, Jeannie McNair, Willa Powless and Rosemary Treetop

Confederated Tribes of Siletz Indians
Address: 201 SE Swan Ave. PO Box 549, Siletz 97380
Phone: 541-444-2532
Email: Kurtisb@ctsi.nsn.us
Web: ctsi.nsn.us
Restoration Date: November 18, 1977
Number of Members: 5,089
Land Base Acreage: 16,655 acres
Reservation Land: 4,010 acres
Number of people employed by the Tribes: 877

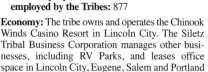

Economy: The tribe owns and operates the Chinook Winds Casino Resort in Lincoln City. The Siletz Tribal Business Corporation manages other businesses, including RV Parks, and leases office space in Lincoln City, Eugene, Salem and Portland

Points of Interest: Chinook Winds Casino and Resort, including an ocean-front hotel, restaurants, arcade and childcare; 18-hole golf course in Lincoln City; Nesika Illahee Pow Wow each August; and the Tribes' Restoration Pow Wow each November

History and Culture: The Confederated Tribes of Siletz Indians (CTSI) is a diverse confederation of 27 Western Oregon, Northern California and Southern Washington bands. A 1.1 million-acre reservation was established by President Franklin Pierce on November 9, 1855, fulfilling the stipulations of eight treaties. Over time, reservation lands were taken away, and CTSI was terminated as a tribe in 1954. In 1977, CTSI was the second tribe in the nation to achieve restoration. In 1980, some reservation lands were reestablished. In spite of mistreatment and displacement, CTSI continues work to recover as much as possible of what was lost.

Since 1980, the tribe has increased its land base to 16,655 acres, which includes 15,977 acres of timberland and 678 acres for cultural preservation, housing, economic purposes and wildlife habitat enhancement. About 56 percent (9,315 acres) of the land base is in Lincoln County. The Siletz Tribal Housing Department currently manages 199 residential units. The tribe partnered on two urban apartment complexes in NE Portland that provides housing for 40 tribal households.

Tribal Court: Tribal Chief Judge Mark B. Williams, PO Box 549, Siletz 97380; 541-444-8228

Tribal Council: Chairperson Delores Pigsley (2025), Vice-Chair Alfred "Bud" Lane III (2025), Treasurer Robert Kentta (2023), Secretary Sharon Edenfield (2024), Members: Loraine Butler (2023), Angela Ramirez (2024), Selene Rilatos (2023), Frank Aspira (2024) and Bonnie Petersen (2025)

Confederated Tribes of the Umatilla Indian Reservation

Address: 46411 Ti'mine Way, Pendleton 97801
Phone: 541-429-7000
Email: info@ctuir.org
Web: ctuir.org
Treaty Date: June 9, 1855; 12 Stat. 945
Number of Members: 3,152
Land Base Acreage: 172,000 acres
Number of people employed by the Tribes: 1,645

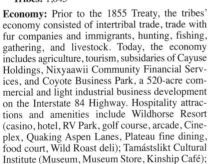

Economy: Prior to the 1855 Treaty, the tribes' economy consisted of intertribal trade, trade with fur companies and immigrants, hunting, fishing, gathering, and livestock. Today, the economy includes agriculture, tourism, subsidaries of Cayuse Holdings, Nixyaawii Community Financial Services, and Coyote Business Park, a 520-acre commercial and light industrial business development on the Interstate 84 Highway. Hospitality attractions and amenities include Wildhorse Resort (casino, hotel, RV Park, golf course, arcade, Cineplex, Quaking Aspen Lanes, Plateau fine dining, food court, Wild Roast deli); Tamástslikt Cultural Institute (Museum, Museum Store, Kinship Café); Hamley's Western Store, Steakhouse, Cafe; The Golf Course at Birch Creek, Arrowhead Travel Plaza, the Mission Market; and the Indian Lake campground. The Umatilla Reservation is also home to the Umatilla National Forest Supervisor's Office, Kenworth Sales Truck Repair, McDonald's,

Subway, Davita Dialysis Center, and Ruby's Indian Crafts & Supplies. The tribes are typically one of the top employers in the region.

Points of Interest: Tamástslikt Cultural Institute, Nixyáwii Warriors Memorial, Crow's Shadow Institute of the Arts, Indian Lake Recreation Area, Oregon National Historic Trail, Lewis & Clark National Historic Trail, seasonal upland game bird and turkey hunting

History and Culture: Three tribes comprise the Confederated Tribes of the Umatilla Indian Reservation (CTUIR): Cayuse, Umatilla, and Walla Walla. They have lived on the Columbia River Plateau for over 10,000 years, in an area of about 6.4 million acres in what is now northeastern Oregon and southeastern Washington. In 1855, the tribes and the United States government concluded a treaty in which the tribes ceded more than 5 million acres, reserving 512,000 acres for their exclusive use in the form of a reservation. Various congressional acts of diminishment resulted in a significantly reduced reservation. In the treaty, the CTUIR reserved their inherent fishing and hunting rights and the right to gather traditional foods and medicines within the ceded areas.

The traditional way of life of the tribes is called "Washat" or "Seven Drums prayer service." The Umatilla, Walla Walla, and Nez Perce languages are spoken and a language preservation program is helping to re-establish use of these languages by youth.

Tribal Court: Chief Judge William Johnson, 46411 Ti'mine Way, Pendleton 97801; 541-276-2046

Tribal Governance: Board of Trustees 2021-2023: Chair Kat Brigham, General Council Chair Lindsey Watchman, Vice-Chair Aaron Ashley, Treasurer Sandra Sampson, Secretary Sally Kosey, Members at Large: Toby Patrick, Lisa Ganuelas, Boots Pond and Corinne Sams

Confederated Tribes of Warm Springs Reservation

Address: PO Box C, Warm Springs 97761
Phone: 541-553-3257
Email: robert.brunoe@wstribes.org
Web: warmsprings-nsn.gov
Treaty Date: June 25, 1855
Number of Members: 5,363
Land Base Acreage: 644,000 acres

Economy: The tribes have established a number of enterprises under the Corporate Charter that are operated independently of tribal government, but

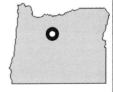

contribute to the economy of the reservation, including Warm Springs Power & Water, Warm Springs Composite Products and Indian Head Casino. Co-owner of PGE Hydro on Deschutes River

Points of Interest: Indian Head Casino and the Museum at Warm Springs; the annual April Welcome Home Vietnam Veterans' Parade and Expo

History and Culture: The 644,000 acre Warm Springs Reservation was established by the Treaty with the Tribes of Middle Oregon of June 25, 1855. In the Treaty, the Tribes ceded to the United States ten million acres of their ancestral homeland in north central Oregon while reserving rights in the ceded area and beyond to fish at their usual and accustomed places, gather berries, dig roots and pasture livestock on unclaimed lands. Today, the tribes eleven member Tribal Council exercises governmental authority over the Reservation and off reservation tribal lands. The tribes' exemption from Public Law 83-280 excludes State jurisdiction on the Reservation. Long before Europeans set foot on the North American continent, the tribes of the Warm Springs Reservation - the Wasco, The Walla Walla (later called the Warm Springs), and the Paiute - had developed societies beside the Columbia River, Cascade Mountains and other parts of Oregon. Prior to settling on the reservation, natural food resources were so plentiful that agriculture was unnecessary. Salmon from the nearby Columbia was a staple for the Wasco and Warm Springs bands. The high-plains Paiutes depended more on deer and other large game. All three tribes took advantage of assorted roots, fruits and other plant life. Salmon were harvested out of the Columbia River and its tributaries with long-handled dip nets. Roots were dug from the ground with specialized digging sticks called kapns. Berries were gathered in ornately-woven baskets. Centuries of practice perfected these methods.

Tribal Council 2022: Chairman Jonathan W. Smith, Sr.; Warm Springs Chief Delvis Heath; Wasco Chief Alfred Smith, Jr.; Paiute Chief Joe Moses; Representatives: Raymond "Captain" Moody, Lincoln Suppah, Carlos Calica, Alvis Smith, III, James Manion, Wilson Wewa Jr. and Rosa Graybael

OREGON CONSULAR CORPS

Many foreign nations maintain consulates in Oregon. Consuls are officials appointed by a government to live in a foreign city to look after the business and interests of the home country. They also assist and protect its nationals within the consular territory, promote a country's trade within the assigned area, assist and protect shipping interests and assist native seamen in distress. Con-

suls may adjudicate shipping matters, administer oaths, legalize ships' papers and foreign documents as required by a country's laws, issue passports and visas and explain a country's policies, cultural achievements and its attractions for tourism.

See this listing by country below.

Barbados
H. Desmond Johnson, M.D., Honorary Consul
Address: 4750 SW Trail Rd., Tualatin 97062
Phone: 503-805-5886
Email: bajandoc@hotmail.com

Belgium
Cyrille Michel, Honorary Consul
Address: 7912 NE 69th St., Vancouver, WA 98662
Phone: 503-803-7534
Email: cyrillebmichel@gmail.com

Canada
Barton Eberwein, Honorary Consul
Address: 3161 NW Cumberland Rd, Portland 97210
Phone: 503-880-7877
Email: eberweinb@gmail.com

Czech Republic
Marie Amicci, Honorary Consul
Address: 12520 SW 68th Ave., Ste B, Tigard 97223
Phone: 503-293-9545
Email: cz_consul_pdx@msn.com

Denmark
Ingolf Noto, Honorary Consul
Address: 888 SW 5th Ave., Ste 1600, Portland 97204
Phone: 503-802-2131
Email: ingolf.noto@tonkon.com

Finland
Veikko Valli, Honorary Consul
Address: 3608 E Burnside St, Portland 97210
Phone: 971-319-2776
Email: veikko.valli@iki.fi

France
Dominiqe Geulin, Honorary Consul
Address: 1922 SE 10th Ave., Portland 97214
Phone: 503-941-8173
Email: consulhonorairePDX@gmail.com

Germany
Blake Peters, Honorary Consul
Address: 3900 SW Murray Blvd., Beaverton 97005
Phone: 503-626-9089
Email: blakepeters.hk@gmail.com

Guatemala
Marta Guembes-Herrera, Honorary Consul
Please contact by email
Phone: 503-530-0046
Email: consulguatemala.or@gmail.com

Italy
Vytas Paul Babusis, Honorary Consul
Address: 5 Centerpointe Dr. Ste 400, Lake Oswego 97035
Phone: 503-593-0082

Email: portland.onorario@esteri.it

Japan
Masaki Shiga, Consul General
Address: 1300 SW Fifth Ave., Ste. 2700, Portland 97201
Phone: 503-221-1811
Email: masaki.shiga@mofa.go.jp

Korea, Republic of
Greg Caldwell, Honorary Consul
Address: 8433 SW 10th Ave., Portland 97219
Phone: 503-768-7457
Email: caldwell@lclark.edu

Susan Soonkeum Cox, Honorary Consul
Address: 3115 Braeman Village, Eugene 97405
Phone: 541-687-2202
Email: coxkoreanconsulate.eug@gmail.com

Latvia, Republic of
Uldis J. Berzins, M.D., Honorary Consul
Address: 6814 SE Reed College Pl., Portland 97202
Phone: 503-689-4705
Email: ujberzins@aol.com

Lithuania
Randolph L. Miller, Honorary Consul
Address: 333 SE Second Ave., Portland 97214
Phone: 503-234-5000
Email: Randy@ProduceRowLLC.com

Luxembourg
Bill Failing, Honorary Consul
Address: 2649 SW Georgian Pl., Portland 97201
Phone: 503-309-2768
Email: wlfailing@gmail.com

Malaysia
John L. Blackwell, Honorary Consul
Address: 4708 SW Fairview Blvd., Portland 97221
Phone: 503-740-8404
Email: johnlblackwell1@gmail.com

Malta
Joseph Micallef, Honorary Consul
Address: 22233 SW Antioch Downs Ct., Tualatin 97062
Phone: 503-638-3949
Email: maltaconsul.portland@gov.mt

Mexico
Carlos Quesnel, Consul General
Address: 1305 SW 12th Ave., Portland 97201
Phone: 503-274-1442
Email: portland@sre.gob.mx

Micronesia
Dominic R. Maluchmai, Acting Consul General
Address: 2625 SE 98th Ave., Portland 97226
Phone: 503-483-7149
Email: cg.portland@gov.fm

Namibia
Lance Mayhew, Honorary Consul
Address: 3519 NE 15th Ave., Portland 97212

Phone: 971-275-0456
Email: lancemayhew@gmail.com

The Netherlands
Pending Appointment
Phone: 971-645-7840
Web: www.oregonconsularcorps.us

New Zealand
Charles Swindells, Honorary Consul
Address: NW 23 Pl., Ste 6, PMB 481, Portland 97210-5580
Phone: 503-803-7129
Email: cjs@theswindells.org

Sweden
Petra Hillberg, Honorary Consul
Address: 14790 NE 95th St. Bldg 8, Redmond, WA 98052
Phone: 206-952-6299
Email: seattle@consulateofsweden.org

Taiwan
Daniel K.C. Chen, Director General
Address: 600 University St., Ste 2020, Seattle, WA 98101
Phone: 206-441-4568
Email: infoseattle@mofa.gov.tw

Thailand
Nicholas J. Stanley, Honorary Consul
Address: 1136 NW Hoyt, Ste. 210, Portland 97209
Phone: 503-221-0440
Email: thai@siaminc.com

Ukraine
Valeriy V. Goloborodko, Honorary Consul
Address: 600 1st Ave., Seattle, WA 98104
Phone: 425-209-0209
Email: hc@uaconsulate.org

United Kingdom
Wilfred Pinfold, Honorary Consul
Address: 2004 NW Irving St., #3, Portland 97209
Phone: 503-709-2975
Email: wp@wilfredpinfold.com

Source: Gale Blessing, Oregon Consular Corps, 971-645-7840; www.oregonconsularcorps.us

STUDENT ESSAY CONTEST WINNER

My Pandemic Experience

Anuva Shah
Allyson Edwards 7th Grade Class
Tumwater Middle School, Portland

When COVID-19 first started affecting me, I was only in fourth grade. I remember hearing rumors, and being quick to ignore them. However, slowly, I started noticing more and more of my friends bringing wipes and sanitizer to school. More whispers of a terrifying, life-changing virus.

Suddenly, spring break was extended, and the rest of the in-person school year canceled. Then, we were to learn on an alien platform called "Zoom". I was excited at first when I realized we had more time for break — clearly remember contacting my friends in the happiness of more freetime. But when the online school year began, I realized how different online school was to the real, in person school I was used to.

There were certainly benefits of online school, considering how I learned ways to better understand technology, and loved being able to have more independent time without my class and teacher. However, COVID-19 impacted me and my life far more negatively than positively. Not being able to communicate with my friends in person was impossible for me, since I was so used to meeting them almost every day of the week. I didn't realize how much of an impact my friends had on me, my mood, and my lifestyle.

Overall, even though the pandemic had negative aspects, like losing much of my in-person social interaction, and not being able to go out without a mask smothering my face, I tried to remember positive parts, like staying in the comfort of my own home, and being able to talk to any of my friends by simply sending them a text or link. The virus changed me thoroughly, and was a vital part of my life. It helped create who I am now, two years from when the pandemic first began.

This drawing by Anuva Shah shows the ups and downs of the COVID-19 restrictions.

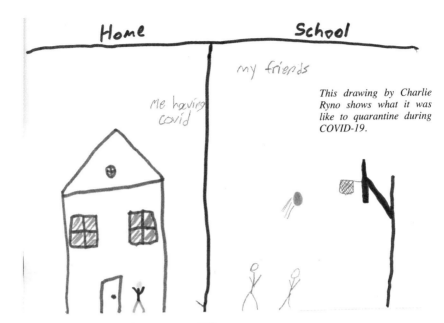

This drawing by Charlie Ryno shows what it was like to quarantine during COVID-19.

STUDENT ESSAY CONTEST WINNER
Friends in Covid

Charlie Ryno
Amy York's 6th Grade Class
Mitchell Middle School, Mitchell

One of the harshest things in the Covid 19 pandemic fo me was not being able to see my friends. When school and sports shut down I was bummed, because those were the two events I saw my friends at the most. When the pandemic was really bad I could only see my friends on Zoom. Once school opened again my family got Covid. That meant I had to stay home from my friends and they also had to quarantine, because they were around me.

I have learned a lot from Covid for example, I know what it feels like to have a pandemic going through the world. I also know that scientists have learned a lot as well.

Local Governments

Oregon offers us a place of rich geographic diversity to establish our communities—from the Pacific Ocean beaches and Coast Range eastward to the Willamette Valley, Klamath Mountains and southwest valleys; on to the Cascade Range; then further east to the Columbia River Plateau, Blue Mountains, the southeast Basin and ranges; and on to the Snake River at our eastern border. This section identifies incorporated cities and towns, counties, regional governments and special districts.

SALEM—
OREGON'S CAPITAL

Salem, with a population of 177,694 is Oregon's state capital and the second largest city. Salem is also the county seat of Marion County, but a small portion contained within its corporate limits of 44 square miles lies across the Willamette River in Polk County. Salem is situated on the 45th geographic parallel in the center of the Willamette Valley—one of the most fertile and agriculturally productive regions in the world—47 miles south of Portland and 64 miles north of Eugene.

Salem serves as the hub of both state government and the surrounding farming communities. State government is the largest employer, with approximately 19,949 state employees and offices for 73 state agencies located in Salem. Salem is also one of the largest food-processing centers in the United States.

In addition, Salem is one of Oregon's oldest cities. The tribal name for the locality was Chemeketa, said to mean "meeting or resting place." It may also have been the name of one of the bands of the Kalapuya Tribe. In 1840–1841, the Jason Lee Mission was moved from the banks of the Willamette River, upstream to a site on Mill Creek. In 1842, missionaries established the Oregon Institute. When the mission was dissolved in 1844, it was decided to lay out a townsite on the Oregon Institute lands. Either David Leslie, one of the trustees who came to Oregon from Salem, Massachusetts, or W. H. Willson, who filed plats in 1850–1851 for what is now the main part of the city, selected the name "Salem." Salem is the Anglicized form of the Hebrew word shalom, meaning peace.*

The location of the Oregon capital caused a spirited contest that lasted nearly 15 years. By a legislative act in 1851, the territorial government moved the capital to Salem from Oregon City. In 1855, it was moved to Corvallis, only to move back to Salem the same year. Destruction of the Capitol Building at Salem on December 31, 1855, was considered an incendiary part of this controversy.

The close proximity of government provides Salem citizens with a distinct opportunity to be involved in the decision-making processes of the state. The citizens of Salem also have a long history of commitment to community improvement, a commitment recognized nationally through the presentation of two All-America City Awards in 1960–1961 and 1982–1983.

*Early Salem history from *Oregon Geographic Names* by Lewis A. McArthur.

INCORPORATED
CITIES AND TOWNS

Source: Patty Mulvihill, Interim Executive Director, League of Oregon Cities
Address: 1201 Court St. NE, Suite 200, Salem 97301, PO Box 928, Salem 97308
Phone: 503-588-6550
Fax: 503-399-4863
Email: loc@orcities.org
Web: orcities.org

There are 241 incorporated cities in Oregon. Cities are centers of population, commerce, education and services. 71% of Oregonians live in cities and nearly 68% of Oregon's property value resides in cities. Economic activity within Oregon's largest cities and urban areas generates 83% of the state's income tax receipts as more than 82% of jobs are located in cities. All of the public institutions of higher education are located in cities, as well as all but two private colleges. All but one of Oregon's 60 hospitals are located within a city. Cities form the heart of Oregon's cultural, educational, service and economic activity.

Among the services city governments typically provide are fire and police protection, streets and street maintenance, sewer and water treatment and collection systems, building permit activities, libraries, parks and recreation activities and other numerous social services determined locally. Cities also have considerable responsibilities for land use planning within their city limits and urban growth boundaries.

City councils serve as the highest authority within city governments in deciding issues of public policy. In open public forums, city councils pass laws (ordinances), adopt resolutions and generally conduct discussions involving the governance of their communities and the welfare of their citizens.

Four forms of city government determine the administrative role of any city council. Most Oregon cities with populations over 2,500 have the council/manager or council/administrator form, in which the council hires a chief executive officer to be responsible for the daily supervision of city affairs. Portland has a commission form of government, where the elected commissioners function collectively as the city council and serve as administrators of city departments. Smaller Oregon cities typically have the mayor/council form, in which the legislative and policy-making body is a popularly-elected council.

City administrators and other city employees often participate in the policy development process but are primarily responsible for effective delivery of municipal services and programs. Under home rule, cities have latitude in managing their affairs, except where the subject matter has been preempted by state government.

Regardless of the form of government, cities find their strength in a cooperative relationship between the citizens, city officials, the private sector and other government entities. Cities recognize the positive impact of working together, both regionally and on a statewide basis, to enhance community livability.

City name origins are available from *Oregon Geographic Names* by Lewis A. McArthur.

Incorporation dates listed below are based on information available.

*County seat

Adair Village
County: Benton
Address: 6030 NE Wm. R. Carr Ave., 97330
Phone: 541-745-5507
Fax: 541-230-5219
Web: adairvillage.org
Elevation: 330'
Incorporated: 5/25/1976
Mayor: William "Bill" Currier

Adams
County: Umatilla
Address: PO Box 20, 190 North Main St., 97810
Phone: 541-566-9380
Fax: 541-566-2077
Web: cityofadamsoregon.com
Elevation: 1,526'
Incorporated: 2/10/1893
Mayor: Graham Alderson

Adrian
County: Malheur
Address: PO Box 226, 97901
Phone: 541-372-2179
Email: cityofadrian@hotmail.com
Elevation: 2,225'
Incorporated: 7/10/1972
Mayor: Carlos Mendoza

*Albany
County: Benton/Linn
Address: PO Box 490, 333 Broadalbin St. SW, 97321
Phone: 541-917-7500
Fax: 541-917-7511
Web: cityofalbany.net
Elevation: 210'
Incorporated: 10/10/1864
Mayor: Alex Johnson II

Amity
County: Yamhill
Address: PO Box 159, 109 Maddox Ave., 97101
Phone: 503-835-3711
Fax: 503-835-3780
Web: cityofamityoregon.org
Elevation: 162'
Incorporated: 10/19/1880
Mayor: Rachel King

Antelope
County: Wasco
Address: PO Box 105, 97001
Phone: 541-489-3201
Web: cityofantelope.us
Elevation: 2,654'
Incorporated: 11/12/1896
Mayor: Sherri Jamison

Arlington
County: Gilliam
Address: PO Box 68, 97812
Phone: 541-454-2743
Fax: 541-454-2753
Web: cityofarlingtonoregon.com
Elevation: 285'
Incorporated: 11/20/1885
Mayor: Jeffery C. Bufton

Ashland
County: Jackson
Address: 20 E Main St., 97520
Phone: 541-488-6002
Fax: 541-488-5311
Web: ashland.or.us
Elevation: 1,949'
Incorporated: 10/13/1874
Mayor: Julie Akins

*Astoria
County: Clatsop
Address: 1095 Duane St., 97103
Phone: 503-325-5821
Fax: 503-325-2997
Web: astoria.or.us
Elevation: 23'
Incorporated: 1/18/1856
Mayor: Bruce Jones

Athena
County: Umatilla
Address: PO Box 686, 302 E Current St., 97813
Phone: 541-566-3862
Fax: 541-566-2781
Web: cityofathena.com
Elevation: 1710'
Incorporated: 2/20/1889
Mayor: Rebecca Schroeder

Aumsville
County: Marion
Address: 595 Main St., 97325
Phone: 503-749-2030
Fax: 503-749-1852
Web: aumsville.us
Elevation: 366'
Incorporated: 8/3/1911
Mayor: Angelica Ceja

Aurora
County: Marion
Address: 21420 Main St. NE, 97002
Phone: 503-678-1283, ext. 2
Fax: 503-678-2758
Web: ci.aurora.or.us
Elevation: 136'
Incorporated: 2/20/1893
Mayor: Brian Asher

*Baker City
County: Baker
Address: PO Box 650, 1655 First St., 97814
Phone: 541-523-6541
Fax: 541-524-2024
Web: bakercity.com
Elevation: 3,451'
Incorporated: 10/13/1874
Mayor: Beverly Calder

Bandon
County: Coos
Address: PO Box 67, 555 Hwy. 101, 97411
Phone: 541-347-2437
Fax: 541-347-1415
Web: cityofbandon.org
Elevation: 20'
Incorporated: 2/18/1891
Mayor: Mary Schamehorn

Banks
County: Washington
Address: 13680 NW Main St., 97106
Phone: 503-324-5112
Fax: 503-324-6674
Web: cityofbanks.org
Elevation: 250'
Incorporated: 1/16/1920
Mayor: Stephanie Jones

Barlow
County: Clackamas
Address: 106 N Main St., 97013
Phone: 503-266-1330
Elevation: 103'

Incorporated: 2/13/1903
Mayor: Michael E. Lundsten

Bay City
County: Tillamook
Address: PO Box 3309, 5525 B St., 97107
Phone: 503-377-2288
Fax: 503-377-4044
Web: ci.bay-city.or.us
Elevation: 17'
Incorporated: 9/13/1910
Mayor: David McCall

Beaverton
County: Washington
Address: PO Box 4755, 12725 SW Millikan Way, 97005
Phone: 503-526-2222
Fax: 503-526-2479
Web: beavertonoregon.gov
Elevation: 189'
Incorporated: 2/10/1893
Mayor: Lacey Beatty

The Tower Theatre in downtown Bend was constructed in 1940. (Oregon State Archives scenic photo)

*Bend
County: Deschutes
Address: PO Box 431, 710 NW Wall St., 97709
Phone: 541-388-5505
Fax: 541-385-6676
Web: bendoregon.gov
Elevation: 3,628'
Incorporated: 1/19/1905
Mayor: Melanie Kebler

Boardman
County: Morrow
Address: PO Box 229, 200 City Center Cir., 97818
Phone: 541-481-9252
Fax: 541-481-3244
Web: cityofboardman.com
Elevation: 308'
Incorporated: 5/20/1921
Mayor: Paul Keefer

Bonanza
County: Klamath

Local Governments

Address: PO Box 297, 97623
Phone: 541-545-6566
Fax: 732-453-7252
Web: townofbonanza.com
Elevation: 4,127'
Incorporated: 2/20/1901
Mayor: Betty Tyre

Brookings
County: Curry
Address: 898 Elk Dr., 97415
Phone: 541-469-2163
Fax: 541-469-3650
Web: brookings.or.us
Elevation: 129'
Incorporated: 10/15/1951
Mayor: Ron Hedenskog

Brownsville
County: Linn
Address: PO Box 188, 255 N Main St., 97327
Phone: 541-466-5880
Fax: 541-466-5118
Web: ci.brownsville.or.us
Elevation: 265'
Incorporated: 10/19/1876
Mayor: Adam Craven

*Burns
County: Harney
Address: 242 S Broadway Ave., 97720
Phone: 541-573-5255
Fax: 541-573-5622
Web: cityofburnsor.gov
Elevation: 4,148'
Incorporated: 2/18/1891
Mayor: Jerry Woodfin

Butte Falls
County: Jackson
Address: PO Box 268, 431 Broad St., 97522
Phone: 541-865-3262
Fax: 541-865-3777
Email: bfcityhall@gmail.com
Elevation: 2,536'
Incorporated: 8/21/1911
Mayor: Trish Callahan

Canby
County: Clackamas
Address: PO Box 930, 222 NE 2nd Ave., 97013
Phone: 503-266-4021
Fax: 503-266-7961
Web: canbyoregon.gov
Elevation: 154'
Incorporated: 2/15/1893
Mayor: Brian Hodson

Cannon Beach
County: Clatsop
Address: PO Box 368, 163 E Gower St., 97110
Phone: 503-436-1581
Fax: 503-436-2050
Web: ci.cannon-beach.or.us
Elevation: 30'

Incorporated: 3/5/1957
Mayor: Barbara Knop

*Canyon City
County: Grant
Address: PO Box 276, 123 S Washington St., 97820
Phone: 541-575-0509
Fax: 541-575-0515
Email: tocc1862@centurylink.net
Elevation: 3,194'
Incorporated: 10/19/1864
Mayor: Steve Fischer

Canyonville
County: Douglas
Address: PO Box 765, 250 N Main, 97417
Phone: 541-839-4258
Fax: 541-839-4680
Web: cityofcanyonville.com
Elevation: 766'
Incorporated: 1/29/1901
Mayor: Christine Morgan

Carlton
County: Yamhill
Address: 191 E Main St., 97111
Phone: 503-852-7575
Fax: 503-852-7761
Web: ci.carlton.or.us
Elevation: 198'
Incorporated: 2/17/1899
Mayor: Linda Watkins

Cascade Locks
County: Hood River
Address: PO Box 308, 140 SW WaNaPa St., 97014
Phone: 541-374-8484
Fax: 541-374-8752
Web: cascade-locks.or.us
Elevation: 170'
Incorporated: 6/19/1935
Mayor: Cathy Fallon

Cave Junction
County: Josephine
Address: PO Box 1396, 222 W Lister St., 97523
Phone: 541-592-2156
Fax: 541-592-6694
Web: cavejunctionoregon.us
Elevation: 1,575'
Incorporated: 9/23/1946
Mayor: Meadow Martell

Central Point
County: Jackson
Address: 140 S Third St., 97502
Phone: 541-664-3321 ext. 231
Fax: 541-664-6384
Web: centralpointoregon.gov
Elevation: 1,272'
Incorporated: 2/25/1889
Mayor: Henry "Hank" Williams

Chiloquin
County: Klamath
Address: PO Box 196, 127 S Second Ave., 97624
Phone: 541-783-2717
Fax: 541-783-2035
Email: chiloquin@centurylink.net
Elevation: 4,180'
Incorporated: 3/3/1926
Mayor: Julie Bettles

Clatskanie
County: Columbia
Address: PO Box 9, 75 S Nehalem St., 97016
Phone: 503-728-2622
Fax: 503-728-3297
Web: cityofclatskanie.com
Elevation: 45'
Incorporated: 2/18/1891
Mayor: Robert "Bob" Brajcich

Coburg
County: Lane
Address: PO Box 8316, 91136 N Willamette St., 97408
Phone: 541-682-7850
Web: coburgoregon.org
Elevation: 398'
Incorporated: 2/10/1893
Mayor: Nancy Bell

Columbia City
County: Columbia
Address: PO Box 189, 1840 Second St., 97018
Phone: 503-397-4010
Fax: 503-366-2870
Web: columbia-city.org
Elevation: 75'
Incorporated: 6/7/1926
Mayor: Susan Ziglinkski

*Condon
County: Gilliam
Address: PO Box 445, 128 S Main St., 97823
Phone: 541-384-2711
Fax: 541-384-2700
Web: cityofcondon.com
Elevation: 2,831'
Incorporated: 2/10/1893
Mayor: Jim Hassing

Coos Bay
County: Coos
Address: 500 Central Ave., 97420
Phone: 541-269-1181
Fax: 541-267-5912
Web: coosbay.org
Elevation: 10'
Incorporated: 10/24/1874
Mayor: Joe Benetti

*Coquille
County: Coos
Address: 851 N Central Blvd., 97423
Phone: 541-396-2115
Fax: 541-396-5125

Web: cityofcoquille.org
Elevation: 40'
Incorporated: 2/25/1885
Mayor: Sam Flaherty

Cornelius
County: Washington
Address: 1355 N Barlow St., 97113
Phone: 503-357-9112
Fax: 503-357-7775
Web: ci.cornelius.or.us
Elevation: 179'
Incorporated: 2/10/1893
Mayor: Jeffrey C. Dalin

*Corvallis
County: Benton
Address: PO Box 1083, 97339, 501 SW Madison Ave., 97333
Phone: 541-766-6900
Fax: 541-766-6946
Web: corvallisoregon.gov
Elevation: 230'
Incorporated: 1/28/1857
Mayor: Charles Maughan

Cottage Grove
County: Lane
Address: 400 E Main St., 97424
Phone: 541-942-5501
Fax: 541-942-1267
Web: cottagegroveor.org
Elevation: 640'
Incorporated: 2/11/1887
Mayor: Candace Lamb Solesbee

Cove
County: Union
Address: PO Box 8, 504 Alder St., 97824
Phone: 541-568-4566
Fax: 541-568-7747
Web: cityofcove.org
Elevation: 2,870'
Incorporated: 3/10/1904
Mayor: Sherry Haeger

Creswell
County: Lane
Address: PO Box 276, 13 South 1st St., 97426
Phone: 541-895-2531
Fax: 541-895-3647
Web: ci.creswell.or.us
Elevation: 542'
Incorporated: 7/16/1909
Mayor: Dave Stram

Culver
County: Jefferson
Address: PO Box 368, 200 First Ave., 97734
Phone: 541-546-6494
Fax: 541-546-3624
Web: cityofculver.net
Elevation: 2,640'
Incorporated: 6/27/1946
Mayor: Bart Carpenter

*Dallas
County: Polk
Address: 187 SE Court St., 97338
Phone: 503-623-2338
Fax: 503-623-2339
Web: dallasor.gov
Elevation: 325'
Incorporated: 2/20/1874
Mayor: Kenneth Woods, Jr.

Dayton
County: Yamhill
Address: PO Box 339, 416 Ferry St., 97114
Phone: 503-864-2221
Fax: 503-864-2956
Web ci.dayton.or.us
Elevation: 280'
Incorporated: 10/15/1880
Mayor: Trini Marquez

Dayville
County: Grant
Address: PO Box 321, 3 Park Ln., 97825
Phone: 541-987-2188
Fax:: 541-987-2187
Email: dville@ortelco.net
Elevation: 2,369'
Incorporated: 10/25/1913
Mayor: Valli Hettinga

Depoe Bay
County: Lincoln
Address: PO Box 8, 570 SE Shell Ave., 97341
Phone: 541-765-2361
Fax: 541-765-2129
Web: cityofdepoebay.org
Elevation: 56'
Incorporated: 12/14/1973
Mayor: Kathy M. Short

Detroit
County: Marion
Address: PO Box 589, 345 Santiam Ave., 97342
Phone: 503-854-3496
Fax: 503-769-2947
Web: detroitoregon.us
Elevation: 1,595'
Incorporated: 9/29/1952
Mayor: James R. Trett

Donald
County: Marion
Address: PO Box 388, 10710 Main St. NE, 97020
Phone: 503-678-5543
Fax: 503-678-2750
Web: donaldoregon.gov
Elevation: 198'
Incorporated: 12/6/1912
Mayor: Rick Olmsted

Drain
County: Douglas
Address: PO Box 158, 431 Payton Ave., 97435
Phone: 541-836-2417
Fax: 541-836-7330

Web: cityofdrain.org
Elevation: 303'
Incorporated: 2/9/1887
Mayor: Erin Sparhawk

The historic Balch Hotel in Dufur preserves the charms of another era. (Oregon State Archives scenic photo)

Dufur
County: Wasco
Address: PO Box 145, 175 NE Third St., 97021
Phone: 541-467-2349
Fax: 541-467-2353
Web: cityofdufur.org
Elevation: 1,345'
Incorporated: 2/10/1893
Mayor: Merle Keys

Dundee
County: Yamhill
Address: PO Box 220, 620 SW Fifth St., 97115
Phone: 503-538-3922
Fax: 503-538-1958
Web: dundeecity.org
Elevation: 189'
Incorporated: 2/21/1895
Mayor: David Russ

Dunes City
County: Lane
Address: PO Box 97, Westlake, 82877 Spruce St., 97493
Phone: 541-997-3338
Fax: 541-997-5751
Web: duneecityhall.com
Elevation: 39'
Incorporated: 6/13/1963
Mayor: Sheldon Meyer

Durham
County: Washington
Address: 17160 SW Upper Boones Ferry Rd., 97224
Phone: 503-639-6851
Fax: 503-598-8595
Elevation: 197'
Incorporated: 7/20/1966
Mayor: Gery Schirado

Eagle Point
County: Jackson
Address: PO Box 779, 17 Buchanan Ave., 97524
Phone: 541-826-4212

Fax: 541-826-6155
Web: cityofeaglepoint.org
Elevation: 1,310'
Incorporated: 2/16/1911
Mayor: Kathy Sell

Echo
County: Umatilla
Address: PO Box 9, 20 S Bonanza St., 97826
Phone: 541-376-6038
Fax: 541-376-6040
Web: echo-oregon.com
Elevation: 635'
Incorporated: 3/9/1904
Mayor: Chad Ray

Elgin
County: Union
Address: PO Box 128, 790 S Eighth Ave., 97827
Phone: 541-437-2253
Fax: 541-437-0131
Web: cityofelginor.org
Elevation: 2,670'
Incorporated: 2/18/1891
Mayor: S. James Johnson

Elkton
County: Douglas
Address: PO Box 508, 366 First St., 97436
Phone: 541-584-2547
Fax: 541-584-2547
Web: elkton-oregon.com
Elevation: 132'
Incorporated: 11/4/1948
Mayor: Daniel Burke

*Enterprise
County: Wallowa
Address: 102 E North St., 97828
Phone: 541-426-4196
Fax: 541-426-3395
Web: enterpriseoregon.org
Elevation: 3,757'
Incorporated: 2/21/1889
Mayor: Ashley Sullivan

Estacada
County: Clackamas
Address: PO Box 958, 475 SE Main St., 97023
Phone: 503-630-8270
Fax: 503-630-8280
Web: cityofestacada.org
Elevation: 468'
Incorporated: 1/31/1905
Mayor: Sean Drinkwine

*Eugene
County: Lane
Address: 101 West 10th, Ave. Suite 203, 97401
Phone: 541-682-5010
Fax: 541-682-5414
Web: eugene-or.gov
Elevation: 430'
Incorporated: 10/17/1862 or 10/22/1864
Mayor: Lucy Vinis

Fairview
County: Multnomah
Address: PO Box 337, 1300 NE Village St., 97024
Phone: 503-665-7929
Fax: 503-666-0888
Web: fairvieworegon.gov
Elevation: 114'
Incorporated: 5/11/1908
Mayor: Brian Cooper

Falls City
County: Polk
Address: 299 Mill St., 97344
Phone: 503-787-3631
Fax: 503-787-3023
Web: fallscityoregon.gov
Elevation: 370'
Incorporated: 2/13/1893
Mayor: TJ Bailey

Florence
County: Lane
Address: 250 Hwy. 101, 97439
Phone: 541-997-3436
Fax: 541-997-6814
Web: ci.florence.or.us
Elevation: 14'
Incorporated: 2/10/1893
Mayor: Rob Ward

Forest Grove
County: Washington
Address: PO Box 326, 1924 Council St., 97116
Phone: 503-992-3200
Fax: 503-992-3207
Web: forestgrove-or.gov
Elevation: 210'
Incorporated: 10/5/1872
Mayor: Malynda Wenzl

*Fossil
County: Wheeler
Address: PO Box 467, 401 Main St., 97830
Phone: 541-763-2698
Fax: 541-763-2124
Web: cityoffossil.com
Elevation: 2,673'
Incorporated: 2/18/1891
Mayor: Terri Hunt

Garibaldi
County: Tillamook
Address: PO Box 708, 107 Sixth St., 97118
Phone: 503-322-3327
Fax: 503-322-3737
Web: ci.garibaldi.or.us
Elevation: 22'
Incorporated: 4/8/1946
Mayor: Tim Hall

Gaston
County: Washington
Address: PO Box 129, 116 Front St., 97119
Phone: 503-985-3340
Fax: 503-985-1014
Email: gaston.city@comcast.net

Elevation: 300'
Incorporated: 12/7/1911
Mayor: David Meeker

Gates
County: Marion
Address: 101 Sorbin Ave. W, 97346
Phone: 503-897-2669
Fax: 503-897-6068
Email: ctygtes@wbcable.net
Elevation: 945'
Incorporated: 7/7/1955
Mayor: Brian Gander

Gearhart
County: Clatsop
Address: PO Box 2510, 698 Pacific Way, 97138
Phone: 503-738-5501
Fax: 503-738-9385
Web: cityofgearhart.com
Elevation: 16'
Incorporated: 1/28/1918
Mayor: Kerry Smith

Gervais
County: Marion
Address: PO Box 329, 592 Fourth St., 97026
Phone: 503-792-4900
Fax: 503-792-3791
Web: gervaisoregon.org
Elevation: 184'
Incorporated: 10/29/1874
Mayor: Andrea "Annie" Gilland

Gladstone
County: Clackamas
Address: 18505 Portland Ave., 97027
Phone: 503-656-5225
Fax: 503-557-2761
Web ci.gladstone.or.us
Elevation: 61'
Incorporated: 1/5/1911
Mayor: Michael Milch

Glendale
County: Douglas
Address: PO Box 361, 124 Third St., 97442
Phone: 541-832-2106
Fax: 541-832-3221
Web: cityofglendaleor.com
Elevation: 1,443'
Incorporated: 2/23/1901
Mayor: Crystal Martin

*Gold Beach
County: Curry
Address: 29592 Ellensburg Ave., 97444
Phone: 541-247-7029
Fax: 541-247-2212
Web: goldbeachoregon.gov
Elevation: 50'
Incorporated: 9/24/1945
Mayor: Tamie Kaufman

Gold Hill
County: Jackson

Address: PO Box 308, 420 Sixth Ave., 97525
Phone: 541-855-1525
Fax: 541-855-4501
Web: ci.goldhill.or.us
Elevation: 1,085'
Incorporated: 2/12/1895
Mayor: Ronald Palmer

Granite
County: Grant
Address: 1378 Main St., 97877
Phone: 541-755-5100
Fax: 541-755-5100
Email: granitecity@pinetel.com
Elevation: 4,695'
Incorporated: 5/17/1900
Mayor: Dorothy Jewell

*Grants Pass
County: Josephine
Address: 101 NW A St., 97526
Phone: 541-450-6000
Fax: 541-479-0812
Web: grantspassoregon.gov
Elevation: 960'
Incorporated: 2/18/1891
Mayor: Sara Bristol

Grass Valley
County: Sherman
Address: PO Box 191, 97029
Phone: 541-333-2434
Fax: 541-333-2276
Email: cityofgv@embarqmail.com
Elevation: 2,275'
Incorporated: 10/8/1900
Mayor: Meinrad Kuettel

Greenhorn
County: Baker
Email: dkadvisoryservicesllc@gmail.com
Elevation: 6,300'
Incorporated: 2/20/1903
Mayor: Dennis Koellermeier

Gresham
County: Multnomah
Address: 1333 NW Eastman Pkwy., 97030
Phone: 503-661-3000
Fax: 503-618-3301
Web: greshamoregon.gov
Elevation: 301'
Incorporated: 6/3/1904
Mayor: Travis Stovall

Haines
County: Baker
Address: PO Box 208, 819 Front St., 97833
Phone: 541-856-3366
Fax: 541-856-3812
Web: cityofhainesor.org
Elevation: 3,341'
Incorporated: 3/11/1902
Mayor: Dennis Anthony

The historic Morrow County Courthouse in Heppner was built in 1903. (Oregon State Archives scenic photo)

Halfway
County: Baker
Address: PO Box 738, 97834
Phone: 541-742-4741
Fax: 541-742-4741
Email: halfwaycity@gmail.com
Elevation: 2,651'
Incorporated: 5/27/1909
Mayor: Nora Aspy

Halsey
County: Linn
Address: PO Box 10, 100 W Halsey St., 97348
Phone: 541-369-2522
Fax: 541-369-2521
Web: cityofhalsey.com
Elevation: 213'
Incorporated: 10/20/1876
Mayor: Jerry Lachenbruch

Happy Valley
County: Clackamas
Address: 16000 SE Misty Dr., 97086-6299
Phone: 503-783-3800
Fax: 503-658-5174
Web: happyvalleyor.gov
Elevation: 377'
Incorporated: 12/4/1965
Mayor: Tom Ellis

Harrisburg
County: Linn
Address: PO Box 378, 120 Smith St., 97446
Phone: 541-995-6655
Fax: 541-995-9244
Web: ci.harrisburg.or.us
Elevation: 309'
Incorporated: 10/24/1866
Mayor: Robert "Bobby" Duncan

Helix
County: Umatilla
Address: PO Box 323, 120 Columbia, 97835
Phone: 541-457-2521
Email: cityofhelix@gmail.com
Elevation: 1,754'
Incorporated: 1/9/1903
Mayor: Kim Herron

*Heppner
County: Morrow
Address: PO Box 756, 111 N Main St., 97836
Phone: 541-676-9618
Fax: 541-676-9650
Web: cityofheppner.com
Elevation: 2,192'
Incorporated: 2/9/1887
Mayor: Corey Sweeney

Hermiston
County: Umatilla
Address: 235 E Gladys Ave., 97838
Phone: 541-567-5521
Fax: 541-567-5530
Web: hermiston.or.us
Elevation: 643'
Incorporated: 7/23/1907
Mayor: Dr. David A. Drotzmann

*Hillsboro
County: Washington
Address: 150 E Main St., 97123
Phone: 503-681-6100
Fax: 503-681-6213
Web: hillsboro-oregon.gov
Elevation: 196'
Incorporated: 10/19/1876
Mayor: Steve Callaway

Hines
County: Harney
Address: PO Box 336, 101 E Barnes Ave., 97738
Phone: 541-573-2251 or 541-573-2244
Fax: 541-573-5827
Web: ci.hines.or.us
Elevation: 4,155'
Incorporated: 12/13/1930
Mayor: Nikki Morgan

*Hood River
County: Hood River
Address: PO Box 1842, 211 Second St., 97031
Phone: 541-386-1488
Fax: 541-387-5289
Web: ci.hood-river.or.us
Elevation: 160'
Incorporated: 2/15/1895
Mayor: Paul Blackburn

Hubbard
County: Marion
Address: PO Box 380, 3720 Second St., 97032
Phone: 503-981-9633
Fax: 503-981-8743
Web: cityofhubbard.org
Elevation: 181'
Incorporated: 2/18/1891
Mayor: Jim Yonally

Huntington
County: Baker
Address: PO Box 369, 50 E Adams, 97907
Phone: 541-869-2202
Fax: 541-869-2550
Email: Huntingtoncityof@gmail.com

Elevation: 2,110'
Incorporated: 2/18/1891
Mayor: Natalie Van Cleave

Idanha
County: Linn/Marion
Address: PO Box 430, 111 Hwy. 22 NW, 97350
Phone: 503-854-3313
Fax: 503-854-3114
Email: cityofid@bmi.net
Elevation: 1,718'
Incorporated: 3/15/1950
Mayor: Robert Weikum

Imbler
County: Union
Address: PO Box 40, 180 Ruckman Ave., 97841
Phone: 541-534-6095
Fax: 541-534-2343
Email: imblercity@oregonwireless.net
Elevation: 2,725'
Incorporated: 3/20/1922
Mayor: Jason M.L. Berglund, Sr.

Independence
County: Polk
Address: PO Box 7, 555 S Main St., 97351
Phone: 503-838-1212
Fax: 503-606-3282
Web: ci.independence.or.us
Elevation: 168'
Incorporated: 10/20/1874
Mayor: John McArdle

A Riverview Park fountain in Independence on the Willamette River. (Oregon State Archives scenic photo)

Ione
County: Morrow
Address: PO Box 361, 385 W Second St., 97843
Phone: 541-422-7414
Fax: 541-422-7179
Elevation: 1,089'
Incorporated: 7/14/1899
Mayor: Michael Skow

Irrigon
County: Morrow
Address: PO Box 428, 500 NE Main St., 97844
Phone: 541-922-3047
Fax: 541-922-9322

Web: ci.irrigon.or.us
Elevation: 297'
Incorporated: 2/28/1957
Mayor: Margaret Anderson

Island City
County: Union
Address: 10605 Island Ave., 97850
Phone: 541-963-5017
Fax: 541-963-3482
Web: islandcityoregon.com
Elevation: 2,743'
Incorporated: 2/12/1904
Mayor: Dave Comfort

Jacksonville
County: Jackson
Address: PO Box 7, 206 N Fifth St., 97530
Phone: 541-899-1231
Fax: 541-899-7882
Web: jacksonvilleor.us
Elevation: 1,569'
Incorporated: 10/19/1860
Mayor: Donna Bowen

Jefferson
County: Marion
Address: PO Box 83, 150 N Second St., 97352
Phone: 541-327-2768
Fax: 541-327-3120
Web: jeffersonoregon.org
Elevation: 240'
Incorporated: 10/29/1870
Mayor: Michael Myers

John Day
County: Grant
Address: 450 E Main St., 97845
Phone: 541-575-0028
Fax: 541-575-3668
Web: cityofjohnday.com
Elevation: 3,087'
Incorporated: 5/9/1900
Mayor: Heather Rookstool

Johnson City
County: Clackamas
Address: 16120 SE 81st Ave., 97267
Phone: 503-655-9710
Fax: 503-723-0317
Email: johnson.city@hotmail.com
Elevation: 114'
Incorporated: 6/23/1970
Mayor: Vincent O. Whitehead, Jr., Mayor Pro Tempore

Jordan Valley
County: Malheur
Address: PO Box 187, 306 Blackaby St., 97910
Phone: 541-586-2460
Fax: 541-586-2460
Web: cityofjordanvalley.com
Elevation: 4,389'
Incorporated: 3/21/1911
Mayor: Lee Ann Conro

Joseph
County: Wallowa
Address: PO Box 15, 201 N Main St., 97846
Phone: 541-432-3832
Fax: 541-432-3833
Web: josephoregon.org
Elevation: 4,200'
Incorporated: 2/9/1887
Mayor: Lisa Collier

Junction City
County: Lane
Address: PO Box 250, 680 Greenwood St., 97448
Phone: 541-998-2153
Fax: 541-998-3140
Web: junctioncityoregon.gov
Elevation: 325'
Incorporated: 10/29/1872
Mayor: Ken Wells

Keizer
County: Marion
Address: PO Box 21000, 930 Chemawa Rd. NE, 97303
Phone: 503-390-3700
Fax: 503-393-9437
Web: keizer.org
Elevation: 132'
Incorporated: 11/16/1982
Mayor: Cathy Clark

King City
County: Washington
Address: 15300 SW 116th Ave., 97224-2693
Phone: 503-639-4082
Fax: 503-639-3771
Web: ci.king-city.or.us
Elevation: 213'
Incorporated: 7/14/1966
Mayor: Jaimie Fender

*Klamath Falls
County: Klamath
Address: PO Box 237, 500 Klamath Ave., 97601
Phone: 541-883-5316
Fax: 541-883-5399
Web: klamathfalls.city
Elevation: 4,099'
Incorporated: 2/6/1893
Mayor: Carol Westfall

*La Grande
County: Union
Address: PO Box 670, 1000 Adams Ave., 97850
Phone: 541-962-1309
Fax: 541-963-3333
Web: cityoflagrande.org
Elevation: 2,785'
Incorporated: 12/18/1865
Mayor: Justin Rock

La Pine
County: Deschutes
Address: PO Box 2460, 16345 Sixth St., 97739

Phone: 541-536-1432
Fax: 541-536-1462
Web: lapineoregon.gov
Elevation: 4,236'
Incorporated: 12/11/2006
Mayor: Daniel L. Richer

Lafayette
County: Yamhill
Address: PO Box 55, 486 Third St., 97127
Phone: 503-864-2451
Fax: 503-864-4501
Web: ci.lafayette.or.us
Elevation: 160'
Incorporated: 10/17/1878
Mayor: Hilary Malcomson

Lake Oswego
County: Clackamas
Address: PO Box 369, 380 A Ave., 97034
Phone: 503-635-0270
Fax: 503-635-0269
Web: ci.oswego.or.us
Elevation: 146'
Incorporated: 1/15/1910
Mayor: Joe Buck

Lakeside
County: Coos
Address: PO Box L, 915 North Lake Rd., 97449
Phone: 541-759-3011
Fax: 541-759-3711
Web: cityoflakeside.org
Elevation: 23'
Incorporated: 6/26/1974
Mayor: Sherry Kinsey

*Lakeview
County: Lake
Address: 525 N First St., 97630
Phone: 541-947-2020
Fax: 541-947-2952
Web: townoflakeview.org
Elevation: 4,802'
Incorporated: 2/10/1893
Mayor: Ray Turner

Lebanon
County: Linn
Address: 925 S Main St., 97355
Phone: 541-258-4900
Fax: 541-258-4950
Web: ci.lebanon.or.us
Elevation: 351'
Incorporated: 10/17/1878
Mayor: Kenneth Jackola

Lexington
County: Morrow
Address: PO Box 416, 425 F St., 97839
Phone: 541-989-8515
Fax: 541-989-8515
Web: lexingtonor.com
Elevation: 1,450'
Incorporated: 2/3/1903
Mayor: Juli Kennedy

Lincoln City
County: Lincoln
Address: PO Box 50, 801 SW Hwy. 101, 97367
Phone: 541-996-2152
Fax: 541-994-7232
Web: lincolncity.org
Elevation: 11'
Incorporated: 2/24/1965
Mayor: Susan Wahlke

Lonerock
County: Gilliam
Address: Lonerock Rte., 104 SE Main St., Condon 97823
Phone: 541-384-2241
Email: lonerock@reagan.com
Elevation: 2,800'
Incorporated: 2/20/1901
Mayor: Shannon Hill

Long Creek
County: Grant
Address: PO Box 489, 250 Hardisty St., 97856
Phone: 541-421-3601
Fax: 541-421-3075
Web: cityoflongcreek.com
Elevation: 3,754'
Incorporated: 2/18/1891
Mayor: Don Porter

Lostine
County: Wallowa
Address: PO Box 181, 128 Hwy 182, 97857
Phone: 541-569-2415
Web: cityoflostine.com
Elevation: 3,200'
Incorporated: 12/28/1903
Mayor: Dusty Tippet

Lowell
County: Lane
Address: PO Box 490, 107 E Third St., 97452
Phone: 541-937-2157
Fax: 541-937-2936
Web: ci.lowell.or.us
Elevation: 742'
Incorporated: 11/24/1954
Mayor: Don Bennett

Lyons
County: Linn
Address: 449 Fifth St., 97358
Phone: 503-859-2167
Fax: 503-859-5167
Web: cityoflyons.org
Elevation: 660'
Incorporated: 12/17/1958
Mayor: Lloyd R. Valentine, Jr.

*Madras
County: Jefferson
Address: 125 SW E St., 97741
Phone: 541-475-2344
Fax: 541-475-7061
Web: ci.madras.or.us
Elevation: 2,242'

Incorporated: 3/29/1910
Mayor: Mike Lepin

Malin
County: Klamath
Address: PO Box 61, 2432 Fourth St., 97632
Phone: 541-723-2021
Fax: 541-723-2011
Web: cityofmalin.org
Elevation: 4,062'
Incorporated: 2/22/1922
Mayor: John Hughto

Manzanita
County: Tillamook
Address: PO Box 129, 167 S 5th Street, 97130
Phone: 503-812-2514
Web: ci.manzanita.or.us
Elevation: 78'
Incorporated: 4/15/1946
Mayor: Deb Simmons

Maupin
County: Wasco
Address: PO Box 308, 408 Deschutes Ave., 97037
Phone: 541-395-2698
Fax: 541-395-2499
Web: cityofmaupin.org
Elevation: 1,047'
Incorporated: 4/17/1922
Mayor: Carol Beatty

Maywood Park
County: Multnomah
Address: 10100 NE Prescott St., Suite 147, Portland 97220
Phone: 503-255-9805
Web: cityofmaywoodpark.com
Elevation: 77'
Incorporated: 10/25/1967
Mayor: Michelle Montross

*McMinnville
County: Yamhill
Address: 230 NE Second St., 97128
Phone: 503-434-7302
Fax: 503-472-4104
Web: mcminnvilleoregon.gov
Elevation: 157'
Incorporated: 10/20/1876
Mayor: Remy Drabkin

*Medford
County: Jackson
Address: 411 W Eighth St., Suite 310, 97501
Phone: 541-774-2000
Fax: 541-618-1700
Web: medfordoregon.gov
Elevation: 1,382'
Incorporated: 2/24/1885
Mayor: Randy Sparacino

Merrill
County: Klamath
Address: PO Box 487, 301 E Second St., 97633
Phone: 541-798-5808

Fax: 541-798-0145
Web: cityofmerrill.org
Elevation: 4,071'
Incorporated: 7/16/1908
Mayor: Joanne Johnson, Mayor Pro Tempore

Metolius
County: Jefferson
Address: 636 Jefferson Ave., 97741
Phone: 541-546-5533
Fax: 541-546-8809
Web: cityofmetolius.org
Elevation: 2,530'
Incorporated: 12/16/1912
Mayor: Patty Wyler

Mill City
County: Linn/Marion
Address: PO Box 256, 444 S First Ave., 97360
Phone: 503-897-2302
Fax: 503-897-3499
Web: ci.mill-city.or.us
Elevation: 862'
Incorporated: 10/15/1947
Mayor: Tim Kirsch

Millersburg
County: Linn
Address: 4222 NE Old Salem Rd., Albany 97321
Phone: 541-928-4523 or 458-233-6300
Fax: 541-928-8945
Web: cityofmillersburg.org
Elevation: 235'
Incorporated: 11/4/1974
Mayor: Scott Cowan

The Milwaukie Masonic Lodge in Milwaukie was constructed in 1925. (Oregon State Archives scenic photo)

Milton-Freewater
County: Umatilla
Address: PO Box 6, 722 S Main St., 97862
Phone: 541-938-5531
Fax: 541-938-8224
Web: mfcity.com
Elevation: 1,071'
Incorporated: 12/4/1950
Mayor: Lewis S. Key

Milwaukie
County: Clackamas
Address: 10722 SE Main St., 97222
Phone: 503-786-7555
Web: milwaukieoregon.gov
Elevation: 50'
Incorporated: 2/4/1903
Mayor: Lisa Batey

Mitchell
County: Wheeler
Address: PO Box 97, 97750
Phone: 541-462-3121
Fax: 541-462-3121
Web: mitchelloregon.us
Elevation: 2,894'
Incorporated: 2/18/1891
Mayor: Steven Tripp

Molalla
County: Clackamas
Address: PO Box 248, 117 N Molalla Ave., 97038
Phone: 503-829-6855
Fax: 503-829-3676
Web: cityofmolalla.com
Elevation: 375'
Incorporated: 8/23/1913
Mayor: Scott Keyser

Monmouth
County: Polk
Address: 151 W Main St., 97361
Phone: 503-838-0722
Fax: 503-838-0725
Web: ci.monmouth.or.us
Elevation: 214'
Incorporated: 10/19/1880
Mayor: Cecelia Koontz

Monroe
County: Benton
Address: PO Box 486, 664 Commercial St., 97456
Phone: 541-847-5175
Fax: 541-847-5177
Web: ci.monroe.or.us
Elevation: 298'
Incorporated: 5/16/1913
Mayor: Daniel Sheets

Monument
County: Grant
Address: PO Box 426, 291 Main St., 97864
Phone: 541-934-2025
Fax: 541-934-2025
Email: cityofmonument@centurytel.net
Elevation: 2,000'
Incorporated: 3/6/1905
Mayor: Sahara Hyder

*Moro
County: Sherman
Address: PO Box 231, 97039
Phone: 541-565-3535
Fax: 541-565-3535

Local Governments

Web: cityofmoro.net
Elevation: 1,870'
Incorporated: 2/17/1899
Mayor: Bert Perisho

Mosier
County: Wasco
Address: PO Box 456, 208 Washington St., 97040
Phone: 541-478-3505
Fax: 541-478-3810
Web: cityofmosier.com
Elevation: 164'
Incorporated: 10/14/1914
Mayor: Witt Anderson

Mount Angel
County: Marion
Address: PO Box 960, 5 N Garfield St., 97362
Phone: 503-845-9291
Fax: 503-845-6261
Web: ci.mt-angel.or.us
Elevation: 168'
Incorporated: 2/10/1893
Mayor: Pete Wall

Mount Vernon
County: Grant
Address: PO Box 647, 290 W Main St., 97865
Phone: 541-932-4688
Fax: 541-932-4222
Email: cmtv@ortelco.net
Elevation: 2,865'
Incorporated: 5/13/1949
Mayor: Kenny Delano

An antique car in downtown Myrtle Creek. (Oregon State Archives scenic photo)

Myrtle Creek
County: Douglas
Address: PO Box 940, 207 NW Pleasant St., 97457
Phone: 541-863-3171
Fax: 541-863-6851
Web: cityofmyrtlecreek.com
Elevation: 650'
Incorporated: 2/13/1893
Mayor: Matthew Hald

Myrtle Point
County: Coos
Address: 424 Fifth St., 97458
Phone: 541-572-2626
Fax: 541-572-3838
Web: ci.myrtlepoint.or.us
Elevation: 131'
Incorporated: 2/4/1887
Mayor: Samantha Clayburn

Nehalem
County: Tillamook
Address: PO Box 143, 35900 Eighth St., 97131
Phone: 503-368-5627
Fax: 503-368-4175
Web: ci.nehalem.or.us
Elevation: 11'
Incorporated: 2/2/1899
Mayor: Phil Chick

Newberg
County: Yamhill
Address: PO Box 970, 414 E First St., 97132
Phone: 503-538-9421
Fax: 503-537-5013
Web: newbergoregon.gov
Elevation: 175'
Incorporated: 2/21/1889
Mayor: Bill Rosacker

*Newport
County: Lincoln
Address: 169 SW Coast Hwy., 97365
Phone: 541-574-0603
Fax: 541-574-0609
Web: newportoregon.gov
Elevation: 134'
Incorporated: 10/23/1882
Mayor: Dean H. Sawyer

North Bend
County: Coos
Address: PO Box B, 835 California St., 97459
Phone: 541-756-8500
Fax: 541-756-8527
Web: northbendoregon.us
Elevation: 41'
Incorporated: 7/6/1903
Mayor: Jessica Engelke

North Plains
County: Washington
Address: 31360 NW Commercial St., 97133
Phone: 503-647-5555
Fax: 503-647-2031
Web: northplains.org
Elevation: 176'
Incorporated: 10/1/1963
Mayor: Teri Lenahan

North Powder
County: Union
Address: PO Box 309, 635 Third St., 97867
Phone: 541-898-2185
Fax: 541-898-2647
Email: cityofnp@eoni.com

Elevation: 3,256'
Incorporated: 7/28/1902
Mayor: John Frieboes

Nyssa
County: Malheur
Address: 301 Main St., 97913
Phone: 541-372-2264
Fax: 541-372-3737
Web: nyssacity.org
Elevation: 2,192'
Incorporated: 2/24/1903
Mayor: Betty Holcomb

Oakland
County: Douglas
Address: 637 NE Locust St., 97462
Phone: 541-459-4531
Fax: 541-459-4472
Web: oaklandoregon.org
Elevation: 484'
Incorporated: 10/17/1878
Mayor: Bette Keehley

Oakridge
County: Lane
Address: PO Box 1410, 48318 E First St., 97463
Phone: 541-782-2258
Fax: 541-782-1081
Web: ci.oakridge.or.us
Elevation: 1,240'
Incorporated: 1/22/1934
Mayor: Bryan Cutchen

Ontario
County: Malheur
Address: 444 SW Fourth St., 97914
Phone: 541-881-3201
Web: ontariooregon.org
Elevation: 2,150'
Incorporated: 9/9/1896
Mayor: Deborah Folden

*Oregon City
County: Clackamas
Address: 625 Center St., 97045
Phone: 503-657-0891
Fax: 503-657-3339
Web: orcity.org
Elevation: 167'
Incorporated: 12/24/1844
Mayor: Denyse McGriff

Paisley
County: Lake
Address: PO Box 100, 705 Chewaucan St., 97636
Phone: 541-943-3173
Fax: 541-943-3982
Web: cityofpaisley.net
Elevation: 4,369'
Incorporated: 11/18/1911
Mayor: Keith Harra

*Pendleton
County: Umatilla
Address: 500 SW Dorion Ave., 97801
Phone: 541-966-0201
Fax: 541-966-0231
Web: pendleton.or.us
Elevation: 1,200'
Incorporated: 10/25/1880
Mayor: John Turner

Philomath
County: Benton
Address: PO Box 400, 980 Applegate St., 97370
Phone: 541-929-6148
Fax: 541-929-3044
Web: ci.philomath.or.us
Elevation: 270'
Incorporated: 10/20/1882
Mayor: Chas Jones

Phoenix
County: Jackson
Address: PO Box 330, 112 W Second St., 97535
Phone: 541-535-1955
Fax: 541-535-5769
Web: phoenixoregon.gov
Elevation: 1,543'
Incorporated: 10/13/1910
Mayor: Terry Baker

Pilot Rock
County: Umatilla
Address: PO Box 130, 144 N Alder Pl., 97868
Phone: 541-443-2811
Fax: 541-443-2253
Web: cityofpilotrock.org
Elevation: 1,637'
Incorporated: 1/10/1902
Mayor: Randy Gawith

Port Orford
County: Curry
Address: PO Box 310, 555 W 20th St., 97465
Phone: 541-332-3681
Fax: 877-281-5307
Web: portorford.org
Elevation: 59'
Incorporated: 12/21/1911
Mayor: Pat Cox

*Portland
County: Clackamas/Multnomah/Washington
Address: 1221 SW Fourth Ave., Rm. 110, 97204
Phone: 503-823-4000
Fax: 503-823-3050
Web: portlandoregon.gov
Elevation: 77'
Incorporated: 1/23/1851
Mayor: Ted Wheeler

Powers
County: Coos
Address: PO Box 250, 275 Fir St., 97466
Phone: 541-439-3331
Email: admin@cityofpowers.com
Elevation: 286'
Incorporated: 12/26/1945
Mayor: Robert Kohn

Prairie City

County: Grant
Address: PO Box 370, 133 S Bridge St., 97869
Phone: 541-820-3605
Fax: 541-820-3566
Elevation: 3,548'
Incorporated: 2/19/1891
Mayor: Scott Officer

Prescott

County: Columbia
Address: 72742 Blakely St., Rainier 97048
Phone: 503-369-4173
Email: blairmlw@gmail.com
Elevation: 30'
Incorporated: 5/9/1949
Mayor: Laurie Blair

*Prineville

County: Crook
Address: 387 NE Third St., 97754
Phone: 541-447-5627
Fax: 541-447-5628
Web: cityofprineville.com
Elevation: 2,868'
Incorporated: 10/23/1880
Mayor: Jason Beebe

Rainier

County: Columbia
Address: PO Box 100, 106 West B St., 97048
Phone: 503-556-7301
Fax: 503-556-3200
Web: cityofrainier.com
Elevation: 45'
Incorporated: 11/25/1885
Mayor: Jerry Cole

Redmond

County: Deschutes
Address: 411 SW 9th St., 97756
Phone: 541-923-7710
Web: ci.redmond.or.us
Elevation: 3,077'
Incorporated: 7/16/1910
Mayor: Ed Fitch

Reedsport

County: Douglas
Address: 451 Winchester Ave., 97467
Phone: 541-271-360
Fax: 541-271-2809
Web: cityofreedsport.org
Elevation: 36'
Incorporated: 8/6/1919
Mayor: Linda R. McCollum

Richland

County: Baker
Address: PO Box 266, 89 Main St., 97870
Phone: 541-893-6141
Fax: 541-893-6267
Email: richcity@eagletelephone.com
Elevation: 2,231'
Incorporated: 8/8/1902
Mayor: Patrick Lattin

Riddle

County: Douglas
Address: PO Box 143, 647 E First Ave., 97469
Phone: 541-874-2571
Fax: 541-874-2625
Email: coriddle@frontiernet.net
Elevation: 685'
Incorporated: 1/30/1893
Mayor: Debbie Carnes

Rivergrove

County: Clackamas/Washington
Address: PO Box 1104, Lake Oswego 97035
Phone: 503-639-6919
Web: cityofrivergrove.org
Elevation: 140'
Incorporated: 3/11/1971
Mayor: Jeff Williams

Rockaway Beach

County: Tillamook
Address: PO Box 5, 276 S Hwy. 101, 97136
Phone: 503-374-1752
Fax: 503-374-0641
Web: corb.us
Elevation: 17'
Incorporated: 7/14/1943
Mayor: Charles McNeilly

Rogue River

County: Jackson
Address: PO Box 1137, 133 Broadway, 97537
Phone: 541-582-4401
Fax: 541-582-0937
Web: cityofrogueriver.org
Elevation: 1,004'
Incorporated: 10/8/1910
Mayor: Pam VanArsdale

*Roseburg

County: Douglas
Address: 900 SE Douglas Ave., 97470
Phone: 541-492-6700
Web: cityofroseburg.org
Elevation: 475'
Incorporated: 10/26/1868
Mayor: Larry Rich

Rufus

County: Sherman
Address: PO Box 27, 304 W Second St., #100, 97050
Phone: 541-739-2321
Fax: 541-739-8229
Web: rufuscityhall.com
Elevation: 235'
Incorporated: 11/3/1964
Mayor: Austin Evans

*Salem

County: Marion/Polk
Address: 555 Liberty St. SE, 97301
Phone: 503-588-6255
Fax: 503-588-6354
Web: cityofsalem.net
Elevation: 154'

Incorporated: 1/13/1857
Mayor: Chris Hoy

Sandy
County: Clackamas
Address: 39250 Pioneer Blvd., 97055
Phone: 503-668-5533
Fax: 503-668-8714
Web: ci.sandy.or.us
Elevation: 992'
Incorporated: 9/11/1911
Mayor: Stan P. Pulliam

Scappoose
County: Columbia
Address: 33568 E Columbia Ave., 97056
Phone: 503-543-7146
Fax: 503-543-7182
Web: ci.scappoose.or.us
Elevation: 64'
Incorporated: 8/13/1921
Mayor: Joe Backus

Scio
County: Linn
Address: PO Box 37, 38957 NW 1st Ave., 97374
Phone: 503-394-3342
Fax: 503-394-2340
Web: ci.scio.or.us
Elevation: 317'
Incorporated: 10/24/1866
Mayor: Debbie Nuber

Scotts Mills
County: Marion
Address: PO Box 220, 265 Fourth St., 97375
Phone: 503-873-5435
Fax: 503-874-4540
Web: scottsmills.org
Elevation: 426'
Incorporated: 8/2/1916
Mayor: Paul Brakeman

Seaside
County: Clatsop
Address: 989 Broadway, 97138
Phone: 503-738-5511
Fax: 503-738-5514
Web: cityofseaside.us

Buildings overlook Silver Creek in downtown Silverton.
(Oregon State Archives scenic photo)

Elevation: 17'
Incorporated: 2/17/1899
Mayor: Steve Wright

Seneca
County: Grant
Address: PO Box 208, 106 A Ave., 97873
Phone: 541-542-2161
Fax: 877-688-0015
Email: admin@senecaoregon.com
Elevation: 4,690'
Incorporated: 8/6/1970
Mayor: Brad Smith

Shady Cove
County: Jackson
Address: PO Box 1210, 22451 Hwy 62, 97539
Phone: 541-878-2225
Fax: 541-878-2226
Web: shadycove.org
Elevation: 1,406'
Incorporated: 11/8/1972
Mayor: Jon Ball

Shaniko
County: Wasco
Address: PO Box 17, 97057
Phone: 541-489-3447
Elevation: 3,344'
Incorporated: 3/13/1901
Mayor: Donald Treanor

Sheridan
County: Yamhill
Address: 120 SW Mill St., 97378
Phone: 503-843-2347
Fax: 503-843-3661
Web: cityofsheridanor.com
Elevation: 189'
Incorporated: 10/25/1880
Mayor: Marianne Thomson

Sherwood
County: Washington
Address: 22560 SW Pine St., 97140
Phone: 503-625-5522
Fax: 503-625-5524
Web: sherwoodoregon.gov
Elevation: 193'
Incorporated: 2/10/1893
Mayor: Tim Rosener

Siletz
County: Lincoln
Address: PO Box 318, 215 W Buford Ave., 97380
Phone: 541-444-2521
Fax: 541-444-7371
Web: cityofsiletz.org
Elevation: 130'
Incorporated: 3/31/1947
Mayor: Will Worman

Silverton
County: Marion
Address: 306 S Water St., 97381

Phone: 503-873-5321
Fax: 503-873-3210
Web: silverton.or.us
Elevation: 252'
Incorporated: 2/16/1885
Mayor: Jason Freilinger

Sisters
County: Deschutes
Address: PO Box 39, 520 E Cascade Ave., 97759
Phone: 541-549-6022
Fax: 541-549-0561
Web: ci.sisters.or.us
Elevation: 3,182'
Incorporated: 4/9/1946
Mayor: Michael Preedin

Sodaville
County: Linn
Address: 30723 Sodaville Rd., 97355
Phone: 541-258-8882
Fax: 541-258-8882
Web: sodaville.org
Elevation: 492'
Incorporated: 10/25/1880
Mayor: Brian Lewis

Spray
County: Wheeler
Address: PO Box 83, 300 Park Ave., 97874
Phone: 541-468-2069
Fax: 541-468-2044
Web: sprayoregon.us
Elevation: 1,801'
Incorporated: 9/18/1958
Mayor: Arcadius St Laurent

Springfield
County: Lane
Address: 225 Fifth St., 97477
Phone: 541-726-3700
Fax: 541-726-2363
Web: springfield-or.gov
Elevation: 456'
Incorporated: 2/25/1885
Mayor: Sean VanGordon

*St, Helens
County: Columbia
Address: PO Box 278, 265 Strand St., 97051
Phone: 503-397-6272
Fax: 503-397-4016
Web: ci.st-helens.or.us
Elevation: 42'
Incorporated: 2/25/1889
Mayor: Rick Scholl

St. Paul
County: Marion
Address: PO Box 7, 20239 Main St., 97137
Phone: 503-633-4971
Fax: 503-633-4972
Email: stpaulcity@stpaultel.com
Elevation: 169'

Incorporated: 2/16/1901
Mayor: Marty Waldo

Stanfield
County: Umatilla
Address: PO Box 369, 160 S Main St., 97875
Phone: 541-449-3831
Fax: 541-449-1828
Web: cityofstanfield.com
Elevation: 592'
Incorporated: 5/13/1910
Mayor: Susan Whelan

Stayton
County: Marion
Address: 362 N Third Ave., 97383
Phone: 503-769-3425
Fax: 503-769-1456
Web: staytonoregon.gov
Elevation: 452'
Incorporated: 2/13/1901
Mayor: Brian Quigley

Sublimity
County: Marion
Address: PO Box 146, 245 NW Johnson St., 97385
Phone: 503-769-5475
Fax: 503-769-2206
Web: cityofsublimity.org
Elevation: 551'
Incorporated: 2/3/1903
Mayor: James Kingsbury

Summerville
County: Union
Address: 301 Main St., 97876
Phone: 541-534-6701
Email: sherirogers46@gmail.com
Elevation: 2,705'
Incorporated: 11/24/1885
Mayor: Sheri Rogers

The St. Helens Marina on the Columbia River in Saint Helens. (Oregon State Archives scenic photo)

Sumpter
County: Baker
Address: PO Box 68, 240 N Mill St., 97877
Phone: 541-894-2314

Web: cityofsumpteror.com
Elevation: 4,429'
Incorporated: 5/5/1898
Mayor: Linda Wise

Sutherlin
County: Douglas
Address: 126 E Central Ave., 97479
Phone: 541-459-2857
Fax: 541-459-9363
Web: ci.sutherlin.or.us
Elevation: 516'
Incorporated: 5/4/1911
Mayor: Michelle Sumner

Sweet Home
County: Linn
Address: 3225 Main Street, 97386
Phone: 541-367-5128
Fax: 541-367-5113
Web: sweethomeor.gov
Elevation: 537'
Incorporated: 2/10/1893
Mayor: Susan Coleman

Talent
County: Jackson
Address: PO Box 445, 110 E Main St., 97540
Phone: 541-535-1566
Fax: 541-535-7423
Web: cityoftalent.org
Elevation: 1,635'
Incorporated: 11/25/1910
Mayor: Darby Ayers-Flood

Tangent
County: Linn
Address: PO Box 251, 32166 Old Oak Dr., 97389
Phone: 541-928-1020
Fax: 541-928-4920
Web: cityoftangent.org
Elevation: 245'
Incorporated: 2/10/1893
Mayor: Loel E. Trulove, Jr.

*The Dalles
County: Wasco
Address: 313 Court St., 97058
Phone: 541-296-5481
Fax: 541-296-6906
Web: thedalles.org
Elevation: 109'
Incorporated: 1/26/1857
Mayor: Rich Mays

Tigard
County: Washington
Address: 13125 SW Hall Blvd., 97223
Phone: 503-639-4171
Fax: 503-684-7297
Web: tigard-or.gov
Elevation: 300'
Incorporated: 10/3/1961
Mayor: Heidi Lueb

*Tillamook
County: Tillamook
Address: 210 Laurel Ave., 97141
Phone: 503-842-2472
Fax: 503-842-3445
Web: tillamookor.gov
Elevation: 24'
Incorporated: 2/18/1891
Mayor: Aaron Burris

Toledo
County: Lincoln
Address: PO Box 220, 206 N Main St., 97391
Phone: 541-336-2247
Fax: 541-363-0362
Web: cityoftoledo.org
Elevation: 59'
Incorporated: 10/11/1893
Mayor: Rod Cross

Troutdale
County: Multnomah
Address: 219 E Historic Columbia River Hwy., 97060
Phone: 503-665-5175
Fax: 503-667-6403
Web: troutdaleoregon.gov
Elevation: 30'–200'
Incorporated: 10/3/1907
Mayor: Randy Lauer

Tualatin
County: Clackamas/Washington
Address: 18880 SW Martinazzi Ave., 97062
Phone: 503-692-2000
Fax: 503-692-5421
Web: tualatinoregon.gov
Elevation: 123'
Incorporated: 5/8/1913
Mayor: Frank Bubenik

Turner
County: Marion
Address: PO Box 456, 5255 Chicago St., SE, 97392
Phone: 503-743-2155
Fax: 503-743-4010
Web: cityofturner.org
Elevation: 287'
Incorporated: 2/10/1905
Mayor: Steve Horning

Ukiah
County: Umatilla
Address: PO Box 265, 97880
Phone: 541-427-3900
Fax: 541-427-3902
Web: cityofukiahoregon.com
Elevation: 3,400'
Incorporated: 5/23/1972
Mayor: Clinton Barber

Umatilla
County: Umatilla
Address: PO Box 130, 700 Sixth St., 97882
Phone: 541-922-3226

Fax: 541-922-5758
Web: umatilla-city.org
Elevation: 322'
Incorporated: 10/24/1864
Mayor: Caden Sipe

Union
County: Union
Address: PO Box 529, 342 S Main, 97883
Phone: 541-562-5197
Fax: 541-562-5196
Web: cityofunion.com
Elevation: 2,791'
Incorporated: 10/19/1878
Mayor: Susan Hawkins

Unity
County: Baker
Address: PO Box 7, 97884
Phone: 541-446-3544
Fax: 541-446-3544
Web: bakercounty.org
Elevation: 4,040'
Incorporated: 7/31/1972
General Manager: Mark Bennett

*Vale
County: Malheur
Address: 150 Longfellow St N., 97918
Phone: 541-473-3133
Fax: 541-473-3895
Web: cityofvale.com
Elevation: 2,343'
Incorporated: 2/21/1889
Mayor: Tom Vialpando

Veneta
County: Lane
Address: PO Box 458, 88184 Eighth St., 97487
Phone: 541-935-2191
Fax: 541-935-1838
Web: venetaoregon.gov
Elevation: 418'
Incorporated: 5/4/1962
Mayor: Keith Weiss

Vernonia
County: Columbia
Address: 1001 Bridge St., 97064
Phone: 503-429-5291
Fax: 503-429-4232
Web: vernonia-or.gov
Elevation: 635'
Incorporated: 2/18/1891
Mayor: Rick Hobart

Waldport
County: Lincoln
Address: PO Box 1120, 355 NW Alder., 97394
Phone: 541-563-3561
Fax: 541-563-1032
Web: waldportoregon.gov
Elevation: 12'
Incorporated: 3/11/1911
Mayor: Greg L. Holland

Wallowa
County: Wallowa
Address: PO Box 487, 97885
Phone: 541-886-2422
Fax: 541-886-4215
Web: https://cityofwallowa.weebly.com
Elevation: 2,950'
Incorporated: 1/18/1909
Mayor: Gary Lee Hulse

Warrenton
County: Clatsop
Address: PO Box 250, 225 S Main Ave., 97146
Phone: 503-861-2233
Fax: 503-861-2351
Web: ci.warrenton.or.us
Elevation: 8'
Incorporated: 2/11/1899
Mayor: Henry Balensifer III

Wasco
County: Sherman
Address: PO Box 26, 1017 Clark St., 97065
Phone: 541-442-5515
Fax: 541-442-5001
Web: http://www.wascooregon.com
Elevation: 1,281'
Incorporated: 4/14/1898
Mayor: Beth McCurdy

Waterloo
County: Linn
Address: PO Box 1066, 31140 First St., Lebanon 97355
Phone: 541-451-2245
Fax: 541-451-3133
Email: main@waterlooor.com
Elevation: 402'
Incorporated: 2/15/1893
Mayor: Justin Cary

West Linn
County: Clackamas
Address: 22500 Salamo Rd., #100, 97068
Phone: 503-657-0331
Fax: 503-650-9041
Web: westlinnoregon.gov
Elevation: 642'
Incorporated: 8/15/1913
Mayor: Rory Bialostosky, Interim Mayor

Westfir
County: Lane
Address: PO Box 296, 47441 Westoak Rd., 97492
Phone: 541-782-3983
Web: westfir-oregon.com
Elevation: 1,075'
Incorporated: 2/6/1979
Mayor: D'Lynn Williams

Weston
County: Umatilla
Address: PO Box 579, 114 Main St., 97886
Phone: 541-566-3313
Fax: 541-566-2792

Web: cityofwestonoregon.com
Elevation: 1,796'
Incorporated: 10/19/1878
Mayor: Duane Thul

An Oregon Coast Scenic Railroad stop in Wheeler. (Oregon State Archives scenic photo)

Wheeler
County: Tillamook
Address: PO Box 177, 775 Nehalem Blvd., 97147
Phone: 503-368-5767
Fax: 503-368-4273
Web: ci.wheeler.or.us
Elevation: 37'
Incorporated: 6/11/1913
Mayor: Doug Honeycutt

Willamina
County: Polk/Yamhill
Address: 411 NE C St., 97396
Phone: 503-876-2242
Fax: 503-876-1121
Web: willaminaoregon.gov
Elevation: 225'
Incorporated: 2/13/1903
Mayor: Ila Skyberg

Wilsonville
County: Clackamas/Washington
Address: 29799 SW Town Center Lp. E, 97070
Phone: 503-682-1011
Fax: 503-682-1015
Web: ci.wilsonville.or.us
Elevation: 179'
Incorporated: 10/10/1968
Mayor: Julie Fitzgerald

Winston
County: Douglas
Address: 201 NW Douglas Blvd., 97496
Phone: 541-679-6739
Fax: 541-679-0794
Web: winstoncity.org
Elevation: 534'
Incorporated: 6/29/1953
Mayor: D. Scott Rutter

Wood Village
County: Multnomah
Address: 24200 NE Halsey, 97060
Phone: 503-667-6211
Fax: 503-669-8723
Web: woodvillageor.gov
Elevation: 90'–330'
Incorporated: 2/9/1951
Mayor: John Miner

Woodburn
County: Marion
Address: 270 Montgomery St., 97071
Phone: 503-982-5228
Fax: 503-982-5243
Web: woodburn-or.gov
Elevation: 197'
Incorporated: 2/20/1889
Mayor: Frank Lonergan

Yachats
County: Lincoln
Address: PO Box 345, 501 Hwy. 101 N, 97498
Phone: 541-547-3565
Fax: 541-547-3063
Web: yachatsoregon.org
Elevation: 45'
Incorporated: 7/18/1966
Mayor: Craig Berdie

Yamhill
County: Yamhill
Address: PO Box 9, 205 S Maple St., 97148
Phone: 503-662-3511
Fax: 503-662-4589
Web: cityofyamhill.org
Elevation: 182'
Incorporated: 2/20/1891
Mayor: Yvette Potter

Yoncalla
County: Douglas
Address: PO Box 508, 2640 Eagle Valley Rd., 97499
Phone: 541-849-2152
Fax: 541-849-2552
Web: cityofyoncalla.org
Elevation: 367'
Incorporated: 2/27/1901
Mayor: Kathleen Ann Wertz

City Populations: 1990–2022

Source: Population Research Center, Portland State University
Phone: 503-725-3922

*Change in population between 2020 and 2022

Cities or counties that share rank numbers are tied in rank.

Rank	City	% Change*	2022	2020	2010	2000	1990
147	Adair Village	19.3	1,318	1,105	840	536	554
203	Adams	4.8	393	375	365	297	223
224	Adrian	-16.3	159	190	175	147	131
11	Albany	4.1	57,199	54,935	50,325	40,852	29,540
130	Amity	6.1	1,809	1,705	1,615	1,478	1,175
237	Antelope	-26	37	50	45	59	34
184	Arlington	5.7	650	615	585	524	425
28	Ashland	2.1	21,554	21,105	20,095	19,522	16,252
54	Astoria	5.4	10,197	9,675	9,475	9,813	10,069
152	Athena	3.6	1,212	1,170	1,125	1,221	997
85	Aumsville	0.5	4,237	4,215	3,605	3,003	1,650
160	Aurora	15	1,133	985	920	655	523
55	Baker City	1.7	10,178	10,010	9,830	9,860	9,140
92	Bandon	7.6	3,470	3,225	3,075	2,833	2,215
129	Banks	-7.4	1,834	1,980	1,775	1,286	563
231	Barlow	-1.5	133	135	135	140	118
142	Bay City	5.1	1,424	1,355	1,290	1,149	1,027
7	Beaverton	-1.5	97,782	99,225	89,925	76,129	53,307
6	Bend	8.7	100,922	92,840	76,740	52,029	20,447
83	Boardman	-5.3	4,338	4,580	3,220	2,855	1,387
202	Bonanza	-11.2	404	455	471	415	323
70	Brookings	2.1	6,809	6,670	6,350	5,447	4,400
133	Brownsville	-1.5	1,705	1,730	1,670	1,449	1,281
105	Burns	-3.2	2,745	2,835	2,805	3,064	2,913
195	Butte Falls	-2.0	451	460	425	439	252
34	Canby	9.0	18,754	17,210	15,830	12,790	8,990
139	Cannon Beach	-13.9	1,498	1,740	1,695	1,588	1,221
181	Canyon City	-5.5	666	705	705	669	648
136	Canyonville	-16.9	1,649	1,985	1,885	1,293	1,219
115	Carlton	-.09	2,270	2,290	2,015	1,514	1,289
143	Cascade Locks	-1.6	1,398	1,420	1,145	1,115	930
119	Cave Junction	8.8	2,149	1,975	1,885	1,363	1,126
31	Central Point	5.1	19,702	18,755	17,185	12,493	7,512
175	Chiloquin	3.7	767	740	735	716	673
131	Clatskanie	-3.9	1,725	1,795	1,735	1,528	1,629
146	Coburg	-3.9	1,322	1,375	1,040	969	763
123	Columbia City	-1.2	1,957	1,980	1,945	1,571	1,003
177	Condon	5.4	722	685	685	759	635
39	Coos Bay	-4.8	16,005	16,810	15,970	15,374	15,076
87	Coquille	2.5	4,018	3,920	3,865	4,184	4,212
41	Cornelius	6.8	13,498	12,635	11,875	9,652	6,148
10	Corvallis	-3.6	57,601	59,730	54,460	49,322	44,757

Rank	City	% Change*	2022	2020	2010	2000	1990
48	Cottage Grove	6.3	10,792	10,155	9,705	8,445	7,403
185	Cove	13	627	555	550	594	507
75	Creswell	1.8	5,684	5,585	5,030	3,579	2,431
137	Culver	4.2	1,636	1,570	1,365	802	570
35	Dallas	4.6	17,320	16,555	14,590	12,459	9,422
106	Dayton	-1.7	2,698	2,745	2,535	2,119	1,526
230	Dayville	-13.6	134	155	150	138	144
138	Depoe Bay	7.5	1,559	1,450	1,400	1,174	870
227	Detroit	-31.2	141	205	205	262	331
163	Donald	1.7	1,012	995	980	625	316
156	Drain	0.8	1,174	1,165	1,155	1,021	1,086
187	Dufur	-2.7	608	625	605	588	527
98	Dundee	-1.3	3,243	3,285	3,170	2,598	1,663
141	Dunes City	6.5	1,454	1,365	1,305	1,241	1,081
124	Durham	3.5	1,950	1,885	1,355	1,382	748
59	Eagle Point	5.1	9,854	9,375	8,470	4,797	3,008
182	Echo	-8.8	657	720	700	650	500
132	Elgin	-0.8	1,717	1,730	1,710	1,654	1,586
219	Elkton	-11.2	182	205	195	147	172
120	Enterprise	4.3	2,080	1,995	1,940	1,895	1,905
80	Estacada	24.3	5,014	4,035	2,730	2,371	2,016
3	Eugene	1.2	175,626	173,620	156,295	137,893	112,733
51	Fairview	10.7	10,446	9,440	8,920	7,561	2,391
161	Falls City	6.4	1,064	1,000	945	966	818
60	Florence	7.6	9,600	8,925	8,465	7,263	5,171
23	Forest Grove	3.2	26,242	25,435	21,130	17,708	13,559
196	Fossil	-5.5	449	475	475	469	399
171	Garibaldi	0.1	831	830	780	899	886
180	Gaston	3.2	676	655	635	600	563
189	Gates	1.5	548	540	475	471	499
128	Gearhart	21.2	1,872	1,545	1,465	995	1,027
108	Gervais	-0.9	2,596	2,620	2,510	2,009	992
44	Gladstone	0.7	12,033	11,945	11,495	11,438	10,152
169	Glendale	0.0	860	860	875	855	707
113	Gold Beach	2.8	2,375	2,310	2,255	1,897	1,546
144	Gold Hill	9.7	1,360	1,240	1,220	1,073	964
238	Granite	-20.0	32	40	40	24	8
14	Grants Pass	4.6	39,475	37,725	34,555	23,003	17,503
226	Grass Valley	-8.5	151	165	165	171	160
241	Greenhorn	50.0	3	2	2	0	0
4	Gresham	1.5	114,361	112,660	105,595	90,205	68,249
204	Haines	-9.4	376	415	415	426	405
207	Halfway	17.3	352	300	290	337	311
166	Halsey	1.5	959	945	910	742	667
24	Happy Valley	14.9	25,738	22,400	14,000	4,519	1,519
88	Harrisburg	-1.0	3,658	3,695	3,565	2,795	1,939
218	Helix	-3.0	194	200	185	183	150
155	Heppner	-8.3	1,187	1,295	1,290	1,395	1,412

Rank	City	% Change*	2022	2020	2010	2000	1990
32	Hermiston	4.9	19,696	18,775	16,795	13,154	10,047
5	Hillsboro	3.3	108,154	104,670	91,970	70,186	37,598
135	Hines	6.1	1,661	1,565	1,565	1,623	1,452
63	Hood River	-3.6	8,259	8,565	7,180	5,831	4,632
91	Hubbard	4.9	3,478	3,315	3,175	2,483	1,881
193	Huntington	13.0	503	445	440	515	522
225	Idanha	0.7	156	155	135	232	289
212	Imbler	-18.4	249	305	305	284	299
56	Independence	4.2	10,081	9,675	8,600	6,035	4,425
208	Ione	2.7	339	330	330	321	255
121	Irrigon	-0.2	2,037	2,040	1,825	1,702	737
159	Island City	0.4	1,144	1,140	1,000	916	696
103	Jacksonville	1.3	3,080	3,040	2,785	2,235	1,896
95	Jefferson	1.8	3,339	3,280	3,115	2,487	1,805
134	John Day	-4.9	1,664	1,750	1,750	1,821	1,836
191	Johnson City	-5.0	537	565	565	634	586
232	Jordan Valley	-25.1	131	175	180	239	364
157	Joseph	3.4	1,158	1,120	1,085	1,054	1,073
69	Junction City	13.4	7,032	6,200	5,430	4,721	3,670
15	Keizer	2.3	39,458	38,585	36,570	32,203	21,884
79	King City	21.1	5,184	4,280	3,115	1,949	2,060
27	Klamath Falls	0.4	22,022	21,940	20,925	19,460	17,737
42	La Grande	-2.8	13,087	13,460	13,095	12,327	11,766
107	La Pine	32.4	2,654	2,005	1,660	--	--
82	Lafayette	7.0	4,446	4,155	3,740	2,586	1,292
13	Lake Oswego	3.4	40,801	39,480	36,620	35,278	30,576
127	Lakeside	8.9	1,906	1,750	1,695	1,421	1,437
111	Lakeview	5.6	2,428	2,300	2,474	2,526	2,770
33	Lebanon	10.3	19,122	17,335	15,525	12,950	10,950
215	Lexington	-10.2	238	265	240	263	286
57	Lincoln City	13.6	10,067	8,865	7,935	7,437	5,908
240	Lonerock	25.0	25	20	20	24	11
220	Long Creek	-11.3	173	195	195	228	244
214	Lostine	12.6	242	215	215	263	231
153	Lowell	11.1	1,211	1,090	1,045	880	785
154	Lyons	0.6	1,207	1,200	1,160	1,008	938
65	Madras	19.3	7,717	6,470	6,050	5,078	3,443
176	Malin	-10.9	731	820	805	640	725
186	Manzanita	-5.6	609	645	600	564	513
199	Maupin	-1.9	427	435	420	411	456
172	Maywood Park	10.5	829	750	750	777	781
18	McMinnville	-1.1	34,251	34,615	32,240	29,499	17,894
8	Medford	5.1	87,353	83,115	74,980	63,687	47,021
173	Merrill	-2.8	821	845	845	897	837
165	Metolius	18.9	981	825	710	729	450
122	Mill City	5.1	2,012	1,915	1,855	1,537	1,555
102	Millersburg	8.5	3,093	2,850	1,345	651	715

Rank	City	% Change*	2022	2020	2010	2000	1990
68	Milton-Freewater	-0.9	7,145	7,210	7,045	6,470	5,533
29	Milwaukie	3.1	21,235	20,600	20,290	20,490	18,670
229	Mitchell	-13.8	138	160	130	170	163
53	Molalla	2.7	10,207	9,910	8,110	5,647	3,651
46	Monmouth	12.1	11,142	9,940	9,545	7,741	6,288
183	Monroe	2.2	654	640	615	607	448
234	Monument	-11.5	115	130	130	151	162
205	Moro	10.0	374	340	325	337	292
194	Mosier	-4.5	468	490	435	410	244
94	Mount Angel	-2.9	3,418	3,520	3,285	3,121	2,778
189	Mount Vernon	4.4	548	525	525	595	549
90	Myrtle Creek	-2.8	3,501	3,600	3,440	3,419	3,063
109	Myrtle Point	-2.2	2,479	2,535	2,515	2,451	2,712
209	Nehalem	-3.2	276	285	270	203	232
25	Newberg	5.2	25,376	24,120	22,110	18,064	13,086
49	Newport	1.8	10,591	10,400	10,030	9,532	8,437
52	North Bend	4	10,375	9,975	9,695	9,544	9,614
93	North Plains	2.6	3,446	3,360	1,970	1,605	997
192	North Powder	13.3	504	445	440	489	448
97	Nyssa	-1.9	3,276	3,340	3,265	3,163	2,629
168	Oakland	-3.4	932	965	925	954	844
99	Oakridge	-2.2	3,238	3,310	3,205	3,172	3,063
45	Ontario	2.6	11,816	11,515	11,365	10,985	9,394
16	Oregon City	5.2	37,737	35,885	31,995	25,754	14,698
213	Paisley	-18.7	244	300	245	247	350
36	Pendleton	0.9	17,169	17,025	16,605	16,354	15,142
76	Philomath	5.8	5,682	5,370	4,590	3,838	2,983
86	Phoenix	-12.1	4,096	4,660	4,540	4,060	3,239
145	Pilot Rock	-11.8	1,328	1,505	1,505	1,532	1,478
158	Port Orford	0.5	1,156	1,150	1,135	1,153	1,025
1	Portland	-0.9	658,773	664,605	583,775	529,121	438,802
178	Powers	1.7	712	700	690	734	682
170	Prairie City	-8.1	841	915	910	1,080	1,117
235	Prescott	50.9	83	55	55	72	63
47	Prineville	6.6	11,042	10,355	9,260	7,358	5,355
126	Rainier	-1.4	1,913	1,940	1,895	1,687	1,674
17	Redmond	12.1	36,122	32,215	26,225	13,481	7,165
84	Reedsport	1.9	4,311	4,430	4,150	4,378	4,796
221	Richland	-5.7	165	175	155	147	161
151	Riddle	2.0	1,214	1,190	1,185	1,014	1,143
188	Rivergrove	8.2	552	510	290	324	294
140	Rockaway Beach	6.2	1,476	1,390	1,315	1,267	970
110	Rogue River	8.2	2,435	2,250	2,135	1,851	1,759
26	Roseburg	-4.9	23,701	24,915	21,660	20,017	17,069
210	Rufus	-5.9	273	290	250	268	295
2	Salem	5.2	177,694	168,970	155,100	136,924	107,793
43	Sandy	10.5	12,869	11,650	9,655	5,385	4,125
64	Scappoose	8.9	8,016	7,360	6,630	4,976	3,529

Rank	City	% Change*	2022	2020	2010	2000	1990
166	Scio	2.0	959	940	840	695	623
198	Scotts Mills	12.0	431	385	355	312	283
67	Seaside	9.0	7,157	6,565	6,460	5,900	5,359
221	Seneca	-17.5	165	200	200	223	191
101	Shady Cove	-1.4	3,095	3,140	2,905	2,307	1,351
239	Shaniko	-14.3	30	35	35	26	26
71	Sheridan	4.5	6,377	6,100	6,125	5,561	3,979
30	Sherwood	3.1	20,496	19,885	18,205	11,791	3,093
148	Siletz	1.1	1,249	1,235	1,210	1,133	992
49	Silverton	0.7	10,591	10,520	9,230	7,414	5,635
96	Sisters	2.1	3,286	3,220	2,040	959	708
206	Sodaville	4.1	360	355	310	290	192
228	Spray	-12.5	140	160	160	140	149
9	Springfield	1.3	62,352	61,535	59,425	52,864	44,464
40	St Helens	4.6	14,560	13,915	12,905	10,019	7,535
197	St Paul	-1.4	434	440	420	354	322
117	Stanfield	-3.5	2,201	2,280	2,045	1,979	1,568
62	Stayton	4.9	8,265	7,880	7,645	6,816	5,011
100	Sublimity	1.8	3,106	3,050	2,680	2,148	1,491
233	Summerville	-11.9	119	135	135	117	147
217	Sumpter	-2.4	205	210	205	171	119
61	Sutherlin	7.9	8,909	8,260	7,840	6,669	5,020
58	Sweet Home	5.1	9,893	9,415	8,945	8,016	6,850
73	Talent	-12.1	5,737	6,530	6,070	5,589	3,274
149	Tangent	-2.7	1,231	1,265	1,165	933	556
38	The Dalles	8.1	16,047	14,845	13,630	12,156	11,021
12	Tigard	2.5	55,854	54,520	48,090	41,223	29,435
77	Tillamook	8.3	5,338	4,930	4,920	4,352	4,001
89	Toledo	2.6	3,611	3,520	3,470	3,472	3,174
37	Troutdale	0.9	16,319	16,180	15,980	13,777	7,852
19	Tualatin	2.6	27,910	27,195	26,060	22,791	14,664
104	Turner	18.9	2,866	2,410	1,855	1,199	1,281
223	Ukiah	-32.1	163	240	185	255	250
66	Umatilla	-1.1	7,520	7,605	6,905	4,978	3,046
118	Union	-1.0	2,153	2,175	2,130	1,926	1,847
236	Unity	-46.7	40	75	70	131	87
125	Vale	2.1	1,914	1,875	1,875	1,976	1,491
78	Veneta	8.8	5,271	4,845	4,565	2,762	2,519
112	Vernonia	13.9	2,403	2,110	2,155	2,228	1,808
114	Waldport	9.2	2,321	2,125	2,035	2,050	1,595
174	Wallowa	-4.9	799	840	810	869	748
72	Warrenton	18.7	6,352	5,350	5,000	4,096	2,681
200	Wasco	-0.2	424	425	410	381	374
216	Waterloo	-5.5	222	235	230	239	191
20	West Linn	5.7	27,452	25,975	25,150	22,261	16,389
211	Westfir	-1.9	260	265	255	280	278
179	Weston	2.3	706	690	670	717	606
201	Wheeler	5.5	422	400	415	391	335
116	Willamina	-1.0	2,248	2,270	2,025	1,844	1,748

Rank	City	% Change*	2022	2020	2010	2000	1990
21	Wilsonville	4.9	27,186	25,915	19,525	13,991	7,106
74	Winston	1.4	5,700	5,620	5,385	4,613	3,773
81	Wood Village	6.9	4,478	4,190	3,875	2,860	2,814
22	Woodburn	4.2	26,250	25,185	24,085	20,100	13,404
164	Yachats	29.5	1,010	780	690	617	533
150	Yamhill	10	1,221	1,110	1,020	794	867
160	Yoncalla	-3.6	1,036	1,075	1,050	1,052	919

COUNTY POPULATIONS: 1990–2022

Rank	County	% Change*	2022	2020	2010	2000	1990
28	Baker	-0.3	16,860	16,910	16,185	16,741	15,317
11	Benton	-0.7	93,976	94,665	85,735	78,153	70,811
3	Clackamas	-0.3	425,316	426,515	376,780	338,391	278,850
19	Clatsop	5	41,428	39,455	37,070	35,630	33,301
17	Columbia	-0.5	53,014	53,280	49,430	43,560	37,557
16	Coos	2.9	65,154	63,315	63,035	62,779	60,273
24	Crook	10.8	25,482	23,440	21,020	19,182	14,111
27	Curry	2.9	23,662	23,005	22,355	21,137	19,327
7	Deschutes	3.2	203,390	197,015	157,905	115,367	74,958
9	Douglas	-0.7	111,694	112,530	107,690	100,399	94,649
34	Gilliam	2.5	2,039	1,990	1,870	1,915	1,717
33	Grant	-1.2	7,226	7,315	7,460	7,935	7,853
31	Harney	3.5	7,537	7,280	7,445	7,609	7,060
26	Hood River	-6.8	23,888	25,640	22,385	20,411	16,903
6	Jackson	0.3	223,827	223,240	203,340	181,269	146,389
25	Jefferson	3.3	24,889	24,105	21,750	19,009	13,676
13	Josephine	2.5	88,728	86,560	82,775	57,726	62,649
15	Klamath	2.6	69,822	68,075	66,505	63,775	57,072
30	Lake	1.3	8,177	8,075	7,890	7,422	7,186
4	Lane	0.3	382,647	381,365	352,010	322,959	282,912
18	Lincoln	5.4	50,903	48,305	46,135	44,479	38,889
8	Linn	2.4	130,440	127,320	116,840	103,069	91,227
20	Malheur	-0.3	31,995	32,105	31,345	31,615	26,038
5	Marion	-0.6	347,182	349,120	315,900	284,834	228,483
29	Morrow	-1.5	12,635	12,825	11,175	710,995	7,625
1	Multnomah	-1.1	820,672	829,560	736,785	660,486	583,887
12	Polk	6.1	88,916	83,805	75,495	62,380	49,541
35	Sherman	6.3	1,908	1,795	1,765	1,934	1,918
21	Tillamook	4.1	27,628	26,530	25,260	24,262	21,570
14	Umatilla	-1.2	80,523	81,495	76,000	70,548	59,249
22	Union	-2	26,295	26,840	25,810	24,530	23,598
32	Wallowa	3.8	7,433	7,160	7,005	7,226	6,911
21	Wasco	-2.6	26,581	27,295	25,235	23,791	21,683
2	Washington	-2.4	605,036	620,080	531,070	445,342	311,554
36	Wheeler	1.1	1,456	1,440	1,440	1,547	1,396
10	Yamhill	-0.3	108,261	108,605	99,405	84,992	65,551
	Oregon	**-0.03**	**4,266,620**	**4,268,005**	**3,837,300**	**3,421,399**	**2,842,321**

COUNTY GOVERNMENT

The word "county" is from the Middle English word "conte." It means the domain of a count. However, the American county, as defined by Merriam-Webster's Dictionary is, "the largest territorial division for local government within a state of the U.S." That definition is based on the Anglo-Saxon County of England dating back to the time of the Norman Conquest. Counties were brought to America by the colonists and were later established in the central and western parts of the nation by the colonizers as they moved westward.

Early Oregon county governments were very limited in the services they provided. Their primary responsibilities were forest and farm-to-market roads, law enforcement, courts, care for the needy and tax collection. In response to demands of a growing population and a more complex society, today's counties provide a wide range of important public services, including public health, mental health, juvenile services, criminal prosecution, hospitals, nursing homes, airports, parks, libraries, land-use planning, building regulations, refuse disposal, elections, air pollution control, veterans' services, economic development, urban renewal, public housing, vector control, county fairs, museums, dog control, civil defense and senior services.

Originally, counties functioned almost exclusively as agents of the state government. Their every activity had to be either authorized or mandated by state law. In 1858, that all changed. An amendment to the Oregon Constitution authorized counties to adopt "home rule" charters. A 1973 state law granted all counties power to exercise broad "home rule" authority. As a result, the national Advisory Commission on Intergovernmental Relations identified county government in Oregon as having the highest degree of local discretionary authority of any state in the nation.

Nine counties have adopted "home rule" charters, wherein voters have the power to adopt and amend their own county government organization. Lane and Washington were the first to adopt "home rule" in 1962, followed by Hood River (1964), Multnomah (1967), Benton (1972), Jackson (1978), Josephine (1980), Clatsop (1988) and Umatilla (1993).

Twenty-nine of Oregon's 36 counties, including the nine with charters, are governed by a board of commissioners comprised of three- to- five elected members. The remaining seven less populated counties are governed by a "county court" consisting of a county judge and two commissioners.

Source: Association of Oregon Counties

Baker County

County Seat: 1995 Third St., Baker City 97814
Phone: 541-523-8203 (General); 541-523-8207 (County Clerk)
Fax: 541-523-8240
Email: skirby@bakercounty.org
Web: bakercounty.org
Established:

Sept. 22, 1862
Elev. at Baker City: 3,471'
Area: 3,089 sq. mi.
Average Temp.: January 25.2° July 66.6°

Assessed Value: $1,850,951,018
Real Market Value: $3,245,165,070 (includes the value of non-taxed properties)
Annual Precipitation: 10.63"
Economy: Agriculture, forest products, manufacturing and recreation
Points of Interest: The Oregon Trail Interpretive Center and Old Oregon Trail, Sumpter Gold Dredge Park and ghost towns, Sumpter Valley Railroad, Baker City Restored Historic District (including Geiser Grand Hotel), Anthony Lakes Ski Resort, Eagle Cap Wilderness area, Brownlee, Oxbow and Hells Canyon Reservoirs, Hells Canyon

Baker County was established from part of Wasco County and named after Colonel Edward D. Baker, a U.S. Senator from Oregon. A Union officer and close friend of President Lincoln, Colonel Baker was the only member of Congress to die in the Civil War. He was killed at Ball's Bluff, Virginia. Auburn, which no longer exists, was the first county seat. Baker City became the county seat in 1868 and was incorporated in 1874.

Before 1861, the majority of immigrants only paused in Baker County on their way west, unaware of its vast agricultural and mineral resources. Then the great gold rush began, and Baker County became one of the Northwest's largest gold producers. Farming, ranching, logging and recreation have become the chief economic bases for an area that displays spectacular scenery, including the world's deepest gorge, Hells Canyon; an outstanding museum with the famous Cavin-Walfel rock collection; and numerous historic buildings with interesting architectural features.

County Officials: Commissioners—Shane Alderson 2027; Bruce Nichols 2025, Christina Witham, 2027; Dist. Atty. Greg M. Baxter 2025; Assess. Kerry Savage 2025; Clerk Stefanie Kirby 2027; Justice of the Peace Brent Kerns 2023; Sheriff Travis Ash 2025; Surv. Tom Hanley 2025; Treas. Alice Durflinger 2027; Co. Admin. Christena Cook; Chief Information Officer Bill Lee

Benton County

County Seat: 205 NW Fifth St., Corvallis 97330
Phone: 541-766-6800 (General); 541-766-6859 (Trial Court Administrator)
Fax: 541-766-6893
Email: webmaster@co.benton.or.us
Web: co.benton.or.us
Established:
Dec. 23, 1847
Elev. at Corvallis:
224'
Area: 679 sq. mi.
Average Temp.:
January 39.3°
July 65.6°

Assessed Value:
$9,990,463,607
Real Market Value: $19,714,966,474
(includes the value of non-taxed properties)
Annual Precipitation: 42.71"
Economy: Agriculture, forest products, research and development, electronics and wineries

Points of Interest: Benton County Courthouse, Oregon State University (OSU) Campus, Benton County Museum (Philomath), Alsea Falls, Mary's Peak, William L. Finley National Wildlife Refuge, Peavy Arboretum, McDonald Forest, Jackson-Frazier Wetland, Beazell Memorial Forest & Education Center

Benton County was created from Polk County by an act of the Provisional Government of Oregon in 1847. It is one of seven counties in the United States to be named after Senator Thomas Hart Benton of Missouri, a longtime advocate of the development of the Oregon Territory. The county is located in an area originally inhabited by the Klickitat Tribe, who rented the area from the Kalapuya Tribe for use as hunting grounds. At that time, the boundaries began at the intersection of Polk County and the Willamette River, ran as far south as the California border and as far west as the Pacific Ocean. Later, portions of Benton County were taken to form Coos, Curry, Douglas, Jackson, Josephine, Lane and Lincoln Counties, leaving it in its present form with 679 square miles of land area.

A substantial portion of the nation's research in forestry, agriculture, engineering, education and the sciences takes place at OSU located at the county seat in Corvallis.
County Officials: Commissioners— Chair Nancy Wyse 2025; Xanthippe (Xan) Augerot 2025, Pat Malone 2027; Dist. Atty. John Haroldson 2025; Assess. Tami Tracy; Clerk James Morales; Sheriff Jefri Van Arsdall 2027; Surv. Joe Mardis; Tax Collector Mary Otley; Public Information Officer Alyssa Rash

Clackamas County

County Seat: County Courthouse, 807 Main St., Oregon City 97045
Phone: 503-655-8581 (General); 503-655-8447 (Court Administrator) 503-655-8447 ext 6 (Records)
Email: bcc@co.clackamas.or.us
Web: clackamas.us
Established:
July 5, 1843
Elev. at Oregon City: 55'
Area: 1,884 sq. mi.
Average Temp.:
January 40.2°
July 68.4°
Assessed Value:
$58,205,791,566
Real Market Value: $110,984,072,418
(includes the value of non-taxed properties)
Annual Precipitation: 48.40"
Economy: Agriculture, metals manufacturing, trucking and warehousing, nursery stock, retail services, wholesale trade and construction
Points of Interest: Mount Hood and Timberline Lodge, Willamette Falls and navigation locks, McLoughlin House, Canby Ferry, Molalla Buckaroo, driving tour of Old Barlow Road, Clackamas Town Center, Museum of the Oregon Territory, North Clackamas Aquatic Park

Clackamas County was named for the resident Clackamas Tribe and was one of the four original Oregon counties created in 1843. Oregon City, the county seat, was the first incorporated city west of the Rocky Mountains, the first capital of the Oregon Territory and the site of the first legislative session.

In 1849, when the city of San Francisco was platted, Oregon City was the site of the only federal court west of the Rockies. The plat was filed in 1850 in the first plat book of the first office of records on the West Coast and are still in Oregon City. The area's early history is featured at the Clackamas County Historical Society and Museum of the Oregon Territory.

From its 55-foot elevation at Oregon City, the county rises to 11,235 feet at the peak of Mount Hood, the only year-round ski resort in the United States and the site of the Timberline Lodge National Historical Landmark. The mountains, rivers and forests offer excellent outdoor recreation activities, from skiing and rafting to fishing and camping.
County Officials: Commissioners—Chair Tootie Smith 2025; Paul Savas 2027, Martha Schrader 2025, Mark Shull 2025, Ben West, 2027; Dist. Atty. John D. Wentworth 2025; Assess. Bronson W Rueda 2027; Clerk Catherine McMullen 2027; Justice of the Peace Karen Brisbin 2029; Sheriff Angela Brandenburg 2025; Surv. Ray Griffin; Treas. Brian T. Nava 2027; Co. Admin. Gary Schmidt

Clatsop County

County Seat: 800 Exchange St., Suite 410, Astoria 97103
Phone: 503-325-1000 (General); 503-325-8555 (Court Administrator)
Fax: 503-325-8325
Email: clerk@co.clatsop.or.us
Web: co.clatsop.or.us
Established:
    June 22, 1844
Elev. at Astoria:
    19'
Area: 1085 sq. mi.
Average Temp.:
    January 41.9°
    July 60.1°
Assessed Value:
    $7,084,305,859
Real Market Value: $11,702,910,802
(includes the value of non-taxed properties)
Annual Precipitation: 66.40"
Economy: Fishing, tourism and forest products
Points of Interest: Astoria Column, Port of Astoria, Flavel Mansion Museum, Lewis and Clark Expedition Salt Cairn, Fort Clatsop, Fort Stevens, Columbia River Maritime Museum

Clatsop County was created from the original Tuality District in 1844 and named for the Clatsop Tribe, one of the many Chinook tribes living in Oregon. *The Journals of Lewis and Clark* mention the tribe. Fort Clatsop, Lewis and Clark's winter headquarters in 1805 and now a national memorial near the mouth of the Columbia River, also took the tribe's name.

Astoria, Oregon's oldest city, was established as a fur trading post in 1811 and named after John Jacob Astor. The first U.S. Post Office west of the Rocky Mountains was also established in Astoria in 1847. The first county courthouse was completed in 1855, and the present courthouse was erected in 1904. Records show that the summer resort of Seaside was founded by Ben Holladay, pioneer Oregon railroad builder, in the early 1870s when he constructed the Seaside House, a famous luxury hotel for which the city was finally named. The Lewis and Clark Expedition reached the Pacific Ocean at this spot.

County Officials: Commissioners—Chair Mark Kujala 2027; Courtney Bangs 2025, John Toyooka 2025, Lianne Thompson 2027, Pamela Wev 2027; Dist. Atty. Ron L. Brown 2027; Assess. Suzanne Johnson; Clerk Tracie Krevanko; Sheriff Matt Phillips 2025; Surv. Vance Swenson; Treas. Jennifer Carlson; County Manager Don Bohn

Columbia County

County Seat: Courthouse, 230 Strand St., Saint Helens 97051
Phone: 503-397-3796 (General); 503-397-7210 (Court Administrator)
Fax: 503-397-7266
Email: Betty.Huser@columbiacountyor.gov
Web: columbiacountyor.gov
Established:
    Jan. 16, 1854
Elev. at Saint
    Helens: 42'
Area: 687 sq. mi.
Average Temp.:
    January 39.0°
    July 68.4°
Assessed Value:
    $6,043,662,288
Real Market Value: $10,815,585,787
(includes the value of non-taxed properties)
Annual Precipitation: 44.60"
Economy: Agriculture, forest products, manufacturing, surface mining and tourism
Points of Interest: Lewis and Clark Heritage Canoe Trail, Vernonia–Banks State Trail, Jewell Elk Refuge, Sauvie Island Wildlife Area, Sand Island Park, Jones Beach near Clatskanie, Prescott Beach Park, Dibblee Beach, Camp Wilkerson, CZ Trail, Big Eddy Park, Vernonia Golf Course, Lewis and Clark Bridge at Rainier, Columbia County Fairgrounds

Chinook and Clatskanie Tribes inhabited this bountiful region centuries before Captain Robert Gray, commanding the *Columbia Rediviva,* landed on Columbia County's timbered shoreline in 1792. The Corps of Discovery expedition, led by Lewis and Clark, traveled and camped along the Columbia River shore in the area later known as Columbia County in late 1805 and early 1806.

The county has 62 miles of Columbia riverfront with deep water ports and premium industrial property. The Columbia River is a major route for ocean-going vessels and is a popular playground for fishing, boating, camping and windsurfing. The county has two marine parks, Sand Island and J. J. Collins Memorial Marine Park. Columbia County's strong economic and cultural heritage is centered on industries such as forest products, shipbuilding, mining and agriculture. Residents enjoy the rural lifestyle and scenic beauty of Columbia County, coupled with its proximity to Portland.

County Officials: Commissioners—Margaret Magruder 2025, Casey Garrett 2025, Kelli Jo Smith 2027; Dist. Atty. Jeffrey D. Auxier 2027; Assess. Andrea Jurkiewicz 2027; Clerk Debbie Klug 2027; Justice of the Peace Diana M. Shera Taylor 2025; Sheriff Brian Pixley 2027; Surv. Nathan Woodward; Treas. Mary Ann Guess 2025

❖ ❖ ❖

Coos County

County Seat: Courthouse, 250 N Baxter, Coquille 97423
Phone: 541-396-7500 (General)
Fax: 541-396-1010
Email: coosclerk@co.coos.or.us
Web: co.coos.or.us
Established:
Dec. 22, 1853
Elev. at Coquille:
40'
Area: 1,629 sq. mi.
Average Temp.:
January 44.2°
July 60.9°
Assessed Value:
$6,201,360,487
Real Market Value: $9,381,043,665
(includes the value of non-taxed properties)
Annual Precipitation: 56.8"
Economy: Forest products, tourism, fishing and agriculture dominate the Coos County economy. Boating, dairy farming, myrtlewood manufacturing, shipbuilding and repair, and agriculture specialty products, including cranberries, also play an important role
Points of Interest: Lumber port, myrtlewood groves, Shore Acres State Park and Botanical Gardens, beaches, Oregon Dunes National Recreation Area, museums, fishing fleets, boat basins, scenic golf courses

Coos County was created by the Territorial Legislature from parts of Umpqua and Jackson counties in 1853 and included Curry County until 1855. The county seat was Empire City until 1896 when it was moved to Coquille. Although trappers had been in the area a quarter century earlier, the first permanent settlement in present day Coos County was established at Empire City, now part of Coos Bay, by members of the Coos Bay Company in 1853. The name "Coos" derives from the Coos Tribe.

The International Port of Coos Bay, considered the best natural harbor between Puget Sound and San Francisco, is the world's largest forest products shipping port.
County Officials: Commissioners—Chair John Sweet 2027, Melissa Cribbins 2023, Robert (Bob) Main 2025; Dist. Atty. Paul R. Frasier 2025; Assess. Steve Jansen 2025; Clerk Julie Brecke 2027; Sheriff Gabe Fabrizio 2027; Surv. Michael Dado 2025; Treas. Megan Simms 2025

Crook County

County Seat: Courthouse, 300 NE Third St., Room 23, Prineville 97754
Phone: 541-447-6553 (General); 541-447-6555 (Court Administrator)
Fax: 541-416-2145
Email: cheryl.seely@co.crook.or.us
Web: co.crook.or.us
Established:
Oct. 24, 1882
Elev. at Prineville:
2,868'
Area: 2,991 sq. mi.
Average Temp.:
January 31.8°
July 64.5°
Assessed Value:
$2,653,128,811
Real Market Value: $4,545,656,769
(includes the value of non-taxed properties)
Annual Precipitation: 10.50"
Economy: Forest products, agriculture, livestock raising, recreation/tourism services, manufacturing and wholesale trade constitute most of Crook County's economy.
Points of Interest: Pine Mills, Crooked River Canyon, Ochoco Mountains, Prineville and Ochoco Reservoirs, rockhound areas, county courthouse, Steins Pillar, Wildland Firefighters Monument, and geological formations

Crook County was formed from Wasco County in 1882 and named for Major General George Crook, U.S. Army. Geographically, the county is in the center of Oregon. It is unique in that it has only one incorporated population center, the city of Prineville founded in 1868. Prineville's colorful past was the scene of tribal raids, range wars between sheep and cattle ranchers and vigilante justice. Other communities in this sparsely settled region are Powell Butte, Post and Paulina.

Thousands of hunters, fishers, boaters, sightseers and rockhounds are annual visitors to its streams, reservoirs and the Ochoco Mountains. Rockhounds can dig for agates, limb casts, jasper and thundereggs on more than 1,000 acres of mining claims provided by the Prineville Chamber of Commerce. Major annual events include the Prineville Rockhound Powwow, Crooked River Roundup, Crook County Fair, Old Fashioned Fourth of July Celebration, High Desert Celtic Festival and the Lord's Acre Sale.
County Officials: County Court—Judge Seth Crawford 2025, Brian Barney 2027, Jerry Brummer 2025; Dist. Atty. Kari Hathorn 2027; Assess. Jon Soliz 2027; Clerk Cheryl Seely 2027; Sheriff John Gautney 2025; Surv. Greg Kelso 2025; Treas. Galan Carter 2027

Curry County

County Seat: 94235 Moore St., Suite 212, Gold Beach 97444
Phone: 541-247-3295 (General); 541-247-4511 (Court Administrator)
Fax: 541-247-6440 (Elections Division)
Email: kolenr@co.curry.or.us
Web: co.curry.or.us
Established:
 Dec. 18, 1855
Elev. at
 Gold Beach: 60'
Area: 1,648 sq. mi.
Average Temp.:
 January 45.0°
 July 65.0°
Assessed Value:
 $3,491,110,599
Real Market Value: $5,574,450,521
(includes the value of non-taxed properties)
Annual Precipitation: 82.67"
Economy: Forest products, agriculture, commercial and sport fishing, recreation and tourism
Points of Interest: Coastal ports, Cape Blanco Lighthouse, Cape Sebastian and Samuel H. Boardman State Parks, Rogue River Japanese Bomb Site, Thomas Creek Bridge near Brookings – Oregon's highest bridge at 345 feet

Named after Territorial Governor George L. Curry, the county was a part of "Coose" County until it was created in 1855. Port Orford was the county seat until 1859 when it was replaced by Ellensburg (later renamed Gold Beach).

Curry County contains valuable standing timber and also offers spectacular coastal scenery, clamming and crabbing, excellent fishing (freshwater and saltwater), upriver scenic boat trips, hiking trails, and gold for the fun of panning. The Port of Brookings is considered one of the safest harbors on the coast.

Agricultural products include sheep and cattle, cranberries, blueberries, Easter lilies and horticultural nursery stock. Curry County is also a prolific producer of myrtlewood.

County Officials: Commissioners—Court Boice 2025, Beth Barker-Hidalgo 2027, John Herzog 2025; Dist. Atty. Joshua A. Spansail 2025; Assess. Jim Kolen 2025; Clerk Reneé Kolen 2025; Sheriff John Ward 2025; Treas. David Barnes 2027

Deschutes County

County Seat: 1300 NW Wall St., Suite 206, Bend 97703
Phone: 541-388-6570 (County Administrator)
Fax: 541-385-3202
Email: Elections@deschutes.org
Web: deschutes.org
Established:
 Dec. 13, 1916
Elev. at Bend:
 3,628'
Area: 3,055 sq. mi.
Average Temp.:
 January 30.5°
 July 65.5°
Assessed Value:
 $28,858,394,563
Real Market Value: $57,139,398,118
(includes the value of non-taxed properties)
Annual Precipitation: 12"
Economy: Tourism, retail trade, forest products, recreational equipment, aviation, software and high technology
Points of Interest: Smith Rock State Park, Mount Bachelor ski area, High Desert Museum, Lava Lands, Cascade Lakes Highway, Lava River Caves State Park, Lava Cast Forests, Newberry Crater, Pilot Butte, Three Sisters Wilderness, Central Oregon Community College, Deschutes County Fairgrounds, Redmond Airport, Pine Mountain Observatory

French-Canadian fur trappers of the Hudson's Bay Company gave the name Riviere des Chutes (River of the Falls) to the Deschutes River, from which Deschutes County took its name. In 1916, Deschutes County was created from a part of Crook County.

Deschutes County, outdoor recreation capital of Oregon, with snow-capped peaks dominating the skyline to the west and the wide-open high desert extending to the east, captivates locals and visitors alike.

Deschutes County has experienced rapid growth largely due to its climate and year-round recreation activities. Central Oregon offers downhill and cross-country skiing, snowboarding, fishing, hunting, hiking, rock climbing, whitewater rafting and golf, among many other opportunities. Deschutes County is the host of diverse annual events, including the Cascade Festival of Music, the Art Hop, Cascade Children's Festival, Pole Pedal Paddle, Sisters Rodeo, Sunriver Sunfest and the Cascade Cycling Classic.

County Officials: Commissioners—Chair Patti Adair 2027; Anthony (Tony) DeBone 2027, Phil Chang 2025; Dist. Atty. Steve Gunnels 2027; Assess. Scot Langton 2027; Clerk Steve Dennison 2027; Sheriff L. Shane Nelson 2025; Surv. Kevin Samuel; Treas. William Kuhn 2027; Justice of the Peace Charles Fadeley 2029; Co. Admin. Nick Lelack

Douglas County

County Seat: Courthouse, 1036 SE Douglas Ave., Roseburg 97470
Phone: 541-672-3311 (General); 541-957-2409 (Court Administrator)
Fax: 541-440-6292
Email: HR@co.douglas.or.us
Web: co.douglas.or.us
Established:
  Jan. 7, 1852
Elev. at Roseburg:
  475'
Area: 5,071 sq. mi.
Average Temp.:
  January 41.2°
  July 68.4°
Assessed Value:
  $10,565,175,743
Real Market Value: $18,117,195,407 (includes the value of non-taxed properties)
Annual Precipitation: 33.35"
Economy: Forest products, mining, agriculture, fishing and recreation
Points of Interest: Winchester Bay, Salmon Harbor, Oregon Dunes National Recreation Area, North Umpqua River, Diamond Lake, historic Oakland, Wildlife Safari, Douglas County Museum, wineries

Douglas County was named for U.S. Senator Stephen A. Douglas, Abraham Lincoln's opponent in the presidential election of 1860 and an ardent congressional advocate for Oregon. Douglas County was created in 1852 from the portion of Umpqua County which lay east of the Coast Range summit. In 1862, Douglas County absorbed what remained of Umpqua County.

Douglas County extends from sea level at the Pacific Ocean to 9,182-foot Mount Thielsen in the Cascade Range. The Umpqua River marks the dividing line between northern and southern Oregon, and its entire watershed lies within the county's boundaries. The county contains nearly 2.8 million acres of commercial forest lands and the largest stand of old growth timber in the world, which still provides the region's main livelihood. Approximately 25 percent of the labor force is employed in the forest products industry. Agriculture includes field crops, orchards and livestock. Over 50 percent of the land area of the county is federal public land.
County Officials: Commissioners—Chair Tim Freeman 2027; Chris Boice 2027, Tom Kress 2027; Dist. Atty. Richard Wesenberg 2025; Assess. Heather Coffel 2027; Clerk Daniel J. Loomis 2025; Justices of the Peace Machelle Briggs-Mayfield 2025 & Kathleen Miller 2025; Sheriff John Hanlin 2025; Surv. Ronald Quimby 2027; Treas. Samuel W. Lee 2025

Gilliam County

County Seat: Courthouse, 221 S Oregon St., Condon 97823-0427
Phone: 541-384-2311 (County Clerk); 541-384-3303 (Court Administrator)
Fax: 541-384-2166 (County Clerk); 541-384-3304 (Courthouse)
Email: ellen.wagenaar@co.gilliam.or.us
Web: co.gilliam.or.us
Established:
  Feb. 25, 1885
Elev. at Condon:
  2,844'
Area: 1,223 sq. mi.
Average Temp.:
  January 31.9°
  July 71.3°
Assessed Value:
  $997,049,835
Real Market Value: $2,409,860,197 (includes the value of non-taxed properties)
Annual Precipitation: 11.39"
Economy: Agriculture, recreation, environmental services, wind power generation, waste management and waste disposal landfills. Hunting, fishing and tourism are secondary industries. The largest individual employers in the county are Chemical Waste Management of the Northwest and Oregon Waste Systems.
Points of Interest: Old Oregon Trail, Arlington Bay and Marina, Lonerock area, Condon historic district, tribal pictographs

Gilliam County was established in 1885 from a portion of Wasco County, and named for Colonel Cornelius Gilliam, a veteran of the Cayuse Indian War. Alkali, now Arlington, was the first county seat. In 1890, voters moved the county seat to Condon, then named "Summit Springs." A brick courthouse was built in Condon in 1903 which was destroyed by fire in 1954. The present courthouse was built on the same site in 1955.

In the heart of the Columbia Plateau wheat area, Gilliam County has an average farm size of about 4,200 acres, principally raising wheat, barley and beef cattle.

With elevations of over 3,000 feet near Condon in the south of the county, and 285 feet at Arlington, 38 miles north, the county offers a variety of climates. Two major rivers, the John Day and Columbia, and Interstate 84 traverse the area east to west. Highway 19 connects the county's major cities north to south and serves as the gateway to the John Day Valley.
County Officials: County Court—Judge Elizabeth A. Farrar-Campbell 2025; Pat Shannon 2025, Leah Watkins 2027; Dist. Atty. Kara Davis 2027; Clerk Ellen Wagenaar 2027; Justice of the Peace Cris Patnode 2027; Sheriff Gary Bettencourt 2027; Surv. Todd Catterson 2027; Treas. Nathan Hammer 2027; Assess. Chet Wilkins 2025

Grant County

County Seat: Courthouse, 201 S Humbolt St., Suite 290, Canyon City 97820
Phone: 541-575-1675 (General); 541-575-0509 (Court Administrator)
Fax: 541-575-2248
Email: percyb@grantcounty-or.gov
Web: grantcountyoregon.net
Established:
  Oct. 14, 1864
Elev. at Canyon City: 3,194'
Area: 4,528 sq. mi.
Average Temp.:
  January 30.7°
  July 68.4°
Assessed Value:
  $666,914,391
Real Market Value: $1,796,275,150 (includes the value of non-taxed properties)
Annual Precipitation: 14.28"
Economy: Forest products, agriculture, hunting, livestock and recreation
Points of Interest: John Day Fossil Beds National Monument, Veterans Memorial, Kam Wah Chung Museum, Joaquin Miller Cabin, Grant County Historical Museum, Sacred Totem Pole, Grant County Historical Mural, Dewitt Museum, Depot Park, Sumpter Valley Railroad, Strawberry Mountain Wilderness, North Fork John Day River Wilderness

Grant County was created in 1864 from Wasco and Umatilla counties and was named for General Ulysses S. Grant. It shares boundaries with more counties (eight) than any other county in Oregon.

Grant County contains the headwaters of the John Day River, which has more miles of Wild and Scenic designation than any other river in the United States. More than 60 percent of the land in the county is in public ownership.

County Officials: County Court—Judge Scott Myers 2025; Commissioners Jim Hamsher 2025, John A Rowell 2027; Dist. Atty. Jim Carpenter 2027; Assess. David Thunell 2025; Clerk Brenda Percy 2027; Justice of the Peace Kathleen Stinnett 2025; Sheriff Todd McKinley 2025; Surv. Mike Springer 2025; Treas. Julie Ellison 2025

Harney County

County Seat: Courthouse, 450 N Buena Vista Ave., Burns 97720
Phone: 541-573-6641 (General); 541-573-5207 (Court Administrator)
Fax: 541-573-8370
Email: derrin.robinson@co.harney.or.us
Web: co.harney.or.us
Established:
  Feb. 25, 1889
Elev. at Burns:
  4,118'
Area: 10,228 sq. mi.
Average Temp.:
  January 27.5°
  July 69.4°
Assessed Value:
  $674,582,043
Real Market Value: $1,720,599,425 (includes the value of non-taxed properties)
Annual Precipitation: 10.13"
Economy: Forest products, manufacturing, livestock and agriculture
Points of Interest: Steens Mountain, Malheur National Wildlife Refuge, Alvord Desert, Alvord Hot Springs, Eastern Oregon Agricultural Research Center, "P" Ranch Round Barn, Frenchglen, Wild Horse Corrals, Delintment Lake, Yellowjacket Lake

In 1826, Peter Skene Ogden became the first white man to explore this area when he led a fur brigade for the Hudson's Bay Company. In 1889, Harney, the largest county in Oregon, was carved out of Grant County and named for Major General William S. Harney, commander of the Department of Oregon, U.S. Army, from 1858–1859. Harney was instrumental in opening areas of Eastern Oregon for settlement.

A fierce political battle, with armed night riders who spirited county records from Harney to Burns, ended with Burns as the county seat in 1890. The courthouse was constructed five years later. Burns' first newspaper was established in 1884, and its first church was established in 1887.

Harney County shares the largest Ponderosa Pine forest in the nation with Grant County and has more than 100,000 beef cattle on its vast ranges. Its abundance of game, campsites, excellent fishing and bird watching have stimulated fast-growing recreational activities.

County Officials: County Court—Judge Bill Hart 2027; Pat Dorroh 2025, Kristen Shelman 2025; Dist. Atty. Ryan Hughes 2025; Assess. Karen Zabala 2025; Clerk Derrin (Dag) Robinson 2025; Justice of the Peace Vicky Clemens 2025; Sheriff Dan Jenkins 2025; Surv. Kenny Delano; Treas. Bobbi Jo Heany 2027

Hood River County

County Seat: 601 State St., Hood River 97031-2093

Phone: 541-386-3970 (General); 541-386-3535 (Court Administrator)

Fax: 541-387-6864

Email: brian.beebe@co.hood-river.or.us

Web: co.hood-river.or.us

Established:
June 23, 1908

Elev. at Hood River: 154'

Area: 533 sq. mi.

Average Temp.:
January 33.6°
July 72°

Assessed Value:
$3,037,742,498

Real Market Value: $5,691,886,784 (includes the value of non-taxed properties)

Annual Precipitation: 30.85"

Economy: Agriculture, industry, tourism and services including health care

Points of Interest: Bridge of the Gods, Cloud Cap Inn, Mount Hood Recreation Area, Mount Hood Meadows Ski Resort, Lost Lake, Hood River Valley Fruit Loop Tour

The first white settlers in Hood River County filed a donation land claim in 1854. The first school was built in 1863, and a road from The Dalles was completed in 1867. By 1880, there were 17 families living in the valley. Hood River County was created in 1908 from Wasco County.

Fruit grown in the fertile valley is of such exceptional quality that the county leads the world in Anjou pear production. There are more than 14,000 acres of commercial orchards growing pears, apples, cherries and peaches. Hood River County also has two ports and two boat basins. Windsurfing and kiteboarding on the Columbia River are very popular sports that attract visitors from all over the world.

County Officials: Commissioners—Chair Jennifer Euwer 2027; Leti Valle Moretti 2027, Ed Weathers 2027, Arthur Babitz 2025, Les Perkins 2025; Dist. Atty. Carrie Rassmussen 2025; Justice of the Peace John Harvey 2027; Sheriff Matt English 2025; Assess./Clerk Brian Beebe; Surv. Bradley Cross; Co. Admin. Jeff Hecksel; Treas. Montina Ruffin

Jackson County

County Seat: Courthouse, 10 S Oakdale Ave., Medford 97501

Phone: 541-774-6029 (General); 541-776-7171 (Court Administrator - Justice Bldg., 100 S Oakdale Ave., Medford 97501)

Fax: 541-774-6455

Email: walkercd@jacksoncounty.org

Web: jacksoncountyor.org

Established:
Jan. 12, 1852

Elev. at Medford:
1,382'

Area: 2,801 sq. mi.

Average Temp.:
January 37.6°
July 72.5°

Assessed Value:
$23,489,281,977

Real Market Value: $38,844,192,957 (includes the value of non-taxed properties)

Annual Precipitation: 19.84"

Economy: Medical, retail, tourism, agriculture, manufacturing and forest products

Points of Interest: Mount Ashland Ski Resort, Historic Jacksonville, Oregon Shakespeare Festival, Peter Britt Music Festival, Southern Oregon University, Pear orchards, Howard Prairie Lake, Emigrant Lake, Hyatt Lake, Fish Lake, Rogue River, Lithia Park, Lost Creek Dam, Butte Creek Mill, Crater Lake Highway, wineries, Rogue Community College

Named for President Andrew Jackson, Jackson County was formed in 1852 from Lane County and the unorganized area south of Douglas and Umpqua Counties. It included lands which now lie in Coos, Curry, Josephine, Klamath and Lake counties. The discovery of gold near Jacksonville in 1852 and completion of a wagon road, which joined the county with California to the south and Douglas County to the north, brought many pioneers.

County Officials: Commissioners—Chair Rick Dyer 2027; Colleen Roberts 2027; Dave Dotterrer 2025; Dist. Atty. Beth Heckert 2025; Assess. David Arrasmith 2025; Clerk Chris Walker 2027; Justice of the Peace Damian Idiart 2027; Sheriff Nathan Sickler 2027; Surv. Scott Fein 2025; Finance Director/Treas. Shannon Bell; Co. Admin. Danny Jordan

Jefferson County

County Seat: 66 SE D St., Madras 97741
Phone: 541-475-4451 (General); 541-475-3317 (Court Administrator)
Fax: 541-325-5018
Email: KZemke@jeffco.net
Web: jeffco.net
Established:
Dec. 12, 1914
Elev. at Madras:
2,242'
Area: 1,791 sq. mi.
Average Temp.:
January 37.4°
July 70.1°
Assessed Value:
$2,066,146,569
Real Market Value: $4,442,739,974 (includes the value of non-taxed properties)
Annual Precipitation: 10.2"
Economy: Agriculture, forest products and recreation
Points of Interest: Mount Jefferson, Warm Springs Indian Reservation, Metolius River, Black Butte, Suttle Lake, Blue Lake, Santiam Summit, Lake Billy Chinook behind Round Butte Dam, Haystack Reservoir, Priday Agate Beds

Jefferson County was established in 1914 from a portion of Crook County. It was named for Mount Jefferson on its western boundary. The county owes much of its agricultural prosperity to the railroad, which arrived in 1911 and to the development of irrigation projects in the late 1930s. The railroad, which links Madras with the Columbia River, was completed after constant feuds and battles between two lines working on opposite sides of the Deschutes River.

Vegetable, grass and flower seeds, garlic, mint and sugar beets are cultivated on some 60,000 irrigated acres. Jefferson County also has vast acres of rangelands and an industrial base related to forest products. With 300 days of sunshine and a low yearly rainfall, fishing, hunting, camping, boating, water-skiing and rock hunting are popular recreations.

County Officials: Commissioners—Chair Kelly Simmelink 2027; Wayne Fording 2025, Mark Wunsch 2027; Dist. Atty. Steven Leriche 2025; Assess. Jean McCloskey 2025; Clerk Kate Zemke 2023; Sheriff Jason Pollock 2027; Treas. Brandie McNamee 2025; Surv. Gary L. DeJarnatt

Josephine County

County Seat: Courthouse, 500 NW Sixth St., Grants Pass; PO Box 69, Grants Pass 97526
Phone: 541-474-5243 (General); 541-476-2309 (Court Administrator)
Fax: 541-474-5246
Email: clerk@co.josephine.or.us
Web: co.josephine.or.us
Established:
Jan. 22, 1856
Elev. at Grants Pass: 948'
Area: 1,641 sq. mi.
Average Temp.:
January 39.9°
July 71.6°
Assessed Value:
$8,826,186,630
Real Market Value: $13,718,465,776 (includes the value of non-taxed properties)
Annual Precipitation: 32.31"
Economy: Tourism, recreation, forest products, electronics and software
Points of Interest: Oregon Caves National Monument, Wolf Creek Tavern, Sunny Valley Covered Bridge and Interpretive Center, Hellgate Canyon-Rogue River, Grants Pass Historic District, Growers Market, Kalmiopsis Wilderness, Rogue Community College, Barnstormers Theater, Rogue Music Theater

Josephine County, named for Virginia "Josephine" Rollins, the first white woman to make this county her home, was established in 1856 out of the western portion of Jackson County. The county seat was originally located in Sailor Diggings (later, Waldo), but in July of 1857 was relocated to Kerbyville, situated on the main route between the port of Crescent City, California and the gold fields.

The discovery of rich placers at Sailor Diggings in 1852 and the resulting gold rush brought the first settlers to this region. Several U.S. Army forts were maintained in the county, and many engagements during the Rogue River Indian War (1855–1858) took place within its boundaries. In 1886, the county seat was finally relocated to Grants Pass, a new town on the railroad that was completed through Oregon that same year. Grants Pass is now the departure point for most Rogue River scenic waterway guided fishing and boat trips. The Illinois River, one of the Rogue's tributaries, has also been designated a scenic waterway.

County Officials: Commissioners— Chair Herman Baertschiger 2025; Dan DeYoung 2025, John West 2027; Dist. Atty. Joshua J. Eastman 2025; Assess. Connie Roach 2025; Clerk Rhiannon Henkels 2023; Sheriff Dave R. Daniel 2027; Surv. Peter D. Allen 2025; Treas. Eva Arce 2025

Klamath County

County Seat: 305 Main St., Klamath Falls 97601-6391
Phone: 541-883-5134 (General); 541-883-5503 (Court Administrator)
Fax: 541-885-6757
Email: rlong@co.klamath.or.us
Web: klamathcounty.org
Established:
Oct. 17, 1882
Elev. at Klamath Falls: 4,105'
Area: 6,135 sq. mi.
Average Temp.:
January 29.8°
July 68.0°
Assessed Value:
$6,528,021,059

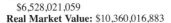

Real Market Value: $10,360,016,883 (includes the value of non-taxed properties)
Annual Precipitation: 14.31"
Economy: Agriculture, renewable energy, tourism/recreation, technology, forest products, and medical services
Points of Interest: Crater Lake National Park, Klamath Lake (Oregon's largest lake), Collier Memorial State Park and Logging Museum, seven National Wildlife Refuges, Oregon Institute of Technology (Oregon Tech), Klamath Community College, Klamath County Museum, Favell Museum of Western Art, Ross Ragland Theatre, Spence Mountain and Moore Park trail systems

Klamath County is the proud home of Kingsley Air Base, that trains F-15 fighter pilots and employs more than 1,000 people, making it the third largest employer in the county.

The Klamath or "Clamitte" Tribe, for which Klamath County was named, has had a presence for thousands of years. The Legislature created Klamath County by dividing Lake County in 1882. Linkville was named county seat, and its name was changed to Klamath Falls in 1893. The railroad came in the early 1900s. Also, work began on the federal Klamath Project, a reclamation which drained much of the 128 square mile Lower Klamath Lake to provide 188,000 acres of irrigable land for agriculture, a major contributor to the basin's economy, despite competing with the tribes and fish for available water.

Klamath boasts more than 300 sunny days a year and is home to dozens of large-scale solar projects. Natural geothermal hot wells provide heat for many homes, businesses and the Oregon Tech campus. Oregon Tech was the first university in the country to be powered completely by renewable energy and is home to Oregon Renewable Energy Center.

County Officials: Commissioners—Chair Kelley Minty-Morris 2027; Dave Henslee 2027, Derrick DeGroot 2025; Dist. Atty. VACANT; Assess. Nathan Bigby 2023; Clerk Rochelle Long 2027; Justice of the Peace Karen Oakes 2027; Sheriff Chris Kaber 2025; Surv. Sheryl Hatcher 2025; Treas. Vickie Noel 2027

Lake County

County Seat: Courthouse, 513 Center St., Lakeview 97630
Phone: 541-947-6006 (General); 541-947-6051 (Court Administrator)
Fax: 541-947-6015
Email: sgeaney@co.lake.or.us
Web: lakecountyor.org
Established:
October 24, 1874
Elev. at Lakeview: 4,800'
Area: 8,359 sq. mi.
Average Temp.:
January 28.4°
July 67.0°
Assessed Value:
$968,362,522
Real Market Value: $2,083,205,062 (includes the value of non-taxed properties)
Annual Precipitation: 15.80"
Economy: Livestock, forest products, agriculture and recreation
Points of Interest: Hart Mountain Antelope Refuge, Fort Rock and Fort Rock Homestead Village Museum, Abert Lake and Rim, Goose Lake, Hunter's Hot Springs, Old Perpetual Geyser, Schminck Memorial Museum and Lake County Museum, Lake County Round-Up Museum, Warner Canyon Ski Area, Gearhart Wilderness, Lost Forest, Crack-in-the-Ground, Sheldon National Wildlife Refuge, Summer Lake Hot Springs, Hole-in-the-Ground, sunstones (Oregon's state gemstone) near Plush, Warner Wetlands, Summer Lake Wildlife Area

Lake County was created from Jackson and Wasco Counties by the 1874 Legislature. It then included the present Klamath County and all of the present Lake County except Warner Valley. In 1882, Klamath was removed, and in 1885, the Warner area from Grant County was added.

Linkville, now Klamath Falls, was the first county seat. M. Bullard gave 20 acres as the Lakeview townsite. In the 1875 election, the county seat was moved to Lakeview. The Hart Mountain Antelope Refuge is a 270,000 acre wildlife haven for antelope, mule deer, bighorn sheep and upland birds. A number of migratory waterfowl flyways converge on Goose Lake, south of Lakeview, the Warner Wetlands near Plush and the Summer Lake Wildlife area. Lakeview has been deemed the hang-gliding capital of the West.

County Officials: Commissioners—Chair James Williams 2027; Mark Albertson 2027, Barry Shullenberger 2025; Dist. Atty. Ted K. Martin 2025; Assess. Dave Knowles 2025; Clerk Stacie Geaney 2025; Sheriff Michael Taylor 2027; Surv. Darryl Anderson 2027; Treas. Ann Crumrine 2025

Lane County

County Seat: Courthouse, 125 E Eighth Ave., Eugene 97401

Phone: 541-682-4203 (General); 541-682-4166 (Court Administrator)

Fax: 541-682-4616

Web: lanecounty.org

Established:
Jan. 28, 1851

Elev. at Eugene:
422'

Area: 4,620 sq. mi.

Average Temp.:
January 40°
July 70°

Assessed Value:
$38,119,932,666

Real Market Value: $77,009,875,845 (includes the value of non-taxed properties)

Annual Precipitation: 46"

Economy: Agriculture, higher education, high technology-manufacturing, forest products, recreation, recreational vehicle manufacturing and tourism

Points of Interest: Twenty historic covered bridges, Bohemia Mines, coastal sand dunes, Darlingtonia Botanical Wayside, Fern Ridge Reservoir, Heceta Head Lighthouse, Hendricks Park Rhododendron Garden, hot springs, Hult Center for the Performing Arts, Lane Community College, Lane ESD Planetarium, Martin Rapids whitewater, McKenzie Pass, Mt. Pisgah Arboretum, Old Town Florence, Pac-12 sports events, Proxy Falls, Sea Lion Caves, University of Oregon, vineyards and wineries, Waldo Lake, Carl G. Washburne State Park tide pools, Willamette Pass ski area

Lane County was named for General Joseph Lane, Oregon's first territorial governor. Pioneers traveling the Oregon Trail in the late 1840s came to Lane County mainly to farm. The county's first district court met under a large oak tree until a clerk's office was built in 1852. A few years later, the first courthouse opened in what is now downtown Eugene. With the building of the railroads, the market for timber opened in the 1880s. Today, wood products are still an important part of the economy in addition to high-technology manufacturing and tourism. Lane County government operates under a home rule charter approved by voters in 1962.

· Although 90 percent of Lane County is forest land, Eugene and Springfield comprise the second largest urban area in Oregon.

County Officials: Commissioners—Chair Pat Farr 2025; Ryan Ceniga 2023, Dave Loveall 2027, Heather Buch 2027, Laurie Trieger 2025; Dist. Atty. Patricia Perlow 2025; Assess. Mary Vuksich-Shafer; Clerk ; Justice of the Peace Rick Brissenden 2027; Sheriff Clifton Harrold 2025; Surv. Jay Blomme; Co. Admin. Steve Mokrohisky

Lincoln County

County Seat: Courthouse, 225 W Olive St., Newport 97365

Phone: 541-265-6611 (General); 541-265-4236 (Court Administrator)

Fax: 541-265-4176

Email: djenkins@co.lincoln.or.us

Web: co.lincoln.or.us

Established:
Feb. 20, 1893

Elev. at Newport:
134'

Area: 992 sq. mi.

Average Temp.:
January 44.4°
July 57.6°

Assessed Value:
$8,892,763,888

Real Market Value: $14,515,065,678 (includes the value of non-taxed properties)

Annual Precipitation: 71.93"

Economy: Tourism, government, services and retail, forest products and fishing

Points of Interest: Agate Beach, Alsea Bay Interpretive Center, Beverly Beach State Park, Boiler Bay, Cape Perpetua Visitors' Center, Cascade Head, Connie Hansen Garden Conservancy, Devil's Lake, Lincoln County Historical Museum, Newport Performing and Visual Arts Centers, OSU Hatfield Marine Science Center and Interpretive Center, Oregon Coast Aquarium, Otter Crest Viewpoint, Seal Rock Park, South Beach State Park, Yaquina Arts Center, Yaquina Bay State Park and Lighthouse, Yaquina Head Outstanding Natural Area

With miles of beach and coastline, Lincoln County is one of the most popular visitor destinations on the Oregon Coast. Named for President Abraham Lincoln, Lincoln County was created by the Oregon Legislature in 1893. Lincoln County has a very temperate climate and a short, but productive, growing season.

Depoe Bay is known as "the whale watching capital of the world." Lincoln City offers more than 2,000 hotel, motel and bed and breakfast rooms and resorts, as well as the Siletz Tribe's Chinook Winds Casino. Newport, known as Oregon's oceanography research center, features numerous interpretive centers and the Oregon Coast Aquarium, along with a large fishing fleet and working bay front. Siletz is the home of the Administration Center and reservation of the Confederated Tribes of Siletz Indians of Oregon. Toledo is known as Lincoln County's industrial center. Waldport features the Alsea Bay Interpretive Center. Yachats is known as the "Gem of the Oregon Coast."

County Officials: Commissioners—Chair Claire Hall 2025; Kaety Jacobson 2027, Casey Miller 2027; Dist. Atty. Lanee Danforth 2025; Assess. Joe Davidson 2025; Clerk Amy Southwell 2027; Sheriff Curtis Landers 2025; Surv. Eli Adam; Treas. Jayne Welch 2027

Linn County

County Seat: Courthouse, 300 SW Fourth Ave., Albany 97321
Phone: 541-967-3825 (General); 541-967-3802 (Court Administrator)
Fax: 541-926-8226
Email: sdruckenmiller@co.linn.or.us
Web: co.linn.or.us
Established:
Dec. 28, 1847
Elev. at Albany:
210'
Area: 2,297 sq. mi.
Average Temp.:
January 39.0°
July 65.6°
Assessed Value:
$11,744,039,973
Real Market Value: $21,193,422,962 (includes the value of non-taxed properties)
Annual Precipitation: 42.55"
Economy: Agriculture, forest products, rare metals, manufacturing and recreation
Points of Interest: Willamette and Santiam Rivers, Foster, Green Peter and Detroit Reservoirs, Cascade Range mountains with Mount Jefferson, Hoodoo Ski Bowl and the Pacific Crest Trail, covered bridges, Fair and Expo Center, Brownsville Museum, Albany historic districts

Linn County was created in 1847 and named for U.S. Senator Lewis F. Linn of Missouri, who was the author of the Donation Land Act which provided free land to settlers in the West. Linn County is in the center of the Willamette Valley, with the Willamette River as its western boundary and the crest of the Cascades as its eastern boundary. The climate and soil conditions provide one of Oregon's most diversified agriculture areas, allowing a wide variety of specialty crops and leading the nation in the production of common and perennial ryegrass. Linn County is also home to major producers of processed food, manufactured homes and motor homes, as well as the traditional logging and wood products industries.

Recreational opportunities are extensive and include hiking, climbing and skiing, picnicking and camping in county and state parks; boating, water skiing and fishing on lakes and rivers; petrified wood and agate beds; covered bridges and historic districts and events.
County Officials: Commissioners— Chair Roger Nyquist 2025; Will Tucker 2027, Sherrie Sprenger 2025; Dist. Atty. Douglas Marteeny 2025; Assess. Andy Stevens 2025; Clerk Steven Druckenmiller 2027; Justice of the Peace Jessica K. Meyer 2027; Sheriff Michelle Duncan 2027; Surv. Thomas Casey 2025; Treas. Michelle Hawkins 2025; Co. Admin. Darrin L. Lane

Malheur County

County Seat: 251 B St. W, Vale 97918
Phone: 541-473-5151 (General); 541-473-5171 (Court Administrator)
Fax: 541-473-5523
Email: CountyClerk@malheurco.org
Web: malheurco.org
Established:
Feb. 17, 1887
Elev. at Vale:
2,243'
Area: 9,926 sq. mi.
Average Temp.:
January 28.7°
July 75.6°
Assessed Value:
$2,438,180,064
Real Market Value: $4,312,983,540 (includes the value of non-taxed properties)
Annual Precipitation: 9.64"
Economy: Agriculture, livestock, food processing and recreation
Points of Interest: Oregon Trail, Keeney Pass, Owyhee Lake, Succor Creek State Park, Leslie Gulch Canyon, Jordan Craters, grave of trapper John Baptiste Charbonneau, Nyssa Agricultural Museum, Vale Oregon Trail Murals, Jordan Valley Basque Pelota Court, Four Rivers Cultural Center

Malheur County was created in 1887 from Baker County. Malheur County derives its name from the "Riviere au Malheur" or "Unfortunate River" (later changed to "Malheur River"), named by French trappers whose property and furs were stolen from their river encampment.

Malheur County is a place filled with fascinating history, diverse landscape and friendly people. The landscape is enchanting and provides for a wide variety of excellent recreation such as hunting, fishing, hiking, rock climbing, rock hounding, boating and water skiing. The county is 94 percent rangeland. Basques, primarily shepherds, settled in Jordan Valley in the 1890s. Irrigated fields in the county's northeast corner, known as Western Treasure Valley, are the center of intensive and diversified farming.
County Officials: County Court—Judge Dan Joyce 2027; Ron Jacobs 2025, Jim Mendiola 2027; Dist. Atty. David M. Goldthorpe 2027; Assess. Dave Ingram 2025; Clerk Gayle Trotter 2027; Justice of the Peace Margaret (Margie) Mahony 2025; Sheriff Brian E. Wolfe 2025; Surv. Tom Edwards; Treas. Jennifer Forsyth 2027; Co. Admin. and Chief Information Officer Lorinda DuBois

Marion County

County Seat: 100 High St. NE, Salem 97301
Phone: 503-588-5225 (General); 503-588-5105 (Court Administrator)
Fax: 503-373-4408
Email: recording@co.marion.or.us
Web: co.marion.or.us
Established:
   July 5, 1843
Elev. at Salem:
   154'
Area: 1,194 sq. mi.
Average Temp.:
   January 39.3°
   July 66.3°
Assessed Value:
   $28,765,707,802
Real Market Value: $49,733,130,631
(includes the value of non-taxed properties)
Annual Precipitation: 40.35"
Economy: Government, agriculture, food processing, forest products, manufacturing, education and tourism
Points of Interest: State Capitol, Champoeg State Park, Silver Falls State Park, The Oregon Garden, Wheatland Ferry, Buena Vista Ferry, Detroit Dam and Santiam River, Breitenbush Hot Springs, Mount Angel Abbey, food processing plants, Willamette University, Chemeketa Community College, Willamette Heritage Center, Bush House, Deepwood House, Gilbert House Children's Museum

Marion County, then called Champooick, was created by the Provisional Government in 1843, sixteen years before Oregon gained statehood. In 1849, the name was changed to Marion in honor of General Francis Marion.

The county, located in the heart of the Willamette Valley, has the Willamette River as its western boundary and the Cascade Range on the east. Salem is the county seat and is one of the valley's oldest cities. Among its public buildings are the Marion County Courthouse, State Capitol, Capitol Mall buildings and Salem Civic Center. The county was presided over by the Marion County Court until January 1, 1963, when the court was abolished and replaced by a Board of Commissioners.

County Officials: Commissioners—Danielle Bethell 2025, Kevin Cameron 2027, Colm Willis 2027; Dist. Atty. Paige Clarkson 2027; Assess. Tom Rohlfing 2025; Clerk Bill Burgess 2025; Justice of the Peace Justin Kidd 2029; Sheriff Joe Kast 2025; Surv. Kent Inman; Treas. Sam Brentano 2027; CFO Janice Fritz

Morrow County

County Seat: Courthouse, 100 S Court St., Heppner; PO Box 788, Heppner 97836
Phone: 541-676-5600 (General); 541-676-2529 (Court Administrator)
Fax: 541-676-5621
Email: bchilders@co.morrow.or.us
Web: co.morrow.or.us
Established:
   Feb. 16, 1885
Elev. at Heppner:
   1,955'
Area: 2,049 sq. mi.
Average Temp.:
   January 33.1°
   July 69.0°
Assessed Value:
   $2,946,622,312
Real Market Value: $8,128,742,745
(includes the value of non-taxed properties)
Annual Precipitation: 12.5"
Economy: Agriculture, food processing, dairies, utilities, forest products, livestock and recreation
Points of Interest: Columbia River, Blue Mountains, Umatilla National Forest, Oregon Trail, Blue Mountain Scenic Byway, Morrow County Museum, Port of Morrow, Lewis and Clark Route

Morrow County was created from Umatilla County in 1885 and is located east of the Cascades in north-central Oregon. It was named for J. L. Morrow, an early resident. Morrow County contains more than one-million acres of gently rolling plains and broad plateaus. This rich agricultural land can be roughly divided into three occupational zones—increasing amounts of irrigation farming in the north, vast fields of wheat yielding to cattle ranches in the center, and timber products in the south. With the advent of center pivot irrigation-technology, Morrow County became one of Oregon's fastest growing areas by population, personal income, and agricultural and industrial development. The Port of Morrow, second largest in the state in terms of tonnage, serves as a gateway to the Pacific Northwest and Pacific Rim markets.

County Officials: Commissioners— David Sykes 2027, Jeff Wenholz 2027, VACANT 2024; Dist. Atty. Justin Nelson 2027; Assess. Mike Gorman 2027; Clerk Bobbi Childers 2025; Justice of the Peace Glen G. Diehl 2027; Sheriff Kenneth Matlack 2025; Surv. Matt Kenny; Treas. Jaylene Papineau 2025

Multnomah County

County Seat: 501 SE Hawthorne Blvd., Portland 97214

Phone: 503-823-4000 (General); 971-274-0500 (Court Administrator)

Web: multco.us

Established:
Dec. 22, 1854

Elev. at Portland:
77'

Area: 465 sq. mi.

Average Temp.:
January 38.9°
July 67.7°

Assessed Value:
$92,500,160,930

Real Market Value: $204,108,620,153 (includes the value of non-taxed properties)

Annual Precipitation: 37.39"

Economy: Manufacturing, transportation, wholesale and retail trade, and tourism

Points of Interest: Oregon Historical Society, Oregon Museum of Science and Industry, Oregon Zoo, Portland Art Museum, Washington Park, International Rose Test Gardens, Japanese Gardens, Columbia River Gorge, Multnomah Falls, Blue Lake Park, Oxbow Park, Pittock Mansion, Port of Portland, Memorial Coliseum and Rose Quarter, Oregon Convention Center, Moda Center Arena, Vista House

Lewis and Clark made note of "Multnomah," the tribal village on Sauvie Island, in 1805 and applied that name to all tribal people of the area. The name is derived from "nematlnomaq," probably meaning "downriver." Multnomah County was created from parts of Washington and Clackamas counties by the Territorial Legislature in 1854, five years before Oregon became a state, because citizens found it inconvenient to travel to Hillsboro to conduct county business.

The county is both the smallest in size and largest in population in Oregon. Over 50 percent of its people live in Portland, a busy metropolis dominated by rivers and greenery. The remaining area includes picturesque rural land, from pastoral farms on Sauvie Island to the rugged Columbia River Gorge and the western slopes of Mount Hood.

County Officials: Commissioners—Chair Jessica Vega Pederson 2027; Sharon Meieran 2025, Susheela Jayapal 2027, Lori Stegmann 2025, Interim Commissioner Diane Rosenbaum 2023; Dist. Atty. Mike Schmidt 2025; Sheriff Nicole Morrisey-O'Donnell 2027; Auditor Jennifer McGuirk 2027; Assess. Michael Vaughn; Elections Director Tim Scott; Surv. James Clayton; Attorney Jenny Madkour

Polk County

County Seat: Courthouse, 850 Main St., Dallas 97338

Phone: 503-623-8173 (General); 503-623-3154 (Court Administrator)

Fax: 503-623-0896

Email: unger.valerie@co.polk.or.us

Web: co.polk.or.us

Established:
Dec. 22, 1845

Elev. at Dallas: 325'

Area: 745 sq. mi.

Average Temp.:
January 39.1°
July 65.6°

Assessed Value:
$7,082,007,884

Real Market Value: $12,819,110,294 (includes the value of non-taxed properties)

Annual Precipitation: 51.66"

Economy: Agriculture, forest products, manufacturing, electronics and education

Points of Interest: Western Oregon University, covered bridges, historic courthouse, Brunk House, Baskett Slough National Wildlife Refuge, mountain scenery, wineries, National Historic Trail, Confederated Tribes of Grand Ronde Headquarters, Spirit Mountain Casino

Polk County was created from the original Yamhill district in 1845 by the Provisional Legislature. It was named for then President James Knox Polk. The first county seat was at Cynthia Ann. City officials later changed its name to Dallas, after Vice-President George M. Dallas, and moved the community about a mile to improve its water supply.

The first courthouse was at Cynthia Ann. A second courthouse burned in 1898 and was replaced with the present building built with sandstone quarried three miles west of Dallas. A three-story office annex was completed in 1966. Polk County Human Services was consolidated in the newly acquired Academy Building in 1989.

Traveling back roads in Polk County will reveal many attractions, from covered bridges and pleasant parks to vineyards, wineries, and bed and breakfast lodgings spotting the surrounding hills. Many roads meander through beautiful fertile valleys from the Willamette River to the timbered foothills of the Coast Range. Polk County was the primary destination of early wagon trains which took the southern route to Oregon. Cities located in Polk County include Dallas, Independence, Monmouth, Falls City and portions of Salem and Willamina.

County Officials: Commissioners—Chair Craig Pope 2027, Jeremy Gordon 2027, Lyle R. Mordhorst 2025; Dist. Atty. Aaron Felton 2025; Assess. Valerie Patoine 2025; Clerk Valerie Unger 2025; Sheriff Mark A. Garton 2025; Surv. Eric Berry; Treas. Steve Milligan 2025; Co. Admin. Greg P. Hansen

Sherman County

County Seat: Courthouse, 500 Court St., Moro 97039

Phone: 541-565-3606 (Clerk); 541-565-3650 (Court Clerk)

Fax: 541-565-3771

Email: countyclerk@shermancounty.net

Web: co.sherman.or.us

Established:
Feb. 25, 1889

Elev. at Moro:
1,807'

Area: 831 sq. mi.

Average Temp.:
January 30.7°
July 67.9°

Assessed Value:
$575,420,343

Real Market Value: $1,687,539,444 (includes the value of non-taxed properties)

Annual Precipitation: 9.15"

Economy: Tourism, wind energy, wheat, barley and cattle

Points of Interest: Historic county courthouse, Sherman County Museum, Gordon Ridge, John Day Dam, Sherar's Grade, Deschutes State Park, LePage Park, Giles French Park, Sherman County Fairgrounds, Recreational Vehicle Park

Sherman County was created in 1889 from the northeast corner of Wasco County and named for General William Tecumseh Sherman. It was separated from Wasco County as much for its unique geological setting as for the settlers' desire to have their own political process. The rolling hills are bordered by the deep canyons of the John Day River to the east, the Columbia River to the north, and the Deschutes River and Buck Hollow to the west and south.

The county was settled in the 1870s by stockmen. By 1881, the homesteaders arrived, permanently changing the area by plowing and fencing the land. Since then, the county has been a wheat-growing area with miles of waving grain on rolling hills of wind-blown glacial silt. The total absence of timber in the county exemplifies the true meaning of the "wide open spaces of the West." Its pastoral landscape has spectacular views of canyons and rivers with mountains silhouetted in the distance. Recreation abounds on the rivers, from the famous and scenic fly-fishing and whitewater rafting stream of the Deschutes to water-skiing, wind-surfing, boating, fishing and rafting on the John Day and Columbia Rivers. Sherman County is one of Oregon's leaders in soil and water conservation.

County Officials: County Court—Judge Joe Dabulskis 2025; Joan Bird 2025, Justin Miller 2027; Dist. Atty. Wade McLeod 2027; Assess. Drew Messenger 2027; Clerk Kristi Weis 2025; Treas. Theresa Olsen 2027; Justice of the Peace Shandie L. Johnson 2027; Sheriff Brad Lohrey 2025; Surv. Daryl Ingebo

Tillamook County

County Seat: Courthouse, 201 Laurel Ave., Tillamook 97141

Phone: 503-842-2034 (General); 503-842-2596, ext. 124 (Court Administrator)

Fax: 503-842-2721

Email: toneil@co.tillamook.or.us

Web: co.tillamook.or.us

Established:
Dec. 15, 1853

Elev. at Tillamook:
22'

Area: 1,125 sq. mi.

Average Temp.:
January 42.2°
July 58.2°

Assessed Value:
$5,723,141,096

Real Market Value: $8,637,807,056 (includes the value of non-taxed properties)

Annual Precipitation: 90.90"

Economy: Agriculture, forest products, fishing and recreation

Points of Interest: Neah-Kah-Nie Mountain; Tillamook, Nehalem, Netarts and Nestucca bays; Oswald West State Park, Nehalem Bay State Park, Bob Straub State Park, Cape Lookout State Park; Pioneer Museum, Blue Heron Cheese Factory, Tillamook Cheese Factory, Naval Air Station Museum, Haystack Rock at Cape Kiwanda, Whalen Island State Park

Tillamook County was formed in 1853 from Yamhill and Clatsop counties. The name Tillamook comes from the Tillamook (or Killamook) Tribe.

Dairy farms dominate the county's fertile valley. It is the home of the world famous Tillamook Cheese Factory. The reforested 355,000-acre "Tillamook Burn" area continues to mature. Commercial thinning will become increasingly evident. With 75 miles of scenic coastline, four bays and nine rivers, Tillamook County offers the finest deep-sea and stream fishing, charter and dory boats, clamming, crabbing, beachcombing and hiking. Its forests also furnish excellent hunting.

County Officials: Commissioners—Chair David Yamamoto 2025; Bill Baertlein 2025, Mary Faith Bell 2027; Dist. Atty. Aubrey Olson 2027; Assess. Denise Vandecoevering 2025; Clerk Tassi O'Neil 2025; Justice of the Peace Ryan Connell 2025; Sheriff Josh Brown 2025; Surv. Michael Rice; Treas. Shawn Blanchard 2027

Umatilla County

County Seat: Courthouse, 216 SE Fourth St., Pendleton 97801
Phone: 541-276-7111 (General); 541-278-0341, Pendleton, 541-667-3020, Hermiston (Court Administrators)
Email: records@umatillacounty.net
Web: co.umatilla.or.us
Established: Sept. 27, 1862
Elev. at Pendleton: 1,069'
Area: 3,231 sq. mi.
Average Temp.: January 31.9° July 73.6°
Assessed Value: $7,051,945,990

Real Market Value: $11,400,636,939 (includes the value of non-taxed properties)
Annual Precipitation: 12.97"
Economy: Agriculture, food processing, forest products, manufacturing, recreation, aggregate production and wind power generation

Tourism is also increasingly important to Umatilla County where "Let-er-Buck" is heard by Pendleton Round-Up crowds.

Points of Interest: Pendleton Round-Up & Happy Canyon Indian Pageant & Wild West Show, Old Town Pendleton, Pendleton Woolen Mills, Pendleton Whisky Music Festival, Pendleton Bike Week, County Historical Society, Pendleton Underground, McNary Dam and Recreation Area, Echo Museum and Historic Area, Hat Rock, Battle Mountain and Emigrant Springs State Parks, Weston Historic District, Frazier Farmstead Museum in Milton-Freewater, North Fork Umatilla Wilderness Area, Tollgate-Spout Springs Recreation Area, Courthouse Clock Tower, Stateline Wind Project, Confederated Tribes of the Umatilla Indian Reservation's Tamastslikt Cultural Center and Wildhorse Casino

Umatilla County traces its creation in 1862 to the regional gold rushes, which spawned the riverport of Umatilla City and brought stockraisers to the lush grasslands.

Although Lewis and Clark and the Oregon Trail pioneers passed through Umatilla County, it did not bloom until the arrival of the railroad in 1881 and the development of dryland wheat farming.

Water in the form of irrigation has been key to economic diversification and growth, most recently in the Hermiston area, where the desert now yields lush watermelons and other products.

County Officials: Commissioners—Chair John Shafer 2027; Dan Dorran 2025, Cindy Timmons 2027; Dist. Atty. Daniel R. Primus 2025; Sheriff Terry Rowan 2025; Assess. Paul Chalmers; Rec. Mgr. Steve Churchill; Surv. David Krumbein; Financial Mgr. Robert Pahl; Admin. Serv. Director Dan Lonai

Union County

County Seat: Union County Commissioners, 1106 K Ave., La Grande 97850
Phone: 541-963-1001 (General); 541-962-9500, ext. 232 (Court Administrator)
Fax: 541-963-1079
Email: rchurch@union-county.org
Web: union-county.org
Established: Oct. 14, 1864
Elev. at La Grande: 2,788'
Area: 2,038 sq. mi.
Average Temp.: January 30.9° July 70.4°
Assessed Value: $2,220,997,404
Real Market Value: $3,797,720,810 (includes the value of non-taxed properties)
Annual Precipitation: 18.79"
Economy: Agriculture, forest products, education and government
Points of Interest: Meacham and Tollgate winter sports areas, Grande Ronde Valley, Eastern Oregon University (La Grande)

Union County was created in 1864 and named for the town of Union, which had been established two years before and named by its founders for patriotic reasons during the Civil War. The county comprised a part of the northern portion of Baker County. In 1899, Union County gave up its eastern portion to Wallowa County.

The Grande Ronde Valley in Union County is nearly table flat and is covered with the rich silt of an old lake bed. Highly diversified, with a 160-day growing season and an annual rainfall of 20 inches, the valley boasts of never having had a general crop failure. The county's 1,092 farms average 473 acres a unit.

Union County's front door opens to the rugged Wallowa Mountains. Its back door faces the Blue Mountains, which attract hikers, skiers and hunters.

County Officials: Commissioners—Chair Paul Anderes 2027, Donna Beverage 2025, Matt Scarfo 2027; Dist. Atty. Kelsie McDaniel 2027; Assess. Cody Vavra 2025; Clerk Lisa Feik 2027; Sheriff Cody Bowen 2025; Surv. Rick G Robinson; Treas. Camee Jensen 2027; Co. Admin. and Chief Info. Officer Shelley Burgess

Wallowa County

County Seat: Courthouse, 101 S River St., Enterprise 97828
Phone: 541-426-4543 ext. 15 (General); 541-426-4991 (Court Administrator)
Fax: 541-426-0582
Email: wcclerk@co.wallowa.or.us
Web: co.wallowa.or.us
Established:
Feb. 11, 1887
Elev. at Enterprise: 3,757'
Area: 3,153 sq. mi.
Average Temp.:
January 24.2°
July 63.0°
Assessed Value: $949,919,533
Real Market Value: $2,605,933,730 (includes the value of non-taxed properties)
Annual Precipitation: 13.08"
Economy: Agriculture, art, livestock, forest products and recreation
Points of Interest: Wallowa Lake, art galleries, Mount Howard gondola, Eagle Cap Wilderness, Hells Canyon National Recreation Area, Minam, Wallowa and Grande Ronde Rivers

This rather isolated area was claimed by the Chief Joseph band of the Nez Perce as its hunting and fishing grounds. The Nez Perce used the word "wallowa" to designate a tripod of poles used to support fish nets. In 1871, the first white settlers came to Wallowa County crossing the mountains in search of livestock feed in the Wallowa Valley. The area had been part of Union County since 1864, but it was carved from that county in 1887 by a legislative act.

Wallowa County is a land of rugged mountains, gentle valleys and deep canyons. Peaks in the Wallowa Mountains soar to almost 10,000 feet in elevation and the Snake River drops over 8,500 feet in elevation over its length. Hells Canyon, carved by the Snake, is the nation's deepest gorge averaging 5,500 feet from rim to river.

The scenery in the county is spectacular and serves as a magnet for tourists. Unrivaled opportunities for outdoor recreation create the county's reputation as a visitors' paradise. Permanent residents enjoy the same recreation opportunities, adding to a high quality of life supported by traditional farm and forest industries, as well as art and tourism.

County Officials: Commissioners—Chair Todd Nash 2025; John Hillock 2027, Susan Roberts 2025; Dist. Atty. Rebecca Frolander 2027; Assess. Randy Wortman 2025; Clerk Sandy Lathrop 2027; Sheriff Joel Fish 2025; Treas. Ginger Goebel-Burns 2027; Surv. Richard Shaver

Wasco County

County Seat: Courthouse, 511 Washington St., The Dalles 97058
Phone: 541-506-2500 (General); 541-506-2700 (Court Administrator)
Fax: 541-506-2531
Email: countyclerk@co.wasco.or.us
Web: co.wasco.or.us
Established:
Jan. 11, 1854
Elev. at The Dalles: 98'
Area: 2,396 sq. mi.
Average Temp.:
January 33.4°
July 73.1°
Assessed Value: $2,716,171,881
Real Market Value: $6,928,713,957 (includes the value of non-taxed properties)
Annual Precipitation: 14.9"
Economy: Agriculture, forest products, manufacturing, electric power, aluminum and transportation
Points of Interest: Columbia and Deschutes Rivers, Fort Dalles Museum, Pulpit Rock, The Dalles Dam, Celilo Converter Station, Confederated Tribes of the Warm Springs Reservation, Mount Hood, Sorosis Park, original Wasco County Courthouse, St. Peter's Landmark, Columbia River Gorge Discovery Center

When the Territorial Legislature created Wasco County in 1854 from parts of Clackamas, Lane, Linn and Marion Counties, it embraced all of Oregon east of the Cascade Range, most of Idaho and parts of Montana and Wyoming. It was named for the Wasco, or Wascopam, Tribe.

Wasco's county seat is The Dalles. Now the trading hub of north-central Oregon, The Dalles gained earlier fame as the town at the end of the Oregon Trail. Thousands of years before that, humans scratched pictographs on rocks overlooking the Columbia River in this area. Later, tribes gathered for generations near Celilo Falls to trade and fish. The county's tribal heritage continues in evidence today.

County Officials: Commissioners—Scott Hege 2027, Steve Kramer 2025, Phil Brady 2027; Dist. Atty. Matthew Ellis 2025; Assess. Jill Filla Amery 2025; Clerk Lisa Gambee 2025; Sheriff Lane Magill 2025; Surv. Brad Cross; Treas. Elijah Preston 2025

Washington County

County Seat: 155 N First Ave., Suite 300, Hillsboro 97124
Phone: 503-846-8611 (General); 503-846-8888 (Court Administrator)
Fax: 503-846-4545
Email: elections@co.washington.or.us
Web: co.washington.or.us
Established:
July 5, 1843

Elev. at Hillsboro:
196'
Area: 727 sq. mi.
Average Temp.:
January 39.9°
July 66.6°
Assessed Value:
$74,371,914,305
Real Market Value: $131,278,858,403
(includes the value of non-taxed properties)
Annual Precipitation: 37.71"
Economy: Agriculture, horticulture, forest products, food processing, high tech, sports equipment and apparel
Points of Interest: Tualatin Valley orchards and vineyards, Pacific University, Wilson River, Sunset Highway, Hagg Lake, Old Scotch Church

The original four counties created by the Provisional Government of Oregon were Twality, Clackamas, Yamhill and Champoick. Twality was changed to Washington in honor of President George Washington by the Territorial Legislature on September 3, 1849. The actual organization of Washington County government followed several years later.

Now one of the state's fastest developing areas, the fertile Tualatin Valley was once filled with beaver and was a favorite hunting ground for Hudson's Bay Company trappers. The first white settlers arrived around 1840, lured by rich soil. Despite its rapid urbanization, the valley still contains prime agricultural land. Many small towns rich in history dot the area. Pacific University, founded as Tualatin Academy in 1849, is one of the oldest colleges in the West. Washington County operates under a home rule charter approved by voters in 1962. The Northwest's largest enclosed shopping center, Washington Square, is located south of Beaverton.

County Officials: Commissioners—Chair Kathryn Harrington 2027; Nafisa Fai 2025, Roy Rogers 2025, Pam Treece 2027, Jerry Willey 2027; Dist. Atty. Kevin Barton 2027; Justice of the Peace Dan Cross 2029; Sheriff Pat Garrett 2025; Auditor Kristine Adams-Wannberg 2027; Assess./Clerk Margaret Garza; Surv. Scott Young; Co. Admin. Tanya Ange; CIOs Phillip Bransford & Julie McCloud

Wheeler County

County Seat: Courthouse, 701 Adams St., Fossil 97830
Phone: 541-763-2400 (General); 541-763-2541 (Court Administrator)
Fax: 541-763-2026
Email: bsnowpotter@co.wheeler.or.us
Web: wheelercountyoregon.com
Established:
Feb. 17, 1899
Elev. at Fossil:
2,654'
Area: 1,715 sq. mi.
Average Temp.:
January 35°
July 66°
Assessed Value:
$163,794,937
Real Market Value: $864,543,150
(includes the value of non-taxed properties)
Annual Precipitation: 14.66"
Economy: Livestock and tourism
Points of Interest: Clarno and Painted Hills Units of the John Day Fossil Bed National Monument, John Day River

Wheeler County was formed by the Oregon Legislature in 1899 from parts of Grant, Gilliam and Crook counties and was named for Henry H. Wheeler, who operated the first mail stage line from The Dalles to Canyon City. The new county consisted of 1,656 square miles with an estimated 46 townships, a population of 1,600 and taxable property worth one million dollars.

Wheeler County is as rugged and uneven as any Oregon county, with the terrain varying widely from sagebrush, juniper and rim rock to stands of pine and fir. Portions of two national forests lie within its boundaries with forest lands covering nearly one-third of the county. The area is probably best known as one of the most outstanding depositories of prehistoric fossils on the North American continent.

County Officials: County Court—Judge Lynn Morley 2027; Clinton Dyer 2025, Rick Shaffer 2027; Dist. Atty. Gretchen M. Ladd 2025; Assess. Auralea Johnson 2027; Clerk Brenda Snow Potter 2025; Justice of the Peace Robin Ordway Campbell 2027; Sheriff Mike Smith 2025; Surv. Michael Springer 2025; Treas. Sandra K. Speer 2027

❖❖❖

Yamhill County

County Seat: Courthouse, 535 NE Fifth St., McMinnville 97128
Phone: 503-434-7501 (General); 503-434-7530 (Court Administrator)
Fax: 503-434-7553
Email: clerk@co.yamhill.or.us
Web: co.yamhill.or.us
Established:
  July 5, 1843
Elev. at
  McMinnville:
  157'
Area: 718 sq. mi.
Average Temp.:
  January 39.0°
  July 65.0°
Assessed Value: $10,457,434,932
Real Market Value: $20,045,715,356
(includes the value of non-taxed properties)
Annual Precipitation: 43.6"
Economy: Agriculture, wine production, manufacturing, forest products, dental instruments, education and health care
Points of Interest: Linfield College, George Fox University, Herbert Hoover House, Yamhill County Historical Museum, Wheatland Ferry, Evergreen Aviation and Space Museum, Rogers Landing

Created in 1843, Yamhill County was one of Oregon's original four districts. Its current boundaries were established in 1860. The county was named after the Yamhelas, members of the Kalapuya Tribe, who lived along the Yamhill River in the western Willamette Valley.

Agriculture is still the county's primary industry. Nursery and greenhouse crops; fruit trees, nuts, wine grapes, berries, hay, silage, field and grass seeds are major agricultural products. Yamhill County ranks sixth among the counties in annual market value of its agricultural production. Yamhill County is also the heart of Oregon's wine industry. Over 80 wineries and 200 vineyards represent the largest concentration of wine growers and producers in any county in the state. One third of the county is covered with commercial timber. The mainstay of the western valley area is logging and timber products. With 276 manufacturers, Yamhill County produces everything from snack foods to rebar, timber products to plastic tubing and textiles to dental equipment.

County Officials: Commissioners—Chair Lindsay Berschauer 2025; Kit Johnson 2027, Mary Starrett 2027; Dist. Atty. Bradley Berry 2025; Assess. Derrick Wharff 2025; Clerk Brian Van Bergen 2025; Sheriff Tim Svenson 2027; Treas. Kris Bledsoe 2025; Surveyor Jason Foose

REGIONAL GOVERNMENTS

Formed in 1984 under ORS Chapter 190, the Oregon Regional Councils Association (ORCA) promotes cooperation among levels of government.

The multi-jurisdictional councils are voluntary associations cooperating on issues and problems which cross city, county, and in some cases, state boundaries. The association provides a forum for exchanging and discussing common issues.

Central Oregon Intergovernmental Council

Contact: Tammy Baney, Executive Director
Address: 334 NE Hawthorne Ave., Bend 97701
Phone: 541-504-3306
Fax: 541-923-3416
Web: coic2.org

Lane Council of Governments

Contact: Brenda Wilson, Executive Director
Address: 859 Willamette St., Suite 500, Eugene 97401
Phone: 541-682-4283
Fax: 541-682-4099
Web: lcog.org

Mid-Willamette Valley Council of Governments

Contact: Renata Wakeley, Executive Director
Address: 100 High St. SE, Suite 200, Salem 97301
Phone: 503-588-6177
Web: mwvcog.org

Northwest Senior and Disability Services

Contact: Melinda Compton, Program Director; Tayna DeHart Operations Director
Address: 3410 Cherry Ave. NE, Salem 97303
Phone: 503-304-3400; Toll-free: 1-800-206-4799
Fax: 503-304-3434
Web: nwsds.org

Oregon Cascades West Council of Governments

Contact: Ryan Vogt, Executive Director
Address: 1400 Queen Ave. SE, Suite 201, Albany 97322
Phone: 541-924-8465
Fax: 541-967-6123
Web: ocwcog.org

Rogue Valley Council of Governments

Contact: Ann Marie Alfrey, Executive Director
Address: 155 N First St., PO Box 3275, Central Point 97502
Phone: 541-423-1334
Fax: 541-664-7927
Web: rvcog.org

METRO

Contact: Andy Shaw, Government Affairs Director
Address: Metro Regional Center, 600 NE Grand Ave., Portland 97232-2736
Phone: 503-797-1700
Fax: 503-797-1799
Web: oregonmetro.gov
Councilors: President Lynn Peterson 2027; Dist. 1 Ashton Simson 2027; Dist. 2 Christine Lewis 2027; Dist. 3 Gerritt Rosenthal 2025; Dist. 4 Juan Carlos Gonzalez 2027; Dist. 5 Mary Nolan 2025; Dist. 6 Duncan Hwang 2027; Auditor Brian Evans 2027

A hippopotamus at the Oregon Zoo in Portland. The zoo is operated by Metro. (Oregon State Archives scenic photo)

Metro is a regional government responsible for managing issues that cross city and county lines. It serves more than 1.6 million residents in the 24 cities and three counties in the Portland area. Metro's core responsibilities include management of the region's garbage, compost and recycling system; support of the economy through management of the Oregon Convention Center and Expo Center; preserving farm and forestland through regional planning and management of the region's urban growth boundary; management of a regional affordable housing and supportive housing program; preservation of our environment through management of 17,000 acres of parks and natural areas; and management of some of the state's top entertainment venues, including the Oregon Zoo and Portland's Centers for the Arts.

An elected seven-member council oversees Metro, and its day-to-day affairs are managed by a chief operating officer, who is appointed by the council.

The council president and auditor are elected regionally. The remaining six councilors are elected by district. All serve four-year terms. The auditor reviews Metro's operations.

The Metropolitan Service District was formed in 1970. The current Metro charter and system of governance was approved in 2002.

PORT DISTRICTS OF OREGON

Port of Alsea, Established 1910

Address: 365 Port St., PO Box 1060, Waldport 97394
Phone: 541-563-3872
Web: portofalsea.com
Commissioners: Chair Rob Bishop; Buster Pankey, Chuck Pavlik, Jan Power, Joe Rohleder; Port Mgr. Roxie Cuellar. Meets third Thursday of the month.

Port of Arlington, Established 1933

Address: 100 Port Island Rd., PO Box 279, Arlington 97812
Phone: 541-454-2868
Web: portofarlington.com
Commissioners: President: Leah Shannon; Vice-President: Ron Wilson; Kathryn Greiner, Rod McGuire, Gibb Wilkins; Port Mgr. Jed Crowther. Meets second Tuesday of the month.

Port of Astoria, Established 1914

Address: 422 Gateway Ave., Suite 100, Astoria 97103
Phone: 503-741-3300
Fax: 503-741-3345
Web: portofastoria.com
Commissioners: President Dirk Rohne; James Campbell, Scott McClaine, Frank Spence, Robert Stevens; Exec. Dir. Will Isom. Meets first Tuesday and third Tuesday of the month (third Tuesday is a workshop).

Port of Bandon, Established 1913

Address: 390 First St. SW, PO Box 206, Bandon 97411
Phone: 541-347-3206
Fax: 541-347-4645
Web: portofbandon.com
Commissioners: President Reg Pullen; Wayne Butler, Rick Goche, Donny Goddard, Rod Taylor; Port Mgr. Jeff Griffin; Harbor Master Shawn Winchell. Meets fourth Thursday of the month at 5:00 p.m.

Port of Brookings Harbor, Established 1956

Address: 16330 Lower Harbor Rd., PO Box 848, Brookings 97415
Phone: 541-469-2218
Fax: 541-359-3999
Web: portofbrookingsharbor.com
Commissioners: President Richard Heap; Sharon Hartung, Larry Jonas, Kenneth Range, Joe Speir; Port Mgr. Gary Dehlinger. Meets third Tuesday of the month.

Port of Cascade Locks, Established 1937
Address: 427 Portage Rd., PO Box 307, Cascade Locks 97014
Phone: 541-374-8619
Fax: 541-374-8428
Web: portofcascadelocks.org
Commissioners: President Jess Groves; Dean Bump, Joeinne Caldwell, Brad Lorang, John Stipan; Port Mgr. Olga Kaganova. Meets first and third Thursdays of the month.

Port of Columbia County, Established 1941
Address: 100 E St., PO Box 190, Columbia City 97018
Phone: 503-397-2888
Fax: 503-397-6924
Web: portofcolumbiacounty.org
Commissioners: President Robert Keyser; Chip Bubl, Brian Fawcett, Chris Iverson, Nancy Ward; Exec. Dir. Sean Clark. Meets second Wednesday of the month.

International Port of Coos Bay, Established 1909
Address: 125 Central Ave., Suite. 300, PO Box 1215, Coos Bay 97420
Phone: 541-267-7678
Fax: 541-269-1475
Web: portofcoosbay.com
Commissioners: President David Kronsteiner; Eric Farm, Robert Garcia, Brianna Hanson, Kyle Stevens; CEO John Burns. Meets third Tuesday of the month at 10:00.

Port of Garibaldi, Established 1910
Address: 402 S Seventh St., PO Box 10, Garibaldi 97118
Phone: 503-322-3292
Fax: 503-322-0029
Web: portofgaribaldi.org
Commissioners: President Valerie Folkema; Kelly Barnett, Robert Browning, Paul Daniels, Jaime Perez; Port Mgr. Michael Saindon. Meets second Wednesday of the month at 7:00.

Port of Gold Beach, Established 1955
Address: 29891 Harbor Way, PO Box 1126, Gold Beach 97444
Phone: 541-247-6269
Fax: 541-247-6268
Web: portofgoldbeach.com
Commissioners: President Bill McNair; Hank Eckardt, Mike Luzmoor, Charles Riddle, Walter Scherbarth; Port Mgr. Andrew Wright. Meets third Thursday of the month.

Port of Hood River, Established 1933
Address: 1000 E Port Marina Dr., Hood River 97031
Phone: 541-386-1645
Web: portofhoodriver.com
Commissioners: President Ben Sheppard; Kristi Chapman, Heather Gehring, Mike Fox, Hoby Streich; Exec. Dir. Kevin Greenwood. Meets first and third Tuesdays of the month at 5:00 p.m.

Port of Morrow, Established 1958
Address: 2 Marine Dr., PO Box 200, Boardman 97818
Phone: 541-481-7678
Fax: 541-481-2679
Web: portofmorrow.com
Commissioners: President Rick Stokoe; Jerry Healy, John Murray, Marv Padberg, Joe Taylor; Exec. Dir Lisa Mittelsdorf. Meets second Wednesday of the month.

Port of Nehalem, Established 1909
Address: 36060 6th St., PO Box 476, Nehalem 97131-0476
Phone: 503-368-7212
Fax: 503-368-7234
Web: portofnehalem.org
Commissioners: President Steve Huber; Dave Devault, Damian Laviolette, Janice Laviolette, Darrell Winegar; Office Manager Camille Hickman. Meets fourth Wednesday of the month, third Wednesday in November and December.

Port of Newport, Established 1910
Address: 600 SE Bay Blvd., Newport 97365
Phone: 541-265-7758
Fax: 541-265-4235
Web: portofnewport.com
Commissioners: President Jim Burke; Walter Chuck, Jeff Lackey, Kelley Retherford, Gil Sylvia; Gen. Manager Paula J Miranda. Meets fourth Tuesday of the month.

Port of Port Orford, Established 1919
Address: 300 Dock Rd., PO Box 490, Port Orford 97465
Phone: 541-332-7121
Web: portofportorford.org
Commissioners: President Aaron Ashdown; Rick Fox, Dave Rickel, Leila Thompson, Brett Webb; Port Mgr. Pat Cox. Meets third Tuesday of the month.

International Port of Portland, Established 1891
Address: 7200 NE Airport Wy., Portland 97208; PO Box 3529, Portland 97218
Phone: 503-415-6000; 1-800-547-8411
Web: portofportland.com
Commissioners: President Alice Cuprill-Comas; Michael Alexander, Katy Coba, Katherine Lam, Richelle Luther, Meg Niemi, Sean O'Halleran, Ketan Sampat, Stuart Strader; Exec. Dir. Curtis Robinhold. Meets second Wednesday of the month.

Port of Siuslaw, Established 1909
Address: 100 Harbor St., Florence 97439
Phone: 541-997-3426
Fax: 541-997-9407
Web: portofsiuslaw.com
Commissioners: President Terry Duman; Mike Buckwald, Bill Meyer, Robert Ward, Craig Zolezzi; Port Mgr. David Huntington. Meets third Wednesday of the month.

The Swan Island Industrial Park on the Willamette River is managed by the Port of Portland. (Oregon State Archives scenic photo)

Port of The Dalles, Established 1933
Address: 3636 Klindt Dr., The Dalles 97058
Phone: 541-298-4148
Web: portofthedalles.com
Commissioners: President Greg Weast; Staci Coburn, David Griffith, Robert Wallace, John D Willer; Exec. Dir. Andrea Klaas. Meets second Wednesday of the month Wednesday of the month.

Port of Tillamook Bay, Established 1953
Address: 4000 Blimp Blvd., Suite 100, Tillamook 97141
Phone: 503-842-2413
Fax: 503-842-3680
Web: potb.org
Commissioners: President Jack Mulder; Bill Baertlein, Sierra Lauder, Matt Mumford, Kevin Stoecker; General Manager Michele Bradley. Meets the third Wednesday of each month, subject to change.

Port of Toledo, Established 1910
Address: 496 NE Hwy. 20, Unit #1, PO Box 428 Toledo 97391-9720
Phone: 541-336-5207
Web: portoftoledo.org
Commissioners: President Chuck Gerttula, Zack Dahl, Rick Graff, Michael Kriz, Penny Ryerson;

Port Mgr. Debbie Scacco. Meets third Tuesday of the month.

Port of Umatilla, Established 1940
Address: 500 Willamette Ave., PO Box 879, Umatilla 97882
Phone: 541-922-3224
Fax: 541-922-5609
Web: portofumatilla.org
Commissioners: President Jerry Baker, Kurt Bendixsen , Bob Blanc, Jerry Imsland, Jerry Simpson, Gen. Mgr. Kim Puzey. Meets Tuesday after first Wednesday of the month.

Port of Umpqua, Established 1913
Address: 1877 Winchester Ave., PO Box 388, Reedsport 97467
Phone: 541-271-2232
Fax: 541-271-2747
Web: portofumpqua.net
Commissioners: President Keith Tymchuk; Eric Boe, Carey Jones, Joe Mulkey, Deborah Yates; Port Mgr. Scott Kent. Meets third Wednesday of the month.

SPECIAL SERVICE DISTRICTS

Contact: Frank Stratton, Executive Director
Address: Special Districts Association of Oregon, PO Box 12613, Salem 97309-0613
Phone: 503-371-8667; Toll-free: 1-800-285-5461
Fax: 503-371-4781
Web: sdao.com
Authorized by: ORS 198.010 and 198.335

Special districts are a form of local government. They are services created by their constituents to fulfill specific community needs. Most districts perform a single function. Fire districts, water districts, and sewer districts are examples of special districts. Find the full list of special district types at sdao.com/what-is-a-special-district.

Special districts are financed through property taxes, fees for services, or a combination thereof. Most special districts are directed by a governing body elected by the voters.

The Special Districts Association of Oregon (SDAO) was formed in 1979. They provide support services to member districts throughout the state in the areas of research and technical assistance, legislative representation, training programs, insurance services, information and reference materials, financing services, and employee benefits programs.

COVID-19 Pandemic Experience

Mieko Soria
Ashley Baker's 4th Grade Class
Yujin Gakuen Japanese Immersion School, Eugene

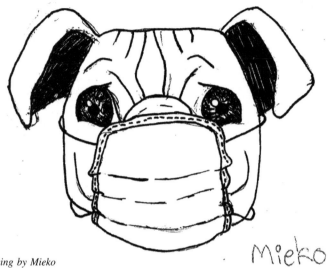

This drawing by Mieko Soria shows a dog wearing a mask during the Covid-19 pandemic.

The pandemic has been hard on everyone. But, like everything else, it has its ups and downs. As we all know it came as a surprise to everyone. We all found ways to keep ourselves busy, and even found new hobbies. Though I didn't find a new hobby I got to know more about the people I loved. Being stuck in a house with three other people and two crazy dogs (for a lot longer than a few days) meant that I would get to know a lot more about them without even realizing it. I even got to know more about my new neighbors!

This may not seem like something very interesting but, the kids next door to me are now some of my best friends! Even though we had a lot of free time on our hands, that didn't mean we didn't have fun. We did some awesome arts and crafts, made delicious desserts and watched movies together! Sometimes I am secretly glad that Covid happened because it meant that I could spend more time with my family. I think I speak for my whole family when I say "You can find light even in the darkest of times." And of course we made unforgettable friends along the way of this long and crazy adventure.

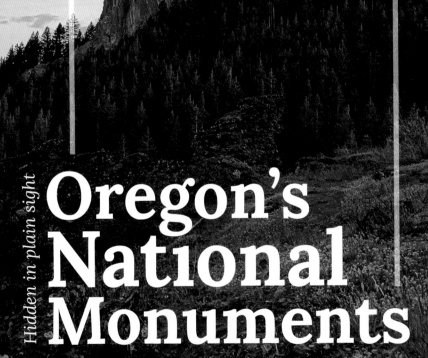

John Day
Fossil Beds

Newberry
Volcanic

Oregon
Caves

Cascade
Siskiyou

Hidden in plain sight

Oregon's National Monuments

Oregonians know our state is full of gorgeous scenery - no matter where you travel, there's always something special to see. We have it all: high deserts stretched under big skies; rugged, snowcapped mountains cradling delicate alpine lakes; magnificent beaches watched over by sea stacks and lighthouses; and lush forests ripe with unique vegetation and thriving with wildlife. But even here among this special setting are places recognized for their rare combination of geologic value, historical significance and uncommon confluence of animal and plant species. These are Oregon's four national monuments.

The John Day Fossil Beds National Monument, Newberry Volcanic National Monument, Oregon Caves National Monument and Preserve and Cascade Siskiyou National Monument each have a story that's as unique as their landscapes.

When you visit, remember to leave any artifacts where you found them, including arrowheads, pottery, fossils, basketry and metal. Once an artifact is moved, important information may be lost forever.

This is also a story of places many Oregonians have yet to discover. Oregon's national monument visitors tend to be, in large part, from outside the state or from other countries. Our hope is this Oregon Blue Book feature will help Oregonians understand the treasures in our own backyard and embrace these places as they have our other important natural spaces.

JOHN DAY PAINTED COVE TRAIL

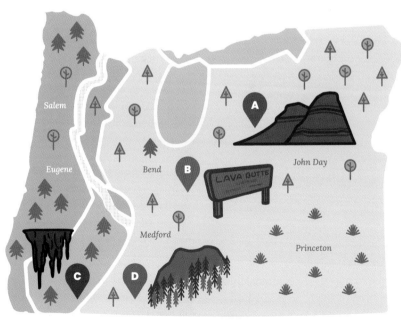

Salem

Eugene

Bend

Medford

John Day

Princeton

A John Day
Fossil Beds

B Newberry
Volcanic

C Oregon
Caves

D Cascade
Siskiyou

Managed by the National Park Service

John Day Fossil Beds

LAYERS IN TIME

Visiting the John Day Fossil Beds National Monument is almost like taking a time machine into the distant past. The three units of the monument hold one of the richest fossil beds on Earth, recording an ancient era, known as the Age of Mammals. Fossils found inside the monument helped define the evolution of many species including horses, cats (felines) and dogs (canines), among others.

The monument holds three distinct units: Clarno, Sheep Rock and Painted Hills. Each of these units tells a piece of the story of the John Day Fossil Beds National Monument.

They display changes in landscape, ecosystems and climate that took place during this fascinating time in the Earth's geologic history.

As you stand back and examine the colored layers and formations of rock, imagine the vast volcanic debris and mudflows that pushed through the landscape. Remind yourself that this was once a subtropical paradise full of lush plants and a wide variety of animals, much like Costa Rica or Veracruz, Mexico today. Underneath these rolling and rugged hills of Eastern Oregon, evidence of ancient history lies within.

CLOSE UP OF PAINTED HILLS

Just ahead – Three national monument units, no waiting...

The incredible scenery and connections to ancient times are just some of the reasons to visit this special place. Take a moment to talk with the scientists and rangers who work at the monument. Their expertise and knowledge can add a whole new layer of wonder to your experience.

CATHEDRAL ROCK

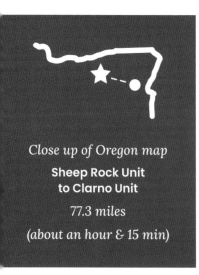

Close up of Oregon map

**Sheep Rock Unit
to Clarno Unit**

77.3 miles

(about an hour & 15 min)

Sheep Rock Unit

The colorful green cliffs at the Sheep Rock Unit occupy several miles of the upper John Day River valley. These noticeable rocks seen as you take in the expanse of the unit date back as far as 95 million years ago. Within the layers of rock not seen from the outside, are remains of plants and animals from 33 to 7 million years ago.

Here you'll find the hub of the monument's operations: the Thomas Condon Paleontology Center. This state-of-the-art facility is dedicated to the study and public understanding of the fossilized remains of prehistoric plants and animals that once covered the John Day region. Visitors can view more than 500 fossilized remains on display. Examples of the tools and materials that paleontologists have used to uncover many of the region's fossils and murals which detail the environments experienced by plants and animals that once lived in the region are also on view. There's even a fishbowl-style laboratory where guests can watch scientists as they study fossils.

THOMAS CONDON PALEONTOLOGY CENTER
Photo courtesy National Park Service

The Sheep Rock fossils are relatively young (as far as fossils go) and reflect millions of years of cooling and drying climate change that would eventually lead to an ice age. Forests gave way to shrub lands, which in turn became grasslands as rain dwindled. Recognizable ancestors to

SHEEP ROCK

many modern animals roamed these grasslands, including prehistoric deer, foxes, short-faced bears and saber-toothed cats, as well as the ancient relatives of camels, elephants and rhinoceroses.

The main hiking spot in the Sheep Rock Unit is Blue Basin, a grey-blue badlands incorporating one of the most important fossil sites in the monument. Visitors hiking the "Island in Time Trail" will see replica fossils embedded into stone, offering a glimpse of what it's like to be a fossil hunter. The "Blue Basin Trail" is longer and more challenging. It leads hikers to a viewpoint with jaw-dropping views of the yellow grasses and undulating crimson hills reminiscent of the Painted Hills.

The Sheep Rock Unit also hosts the Cant Ranch Historic Home & Museum. The Cant family emigrated to Oregon from Scotland in 1910. The museum provides details about the life of this immigrant family, along with the story of what it was like to build, maintain and run a ranch in the 1900s.

BLUE BASIN
*Photo courtesy
National Park Service*

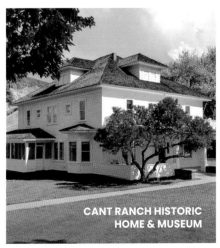

CANT RANCH HISTORIC
HOME & MUSEUM

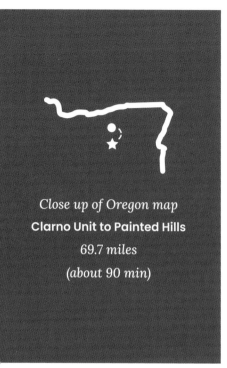

Close up of Oregon map
Clarno Unit to Painted Hills
69.7 miles
(about 90 min)

THE PALISADES

Clarno Unit

When visiting the Clarno Unit, the first thing you might notice is the quiet. Clarno sees fewer visitors, which means those who enjoy solace while among ancient rocks have a place to call their own.

The real draw to the Clarno Unit are the towering Palisades, which stand tall along the hills like guardians watching over the landscape. These formations are the remains of volcanic mud and ash flows called lahars, which flowed down the volcano 54 to 40 million years ago. During that time, the landscape was a semi-tropical rain forest rich with animal and plant life.

Plants and animals in the way of the volcanic lahars were mowed down and often captured by the flows. When you visit the Clarno Unit, see if you can spot some fossilized plants embedded into cliff walls. As you hike the trails, notice the boulders situated alongside; you might spy fossils there as well. But remember, pictures only. Please leave any fossils you locate right where you found them. It's illegal to remove fossils from any of the John Day Fossil Beds National Monument's three units.

The unit's three short trails take visitors around to view the Palisades from different angles. One of these trails is known as the "Geologic Time Trail." It includes signs along the way that help tell the landscape's 50-million-year-old story.

CLOSE UP OF THE PALISADES

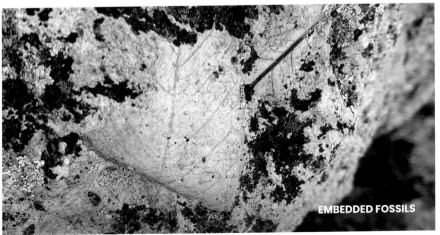

EMBEDDED FOSSILS

Painted Hills Unit

The Painted Hills Unit is the spectacular crown jewel of the John Day Fossil Beds National Monument. Its otherworldly, undulating folds of scarlet, yellow and olive open as you come around the bend along the gravel road that leads to the parking area. In the golden light of late afternoon, the sunset colors of the hills intensify.

Songs of local birds and the smell of sage make the Painted Hills Unit a multi-sensory experience. On sunny days, the soils on the hills come alive with color. On overcast days the stripes are richly maroon and ochre. Of all the units, Painted Hills is the most visited. It's easy to see why.

This area is a preserve showing a sequence of past climate change. The colors of the soil hold the key to understanding the wet and dry periods, along with their different ecosystems. Visitors here should take notice of more than just the color,

however. The hills are full of crumbly textures and patterns.

Fossils in the Painted Hills Unit are from around 30 million years ago, when central Oregon was drying out as the planet slowly cooled. Jungles diminished and shrublands appeared, along with long-limbed running animals. Three-toed horses and sheep-like *oreodonts* were hunted by carnivorous bear-dogs, catlike *nimravids* and giant pig-like *entelodonts* related to modern hippos. Hardwood forests covered the land, competing for canopy space with the coniferous "Dawn Redwood" (*metasequoia*) which is Oregon's state fossil. Surviving populations of this tree still thrive in China.

The overlook area is just one of the stops at The Painted Hills Unit. There are five short trails scattered within, some with interpretive signs along the way. Others offer looks at the

PAINTED HILLS OVERLOOK

amazing palette of vibrant rocks. At all times, stay on the trails. The soils are sensitive.

PAINTED COVE

Salem to Newberry
National Volcanic
Monument, Lava Lands
Visitor Center:

143 miles

(about 2 hours, 40 min)

Managed by the U.S. Forest Service

Newberry National Volcanic Monument

THE SLEEPING GIANT

Oregon's Newberry Volcano is almost the definition of something "hidden in plain sight." It's not a traditional cone-style volcano, but instead is flatter and more expansive. Visitors to this national monument have the chance to explore Central Oregon's fiery past. It began 500,000 years ago (practically yesterday in geologic terms) with a massive lava flow that spanned hundreds of miles producing lava tubes, cinder cones and volcanic vents during its active periods.

Newberry is the largest volcano by volume in the Cascades, covering 1,200 square miles or an area about the size of Rhode Island. It's also much different from other Cascade volcanoes like South Sister near Bend or Mt. Rainier in Washington. Newberry is a "composite" volcano, formed by diverse types of eruptions.

Newberry is shaped more like a shield than the familiar cone seen in other places. A volcanic depression, or caldera, was created over tens of thousands of years as a result of major explosions and collapses. The last eruption at Newberry was about 1,300

BIG OBSIDIAN FLOW
Photo by Kevin Sperl, US Forest Service

years ago. Present-day hot springs and relatively young lava flows have scientists keeping a close watch on the area, as it could erupt again at any time.

Take time to stop at the Lava Lands Visitors Center. It's a good spot to get yourself familiar with all the monument has to offer. Engage with the rangers and volunteers, whose passion for this place and unique knowledge of the area make the experience extra special.

Around the monument, waterfalls, peaks, lakes and more than 110 miles of trails are waiting to be explored. The monument offers lots of recreation options for visitors, including hiking, biking, fishing, swimming, boating and wildlife viewing. Camping facilities, lodging and dining are also available inside the monument.

In the pages to come, we'll cover a few of the don't-miss spots.

LAVA LANDS VISITOR CENTER HIKE

LAVA LANDS VISITOR CENTER HIKE

LAVA VOLCANIC BUTTE

Lava Volcanic Butte

Standing at the 500-foot summit of Lava Butte feels a little like being at the top of Central Oregon. Bring your camera to capture panoramic views showing off the Cascade volcanoes to the north – Mt. Bachelor, Broken Top and the Three Sisters. To the south you'll see the entire Newberry National Monument laid out before you. A very short path and a 1.5-mile road help visitors more fully explore the area.

LAVA VOLCANIC BUTTE

LAVA CAST FOREST
Photo by Kevin Sperl, US Forest Service

Lava Cast Forest

Just over 7,000 years ago, this was an old growth forest. Towering ancient trees shaded the forest floor. Then Newberry Volcano erupted, sending molten lava flows to the forest, swallowing up trees, leaving solid tree molds. Steam from the burning wood cooled the lava, creating hollow channels where trees once lay. A mile-long interpretive trail helps you explore the ghostly landscape, littered with basalt casts of trees, logs and lakes.

PAULINA LAKE

Newberry Caldera

The Newberry Caldera holds the crystal blue waters of East and Paulina Lakes. The caldera is about four by five miles across, covering a volcano 20 miles in diameter. The last eruption here was 1,300 years ago. It remains geothermally and seismically active. Paulina Lake to the west is much deeper, reaching 250 feet down. Fed by rain, snowmelt and hot springs, these lakes drain out through the spectacular Paulina Falls.

Lava River Cave

Lava River Cave is a mile-long lava tube, the longest continuous tube in Oregon. It was formed during Newberry Crater's massive eruption about 80,000 years ago. It stays a cool 42-degrees Fahrenheit year-round inside the cave, so bring a jacket and be ready to see bats, who've created a colony there. These tiny creatures are vital to the local ecosystem, so it is important to heed the advice of rangers when visiting their underground homes.

Big Obsidian Flow

Here you'll find Oregon's youngest lava flow. Stretching just over a square mile, the big obsidian flow moved across the high desert only 1,300 years ago. There's a mile-long interpretive trail to help you explore. This site hosts ranger talks throughout the summer, so you can dig even deeper into this "hot spot" of shining volcanic glass.

PAULINA PEAK

Paulina Peak

This 7,984-foot summit crowns Newberry Caldera. Spectacular views of the south and west flanks of Newberry Volcano can be seen from the top. You can also see Fort Rock 25 miles to the south and an expanse of Central Oregon farther on. Visitors can drive to the top where they can also access additional hiking trails.

Paulina Falls

A short, accessible path leads visitors to a viewpoint where they witness the lowest point of Newberry Caldera. These twin falls spill over, tumbling 80 feet out of the caldera. At over 6,000 feet above sea level, these falls freeze in the winter, sending long icicles trailing down the cliffs.

Salem to Oregon Caves National Monument and Preserve entrance:

246 miles

(about 4 hours, 20 minutes)

Oregon Caves

INTERIOR OF CAVES

OREGON'S MARBLE HALLS

When visiting Oregon Caves National Monument and Preserve, visitors might find themselves asking, "What's a speleothem?" and "Why does phenology matter?" That's because this 4,600-acre area leans hard on science, featuring complicated marble cave systems and a rare combination of plant and animal species.

What lures most visitors to Oregon Caves National Monument and Preserve? A chance to explore a mountain inside and out. Wind along a ranger-guided tour of smooth flowstones, stalactites, stalagmites and yes, speleothems inside

INTERIOR OF THE OREGON CAVES

BIG LOOP TRAIL VIEW

**Next up –
Where to go and
what to see
at Oregon Caves.**

the caves. Then wander your way through groves of ancient trees and meadows of flowering plants. Besides getting to know the cave, get to know the ranger who guides your tour. You'll find yourself learning not just about the rock formations, but about a person who has dedicated themselves to understanding this very special place.

The monument and preserve are also home to a remnant old growth forest with towering conifers, including Oregon's widest-circumference Douglas Fir. A multitude of hiking options are available, from short trails with stunning views of the Illinois Valley to a full-day hike through peaceful meadows and lakes. Lucky hikers might have the chance to practice some phenology (how plants and animals react to their environment) by studying wildflowers along the way.

OREGON CAVES CHATEAU

Oregon Caves Chateau

Counted as one of the National Park's Great Lodges and a National Historic Landmark, the Chateau at Oregon Caves is a six-story lodge with two restaurants and lots of charm. The Chateau is undergoing a full restoration and rehabilitation, so it's currently closed to visitors. It was designed by self-taught architect Gust Limm and completed in 1934. Interior furnishings include uniquely hand-crafted Monterey furniture, mostly made from Oregon alder wood. The outside looks like many national park buildings: rustic and homey.

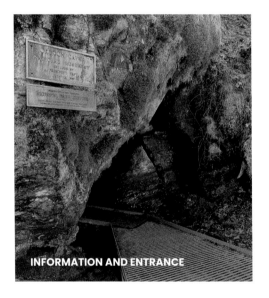

INFORMATION AND ENTRANCE

In terms of geology, the Oregon Caves are a few million years old. It's believed that Indigenous tribes lived near the caves for thousands of years, but white settlers didn't locate them until 1874. President William Howard Taft established the Oregon Caves National Monument in 1909 and by 1935, tens of thousands visited the cave each year.

Oregon Caves Visitor Center

This wooded location offers visitors the chance to study up on the caves and other information about the area through a series of exhibits. It's also the trail juncture for Cliff Nature and Big Tree Trails. Here you'll find the Junior Ranger Program and some of the extremely knowledgeable rangers and volunteers who can help enhance your experience at the monument.

Illinois Valley Visitor Center

Visitors to the area who are looking to be well prepared should consider Illinois Valley Visitor Center as their first stop. The center offers information about the region, including up-to-the-moment cave tour reports at the Oregon Caves National Monument and Preserve. The visitor center also sells same-day cave tour tickets, which can be handy during the busy summer season when tour lines are long.

ILLINOIS VALLEY
VISITOR CENTER

TRAIL SIGNAGE

Hikes

Oregon Caves National Monument and Preserve has six hiking trails that range from about an hour round trip to a full day. You can choose from the Big Tree (where you'll find the thickest Doug Fir in Oregon at 13 feet), Cliff Nature, Mt. Elijah, Old Growth, No Name and Cave Creek trails. Here's where you'll explore the outside of the mountain as you walk through groves of Port Orford Cedar and some of the largest Douglas Firs in Oregon.

INTERIOR OF
OREGON CAVE

Oregon Caves Tour

The first thing to know about the Oregon Caves tour is that it's cold. Whether touring in the heat of summer or the dead of winter, the interior of the cave stays at a chilly 44 degrees Fahrenheit (7 degrees Celsius). Wear warm clothing and good walking shoes. Once inside you'll stoop, explore and discover a labyrinth of marble passageways, cruise by glassy flowstones and visit a room 220 feet beneath the surface. This 90-minute, ranger-guided tour has something for everyone who loves rocks, fossils, wildlife and bats.

Salem to Cascade
Siskiyou National
Monument, Hyatt Lake

263 miles

*(or about 4 hours,
25 minutes)*

Managed by the Bureau of Land Management

Cascade Siskiyou National Monument

PILOT ROCK

OREGON'S ECOLOGICAL WONDERLAND

Many national monuments and parks have an iconic spot, that instantly recognizable view that indicates the location. For Cascade Siskiyou National Monument, that spot is Pilot Rock. The Takelma people called it "Tan-ts'at-seniptha," meaning "Stone Standing Up." It rises 570 feet up and is visible from parts of the Rogue Valley, and much of Shasta Valley in northern California.

TABLE MOUNTAIN

VIEW OF MT SHASTA FROM PILOT ROCK

Stretching out from below Pilot Rock lies a breathtaking landscape with a short trail that winds through a moss-covered forest and leads to a boulder and wildflower meadow, dotted with colorful butterflies. From the meadow, the wide expanse of the Shasta Valley and the imposing face of Mt. Shasta are laid out with stunning views.

Next up: Ways to explore

SUCCULENTS

LARGE FLOWERED BLUE EYED MARY

Each of these parts: the rock, plants, volcanoes, valleys and butterflies are pieces of the unique ecological story of Cascade Siskiyou National Monument. The complex geology provides the foundation for a variety of soils and habitats. Multiple combinations of geology, soils, climate and vegetation; known as ecoregions, are jumbled together here. Animals usually found east of the Cascades like nuthatches and kangaroo rats, share habitat with western species like rough-skinned newts and northern spotted owls.

This rare and special intersection of rock and life prompted the effort to preserve this area for study, recreation and generations to come.

NORTHERN SPOTTED OWL
Bureau of Land Management, Photo by Kyle Sullivan

PACIFIC CREST TRAIL

The Pacific Crest Trail

A stunning 41-mile stretch of the Pacific Crest Trail bisects Cascade Siskiyou. Multiple access points provide everything from fishing at Hyatt Lake to jaw-dropping views at Pilot Rock. These trails are rarely crowded, even in summer.

HOBART BLUFF TRAIL
Bureau of Land Management, Photo by Kyle Sullivan

Hobart Bluff

A 1.5-mile trail leads visitors to an incredible 360-degree view that includes the snowy peak of Mt. Shasta to the woodsy and lush Rogue River Valley to the high desert Klamath Basin. The hike itself offers great views of all the nearby mountains including Mount Ashland, Mt. McLoughlin and Pilot Rock.

PILOT ROCK
Bureau of Land Management, Photo by Kyle Sullivan

Highway 66 Scenic Drive

Historic Highway 66 roams through an area called the Greensprings, traditionally a seasonal gathering place for Indigenous tribes. The Applegate Trail brought white settlers to the area, along with houses and businesses. Highway 66 provides a series of scenic and informative stops, along with local restaurants and lodging.

Soda Mountain

The hike to Soda Mountain is more challenging than some in the monument, but the payoff is the chance to take in the view from the lookout tower. Here you can spy Pilot Rock and a vast expanse of the Klamath Basin.

HYATT LAKE
Bureau of Land Management, Photo by Kyle Sullivan

Hyatt Lake

This reservoir is one of the most accessible parts of the monument. A bit more than 50 tent camping spots dot the area. Mt. McLoughlin looks down over the azure water. Boat ramps and a dock make Hyatt Lake an excellent spot for fishing, kayaking and swimming.

LOST CREEK FALLS

SUCCULENTS

MT SHASTA
Bureau of Land Management, Photo by Kyle Sullivan

All images by the Oregon State Archives unless otherwise stated.

Oregon State Symbols

State Flag: The front of the Oregon ceremonial flag. Navy blue and gold are the state colors.
(Oregon State Archives)

State Flag: The reverse of the ceremonial flag. Oregon is the only state to have different designs on two sides of the flag.
(Oregon State Archives)

State Seal: The seal of the State of Oregon.
(Oregon State Archives)

State Animal: American Beaver *(Castor canadensis)* *(Oregon Department of Fish and Wildlife)*

State Gemstone: Oregon Sunstone *(Oregon Department of Geology and Mineral Industries)*

State Insect: Oregon Swallowtail *(Papilio oregonius)* *(Neil Björklund)*

State Mushroom: Pacific Golden Chanterelle *(Cantharellus formosus)* *(Richard F. Bishop)*

State Nut: Hazelnut *(Corylus avellana)* *(Oregon State Archives)*

State Shell: Hairy Triton *(Fusitriton oregonesis)* *(Bill Hanshumaker, Hatfield Marine Science Center)*

State Crustacean: Dungeness Crab
(Metacarcinus magister)
(Dungeness Crab Commission)

State Bird: Western Meadowlark *(Sturnella neglecta)*
(Jim Leonard)

State Rock: Thunderegg (geode)
(Oregon Department of Geology and Mineral Industries)

State Fruit: Pear *(Pyrus communis)*
(Pear Bureau Northwest)

State Flower: Oregon Grape
(Mahonia Aquifolium)
(Oregon State Archives)

State Fossil: Dawn Redwood
(Metasequoia glyptostroboides)
(National Park Service, John Day Fossil Beds National Monument)

State Fish: Chinook Salmon *(Oncorhynchus tshawytscha)*
(Oregon Department of Fish and Wildlife)

State Raptor: Osprey *(Pandion haliaetus)*
(Jim Leonard)

State Tree: Douglas Fir *(Pseudotsuga menziesii)*
(Oregon State Archives)

The State Capitol decorated with special lighting to celebrate the 75th Anniversary of the building in 2013. *(Oregon State Archives)*

Physical Features Map

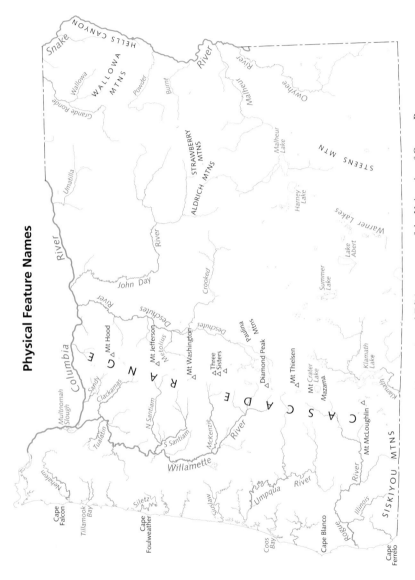

Physical Feature Names

Snake River · HELLS CANYON · WALLOWA MTNS · Wallowa · Powder · Burnt · River · River · Malheur · Owyhee · Grande Ronde · STRAWBERRY MTNS · ALDRICH MTNS · Malheur Lake · STEENS MTN · Umatilla · River · Harney Lake · Warner Lakes · Lake Abert · Crooked · John Day · Summer Lake · Deschutes · Deschutes · River · River · Mt Hood · Mt Jefferson · Metolius · Mt Washington · Paulina Mtns · Diamond Peak · Mt Thielsen · Klamath Lake · Columbia · River · Sandy · Clackamas · N Santiam · Three Sisters · Mt Crater Lake · Mazama · Klamath · Multnomah Slough · Tualatin · S Santiam · Mckenzie · River · Mt McLoughlin · Willamette · River · SISKIYOU MTNS · Nehalem · Siletz · Siuslaw · Umpqua · River · River · Cape Falcon · Tillamook Bay · Cape Foulweather · Coos Bay · Cape Blanco · Illinois · Rogue · Cape Ferrelo

Image reproduced from the *Atlas of Oregon, Second Edition* courtesy of the University of Oregon Press. © 2001 University of Oregon Press.

Elections and Records

The "Oregon System"—procedures for initiative, referendum and recall—gained Oregon national recognition for the degree of citizen involvement in the processes of self-government. Most recently, vote by mail and the Oregon Motor Voter processes have drawn national attention to Oregon. This detailed history of elections in Oregon illustrates the tangible results of participation in our government.

VOTING AND VOTER REGISTRATION

Source: Office of the Secretary of State, Elections Division
Address: 255 Capitol St. NE, Suite 501, Salem 97310
Phone: 503-986-1518
Web: oregonvotes.gov

Elections in Oregon

All regular elections in Oregon are held on one of four days each year, except in cases of emergency. The election days are the second Tuesday in March, the third Tuesday in May, the third Tuesday in September and the first Tuesday after the first Monday in November. Elections are conducted exclusively by mail. Voters who are registered as of the 21st day before an election are mailed a ballot to vote and return by election day.

The use of vote by mail was first approved on a limited basis by the Legislature in 1981 and was made a permanent feature of some elections in 1987. In 1998, Oregon voters amended state law to require that the primary and general elections in May and November of even-numbered years also be conducted through vote by mail. Beginning in 2000, primary and general elections have been conducted by mail. In 2007, the Legislature provided that all elections be conducted by mail. In 2019, the Legislature approved funding for postage paid envelopes to be provided for returning ballots starting in 2020.

Major political parties use the primary election to nominate candidates to run for partisan office in the general election. Minor political parties nominate candidates to run for partisan office in the general election according to party rule, and those candidates do not appear on the primary election ballot. Partisan offices include U.S. President, U.S. Senator, U.S. Representative, Governor, Secretary of State, State Treasurer, Attorney General, State Senator and State Representative.

Oregon's primary is closed, meaning only registered voters of a major political party can vote for candidates of the same party. At the primary election, voters who are not registered in one of the major political parties would receive a ballot containing nonpartisan contests, such as judicial elections, which all registered voters may vote on.

At the general election, voters will receive a ballot containing both partisan and nonpartisan offices and can vote for any candidate even if they are not of the same party. Most statewide ballot measures are on the general election ballot.

Registering to Vote

Every Oregonian who is at least 16 years old, a U.S. citizen and an Oregon resident can register to vote. To participate in an election a voter must be registered at least 21 days before the election. Persons registered to vote in other states may not transfer their voter registration to Oregon.

There are three ways to register to vote in Oregon, Oregon Motor Voter automatic voter registration, online voter registration and paper registration.

The Oregon Motor Voter (OMV) registration law took effect on January 1, 2016, making Oregon the first state in the nation to implement automatic voter registration. Automatic registration is available to those who apply for an original, renewal or replacement driver's license, permit or identification card and provide evidence of citizenship at a Driver and Motor Vehicle Division (DMV) office.

The OMV registration process takes approximately three weeks until a voter's registration is effective. If an election will occur in the two months following the DMV interaction, one of the other methods of registering to vote should be used to ensure the voter will be eligible to vote.

Paper voter registration forms can also be mailed or hand-delivered to a county election office, or a voter can complete the form electronically at oregonvotes.gov. Forms are located in many public buildings, in every county elections office and in many state agencies including the Office of the Secretary of State, Elections Division.

Registration Deadlines

A completed registration form must be postmarked or delivered to a county elections office or voter registration agency (e.g., DMV) no later than 21 days before the election. Electronic registrations must be completed no later than 11:59 p.m. 21 days before the election. Oregon residents who are not U.S. citizens by the deadline to register to vote, but who will be citizens by election day, should contact their county elections office for information about how to register to vote.

Persons who become residents of Oregon after the deadline to register for a U.S. presidential election may be eligible to vote for U.S. president and vice-president. Contact your county elections office for more information.

Maintaining a Current Voter Registration

Registered voters should update their registration if their home address or mailing address changes, their name or signature changes, if they want to change or select a political party or will be away from home on election day.

A registered voter can provide the new information online at www.oregonvotes.gov or by completing and returning a voter registration card to a county elections office or voter registration agency (e.g., DMV).

With the exception of changes to a voter's political party affiliation, updates can be made at any time including as late as election day in order to vote in that election. Political party changes, which determine the type of ballot a voter receives for the primary election, must be made no later than 21 days before the election.

Voting Absentee

Absentee ballots are mailed to military and other out-of-state voters in advance of the regular mailing of ballots. Voters should contact their local elections office to obtain an absentee ballot if they will be away from home on election day.

Voters' Pamphlets

For each primary and general election and for most special elections, the Elections Division produces and distributes to every household, a pamphlet containing information about candidates and measures that will appear on the ballot at the election. Many counties also produce pamphlets that contain information about local candidates and measures.

2024 FILING DEADLINES

Primary Election: The candidate filing period for the May 21, 2024, primary election begins on September 14, 2023, and ends on March 14, 2024. The deadline for filing *Voters' Pamphlet* material with the Elections Division is no sooner than January 22, 2024, and no later than March 14, 2024.

General Election: The candidate filing period for the November 21, 2024, general election begins on June 5, 2024, and ends on August 27, 2024. The deadline for filing *Voters' Pamphlet* material with the Elections Division is not sooner than July 8, 2024, and no later than August 27, 2024.

RECENT ELECTION HISTORY

2022 Primary Election

Election Date: May 17, 2022
Source: Abstracts of Votes, available from the Office of the Secretary of State, Elections Division, 255 Capitol St. NE, Suite 501, Salem 97310
Web: oregonvotes.gov
Key: *Nominated; **Elected

United States Senator

Democrat	Total
Barlow III, William E.	35,025
Thompson, Brent	17,197
Wyden, Ron*	439,665
Miscellaneous	3,279
Republican	
Beebe, Jason	39,456
Christensen, Christopher C.	28,433
Fleming, Robert M.	6,821
Harbick, Darin	107,506
Palmer, Sam	42,703
Perkins, Jo Rae*	115,701
Taher, Ibra A.	6,659
Miscellaneous	3,024

United States Representative

1st Congressional District

Democrat	Total
Bonamici, Suzanne*	80,317
Phillips, Scott	7,832
Robertson, Christian	2,625
Miscellaneous	287
Republican	
Mann, Christopher A.*	19,605
Murray, Armidia (Army)	9,047
Miscellaneous	671

2nd Congressional District

Democrat	Total
Prine, Adam	11,669
Yetter, Joe*	27,814
Miscellaneous	788
Republican	
Bentz, Cliff*	67,051
Cavener, Mark	17,372
Gallant, Katherine M.	4,598
Miscellaneous	386

3rd Congressional District

Democrat	Total
Blumenauer, Earl*	96,386
Polhemus, Jonathan E.	5,392
Miscellaneous	428
Republican	
Harbour, Joanna*	18,031
Miscellaneous	429

4th Congressional District

Democrat	Total
Al-Abdrabbuh, Sami	6,080
Canning, Doyle E.	14,245
Hoyle, Val*	56,153
Kalloch, Andrew	4,322
Laible, Steve William	292
Matthews, Jake	607
Selker, John S.	4,738
Smith, G. Tommy	1,278
Miscellaneous	663
Republican	
Skarlatos, Alek*	58,655
Miscellaneous	1,021

5th Congressional District

Democrat	Total
McLeod-Skinner, Jamie*	47,148
Schrader, Kurt	38,726
Miscellaneous	537
Republican	
Chavez-DeRemer, Lori*	30,438
Crumpacker, Jimmy	20,631
Di Paola, John	11,486
Oatman, Madison	1,863
Roses, Laurel L.	6,321
Miscellaneous	429

6th Congressional District

Democrat	Total
Alonso Leon, Teresa	4,626
Barajas, Ricky	292
Flynn, Carrick	13,052
Goodwin, Greg	217
Harder, Kathleen	5,510
Reynolds, Cody	7,951
Salinas, Andrea*	26,101
Smith, Loretta	7,064
West, Matt	5,658
Miscellaneous	508
Republican	
Bunn, Jim	6,340
Erickson, Mike*	21,675
Noble, Ron	10,980
Plowhead, Angela	8,271
Russ, David	2,398
Ryan Courser, Amy L.	10,176
Sandvig, Nathan A.	2,222
Miscellaneous	432

Governor

Democrat	Total
Beem, David	1,308
Bell, Julian	3,926
Bright, Wilson R.	2,316
Carrillo, George L.	9,365
Cross, Michael	1,342
Diru, Ifeanyichukwu C.	1,780
Hall, Peter W.	982
Kotek, Tina*	275,301
Merchant, Keisha Lanell	1,755
Read, Tobias	156,017
Starnes, Patrick E.	10,524
Stauffer, Dave W.	2,302
Sweeney, John	4,193
Trimble, Michael	5,000
Wilson, H. Genevieve	1,588
Miscellaneous	13,746
Republican	
Baldwin, Raymond	459
Barton, Bridget	40,886
Boice, Court	4,040
Burch, David A.	406
Christensen, Reed	3,082
Drazan, Christine*	85,255
Gomez, Jessica	9,970
Hess, Nick	4,287
McCloud, Tim	4,400
McQuisten, Kerry	28,727
Merritt, Brandon C.	3,615
Pierce, Bud	32,965
Presco, John G.	174
Pulliam, Stan	41,123
Richardson, Amber R.	1,924
Sizemore, Bill	13,261
Strek (Stregoi), Stefan G.	171
Thielman, Marc	30,076
Tiernan, Bob	66,089
Miscellaneous	7,407

Commissioner of the Bureau of Labor and Industries

Nonpartisan	Total
Baca, Aaron R.	14,217
Barker, Brent T.	101,576
Helt, Cheri*	171,168
Henry, Chris	22,936
Kulla, Casey M.	126,036
Neuman, Robert	32,331
Stephenson, Christina E.*	421,619
Miscellaneous	3,922

Judge of the Supreme Court

Nonpartisan	Total

Position 6

	Total
DeHoog, Roger J.**	613,950
Miscellaneous	11,515

Elections and Records

Judge of the Court of Appeals

Nonpartisan	Total

Position 3

Day, Vance	330,454
Ortega, Darleen**	547,660
Miscellaneous	2,473

Position 5

Shorr, Scott A.**	611,050
Miscellaneous	10,105

Position 8

Pagán, Ramón A.**	603,936
Miscellaneous	10,625

Judge of the Circuit Court

Nonpartisan	Total

2nd District, Position 5

Morgan, Stephen W.**	49,815
Miscellaneous	767

2nd District, Position 9

Fennerty, Erin A.**	50,149
Miscellaneous	747

2nd District, Position 11

Holland, Lauren S.**	50,575
Miscellaneous	763

2nd District, Position 13

McIntyre, Karrie**	49,977
Miscellaneous	734

3rd District, Position 1

Bennett, Channing**	43,520
Miscellaneous	631

3rd District, Position 4

Bureta, Jodie A.**	42,255
Miscellaneous	618

3rd District, Position 6

Edmonds, James (Jim)**	42,894
Miscellaneous	484

3rd District, Position 7

Armstrong, Sean E.**	42,571
Miscellaneous	516

3rd District, Position 9

Broyles, Audrey J.**	41,515
Miscellaneous	515

3rd District, Position 13

Hart, Tom**	42,178
Miscellaneous	514

4th District, Position 6

Bottomly, Leslie G.**	106,152
Miscellaneous	1,451

4th District, Position 9

Rees, David F.**	104,899
Miscellaneous	1,402

4th District, Position 17

Skye, Kelly**	105,141
Miscellaneous	1,407

4th District, Position 20

Bloch, Eric J.**	105,051
Miscellaneous	1,342

4th District, Position 22

Sinlapasai, Chanpone**	105,005
Miscellaneous	1,303

4th District, Position 24

Dahlin, Eric L.**	107,675
Miscellaneous	1,207

4th District, Position 25

Gates, Maurisa R.**	108,903
Miscellaneous	1,163

4th District, Position 35

Henry, Patrick W.**	103,944
Miscellaneous	1,287

5th District, Position 4

Weston, Cody M.**	59,109
Miscellaneous	808

5th District, Position 5

Weber, Katherine**	57,384
Miscellaneous	877

5th District, Position 10

Rastetter, Thomas J.**	57,526
Miscellaneous	813

6th District, Position 2

Lieuallen, Jon**	10,005
Miscellaneous	107

6th District, Position 3

Hill, Daniel J.**	10,395
Miscellaneous	105

7th District, Position 2

Weatherford, Marion T.**	9,039
Miscellaneous	144

7th District, Position 4

Berthelsen, Caleb M.	5,956
Wolf, John A.**	6,893
Miscellaneous	38

9th District, Position 1

Landis, Erin**	4,010
Miscellaneous	43

11th District, Position 3

Flint, Bethany P.**	35,137
Miscellaneous	491

11th District, Position 6

Ashby, Wells B.**	35,484
Miscellaneous	442

11th District, Position 8

McIver, Michelle A.**	35,389
Miscellaneous	460

11th District, Position 9

Herriott, Alycia M.**	35,059
Miscellaneous	400

12th District, Position 2

Campbell, Monte S.**	15,706
Miscellaneous	164

13th District, Position 1

Janney, Andrea M.**	10,034
Miscellaneous	145

13th District, Position 3

Adkisson, Marci W.**	11,909
Hedrick, Valerie B.	3,230
Miscellaneous	35

13th District, Position 4

Kritzer, Kelly**	9,803
Miscellaneous	133

13th District, Position 5

Bunch, Dan**	10,791
Miscellaneous	115

15th District, Position 1

Stone, Martin**	16,899
Miscellaneous	173

15th District, Position 4

Jacquot, Megan L.**	14,754
Miscellaneous	209

16th District, Position 2

Hoddle, Steve H.**	20,139
Miscellaneous	327

16th District, Position 3

Johnson, Kathleen E.**	19,767
Miscellaneous	397

16th District, Position 4

Johnson, Robert B.**	16,985
Thomas, Jason	10,306
Miscellaneous	153

18th District, Position 2

McIntosh, Dawn M.**	7,174
Miscellaneous	110

20th District, Position 1

Sims, Ted**	79,958
Miscellaneous	1,441

20th District, Position 4

Butterfield, Eric E.**	76,017
Miscellaneous	1,626

20th District, Position 14

Summer, Miranda**	79,158
Miscellaneous	1,541

23rd District, Position 5

McHill, Tom**	18,688
Miscellaneous	459

25th District, Position 1

Kaufman Noble, Cynthia**	17,178
Miscellaneous	233

25th District, Position 3

Easterday, Cynthia L.**	17,695
Miscellaneous	261

27th District, Position 1

Hill, Jonathan R.**	5,533
Miscellaneous	149

2022 General Election

Election Date: November 8, 2022
Source: *Abstracts of Votes,* available from the Office of the Secretary of State, Elections Division, 255 Capitol St. NE, Suite 501, Salem 97310
Web: oregonvotes.gov

Key: *Elected
C = Constitution Party
D = Democratic Party
I = Independent Party
L = Libertarian Party
NAV = Nonaffiliated
PG = Pacific Green Party
P = Progressive Party
R = Republican Party
WF = Working Families Party

United States Senator

	Total
Henry, Chris—P	36,881
Perkins, Jo Rae—R	788,991
Pulju, Dan—PG	23,454
Wyden, Ron—D*	1,076,424
Miscellaneous	2,196

United States Representative

1st Congressional District

	Total
Bonamici, Suzanne—D*	210,682
Mann, Christopher A.—R	99,042
Miscellaneous	519

2nd Congressional District

	Total
Bentz, Cliff S.—R*	208,369
Yetter, Joe—D	99,882
Miscellaneous	425

3rd Congressional District

	Total
Blumenauer, Earl—D*	212,119
Delk, David E.—P	10,982
Harbour, Joanna—R	79,766
Miscellaneous	467

4th Congressional District

	Total
Beilstein, Mike—PG	6,033
Howard, Jim—C	6,075
Hoyle, Val—D*	171,372
Leatherberry, Levi—I	9,052
Skarlatos, Alek—R	146,055
Miscellaneous	490

5th Congressional District

	Total
Chavez-DeRemer, Lori—R*	178,813
McLeod-Skinner, Jamie—D	171,514
Miscellaneous	906

6th Congressional District

	Total
Erickson, Mike—R	139,946
McFarland, Larry D.—C	6,762
Salinas, Andrea—D*	147,156
Miscellaneous	513

Governor

	Total
Drazan, Christine—R	850,347
Johnson, Betsy—NAV	168,431
Kotek, Tina—D*	917,074
Noble, R. Leon—L	6,867
Smith, Donice Noelle—C	8,051
Miscellaneous	2,113

Commissioner of the Bureau of Labor and Industries

Nonpartisan	Total
Helt, Cheri	582,609
Stephenson, Christina E.*	916,455
Miscellaneous	9,826

Judge of the Court of Appeals

Nonpartisan	Total

Position 10

Hellman, Kristina*	1,093,911
Miscellaneous	22,646

Position 11

Anna M. Joyce*	1,042,573
Miscellaneous	21,843

Judge of the Circuit Court

Nonpartisan	Total

2nd District—Position 2

Bassi, Michelle*	91,353
Miscellaneous	2,050

2nd District—Position 11

Grace, Beatrice*	81,099
Wilde, Marty	50,888
Miscellaneous	1,084

3rd District—Position 3

Gardiner, Jennifer K.*	70,257
Miscellaneous	1,359

3rd District—Position 14

Johnson Jr., Erious*	45,834
Queen, Amy	56,759
Miscellaneous	454

4th District—Position 3

Alarcon, Jacqueline L.*	199,360
Miscellaneous	4,018

4th District—Position 8

Howes, Celia*	199,051
Miscellaneous	3,995

4th District—Position 37

Plank, Jenna R.*	198,539
Miscellaneous	3,877

17th District—Position 3

Benjamin, Amanda*	15,802
Miscellaneous	193

18th District—Position 3

Wintermute, Kirk*	11,710
Miscellaneous	99

19th District—Position 2

Keppinger, Denise E.*	16,298
Miscellaneous	346

20th District—Position 13

Rini, Michele C.*	145,214
Miscellaneous	3,399

22nd District—Position 2

Whiting, Wade L.*	14,804
Miscellaneous	276

23rd District—Position 2

Stein, Keith B.*	33,114
Miscellaneous	724

Voter Participation 1992–2022

*Presidential election year

Primary Election

Year	Registered Voters	Voted	Percent
1992*	1,543,315	758,459	49.1
1994	1,730,562	661,717	38.2
1996*	1,851,499	698,990	37.8
1998	1,906,677	665,340	34.9
2000*	1,808,080	927,351	51.3
2002	1,839,072	858,524	46.7
2004*	1,862,919	864,833	46.4
2006	1,965,875	758,357	38.6
2008*	2,008,957	1,170,526	58.3
2010	2,033,951	846,515	41.6
2012*	2,021,263	787,847	39.0
2014	2,113,430	758,604	35.9
2016*	2,281,555	1,231,843	54.0
2018	2,660,267	908,168	34.1
2020*	2,833,716	1,334,490	47.1
2022	2,943,071	1,111, 233	37.8

General Election

Year	Registered Voters	Voted	Percent
1992*	1,775,416	1,498,959	84.4
1994	1,832,774	1,254,265	68.4
1996*	1,962,155	1,399,180	71.3
1998	1,965,981	1,160,400	59.0
2000*	1,954,006	1,559,215	79.8
2002	1,872,615	1,293,761	69.1
2004*	2,141,249	1,851,669	86.5
2006	1,976,669	1,399,290	70.8
2008*	2,153,914	1,845,251	85.7
2010	2,068,798	1,487,190	71.9
2012*	2,199,360	1,820,507	82.8
2014	2,174,763	1,541,782	70.9
2016*	2,553,806	2,051,448	80.3
2018	2,748,232	1,914,923	69.7
2020*	2,944,588	2,413,890	82.0
2022	2,985,820	1,997,689	66.9

Voter Registration by County—November 8, 2022

County	Democrat	Republican	*Nonaffiliated	**Other	Total
Baker	1,948	5,869	4,235	905	12,957
Benton	26,069	12,438	18,504	3,895	60,906
Clackamas	104,501	84,246	102,833	22,291	313,871
Clatsop	10,195	7,354	11,355	2,241	31,145
Columbia	11,897	11,483	15,176	3,000	41,556
Coos	11,600	15,628	18,428	3,537	49,193
Crook	3,240	9,189	6,916	1,474	20,819
Curry	4,334	6,196	7,215	1,438	19,183
Deschutes	47,859	44,366	51,160	11,914	155,299
Douglas	16,509	33,798	31,121	6,330	87,758
Gilliam	251	598	468	96	1,413
Grant	845	2,759	1,665	374	5,643
Harney	767	2,766	1,731	347	5,611
Hood River	6,413	3,068	5,762	1,018	16,261
Jackson	43,842	49,167	55,472	11,348	159,829
Jefferson	3,382	5,635	6,762	1,223	17,002

County	Democrat	Republican	*Nonaffiliated	**Other	Total
Josephine	14,181	24,896	25,556	5,080	69,713
Klamath	8,198	19,830	18,892	3,511	50,431
Lake	632	2,822	1,807	343	5,604
Lane	102,743	60,845	89,918	19,230	272,736
Lincoln	13,404	8,626	14,578	2,901	39,509
Linn	22,054	33,356	35,198	6,934	97,542
Malheur	2,334	6,271	8,104	845	17,554
Marion	61,879	61,774	83,067	14,299	221,019
Morrow	1,093	2,455	2,998	464	7,010
Multnomah	290,223	59,344	182,513	34,359	566,439
Polk	17,674	19,231	21,674	4,290	62,869
Sherman	244	691	429	92	1,456
Tillamook	6,333	6,039	7,419	1,416	21,207
Umatilla	8,496	15,697	21,284	3,078	48,555
Union	3,427	8,275	6,232	1,283	19,217
Wallowa	1,244	2,881	1,821	377	6,323
Wasco	5,117	5,078	7,085	1,268	18,548
Washington	143,570	75,592	142,856	23,792	385,810
Wheeler	209	522	282	61	1,074
Yamhill	20,344	22,961	26,087	5,366	74,758
Totals	**1,017,051**	**731,746**	**1,036,603**	**200,420**	**2,985,820**

*A "nonaffiliated" voter is one who has chosen not to be a member of any political party and has indicated this on his or her voter registration card.

**"Other" includes all voters registered with minor political parties.

OREGON ELECTION HISTORY

Voter Registration for General Elections 1992–2022

Year	Democrat	Republican	*Other	Total
1992	792,551	642,206	340,659	1,775,416
1994	786,990	665,956	379,828	1,832,774
1996	805,286	714,548	442,321	1,962,155
1998	791,970	704,593	469,418	1,965,981
2000	769,195	699,179	485,632	1,954,006
2002	729,460	680,444	462,711	1,872,615
2004	829,193	761,715	550,335	2,141,249
2006	767,562	706,365	502,742	1,976,669
2008	929,741	695,677	528,496	2,153,914
2010	863,322	664,123	541,353	2,068,798
2012	872,361	684,858	642,141	2,199,360
2014	825,701	653,048	696,014	2,174,763

Year	Democrat	Republican	Independent	*Other	Total
2016	981,153	717,497	117,389	745,618	2,553,806
2018	976,908	705,833	124,187	941,304	2,748,232

Year	Democrat	Republican	*Other	Total
2020	1,051,119	753,590	1,139,879	2,944,588
2022	1,017,051	731,746	1,237,023	2,985,820

*"Other" includes all voters registered with minor political parties and nonaffiliated voters.

Votes Cast in Oregon for United States President 1860–2022

Key: *Elected; **Received highest vote in Oregon but lost election nationwide

Year	Candidate	Party	Votes
1860	John Bell	Constitutional Union	212
	John C. Breckenridge	Democrat	5,074
	Stephen Douglas	Douglas Democrat	4,131
	Abraham Lincoln*	Republican	5,344
1864	Abraham Lincoln*	Republican	9,888
	George McClellan	Democrat	8,457
1868	U.S. Grant*	Republican	10,961
	Horatio Seymour**	Democrat	11,125
1872	U.S. Grant*	Republican	11,818
	Horace Greeley	Democrat-Liberal Republicans	7,742
	Charles O'Connor	National Labor Reformers	587
1876	Peter Cooper	Greenback	510
	Rutherford B. Hayes*	Republican	15,214
	Samuel Tilden	Democrat	14,157
1880	James A. Garfield*	Republican	20,619
	Winfield Hancock	Democrat	19,955
	James B. Weaver	Greenback Labor	249
1884	James G. Blaine**	Republican	26,860
	General B.F. Butler	Greenback Labor (Workingman)	726
	Grover Cleveland*	Democrat	24,604
	John P. St. John	Prohibition	492
1888	Grover Cleveland	Democrat	26,522
	Robert H. Cowdrey	United Labor	363
	Clinton B. Fisk	Prohibition	1,677
	Benjamin Harrison*	Republican	33,291
1892	John Bidwell	Prohibition	2,281
	Grover Cleveland*	Democrat	14,243
	Benjamin Harrison**	Republican	35,002
	James B. Weaver[1]	Populist	26,965
1896	William J. Bryan	Democrat, People's Party and Silver Republican	46,739
	Joshua Levering	Prohibition	919
	William McKinley*	Republican	48,779
	John M. Palmer	National (Gold) Democrat	977
1900	Wharton Barker	Regular People's	275
	William J. Bryan	Democrat People's	33,385
	Eugene V. Debs	Social-Democrats	1,494
	William McKinley*	Republican	46,526
	John G. Woolley	Prohibition	2,536
1904	Eugene V. Debs	Socialist	7,619
	Alton Parker	Democrat	17,327
	Theodore Roosevelt*	Republican	60,455
	Silas C. Swallow	Prohibition	3,806
	Thomas E. Watson	People's	753
1908	William J. Bryan	Democrat	38,049
	Eugene W. Chafin	Prohibition	2,682
	Eugene V. Debs	Socialist	7,339
	Thomas L. Hisgen	Independence	289
	William H. Taft*	Republican	62,530
1912	Eugene W. Chafin	Prohibition	4,360
	Eugene V. Debs	Socialist	13,343
	Theodore Roosevelt	Progressive	37,600
	William H. Taft	Republican	34,673
	Woodrow Wilson*	Democrat	47,064
1916	Allan L. Benson	Socialist	9,711
	J. Frank Hanley	Prohibition	4,729
	Charles Evans Hughes**	Republican	126,813

Year	Candidate	Party	Votes
	John M. Parker[2]	Progressive	310
	Woodrow Wilson*	Democrat	120,087
1920	James M. Cox	Democrat	80,019
	William W. Cox	Industrial Labor	1,515
	Eugene V. Debs	Socialist	9,801
	Warren G. Harding*	Republican	143,592
	Aaron S. Watkins	Prohibition	3,595
1924	Calvin Coolidge*	Republican	142,579
	John W. Davis	Democrat	67,589
	Frank T. Johns	Socialist Labor	917
	Robert M. LaFollette	Independent	68,403
1928	William Z. Foster	Independent	1,094
	Herbert Hoover*	Republican	205,341
	Verne L. Reynolds	Socialist Labor	1,564
	Alfred E. Smith	Democrat	109,223
	Norman Thomas	Socialist Principles-Independent	2,720
1932	William Z. Foster	Communist	1,681
	Herbert Hoover	Republican	136,019
	Verne L. Reynolds	Socialist Labor	1,730
	Franklin D. Roosevelt*	Democrat	213,871
	Norman Thomas	Socialist	15,450
1936	John W. Aiken	Socialist Labor	500
	Alfred M. Landon	Republican	122,706
	William Lemke	Independent	21,831
	Franklin D. Roosevelt*	Democrat	266,733
	Norman Thomas	Independent	2,143
1940	John W. Aiken	Socialist Labor	2,487
	Franklin D. Roosevelt*	Democrat	258,415
	Wendell L. Willkie	Republican	219,555
1944	Thomas E. Dewey	Republican	225,365
	Franklin D. Roosevelt*	Democrat	248,635
	Norman Thomas	Independent	3,785
	Claude A. Watson	Independent	2,362
1948	Thomas E. Dewey**	Republican	260,904
	Norman Thomas	Independent	5,051
	Harry S. Truman*	Democrat	243,147
	Henry A. Wallace	Progressive	14,978
1952	Dwight D. Eisenhower*	Republican	420,815
	Vincent Hallinan	Independent	3,665
	Adlai Stevenson	Democrat	270,579
1956	Dwight D. Eisenhower*	Republican	406,393
	Adlai Stevenson	Democrat	329,204
1960	John F. Kennedy*	Democrat	367,402
	Richard M. Nixon**	Republican	408,060
1964	Barry M. Goldwater	Republican	282,779
	Lyndon B. Johnson*	Democrat	501,017
1968	Hubert H. Humphrey	Democrat	358,866
	Richard M. Nixon*	Republican	408,433
	George C. Wallace	Independent	49,683
1972	George S. McGovern	Democrat	392,760
	Richard M. Nixon*	Republican	486,686
	John G. Schmitz	Independent	46,211
1976	Jimmy Carter*	Democrat	490,407
	Gerald Ford**	Republican	492,120
	Eugene J. McCarthy	Independent	40,207
1980	John Anderson	Independent	112,389
	Jimmy Carter	Democrat	456,890
	Ed Clark	Libertarian	25,838
	Barry Commoner	Independent	13,642
	Ronald Reagan*	Republican	571,044

Year	Candidate	Party	Votes
1984	Walter F. Mondale	Democrat	536,479
	Ronald Reagan*	Republican	685,700
1988	George Bush*	Republican	560,126
	Michael S. Dukakis**	Democrat	616,206
	Lenora B. Fulani	Independent	6,487
	Ron Paul	Libertarian	14,811
1992	George Bush	Republican	475,757
	Bill Clinton*	Democrat	621,314
	Lenora Fulani	New Alliance Party	3,030
	Andre Marrou	Libertarian	4,277
	Ross Perot	Independent Initiative Party of Oregon	354,091
1996	Harry Browne	Libertarian	8,903
	Bill Clinton*	Democrat	649,641
	Bob Dole	Republican	538,152
	John Hagelin	Natural Law	2,798
	Mary Cal Hollis	Socialist	1,922
	Ralph Nader	Pacific	49,415
	Ross Perot	Reform	121,221
	Howard Phillips	U.S. Taxpayers	3,379
2000	Harry Browne	Libertarian	7,447
	Patrick J. Buchanan	Independent	7,063
	George W. Bush*	Republican	713,577
	Al Gore**	Democrat	720,342
	John Hagelin	Reform	2,574
	Ralph Nader	Pacific Green	77,357
	Howard Phillips	Constitution	2,189
2004	Michael Badnarik	Libertarian	7,260
	George W. Bush*	Republican	866,831
	David Cobb	Pacific Green	5,315
	John F. Kerry**	Democrat	943,163
	Michael Anthony Peroutka	Constitution	5,257
2008	Baldwin, Chuck	Constitution	7,693
	Barr, Bob	Libertarian	7,635
	McCain, John	Republican	738,475
	McKinney, Cynthia	Pacific Green	4,543
	Nader, Ralph	Peace	18,614
	Obama, Barack*	Democrat	1,037,291
2012	Anderson, Ross C. (Rocky)	Progressive	3,384
	Christensen, Will	Constitution	4,432
	Johnson, Gary	Libertarian	24,089
	Obama, Barack*	Democrat	970,488
	Romney, Mitt	Republican	754,175
	Stein, Jill	Pacific Green	19,427
2016	Clinton, Hillary**	Democrat	1,002,106
	Johnson, Gary	Libertarian	94,231
	Stein, Jill	Pacific Green	50,002
	Trump, Donald J.*	Republican	782,403
2020	Biden, Joseph R.*	Democrat	1,340,383
	Hawkins, Howie	Pacific Green	11,831
	Hunter, Dario	Progressive	4,988
	Jorgensen, Jo	Libertarian	41,582
	Trump, Donald J	Republican	958,448

[1]One Weaver elector was endorsed by the Democrats and elected as a Fusionist, receiving 35,811 votes.

[2]Vice-presidential candidate

Initiative, Referendum and Recall

In 1902, Oregon voters overwhelmingly approved a legislatively referred ballot measure that created Oregon's initiative and referendum process. In 1904, voters enacted the direct primary and in 1908, Oregon's Constitution was amended to allow for recall of public officials. These were the culmination of efforts by the Direct Legislation League, a group of political activists that progressive leader William S. U'Ren founded in 1898.

This system of empowering the people to propose new laws or change the Constitution of Oregon through a general election ballot measure became nationally known as "the Oregon System."

Initiative: Petition process that allows registered voters to propose amendments to the Oregon Constitution or changes to the Oregon Revised Statutes (ORS).

Referendum: Petition process that allows registered voters to adopt or reject any nonemergency Act or portion of a nonemergency Act passed by the Legislature.

Referral: Process that allows the Legislature to place on the ballot for voters' approval, any bill it passes. Any amendment to the Oregon Constitution proposed by the Legislature must be placed on the ballot for voters to approve or reject.

Since 1902, the people have passed 132 of the 377 initiative measures placed on the ballot and 24 of the 66 referenda on the ballot. During the same period, the Legislature has referred 436 measures to the people, of which 255 have passed.

Both houses of the Legislature must vote to refer a statute or constitutional amendment for popular vote. Such referrals cannot be vetoed by the governor.

To place an initiative or referendum on the ballot, supporters must obtain a specified number of signatures from registered voters. The number required is determined by a fixed percentage of the votes cast for all candidates for governor at the last general election where the governor was elected to a full term. In the 2022 General Election, 1,952,883 votes were cast for governor. Therefore, referendum petitions require 4%, or 78,116 signatures; initiative petitions for statutory enactments require 6%, or 117,173 signatures; and initiative petitions for constitutional amendments require 8%, or 156,231 signatures.

The original constitutional amendment, passed in 1902, provided that a fixed percentage of the votes cast for justice of the Supreme Court would determine the number of signatures required to place an initiative or referendum on the ballot. Both a statutory enactment and a constitutional amendment required 8% of the votes cast, while a referendum required 5% of the votes cast. In 1954, the people amended the Oregon Constitution to increase the required number of signatures to 10% for a constitutional amendment. In 1968, a vote of the people established the current requirements.

Prior to 1954, measures on the ballot were not numbered. They are listed below in order of appearance on the ballot. The 2001 Legislature amended state law to require that ballot measure numbers not repeat in any subsequent election. Numbers assigned for each election begin with the next number after the last number assigned in the previous election.

Key: *Adopted; L = Referred by the Legislature; I = Submitted by initiative petition;
R = Referendum by petition; (Also see footnotes on pp. 268–269)

Election Date/Measure Number/Ballot Title	Yes	No
June 2, 1902		
1. Limits Uses Initiative and Referendum—L[1]	*62,024	5,668
June 6, 1904		
1. Office of State Printer—L[1]	*45,334	14,031
2. Direct Primary Nominating Convention Law—I[2]	*56,205	16,354
3. Local Option Liquor Law—I[2]	*43,316	40,198
June 4, 1906		
1. Shall act appropriating money maintaining Insane Asylum, Penitentiary, Deaf-Mute, Blind School, University, Agricultural College, and Normal Schools be approved—R	*43,918	26,758
2. Equal Suffrage Constitutional Amendment—I[1]	36,902	47,075
3. Amendment to local option law giving anti-prohibitionists and prohibitionists equal privileges—I[2]	35,297	45,144
4. Law to abolish tolls on the Mount Hood and Barlow Road and providing for its ownership by the State—I[2]	31,525	44,527
5. Constitutional amendment providing method of amending constitution and applying the referendum to all laws affecting constitutional conventions and amendments—I[1]	*47,661	18,751
6. Constitutional amendment giving cities and towns exclusive power to enact and amend their charters—I[1]	*52,567	19,852

Election Date/Measure Number/Ballot Title	Yes	No
7. Constitutional amendment to allow the state printing, binding, and Printers' compensation to be regulated by law at any time—I^1	*63,749	9,571
8. Constitutional amendment for the initiative and referendum on local, special and municipal laws and parts of laws—I^1	*47,678	16,735
9. Bill for a law prohibiting free passes and discrimination by railroad companies and other public service corporations—I^2	*57,281	16,779
10. An act requiring sleeping car companies, refrigerator car companies and oil companies to pay an annual license upon gross earnings—I^2	*69,635	6,441
11. An act requiring express companies, telegraph companies and telephone companies to pay an annual license upon gross earnings—I^2	*70,872	6,360

June 1, 1908

	Yes	No
1. To Increase Compensation of Legislators from $120 to $400 Per Session—$L^1$	19,691	68,892
2. Permitting Location of State Institutions at Places Other than the State Capitol—L^1	*41,975	40,868
3. Reorganization System of Courts and Increasing the Number of Supreme Judges from Three to Five—L^1	30,243	50,591
4. Changing Date of General Elections from June to November—L^1	*65,728	18,590
5. Giving Sheriffs Control of County Prisoners—R	*60,443	30,033
6. Requiring Railroads to Give Public Officials Free Passes—R	28,856	59,406
7. Appropriating $100,000 for Building Armories—R	33,507	54,848
8. Increasing Annual Appropriation for University of Oregon from $47,500 to $125,000—R	*44,115	40,535
9. Equal Suffrage—I^1	36,858	58,670
10. Fishery Law Proposed by Fishwheel Operators—I^2	*46,582	40,720
11. Giving Cities Control of Liquor Selling, Poolrooms, Theaters, etc., subject to local option law—I^1	39,442	52,346
12. Modified Form of Single Tax Amendment—I^1	32,066	60,871
13. Recall Power on Public Officials—I^1	*58,381	31,002
14. Instructing Legislature to Vote for People's Choice for United States Senator—I^2	*69,668	21,162
15. Authorizing Proportional Representation Law—I^1	*48,868	34,128
16. Corrupt Practices Act Governing Elections—I^2	*54,042	31,301
17. Fishery Law Proposed by Gillnet Operators—I^2	*56,130	30,280
18. Requiring Indictment To Be By Grand Jury—I^1	*52,214	28,487
19. Creating Hood River County—I^2	*43,948	26,778

November 8, 1910

	Yes	No
1. Permitting Female Taxpayers to Vote—I^1	35,270	59,065
2. Establishing Branch Insane Asylum in Eastern Oregon—L^2	*50,134	41,504
3. Calling Convention to Revise State Constitution—L^2	23,143	59,974
4. Providing Separate Districts for Election of Each State Senator and Representative—L^1	24,000	54,252
5. Repealing Requirements That All Taxes Shall Be Equal and Uniform—L^1	37,619	40,172
6. Permitting Organized Districts to Vote Bonds for Construction of Railroads by Such Districts—L^1	32,884	46,070
7. Authorizing Collection of State and County Taxes on Separate Classes of Property—L^1	31,629	41,692
8. Requiring Baker County to Pay $1,000 a Year to Circuit Judge in Addition to His State Salary—R	13,161	71,503
9. Creating Nesmith County From Parts of Lane and Douglas—I^2	22,866	60,951
10. To Establish a State Normal School at Monmouth—I^2	*50,191	40,044
11. Creating Otis County From Parts of Harney, Malheur and Grant—I^2	17,426	62,016
12. Annexing Part of Clackamas County to Multnomah—I^2	16,250	69,002
13. Creating Williams County From Parts of Lane and Douglas—I^2	14,508	64,090
14. Permitting People of Each County to Regulate Taxation for County Purposes and Abolishing Poll Taxes—I^1	*44,171	42,127
15. Giving Cities and Towns Exclusive Power to Regulate Liquor Traffic Within Their Limits—I^1	*53,321	50,779

Election Date/Measure Number/Ballot Title	Yes	No
16. For Protection of Laborers in Hazardous Employment, Fixing Employers' Liability, etc.—I²	*56,258	33,943
17. Creating Orchard County From Part of Umatilla—I²	15,664	62,712
18. Creating Clark County From Part of Grant—I²	15,613	61,704
19. To Establish State Normal School at Weston—I²	40,898	46,201
20. To Annex Part of Washington County to Multnomah—I²	14,047	68,221
21. To Establish State Normal School at Ashland—I²	38,473	48,655
22. Prohibiting Liquor Traffic—I¹	43,540	61,221
23. Prohibiting the Sale of Liquors and Regulating Shipments of Same, and Providing for Search for Liquor—I²	42,651	63,564
24. Creating Board to Draft Employers' Liability Law for Submission to Legislature—I²	32,224	51,719
25. Prohibiting Taking of Fish in Rogue River Except With Hook and Line—I²	*49,712	33,397
26. Creating Deschutes County Out of Part of Crook—I²	17,592	60,486
27. Bill for General Law Under Which New Counties May Be Created or Boundaries Changed—I²	37,129	42,327
28. Permitting Counties to Vote Bonds for Permanent Road Improvement—I¹	*51,275	32,906
29. Permitting Voters in Direct Primaries to Express Choice for President and Vice President, to Select Delegates to National Convention and Nominate Candidates for Presidential Electors—I²	*43,353	41,624
30. Creating Board of People's Inspectors of Government, Providing for Reports of Board in Official State Gazette to be Mailed to All Registered Voters Bi-monthly—I²	29,955	52,538
31. Extending Initiative and Referendum, Making Term of Members of Legislature Six Years, Increasing Salaries, Requiring Proportional Representation in Legislature, Election of President of Senate and Speaker of House Outside of Members, etc.—I¹	37,031	44,366
32. Permitting Three-Fourths Verdict in Civil Cases—I¹	*44,538	39,399

November 5, 1912

	Yes	No
1. Equal Suffrage Amendment—I¹	*61,265	57,104
2. Creating Office of Lieutenant Governor—L¹	50,562	61,644
3. Divorce of Local and State Taxation—L¹	51,582	56,671
4. Permitting Different Tax Rates on Classes of Property—L¹	52,045	54,483
5. Repeal of County Tax Option—L¹	*63,881	47,150
6. Majority Rule on Constitutional Amendments—L¹	32,934	70,325
7. Double Liability on Bank Stockholders—L¹	*82,981	21,738
8. Statewide Public Utilities Regulation—R	*65,985	40,956
9. Creating Cascade County—I²	26,463	71,239
10. Millage Tax for University and Agricultural College—I²	48,701	57,279
11. Majority Rule on Initiated Laws—I¹	35,721	68,861
12. County Bond and Road Construction Act—Grange Bill—I²	49,699	56,713
13. Creating State Highway Department—Grange Bill—I²	23,872	83,846
14. Changing Date State Printer Bill Becomes Effective—I²	34,793	69,542
15. Creating Office of Hotel Inspector—I²	16,910	91,995
16. Eight-hour Day on Public Works—I²	*64,508	48,078
17. Blue Sky Law—I²	48,765	57,293
18. Relating to Employment of State Prisoners—I²	*73,800	37,492
19. Relating to Employment of County and City Prisoners—I²	*71,367	37,731
20. State Road Bonding Act—I²	30,897	75,590
21. Limiting State Road Indebtedness—I¹	*59,452	43,447
22. County Bonding Act—I²	43,611	60,210
23. Limiting County Road Indebtedness—I¹	*57,258	43,858
24. Providing Method for Consolidating Cities and Creating New Counties—I²	40,199	56,992
25. Income Tax Amendment—I¹	52,702	52,948
26. Tax Exemption on Household Effects—I²	*60,357	51,826
27. Tax Exemption on Moneys and Credits—I²	42,491	66,540
28. Revising Inheritance Tax Laws—I²	38,609	63,839

Election Date/Measure Number/Ballot Title	Yes	No
29. Freight Rates Act—I^2	*58,306	45,534
30. County Road Bonding Act—I^1	38,568	63,481
31. Abolishing Senate; Proxy Voting; U'Ren Constitution—I^1	31,020	71,183
32. Statewide Single Tax with Graduated Tax Provision—I^1	31,534	82,015
33. Abolishing Capital Punishment—I^2	41,951	64,578
34. Prohibits Boycotts and Pickets—I^2	49,826	60,560
35. Prohibits Use of Public Streets, Parks and Grounds in Cities over 5,000 Without Permit—I^2	48,987	62,532
36. Appropriation for University of Oregon—R	29,437	78,985
37. Appropriation for University of Oregon—R	27,310	79,376
November 4, 1913 (Special Referendum Election)		
1. State University Building Repair Fund—R	*56,659	40,600
2. University of Oregon New Building Appropriation—R	*53,569	43,014
3. Sterilization Act—R	41,767	53,319
4. County Attorney Act—R	*54,179	38,159
5. Workmen's Compensation Act—R	*67,814	28,608
November 3, 1914		
1. Requiring Voters to be Citizens of the United States—L^1	*164,879	39,847
2. Creating Office of Lieutenant Governor—L^1	52,040	143,804
3. Permitting Certain City and County Boundaries to be Made Identical, and Governments Consolidated—L^1	77,392	103,194
4. Permitting State to Create an Indebtedness Not to Exceed Two Percent of Assessed Valuation for Irrigation and Power Projects and Development of Untilled Lands—L^1	49,759	135,550
5. Omitting Requirement that "All Taxation Shall Be Equal And Uniform"—L^1	59,206	116,490
6. Changing Existing Rule of Uniformity and Equality of Taxation— Authorizing Classification of Property for Taxation Purposes—L^1	52,362	122,704
7. To Establish State Normal School at Ashland—L^2	84,041	109,643
8. Enabling Incorporated Municipalities to Surrender Charters and To Be Merged in Adjoining City or Town—L^1	*96,116	77,671
9. To Establish State Normal School at Weston—L^2	87,450	105,345
10. Providing Compensation for Members of Legislature at Five Dollars Per Day—L^1	41,087	146,278
11. Universal Constitutional Eight Hour Day Amendment—I^1	49,360	167,888
12. Eight-hour Day and Room-Ventilation Law for Female Workers—I^2	88,480	120,296
13. Nonpartisan Judiciary Bill Prohibiting Party Nominations for Judicial Officers—I^2	74,323	107,263
14. $1,500 Tax Exemption Amendment—I^1	65,495	136,193
15. Public Docks and Water Frontage Amendment—I^1	67,128	114,564
16. Municipal Wharves and Docks Bill—I^2	67,110	111,113
17. Prohibition Constitutional Amendment—I^1	*136,842	100,362
18. Abolishing Death Penalty—I^1	*100,552	100,395
19. Specific Personal Graduated Extra-tax Amendment of Article IX, Oregon Constitution—I^1	59,186	124,943
20. Consolidating Corporation and Insurance Departments—I^2	55,469	120,154
21. Dentistry Bill—I^2	92,722	110,404
22. County Officers Term Amendment—I^1	82,841	107,039
23. A Tax Code Commission Bill—I^2	34,436	143,468
24. Abolishing Desert Land Board and Reorganizing Certain State Offices—I^2	32,701	143,366
25. Proportional Representation Amendment to Oregon Constitution—I^1	39,740	137,116
26. State Senate Constitutional Amendment—I^1	62,376	123,429
27. Department of Industry and Public Works Amendment—I^1	57,859	126,201
28. Primary Delegate Election Bill—I^2	25,058	153,638
29. Equal Assessment and Taxation and $300 Exemption Amendment—I^1	43,280	140,507
November 7, 1916		
1. Single Item Veto Amendment—L^1	*141,773	53,207
2. Ship Tax Exemption Amendment—L^1	*119,652	65,410
3. Negro and Mulatto Suffrage Amendment—L^1	100,027	100,701

Elections and Records

Election Date/Measure Number/Ballot Title	Yes	No
4. Full Rental Value Land Tax and Homemakers' Loan Fund Amendment—I[1]	43,390	154,980
5. For Pendleton Normal School and Ratifying Location Certain State Institutions—I[1]	96,829	109,523
6. Anti-compulsory Vaccination Bill—I[2]	99,745	100,119
7. Bill Repealing and Abolishing the Sunday Closing Law—I[2]	*125,836	93,076
8. Permitting Manufacture and Regulating Sale 4 Percent Malt Liquors—I[1]	85,973	140,599
9. Prohibition Amendment Forbidding Importation of Intoxicating Liquors for Beverage Purposes—I[1]	*114,932	109,671
10. Rural Credits Amendment—I[1]	*107,488	83,887
11. State-wide Tax and Indebtedness Limitation Amendment—I[1]	*99,536	84,031

June 4, 1917 (Special Election)

	Yes	No
1. Authorizing Ports to Create Limited Indebtedness to Encourage Water Transportation—L[1]	*67,445	54,864
2. Limiting Number of Bills Introduced and Increasing Pay of Legislators—L[1]	22,276	103,238
3. Declaration Against Implied Repeal of Constitutional Provisions by Amendments Thereto—L[1]	37,187	72,445
4. Uniform Tax Classification Amendment—L[1]	*62,118	53,245
5. Requiring Election City, Town and State Officers at Same Time—L[1]	*83,630	42,296
6. Four Hundred Thousand Dollar Tax Levy for a New Penitentiary—L[2]	46,666	86,165
7. Six Million Dollar State Road Bond Issue and Highway Bill—L[2]	*77,316	63,803

November 5, 1918

	Yes	No
1. Establishing and Maintaining Southern and Eastern Oregon Normal Schools—L[1]	49,935	66,070
2. Establishing Dependent, Delinquent and Defective Children's Home, Appropriating Money Therefor—L[2]	43,441	65,299
3. Prohibiting Seine and Setnet Fishing in Rogue River and Tributaries—R	45,511	50,227
4. Closing the Willamette River to Commercial Fishing South of Oswego—R	*55,555	40,908
5. Delinquent Tax Notice Bill—I[2]	*66,652	41,594
6. Fixing Compensation for Publication of Legal Notice—I[2]	*50,073	41,816
7. Authorizing Increase in Amount of Levy of State Taxes for Year 1919 (submitted by state tax commission under chapter 150, Laws 1917)	41,364	56,974

June 3, 1919 (Special Election)

	Yes	No
1. Six Percent County Indebtedness for Permanent Roads Amendment—L[1]	*49,728	33,561
2. Industrial and Reconstruction Hospital Amendment—L[1]	38,204	40,707
3. State Bond Payment of Irrigation and Drainage District Bond Interest—L[1]	*43,010	35,948
4. Five Million Dollar Reconstruction Bonding Amendment—L[1]	39,130	40,580
5. Lieutenant Governor Constitutional Amendment—L[1]	32,653	46,861
6. The Roosevelt Coast Military Highway Bill—L[2]	*56,966	29,159
7. Reconstruction Bonding Bill—L[2]	37,294	42,792
8. Soldiers', Sailors' and Marines' Educational Financial Aid Bill—L[2]	*49,158	33,513
9. Market Roads Tax Bill—L[2]	*53,191	28,039

May 21, 1920 (Special Election)

	Yes	No
1. Extending Eminent Domain Over Roads and Ways—L[1]	*100,256	35,655
2. Limitation of 4 Percent State Indebtedness for Permanent Roads—L[1]	*93,392	46,084
3. Restoring Capital Punishment—L[1]	*81,756	64,589
4. Crook and Curry Counties Bonding Amendment—L[1]	*72,378	36,699
5. Successor to Governor—L[1]	*78,241	56,946
6. Higher Educational Tax Act—L[2]	*102,722	46,577
7. Soldiers', Sailors' and Marines' Educational Aid Revenue Bill—L[2]	*91,294	50,482
8. State Elementary School Fund Tax—L[2]	*110,263	39,593
9. Blind School Tax Measure—L[2]	*115,337	30,739

November 2, 1920

	Yes	No
1. Compulsory Voting and Registration Amendment—L[1]	61,258	131,603
2. Constitutional Amendment Regulating Legislative Sessions and the Payment of Legislators—L[1]	80,342	85,524

Election Date/Measure Number/Ballot Title	Yes	No
3. Oleomargarine Bills—R	67,101	119,126
4. Single Tax Constitutional Amendment—I[1]	37,283	147,426
5. Fixing Term of Certain County Officers—I[1]	*97,854	80,983
6. Port of Portland Dock Commission Consolidation—I[2]	80,493	84,830
7. Anti-compulsory Vaccination Amendment—I[1]	63,018	127,570
8. Constitutional Amendment Fixing Legal Rate of Interest in Oregon—I[1]	28,976	158,673
9. Roosevelt Bird Refuge—I[2]	78,961	107,383
10. Divided Legislative Session Constitutional Amendment—I[1]	57,791	101,179
11. State Market Commission Act—I[2]	51,605	119,464

June 7, 1921 (Special Election)

	Yes	No
1. Legislative Regulation and Compensation Amendment—L[1]	42,924	72,596
2. World War Veterans' State Aid Fund, Constitutional Amendment—L[1]	*88,219	37,866
3. Emergency Clause Veto Constitutional Amendment—L[1]	*62,621	45,537
4. Hygiene Marriage Examination and License Bill—L[2]	56,858	65,793
5. Women Jurors and Revised Jury Law—L[2]	*59,882	59,265

November 7, 1922

	Yes	No
1. Amendment Permitting Linn County Tax Levy to Pay Outstanding Warrants—L	*89,177	57,049
2. Amendment Permitting Linn and Benton Counties to Pay Outstanding Warrants—L[1]	*86,547	53,844
3. Single Tax Amendment—I[1]	39,231	132,021
4. 1925 Exposition Tax Amendment—I[2]	82,837	95,587
5. Income Tax Amendment—I[2]	54,803	112,197
6. Compulsory Education Bill—I[2]	*115,506	103,685

November 6, 1923 (Special Election)

	Yes	No
1. Income Tax Act—L[2]	*58,647	58,131

November 4, 1924

	Yes	No
1. Voters' Literacy Amendment—L[1]	*184,031	48,645
2. Public Use and Welfare Amendment—L[1]	*134,071	65,133
3. Bonus Amendment—L[1]	*131,199	92,446
4. Oleomargarine Condensed Milk Bill—R	91,597	157,324
5. Naturopath Bill—I[2]	75,159	122,839
6. Workmen's Compulsory Compensation Law for Hazardous Occupations—I[1]	73,270	151,862
7. Income Tax Repeal—I[2]	*123,799	111,055

November 2, 1926

	Yes	No
1. Klamath County Bonding Amendment—L[1]	*81,954	68,128
2. Six Percent Limitation Amendment—L[1]	54,624	99,125
3. Repeal of Free Negro and Mulatto Section of the Constitution—L[1]	*108,332	64,954
4. Amendment Prohibiting Inheritance and Income Taxes—L[1]	59,442	121,973
5. The Seaside Normal School Act—L[2]	47,878	124,811
6. The Eastern Oregon State Normal School Act—L[2]	*101,327	80,084
7. The Recall Amendment—L[1]	*100,324	61,307
8 Curry County Bonding or Tax Levy Amendment—L[1]	*78,823	61,472
9. Amendment Relating to Elections to Fill Vacancies in Public Offices—L[1]	*100,397	54,474
10. Klamath and Clackamas County Bonding Amendment—L[1]	*75,229	61,718
11. The Eastern Oregon Tuberculosis Hospital Act—L[2]	*131,296	48,490
12. Cigarette and Tobacco Tax Bill—R	62,254	123,208
13. Motor Bus and Truck Bill—R	*99,746	78,685
14. Act Appropriating Ten Percent of Self-sustaining Boards' Receipts—R	46,389	97,460
15. Income Tax Bill With Property Tax Offset—I[2]	50,199	122,512
16. Bus and Truck Operating License Bill—I[2]	76,164	94,533
17. Fish Wheel, Trap, Seine and Gillnet Bill—I[2]	*102,119	73,086
18. Income Tax Bill—I[2]	83,991	93,997
19. Oregon Water and Power Board Development Measure—I[1]	35,313	147,092
20. Amendment Fixing Salaries of County Officers of Umatilla County—L[2]	1,988	2,646
21. To Provide Salaries for Certain Officials of Clackamas County—L[2]	2,826	6,199

Election Date/Measure Number/Ballot Title	Yes	No
June 28, 1927 (Special Election)		
1. Repeal of Negro, Chinaman and Mulatto Suffrage Section of Constitution—L[1]	*69,373	41,887
2. Portland School District Tax Levy Amendment—L[1]	46,784	55,817
3. Criminal Information Amendment—L[1]	*64,956	38,774
4. Legislators' Pay Amendment—L[1]	28,380	81,215
5. Voters' Registration Amendment—L[1]	*55,802	49,682
6. State and County Officers, Salary Amendment—L[1]	46,999	61,838
7. City and County Consolidation Amendment—L[1]	41,309	57,613
8. Veterans' Memorial and Armory Amendment—L[1]	25,180	80,476
9. State Tax Limitation Amendment—L[1]	19,393	84,697
10. Income Tax Bill—L[2]	48,745	67,039
11. Property Assessment and Taxation Enforcement Bill—L[2]	31,957	70,871
12. Nestucca Bay Fish Closing Bill—R	*53,684	47,552
November 6, 1928		
1. Five Cent Gasoline Tax Bill—I[1]	71,824	198,798
2. Bill for Reduction of Motor Vehicle License Fees—I[1]	98,248	174,219
3. Income Tax Bill—I[2]	118,696	132,961
4. Limiting Power of Legislature Over Laws Approved by the People—I[1]	108,230	124,200
5. Deschutes River Water and Fish Bill—I[2]	78,317	157,398
6. Rogue River Water and Fish Bill—I[2]	79,028	156,009
7. Umpqua River Water and Fish Bill—I[2]	76,108	154,345
8. McKenzie River Water and Fish Bill—I[2]	77,974	153,418
November 4, 1930		
1. Repeal of State Payment of Irrigation and Drainage District Interest—L[1]	*96,061	74,892
2. State Cabinet Form of Government Constitutional Amendment—L[1]	51,248	135,412
3. Bonus Loan Constitutional Amendment—L[1]	92,602	101,785
4. Motor Vehicle License Tax Constitutional Amendment—L[1]	71,557	115,480
5. Motor Vehicle License Tax Constitutional Amendment—L[1]	63,683	111,441
6. Constitutional Amendment for Filling Vacancies in the Legislature—L[1]	*85,836	76,455
7. Legislators' Compensation Constitutional Amendment—L[1]	70,937	108,070
8. Two Additional Circuit Judges Bill—R	39,770	137,549
9. Income Tax Bill—R	*105,189	95,207
10. Anti-cigarette Constitutional Amendment—I[1]	54,231	156,265
11. Rogue River Fishing Constitutional Amendment—I[1]	96,596	99,490
12. Lieutenant Governor Constitutional Amendment—I[1]	92,707	95,277
13. People's Water and Power Utility Districts Constitutional Amendment—I[1]	*117,776	84,778
November 8, 1932		
1. Taxpayer Voting Qualification Amendment—L[1]	*189,321	124,160
2. Amendment Authorizing Criminal Trials Without Juries by Consent of Accused—L[1]	*191,042	111,872
3. Six Percent Tax Limitation Amendment—L[1]	*149,833	121,852
4. Oleomargarine Tax Bill—R	131,273	200,496
5. Bill Prohibiting Commercial Fishing on the Rogue River—R	127,445	180,527
6. Higher Education Appropriation Bill—R	58,076	237,218
7. Bill to Repeal State Prohibition Law of Oregon—I[2]	*206,619	138,775
8. The Freight Truck and Bus Bill—I[2]	151,790	180,609
9. Bill Moving University, Normal and Law Schools, Establishing Junior Colleges—I[2]	47,275	292,486
10. Tax and Debt Control Constitutional Amendment—I[1]	99,171	162,552
11. Tax Supervising and Conservation Bill—I[2]	117,940	154,206
12. Personal Income Tax Law Amendment—I[2]	144,502	162,468
13. State Water Power and Hydroelectric Constitutional Amendment—I[1]	*168,937	130,494
July 21, 1933 (Special Election)		
1. An Amendment to the Constitution of the United States of America—L[0]	*136,713	72,854
2. Soldiers and Sailors Bonus Limitation Amendment—L[1]	*113,267	75,476
3. County Manager Form of Government Constitutional Amendment—L[1]	66,425	117,148

Election Date/Measure Number/Ballot Title	Yes	No
4. Prosecution by Information and Grand Jury Modification Amendment—L[1]	67,192	110,755
5. Debt and Taxation Limitations for Municipal Corporations Constitutional Amendment—L[1]	82,996	91,671
6. State Power Fund Bonds—L[2]	73,756	106,153
7. Sales Tax Bill—L[2]	45,603	167,512
8. Repeal of Oregon Prohibition Constitutional Amendment—L[1]	*143,044	72,745
9. Oleomargarine Tax Bill—R	66,880	144,542
May 18, 1934 (Special Election)		
1. County Indebtedness and Funding Bond Constitutional Amendment—L[1]	83,424	96,629
2. Criminal Trial Without Jury and Non-unanimous Verdict Constitutional Amendment—L[1]	*117,446	83,430
3. Bill Authorizing a State Tuberculosis Hospital in Multnomah County—L[2]	*104,459	98,815
4. Bill Authorizing a State Insane Hospital in Multnomah County—L[2]	92,575	108,816
5. School Relief Sales Tax Bill—R	64,677	156,182
November 6, 1934		
1. Grange Power Bill—R	124,518	139,283
2. Limitations of Taxes on Taxable Property Constitutional Amendment—I[1]	100,565	161,644
3. Healing Arts Constitutional Amendment—I[1]	70,626	191,836
January 31, 1936 (Special Election)		
1. Bill Changing Primary Elections to September With Other Resulting Changes—L[2]	61,270	155,922
2. Compensation of Members of the Legislature Constitutional Amendment—L[1]	28,661	184,332
3. Sales Tax Bill—L[2]	32,106	187,319
4. Bill Authorizing Student Activity Fees in State Higher Educational Institutions—R	50,971	163,191
November 3, 1936		
1. Bill Amending Old Age Assistance Act of 1935—R	174,293	179,236
2. Amendment Forbidding Prevention or Regulation of Certain Advertising If Truthful—I[1]	100,141	222,897
3. Tax Limitation Constitutional Amendment for School Districts Having 100,000 Population—I[1]	112,546	203,693
4. Noncompulsory Military Training Bill—I[2]	131,917	214,246
5. Amendment Limiting and Reducing Permissible Taxes on Tangible Property—I[1]	79,604	241,042
6. State Power Bill—I[2]	131,489	208,179
7. State Hydroelectric Temporary Administrative Board Constitutional Amendment—I[1]	100,356	208,741
8. State Bank Bill—I[2]	82,869	250,777
November 8, 1938		
1. Governor's 20-day Bill Consideration Amendment—L[1]	*233,384	93,752
2. Amendment Repealing the Double Liability of Stockholders in Banking Corporations—L[1]	133,525	165,797
3. Legislators Compensation Constitutional Amendments—L[1]	149,356	169,131
4. Bill Requiring Marriage License Applicants Medically Examined; Physically and Mentally—L[2]	*277,099	66,484
5. Slot Machines Seizure by Sheriffs and Destruction on Court Order—R	*204,561	126,580
6. Prohibiting Slot Machines, Pin-ball, Dart and Other Similar Games—R	*197,912	129,043
7. Townsend Plan Bill—I[3]	*183,781	149,711
8. Citizens' Retirement Annuity Bill; Levying Transactions Tax to Provide Fund—I[2]	112,172	219,557
9. Bill Regulating Picketing and Boycotting by Labor Groups and Organizations—I[2]	*197,771	148,460
10. Water Purification and Prevention of Pollution Bill—I[2]	*247,685	75,295
11. Bill Regulating Sale of Alcoholic Liquor for Beverage Purposes—I[2]	118,282	222,221

Elections and Records — vertical margin text

Election Date/Measure Number/Ballot Title	Yes	No
12. Constitutional Amendment Legalizing Certain Lotteries and Other Forms of Gambling—I[1]	141,792	180,329
November 5, 1940		
1. Amendment Removing Office Time Limit of State Secretary and Treasurer—L[1]	163,942	213,797
2. Amendment Making Three Years' Average People's Voted Levies, Tax Base—L[1]	129,699	183,488
3. Amendment Repealing the Double Liability of Stockholders of State Banks—L[1]	157,891	191,290
4. Legislators' Compensation Constitutional Amendment—L[1]	186,830	188,031
5. Bill Changing the Primary Nominating Elections from May to September—R	156,421	221,203
6. Bill to Further Regulate Sale and Use of Alcoholic Liquor—R	158,004	235,128
7. Bill Repealing Present Liquor Law; Authorizing Private Sale, Licensed, Taxed—I[2]	90,681	309,183
8. Amendment Legalizing Certain Gambling and Gaming Devices and Certain Lotteries—I[1]	150,157	258,010
9. Bill to Repeal the Oregon Milk Control Law—I[2]	201,983	213,838
November 3, 1942		
1. Legislators' Compensation Constitutional Amendment—L[1]	*129,318	109,898
2. Rural Credits Loan Fund Repeal Amendment—L[1]	*101,425	88,857
3. Amendment Specifying Exclusive Uses of Gasoline and Motor Vehicle Taxes—L[1]	*125,990	86,332
4. Amendment Authorizing Regulation by Law of Voting Privilege Forfeiture—L[1]	101,508	103,404
5. Cigarette Tax Bill—R	110,643	127,366
6. Bill Restricting and Prohibiting Net Fishing Coastal Streams and Bays—R	97,212	137,177
7. Bill Distributing Surplus Funds to School Districts, Reducing Taxes Therein—I[2]	*136,321	92,623
November 7, 1944		
1. Amendment To Provide Alternative Means for Securing Bank Deposits—L[1]	*228,744	115,745
2. Amendment Authorizing Change to Managerial Form of County Government—L[1]	*175,716	154,504
3. Amendment Authorizing "Oregon War Veterans' Fund," Providing Tax Therefor—L[1]	*190,520	178,581
4. Amendment to Authorize Legislative Regulation of Voting Privilege Forfeiture—L[1]	*183,855	156,219
5. Bill Providing Educational Aid to Certain Veterans World War II—L[2]	*238,350	135,317
6. Bill Imposing Tax on Retail Sales of Tangible Personal Property—L[2]	96,697	269,276
7. Burke Bill; Only State Selling Liquor over 14 Hundredths Alcohol—R	*228,853	180,158
8. Constitutional Amendment Increasing State Tax Fund for Public School Support—I[1]	177,153	186,976
9. Constitutional Amendment Providing Monthly Annuities From a Gross Income Tax—I[1]	180,691	219,981
June 22, 1945 (Special Election)		
1. Bill Authorizing Tax Levy for State Building Fund—L[2]	*78,269	49,565
2. Bill Authorizing Cigarette Tax to Support Public Schools—L[2]	60,321	67,542
November 5, 1946		
1. Constitutional Amendment Providing for Succession to Office of Governor—L[1]	*221,547	70,322
2. Bill Authorizing Tax for Construction and Equipment of State Armories—L[2]	75,693	219,006
3. Bill Establishing Rural School Districts and School Boards—L[2]	*155,733	134,673
4. Bill Authorizing Chinamen to Hold Real Estate and Mining Claims—L[1]	*161,865	133,111
5. Amendment Permitting Legislative Bills to be Read by Title Only—L[1]	*145,248	113,279

Election Date/Measure Number/Ballot Title	Yes	No
6. Constitutional Amendment Increasing Number of Senators to Thirty-one—L[1]	88,717	185,247
7. Bill Regulating Fishing in Coastal Streams and Inland Waters—R	*196,195	101,398
8. To Create State Old-age and Disability Pension Fund—I[2]	86,374	244,960
9. To Create Basic School Support Fund by Annual Tax Levy—I[2]	*157,904	151,765
October 7, 1947 (Special Election)		
1. Bill Taxing Retail Sales for School, Welfare and Governmental Purposes—L[2]	67,514	180,333
2. Cigarette Tax Bill—R	103,794	140,876
November 2, 1948		
1. Constitutional Six Percent Tax Limitation Amendment—L[1]	150,032	268,155
2. Constitutional Amendment Authorizing Indebtedness for State Forestation—L[1]	*211,912	209,317
3. Bill Authorizing State Boys' Camp Near Timber, Oregon—L[2]	*227,638	219,196
4. Bill Amending Licensing and Acquisition Provisions for Hydroelectric Commission Act—R	173,004	242,100
5. Constitutional Amendment Fixing Qualifications of Voters in School Elections—I[1]	*284,776	164,025
6. Oregon Old Age Pension Act—I[2]	*313,212	172,531
7. Bill Increasing Personal Income Tax Exemptions—I[2]	*405,842	63,373
8. Oregon Liquor Dispensing Licensing Act—I[2]	210,108	273,621
9. World War II Veterans' Bonus Amendment—I[1]	198,283	265,805
10. Prohibiting Salmon Fishing in Columbia River With Fixed Appliances—I[2]	*273,140	184,834
11. Question of Authorizing Additional State Tax, to be Offset by Income Tax Funds—R	143,856	256,167
November 7, 1950		
1. Constitutional Amendment Fixing Legislators' Annual Compensation—L[1]	*243,518	205,361
2. Constitutional Amendment Lending State Tax Credit for Higher Education Buildings—L[1]	*256,895	192,573
3. Constitutional Amendment Augmenting "Oregon War Veterans' Fund"—L[1]	*268,171	183,724
4. Increasing Basic School Support Fund by Annual Tax Levy—L[2]	*234,394	231,856
5. Needy Aged Persons Public Assistance Act—R	*310,143	158,939
6. Providing Uniform Standard Time in Oregon—R	*277,633	195,319
7. World War II Veterans' Compensation Fund—I[1]	*239,553	216,958
8. Constitutional Amendment for Legislative Representation Reapportionment—I[1]	190,992	215,302
9. Making Sale of Promotively Advertised Alcoholic Beverage Unlawful—I[2]	113,524	378,732
November 4, 1952		
1. Amendment Making Superintendent of Public Instruction Appointive—L[1]	282,882	326,199
2. World War Veterans' State Aid Sinking Fund Repeal—L[1]	*454,898	147,128
3. Act Authorizing Domiciliary State Hospital for Aged Mentally Ill—L[2]	*480,479	153,402
4. Amendment Legal Voters of Taxing Unit Establish Tax Base—L[1]	*355,136	210,373
5. Amendment to Augment Oregon War Veterans' Fund—L[1]	*465,605	132,363
6. Amendment Creating Legislative Assembly Emergency Committee—L[1]	*364,539	194,492
7. Amendment Fixing Elective Terms of State Senators and Representatives—L[1]	*483,356	103,357
8. Amendatory Act Title Subject Amendment—L[1]	*315,071	191,087
9. Act Limiting State Property Tax—L[2]	*318,948	272,145
10. Motor Carrier Highway Transportation Tax Act—R	*409,588	230,241
11. School District Reorganization Act—R	295,700	301,974
12. Cigarette Stamp Tax Revenue Act—R	233,226	413,137
13. Establishing United States Standard Time in Oregon—I[2]	*399,981	256,981
14. Constitutional Amendment Prohibiting Lotteries, Bookmaking, Pari-mutuel Betting on Animal Racing—I[1]	230,097	411,884

Elections and Records — side tab

Election Date/Measure Number/Ballot Title	Yes	No
15. Constitutional Amendment Authorizing Alcoholic Liquor Sale by Individual Glass—I[1]	*369,127	285,446
16. Constitutional Amendment Providing Equitable Taxing Method for Use of Highways—I[1]	135,468	484,730
17. Milk Production and Marketing Act Bill—I[2]	313,629	337,750
18. Constitutional Legislative Senator and Representative Apportionment Enforcement Amendment—I[1]	*357,550	194,292
November 2, 1954		
1. Salaries of State Legislators—L[1]	216,545	296,008
2. Subdividing Counties for Electing State Legislators—L[1]	*268,337	208,077
3. Mental Hospital In or Near Portland—L[2]	*397,625	128,685
4. Constitutional Amendments—How Proposed by People—L[1]	*251,078	230,770
5. State Property Tax—L[1]	208,419	264,569
6. Establishing Daylight Saving Time—I[2]	252,305	300,007
7. Prohibiting Certain Fishing in Coastal Streams—I[2]	232,775	278,805
8. Repealing Milk Control Law—I[2]	*293,745	247,591
November 6, 1956		
1. State Tax Laws—Immediate Effect Authorized—L[1]	175,932	487,550
2. Authorizing State Acceptance of Certain Gifts—L[1]	*498,633	153,033
3. Salaries of Certain State Officers—L[1]	*390,338	263,155
4. Qualifications for County Coroner and Surveyor—L[1]	*455,485	182,550
5. Salaries of State Legislators—L[1]	320,741	338,365
6. Cigarette Tax—R	280,055	414,613
7. Prohibiting Certain Fishing in Coastal Streams—I[2]	*401,882	259,309
November 4, 1958		
1. Fixing State Boundaries—L[1]	*399,396	114,318
2. Increasing Funds for War Veterans' Loans—L[1]	232,246	318,685
3. Salaries of State Legislators—L[1]	236,000	316,437
4. Capital Punishment Bill—L[1]	264,434	276,487
5. Financing Urban Redevelopment Projects—L[1]	221,330	268,716
6. Modifying County Debt Limitation—L[1]	*252,347	224,426
7. Special Grand Jury Bill—L[1]	*357,792	136,745
8. Authorizes Different Use of State Institution—L[1]	*303,282	193,177
9. Temporary Appointment and Assignment of Judges—L[1]	*373,466	125,898
10. State Power Development—L[1]	218,662	291,210
11. County Home Rule Amendment—L[1]	*311,516	157,023
12. Authorizing Discontinuing Certain State Tuberculosis Hospitals—L[1]	*319,790	195,945
13. Persons Eligible to Serve in Legislature—I[1]	*320,751	201,700
May 20, 1960		
1. Salaries of State Legislators—L[1]	250,456	281,542
November 8, 1960		
1. Fixing Commencement of Legislators' Term—L[1]	*579,022	92,187
2. Daylight Saving Time—L[2]	357,499	393,652
3. Financing Urban Redevelopment Projects—L[1]	*335,792	312,187
4. Permitting Prosecution by Information or Indictment—L[1]	306,190	340,197
5. Authorizing Legislature to Propose Revised Constitution—L[1]	*358,367	289,895
6. State Bonds for Higher Education Facilities—L[1]	*467,557	233,759
7. Voter Qualification Amendment—L[1]	*508,108	183,977
8. Authorizing Bonds for State Building Program—L[1]	232,250	433,515
9. Compulsory Retirement for Judges—L[1]	*578,471	123,283
10. Elective Offices: When to Become Vacant—L[1]	*486,019	169,865
11. Financing Improvements in Home Rule Counties—L[1]	*399,210	222,736
12. Continuity of Government in Enemy Attack—L[1]	*578,266	88,995
13. War Veterans' Bonding and Loan Amendment—L[1]	*415,931	266,630
14. Personal Income Tax Bill—R	115,610	570,025
15. Billboard Control Measure—I[2]	261,735	475,290
May 18, 1962		
1. Six Percent Limitation Amendment—L[1]	141,728	262,140
2. Salaries of State Legislators—L[1]	*241,171	178,749

Election Date/Measure Number/Ballot Title	Yes	No
November 6, 1962		
1. Reorganize State Militia—L[1]	*312,680	234,440
2. Forest Rehabilitation Debt Limit Amendment—L[1]	*323,799	199,174
3. Permanent Road Debt Limit Amendment—L[1]	*319,956	200,236
4. Power Development Debt Limit Amendment—L[1]	*298,255	208,755
5. State Courts Creation and Jurisdiction—L[1]	*307,855	193,487
6. Daylight Saving Time—L[2]	*388,154	229,661
7. Constitutional Six Percent Limitation Amendment—L[1]	*270,637	219,509
8. Legislative Apportionment Constitutional Amendment—I[1]	197,322	325,182
9. Repeals School District Reorganization Law—I[2]	206,540	320,917
October 15, 1963 (Special Election)		
1. Personal and Corporation Income Tax Bill—R	103,737	362,845
May 15, 1964		
1. Authorizing Bonds for Education Building Program—L[1]	*327,220	252,372
November 3, 1964		
1. Capital Punishment Bill—L[1]	*455,654	302,105
2. Leasing Property for State Use—L[1]	*477,031	238,241
3. Amending State Workmen's Compensation Law—I[2]	205,182	549,414
4. Prohibiting Commercial Fishing for Salmon, Steelhead—I[2]	221,797	534,731
May 24, 1966		
1. Cigarette Tax Bill—L[2]	*310,743	181,957
2. Superintendent of Public Instruction Constitutional Amendment—L[1]	197,096	267,319
November 8, 1966		
1. Public Transportation System Employes Constitutional Amendment—L[1]	*468,103	123,964
2. State Bonds for Educational Facilities—L[1]	237,282	332,983
May 28, 1968		
1. Common School Fund Constitutional Amendment—L[1]	*372,915	226,191
2. Constitutional Amendment Changing Initiative — Referendum Requirements—L[1]	*321,731	244,750
3. Higher Education and Community College Bonds—L[1]	*353,383	261,014
November 5, 1968		
1. Constitutional Amendment Broadening Veterans Loan Eligibility—L[1]	*651,250	96,065
2. Constitutional Amendment for Removal of Judges—L[1]	*690,989	56,973
3. Empowering Legislature to Extend Ocean Boundaries—L[1]	*588,166	143,768
4. Constitutional Amendment Broadening County Debt Limitation—L[1]	331,617	348,866
5. Government Consolidation City-County Over 300,000—L[1]	*393,789	278,483
6. Bond Issue to Acquire Ocean Beaches—I[1]	315,175	464,140
7. Constitutional Amendment Changing Property Tax Limitation—I[1]	276,451	503,443
June 3, 1969 (Special Election)		
1. Property Tax Relief and Sales Tax—L[1]	65,077	504,274
May 26, 1970		
1. Capital Construction Bonds for State Government—L[1]	190,257	300,126
2. Repeals "White Foreigner" Section of Constitution—L[1]	*326,374	168,464
3. Revised Constitution for Oregon—L[1]	182,074	322,682
4. Pollution Control Bonds—L[1]	*292,234	213,835
5. Lowers Oregon Voting Age to 19—L[1]	202,018	336,527
6. Local School Property Tax Equalization Measure—L[1]	180,602	323,189
November 3, 1970		
1. Constitutional Amendment Concerning Convening of Legislature—L[1]	261,428	340,104
2. Automatic Adoption, Federal Income Tax Amendments—L[1]	*342,138	269,467
3. Constitutional Amendment Concerning County Debt Limitation—L[1]	283,659	294,186
4. Investing Funds Donated to Higher Education—L[1]	*332,188	268,588
5. Veterans' Loan Amendment—L[1]	*481,031	133,564
6. Limits Term of Defeated Incumbents—L[1]	*436,897	158,409
7. Constitutional Amendment Authorizing Education Bonds—L[1]	269,372	318,651
8. Allows Penal Institutions Anywhere in Oregon—L[1]	*352,771	260,100
9. Scenic Waterways Bill—I[2]	*406,315	214,243
10. New Property Tax Bases for Schools—I[1]	223,735	405,437
11. Restricts Governmental Powers Over Rural Property—I[1]	272,765	342,503

Elections and Records

Election Date/Measure Number/Ballot Title	Yes	No
January 18, 1972 (Special Election)		
1. Increases Cigarette Tax — R	*245,717	236,937
May 23, 1972		
1. Eliminates Literacy Requirement; Lowers Voting Age — L[1]	327,231	349,746
2. Repeals Requirement for Decennial State Census — L[1]	*420,568	206,436
3. Allows Legislators to Call Special Sessions — L[1]	241,371	391,698
4. Capital Construction Bonds for State Government — L[1]	232,391	364,323
5. Irrigation and Water Development Bonds — L[1]	233,175	374,295
6. Enabling County-City Vehicle Registration Tax — R	120,027	491,551
November 7, 1972		
1. Eliminates Location Requirements for State Institutions — L[1]	*594,080	232,948
2. Qualifications for Sheriff Set By Legislature — L[1]	*572,619	281,720
3. Amends County Purchase and Lease Limitations — L[1]	329,669	462,932
4. Changes State Constitution Provision Regarding Religion — L[1]	336,382	519,196
5. Minimum Jury Size of Six Members — L[1]	*591,191	265,636
6. Broadens Eligibility for Veterans' Loans — L[1]	*736,802	133,139
7. Repeals Governor's Retirement Act — I[2]	*571,959	292,561
8. Changes Succession to Office of Governor — I[1]	*697,297	151,174
9. Prohibits Property Tax for School Operations — I[1]	342,885	558,136
May 1, 1973 (Special Election)		
1. Property Tax Limitation; School Tax Revision — L[2]	253,682	358,219
May 28, 1974		
1. Income, Corporate Tax, School Support Increase — L[2]	136,851	410,733
2. Highway Fund Use for Mass Transit — L[1]	190,899	369,038
3. New School District Tax Base Limitation — L[1]	166,363	371,897
4. Authorizes Bonds for Water Development Fund — L[1]	198,563	328,221
5. Increases Veterans' Loan Bonding Authority — L[1]	*381,559	164,953
6. Permits Legislature to Call Special Session — L[1]	246,525	298,373
November 5, 1974		
1. Liquor Licenses for Public Passenger Carriers — L[1]	353,357	384,521
2. Opens All Legislative Deliberations to Public — L[1]	*546,255	165,778
3. Revises Constitutional Requirements for Grand Juries — L[1]	*437,557	246,902
4. Governor Vacancy Successor Age Requirement Eliminated — L[1]	*381,593	331,756
5. The measure designated as Number 5 by the 1973 Legislature was moved to the May 28, 1974 primary election by the 1974 special session. On the advice of the Attorney General, this measure number was left blank.		
6. Permits Establishing Qualifications for County Assessors — L[1]	*552,737	146,364
7. Tax Base Includes Revenue Sharing Money — L[1]	322,023	329,858
8. Revises School District Election Voting Requirements — L[1]	337,565	378,071
9. Permits State Employes to be Legislators — L[1]	218,846	476,547
10. Revises Oregon Voter Qualification Requirements — L[1]	*362,731	355,506
11. Right to Jury in Civil Cases — L[1]	*480,631	216,853
12. Community Development Fund Bonds — L[1]	277,723	376,747
13. Obscenity and Sexual Conduct Bill — R	*393,743	352,958
14. Public Officials' Financial Ethics and Reporting. This measure was also referred to all 36 counties, with 30 voting yes and 6 voting no; and all cities with governing bodies, with 153 voting yes and 90 voting no. — L[2]	*498,002	177,946
15. Prohibits Purchase or Sale of Steelhead — I[2]	*458,417	274,182
May 25, 1976		
1. Expands Veterans' Home-Farm Loan Eligibility — L[1]	*549,553	158,997
2. Discipline of Judges — L[1]	*639,977	59,774
3. Housing Bonds — L[1]	*315,588	362,414
4. Authorizes Vehicle Tax Mass Transit Use — L[1]	170,331	531,219
November 2, 1976		
1. Validates Inadvertently Superseded Statutory Amendments — L[1]	*607,325	247,843
2. Allows Changing City, County Election Days — L[1]	376,489	536,967
3. Lowers Minimum Age for Legislative Service — L[1]	285,777	679,517

Election Date/Measure Number/Ballot Title	Yes	No
4. Repeals Emergency Succession Provision—L[1]	*507,308	368,646
5. Permits Legislature to Call Special Session—L[1]	*549,126	377,354
6. Allows Charitable, Fraternal, Religious Organizations Bingo—L[1]	*682,252	281,696
7. Partial Public Funding of Election Campaigns—L[2]	263,738	659,327
8. Increases Motor Fuel, Ton-Mile Taxes—R	465,143	505,124
9. Regulates Nuclear Power Plant Construction Approval—I[2]	423,008	584,845
10. Repeals Land Use Planning Coordination Statutes—I[2]	402,608	536,502
11. Prohibits Adding Fluorides to Water Systems—I[2]	419,567	555,981
12. Repeals Intergovernmental Cooperation, Planning District Statutes—I[2]	333,933	525,868
May 17, 1977 (Special Election)		
1. School Operating Levy Measure—L[1]	112,570	252,061
2. Authorizes Additional Veterans' Fund Uses—L[1]	*200,270	158,436
3. Increases Veterans' Loan Bonding Authority—L[1]	*250,783	106,953
November 8, 1977 (Special Election)		
1. Water Development Loan Fund Created—L[1]	*124,484	118,953
2. Development of Nonnuclear Energy Resources—L[1]	105,219	137,693
May 23, 1978		
1. Home Rule County Initiative-Referendum Requirements—L[1]	*306,506	156,623
2. Open Meetings Rules for Legislature—L[1]	*435,338	80,176
3. Housing for Low Income Elderly—L[1]	*291,778	250,810
4. Domestic Water Fund Created—L[1]	148,822	351,843
5. Highway Repair Priority, Gas Tax Increase—L[2]	190,301	365,170
6. Reorganizes Metropolitan Service District, Abolishes CRAG—L[2,4]	*110,600	91,090
November 7, 1978		
1. Appellate Judge Selection, Running on Record—L[1]	358,504	449,132
2. Authorizes Senate Confirmation of Governor's Appointments—L[1]	*468,458	349,604
3. Vehicle and Fee Increase Referendum—R	208,722	673,802
4. Shortens Formation Procedures for People's Utility Districts—I[2]	375,587	471,027
5. Authorizes, Regulates Practice of Denture Technology—I[2]	*704,480	201,463
6. Limitations on Ad Valorem Property Taxes—I[1]	424,029	453,741
7. Prohibits State Expenditures, Programs or Services for Abortion—I[1]	431,577	461,542
8. Requires Death Penalty for Murder under Specified Conditions—I[2]	*573,707	318,610
9. Limitations on Public Utility Rate Base—I[2]	*589,361	267,132
10. Land Use Planning, Zoning Constitutional Amendment—I[1]	334,523	515,138
11. Reduces Property Tax Payable by Homeowner and Renter—L[1]	383,532	467,765
12. Support of Constitutional Amendment (Federal) Requires Balance Budget—L[5]	*641,862	134,758
May 20, 1980		
1. Constitutional Amendment Limits Uses of Gasoline and Highway User Taxes—L[1]	*451,695	257,230
2. Amends Liquor by the Drink Constitutional Provision—L[1]	325,030	384,346
3. State Bonds for Small Scale Local Energy Project Loan Fund—L[1]	*394,466	278,125
4. Veterans' Home and Farm Loan Eligibility Changes—L[1]	*574,148	130,452
5. Continues Tax Reduction Program—L[2]	*636,565	64,979
6. Definition of Multifamily Low Income Elderly Housing—L[1]	*536,002	138,675
November 4, 1980		
1. Repeal of Constitutional Provision Requiring Elected Superintendent of Public Instruction—L[1]	291,142	820,892
2. Guarantees Mentally Handicapped Voting Rights, Unless Adjudged Incompetent to Vote—L[1]	*678,573	455,020
3. Dedicates Oil, Natural Gas Taxes to Common School Fund—L[1]	*594,520	500,586
4. Increases Gas Tax from Seven to Nine Cents per Gallon—L[2]	298,421	849,745
5. Forbids Use, Sale of Snare, Leghold Traps for Most Purposes—I[2]	425,890	728,173
6. Constitutional Real Property Tax Limit Preserving 85% Districts' 1977 Revenue—I[1]	416,029	711,617
7. Nuclear Plant Licensing Requires Voter Approval, Waste Disposal Facility Existence—I[2]	*608,412	535,049
8. State Bonds for Fund to Finance Correctional Facilities—L[1]	523,955	551,383

Election Date/Measure Number/Ballot Title	Yes	No
May 18, 1982		
1. Use of State Bond Proceeds to Finance Municipal Water Projects—L[1]	*333,656	267,137
2. Multifamily Housing for Elderly and Disabled Persons—L[1]	*389,820	229,049
3. State Bonds for Fund to Finance Corrections Facilities—L[1]	281,548	333,476
4. Raises Taxes on Commercial Vehicles, Motor Vehicles Fuels for Roads—L[2]	308,574	323,268
5. Governor to Appoint Chief Justice of Oregon Supreme Court—L[2]	159,811	453,415
November 2, 1982		
1. Increases Tax Base When New Property Construction Increases District's Value—L[1]	219,034	768,150
2. Lengthens Governor's Time for Postsession Veto or Approval of Bills—L[1]	385,672	604,864
3. Constitutional Real Property Tax Limit Preserving 85% Districts' 1979 Revenue—I[1]	504,836	515,626
4. Permits Self-Service Dispensing of Motor Vehicle Fuel at Retail—I[2]	440,824	597,970
5. People of Oregon Urge Mutual Freeze on Nuclear Weapons Development—I[3]	*623,089	387,907
6. Ends State's Land Use Planning Powers, Retains Local Planning—I[2]	461,271	565,056
May 15, 1984		
1. State May Borrow and Lend Money for Public Works Projects—L[1]	332,175	365,571
2. Increases Fees for Licensing and Registration of Motor Vehicles—L[2]	234,060	487,457
November 6, 1984		
1. Changes Minimum Requirements for Recall of Public Officers—L[1]	*664,464	470,139
2. Constitutional Real Property Tax Limit—I[1]	599,424	616,252
3. Creates Citizens' Utility Board to Represent Interests of Utility Consumers—I[2]	*637,968	556,826
4. Constitutional Amendment Establishes State Lottery, Commission; Profits for Economic Development—I[1]	*794,441	412,341
5. Statutory Provisions for State Operated Lottery if Constitutionally Authorized—I[2]	*786,933	399,231
6. Exempts Death Sentences from Constitutional Guarantees Against Cruel, Vindictive Punishments—I[1]	*653,009	521,687
7. Requires by Statute Death or Mandatory Imprisonment for Aggravated Murder—I[2]	*893,818	295,988
8. Revises Numerous Criminal Laws Concerning Police Powers, Trials, Evidence, Sentencing—I[2]	552,410	597,964
9. Adds Requirements for Disposing Wastes Containing Naturally Occurring Radioactive Isotopes—I[2]	*655,973	524,214
September 17, 1985 (Special Election)		
1. Amends Constitution. Approves Limited 5% Sales Tax for Local Education—L[1]	189,733	664,365
May 20, 1986		
1. Constitutional Amendment: Bans Income Tax on Social Security Benefits—L[1]	*534,476	118,766
2. Constitutional Amendment: Effect on Merger of Taxing Units on Tax Base—L[1]	*333,277	230,886
3. Constitutional Amendment: Verification of Signatures on Initiative and Referendum Petitions—L[1]	*460,148	132,101
4. Requires Special Election for U.S. Senator Vacancy, Removes Constitutional Provision—L[1]	*343,005	269,305
5. Constitutional Amendment: $96 Million Bonds for State-County Prison Buildings—L[1]	300,674	330,429
November 4, 1986		
1. Deletes Constitutional Requirement that Secretary of State Live in Salem—L[1]	*771,959	265,999
2. Constitutional Amendment Revising Legislative District Reapportionment Procedures After Federal Census—L[1]	*637,410	291,355
3. Constitutional Amendment Allows Charitable, Fraternal, Religious Organizations to Conduct Raffles—L[1]	*736,739	302,957

Election Date/Measure Number/Ballot Title	Yes	No
4. Replaces Public Utility Commissioner with Three Member Public Utility Commission—L^2	*724,577	297,973
5. Legalizes Private Possession and Growing of Marijuana for Personal Use—I^2	279,479	781,922
6. Constitutional Amendment Prohibits State Funding Abortions. Exception: Prevent Mother's Death—I^1	477,920	580,163
7. Constitutional 5% Sales Tax, Funds Schools, Reduces Property Tax—I^1	234,804	816,369
8. Prohibits Mandatory Local Measured Telephone Service Except Mobile Phone Service—I^2	*802,099	201,918
9. Amends Constitution. Limits Property Tax Rates and Assessed Value Increases—I^1	449,548	584,396
10. Revises Many Criminal Laws Concerning Victims' Rights, Evidence, Sentencing, Parole—I^2	*774,766	251,509
11. Homeowner's, Renter's Property Tax Relief Program; Sales Tax Limitation Measure—I^1	381,727	639,034
12. State Income Tax Changes, Increased Revenue to Property Tax Relief—I^2	299,551	720,034
13. Constitutional Amendment: Twenty Day Pre-election Voter Registration Cutoff—I^1	*693,460	343,450
14. Prohibits Nuclear Power Plant Operation Until Permanent Waste Site Licensed—I^2	375,241	674,641
15. Supersedes "Radioactive Waste" Definition; Changes Energy Facility Payment Procedure—I^2	424,099	558,741
16. Phases Out Nuclear Weapons Manufactured With Tax Credits, Civil Penalty—I^2	400,119	590,971
May 19, 1987 (Special Election)		
1. State Role In Selection of High-Level Nuclear Waste Repository Site—L^2	*299,581	100,854
2. Continues Existing Levies To Prevent School Closures: Tax Base Elections—L^1	*223,417	178,839
May 17, 1988		
1. Authorizes Water Development Fund Loans for Fish Protection, Watershed Restoration—L^1	*485,629	191,008
2. Protective Headgear for Motorcycle Operators and Passengers and Moped Riders—L^2	*486,401	224,655
November 8, 1988		
1. Extends Governor's Veto Deadline After Legislature Adjourns; Requires Prior Announcement—L^1	*615,012	520,939
2. Common School Fund Investments; Using Income for State Lands Management—L^1	*621,894	510,694
3. Requires the Use of Safety Belts—L^2	528,324	684,747
4. Requires Full Sentences Without Parole, Probation for Certain Repeat Felonies—I^2	*947,805	252,985
5. Finances Intercollegiate Athletic Fund by Increasing Malt Beverage, Cigarette Taxes—I^2	449,797	759,360
6. Indoor Clean Air Law Revisions Banning Public Smoking—I^2	430,147	737,779
7. Oregon Scenic Waterway System—I^2	*663,604	516,998
8. Revokes Ban on Sexual Orientation Discrimination in State Executive Branch—I^2	*626,751	561,355
May 16, 1989 (Special Election)		
1. Establishes New Tax Base Limits on Schools—L^1	183,818	263,283
June 27, 1989 (Special Election)		
1. Removes Constitutional Limitation on Use of Property Forfeited To State—L^1	*340,506	141,649
2. Prohibits Selling/Exporting Timber from State Lands Unless Oregon Processed—L^1	*446,151	48,558

Elections and Records

Election Date/Measure Number/Ballot Title	Yes	No
May 15, 1990		
1. Permits Using Local Vehicle Taxes for Transit if Voters Approve—L[1]	294,099	324,458
2. Amends Constitution; Allows Pollution Control Bond Use for Related Activities—L[1]	*352,922	248,123
3. Amends State Constitution; Requires Annual Legislative Sessions of Limited Duration—L[1]	294,664	299,831
4. Amends Laws on Organization of International Port of Coos Bay—L[2]	4,234	4,745
5A. Advisory Vote: Changing the School Finance System—L[5]	*462,090	140,747
5B. Advisory Vote: Income Tax Increase Reducing Homeowner School Property Taxes—L[5]	177,964	408,842
5C. Advisory Vote: Income Tax Increase Eliminating Homeowner School Property Taxes—L[5]	128,642	449,725
5D. Advisory Vote: Sales Tax Reducing School Property Taxes—L[5]	202,367	385,820
5E. Advisory Vote: Sales Tax Eliminating School Property Taxes—L[5]	222,611	374,466
November 6, 1990		
1. Grants Metropolitan Service District Electors Right to Home Rule—L[1]	*510,947	491,170
2. Constitutional Amendment Allows Merged School Districts to Combine Tax Bases—L[1]	*680,463	354,288
3. Repeals Tax Exemption, Grants Additional Benefit Payments for PERS Retirees—R	406,372	617,586
4. Prohibits Trojan Operation Until Nuclear Waste, Cost, Earthquake Standards Met—I[2]	446,795	660,992
5. State Constitutional Limit on Property Taxes for Schools, Government Operations—I[1]	*574,833	522,022
6. Product Packaging Must Meet Recycling Standards or Receive Hardship Waiver—I[2]	467,418	636,804
7. Six-County Work in Lieu of Welfare Benefits Pilot Program—I[2]	*624,744	452,853
8. Amends Oregon Constitution to Prohibit Abortion With Three Exceptions—I[1]	355,963	747,599
9. Requires the Use of Safety Belts—I[2]	*598,460	512,872
10. Doctor Must Give Parent Notice Before Minor's Abortion—I[2]	530,851	577,806
11. School Choice System, Tax Credit for Education Outside Public Schools—I[1]	351,977	741,863
May 19, 1992		
1. Amends Constitution: Future Fuel Taxes May Go to Police—L[1]	244,173	451,715
November 3, 1992		
1. Bonds May be Issued for State Parks—L[1]	653,062	786,017
2. Future Fuel Taxes May Go to Parks—L[1]	399,259	1,039,322
3. Limits Terms for Legislature, Statewide Offices, Congressional Offices—I[1]	*1,003,706	439,694
4. Bans Operation of Triple Truck-Trailer Combinations on Oregon Highways—I[2]	567,467	896,778
5. Closes Trojan Until Nuclear Waste, Cost, Earthquake, Health Conditions Met—I[2]	585,051	874,636
6. Bans Trojan Power Operation Unless Earthquake, Waste Storage Conditions Met—I[2]	619,329	830,850
7. Raises Tax Limit on Certain Property; Residential Renters' Tax Relief—I[1]	362,621	1,077,206
8. Restricts Lower Columbia Fish Harvests to Most Selective Means Available—I[2]	576,633	828,096
9. Government Cannot Facilitate, Must Discourage Homosexuality, Other "Behaviors"—I[1]	638,527	828,290
June 29, 1993 (Special Election)		
1. Allows Voter Approval of Urban Renewal Bond Repayment Outside Limit—L[1]	180,070	482,714
November 9, 1993 (Special Election)		
1. Should We Pass A 5% Sales Tax for Public Schools with these Restrictions?—L[1]	240,991	721,930

Election Date/Measure Number/Ballot Title	Yes	No
May 17, 1994		
2. Allows New Motor Vehicle Fuel Revenues for Dedicated Purposes—L[1]	158,028	446,665
November 8, 1994		
3. Amends Constitution: Changes Deadline for Filling Vacancies at General Election—L[1]	*776,197	382,126
4. Amends Constitution: Creates Vacancy if State Legislator Convicted of Felony—L[1]	*1,055,111	145,499
5. Amends Constitution: Bars New or Increased Taxes without Voter Approval—I[1]	543,302	671,025
6. Amends Constitution: Candidates May Use Only Contributions from District Residents—I[1]	*628,180	555,019
7. Amends Constitution: Guarantees Equal Protection: Lists Prohibited Grounds of Discrimination—I[1]	512,980	671,021
8. Amends Constitution: Public Employees Pay Part of Salary for Pension—I[1]	*611,760	610,776
9. Adopts Contribution and Spending Limits, Other Campaign Finance Law Changes—I[2]	*851,014	324,224
10. Amends Constitution: Legislature Cannot Reduce Voter-Approved Sentence Without 2/3 Vote—I[1]	*763,507	415,678
11. Mandatory Sentences for Listed Felonies; Covers Persons 15 and Up—I[2]	*788,695	412,816
12. Repeals Prevailing Rate Wage Requirement for Workers on Public Works—I[2]	450,553	731,146
13. Amends Constitution: Governments Cannot Approve, Create Classifications Based on, Homosexuality—I[1]	592,746	630,628
14. Amends Chemical Process Mining Laws: Adds Requirements, Prohibitions, Standards, Fees—I[1]	500,005	679,936
15. Amends Constitution: State Must Maintain Funding for Schools, Community Colleges—I[1]	438,018	760,853
16. Allows Terminally Ill Adults to Obtain Prescription for Lethal Drugs—I[2]	*627,980	596,018
17. Amends Constitution: Requires State Prison Inmates to Work Full Time—I[1]	*859,896	350,541
18. Bans Hunting Bears with Bait, Hunting Bears, Cougars with Dogs—I[2]	*629,527	586,026
19. Amends Constitution: No Free Speech Protection for Obscenity, Child Pornography—I[1]	549,754	652,139
20. Amends Constitution: "Equal Tax" on Trade Replaces Current Taxes—I[1]	284,195	898,416
May 16, 1995 (Special Election)		
21. Dedication of Lottery Funds to Education—L[1]	*671,027	99,728
22. Inhabitancy in State Legislative Districts—L[1]	*709,931	45,311
May 21, 1996		
23. Amends Constitution: Increases Minimum Value in Controversy Required to Obtain Jury Trial—L[1]	*466,580	177,218
24. Amends Constitution: Initiative Petition Signatures Must Be Collected From Each Congressional District—L[1]	279,399	360,592
25. Amends Constitution: Requires 3/5 Majority in Legislature to Pass Revenue-Raising Bills—L[1]	*349,918	289,930
November 5, 1996		
26. Amends Constitution: Changes the Principles that Govern Laws for Punishment of Crime—L[1]	*878,677	440,283
27. Amends Constitution: Grants Legislature New Power Over Both New, Existing Administrative Rules—L[1]	349,050	938,819
28. Amends Constitution: Repeals Certain Residency Requirements for State Veterans' Loans—L[1]	*708,341	593,136
29. Amends Constitution: Governor's Appointees Must Vacate Office If Successor Not Timely Confirmed—L[1]	335,057	958,947
30. Amends Constitution: State Must Pay Local Governments Costs of State-Mandated Programs—L[1]	*731,127	566,168
31. Amends Constitution: Obscenity May Receive No Greater Protection Than Under Federal Constitution—L[1]	630,980	706,974

Election Date/Measure Number/Ballot Title	Yes	No
32. Authorizes Bonds for Portland Region Light Rail, Transportation Projects Elsewhere—R[2]	622,764	704,970
33. Amends Constitution: Limits Legislative Change to Statutes Passed by Voters—I[1]	638,824	652,811
34. Wildlife Management Exclusive to Commission; Repeals 1994 Bear/Cougar Initiative—I[2]	570,803	762,979
35. Restricts Bases for Providers to Receive Pay for Health Care—I[2]	441,108	807,987
36. Increases Minimum Hourly Wage to $6.50 Over Three Years—I[2]	*769,725	584,303
37. Broadens Types of Beverage Containers Requiring Deposit and Refund Value—I[2]	540,645	818,336
38. Prohibits Livestock in Certain Polluted Waters or on Adjacent Lands—I[2]	479,921	852,661
39. Amends Constitution: Government, Private Entities Cannot Discriminate Among Health Care Provider Categories—I[1]	569,037	726,824
40. Amends Constitution: Gives Crime Victims Rights, Expands Admissible Evidence, Limits Pretrial Release—I[1]	*778,574	544,301
41. Amends Constitution: States How Public Employee Earnings Must Be Expressed—I[1]	446,115	838,088
42. Amends Constitution: Requires Testing of Public School Students; Public Report—I[1]	460,553	857,878
43. Amends Collective Bargaining Law for Public Safety Employees—I[2]	547,131	707,586
44. Increases, Adds Cigarette and Tobacco Taxes; Changes Tax Revenue Distribution—I[2]	*759,048	598,543
45. Amends Constitution: Raises Public Employees' Normal Retirement Age; Reduces Benefits—I[1]	458,238	866,461
46. Amends Constitution: Counts Non-Voters As "No" Votes on Tax Measures—I[1]	158,555	1,180,148
47. Amends Constitution: Reduces and Limits Property Taxes; Limits Local Revenues, Replacement Fees—I[1]	*704,554	642,613
48. Amends Constitution: Instructs State, Federal Legislators to Vote for Congressional Term Limits—I[1,3]	624,771	671,095
May 20, 1997 (Special Election)		
49. Amends Constitution: Restricts Inmate Lawsuits; Allows Interstate Shipment of Prison Made Products—L[1]	*699,813	70,940
50. Amends Constitution: Limits Assessed Value of Property for Tax Purposes; Limits Property Tax Rates—L[1]	*429,943	341,781
November 4, 1997 (Special Election)		
51. Repeals Law Allowing Terminally Ill Adults To Obtain Lethal Prescription—L[2]	445,830	666,275
52. Authorizes State Lottery Bond Program To Finance Public School Projects—L[2]	*805,742	293,425
May 19, 1998		
53. Amends Constitution: Eliminates Voter Turnout Requirement For Passing Certain Property Tax Measures—L[1]	303,539	319,871
November 3, 1998		
54. Amends Constitution: Authorizes State To Guarantee Bonded Indebtedness Of Certain Education Districts—L[1]	*569,982	474,727
55. Amends Constitution: Permits State To Guarantee Earnings On Prepaid Tuition Trust Fund—L[1]	456,464	579,251
56. Expands Notice To Landowners Regarding Changes To Land Use Laws—L[2]	*874,547	212,737
57. Makes Possession Of Limited Amount Of Marijuana Class C Misdemeanor—R[2]	371,967	736,968
58. Requires Issuing Copy Of Original Oregon Birth Certificate to Adoptees—I[2]	*621,832	462,084
59. Amends Constitution: Prohibits Using Public Resources To Collect Money For Political Purposes—I[1]	539,757	561,952
60. Requires Vote By Mail In Biennial Primary, General Elections—I[2]	*757,204	334,021
61. Vote Not Tallied By Court Order		
62. Amends Constitution: Requires Campaign Finance Disclosures; Regulates Signature Gathering; Guarantees Contribution Methods—I[1]	*721,448	347,112

Election Date/Measure Number/Ballot Title	Yes	No
63. Amends Constitution: Measures Proposing Supermajority Voting Requirements Require Same Supermajority For Passage—I[1]	*566,064	457,762
64. Prohibits Many Present Timber Harvest Practices, Imposes More Restrictive Regulations—I[2]	215,491	897,535
65. Amends Constitution: Creates Process For Requiring Legislature To Review Administrative Rules—I[1]	483,811	533,948
66. Amends Constitution: Dedicates Some Lottery Funding To Parks, Beaches; Habitat, Watershed Protection—I[1]	*742,038	362,247
67. Allows Medical Use Of Marijuana Within Limits; Establishes Permit System—I[2]	*611,190	508,263

November 2, 1999 (Special Election)

68. Amends Constitution: Allows Protecting Business, Certain Government Programs From Prison Work Programs—L[1]	*406,526	289,407
69. Amends Constitution: Grants Victims Constitutional Rights In Criminal Prosecutions, Juvenile Court Delinquency Proceedings—L[1]	*406,393	292,419
70. Amends Constitution: Gives Public, Through Prosecutor, Right To Demand Jury Trial In Criminal Cases—L[1]	289,783	407,429
71. Amends Constitution: Limits Pretrial Release Of Accused Person To Protect Victims, Public—L[1]	*404,404	292,696
72. Amends Constitution: Allows Murder Conviction By 11 To 1 Jury Verdict—L[1]	316,351	382,685
73. Amends Constitution: Limits Immunity From Criminal Prosecution Of Person Ordered To Testify About His Or Her Conduct—L[1]	320,160	369,843
74. Amends Constitution: Requires Terms Of Imprisonment Announced In Court Be Fully Served, With Exceptions—L[1]	*368,899	325,078
75. Amends Constitution: Persons Convicted Of Certain Crimes Cannot Serve On Grand Juries, Criminal Trial Juries—L[1]	*399,671	292,445
76. Amends Constitution: Requires Light, Heavy Motor Vehicle Classes Proportionately Share Highway Costs—L[1]	*372,613	314,351

May 16, 2000

77. Amends Constitution: Makes Certain Local Taxing Districts' Temporary Property Tax Authority Permanent—L[1]	336,253	432,541
78. Amends Constitution: Lengthens Period For Verifying Signatures On Initiative And Referendum Petitions—L[1]	*528,129	327,440
79. Amends Constitution: Increases Signatures Required To Place Initiative Amending Constitution On Ballot—L[1]	356,912	505,081
80. Amends Constitution: Authorizes Using Fuel Tax, Vehicle Fees For Increasing Highway Policing—L[1]	310,640	559,941
81. Amends Constitution: Allows Legislature To Limit Recovery Of Damages In Civil Actions—L[1]	219,009	650,348
82. Repeals Truck Weight-Mile Tax; Establishes And Increases Fuel Taxes—R[2]	109,741	767,329

November 7, 2000

83. Amends Constitution: Authorizes New Standards, Priorities For Veterans' Loans; Expands Qualified Recipients—L[1]	*1,084,870	365,203
84. Amends Constitution: State Must Continue Paying Local Governments For State-Mandated Programs—L[1]	*1,211,384	222,723
85. Amends Constitution: Modifies Population, Minimum Area Requirements For Formation Of New Counties—L[1]	634,307	767,366
86. Amends Constitution: Requires Refunding General Fund Revenues Exceeding State Estimates To Taxpayers—L[1]	*898,793	550,304
87. Amends Constitution: Allows Regulation Of Location Of Sexually Oriented Businesses Through Zoning—L[1]	694,410	771,901
88. Increases Maximum Deductible In Oregon For Federal Income Taxes Paid—L[2]	*739,270	724,097
89. Dedicates Tobacco Settlement Proceeds To Specified Health, Housing, Transportation Programs—L[2]	622,814	828,117
90. Authorizes Rates Giving Utilities Return On Investments In Retired Property—R[2]	158,810	1,208,545

Election Date/Measure Number/Ballot Title	Yes	No
91. Amends Constitution: Makes Federal Income Taxes Fully Deductible On Oregon Tax Returns—I[1]	661,342	814,885
92. Amends Constitution: Prohibits Payroll Deductions For Political Purposes Without Specific Written Authorization—I[1]	656,250	815,338
93. Amends Constitution: Voters Must Approve Most Taxes, Fees; Requires Certain Approval Percentage—I[1]	581,186	865,091
94. Repeals Mandatory Minimum Sentences For Certain Felonies, Requires Resentencing—I[2]	387,068	1,073,275
95. Amends Constitution: Student Learning Determines Teacher Pay; Qualifications, Not Seniority, Determine Retention—I[1]	514,926	962,250
96. Amends Constitution: Prohibits Making Initiative Process Harder, Except Through Initiative; Applies Retroactively—I[1]	527,613	866,588
97. Bans Body-Gripping Animal Traps, Some Poisons; Restricts Fur Commerce—I[2]	606,939	867,219
98. Amends Constitution: Prohibits Using Public Resources For Political Purposes; Limits Payroll Deductions—I[1]	678,024	776,489
99. Amends Constitution: Creates Commission Ensuring Quality Home Care Services For Elderly, Disabled—I[1]	*911,217	539,414
1. Amends Constitution: Legislature Must Fund School Quality Goals Adequately; Report; Establish Grants—I[1]	*940,223	477,461
2. Amends Constitution: Creates Process For Requiring Legislature To Review Administrative Rules—I[1]	605,575	779,190
3. Amends Constitution: Requires Conviction Before Forfeiture; Restricts Proceeds Usage; Requires Reporting, Penalty—I[1]	*952,792	465,081
4. Dedicates Tobacco-Settlement Proceeds; Earnings Fund Low-Income Health Care—I[2]	650,850	789,543
5. Expands Circumstances Requiring Background Checks Before Transfer Of Firearm—I[2]	*921,926	569,996
6. Provides Public Funding To Candidates Who Limit Spending, Private Contributions—I[2]	586,910	838,011
7. The Secretary of State has been enjoined from canvassing the votes for this measure—I[1]		
8. Amends Constitution: Limits State Appropriations To Percentage Of State's Prior Personal Income—I[1]	608,090	789,699
9. Prohibits Public School Instruction Encouraging, Promoting, Sanctioning Homosexual, Bisexual Behaviors—I[2]	702,572	788,691
May 21, 2002		
10. Amends Constitution: Allows Public Universities to Receive Equity in Private Companies as Compensation for Publicly Created Technology—L[1]	*608,640	177,004
11. Amends Constitution: Authorizes Less Expensive General Obligation Bond financing for OHSU Medical Research and other Capital Costs—L[1]	*589,869	190,226
12. Removed from Ballot		
13. Amends Constitution: Authorizes Using Education Fund Principal in Specified Circumstances; Transfers $220 Million to School Fund—L[1]	376,605	411,923
September 17, 2002 (Special Election, see Note below)		
19. Amends Constitution: Authorizes Using Education Stability Fund Principal in Specified Circumstances; Transfers $150 Million to State School Fund; Creates School Capital Matching Subaccount in Stability Fund—L[1]	*496,815	306,440
20. Increases Cigarette Tax; Uses Revenue for Health Plan, Other Programs—L[2]	*522,613	289,119
November 5, 2002		
14. Amends Constitution: Removes Historical Racial References in Obsolete Sections of Constitution—L[1]	*867,901	352,027
15. Amends Constitution: Authorizes State to Issue General Obligation Bonds for Seismic Rehabilitation of Public Education Buildings—L[1]	*671,640	535,638
16. Amends Constitution: Authorizes State to Issue General Obligation Bonds for Seismic Rehabilitation of Emergency Services Buildings—L[1]	*669,451	530,587
17. Amends Constitution: Reduces Minimum Age Requirement to Serve as State Legislator from 21 Years to 18 Years—L[1]	341,717	910,331

Election Date/Measure Number/Ballot Title	Yes	No
18. Amends Constitution: Allows Certain Tax Districts to Establish Permanent Property Tax Rates and Divide into Tax Zones—L[1]	450,444	704,116
Note: An early Special Election was held for Measures 19 and 20 (see above)		
21. Amends Constitution: Revises Procedure for Filling Judicial Vacancies, Electing Judges; Allows Vote for "None of the Above"—I[1]	526,450	668,256
22. Amends Constitution: Requires Supreme Court Judges and Court of Appeals Judges to be Elected by District—I[1]	595,936	610,063
23. Creates Health Care Finance Plan for Medically Necessary Services; Creates Additional Income, Payroll Taxes—I[2]	265,310	969,537
24. Allows Licensed Denturists to Install Partial Dentures; Authorizes Cooperative Dentist-Denturist Business Ventures—I[2]	*907,979	286,492
25. Increases Minimum Wage to $6.90 in 2003; Increases for Inflation in Future Years—I[2]	*645,016	611,658
26. Amends Constitution: Prohibits Payment, Receipt of Payment Based on the Number of Initiative, Referendum Petition Signatures Obtained—I[1]	*921,606	301,415
27. Requires Labeling of Genetically-Engineered Foods Sold or Distributed in or from Oregon—I[2]	371,851	886,806
January 28, 2003 (Special Election)		
28. Temporarily Increases Income Tax Rates—L[2]	575,846	676,312
September 16, 2003 (Special Election)		
29. Amends Constitution: Authorizes State of Oregon to Incur General Obligation Debt for Savings on Pension Liabilities—L[1]	*360,209	291,778
February 3, 2004 (Special Election)		
30. Enacts Temporary Personal Income Tax Surcharge; Increases, Changes Corporate, Other Taxes; Avoids Specific Budget Cuts—R[2]	481,315	691,462
November 2, 2004		
31. Amends Constitution: Authorizes Law Permitting Postponement of Election for Particular Public Office When Nominee for Office Dies—L[1]	*1,122,852	588,502
32. Amends Constitution: Deletes Reference to Mobile Homes from Provision Dealing with Taxes and Fees on Motor Vehicles—L[1]	*1,048,090	661,576
33. Amends Medical Marijuana Act: Requires Marijuana Dispensaries for Supplying Patients/Caregivers; Raises Patients' Possession Limit—I[2]	764,015	1,021,814
34. Requires Balancing Timber Production, Resource Conservation/Preservation in Managing State Forests; Specifically Addresses Two Forests—I[2]	659,467	1,060,496
35. Amends Constitution: Limits Noneconomic Damages (Defined) Recoverable for Patient Injuries Caused by Healthcare Provider's Negligence or Recklessness—I[1]	869,054	896,857
36. Amends Constitution: Only Marriage Between One Man and One Woman Is Valid or Legally Recognized as Marriage—I[1]	*1,028,546	787,556
37. Governments Must Pay Owners, or Forgo Enforcement, when Certain Land Use Restrictions Reduce Property Value—I[2]	*1,054,589	685,079
38. Abolishes SAIF; State Must Reinsure, Satisfy SAIF's Obligations; Dedicates Proceeds, Potential Surplus to Public Purposes—I[2]	670,935	1,037,722
November 7, 2006		
39. Prohibits Public Body from Condemning Private Real Property If Intends to Convey to Private Party—I[2]	*881,820	431,844
40. Amends Constitution: Requires Oregon Supreme Court Judges and Court of Appeals Judges To Be Elected by District—I[1]	576,153	749,404
41. Allows Income Tax Deduction Equal to Federal Exemptions Deduction to Substitute for State Exemption Credit—I[2]	483,443	818,452
42. Prohibits Insurance Companies from Using Credit Score or "Credit Worthiness" in Calculating Rates or Premiums—I[2]	479,935	876,075
43. Requires 48-Hour Notice to Unemancipated Minor's Parent Before Providing Abortion; Authorizes Lawsuits, Physician Discipline—I[2]	616,876	746,606
44. Allows Any Oregon Resident Without Prescription Drug Coverage to Participate in Oregon Prescription Drug Program—I[2]	*1,049,594	296,649
45. Amends Constitution: Limits State Legislators: Six Years as Representative, Eight Years as Senator, Fourteen Years in Legislature—I[1]	555,016	788,895
46. Amends Constitution: Allows Laws Regulating Election Contributions, Expenditures Adopted by Initiative or 3/4 of Both Legislative Houses—I[1]	520,342	770,251

Elections and Records

Election Date/Measure Number/Ballot Title	Yes	No
47. Revises Campaign Finance Laws: Limits or Prohibits Contributions and Expenditures; Adds Disclosure, New Reporting Requirements—I[2]	*694,918	615,256
48. Amends Constitution: Limits Biennial Percentage Increase in State Spending to Percentage Increase in State Population, Plus Inflation—I[1]	379,971	923,629
November 6, 2007 (Special Election)		
49. Modifies Measure 37: Clarifies Right to Build Homes; Limits Large Developments; Protects Farms, Forests, Groundwater—L[2]	*718,023	437,351
50. Amends Constitution: Dedicates Funds to Provide Health Care for Children, Fund Tobacco Prevention, Through Increased Tobacco Tax—L[1]	472,063	686,470
May 20, 2008		
51. Amends Constitution: Enables Crime Victims to Enforce Existing Constitutional Rights in Prosecutions, Delinquency Proceedings; Authorizes Implementing Legislation—L[1]	*744,195	249,143
52. Amends Constitution: Enables Crime Victims to Enforce Existing Constitutional Rights in Prosecutions, Delinquency Proceedings; Authorizes Implementing Legislation—L[1]	*738,092	247,738
53. Amends Constitution: Modifies Provisions Governing Civil Forfeitures Related to Crimes; Permits Use of Proceeds by Law Enforcement—L[1]	*490,158	489,477
November 4, 2008		
54. Amends Constitution: Standardizes Voting Eligibility for School Board Elections with Other State and Local Elections—L[1]	*1,194,173	450,979
55. Amends Constitution: Changes Operative Date of Redistricting Plans; Allows Affected Legislators to Finish Term in Original District—L[1]	*1,251,478	364,993
56. Amends Constitution: Provides that May and November Property Tax Elections are Decided by Majority of Voters Voting—L[1]	*959,118	735,500
57. Increases Sentences for Drug Trafficking, Theft Against Elderly and Specified Repeat Property and Identity Theft Crimes; Requires Addiction Treatment for Certain Offenders—L[2]	*1,058,955	665,942
58. Prohibits Teaching Public School Student in Language Other Than English for More Than Two Years—I[2]	756,903	977,696
59. Creates an Unlimited Deduction for Federal Income Taxes on Individual Taxpayers' Oregon Income-Tax Returns—I[2]	615,894	1,084,422
60. Teacher "Classroom Performance," Not Seniority, Determines Pay Raises; "Most Qualified" Teachers Retained, Regardless of Seniority—I[2]	673,296	1,070,682
61. Creates Mandatory Minimum Prison Sentences for Certain Theft, Identity Theft, Forgery, Drug, and Burglary Crimes—I[2]	848,901	887,165
62. Amends Constitution: Allocates 15% of Lottery Proceeds to Public Safety Fund for Crime Prevention, Investigation, Prosecution—I[2]	674,428	1,035,756
63. Exempts Specified Property Owners From Building Permit Requirements for Improvements Valued At/Under 35,000 Dollars—I[2]	784,376	928,721
64. Penalizes Person, Entity for Using Funds Collected with "Public Resource" (Defined) for "Political Purpose"—I[2]	835,563	854,327
65. Changes General Election Nomination Processes for Major/Minor Party, Independent Candidates for Most Partisan Offices—I[2]	553,640	1,070,580
January 26, 2010 (Special Election)		
66. Raises tax on household income at and above $250,000 (and $125,000 for individual filers). Reduces income taxes on unemployment benefits in 2009. Provides funds currently budgeted for education, health care, public safety, other services—R[2]	*692,687	583,707
67. Raises $10 corporate minimum tax, business minimum tax, corporate profits tax. Provides funds currently budgeted for education, health care, public safety, other services—R[2]	*682,720	591,188
May 18, 2010		
68. Revises Constitution: Allows State To Issue Bonds To Match Voter Approved School District Bonds For School Capital Costs—L[1]	*498,073	267,052
69. Amends Constitution: Continues And Modernizes Authority For Lowest Cost Borrowing For Community Colleges And Public Universities—L[1]	*546,649	216,157

Election Date/Measure Number/Ballot Title	Yes	No
November 2, 2010		
70. Amends Constitution: Expands availability of home ownership loans for Oregon veterans through Oregon War Veterans' Fund—L[1]	*1,180,933	217,679
71. Amends Constitution: Requires legislature to meet annually; limits length of legislative sessions; provides exceptions—L[1]	*919,040	435,776
72. Amends Constitution: Authorizes exception to $50,000 state borrowing limit for state's real and personal property projects—L[1]	*774,582	536,204
73. Requires increased minimum sentences for certain repeated sex crimes, incarceration for repeated driving under influence—I[2]	*802,388	608,317
74. Establishes medical marijuana supply system and assistance and research programs; allows limited selling of marijuana—I[2]	627,016	791,186
75. Authorizes Multnomah County casino; casino to contribute monthly revenue percentage to state for specified purposes—I[2]	448,162	959,342
76. Amends Constitution: Continues lottery funding for parks, beaches, wildlife habitat, watershed protection beyond 2014; modifies funding process—I[1]	*972,825	432,552
November 6, 2012		
77. Amends Constitution: Governor may declare "catastrophic disaster" (defined); requires legislative session; authorizes suspending specified constitutional spending restrictions—L[1]	*957,646	673,468
78. Amends Constitution: Changes constitutional language describing governmental system of separation of powers; makes grammatical and spelling changes—L[1]	*1,165,963	458,509
79. Amends Constitution: Prohibits real estate transfer taxes, fees, other assessments, except those operative on December 31, 2009—I[1]	*976,587	679,710
80. Allows personal marijuana, hemp cultivation/use without license; commission to regulate commercial marijuana cultivation/sale—I[2]	810,538	923,071
81. Prohibits commercial non-tribal fishing with gillnets in Oregon "inland waters," allows use of seine nets—I[2]	567,996	1,072,614
82. Amends Constitution: Authorizes establishment of privately-owned casinos; mandates percentage of revenues payable to dedicated state fund—I[1]	485,240	1,226,331
83. Authorizes privately-owned Wood Village casino; mandates percentage of revenues payable to dedicated state fund—I[2]	500,123	1,207,508
84. Phases out existing inheritance taxes on large estates, and all taxes on intra-family property transfers—I[2]	776,143	912,541
85. Amends Constitution: Allocates corporate income/excise tax "kicker" refund to additionally fund K through 12 public education—I[1]	*1,007,122	672,586
November 4, 2014		
86. Amends Constitution: Requires creation of fund for Oregonians pursuing post-secondary education, authorizes state indebtedness to finance fund—L[1]	614,439	821,596
87. Amends Constitution: Permits employment of state judges by National Guard (military service) and state public universities (teaching)—L[1]	*817,709	600,015
88. Provides Oregon resident "driver card" without requiring proof of legal presence in the United States—R[2]	506,751	983,576
89. Amends Constitution: State/political subdivision shall not deny or abridge equality of rights on account of sex—I[1]	*925,892	514,907
90. Changes general election nomination processes: provides for single primary ballot listing candidates; top two advance—I[2]	459,629	987,050
91. Allows possession, manufacture, sale of marijuana by/to adults, subject to state licensing, regulation, taxation—I[2]	*847,865	663,346
92. Requires food manufacturers, retailers to label "genetically engineered" foods as such; state, citizens may enforce—I[2]	752,737	753,574
May 17, 2016		
93. Majority yes vote disincorporates City of Damascus; property to Clackamas County, net assets to taxpayers—L[6]	*2,834	1,400
November 8, 2016		
94. Amends Constitution: Eliminates mandatory retirement age for state judges—L[1]	699,689	1,194,167

Elections and Records

Election Date/Measure Number/Ballot Title	Yes	No
95. Amends Constitution: Allows investments in equities by public universities to reduce financial risk and increase investments to benefit students—L[1]	*1,301,183	546,919
96. Amends Constitution: Dedicates 1.5% of state lottery net proceeds to funding support services for Oregon veterans—L[1]	*1,611,367	312,526
97. Increases corporate minimum tax when sales exceed $25 million; funds education, healthcare, senior services—I[2]	808,310	1,164,658
98. Requires state funding for dropout-prevention, career and college readiness programs in Oregon high schools—I[2]	*1,260,163	650,347
99. Creates "Outdoor School Education Fund," continuously funded through Lottery, to provide outdoor school programs statewide—I[2]	*1,287,095	630,735
100. Prohibits purchase or sale of parts or products from certain wildlife species; exceptions; civil penalties—I[2]	*1,306,213	574,631

January 23, 2018 (Special Election)

	Yes	No
101 Approves temporary assessments to fund health care for low-income individuals and families, and to stabilize health insurance premiums. Temporary assessments on insurance companies, some hospitals, and other providers of insurance or health care coverage. Insurers may not increase rates on health insurance premiums by more than 1.5 percent as a result of these assessments—R[2]	*657,117	408,387

November 6, 2018

	Yes	No
102 Amends Constitution: Allows local bonds for financing affordable housing with nongovernmental entities. Requires voter approval, annual audits—L[1]	*1,037,922	786,225
103 Amends Constitution: Prohibits taxes/fees based on transactions for "groceries" (defined) enacted or amended after September 2017—I[1]	791,687	1,062,752
104 Amends Constitution: Expands (beyond taxes) application of requirement that three-fifths legislative majority approve bills raising revenue—I[1]	631,211	1,182,023
105 Repeals law limiting use of state/local law enforcement resources to enforce federal immigration laws—I[2]	675,389	1,172,774
106 Amends Constitution: Prohibits spending "public funds" (defined) directly/indirectly for "abortion" (defined); exceptions; reduces abortion access—I[1]	658,793	1,195,718

November 3, 2020

	Yes	No
107 Amends Constitution: Allows laws limiting political campaign contributions and expenditures, requiring disclosure of political campaign contributions and expenditures, and requiring political campaign advertisements to identify who paid for them—L[1]	*1,763,276	488,413
108 Increases cigarette and cigar taxes. Establishes tax on e-cigarettes and nicotine vaping devices. Funds health programs.—L[2]	*1,535,866	779,311
109 Allows manufacture, delivery, administration of psilocybin at supervised, licensed facilities; imposes two-year development period—I[2]	*1,270,057	1,008,199
110 Provides statewide addiction/recovery services; marijuana taxes partially finance; reclassifies possession/penalties for specified drugs—I[2]	*1,333,268	947,313

November 8, 2022

	Yes	No
111 Amends Constitution: State must ensure affordable healthcare access, balanced against requirement to fund schools, other essential services—L[1]	*951,446	924,231
112 Amends Constitution: Removes language allowing slavery and involuntary servitude as punishment for crime—L[1]	*1,047,028	836,295
113 Amends Constitution: Legislators with ten unexcused absences from floor sessions disqualified from holding next term of office—I[1]	*1,292,127	599,204
114 Requires permit to acquire firearms; police maintain permit/firearm database; criminally prohibits certain ammunition magazines—I[2]	*975,862	950,891

[0]Repeal of federal prohibition amendment
[1]Constitutional amendment
[2]Statutory enactment

3Required communication to federal officials on behalf of people of Oregon
4Tri-county measure voted on in Clackamas, Multnomah and Washington Counties
5Advisory vote for legislators' information
6Voted on in Clackamas County

Earliest Authorities in Oregon

Pacific Fur Company*
Fort Astoria

Name	Term of Service	By What Authority/Remarks
McDougall, Duncan	Mar. 22, 1811–Feb. 15, 1812 Aug. 4, 1812–Aug. 20, 1813 Aug. 26, 1813–Oct. 16, 1813	Acting agent and partner; served in absence of Wilson Price Hunt by agreement with partners
Hunt, Wilson Price	Feb. 15, 1812–Aug. 4, 1812 Aug. 20, 1813–Aug. 26, 1813	Agent and partner by Articles of Agreement, June 23, 1810, Article 21

*Sold to John George McTavish and John Stuart, partners of the North West Company, Oct. 16, 1813; sale confirmed by Wilson Price Hunt, agent, March 10, 1814.

North West Company
Headquarters, Columbia District, Fort George (Astoria)

Name	Term of Service	By What Authority/Remarks
McTavish, John George	Oct. 16, 1813–Dec. 1, 1813	Acting governor and partner
McDonald, John (of Garth)	Dec. 1, 1813–Apr. 4, 1814	Governor and partner, Alexander Henry, trader
McTavish, Donald	Apr. 23, 1814–May 22, 1814	Governor and partner; with Alexander Henry, drowned in the Columbia River
Keith, James	May 22, 1814–June 7, 1816	Acting governor and partner

Chief of the Coast	Term of Service	Chief of the Interior
Keith, James	June 7, 1816–Mar. 21, 1821	McKenzie, Donald

Hudson's Bay Company*
Headquarters, Columbia District, Fort George (Astoria) 1821–1825; Fort Vancouver, 1825–1846

Chief Factor	Term of Service	Junior Chief Factor
McMillan, James	Spring, 1821–Fall, 1821	Cameron, John Dougald
Cameron, John Dougald	Fall, 1821–Spring, 1824	Kennedy, Alexander
Kennedy, Alexander	Spring, 1824–Mar. 18, 1825	McLoughlin, John
McLoughlin, John	Mar. 18, 1825–May 31, 1845	None appointed

*Appointments in 1821 by agreement with North West Company; and 1822–1825 by council of Northern Department, Sir George Simpson, Governor

Oregon (Walamet) Mission of the Methodist Episcopal Church
Mission Bottom 1834–1841; Chemeketa (Salem) 1841–1847

Name	Term of Service	Position
Lee, Jason	Oct. 6, 1834–Mar. 26, 1838	Appointed superintendent upon recommendation of the Board of Managers of the Missionary Society
Leslie, David	Mar. 26, 1838–May 27, 1840	Acting superintendent in absence of Lee
Lee, Jason	May 27, 1840–Dec. 25, 1843	Superintendent
Leslie, David	Dec. 25, 1843–June 1, 1844	Acting superintendent in absence of Lee
Gary, George	June 1, 1844–July 18, 1847	Appointed superintendent; instructed to dissolve the mission properties

Provisional Government Executive Committee

Name	Term of Service	By What Authority/Remarks
Hill, David; Beers, Alanson; Gale, Joseph	July 5, 1843–May 25, 1844	Elected by meeting of inhabitants of the Oregon Territory
Stewart, P.G.; Russell Osborn; Bailey, W.J.	May 25, 1844–July 14, 1845	By vote of the people

Governors of Oregon

Under Provisional Government

Name	Term of Service	By What Authority/Remarks
Abernethy, George	July 14, 1845–Mar. 3, 1849	By people at 1845 general election; reelected 1848

Under Territorial Government

Name/Political Party[1]	Term of Service	By What Authority/Remarks
Lane, Joseph—D	Mar. 3, 1849–June 18, 1850	Appointed by President Polk; resigned
Prichette, Kintzing—D	June 18, 1850–Aug. 18, 1850	Acting governor, was secretary
Gaines, John P.—W	Aug. 18, 1850–May 16, 1853	Appointed by President Taylor
Lane, Joseph—D	May 16, 1853–May 19, 1853	Appointed by President Pierce; resigned
Curry, George L.—D	May 19, 1853–Dec. 2, 1853	Acting governor, was secretary
Davis, John W.—D	Dec. 2, 1853–Aug. 1, 1854	Appointed by President Pierce; resigned
Curry, George L.—D	Aug. 1, 1854–Mar. 3, 1859	Acting governor, was secretary; appointed by President Pierce, Nov. 1, 1854

Under State Government

Name/Political Party[1]	Term of Service	By What Authority/Remarks
Whiteaker, John—D	Mar. 3, 1859–Sept. 10, 1862	Elected 1858
Gibbs, A.C.—R	Sept. 10, 1862–Sept. 12, 1866	Elected 1862
Woods, George L.—R	Sept. 12, 1866–Sept. 14, 1870	Elected 1866
Grover, LaFayette—D	Sept. 14, 1870–Feb. 1, 1877	Elected 1870; reelected 1874; resigned
Chadwick, Stephen F.—D	Feb. 1, 1877–Sept. 11, 1878	Was secretary of state
Thayer, W.W.—D	Sept. 11, 1878–Sept. 13, 1882	Elected 1878
Moody, Z.F.—R	Sept. 13, 1882–Jan. 12, 1887	Elected 1882
Pennoyer, Sylvester—DP	Jan. 12, 1887–Jan. 14, 1895	Elected 1886; reelected 1890
Lord, William Paine—R	Jan. 14, 1895–Jan. 9, 1899	Elected 1894
Geer, T.T.—R	Jan. 9, 1899–Jan. 14, 1903	Elected 1898
Chamberlain, George E.—D	Jan. 15, 1903–Feb. 28, 1909	Elected 1902; reelected 1906; resigned
Benson, Frank W.—R	Mar. 1, 1909–June 17, 1910	Was secretary of state; resigned
Bowerman, Jay[2]—R	June 17, 1910–Jan. 8, 1911	Was president of Senate
West, Oswald—D	Jan. 11, 1911–Jan. 12, 1915	Elected 1910
Withycombe, James—R	Jan. 12, 1915–Mar. 3, 1919	Elected 1914; reelected 1918; died in office
Olcott, Ben W.—R	Mar. 3, 1919–Jan. 8, 1923	Was secretary of state
Pierce, Walter M.—D	Jan. 8, 1923–Jan. 10, 1927	Elected 1922
Patterson, I.L.—R	Jan. 10, 1927–Dec. 21, 1929	Elected 1926; died in office
Norblad, A.W.[3]—R	Dec. 22, 1929–Jan. 12, 1931	Was president of Senate
Meier, Julius L.—I	Jan. 12, 1931–Jan. 14, 1935	Elected 1930
Martin, Charles H.—D	Jan. 14, 1935–Jan. 9, 1939	Elected 1934
Sprague, Charles A.—R	Jan. 9, 1939–Jan. 11, 1943	Elected 1938
Snell, Earl—R	Jan. 11, 1943–Oct. 28, 1947	Elected 1942; reelected 1946; died in office
Hall, John H.[4]—R	Oct. 30, 1947–Jan. 10, 1949	Was speaker of House
McKay, Douglas—R	Jan. 10, 1949–Dec. 27, 1952	Elected 1948; reelected 1950; resigned

Name/Political Party[1]	Term of Service	By What Authority/Remarks
Patterson, Paul L.—R	Dec. 27, 1952–Jan. 31, 1956	Was president of Senate; elected 1954; died in office
Smith, Elmo—R	Feb. 1, 1956–Jan. 14, 1957	Was president of Senate
Holmes, Robert D.—D	Jan. 14, 1957–Jan. 12, 1959	Elected 1956
Hatfield, Mark O.—R	Jan. 12, 1959–Jan. 9, 1967	Elected 1958; reelected 1962
McCall, Tom—R	Jan. 9, 1967–Jan 13, 1975	Elected 1966; reelected 1970
Straub, Robert W.—D	Jan. 13, 1975–Jan. 8, 1979	Elected 1974
Atiyeh, Victor G.—R	Jan. 8, 1979–Jan. 12, 1987	Elected 1978; reelected 1982
Goldschmidt, Neil—D	Jan. 12, 1987–Jan. 14, 1991	Elected 1986
Roberts, Barbara—D	Jan. 14, 1991–Jan. 9, 1995	Elected 1990
Kitzhaber, John—D	Jan. 9, 1995–Jan. 13, 2003	Elected 1994; reelected 1998
Kulongoski, Theodore R.—D	Jan. 13, 2003–Jan. 10, 2011	Elected 2002; reelected 2006
Kitzhaber, John—D	Jan. 10, 2011–Feb. 18, 2015	Elected 2010; reelected 2014; resigned
Brown, Kate[5]—D	Feb. 18, 2015–Jan. 9, 2023	Succeeded Kitzhaber; elected 2016; reelected 2018
Kotek, Tina—D	Jan. 9, 2023–	Elected 2022

[1]D = Democrat; R = Republican; DP = Democrat People's; I = Independent; W = Whig

[2]Jay Bowerman became governor when Frank Benson, who was serving as both governor and secretary of state, became incapacitated. Benson resigned as governor but continued as secretary of state until his death.

[3]In 1920, the Constitution was changed to allow the president of the Senate to succeed as governor.

[4]A plane crash on October 28, 1947, killed Governor Earl Snell, Secretary of State Robert S. Farrell, Jr., President of the Senate Marshall E. Cornett and the pilot, Cliff Hogue. John H. Hall, Speaker of the House and next in line of succession, automatically became governor. Earl Newbry was appointed by John H. Hall to the position of secretary of state.

[5]Kate Brown was serving as secretary of state when John Kitzhaber vacated the office of governor. The Oregon Constitution requires that the secretary of state is next in line to fill the vacancy. In 2016, Brown was elected to serve the remaining two years of Kitzhaber's term.

Secretaries of State of Oregon

Under Provisional Government

Name/Political Party	Term of Service	By What Authority/Remarks
LeBreton, George W.	Feb. 18, 1841–Mar. 4, 1844	Elected by meeting of inhabitants of the Willamette Valley to office of clerk of courts and public recorder, thus served as first secretary; reelected 1843; died in office
Johnson, Overton	Mar. 4, 1844–May 25, 1844	Appointed clerk and recorder
Long, Dr. John E.	May 25, 1844–June 21, 1846	Elected clerk and recorder by people at first 1844 general election; reelected 1845 general election; reelected 1845 by Legislature; drowned
Prigg, Frederick	June 26, 1846–Sept. 16, 1848	Appointed secretary to succeed Long; elected 1846 by Legislature; resigned
Holderness, Samuel M.	Sept. 19, 1848–Mar. 10, 1849	Appointed to succeed Prigg; elected 1848 by Legislature

Under Territorial Government

Magruder, Theophilus	Mar. 10, 1849–Apr. 9, 1849	Elected by Legislature
Prichette, Kintzing—D	Apr. 9, 1849–Sept. 18, 1850	Appointed by President Polk
Hamilton, Gen. E.D.—W	Sept. 18, 1850–May 14, 1853	Appointed by President Taylor
Curry, George L.—D	May 14, 1853–Jan. 27, 1855	Appointed by President Pierce
Harding, Benjamin—D	Jan. 27, 1855–Mar. 3, 1859	Appointed by President Pierce

Name/Political Party	Term of Service	By What Authority/Remarks
Under State Government		
Heath, Lucien—D	Mar. 3, 1859–Sept. 8, 1862	Elected 1858
May, Samuel E.—R	Sept. 8, 1862–Sept. 10, 1870	Elected 1862; reelected 1866
Chadwick, Stephen F.[1]—D	Sept. 10, 1870–Sept. 2, 1878	Elected 1870; reelected 1874
Earhart, R.P.—R	Sept. 2, 1878–Jan. 10, 1887	Elected 1878; reelected 1882
McBride, George W.—R	Jan. 10, 1887–Jan. 14, 1895	Elected 1886; reelected 1890
Kincaid, Harrison R.—R	Jan. 14, 1895–Jan. 9, 1899	Elected 1894
Dunbar, Frank I.—R	Jan. 9, 1899–Jan. 14, 1907	Elected 1898; reelected 1902
Benson, Frank W.[2]—R	Jan. 15, 1907–Apr. 14, 1911	Elected 1906; reelected 1910; died in office
Olcott, Ben W.[3]—R	Apr. 17, 1911–May 28, 1920	Appointed by Governor West; elected 1912; reelected 1916; resigned
Kozer, Sam A.—R	May 28, 1920–Sept. 24, 1928	Appointed by Governor Olcott; elected 1920; reelected 1924; resigned
Hoss, Hal E.—R	Sept. 24, 1928–Feb. 6, 1934	Appointed by Governor Patterson; elected 1928; reelected 1932; died in office
Stadelman, P.J.—R	Feb. 9, 1934–Jan. 7, 1935	Appointed by Governor Meier
Snell, Earl—R	Jan. 7, 1935–Jan. 4, 1943	Elected 1934; reelected 1938
Farrell, Robert S., Jr.—R	Jan. 4, 1943–Oct. 28, 1947	Elected 1942; reelected 1946; died in office
Newbry, Earl T.—R	Nov. 3, 1947–Jan. 7, 1957	Appointed by Governor Hall; elected 1948; reelected 1952
Hatfield, Mark O.—R	Jan. 7, 1957–Jan. 12, 1959	Elected 1956; resigned
Appling, Howell, Jr.—R	Jan. 12, 1959–Jan. 4, 1965	Appointed by Governor Hatfield; elected 1960
McCall, Tom—R	Jan. 4, 1965–Jan. 9, 1967	Elected 1964; resigned
Myers, Clay—R	Jan. 9, 1967–Jan. 3, 1977	Appointed by Governor McCall; elected 1968; reelected 1972
Paulus, Norma—R	Jan. 3, 1977–Jan. 7, 1985	Elected 1976; reelected 1980
Roberts, Barbara—D	Jan. 7, 1985–Jan. 14, 1991	Elected 1984; reelected 1988; resigned
Keisling, Phil—D	Jan. 14, 1991–Nov. 8, 1999	Appointed by Governor Roberts; elected 1992; reelected 1996; resigned
Bradbury, Bill—D	Nov. 8, 1999–Jan. 5, 2009	Appointed by Governor Kitzhaber; elected 2000; reelected 2004
Brown, Kate[4]—D	Jan. 5, 2009–Feb. 17, 2015	Elected 2008; reelected 2012; succeeded Governor Kitzhaber
Atkins, Jeanne P.—D	Mar. 11, 2015–Jan. 2, 2017	Appointed by Governor Brown
Richardson, Dennis—R	Jan. 2, 2017–Feb. 26, 2019	Elected 2016; died in office
Bev Clarno[5]—R	March 31, 2019–Jan. 2, 2021	Appointed by Governor Brown
Shemia Fagan—D	Jan. 4, 2021–	Elected 2020

[1]When Stephen Chadwick succeeded L. F. Grover as governor in 1877, he did not resign as secretary of state. He signed documents and proclamations twice—as governor and as secretary of state—until September 1878.

[2]Frank Benson served as both secretary of state and governor. See Footnote 2 under Governors of Oregon.

[3]When James Withycombe died in office on March 3, 1919, Ben W. Olcott succeeded him as governor. However, Governor Olcott did not resign or appoint a new secretary of state until May 28, 1920.

[4]When Governor John Kitzhaber resigned during office, Secretary of State Kate Brown became governor according to the order of succession required by the Oregon Constitution.

[5]When Dennis Richardson died in office on Feb. 26, 2019, his deputy Leslie Cummings served as acting secretary until Governor Kate Brown appointed Bev Clarno.

Treasurers of Oregon

Under Provisional Government

Name/Political Party	Term of Service	By What Authority/Remarks
Gray, W.H.	Mar. 1, 1843–July 5, 1843	Elected by meeting of citizens of the Willamette Valley
Willson, W.H.	July 5, 1843–May 14, 1844	Elected by meeting of the inhabitants of the Willamette settlements
Foster, Phillip	July 2, 1844–July 7, 1845	Elected by people at first 1844 general election
Ermatinger, Francis	July 7, 1845–Mar. 3, 1846	Elected by people at 1845 general election; reelected 1845 by Legislature; resigned
Couch, John H.	Mar. 4, 1846–Sept. 27, 1847	Appointed to succeed Ermatinger; elected by Legislature 1846; resigned
Kilbourn, William K.	Oct. 11, 1847–Sept. 28, 1849	Appointed to succeed Couch; elected by Legislature 1849

Under Territorial Government

Taylor, James	Sept. 28, 1849–Feb. 8, 1851	Elected by Legislature
Rice, L.A.	Feb. 8, 1851–Sept. 22, 1851	Elected by Legislature; resigned
Buck, William W.	Sept. 27, 1851–Dec. 16, 1851	Appointed to succeed Rice
Boon, John D.—D	Dec. 16, 1851–Mar. 1, 1855	Elected by Legislature
Lane, Nat H.—D	Mar. 1, 1855–Jan. 10, 1856	Elected by Legislature
Boon, John D.—D	Jan. 10, 1856–Mar. 3, 1859	Elected by Legislature

Under State Government

Boon, John D.—D	Mar. 3, 1859–Sept. 8, 1862	Elected 1858
Cooke, E.N.—R	Sept. 8, 1862–Sept. 12, 1870	Elected 1862; reelected 1866
Fleischner, L.—D	Sept. 12, 1870–Sept. 14, 1874	Elected 1870
Brown, A.H.—D	Sept. 14, 1874–Sept. 9, 1878	Elected 1874
Hirsch, E.—R	Sept. 9, 1878–Jan. 10, 1887	Elected 1878; reelected 1882
Webb, G.W.—D	Jan. 10, 1887–Jan. 12, 1891	Elected 1886
Metschan, Phil—R	Jan. 12, 1891–Jan. 9, 1899	Elected 1890; reelected 1894
Moore, Charles S.—R	Jan. 9, 1899–Jan. 14, 1907	Elected 1898; reelected 1902
Steel, George A.—R	Jan. 15, 1907–Jan. 3, 1911	Elected 1906
Kay, Thomas B.—R	Jan. 4, 1911–Jan. 6, 1919	Elected 1910; reelected 1914
Hoff, O.P.—R	Jan. 6, 1919–Mar. 18, 1924	Elected 1918; reelected 1922; died in office
Myers, Jefferson—D	Mar. 18, 1924–Jan. 4, 1925	Appointed by Governor Pierce
Kay, Thomas B.—R	Jan. 4, 1925–April 29, 1931	Elected 1924; reelected 1928; died in office
Holman, Rufus C.—R	May 1, 1931–Dec. 27, 1938	Appointed by Governor Meier; elected 1932; reelected 1936; resigned
Pearson, Walter E.—D	Dec. 27, 1938–Jan. 6, 1941	Appointed by Governor Martin
Scott, Leslie M.—R	Jan. 6, 1941–Jan. 3, 1949	Elected 1940; reelected 1944
Pearson, Walter J.—D	Jan. 3, 1949–Jan. 5, 1953	Elected 1948
Unander, Sig—R	Jan. 5, 1953–Dec. 31, 1959	Elected 1952; reelected 1956; resigned
Belton, Howard C.—R	Jan. 4, 1960–Jan. 4, 1965	Appointed by Governor Hatfield; elected 1960
Straub, Robert—D	Jan. 4, 1965–Jan. 1, 1973	Elected 1964; reelected 1968
Redden, James A.—D	Jan. 1, 1973–Jan. 3, 1977	Elected 1972
Myers, Clay—R	Jan. 3, 1977–Apr. 1, 1984	Elected 1976; reelected 1980; resigned
Rutherford, Bill—R	Apr. 1, 1984–July 9, 1987	Appointed by Governor Atiyeh; elected 1984; resigned
Meeker, Tony—R	July 9, 1987–Jan. 4, 1993	Appointed by Governor Goldschmidt; elected 1988
Hill, Jim—D	Jan. 4, 1993–Jan. 1, 2001	Elected 1992; reelected 1996
Edwards, Randall—D	Jan. 1, 2001–Jan. 5, 2009	Elected 2000; reelected 2004
Westlund, Ben—D	Jan. 5, 2009–Mar. 7, 2010	Elected 2008; died in office

Name/Political Party	Term of Service	By What Authority/Remarks
Ted Wheeler—D	Mar. 11, 2010–Jan. 2, 2017	Appointed by Governor Kulongoski; elected 2010; reelected 2012
Read, Tobias—D	Jan. 2, 2017–	Elected 2016; reelected 2020

Oregon Supreme Court Justices[1]

Under Provisional Government

Name	Term of Service	By What Authority/Remarks
Babcock, Dr. Ira L.	Feb. 18, 1841–May 1, 1843	Supreme judge with probate powers elected at meeting of inhabitants of the Willamette Valley
Wilson, W.E.	No record of service	Supreme judge with probate powers; elected at meeting of inhabitants of the Willamette Settlements, May 2, 1843
Russell, Osborn	Oct. 2, 1843–May 14, 1844	Supreme judge and probate judge; appointed by the Executive Committee
Babcock, Dr. Ira L.	June 27, 1844–Nov. 11, 1844	Presiding judge, Circuit Court; elected at first general election May 1844; resigned
Nesmith, James W.	Dec. 25, 1844–Aug. 9, 1845	Presiding judge, Circuit Court; appointed by Executive Committee; elected by people 1845
Ford, Nathaniel	Declined service	Supreme judge; elected by Legislature Aug. 9, 1845; declined to serve
Burnett, Peter H.	Sept. 6, 1845–Dec. 29, 1846	Supreme judge; elected by Legislature; declined appointment to Supreme Court 1848
Thornton, J. Quinn	Feb. 20, 1847–Nov. 9, 1847	Supreme judge; appointed by Governor Abernethy; resigned
Lancaster, Columbia	Nov. 30, 1847–Apr. 9, 1849	Supreme judge; appointed by Governor Abernethy
Lovejoy, A.L.	No record of service	Supreme judge; elected by Legislature Feb. 16, 1849

Under Territorial[2] and State Government[3]

Name	Term of Service	By What Authority/Remarks
Bryant, William P.	1848–1850	Appointed 1848; resigned 1850; chief justice 1848–1850
Pratt, Orville C.	1848–1852	Appointed 1848; term ended 1852
Nelson, Thomas	1850–1853	Appointed 1850 to succeed Bryant; term ended 1853; chief justice 1850–1853
Strong, William	1850–1853	Appointed 1850 to succeed Burnett; term ended 1853
Williams, George H.	1853–1858	Appointed 1853, 1857; resigned 1858; chief justice 1853–1858
Olney, Cyrus	1853–1858	Appointed 1853, 1857; resigned 1858
Deady, Matthew P.	1853–1859	Appointed 1853, 1857; elected 1858; resigned 1859
McFadden, Obadiah B.	1853–1854	Appointed 1853; term ended 1854
Boise, Reuben P.	1858–1870, 1876–1880	Appointed 1858 to succeed Olney; elected 1859; reelected 1864; term ended 1870; elected 1876; term ended 1878; appointed 1878; term ended 1880; chief justice 1862–1864, 1867–1870
Wait, Aaron E.	1859–1862	Elected 1858; resigned May 1, 1862; chief justice 1859–1862
Stratton, Riley E.	1859–1866	Elected 1858, 1864; died Dec. 26, 1866
Prim, Paine Page	1859–1880	Appointed 1859 to succeed Deady; elected 1860; reelected 1866, 1872; term ended 1878; appointed 1878; term ended 1880; chief justice 1864–1866, 1870–1872, 1876–1878
Page, William W.	1862	Appointed May 1862 to succeed Wait; term ended Sept. 1862
Shattuck, Erasmus D.	1862–1867,	Elected 1862; resigned Dec. 1867; elected 1874;

Name	Term of Service	By What Authority/Remarks
	1874–1878	term ended 1878; chief justice 1866–1867
Wilson, Joseph G.	1862–1870	New appointment Oct. 17, 1862; elected 1864; resigned May 1870
Skinner, Alonzo A.	1866–1867	Appointed 1866 to succeed Stratton; term ended 1867
Upton, William W.	1867–1874	Appointed Dec. 1867 to succeed Shattuck; elected 1868; term ended 1874; chief justice 1872–1874
Kelsay, John	1868–1870	Elected 1868 to succeed Stratton; term ended 1870
Whitten, Benoni	1870	Appointed May 1870 to succeed Wilson; term ended Sept. 1870
McArthur, Lewis L.	1870–1878	Elected 1870; reelected 1876; term ended 1878
Thayer, Andrew J.	1870–1873	Elected 1870; died Apr. 26, 1873
Bonham, Benjamin F.	1870–1876	Elected 1870; term ended 1876; chief justice 1874–1876
Moser, Lafayette F.	1873–1874	Appointed May 1873 to succeed A.J. Thayer; term ended 1874
Burnett, John	1874–1876	Elected 1874; term ended 1876
Watson, James F.	1876–1878	Elected 1876; term ended 1878
Kelly, James K.	1878–1880	Appointed 1878; term ended 1880; chief justice 1878–1880
Lord, William P.	1880–1894	Elected 1880; reelected 1882, 1888; term ended 1894; chief justice 1880–1882, 1886–1888, 1892–1894
Watson, Edward B.	1880–1884	Elected 1880; term ended 1884; chief justice 1882–1884
Waldo, John B.	1880–1886	Elected 1880; term ended 1886; chief justice 1884–1886
Thayer, William W.	1884–1890	Elected 1884; term ended 1890; chief justice 1888–1890
Strahan, Reuben S.	1886–1892	Elected 1886; term ended 1892; chief justice 1890–1892
Bean, Robert S.	1890–1909	Elected 1890; reelected 1896, 1902, 1908; resigned May 1, 1909; chief justice 1894–1896, 1900–1902, 1905–1909
Moore, Frank A.	1892–1918	Elected 1892; reelected 1898, 1904, 1910, 1916; died Sept. 25, 1918; chief justice 1896–1898, 1902–1905, 1909–1911, 1915–1917
Wolverton, Charles E.	1894–1905	Elected 1894, 1900; resigned Dec. 4, 1905; chief justice 1898–1900, 1905
Hailey, Thomas G.	1905–1907	Appointed Dec. 5, 1905 to succeed Wolverton; term ended Jan. 15, 1907
Eakin, Robert	1907–1917	Elected 1906, 1912; resigned Jan. 8, 1917; chief justice 1911–1913
King, William R.	1909–1911	Appointed Feb. 12, 1909; term ended Jan. 1, 1911
Slater, Woodson T.	1909–1911	Appointed Feb. 12, 1909; term ended Jan. 1, 1911
McBride, Thomas A.	1909–1930	Appointed May 1, 1909 to succeed Robert S. Bean; elected 1914; reelected 1920, 1926; died Sept. 9, 1930; chief justice 1913–1915, 1917–1921, 1923–1927
Bean, Henry J.	1911–1941	Elected 1910; reelected 1914, 1920, 1926, 1932, 1938; died May 8, 1941; chief justice 1931–1933, 1937–1939
Burnett, George H.	1911–1927	Elected 1910; reelected 1916, 1922; died Sept. 10, 1927; chief justice 1921–1923, 1927
McNary, Charles L.	1913–1915	Appointed June 3, 1913; term ended Jan. 4, 1915
Ramsey, William M.	1913–1915	Appointed June 3, 1913; term ended Jan. 4, 1915
Benson, Henry L.	1915–1921	Elected 1914; reelected 1920; died Oct. 16, 1921
Harris, Lawrence T.	1915–1924	Elected 1914; reelected 1920; resigned Jan. 15, 1924
McCamant, Wallace	1917–1918	Appointed Jan. 8, 1917 to succeed Eakin; resigned June 4, 1918

Name	Term of Service	By What Authority/Remarks
Johns, Charles A.	1918–1921	Appointed June 4, 1918 to succeed McCamant; elected 1918; resigned Oct. 7, 1921
Olson, Conrad P.	1918–1919	Appointed Sept. 27, 1918 to succeed Moore; term ended Jan. 7, 1919
Bennett, Alfred S.	1919–1920	Elected 1918; resigned Oct. 5, 1920
Brown, George M.	1920–1933	Appointed Oct. 14, 1920 to succeed Bennett; elected 1920; reelected 1926; term ended 1933
McCourt, John	1921–1924	Appointed Oct. 8, 1921 to succeed Johns; elected 1922; died Sept. 12, 1924
Rand, John L.	1921–1942	Appointed Oct. 18, 1921 to succeed Benson; elected 1922; reelected 1928, 1934, 1940; died Nov. 19, 1942; chief justice 1927–1929, 1933–1935, 1939–1941
Coshow, Oliver P.	1924–1931	Appointed Jan. 15, 1924 to succeed Harris; elected 1924; term ended 1931; chief justice 1929–1931
Pipes, Martin L.	1924	Appointed Sept. 1924 to succeed McCourt; term ended Dec. 31, 1924
Belt, Harry H.	1925–1950	Elected 1924; reelected 1930, 1936, 1942, 1948; died Aug. 6, 1950; chief justice 1945–1947
Rossman, George	1927–1965	Appointed Sept. 13, 1927 to succeed George H. Burnett; elected 1928; reelected 1934, 1940, 1946, 1952, 1958; term ended 1965; chief justice 1947–1949
Kelly, Percy R.	1930–1949	Appointed Sept. 24, 1930 to succeed McBride; elected 1930; reelected 1936, 1942, 1948; died June 14, 1949; chief justice 1941–1943
Campbell, James U.	1931–1937	Elected 1930; reelected 1936; died July 16, 1937; chief justice 1935–1937
Bailey, John O.	1933–1950	Elected 1932; reelected 1938, 1944; resigned Nov. 15, 1950; chief justice 1943–1945
Lusk, Hall S.	1937–1960	Appointed July 22, 1937 to succeed Campbell; elected 1938; reelected 1944, 1950, 1956; resigned Mar. 15, 1960; 1961–1968 recalled to temporary active service 1961 through 1968; chief justice 1949–1951
Brand, James T.	1941–1958	Appointed May 14, 1941 to succeed Henry J. Bean; elected 1942; reelected 1948, 1954; resigned June 30, 1958; chief justice 1951–1953
Hay, Arthur D.	1942–1952	Appointed Nov. 28, 1942 to succeed Rand; elected 1944; reelected 1950; died Dec. 19, 1952
Page, E.M.	1949–1950	Appointed July 8, 1949 to succeed Percy R. Kelly; resigned Jan. 18, 1950
Latourette, Earl C.	1950–1956	Appointed Jan. 19, 1950 to succeed E.M. Page; elected 1950; died Aug. 18, 1956; chief justice 1953–1955
Warner, Harold J.	1950–1963	Appointed Sept. 5, 1950 to succeed Belt; elected 1950; reelected 1956; term ended 1963; chief justice 1955–1957
Tooze, Walter L.	1950–1956	Appointed Nov. 16, 1950 to succeed Bailey; elected 1950; reelected 1956; died Dec. 21, 1956
Perry, William C.	1952–1970	Appointed Dec. 26, 1952 to succeed Hay; elected 1954; reelected 1960, 1966; resigned June 1, 1970; chief justice 1957–1959, 1967–1970
McAllister, William M.	1956–1976	Appointed Aug. 24, 1956 to succeed Latourette; elected 1956; reelected 1962, 1968, 1974; resigned Dec. 31, 1976; chief justice 1959–1967
Kester, Randall B.	1957–1958	Appointed Jan. 3, 1957 to succeed Tooze; resigned Mar. 1, 1958
Sloan, Gordon	1958–1970	Appointed Mar. 1, 1958 to succeed Kester; elected 1958; reelected 1964; resigned Oct. 1, 1970
O'Connell, Kenneth J.	1958–1977	Appointed July 1, 1958 to succeed Brand; elected 1958; reelected 1964, 1970; term ended 1977; chief justice 1970–1976

Name	Term of Service	By What Authority/Remarks
Goodwin, Alfred T.	1960–1969	Appointed Mar. 18, 1960 to succeed Lusk; elected 1960; reelected 1966; resigned Dec. 19, 1969
Denecke, Arno H.	1963–1982	Elected 1962; reelected 1968, 1974, 1980; resigned June 30, 1982; chief justice 1976–1982
Holman, Ralph M.	1965–1980	Elected 1964; reelected 1970, 1976; resigned Jan. 20, 1980
Tongue, Thomas H.	1969–1982	Appointed Dec. 29, 1969 to succeed Goodwin; elected 1970; reelected 1976; resigned Feb. 7, 1982
Howell, Edward H.	1970–1980	Appointed June 1, 1970 to succeed Perry; elected 1970; reelected 1976; resigned Nov. 30, 1980
Bryson, Dean F.	1970–1979	Elected 1970; appointed Oct. 23, 1970 (before elective term began) to succeed Sloan; reelected 1976; resigned April 1, 1979
Lent, Berkeley	1977–1988	Elected 1976; reelected 1982; resigned Sept. 30, 1988; chief justice 1982–1983
Linde, Hans	1977–1990	Appointed Jan. 3, 1977 to succeed McAllister; elected 1978; reelected 1984; resigned Jan. 31, 1990
Peterson, Edwin J.	1979–1993	Appointed May 15, 1979 to succeed Bryson; elected 1980; reelected 1986, 1992; resigned Dec. 31, 1993; chief justice 1983–1991
Tanzer, Jacob	1980–1982	Appointed Jan. 21, 1980 to succeed Holman; elected 1980; resigned Dec. 31, 1982
Campbell, J.R.	1980–1988	Appointed Dec. 1, 1980 to succeed Howell; elected 1982; resigned Dec. 31, 1988
Roberts, Betty	1982–1986	Appointed Feb. 8, 1982 to succeed Tongue; elected 1982; resigned Feb. 7, 1986
Carson, Wallace P., Jr.	1982–2006	Appointed July 14, 1982 to succeed Denecke; elected 1982; reelected 1988, 1994, 2000; chief justice 1991–2005; resigned Dec. 31, 2006
Jones, Robert E.	1983–1990	Appointed Dec. 16, 1982 to succeed Tanzer; elected 1984; resigned April 30, 1990
Gillette, W. Michael	1986–2011	Appointed Feb. 10, 1986 to succeed Roberts; elected 1986; reelected 1992, 1998, 2004
Van Hoomissen, George	1988–2001	Elected May 17, 1988 to succeed Lent; reelected 1994; resigned Dec. 31, 2000
Fadeley, Edward N.	1988–1998	Elected Nov. 8, 1988 to succeed Campbell; reelected 1994; resigned Jan. 31, 1998
Unis, Richard	1990–1996	Appointed Feb. 1, 1990 to succeed Linde; elected 1990; resigned June 30, 1996
Graber, Susan P.[4]	1990–1998	Appointed May 2, 1990 and Jan. 7, 1991 to succeed Jones; elected 1992; resigned April 1, 1998
Durham, Robert D.	1994–2013	Appointed Jan. 4, 1994 to succeed Peterson; elected 1994; reelected 2000, 2006
Kulongoski, Ted	1997–2001	Elected May, 1996; resigned June 14, 2001
Leeson, Susan M.	1998–2003	Appointed Feb. 26, 1998 to succeed Fadeley; elected 1998; resigned Jan. 31, 2003
Riggs, R. William	1998–2006	Appointed Sept. 8, 1998 to succeed Graber; elected 1998; reelected 2004, resigned Sept. 30, 2006
De Muniz, Paul J.	2001–2013	Elected Nov. 7, 2000 to succeed Van Hoomissen; reelected 2006; chief justice 2006–2012
Balmer, Thomas A.	2001–	Appointed Sept. 20, 2001 to succeed Kulongoski; elected 2002; reelected 2008, 2014; chief justice 2012–2018; reelected 2020; retired Dec. 31, 2022
Kistler, Rives	2003–2018	Appointed Aug. 15, 2003 to succeed Leeson; elected 2004; reelected 2010, 2016; retired Dec. 31, 2018
Walters, Martha Lee	2006–	Appointed Oct. 1, 2006 to succeed Riggs; elected 2008; reelected 2014, 2020; resigned Dec. 31, 2022
Linder, Virginia L.	2007–2015	Elected Nov. 7, 2006 to succeed Carson; reelected 2012; retired Dec. 31, 2015
Landau, Jack L.	2011–2017	Elected 2010 to succeed Gillette; reelected 2016; retired Dec. 31, 2017

Name	Term of Service	By What Authority/Remarks
Brewer, Dave	2013–2017	Elected 2012 to succeed De Muniz; retired June 30, 2017
Baldwin, Richard C.	2013–2017	Elected 2012 to succeed Durham; retired March 31, 2017
Nakamoto, Lynn	2016–2021	Appointed Jan. 1, 2016 to succeed Linder; elected 2016; retired Dec. 31, 2021
Duncan, Rebecca	2017–	Appointed July 6, 2017 to succeed Brewer; elected 2018
Flynn, Meagan A.	2017–	Appointed April 4, 2017 to succeed Baldwin; elected 2018; chief justice 2023 to date
Nelson, Adrienne C.	2018–	Appointed Jan. 2, 2018 to succeed Landau; elected 2018
Garrett, Chris	2019–	Appointed Jan. 2, 2019 to succeed Kistler; elected 2020
DeHoog, Roger J.	2022–	Appointed Jan. 19, 2022 to succeed Nakamoto; Elected 2022
Bushong, Stephen K.	2023–	Appointed Jan. 3, 2023 to succeed Balmer
James, Bronson D.	2023–	Appointed Jan. 3, 2023 to succeed Walters

[1]Unless otherwise noted, justices took office in the year in which elected until 1905. Since then, terms have started on the first Monday in January and continued until the first Monday six years hence or until a successor has been sworn in, if later.

[2]Appointments under territorial government were made by the president of the United States.

[3]From 1859 to 1862, there were four Supreme Court justices. In 1862, a fifth justice was added. The justices at that time also rode circuit. In 1878, the Supreme Court and Circuit Court were separated; the Supreme Court then had three justices. In 1910, the number increased to five. The final increase to the present seven occurred in 1913.

[4]When Justice Jones resigned, he had already filed to run for another term and his name appeared on the ballot at the 1990 primary election. Because he was elected for another term, which began January 7, 1991, he had to resign from his new term, and Justice Graber was appointed again at that time.

Judges of the Oregon Court of Appeals

The Oregon Court of Appeals was established July 1, 1969 with five members, expanded to six members October 5, 1973 and to ten members September 1, 1977.

Name	Term of Service	By What Authority/Remarks
Langtry, Virgil	1969–1976	Appointed July 1, 1969; elected 1970; resigned Sept. 15, 1976
Foley, Robert H.	1969–1976	Appointed July 1, 1969; elected 1970; resigned Aug. 16, 1976
Schwab, Herbert M.	1969–1980	Appointed July 1, 1969; elected 1970; reelected 1976; resigned Dec. 31, 1980; chief judge 1969–1980
Fort, William S.	1969–1977	Appointed July 1, 1969; elected 1970; term ended 1977
Branchfield, Edward	1969–1971	Appointed July 1, 1969; term ended 1971
Thornton, Robert Y.	1971–1983	Elected 1970; reelected 1976; term ended 1983
Tanzer, Jacob	1973–1975, 1976–1980	Appointed to new seat Oct. 5, 1973; term ended Jan. 6, 1975; elected 1976; appointed Aug. 16, 1976 (before elective term began) to succeed Foley; resigned Jan. 21, 1980
Lee, Jason	1975–1980	Elected 1974; died Feb. 19, 1980
Johnson, Lee	1977–1978	Elected 1976; resigned Dec. 18, 1978
Richardson, William L.	1976–1997	Elected 1976; appointed Oct. 15, 1976 (before elective term began) to succeed Langtry; reelected 1982, 1988, 1994; chief judge 1993–1997; resigned June 30, 1997
Buttler, John H.	1977–1992	Appointed to new seat Sept. 1, 1977; elected 1978; reelected 1984, 1990; resigned Dec. 31, 1992

Name	Term of Service	By What Authority/Remarks
Joseph, George M.	1977–1992	Appointed to new seat Sept. 1, 1977; elected 1978; reelected 1984, 1990; resigned Dec. 31, 1992; chief judge 1981–1992
Gillette, W. Michael	1977–1986	Appointed to new seat Sept. 1, 1977; elected 1978; reelected 1984; resigned Feb. 10, 1986
Roberts, Betty	1977–1982	Appointed to new seat Sept. 1, 1977; elected 1978; resigned Feb. 8, 1982
Campbell, J.R.	1979–1980	Appointed Mar. 19, 1979 to succeed Johnson; elected 1980; resigned Nov. 30, 1980
Warden, John C.	1980–1988	Appointed Feb. 19, 1980 to succeed Tanzer; term ended Jan. 5, 1981; appointed Jan. 6, 1981 to succeed Schwab; elected 1982; resigned Dec. 30, 1988
Warren, Edward H.	1980–1999	Appointed Mar. 10, 1980 to succeed Lee; elected 1980; reelected 1986, 1992, 1998; resigned 1999
Van Hoomissen, George A.	1981–1988	Elected 1980; reelected 1986; resigned Sept. 30, 1988
Young, Thomas F.	1981–1988	Appointed Jan. 5, 1981 to succeed Campbell; elected 1982; died Jan. 3, 1988
Rossman, Kurt C.	1982–1994	Appointed Mar. 2, 1982 to succeed Roberts; elected 1982; reelected 1988; resigned Dec. 31, 1994
Newman, Jonathan	1983–1991	Elected 1982; reelected 1988; resigned Aug. 31, 1991
Deits, Mary J.	1986–2004	Appointed Feb. 28, 1986 to succeed Gillette; elected 1986; reelected 1992, 1998; chief judge 1997–2004; resigned Oct. 31, 2004
Riggs, R. William	1988–1998	Appointed Oct. 24, 1988 to fill Van Hoomissen position; elected 1988 to succeed Warden; reelected 1994; resigned Sept. 8, 1998
Graber, Susan P.	1988–1990	Appointed Feb. 11, 1988 to succeed Young; elected 1988; resigned May 2, 1990
Edmonds, Walter I., Jr.	1989–2009	Appointed Jan. 1, 1989 to succeed Van Hoomissen; elected 1990; reelected 1996, 2002, 2008; retired Dec. 31, 2009
De Muniz, Paul J.	1990–2000	Appointed May 11, 1990 to succeed Graber; elected 1990; reelected 1996; resigned Dec. 29, 2000
Durham, Robert D.	1991–1994	Appointed Nov. 14, 1991 to succeed Newman; elected 1992; resigned Jan. 4, 1994
Landau, Jack L.	1993–2011	Appointed Dec. 15, 1992 to succeed Joseph; elected 1994; reelected 2000, 2006; resigned Jan. 3, 2011
Leeson, Susan M.	1993–1998	Appointed Dec. 15, 1992 to succeed Buttler; elected 1994; resigned Feb. 26, 1998
Haselton, Rick T.	1994–2015	Appointed Mar. 4, 1994 to succeed Durham; elected 1994; reelected 2000, 2006, 2012; chief judge 2012–2015; retired Dec. 31, 2015
Armstrong, Rex	1995–2021	Elected 1994; reelected 2000, 2006, 2012, 2018; retired Dec. 31, 2021
Linder, Virginia L.	1997–2007	Appointed Sept. 24, 1997 to succeed Richardson; elected 1998; reelected 2004; resigned Jan. 2, 2007
Wollheim, Robert D.	1998–2014	Appointed Feb. 27, 1998 to succeed Leeson; elected 1998; reelected 2004, 2010; retired Oct. 31, 2014
Brewer, Dave	1999–2012	Appointed Jan. 14, 1999 to succeed Warren; elected 2000; reelected 2006; chief judge 2004–2012
Kistler, Rives	1999–2003	Appointed Jan. 14, 1999 to succeed Riggs; elected 2000; resigned Aug. 14, 2003
Schuman, David	2001–2014	Appointed March 19, 2001 to succeed De Muniz; elected 2002; reelected 2008; retired Jan. 31, 2014
Ortega, Darleen	2003–	Appointed Oct. 13, 2003 to succeed Kistler; elected 2004; reelected 2010, 2016, 2022

Name	Term of Service	By What Authority/Remarks
Rosenblum, Ellen F.	2007–2011	Elected 2006; retired May 1, 2011
Sercombe, Timothy	2007–2017	Appointed March 26, 2007 to succeed Linder; elected 2008; reelected 2014; retired July 1, 2017
Duncan, Rebecca	2010–2017	Appointed Jan. 7, 2010 to succeed Edmonds; elected 2010; reelected 2016; resigned 2017
Nakamoto, Lynn	2011–2015	Appointed Dec. 7, 2010 to succeed Landau; elected 2012; resigned Dec. 31, 2015
Hadlock, Erika	2011–2019	Appointed July 7, 2011 to succeed Rosenblum; elected 2012; chief judge 2016–2017; reelected 2018; retired Oct. 31, 2019
Egan, James C.	2013–	Elected 2012; reelected 2018; chief judge 2018 to date
DeVore, Joel	2013–	Appointed Oct. 17, 2013; elected 2014; reelected 2020; resigned Dec. 31, 2021
Lagesen, Erin C.	2013–	Appointed Oct. 17, 2013; elected 2014; reelected 2020
Tookey, Douglas L.	2013–	Appointed Oct. 17, 2013; elected 2014; reelected 2020
Garrett, Chris	2014–2018	Appointed Dec. 24, 2013 to succeed Schuman; elected 2014; resigned Jan. 1, 2019
Flynn, Meagan A.	2014–2017	Appointed Sept. 25, 2014 to succeed Wollheim; elected 2016; resigned April 3, 2017
DeHoog, Roger J.	2016–	Appointed Dec. 7, 2015 to succeed Nakamoto; elected 2016; resigned Jan. 25, 2022
Shorr, Scott A.	2016–	Appointed Dec. 7, 2015 to succeed Haselton; elected 2016; reelected 2022
James, Bronson D.	2017–	Appointed July 17, 2017 to succeed Duncan; elected 2018; resigned Jan. 3, 2023
Aoyagi, Robyn Ridler	2017–	Appointed July 17, 2017 to succeed Sercombe; elected 2018
Powers, Steven R.	2017–	Appointed July 20, 2017 to succeed Flynn; elected 2018
Mooney, Josephine H.	2019–	Appointed June 3, 2019 to succeed Garrett; elected 2020
Kamins, Jacqueline S.	2020–	Appointed February 10, 2020 to succeed Hadlock; elected 2020
Pagán, Ramón A.	2022–	Appointed January 19, 2022 to succeed DeHoog; Elected 2022
Hellman, Kristina	2022–	Appointed January 19, 2022 to succeed Armstrong; Elected 2022
Joyce, Anna M.	2022–	Appointed January 19, 2022 to succeed DeVore; Elected 2022
Jacquot, Megan L.	2023–	Appointed January 6, 2023 to succeed James

Judges of the Oregon Tax Court

The Oregon Tax Court was established January 1, 1962.

Name	Term of Service	By What Authority/Remarks
Gunnar, Peter M.	1962–1965	Appointed by Governor Hatfield Jan. 1, 1962; elected 1962; resigned Feb. 18, 1965
Howell, Edward H.	1965–1970	Appointed by Governor Hatfield Feb. 19, 1965; elected 1966; resigned May 31, 1970
Roberts, Carlisle B.	1970–1983	Appointed by Governor McCall June 1, 1970; elected 1970; reelected 1976; term ended 1983
Stewart, Samuel B.	1983–1985	Elected 1982; died Feb. 25, 1985
Byers, Carl N.	1985–2001	Appointed by Governor Atiyeh Mar. 6, 1985; elected 1986; reelected 1992, 1998; retired 2001
Breithaupt, Henry C.	2001–2017	Appointed by Governor Kitzhaber June 29, 2001 to succeed Byers; elected 2002; reelected 2008, 2014; retired Dec. 31, 2017

Name	Term of Service	By What Authority/Remarks
Manicke, Robert	2018–	Appointed by Governor Brown Jan 1, 2018 to succeed Breithaupt; elected 2018

Attorneys General of Oregon

Name/Political Party	Term of Service	By What Authority/Remarks
Chamberlain, George E.—D	May 20, 1891–Jan. 14, 1895	Appointed by Governor Pennoyer; elected June 1892
Idleman, Cicero M.—R	Jan. 14, 1895–Jan. 9, 1899	Elected 1894
Blackburn, D.R.N.—R	Jan. 9, 1899–Jan. 12, 1903	Elected 1898
Crawford, Andrew M.—R	Jan. 13, 1903–Jan. 3, 1915	Elected 1902; reelected 1906, 1910
Brown, George M.—R	Jan. 4, 1915–Oct. 14, 1920	Elected 1914; reelected 1918; resigned
Van Winkle, Isaac H.—R	Oct. 14, 1920–Dec. 14, 1943	Appointed by Governor Olcott; elected 1920; reelected 1924, 1928, 1932, 1936, 1940; died in office
Neuner, George—R	Dec. 21, 1943–Jan. 5, 1953	Appointed by Governor Snell; elected 1944; reelected 1948
Thornton, Robert Y.—D	Jan. 5, 1953–May 20, 1969	Elected 1952; reelected 1956, 1960, 1964

Name/Political Party	Term of Service	By What Authority/Remarks
Johnson, Lee—R	May 20, 1969–Jan. 3, 1977	Elected 1968; reelected 1972
Redden, James—D	Jan. 3, 1977–Mar. 24, 1980	Elected 1976
Brown, James M.—D	Mar. 24, 1980–Jan. 4, 1981	Appointed by Governor Atiyeh
Frohnmayer, David B.—R	Jan. 5, 1981–Dec. 31, 1991	Elected 1980; reelected 1984, 1988; resigned 1991
Crookham, Charles S.—R	Jan. 2, 1992–Jan. 3, 1993	Appointed by Governor Roberts
Kulongoski, Ted—D	Jan. 4, 1993–Jan. 4, 1997	Elected 1992
Myers, Hardy—D	Jan. 6, 1997–Jan. 5, 2009	Elected 1996; reelected 2000, 2004
Kroger, John R.—D	Jan. 5, 2009–June 29, 2012	Elected 2008; resigned 2012
Rosenblum, Ellen—D	June 29, 2012–	Appointed by Governor Kitzhaber; elected 2012; reelected 2016, 2020

Commissioners of the Bureau of Labor and Industries[1]

Name/Political Party	Term of Service	By What Authority/Remarks
Hoff, O.P.—R	June 2, 1903–Jan. 6, 1919	Appointed by Governor Chamberlain; elected 1906; reelected 1910, 1914
Gram, C.H.—R	Jan. 6, 1919–Jan. 4, 1943	Elected 1918; reelected 1922, 1926, 1930, 1934, 1938
Kimsey, W.E.—R	Jan. 4, 1943–Jan. 3, 1955	Elected 1942; reelected 1946, 1950
Nilsen, Norman O.—D	Jan. 3, 1955–Jan. 6, 1975	Elected 1954; reelected 1958, 1962, 1966, 1970
Stevenson, Bill—D	Jan. 6, 1975–Jan. 1, 1979	Elected 1974
Roberts, Mary Wendy—D.	Jan. 1, 1979–Jan 2, 1995	Elected 1978; reelected 1982, 1986, 1990
Roberts, Jack—R	Jan. 2, 1995–Jan. 6, 2003	Elected 1994; reelected 1998
Gardner, Dan[2]	Jan. 6, 2003–April 7, 2008	Elected 2002; reelected 2006; resigned 2008
Avakian, Brad[3]	Apr. 8, 2008–Jan. 6, 2019	Appointed by Governor Kulongoski; elected 2008; reelected 2012, 2014
Hoyle, Val	Jan. 7, 2019–Dec. 16, 2022	Elected 2018
Stephenson, Christina E.	Dec. 16, 2022–	Elected 2022

[1]This position, originally called Labor Commissioner, was changed to Commissioner of the Bureau of Labor Statistics and Inspector of Factories and Workshops in 1918. In 1930, the name changed to Commissioner of the Bureau of Labor. The 1979 Legislature changed the name to Commissioner of the Bureau of Labor and Industries.

[2]The 1995 Legislature made this position nonpartisan, and the 1998 election was the first for this position after the change.

[3]Due to the appointment and election of Brad Avakian in 2008, the 2009 Legislature's House Bill 2095 provided that the Commissioner of the Bureau of Labor and Industries position be placed on the 2012 ballot for a two-year term. This restored the position to its regular election schedule in 2014.

Superintendents of Public Instruction[1]

Name/Political Party	Term of Service	By What Authority/Remarks
Simpson, Sylvester C.—D	Jan. 29, 1873–Sept. 14, 1874	Appointed by Governor Grover
Rowland, L.L.—R	Sept. 14, 1874–Sept. 9, 1878	Elected 1874
Powell, J.L.—R	Sept. 9, 1878–Sept. 11, 1882	Elected 1878
McElroy, E.B.—R	Sept. 11, 1882–Jan. 14, 1895	Elected 1882; reelected 1886, 1890
Irwin, G.M.—R	Jan. 14, 1895–Jan. 9, 1899	Elected 1894
Ackerman, J.H.—R	Jan. 9, 1899–Jan. 3, 1911	Elected 1898; reelected 1902, 1906
Alderman, L.R.—R	Jan. 4, 1911–Jan. 28, 1913	Elected 1910; resigned
Churchill, J.A.—R	July 1, 1913–June 1, 1926	Appointed by Governor West; elected 1914; reelected 1918, 1922; resigned
Turner, R.R.—D	June 1, 1926–Jan. 3, 1927	Appointed by Governor Pierce
Howard, Charles A.—R	Jan. 3, 1927–Sept. 1, 1937	Elected 1926; reelected 1930, 1934; resigned
Putnam, Rex—D	Sept. 1, 1937–Jan. 31, 1961	Appointed by Governor Martin; elected 1938; reelected 1942, 1946, 1950, 1954, 1958; resigned
Minear, Leon P.	Feb. 1, 1961–Mar. 31, 1968	Appointed by Governor Hatfield; elected 1966; resigned
Fasold, Jesse V.	Apr. 8, 1968–June 30, 1968	Appointed by Governor McCall; resigned
Parnell, Dale	July 1, 1968–Mar. 31, 1974	Appointed by Governor McCall; elected 1968; reelected 1970; resigned
Fasold, Jesse V.	Apr. 1, 1974–Jan. 6, 1975	Appointed by Governor McCall
Duncan, Verne A.	Jan. 6, 1975–Nov. 15, 1989	Elected 1974; reelected 1978, 1982, 1986; resigned 1989
Erickson, John	Dec. 18, 1989–Sept. 30, 1990	Appointed by Governor Goldschmidt; resigned
Paulus, Norma	Oct. 1, 1990–Jan. 4, 1999	Elected 1990; appointed by Governor Goldschmidt (before elective term began); reelected 1994
Bunn, Stan	Jan. 4, 1999–Jan. 6, 2003	Elected 1998
Castillo, Susan[2]	Jan. 6, 2003–June 29, 2012	Elected 2002; reelected 2006, 2010; resigned 2012

[1]From 1942 to 1961, this office was filled by election on nonpartisan ballot. In 1961, the state Legislature passed a statute making the office appointive by the State Board of Education. The Supreme Court declared this unconstitutional in 1965, and a constitutional amendment to place the method of selection in the hands of the state Legislature was defeated in 1966. Another attempt to repeal the constitutional provision requiring election was defeated in 1980.

[2]In 2011, Senate Bill 552 created a new statutory provision naming the governor as Superintendent of Public Instruction. Susan Castillo served until her 2012 resignation as the last elected superintendent.

Presidents of the Senate

Session	Name/Political Party	City	County
1860	Elkins, Luther—D		Linn
1862	Bowlby, Wilson—R		Washington
1864	Mitchell, J.H.—R	Portland	Multnomah
1865[1]	Mitchell, J.H.—R	Portland	Multnomah
1866	Cornelius, T.R.—R		Washington
1868	Burch, B.F.—D		Polk
1870	Fay, James D.—D		Jackson
1872	Fay, James D.—D		Jackson
1874	Cochran, R.B.—D		Lane
1876	Whiteaker, John—D		Lane
1878	Whiteaker, John—D		Lane

Session	Name/Political Party	City	County
1880	Hirsch, Sol—R	Portland	Multnomah
1882	McConnell, W.J.—R		Yamhill
1885[2]	Waldo, William—R	Salem	Marion
1887	Carson, John C.—R	Portland	Multnomah
1889	Simon, Joseph—R	Portland	Multnomah
1891	Simon, Joseph—R	Portland	Multnomah
1893	Fulton, C.W.—R	Astoria	Clatsop
1895	Simon, Joseph—R	Portland	Multnomah
1897	Simon, Joseph—R	Portland	Multnomah
1898[1]	Simon, Joseph—R	Portland	Multnomah
1899	Taylor, T.C.—R	Pendleton	Umatilla
1901	Fulton, C.W.—R	Astoria	Clatsop
1903[2]	Brownell, George C.—R	Oregon City	Clackamas
1905	Kuykendall, W.—R	Eugene	Lane
1907	Haines, E.W.—R	Forest Grove	Washington
1909[2]	Bowerman, Jay—R	Condon	Gilliam
1911	Selling, Ben—R	Portland	Multnomah
1913	Malarkey, Dan J.—R	Portland	Multnomah
1915	Thompson, W. Lair—R	Lakeview	Lake
1917	Moser, Gus C.—R	Portland	Multnomah
1919	Vinton, W.T.—R	McMinnville	Yamhill
1920[1]	Vinton, W.T.—R	McMinnville	Yamhill
1921[2]	Ritner, Roy W.—R	Pendleton	Umatilla
1923	Upton, Jay—R	Prineville	Crook
1925	Moser, Gus C.—R	Portland	Multnomah
1927	Corbett, Henry L.—R	Portland	Multnomah
1929	Norblad, A.W.—R	Astoria	Clatsop
1931	Marks, Willard L.—R	Albany	Linn
1933[3]	Kiddle, Fred E.—R	Island City	Union
1935[2]	Corbett, Henry L.—R	Portland	Multnomah
1937	Franciscovich, F.M.—R	Astoria	Clatsop
1939	Duncan, Robert M.—R	Burns	Harney
1941	Walker, Dean H.—R	Independence	Polk
1943	Steiwer, W.H.—R	Fossil	Wheeler
1945	Belton, Howard C.—R	Canby	Clackamas
1947	Cornett, Marshall E.—R	Klamath Falls	Klamath
1949	Walsh, William E.—R	Coos Bay	Coos
1951	Patterson, Paul L.—R	Hillsboro	Washington
1953	Marsh, Eugene E.—R	McMinnville	Yamhill
1955	Smith, Elmo—R	John Day	Grant
1957[2]	Overhulse, Boyd R.—D	Madras	Jefferson
1959	Pearson, Walter J.—D	Portland	Multnomah
1961	Boivin, Harry D.—D	Klamath Falls	Klamath
1963[2]	Musa, Ben—D	The Dalles	Wasco
1965[2]	Boivin, Harry D.—D	Klamath Falls	Klamath
1967[2]	Potts, E.D.—D	Grants Pass	Josephine
1969	Potts, E.D.—D	Grants Pass	Josephine
1971[2]	Burns, John D.—D	Portland	Multnomah
1973	Boe, Jason—D	Reedsport	Douglas
1974[1]	Boe, Jason—D	Reedsport	Douglas
1975	Boe, Jason—D	Reedsport	Douglas
1977	Boe, Jason—D	Reedsport	Douglas
1978[1]	Boe, Jason—D	Reedsport	Douglas
1979	Boe, Jason—D	Reedsport	Douglas
1980[1]	Boe, Jason—D	Reedsport	Douglas
1981[4]	Heard, Fred W.—D	Klamath Falls	Klamath
1983[3]	Fadeley, Edward N.—D	Eugene	Lane
1985	Kitzhaber, M.D., John A.—D	Roseburg	Douglas
1987	Kitzhaber, M.D., John A.—D	Roseburg	Douglas
1989[2]	Kitzhaber, M.D., John A.—D	Roseburg	Douglas
1991	Kitzhaber, M.D., John A.—D	Roseburg	Douglas

Session	Name/Political Party	City	County
1993	Bradbury, Bill—D	Bandon	Coos
1995[2]	Smith, Gordon H.—R	Pendleton	Umatilla
1997	Adams, Brady—R	Grants Pass	Josephine
1999	Adams, Brady—R	Grants Pass	Josephine
2001[5]	Derfler, Gene—R	Salem	Marion
2003	Courtney, Peter—D	Salem	Marion
2005	Courtney, Peter—D	Salem	Marion
2007	Courtney, Peter—D	Salem	Marion
2009	Courtney, Peter—D	Salem	Marion
2011	Courtney, Peter—D	Salem	Marion
2013	Courtney, Peter—D	Salem	Marion
2015	Courtney, Peter—D	Salem	Marion
2017	Courtney, Peter—D	Salem	Marion
2019	Courtney, Peter—D	Salem	Marion
2021	Courtney, Peter—D	Salem	Marion
2022	Wagner, Rob—D	Salem	Clackamas, Multnomah, Washington

[1]Special session
[2]Regular and special session
[3]Regular and two special sessions
[4]Regular and four special sessions
[5]Regular and five special sessions

Speakers of the House of Representatives

Session	Name/Political Party	City	County
1860	Harding, B.F.—D		Marion
1862	Palmer, Joel—R		Yamhill
1864	Moores, I.R.—R		Marion
1865[1]	Moores, I.R.—R		Marion
1866	Chenoweth, F.A.—R		Benton
1868	Whiteaker, John J.—D		Lane
1870	Hayden, Benjamin—D		Polk
1872	Mallory, Rufus—R		Marion
1874	Drain, J.C.—D		Douglas
1876	Weatherford, J.K.—D	Albany	Linn
1878	Thompson, J.M.—D		Lane
1880	Moody, Z.F.—R	The Dalles	Wasco
1882	McBride, George W.—R		Columbia
1885[2]	Keady, W.P.—R	Corvallis	Benton
1887	Gregg, J.T.—R	Salem	Marion
1889	Smith, E.L.—R	Hood River	Hood River
1891	Geer, T.T.—R	Macleay	Marion
1893	Keady, W.P.—R	Portland	Multnomah
1895	Moores, C.B.—R	Salem	Marion
1897[4]	House failed to organize		
1898[1]	Carter, E.V.—R	Ashland	Jackson
1899	Carter, E.V.—R	Ashland	Jackson
1901	Reeder, L.B.—R	Pendleton	Umatilla
1903[2]	Harris, L.T.—R	Eugene	Lane
1905	Mills, A.L.—R	Portland	Multnomah
1907	Davey, Frank—R	Salem	Marion
1909[2]	McArthur, C.N.—R	Portland	Multnomah
1911	Rusk, John P.—R	Joseph	Wallowa
1913	McArthur, C.N.—R	Portland	Multnomah
1915	Selling, Ben—R	Portland	Multnomah
1917	Stanfield, R.N.—R	Stanfield	Umatilla
1919	Jones, Seymour—R	Salem	Marion
1920[1]	Jones, Seymour—R	Salem	Marion

Session	Name/Political Party	City	County
1921[2]	Bean, Louis E.—R	Eugene	Lane
1923	Kubli, K.K.—R	Portland	Multnomah
1925	Burdick, Denton G.—R	Redmond	Deschutes
1927	Carkin, John H.—R	Medford	Jackson
1929	Hamilton, R.S.—R	Bend	Deschutes
1931	Lonergan, Frank J.—R	Portland	Multnomah
1933[3]	Snell, Earl W.—R	Arlington	Gilliam
1935	Cooter, John E.—D	Toledo	Lincoln
1935[1]	Latourette, Howard—D	Portland	Multnomah
1937	Boivin, Harry D.—D	Klamath Falls	Klamath
1939	Fatland, Ernest R.—R	Condon	Gilliam
1941	Farrell, Robert S., Jr.—R	Portland	Multnomah
1943	McAllister, William M.—R	Medford	Jackson
1945	Marsh, Eugene E.—R	McMinnville	Yamhill
1947	Hall, John H.—R	Portland	Multnomah
1949	Van Dyke, Frank J.—R	Medford	Jackson
1951	Steelhammer, John F.—R	Salem	Marion
1953	Wilhelm, Rudie, Jr.—R	Portland	Multnomah
1955	Geary, Edward A.—R	Klamath Falls	Klamath
1957[2]	Dooley, Pat—D	Portland	Multnomah
1959	Duncan, Robert B.—D	Medford	Jackson
1961	Duncan, Robert B.—D	Medford	Jackson
1963[2]	Barton, Clarence—D	Coquille	Coos
1965[2]	Montgomery, F.F.—R	Eugene	Lane
1967[2]	Montgomery, F.F.—R	Eugene	Lane
1969	Smith, Robert F.—R	Burns	Harney
1971[2]	Smith, Robert F.—R	Burns	Harney
1973	Eymann, Richard O.—D	Springfield	Lane
1974[1]	Eymann, Richard O.—D	Springfield	Lane
1975	Lang, Philip D.—D	Portland	Multnomah
1977	Lang, Philip D.—D	Portland	Multnomah
1978[1]	Lang, Philip D.—D	Portland	Multnomah
1979	Myers, Hardy—D	Portland	Multnomah
1980[1]	Myers, Hardy—D	Portland	Multnomah
1981[5]	Myers, Hardy—D	Portland	Multnomah
1983[3]	Kerans, Grattan—D	Eugene	Lane
1985	Katz, Vera—D	Portland	Multnomah
1987	Katz, Vera—D	Portland	Multnomah
1989[2]	Katz, Vera—D	Portland	Multnomah
1991	Campbell, Larry—R	Eugene	Lane
1993	Campbell, Larry—R	Eugene	Lane
1995[2]	Clarno, Bev—R	Bend	Deschutes
1997	Lundquist, Lynn—R	Powell Butte	Deschutes
1999	Snodgrass, Lynn—R	Boring	Clackamas
2001[6]	Simmons, Mark—R	Elgin	Union
2003	Minnis, Karen—R	Wood Village	Multnomah
2005	Minnis, Karen—R	Wood Village	Multnomah
2007	Merkley, Jeff—D	Portland	Multnomah
2009	Hunt, Dave—D	Gladstone	Clackamas
2011	Hanna, Bruce (co-speaker)—R	Roseburg	Douglas, Lane
2011	Roblan, Arnie (co-speaker)—D	Coos Bay	Coos, Douglas, Lane
2013	Kotek, Tina—D	Portland	Multnomah
2015	Kotek, Tina—D	Portland	Multnomah
2017	Kotek, Tina—D	Portland	Multnomah
2019	Kotek, Tina—D	Portland	Multnomah
2021	Kotek, Tina—D	Portland	Multnomah
2022	Rayfield, Dan—D	Salem	Benton

[1]Special session
[2]Regular and special session
[3]Regular and two special sessions

E.J. Davis was elected speaker by less than a quorum. Subsequently, Henry L. Benson was elected speaker by less than a quorum. The Supreme Court revised an 1871 decision and ordered the secretary of state to audit claims and draw warrants for all claims which the Legislature, through its enactments, permitted and directed, either expressly or by implication.

[5]Regular and four special sessions

[6]Regular and five special sessions

U.S. Senators from Oregon

First Position[2]

Name/Political Party	Term of Service[1]	By What Authority/Remarks
Smith, Delazon[3]—D	Feb. 14–Mar. 3, 1859	Elected by Legislature 1858
Baker, Edward[4]—R	Dec. 5, 1860–Oct. 21, 1861	Elected by Legislature 1860; died in office
Stark, Benjamin—D	Oct. 29, 1861–Sept. 11, 1862	Appointed by Governor Whiteaker to succeed Baker
Harding, Benjamin F.—D	Sept. 11, 1862–1865	Elected by Legislature to succeed Baker
Williams, George H.—R	1865–1871	Elected by Legislature 1864
Kelly, James K.—D	1871–1877	Elected by Legislature 1870
Grover, LaFayette—D	1877–1883	Elected by Legislature 1876
Dolph, Joseph N.—R	1883–1895	Elected by Legislature 1882; reelected 1889
McBride, George W.—R	1895–1901	Elected by Legislature 1895
Mitchell, John H.—R	1901–1905	Elected by Legislature 1901; died in office Dec. 8, 1905
Gearin, John M.—D	Dec. 12, 1905–Jan. 23, 1907	Appointed by Governor Chamberlain to succeed Mitchell
Mulkey, Fred W.—R	Jan. 23–Mar. 2, 1907	Selected by general election 1906 for short term; elected by Legislature to serve remaining term of Mitchell and Gearin
Bourne, Jonathan, Jr.—R	1907–1913	Selected by general election1906; elected by Legislature 1907
Lane, Harry—D	1913–May 23, 1917	Selected by general election 1912; elected by Legislature 1913; died in office
McNary, Charles L.—R	May 29, 1917–Nov. 5, 1918	Appointed by Governor Withycombe to succeed Lane
Mulkey, Fred W.—R	Nov. 5–Dec. 17, 1918	Elected 1918 for short term; resigned to permit reappointment of McNary
McNary, Charles L.—R	Dec. 17, 1918–Feb. 24, 1944	Appointed 1918 for unexpired short term; elected 1918; reelected 1924, 1930, 1936, 1942; died in office
Cordon, Guy—R	Mar. 4, 1944–1955	Appointed by Governor Snell to succeed McNary; elected 1944; reelected 1948
Neuberger, Richard L.—D	1955–Mar. 9, 1960	Elected 1954; died in office
Lusk, Hall S.—D	Mar. 16, 1960–Nov. 8, 1960	Appointed by Governor Hatfield to succeed Neuberger
Neuberger, Maurine—D	Nov. 8, 1960–1967	Elected 1960 for short and full terms
Hatfield, Mark O.—R	1967–1997	Elected 1966; reelected 1972, 1978, 1984, 1990
Smith, Gordon H.—R	1997–2009	Elected 1996; reelected 2002
Merkley, Jeff—D	2009–	Elected 2008; reelected 2014, 2020

Second Position[2]

Name/Political Party	Term of Service	By What Authority/Remarks
Lane, Joseph—D	Feb. 14, 1859–1861	Elected by Legislature 1858
Nesmith, James W.—D	1861–1867	Elected by Legislature 1860
Corbett, Henry W.—R	1867–1873	Elected by Legislature 1866
Mitchell, John H.—R	1873–1879	Elected by Legislature 1872

Name/Political Party	Term of Service[1]	By What Authority/Remarks
Slater, James H.—D	1879–1885	Elected by Legislature 1878
Mitchell, John H.—R	1885–1897	Elected by Legislature 1885; reelected 1891
Corbett, Henry W.—R[5]	March, 1897	Appointed by Governor Lord, not seated
Simon, Joseph—R	Oct. 6, 1898–1903	Elected by Legislature to fill vacancy
Fulton, Charles W.—R	1903–1909	Elected by Legislature 1903
Chamberlain, George E.—D[6]	1909–1921	Selected by general election 1908; elected by Legislature; reelected by people 1914
Stanfield, Robert N.—R	1921–1927	Elected 1920
Steiwer, Frederick—R	1927–Feb. 1, 1938	Elected 1926; reelected 1932; resigned
Reames, Alfred Evan—D	Feb. 1–Nov. 9, 1938	Appointed by Governor Martin to succeed Steiwer
Barry, Alex G.—R	Nov. 9, 1938–1939	Elected 1938 for short term
Holman, Rufus C.—R	1939–1945	Elected 1938
Morse, Wayne[7]—D	1945–1969	Elected 1944; reelected 1950, 1956, 1962
Packwood, Robert—R	1969–1995	Elected 1968; reelected 1974, 1980, 1986, 1992; resigned 1995
Wyden, Ron[8]—D	1996–	Elected 1996; reelected 1998, 2004, 2010, 2016, 2022

[1]Unless otherwise noted, normal terms of office began on the fourth day of March and ended on the third day of March until 1933 when terms were changed to begin and end on the third day of January, unless a different date was set by Congress.

[2]Delazon Smith and Joseph Lane drew lots in 1859 for the short and long term senate seats. Smith won the short term of only 17 days expiring March 3, 1859 (designated first position). Lane won the long term expiring March 3, 1861 (designated second position).

[3]When the Legislature first met after statehood in May 1859, Smith was defeated for reelection, and no successor was named. Consequently, Oregon had only one U.S. senator from March 3, 1859 until Baker was elected October 1, 1860.

[4]Senator Edward Baker was killed in the Battle of Balls Bluff, Virginia while serving as a colonel in the Civil War, the only U.S. senator to serve in military action while a senator. His statue, cast of horatio stone and marble, stands 6 ft. 5 in. tall in the Capitol rotunda in Washington, D.C.

[5]When the Legislature failed to elect a successor to Mitchell, Governor Lord appointed Henry Corbett. After conflict, however, the U.S. Senate decided the governor did not have this authority and refused to seat Corbett. Therefore, Oregon was represented by only one U.S. senator from March 4, 1897 to October 6, 1898.

[6]Direct election of U.S. senators resulted from Oregon's ratification of Article XVII of the U.S. Constitution on January 23, 1913 (effective May 31, 1913). Oregon initiated a direct primary for selecting candidates in 1904.

[7]Wayne Morse was elected as a Republican in 1944 and reelected as a Republican in 1950. He changed to Independent in 1952, and to Democrat in 1955. He was reelected as a Democrat in 1956 and 1962.

[8]Elected to fill the unexpired term of Robert Packwood due to Senator Packwood's resignation. The elections, both primary and general, to fill Senator Packwood's seat were conducted by mail. The special primary and general elections were the first statewide vote-by-mail elections to fill a federal office in United States history.

U.S. Representatives from Oregon

Name/Political Party	Term of Service[1]	By What Authority/Remarks
Thurston, Samuel R.—D	June 6, 1849–Apr. 9, 1851	Territorial Delegate elected 1849; died at sea returning home from first session
Lane, Joseph—D	June 2, 1851–Feb. 14, 1859	Territorial Delegate elected 1851; reelected 1853, 1855, 1857
Grover, LaFayette—D	Feb. 15–Mar. 3, 1859	First Representative at large, elected 1858 for short term

Name/Political Party	Term of Service[1]	By What Authority/Remarks
Stout, Lansing—D	1859–1861	Elected 1858
Shiel, George K.—D	1861–1863	Elected 1860
McBride, John R.—R	1863–1865	Elected 1862
Henderson, J.H.D.—R	1865–1867	Elected 1864
Mallory, Rufus—R	1867–1869	Elected 1866
Smith, Joseph S.—D	1869–1871	Elected 1868
Slater, James H.—D	1871–1873	Elected 1870
Wilson, Joseph G.—R	1873	Elected 1872; died in July, 1873 before qualifying
Nesmith, James W.—D	1873–1875	Elected 1873
La Dow, George A.—D	1875	Elected 1874; died Mar. 4, 1875 before qualifying
Lane, Lafayette—D	Oct. 25, 1875–1877	Elected 1875
Williams, Richard—R	1877–1879	Elected 1876
Whiteaker, John—D	1879–1881	Elected 1878
George, Melvin C.—R	1881–1885	Elected 1880; reelected 1882
Hermann, Binger—R	1885–1893	Elected 1884; reelected 1886, 1888, 1890

1st District

Hermann, Binger—R	1893–1897	Elected 1892; reelected 1894
Tongue, Thomas H.—R	1897–Jan. 11, 1903	Elected 1896; reelected 1898, 1900, 1902; died in office
Hermann, Binger—R	June 1, 1903–1907	Elected 1903 to succeed Tongue; reelected 1904
Hawley, Willis C.—R	1907–1933	Elected 1906; reelected 1908, 1910, 1912, 1914, 1916, 1918, 1920, 1922, 1924, 1926, 1928, 1930
Mott, James W.—R	1933–Nov. 12, 1945	Elected 1932; reelected 1934, 1936, 1938, 1940, 1942, 1944; died in office
Norblad, A. Walter, Jr.—R	Jan. 11, 1946–Sept. 20, 1964	Elected 1945 to succeed Mott; reelected 1946, 1948, 1950, 1952, 1954, 1956, 1958, 1960, 1962; died in office
Wyatt, Wendell—R	Nov. 3, 1964–1975	Elected 1964 to succeed Norblad; reelected 1966, 1968, 1970, 1972
AuCoin, Les—D	1975–1993	Elected 1974; reelected 1976, 1978, 1980, 1982, 1984, 1986, 1988, 1990
Furse, Elizabeth—D	1993–1999	Elected 1992; reelected 1994, 1996
Wu, David—D	1999–2011	Elected 1998; reelected 2000, 2002, 2004, 2006, 2008, 2010; resigned 2011
Bonamici, Suzanne—D[2]	2012–	Elected 2012; reelected 2012, 2014, 2016, 2018, 2020, 2022

2nd District

Ellis, William R.—R	1893–1899	Elected 1892; reelected 1894, 1896
Moody, Malcolm A.—R	1899–1903	Elected 1898; reelected 1900
Williamson, John N.—R	1903–1907	Elected 1902; reelected 1904
Ellis, William R.—R	1907–1911	Elected 1906; reelected 1908
Lafferty, Abraham W.—R.	1911–1913	Elected 1910
Sinnott, N.J.—R	1913–May 31, 1928	Elected 1912; reelected 1914, 1916, 1918, 1920, 1922, 1924, 1926; resigned
Butler, Robert R.—R	Nov. 6, 1928–Jan. 7, 1933	Elected 1928 to succeed Sinnott; reelected 1930; died in office
Pierce, Walter M.—D	1933–1943	Elected 1932; reelected 1934, 1936, 1938, 1940

Name/Political Party	Term of Service[1]	By What Authority/Remarks
Stockman, Lowell—R	1943–1953	Elected 1942; reelected 1944, 1946, 1948, 1950
Coon, Samuel H.—R	1953–1957	Elected 1952; reelected 1954
Ullman, Albert C.—D	1957–1981	Elected 1956; reelected 1958, 1960, 1962, 1964, 1966, 1968, 1970, 1972, 1974, 1976,1978
Smith, Denny—R	1981–1983	Elected 1980
Smith, Robert F.—R	1983–1995	Elected 1982; reelected 1984, 1986, 1988, 1990, 1992
Cooley, Wes—R	1995–1997	Elected 1994
Smith, Robert F.—R	1997–1999	Elected 1996
Walden, Greg—R	1999–2020	Elected 1998; reelected 2000, 2002, 2004, 2006, 2008, 2010, 2012, 2014, 2016, 2018
Bentz, Cliff—R	2021–	Elected 2020; reelected 2022

3rd District

Lafferty, Abraham W.—R	1913–1915	Elected 1912
McArthur, Clifton N.—R	1915–1923	Elected 1914; reelected 1916, 1918, 1920
Watkins, Elton—D	1923–1925	Elected 1922
Crumpacker, Maurice E.—R	1925–July 25, 1927	Elected 1924; reelected 1926; died in office
Korell, Franklin F.—R	Oct. 18, 1927–1931	Elected 1927; reelected 1928
Martin, Charles H.—D	1931–1935	Elected 1930; reelected 1932
Ekwall, William A.—R	1935–1937	Elected 1934
Honeyman, Nan Wood—D	1937–1939	Elected 1936
Angell, Homer D.—R	1939–1955	Elected 1938; reelected 1940, 1942, 1944, 1946, 1948, 1950, 1952
Green, Edith S.—D	1955–1975	Elected 1954; reelected 1956, 1958, 1960, 1962, 1964, 1966, 1968, 1970, 1972
Duncan, Robert B.—D	1975–1981	Elected 1974; reelected 1976, 1978
Wyden, Ron—D	1981–1996	Elected 1980; reelected 1982, 1984, 1986, 1988, 1990, 1992, 1994
Blumenauer, Earl—D[3]	1996–	Elected 1996; reelected 1998, 2000, 2002, 2004, 2006, 2008, 2010, 2012, 2014, 2016, 2018, 2020, 2022

4th District

Ellsworth, Harris—R	1943–1957	Elected 1942; reelected 1944, 1946, 1948, 1950, 1952, 1954
Porter, Charles O.—D	1957–1961	Elected 1956; reelected 1958
Durno, Edwin R.—R	1961–1963	Elected 1960
Duncan, Robert B.—D	1963–1967	Elected 1962; reelected 1964
Dellenback, John—R	1967–1975	Elected 1966; reelected 1968, 1970, 1972
Weaver, James—D	1975–1987	Elected 1974; reelected 1976, 1978, 1980, 1982, 1984
DeFazio, Peter A.—D	1987–2022	Elected 1986; reelected 1988, 1990, 1992, 1994, 1996, 1998, 2000, 2002, 2004, 2006, 2008, 2010, 2012, 2014, 2016, 2018, 2020
Hoyle. Val—D	2023–	Elected 2022

5th District

Smith, Denny—R	1983–1991	Elected 1982; reelected 1984, 1986, 1988
Kopetski, Mike	1991–1995	Elected 1990; reelected 1992
Bunn, Jim—R	1995–1997	Elected 1994
Hooley, Darlene—D	1997–2009	Elected 1996; reelected 1998, 2000, 2002, 2004, 2006

Name/Political Party	Term of Service[1]	By What Authority/Remarks
Schrader, Kurt—D	2009–	Elected 2008, reelected 2010, 2012, 2014, 2016, 2018, 2020
Chavez-DeRemer, Lori—R	2023–	Elected 2022

6th District

Salinas, Andrea—D	2023–	Elected 2022

[1]Unless otherwise noted, normal terms of office began on the fourth day of March and ended on the third day of March until 1933 when terms were changed to begin and end on the third day of January, unless a different date was set by Congress.

[2]Elected in the January 31, 2012, Special Election to finish the unexpired term of Representative David Wu.

[3]Elected in 1996 to finish the unexpired term of Representative Ron Wyden. Reelected to a full term at the November 5, 1996, General Election.

History

Historian Bob Reinhardt's essay introduces readers to the myriad ways that different people interacted with their environments to create this place we know as Oregon — from the Native people who made this land their home for thousands of years before Lewis and Clark, to the complex challenges rural and urban Oregonians alike will grapple with in the coming decades.

OREGON HISTORY

Oregon Environments, Oregon People: A History

Written by Bob H. Reinhardt, Ph.D.

Assistant Professor of History at Boise State University, where he works in the fields of environmental history and the history of the American West.

Oregonians have a long and complex relationship with the extraordinary environments and natural worlds in which they live. Take predators like coyotes and wolves, for example. In the oral traditions of many Oregon Native peoples, Coyote is a clever trickster whose adventures teach moral lessons that deserve respect and understanding. Wolves commanded respect from the British, French-Canadians, and Americans living in Oregon in the mid-19th century, too. Their fear of wolves brought them together along the banks of the Willamette River for the "Wolf Meetings" in 1843, to discuss how to eliminate predators (additionally, they created Oregon's first government). That anxiety faded in the following decades as Oregonians developed the ability to control wolves, which disappeared from the state by the 1940s. But when wolves returned to Oregon at the end of the 20th century, they once again warranted the respect of Oregonians: many rural residents regarded the animals as a continued dangerous threat to life and property, while city-dwellers often saw them as noble, wild creatures deserving protection.

These wolf stories provide a glimpse into many aspects of Oregon's history: the long presence of humans, the variety of communities that have made this place home, the combination of pragmatism and ideology that characterizes Oregon politics, the tension between the state's urban and rural populations and the spirit of cooperation and compromise that often brings Oregonians together. Through it all, a larger theme emerges: the changing relationship between Oregonians and nature. For millennia, Oregon's landscape demanded respect and adaptation from the people who lived here. That changed in the late 19th

century as Oregonians developed tools and methods to manipulate and to try to master their environments. Over time, many Oregonians came to question the destructive effects of such manipulation and instead developed an interest in the aesthetic, the recreational and even the inherent value of Oregon's landscape. Understanding Oregon's history requires understanding how Oregonians have related to their environments — and to each other.

Traditional stories of Native peoples told of the eruption of Mount Mazama, which created Crater Lake. (Oregon State Archives scenic photo)

Original Oregonians

Modern geology and archaeology hold that humans arrived in Oregon at least 14,000 years ago, after a centuries-long migration from Asia via the Bering Strait land bridge and sea-borne routes along the coast. But there are other origin stories, too. Oral traditions from the Klamath and Modoc Native peoples, for instance, speak of beings who dug tunnels under the earth, created the marshes and rivers, made the people, and caused the eruption of Mount Mazama and the creation of Crater Lake. The stories told by science and tradition both emphasize the importance of environmental change at a variety of scales: geological shifts producing the Cascade Mountains, the Missoula floods that raged through the Columbia Basin between 13,000 and 15,000 years ago, and volcanic eruptions like that of Mount Mazama around

7,000 years ago. Such forces and transformations produced evolving ecosystems that dozens of American Indian groups both adapted to and changed. To make sense of this diversity, historians and anthropologists often refer to three (occasionally four) culture areas in Oregon: the Great Basin; the Columbia Plateau; the Northwest Coast which also includes the "western interior" of the Willamette Valley; and Southern Oregon.

Northern Paiute peoples thrived in a range of Great Basin environments such as the Alvord Desert. (Oregon State Archives scenic photo)

To an outsider, the Great Basin might seem desolate and even barren. But the Northern Paiute peoples and their ancestors created life and opportunity in this home. Encompassing the southeast quarter of Oregon and stretching far beyond the state, the Great Basin includes Steens Mountain, the Alvord Desert, and Harney and Malheur lakes. Those who knew the landscape, manipulated and made sense of these environments not just to survive, but to thrive. That knowledge started with a deep understanding of the location and development of food and other resource production in different places at different times of the year. Northern Paiute peoples made "seasonal rounds" throughout the diverse landscapes of the Great Basin, migrating to places where they knew they would find resources. In the spring, women and children dug up and dried *tsuga* (biscuitroot), which they made into loaves; men speared and trapped salmon at the headwaters of the Malheur River. Summertime saw the Northern Paiute peoples travelling widely to the north and south in pursuit of deer, elk, groundhogs, and other game, as well as a variety of plants, such as huckleberries and chokecherries. The work continued into the fall, when the Wada'Tika band of Northern Paiutes along the shores of Malheur Lake harvested *waada* (seepweed), extracting the plant's nutritious seeds that were stored for the winter. As the days turned shorter and colder, the Northern Paiute peoples gathered at their winter encampments near lakes, living in homes they made of willow branches and tule plants. Along the eastern side of the Cascade mountains in southern Oregon, the Klamath peoples of the Klamath Basin cultivated the additional resources of that area, such as different kinds of fish and waterfowl. Through their knowledge, expertise

and the labor represented in their seasonal rounds and the homes they made, these peoples — including today's Burns Paiute Tribe, the Paiutes of the Confederated Tribes of Warm Springs, and the Yahooskin band of Paiutes of the Klamath — sustained complex and enriching lives in the Great Basin environment.

North of the Great Basin lies the Columbia Plateau, a region defined by the Columbia River's drainage system east of the Cascade Mountains into northeastern Oregon and beyond to Washington, Idaho, Montana, and British Columbia. The *Nimiipuu* (Nez Perce), Umatilla, Cayuse, and other peoples of the Plateau developed sophisticated seasonal rounds that ranged throughout the region's different ecological zones, each providing a variety of foods and other resources. Plateau peoples spent their winters in villages along the upper Columbia River and its tributaries, living in longhouses made of tule mats and consuming carefully-preserved food. They crafted baskets, digging implements, fishing spears and nets, weapons and other kinds of technologies. Those tools were put to good use in the spring, first with the gathering of *qém'es* (camas) and other plants, and then with the expert harvesting of spring *nacó'x* (salmon). Fishing continued into the summer with steelhead and sockeye salmon runs, along with harvests of *cemíitx* (huckleberries), *mi'ttip* (elderberry), and other fruits. The fall meant more plant harvests, supplemented by the hunting of mule deer and the taking of fall *nacó'x*, which was carefully dried and processed into nutritious and long-lasting pemmican.

These foods also served as valuable trade goods, contributing to a vast network of exchange that connected the Plateau people to other Native peoples throughout and beyond the Columbia River watershed. *Wyam* (Celilo Falls) on the Columbia River was the largest trading site in what would become Oregon. There, where the river's power and its huge salmon runs squeezed through narrow passages, Native peoples built communities — including Celilo Village, the oldest continuously-occupied site in Oregon — and cultures that merged traditions from the lower and upper Columbia. Wyam drew people not just for the harvesting of salmon, which became disoriented in the rapids, but also for the trade of an astonishing variety of goods from far-flung locales: whale oil and shells from the west, bison meat and robes from the east, obsidian and weapons from the south, skins and baskets from the north and more. The diversity of goods available at Wyam and at other trading sites indicates the depth and breadth of the material abundance, societies and cultures created by Native peoples.

Some of those who gathered at Wyam came from the Northwest Coast, a cultural region stretching from Alaska to California and defined by mild climate, dense forests and wetness from rain, fog and rivers. In Oregon, Coastal Indian groups included the Clatsop, Tillamook, Siletz, Siuslaw, Coos and Chetco, each developing sophisticated adaptations to and manipulations of their environments. Coastal peoples moved far less frequently or widely compared to the peoples of the Columbia Plateau and Great Basin, instead drawing on and cultivating the rich resources of their local and remarkably diverse environments, including the Pacific Ocean, coastal estuaries, freshwater rivers, plains and mountain ranges. From *ghvs-t'utlh* (cedar), they crafted clothing, dugout canoes, and houses, and they lived in permanent and often large villages at the mouths of rivers. From those rivers, Coastal Indians drew many different kinds of fish, including *luuk'e* (salmon), which at times so filled the streams that a person could cross the water on their backs — or so it was said. Knowing and understanding the seasonal rhythms by which salmon came and went, Coastal Indians developed elaborate ceremonies of respect that had the effect of maintaining salmon populations, while allowing them to harvest enough so that each person living in the region ate on average one pound of salmon per day.

The Coast Range Mountains divided the homelands of Coastal Indian groups from the Native peoples of the Western Interior. (Oregon State Archives scenic photo)

East and south of the coastal mountain ranges and in the valleys of the Willamette, Umpqua and Rogue rivers, the Native peoples of the Western Interior created lives that in many ways merged those of Coastal, Great Basin and Plateau Indians. Salmon and other fish contributed to the diets of these peoples, including the Kalapuya and Upper Umpqua, but expert hunting of *amu'ki'* (deer) and *antká'* (elk) were also common sources of protein. Their seasonal rounds did not range as far as those of the Plateau and Great Basin peoples, but their knowledge of different environments and opportunities was just as sophisticated, particularly in their harvesting and processing of edible plants, including *dinibgwi' ampgwi'* (hazelnuts), many types of berries, and, most importantly, *dinidi "p* (camas). Western Interior Indians developed the knowledge to harvest the camas bulb and roast it in preparation for both storage as well as, in large amounts, trading; they, like other Native peoples, also regularly burned prairies and savannahs, which assisted in plant propagation. Fire also facilitated berry and acorn collection by creating open areas, assisted in the harvest of tarweed seeds in the fall, and developed fringe environments on the edges of prairies and forests that attracted game for hunting. Those foods, carefully preserved, carried the peoples of the valleys through the cooler and wetter months of winter, when they returned to permanent villages, often close to lakes.

The original Oregonians participated in worlds of cycle and tradition, but also of change. Major disruptions, such as the eruption of Mount Mazama or earthquakes in the Pacific that produced enormous tidal waves, led to significant changes for Native peoples, including displacement. Less dramatic changes, such as the gradual cooling of the climate 4,000 years ago, also led to migration and further adaptation. Seasonal rounds took Native peoples to familiar grounds, but their travels changed for a variety of reasons: a particularly dry or wet season that delayed or accelerated root and edible plant production, for example, or the development and improvement of new tools and technologies such as weirs for harvesting fish. Native societies expanded, contracted and evolved in response to new goods, ideas and people incorporated through trade networks. These networks also brought horses, which arrived on the Columbia Plateau in the 1700s, leading to more mobility and significant social change among the Cayuse, Nimiipuu and Umatilla. These animals, reintroduced to North America by the Spanish, were one of the most significant manifestations of a new connection to Europe, from which trade goods, diseases and eventually people soon would enter the worlds of the original people of Oregon.

Oregon and Imperial Ambition

The Europeans who came to Oregon beginning in the 1500s recognized in their own ways the power of the nonhuman world. They arrived by means of the Pacific Ocean, an immensely powerful force that regularly destroyed ships and stole lives. But thirst for knowledge, hunger for wealth and imperial ambitions drove Europeans and Euro-Americans to try to overcome and control the forces of nature. The Pacific Ocean offered not only danger, but also economic and political opportunities, especially if one could find a water route through North America that would facilitate global trade between Europe and Asia. Spain was the first European empire to send ships to Oregon: initially, in the mid-1500s, in purposeful pursuit of a water route through the continent; then, throughout the 1600s, by accident as galleons travelling the Pacific occasionally wrecked off the Oregon coast; and finally, in the mid-1700s, with a series of naval expeditions meant to establish Spain's claim to the entire Pacific Coast and defend its colonies, mines and other imperial interests in Mexico. Spain imagined competition from Russian fur traders in the north, who had by the late-1700s established extensive operations in Alaska. But Russia never posed a real threat to Spain's claims to the Pacific Northwest. The wealth of nature, both in the imagined water trade route through North

America and the real riches in animal pelts, drew a much more formidable opponent toward Oregon.

The English first came to the Pacific Northwest in search of the mythical Northwest Passage bridging the Pacific and Atlantic, but they returned because of the real and profitable pelts of sea otters, beavers and other fur-bearing animals. England's interest in the Pacific Northwest began in earnest with Captain James Cook, whose 1776–1780 voyage not only made landfall on the Oregon coast, but also established and publicized the enormous profits available in the sea otter fur trade. British traders soon were plying the Northwest coastline for ports, and trading with Native peoples, directly challenging Spain's claims to the entire Pacific coast. In 1790, Spain finally relinquished those claims, and British mariners and merchants asserted their dominance to explore and trade in the region. In another attempt to find a water passage through North America, the British admiralty sent Captain George Vancouver to the Pacific coast in 1792. Vancouver's ships carefully probed the coastline over the course of three years, creating detailed maps, gathering information on Native peoples and their environments, and establishing with certainty that no sea route through North America existed. The British still exploited fur-bearing animals for enormous profit, but doing so required crossing the continent by land and multiple rivers, such as the Columbia, which Vancouver's expedition traveled through and officially claimed for Great Britain.

Vancouver had a strong imperial claim to the Columbia River, but it was not the only such claim, and it would not be enough to hold the Oregon Country for Great Britain. The American sea captain Robert Gray first traveled to the Oregon coast in 1788, when he traded and fought with the Tillamook people at Tillamook Bay. He returned four years later, taking his ship *Columbia Rediviva* into the mouth of a great river that Vancouver had bypassed just two weeks earlier. Gray named the river after his ship, traded for a few hundred pelts and left, neglecting to officially take possession of the river for the United States. It hardly mattered. News of Gray's voyages, as well as reports from Vancouver and other expeditions, traveled quickly, attracting dozens of American ships to the Pacific Northwest and challenging British claims to sovereignty and the wealth of the fur trade. Although these ships flew under different flags, Americans and Britons shared the view that Oregon's environments could be known and owned, and that they should extract wealth from those environments.

For the first two decades of the 19th century, British and American merchants and traders, with the support of their respective governments, competed over Oregon's wealth. Lewis and Clark's famous expedition of 1805–06 brought official agents of the United States into Oregon Country, seeking a navigable route to the Pacific, scientific knowledge, economic opportunities for trade with

Native peoples, and stronger claims to land that President Thomas Jefferson hoped might extend the American "empire of liberty." Four years later, the Boston entrepreneur John Jacob Astor sent two parties, one by land and one by sea, toward Oregon Country to found an ambitious global fur empire called the Pacific Fur Company. These parties established Fort Astoria in 1811, but it (and the Pacific Fur Company) only lasted until 1813, when the British North West Company bought Astor's fort and renamed it Fort George, incorporating it into their extensive network of fur trading posts in the Pacific Northwest. While American and British negotiators agreed in 1818 to jointly occupy Oregon, British fur traders established their dominance, particularly after the Hudson's Bay Company (HBC) acquired the North West Company in 1821. Under the leadership of Dr. John McLoughlin, from its new Columbia District headquarters at Fort Vancouver, the HBC vigorously pursued its vision for Oregon Country. While cultivating trade relationships with Native trappers west of the Cascades, the HBC urged trappers in the east to hunt beavers into extinction, hoping to create a "fur desert" that would discourage American traders and trappers.

This strategy failed to reckon with the power of another view of Oregon's environment: its potential for agriculture. While the fur trade offered short-term profits by extracting nature's wealth, many Euro-Americans looked to agriculture for long-term progress through cultivation and "improvement" of nature. The Lewis and Clark expedition recorded the remarkable diversity of Oregon's environments, particularly the farming opportunities in the Willamette Valley. The expedition's journals and other reports on Oregon suggested that Euro-American farmers could and should fulfill what they believed to be Oregon's true destiny as an agricultural paradise. Especially among Americans in the Midwest looking for a better life, Oregon became a place in which to live, thrive and make one's home. That view had been present even before Americans came to Oregon: some former fur trappers and HBC employees built farms and set down roots in the Willamette Valley, including the company's chief factor, McLoughlin, who claimed land for a home in what is now Oregon City. But McLoughlin and his fellow British citizens were increasingly joined — and soon were outnumbered by — Americans who saw in Oregon not just the possibility, but the inevitability of agricultural settlement under the U.S. flag.

Oregon Becomes American

The Americans' belief in the righteousness of managing nature through agriculture, coupled with a belief in the righteousness of Christianity, confronted the lifeways and worldviews of Native peoples in Oregon. While McLoughlin developed his claim in the area around Willamette Falls, American newspapers in 1833 circulated reports of a small group of Nimiipuu who came to St. Louis looking for Bibles and Christianity. For Americans steeped in the evangelical fervor of the Second Great Awakening, such reports confirmed their calling to spread the Gospel. The Methodists first answered the call in 1834, sending the preacher Jason Lee, his nephew Daniel, and three laymen, who established a mission on the Willamette River about 13 miles north of what is now Salem. Two years later, an ecumenical Protestant party led by Dr. Marcus Whitman and his wife, Narcissa, settled near the Blue Mountains of northeastern Oregon to evangelize among the Cayuse, Umatilla and Nimiipuu. Fathers Francois Blanchet and Modeste Demers arrived in Oregon in 1838, establishing Catholic missions first on the Cowlitz River and then among retired French-Canadian HBC employees and their families living at French Prairie, in what is now St. Paul. These missionaries brought not only Bibles and Christianity, but also farming tools and agricultural practices: the gospel of progress through management of nature.

These evangelizing efforts failed to convert Oregon's Native peoples to a new faith in great numbers, but the missions drastically changed life in Oregon. Protestant missionaries in particular critiqued Native belief systems and insisted on the superiority of White agricultural settlement rather than Native seasonal rounds. They also contributed to the spread of disease and death among Native peoples. Even prior to regular contact with White explorers, fur traders, sailors and farmers, Native peoples experienced the devastating effects of smallpox, measles and other Old World diseases. That devastation increased in the early 1830s, when a series of malaria epidemics decimated Chinookan and Kalapuyan societies along the lower Columbia River and in the Willamette Valley, killing perhaps 90 percent of the Native population. Missionaries and their families contributed to these epidemics both through their own biological presence, and by facilitating the immigration of more White families and the diseases they brought with them. Their reports and public presentations delivered back east trumpeted the agricultural potential of the Willamette Valley, where diseases had decimated Native populations, leaving behind the rich, open fields produced by Native burning practices. Those reports, along with other positive accounts from Oregon boosters like Hall Jackson Kelley and John Wyeth, drew more and more settlers to the Willamette Valley, which held an estimated 150 Americans in 1841. The next year, more than 100 Americans migrated to Oregon, and approximately 900 more came the year after that. By 1845 — just 11 years after Jason Lee arrived — the Willamette Valley was home to approximately 6,000 Euro-Americans and just 500 Kalapuyans. These emigrants to Oregon were part of a wave of mass migration that washed over the globe during the nineteenth century, when millions of settlers and workers from Europe and Asia descended on the American West, Australia, South Africa and elsewhere.

Thousands of Americans packed their possessions into covered wagons and traveled the Oregon Trail in the 1840s. (Oregon State Archives scenic photo)

The Americans who came over the Oregon Trail in the 1840s traveled relatively lightly but carried weighty hopes for the future and strong beliefs about religion, society and nature. They came from the newer states of the Midwest and the Upper South — Illinois, Indiana, Ohio, Kentucky and Missouri, especially. Most were Protestants, and they found in Oregon spiritual and material support from the missions that had shifted from saving Indian souls to encouraging White settlement. They traveled the Oregon Trail and settled in Oregon as patriarchal families, establishing extensive kin networks with distinct roles for women and men in family and work. These new Oregonians also had particularly strong ideas about racial hierarchies. Although very few held slaves, nearly all White Americans in Oregon believed that Blacks were inferior. White Oregonians also helped quicken the decline of Native populations. They poured into the Willamette Valley and took Kalapuyan land by "squatting," claiming land for homesteads by virtue of the advances of American civilization and agriculture, preceding any legal action by the United States government towards Native lands.

The new Oregonians brought with them plants, livestock, and agricultural techniques that remade the landscape in the image of the farms they had left behind back east. Americans tilled the land and built fences; they planted corn, wheat and vegetable gardens; they raised cattle, oxen and hogs. This resettlement of Oregon – for the country had once been the settled home of Native people – depended on the labor of Native peoples, hired to work fields that had been cleared by the burning practices of their parents, grandparents and ancestors. American resettlers concentrated on establishing subsistence farmsteads that would sustain their families and future generations. But the new Oregonians gradually cleared larger fields, built longer fences, and established sawmills, gristmills and granaries to prepare their products for market; these processes accelerated and expanded as farming and transportation technologies improved over the 19th century. These new Oregonians found willing buyers, too, especially when the California Gold Rush increased demand for Oregon's wheat and wood. But even before 1849, American resettlers had remade the environment of the Willamette Valley with homesteads, vegetable gardens, tilled fields, fruit orchards and other signs of Euro-American cultivation and culture. In so doing, these new Oregonians acted out another aspect of their mid-19th century religious ideology: their understanding of the Biblical instruction to "have dominion" over nature. The changes they wrought transformed the environments upon which Native peoples had developed their seasonal rounds and other ways of thriving in their lands.

These White resettlers quickly turned to economic and political organization to reaffirm their view of nature and their ambitious claims to Oregon. They especially valued domesticated animals, which not only provided meat and milk, but also represented control over the wild nature that surrounded them. In 1837, a group of settlers formed the Willamette Cattle Company and sent a party led by former fur trapper Ewing Young to California to buy cattle. Young returned with more than 600 longhorns, which increased the availability of valuable livestock, transformed the valley's landscapes by eating native plants and enriched the company's investors, including Young. He died in 1841 without a will or any heirs, causing a minor legal emergency. To determine what to do with Young's cattle-based estate, White settlers elected a judge and three law enforcement officials. In short, cattle — more specifically, the value White settlers placed on them — gave birth to political organization in Oregon country.

A State Capitol mural of the 1843 "Wolf Meetings."
(Oregon State Archives scenic photo)

Livestock also instigated the next big move toward government in 1843, during what would later be known as the "Wolf Meetings." During those meetings, Willamette Valley settlers not only created a tax-funded bounty system meant to destroy wolves, bears, and other predators preying on livestock, but also decided to found a Provisional

Government. The Wolf Meetings alienated many British citizens living in Oregon, and nearly all Britons abandoned the meetings, rejecting what was a clearly an American-led effort to establish American-style government in anticipation of the official extension of American authority. Those settlers were soon overwhelmed by rapidly-increasing numbers of Americans, who expanded the role of the Provisional Government and called on the United States to assert more authority in Oregon. The Americans especially wanted to guarantee their extensive land claims: up to a full square mile of land under the Provisional Government's code of laws — which, of course, were not recognized by Great Britain, which still jointly occupied Oregon with the United States. The Oregon Treaty of 1846 provided some security by finally settling the boundary between U.S. and British claims at the 49th parallel. But Americans in Oregon wanted more: to become a U.S. territory, which would bring federal recognition of their land claims and, more importantly, federal intervention against Native peoples. It was their and the nation's "Manifest Destiny" — the popular mid-century explanation of and justification for what many White Americans believed was the natural, inevitable and righteous expansion of the United States to the Pacific Ocean.

A deadly conflict with the Cayuse people of the Columbia Plateau brought Americans in Oregon the territorial status, recognition and intervention they wanted. Since its founding in 1838, the Whitman Mission had produced more conflict than conversion: the Whitmans accused the Cayuse, Nimiipu, and Umatilla peoples of laziness and backwardness, while the Native peoples became frustrated with the missionaries' abusive evangelism and the ecological destruction caused by increasing numbers of American settlers and travelers. In 1847, the tension boiled over into war. A group of Cayuse and Umatilla, suspecting Marcus Whitman of causing a measles epidemic that killed more than 200 of their people, attacked the mission, killing a dozen Whites (including the Whitmans) and taking 53 hostages. They eventually released the hostages, but not before White settlers in the Willamette Valley sent a volunteer militia on raids against the Cayuse demanding federal action and protection. The federal government responded in 1848 by passing the Organic Act, which created Oregon Territory, and by sending the U.S. Army to assist the White vigilantes, who returned to Oregon with five of the Cayuses involved in the Whitman attack. On May 24, 1850, after a two-day trial and 75 minutes of deliberation, a jury of twelve White men convicted the five Cayuses of murder, and they were executed on June 3. That same year, the U.S. Congress passed the Oregon Donation Land Law, which legitimized existing land claims and allowed new White immigrant families arriving before Dec. 1, 1850 to claim up to 640 acres (later arrivals would get half as much land). Congress also authorized treaty commissioners to negotiate with Oregon tribes for their land, although that work did not commence until 1851, well after Congressional authorization of the distribution of Native lands. With official incorporation into the United States, the federal government's commitment to obtaining Native lands, and their own land claims secured, the new Oregonians could continue to pursue their hopes for a better future and their vision for Oregon's landscapes.

Creating an Exclusive Paradise

Other peoples and cultures would have to make way for that particular vision. In the 1850s and 1860s, U.S. Indian agents and treaty commissioners secured agreements with dozens of Native tribes and bands throughout Oregon, sometimes through honest negotiations, but often by means of dishonest or willfully ignorant negotiations. These forced treaties ceded enormous amounts of Native lands and confined Native peoples to marginal territories on reservations. Treaties that were regarded as insufficiently generous to White interests often went unratified or simply ignored until government officials secured harsher terms requiring the sacrifice of more Native land. In addition to establishing reservations, the U.S. government also built military posts throughout Oregon to keep Native peoples separated from the growing numbers of White settlers. Devastated by disease and displacement, many Native peoples were forced to move to reservations, where some adopted sedentary agriculture and accepted as a necessity poorly-paid wage labor, while attempting to preserve their families, societies and cultures as much as possible.

Other Native peoples refused to tolerate White aggression and the ecological havoc wrought by Whites and the invasive plants and animals that came with them. In the 1850s in southwestern Oregon, bands of Shasta, Tututni, and other Native groups attacked White settlers and miners, responding to years of raids and violence against Native peoples and the destruction of the plants and animals on which they depended. The ensuing Rogue River Wars lasted until 1856, when the U.S. Army forcibly removed Native peoples to far-off reservations on the western side of the coastal mountain range. In the Great Basin in the 1860s, Northern Paiute bands raided miners, ranchers and other overland travelers who strained the region's scarce resources. After a vigorous campaign by the U.S. Army in 1866–68, most Northern Paiute surrendered and moved to reservations, although some later joined the Bannock people of Idaho in their resistance to federal authority. Further south on the Oregon-California border, the Modoc War of 1872 pitted more than 1,000 U.S. soldiers against a few dozen Modoc warriors who could no longer tolerate the poor conditions at the Klamath Reservation. The Modocs held out for nearly six months before the U.S. Army finally chased them down,

executing some of the leaders and sending the rest to far-away Indian Territory in Oklahoma. On the Columbia Plateau, White travelers, settlers and miners continued to strain the environment on which the Cayuse, Umatilla and Nimiipuu depended, leading to a series of treaties, reservations and finally conflicts: the Yakima War of 1855–58, the Nez Perce War of 1877, and the Bannock War of 1878.

The Warm Springs River flows through the Warm Springs Indian Reservation. (Oregon State Archives scenic photo)

By the end of the 1880s, multiple methods of force — treaties, displacement to reservations and violence — had removed Native peoples from their homes throughout Oregon. The Nimiipuu were scattered to different places: the Warm Springs and Umatilla Indian Reservations in Oregon, Colville Indian Reservation in Washington and Nez Perce Indian Reservation in Idaho. Some Northern Paiutes remained in the Burns area, while others moved to the Warm Springs Reservation, joining Wascoes and other people from the Columbia Plateau; other Plateau peoples were forcibly moved to the Umatilla Indian reservations, as well as at the Klamath, Grand Ronde, and Siletz Reservations. Still other Native peoples, together as small communities or families or individually, lived away from reservations in or close to towns and urban areas. Hundreds of Native children were forced to attend and live at the Chemawa Indian School, established in Forest Grove in 1880 and moved to its present location north of Salem in 1885. In such challenging situations and environments, Native peoples would continue to claim their place in Oregon's history, while their homelands became subject to the exclusive possession and control of White resettlers, prospectors and speculators.

The vision of civilization, agriculture, and progress embraced by White Oregonians also excluded other nonwhite peoples. From the earliest stages of American political organization in Oregon, White settlers took deliberate steps to keep out people of color. Even before Oregon became a U.S. territory, the Provisional Government enacted laws that banned both free and enslaved Blacks from

Oregon and threatened to whip those who stayed. The territorial government reinforced these exclusionary efforts by barring nonwhites from testifying in court, and the Oregon Donation Land Law of 1850 excluded Blacks from its generous provisions. At the critical moment of statehood in 1857, Whites once again attempted to keep out Blacks: voters rejected slavery, but by an even greater margin they also reaffirmed the exclusion of Blacks from Oregon. The Oregon constitution thereby became the first state constitution to explicitly exclude free Blacks. White Oregonians made it clear that other nonwhite peoples also were not welcome: the Donation Land Law excluded Hawaiians, who had worked and lived in Oregon since the early 1800s, and the state constitution barred Chinese people from voting. White Oregonians wanted a White state, and they got one: according to the 1860 census, they made up more than 90 percent of the state's 52,465 inhabitants, although that figure did not fully record the state's Native population.

The Civil War and its aftermath confirmed that Oregon's environments would be owned, cultivated and manipulated by Whites only. Oregon's Democratic, Whig, Know-Nothing and Republican party leaders shouted at each other about abstract issues such as property rights and self-determination, but like their White male constituents who approved the exclusionary Oregon constitution, they generally agreed that the state must exclude both slavery and free Blacks. While other parts of the United States violently divided over slavery, the Civil War most directly affected Oregon by temporarily restricting the federal government's negotiations and conflicts with Oregon's Native peoples. Watching the Civil War from a distance, White Oregonians generally approved of the Union's success, with isolated but notable expressions of Southern sympathy in Jacksonville and Eugene. But White Oregonians did not embrace the Civil War's greater meaning for rights and equality. Instead, Oregonians passed laws that banned interracial marriage and required nonwhites to pay extra taxes. In 1870, they rejected the 15th Amendment, which protected the right to vote for all men, regardless of "race, color, or previous condition of servitude." White American settlers jealously guarded their agricultural paradise in Oregon.

Expanding into New Environments

In the 1840s and 1850s, that agricultural paradise centered on the Willamette Valley, where the landscape most easily accommodated the immigrants' efforts to create market-oriented, subsistence-based family farms. But even before Oregon joined the United States in 1859, new challenges and opportunities drew recent arrivals out into Oregon's diverse environments. One challenge was finding land: thanks to the generous provisions of the Donation Land Law, early White immigrants had gobbled up most of the good free land in the Willamette Valley, so new immigrants either paid premiums for a farm

there or were pushed out to unclaimed, less-ideal land elsewhere. New opportunities in Oregon's environments also pulled immigrants to other parts of the state. Discoveries of gold drew not only prospectors hoping for a quick strike, but also miners, traders and settlers who tried to turn temporary gold boom towns into permanent settlements. As American settlers and the federal government increased their pressure on Native peoples, especially after the Civil War, more land opened up in different parts of the state for different kinds of work, including ranching and logging. No matter where they went or how they tried to make a living, these Oregonians, like those who settled in the Willamette Valley, brought with them both anxiety about the environments they confronted and a desire to turn those challenges into opportunities.

Even before the Willamette Valley filled up, some American settlers headed to southwestern Oregon to farm or find faster ways to profit off the land. In 1846, a party led by Jesse and Lindsay Applegate blazed a new trail to the Willamette Valley that passed through southern Oregon, and a few years later, the Applegate party families moved south and settled in the Umpqua River Valley. Other farmers followed them there and later moved into other river valleys in southwestern Oregon, including the Rogue River area. Miners and traders soon joined them, first on their way to and from the gold fields of California, and then to make their own claims after the discovery of gold in the Rogue River Valley in 1851. Prospectors spread throughout southwestern Oregon, sifting, digging and blasting for gold from the broad coastal beaches to the smallest tributaries of the Rogue and Umpqua rivers. Many of the miners stayed after the boom years, establishing their own small farmsteads or continuing to squeeze ever-smaller amounts of gold out the streams and hillsides. Among these miners were Chinese migrants, who worked creeks and streams throughout southwest Oregon, ran merchant businesses, and established communities, such as Jacksonville's Chinatown. Southwestern Oregon landscapes also offered another source of riches: ancient forests full of timber, ready to be cut, processed and shipped off to California markets. By 1870, the lure of timber, gold and soil had drawn 15 percent of Oregon's population to southwestern Oregon.

American immigrants initially avoided eastern Oregon, where the climate and landscape challenged their agricultural pursuits. But gold, free land and ranching opportunities soon pulled American speculators and settlers east of the Cascades. Methodist missionaries established a station at The Dalles in 1838, and soon emigrants on the Oregon Trail were stopping there to rest before continuing on to the Willamette Valley, occasionally by way of the Barlow Road around Mount Hood. Some American settlers stayed in The Dalles, and the town developed into a small but important trading link between the west and east sides of the Cascades, much as it had

The Dalles on the Columbia River became an important transportation center on the Oregon Trail, as this mural detail in The Dalles by Don Crook depicts. (Oregon State Archives scenic photo)

been for the Native peoples of the Columbia Plateau and western valleys. The White population of eastern Oregon remained very small — only 3 percent of the state's Whites lived there in 1860 — until the discovery of gold in 1861 in the John Day and Powder River valleys. As in southwestern Oregon, thousands of prospectors followed the rumors of gold, scouring the hillsides and streambeds and establishing dozens of short-lived mining towns. The rush also contributed to the economic growth of The Dalles, Umatilla Landing, La Grande and other trading and shipping sites on the Columbia River and the surrounding valleys. That growth was shaped by a growing Chinese population of miners, merchants, physicians and more, who built thriving communities in John Day, The Dalles, Baker City and elsewhere in northeastern Oregon.

To serve the appetites of those miners and communities, another form of resource extraction developed: raising and grazing cattle and sheep, which thrived on the semi-arid lands east of the Cascades. Recent Willamette Valley settlers and their children looking for open lands and new economic opportunities led these initial ranching efforts, which continued even after the gold booms went bust. In a few pockets in eastern Oregon, including Harney Basin, some subsistence farming families established homesteads and adapted their agricultural practices to the higher altitude and drier climate. But the landscapes east of the Cascades presented a few too many challenges to White settlers, and the area remained sparsely populated, with just 14 percent of the state's White population in 1870.

As White settlers spread throughout the state, they redefined, remade, and, to some degree, overcame Oregon's environments. Americans drew the territory and state of Oregon with straight eastern and southern boundaries that recognized political interests rather than ecological reality. As they claimed land through the Donation Land Law and successive legislation, White settlers imprinted on

the landscape a peculiar patchwork of square and rectangular homesteads. Farmers eliminated some predators and raised imported plants and livestock that pushed out existing flora and fauna. Miners rearranged streams and dug into hillsides, loggers cut down trees and ranchers grazed cattle and sheep on native grasslands. Despite such changes, the new Oregonians recognized some limits to their efforts to overcome nature. They relied on manual and animal labor and used relatively simple tools, limiting the extent and intensity of ecological transformations. They depended on and remained vulnerable to seasonal cycles, hoping for enough rain to grow crops, but not so much as to flood them out of home and farm. Even political boundaries and land claims bent to the realities of nature: the Pacific Ocean and Columbia River bounded the state to the west and north, and environmental obstacles, such as rivers and mountains, often defined the practical limits of where farmers could plant crops. In short, the first generation of new Oregonians accepted the power of nature. Many of their children would have a different view of their relationship to Oregon's environments.

Section II: Confidence in Control of Oregon's Environments

Connecting Oregon

Transportation improvements provided the key not only to overcoming nature, but to controlling it. Oregon's environments presented a variety of transportation challenges, from the sheer size of the state to natural obstacles like rivers, mountains and canyons. These obstacles hindered the movement of people, ideas, goods and investment capital, slowing efforts to develop Oregon's environments. Roads offered the first and generally least-effective measure for overcoming these challenges. Backed by investors and state charters guaranteeing a monopoly, private toll road companies transformed old trails and rough wagon paths into "improved" roads made of dirt tracks, planks and bridges. Some companies failed; the Portland & Valley Plank Road Company, for example, went bust within two years. Others thrived, especially when they received federal and state land grants to sell or lease, supposedly to help pay for what they called "military wagon roads." In reality, speculators took most of the profits from the land grants, which totaled nearly 2.5 million acres, and farmers, not soldiers, primarily used the roads. That, after all, was the point: to move people, ideas, goods and capital more quickly throughout the state and accelerate the transformation of Oregon's environments into profitable natural resources. But these connections were unreliable, difficult and slow, as bridges collapsed, planks decayed, and rain turned dirt paths into impassable mud pits. Oregonians seeking to get their products to market looked beyond wagon roads for their transportation solutions.

Oregon's waterways offered faster and easier transportation options, especially as they became better understood and even managed. By 1851, steam-powered ships traveled up and down the Willamette and Columbia rivers and cruised along the Oregon coastline, delivering wheat, wood and other products to internal and external markets, especially in San Francisco. But water transportation could be difficult, unreliable and dangerous. When European and American ships began plying the Columbia River in the early nineteenth century, they relied heavily on the expertise of Native guides to find their way around the river's bars and other hazards. Throughout the 1800s, the U.S. government invested heavily in the safety and navigability of the Oregon coastline, building lighthouses and lifesaving stations and producing reliable charts of anchorages and safe passages into the Coos Bay estuary, Tillamook Bay, and other ports and rivers. Meanwhile, exploration and first-hand experience on the Columbia and Willamette rivers provided important information for shippers: the location of sandbars and other hazards, the routes through the rivers' deepest and safest passages, and the times of year when water ran high and fast enough to allow transportation.

But knowledge of natural waterways was not enough. To increase the reliability and speed of water transportation, Oregonians changed waterways by deepening bars at harbor entrances, rerouting streams into straighter and faster canals, and using dynamite and specially-designed boats to remove snags and trees from rivers. There were significant limits, though: river transportation depended on rainfall and snowmelt to keep water levels high enough for boats and ships, major falls like those at Oregon City and The Dalles remained impassable, and eastern Oregon offered essentially no water transportation options. Waterways, like wagon roads, could only move Oregonians so far and fast towards their goal of controlling nature.

Even as they built and maintained wagon roads and waterways, Oregonians eagerly anticipated the arrival of an even more powerful and transformative force: railroads. Railroads offered many promises to Oregonians eager to free themselves from the constraints of nature. While floods or low flow stopped water transportation on the Willamette River and other streams, and heavy rains washed out the Great Plank Road and other wagon roads, trains could run almost without regard to weather or season. Railroads could reach every corner of the state, including east of the Cascades where the lack of navigable waterways cut off farmers, ranchers, and other producers from markets. Most importantly, trains promised amazing speeds that seemed to smash through the natural barriers of time and distance. Within just a few years of statehood, railroads had spread through every region of Oregon: in 1862, the Oregon Steam Navigation Company built tracks along the Columbia River at the Cascades and Celilo Falls; the Oregon & California Railroad connected Portland to Eugene by 1871 and reached California in 1887; and in 1883, transcontinental train transportation came to Oregon via the Northern Pacific Railroad. As with wagon roads and water transportation, federal investment helped speed railroad construction: federal surveyors started exploring the best routes in the 1850s, and the federal government gave away millions of acres to railroad companies, including 3.7 million acres to the Oregon & California Railroad.

This Carleton Watkins photo shows a railroad train at Upper Cascades on the Columbia River in the 1860s. (Oregon State Archives photo)

By the end of the century, 1,850 miles of railroad track crisscrossed Oregon, utterly transforming the state's environments. This dramatic transformation was made possible by immigrants, first and most prominently from China, but also Greece, Italy, Japan and elsewhere. Construction crews built bridges across rivers and canyons and blasted away mountainsides to make room for railroad beds, ties and rails. Those wooden ties came by cutting and processing millions of trees from surrounding forests. Once built, the tracks allowed and encouraged Oregonians to accelerate environmental transformation: plant more wheat to send to distant markets, process more timber to transport on the railroads, and graze more cattle to herd towards rail shipping points. Trains carried not only the products of Oregon's environments, but also the increasingly efficient and expensive agricultural equipment, logging machinery, and other industrial tools used to transform nature. And, of course, the railroads carried people: old and new immigrants, including people of color, moving through and throughout the state in pursuit of a better life. Along with water transportation routes, which remained vitally important, railroads helped incorporate Oregon, connecting farmers, ranchers, miners and loggers to land, resources and markets.

Industrialization and Urbanization

Transportation revolutions in Oregon accelerated ongoing transformations of the state's environment. Oregon's farmers and ranchers expanded and intensified their tilling, planting, grazing and other productive efforts. West of the Cascades, plentiful water created a lush and fruitful environment, but it caused farmers plenty of problems, too. Abundant rain and overflowing streams soaked the soil and ruined crops, and farmers could not extend their fields into marshes, wetlands and commonly flooded areas. Although they could not control the water falling from the sky, farmers managed it once it hit the ground: they built protective dikes to restrain rivers and dug ditches and ran underground pipes to drain water from fields, creating more cultivable land planted with wheat and other crops for market. East of the Cascades on the Columbia Plateau, insufficient water meant fewer transportation options and the inability to grow the thirsty crops that thrived in the Willamette Valley. Railroads, financed and controlled by capitalists and managers in Eastern centers of capital, helped solve the first problem; farmers overcame the second by developing small-scale irrigation projects and by planting winter wheat, a hardier but still profitable crop. Farmers on the Columbia Plateau were soon growing more wheat than their competitors west of the Cascades. Southeastern Oregon was too remote and too dry for wheat, but cattle and sheep ranching grew and flourished on a massive scale. By 1900, more than 15,000 cattle and 400,000 sheep roamed Harney and Malheur counties. Again, railroads allowed and encouraged this expansion. The Central Pacific's shipping facility at Winnemucca, Nevada and the Union Pacific's tracks into eastern Oregon gave ranchers access to markets in San Francisco, Chicago and beyond.

As Oregon's fields and rangelands industrialized, so did its hillsides, forests, rivers and ocean. Equipped with new technology, often powered by steam, miners, loggers, fishers and manufacturers asserted more control over Oregon's environments and the wealth they contained. After the placer miners had taken all the "easy" gold from southern and eastern Oregon stream beds during the early mining booms, larger-scale operations took their place. Industrial miners, working for corporations overseen by external investors, dynamited their way into mountains and then used machines to crush and smelt precious mineral-bearing ore, or rechanneled streams and built high-pressure water cannons to wash away hillsides that were then sifted through for gold. Industrial technology and market forces increased timber production, too. Strong cross-cut saws replaced axes to fell trees, small railroads and "steam donkey" machines replaced real animals pulling logs out of forests, and steam-powered mills replaced water-powered mills to turn logs into marketable timber.

New technologies made logging and other industries more efficient in the years around 1900. (Oregon State Archives scenic photo)

Equipped with such technology, timber companies with headquarters in Minneapolis, San Francisco, the Puget Sound and elsewhere reached into previously inaccessible forests — stands of Douglas fir in the Nehalem Valley, for example, and Ponderosa pine in Klamath and Deschutes counties — and cut down as many trees as the market could handle. Oregon's rivers also became industrial sites for the harvesting and processing of salmon traveling to and from the Pacific Ocean. In the last quarter of the 1800s, fishers constructed a gauntlet of salmon harvesting technologies on the Columbia River: nets, traps, weirs, seines and fish wheels that took out hundreds of thousands of pounds of salmon. Oregon's salmon canning industry grew quickly, from 4,000 cases in 1866 to a high of 620,000 in 1884. The state took a variety of measures to conserve fish populations; for example, in 1898, the state legislature passed a law that regulated salmon fishing and encouraged salmon propagation through hatcheries and the removal of fish passage barriers. Such efforts sought to allay concerns about the potential exhaustion of natural resources that might result from the transformation of Oregon's rivers, forests, hillsides and fields.

The timber, ore, grains and fish coming out of Oregon's environments traveled on railroads and waterways toward Oregon's growing and increasingly diverse cities and towns. Portland quickly became Oregon's largest city and commercial hub, thanks to its location at the confluence of the

Willamette and Columbia rivers and its citizens' aggressive and successful efforts to attract railroads to the city. From a population of less than 3,000 in 1860, Portland grew into a metropolis of 90,426 by 1900. The state's financial power also centered on Portland, home to the state's first bank and its richest citizens. Other cities and towns developed along rivers and railroads during the 1800s, too, including Astoria (population 8,381 in 1900), Baker City (6,663), Pendleton (4,406), and Salem (4,258). In towns both big and small, Oregonians busily transformed the products of the state's environments. To serve markets near and far, a variety of manufacturing and processing industries developed, from flour and woolen mills to fish canneries and brick factories. Urban areas also offered many other commercial and retail services: printers, blacksmiths, bankers, launderers, bakers, carpenters, photographers and more, depending on the size and age of the town.

While power over these industries and enterprises rested in the hands of elites in Portland, San Francisco, New York, and other centers of capital, the actual transformation of environments came at the hands of old and new immigrants alike, drawn to natural resource extraction work in the countryside and commercial and manufacturing jobs in Oregon's cities. Oregonians of western European descent generally welcomed and quickly integrated other immigrants from the countries of their homeland, including the United Kingdom, Germany, and Scandinavian nations. Other immigrant groups remained more distinct and subject to exclusion. Groups of Chinese immigrants initially came to Oregon to work in and around mines and on railroads; later, they worked in fish canneries and in cities as launderers, gardeners, grocers and other service workers. Immigrants from Japan and southern and eastern Europe also arrived in the late 1800s, adding to the ethnic diversity of Oregon's towns, especially Portland. Portland was also home to most of Oregon's Black population, who worked for railroads and as domestic workers in hotels and the homes of the well-to-do. People of color and immigrants often faced severe discrimination; Chinese immigrants, for example, were forced to pay special taxes and were confronted by violent White rioters during the 1880s. These marginalized groups persevered through these challenges, and of the 413,536 inhabitants of Oregon counted by the 1900 census, 4.5 percent were listed as other than White, and 15.9 percent had been born outside of the United States. Transforming Oregon's environments, it turned out, required the hard work of people from all over the world.

Reforming Industrial Oregon

Some Oregonians worried about the effects of these transformations: the potential exhaustion of natural resources, the concentrated power of political and economic actors, community and social disruption, and more. They had a different vision for Oregon, and at the end of the 1800s and beginning of the 1900s, they tried to reform Oregon politics, government, society and environments. Many of these efforts originated among farmers and workers who experienced first-hand the transformation of Oregon's environments. Frustrated with high interest rates on bank loans, expensive shipping costs, and the low prices their crops got at market, farmers joined the Patrons of Husbandry — the Grange, established in 1873 — and local chapters of the Farmers' Alliance, an advocacy organization that appeared in Oregon in 1891. Laborers in Oregon's cities, forests, farms, mines and fisheries had their own frustrations, including low pay, poor and often dangerous working conditions and long hours. Beginning in 1880, White workers organized into chapters of the Knights of Labor, a union that advocated for better pay and working conditions, and also supported legislation and violence directed against Chinese workers. Entrenched political and economic interests stymied these reform organizations, and so these farmers and workers stepped into Oregon politics with the formation of the People's Party, or Populists, in 1892 and the Union Party in 1899. The People's Party quickly fragmented and disintegrated, but enthusiasm for reform continued and grew. In the 1910s, reformers secured a series of transformative laws, including the initiative and referendum process, direct election of senators, and the recall of elected officials. This package of reforms became known as the Oregon System — a set of political tools that put more power directly in the hands of the electorate.

During the first two decades of the 1900s, activists used the Oregon System to implement a variety of reforms. Voters approved initiatives that taxed telephone, telegraph and railroad companies, prohibited railroads from bribing public officials with free passes and regulated shipping rates. Oregon established a minimum wage, workers' compensation, an eight-hour work day for public works projects and maximum hours and other protections for women workers. Some reformers also tried to address broader social issues with anti-prostitution and gambling campaigns, and, most famously and controversially, the prohibition of alcohol by constitutional amendment in 1914. Women led the prohibition campaign and many other reform efforts that sought to improve their communities by encouraging safer, more sanitary and more healthy environments. Through the Woman's Christian Temperance Union, the Oregon Federation of Women's Clubs and other organizations, as well as individually, women reformers asserted a powerful role in public life. In contrast to the racism and nativism that sometimes paired with Progressive Era reform efforts, the movement for women's suffrage in Oregon relied on partnerships between White women and women of color in groups such as the Colored Women's Equal Suffrage Association. The struggle to secure the right of women to vote took decades, failing five times before finally succeeding by initiative in 1912, eight years before it passed nationally. Women's suffrage represented perhaps the most significant reform, while other ambitious and even radical efforts failed or quickly faded away. Despite long and intense efforts, advocates of the "single tax" — a 100 percent tax on the unearned value and profits on land — failed every time they went to the ballot. The Socialist Party of Oregon found limited but often enthusiastic support, especially in Portland and in southwestern Oregon; the citizens of Coquille, for example, elected a socialist mayor, although the party's statewide efforts had little success. Though not quite the radical transformation that some Oregonians wanted, reform efforts significantly changed Oregon society.

Oregon women march in the first national suffrage parade in Washington D.C. in 1913. (Courtesy of Library of Congress)

Oregonians also directed reform efforts toward the state's environments. Reformers believed that Oregon's forests, fisheries and other natural resources should be conserved and preserved for the public good, rather than exclusively possessed and exploited by private individuals and companies. The Oregon Land Fraud Trials (1904–1910) led to the prosecution of private speculators, government employees and elected officials who had abused homestead laws to illegally claim public land in Oregon and then sell it cheaply to timber and livestock companies. In 1911, the state legislature created the Oregon Board of Forestry and Department of Forestry, tasked with reducing forest fires, encouraging reforestation and enforcing other conservation measures. The federal government assisted reform efforts by setting aside land for preservation and conservation: it established Crater Lake National Park (1902) and Oregon Caves National Monument (1909), returned unsold Oregon & California Railroad land grants to the government (1914) and created millions of acres of national forest reserves. Reformers focused on Oregon's oceans and rivers, too, asserting open public access to the state's beaches (1913) and passing initiatives meant to conserve fish populations on the Rogue and Columbia Rivers.

Even as they slowed or stopped some transformations of Oregon's environments, reformers encouraged other "improvements." These changes were particularly visible on the Columbia River, where the Army Corps of Engineers completed the Cascade Locks in 1896 and Celilo Locks and Canal in 1916 to improve navigation and shipping. Reclamation projects — draining swampy land or irrigating dry land to "reclaim" it for farming — had an even greater effect in southern Oregon. Beginning in 1905, the federal Bureau of Reclamation built a complex system of dams, ditches, canals and other mechanisms that created more than 200,000 acres of farmland in the Klamath Basin while damaging the basin's wetland ecosystems. The Klamath Irrigation Project and Columbia River locks and canals set the stage for even more ambitious reconfigurations of river systems later in the century. These developments, coupled with successful reform efforts, reinforced the view that Oregonians could and should control the state's environments.

World War I and Reactionary Oregon

World War I turned Oregonians away from reform and back to more intense environmental transformations for the purposes of economic growth and war production. Heightened European demand for wheat and wood led to increased production in the fields and forests of Oregon. Airplane manufacturers wanted the light and strong wood of Sitka spruce trees, which grew especially well in coastal environments, including on lands that the U.S. government had removed from the Siletz and Grand Ronde Indian Reservations and sold to timber companies. To supplement private timber company production, the federal government in 1917 established the United States Spruce Production Division, which sent more than 7,500 soldiers into Oregon coastal forests to cut down spruce trees for the war effort. The war also brought changes to the ports of Astoria, Coos Bay, Tillamook and elsewhere on Oregon's coast and the Columbia River, as the federal government's Emergency Fleet Corporation contracted with a dozen shipyards to build wooden and steel ships. The increased demand for wartime material led to a shortage of labor, which briefly empowered workers and their unions. Timber workers in the Industrial Workers of the World (IWW) went on strike in the summer of 1917, demanding shorter hours, more pay and better working and living conditions. Timber companies refused, and the federal government stepped in, creating the Loyal Legion of Loggers and Lumbermen (the 4-L), an industry-wide, timber company-friendly union that prohibited strikes, demanded loyalty pledges and instituted eight-hour days and better conditions. The 4-L undermined support for the IWW while government officials, politicians, law enforcement and vigilante groups attacked union members and officials. Workers suffered further with the end of the war in

1918: the international market for wood and wheat contracted, economic growth slowed and more workers competed for fewer jobs. The economic boom was over, but wartime production left behind logging equipment, shipyards, agricultural machinery and other tools and infrastructure that soon would transform Oregon's environments again.

The Ku Klux Klan grew in power in Oregon in the aftermath of World War I. (Courtesy of Library of Congress)

The immediate postwar period in Oregon brought a reaction against progressive reform and expanded efforts by some Oregonians to marginalize and exclude others. By 1920, the momentum for reform had slowed. In the 10 years following World War I, Oregonians voted on 89 ballot measures, compared to 147 measures in the decade before the war. Some of those initiatives, along with a variety of other laws and actions, sought to more closely define which peoples and cultures did and did not belong in Oregon. In 1922, voters approved the Compulsory School Bill, which required all students to attend public schools — a direct attack on Catholic schools and Oregon's Catholic communities. The next year, the state legislature passed discriminatory laws that banned religious garb in schools (another assault on Catholic culture) and allowed city governments to deny business licenses to Japanese immigrants. The state legislature also passed a law prohibiting "aliens ineligible for citizenship" — especially Japanese immigrants — from purchasing or leasing land, an act that denied such immigrants equal participation and ownership in the agricultural transformation of Oregon's environments. A variety of organized groups and civic associations supported these exclusionary efforts, including the American Legion and, most infamously, the Ku Klux Klan, which became a powerful political and social force in Oregon beginning in 1921. Some of this reactionary tide was pulled back — the Supreme Court ruled the Compulsory School Bill unconstitutional in 1924, and the Oregon Klan disintegrated by the end of the decade — but these exclusionary efforts left a hateful mark on the state's history.

Discrimination also took more violent forms. The laws directed against Japanese Oregonians stayed in effect, and Japanese communities faced repeated harassment and violence, such as a 1925

incident in which a mob expelled Japanese workers from Toledo. Black Oregonians faced similar discrimination, including legal segregation, "sundown laws" that threatened them with violence if they remained in certain towns after dark, and real estate practices that restricted where they could live. Native Oregonians, too, were further marginalized. Native peoples were ineligible for American citizenship until 1924; Native children were forced into boarding and day schools that prohibited Native languages and dress; and Native peoples were prohibited from leaving reservations, which in western Oregon dramatically shrank in the aftermath of the Dawes Allotment Act of 1887, which allocated some reservation lands for ownership by tribal members, but sold most of the land as "surplus" to the highest bidder.

These Oregonians resisted such marginalization. Native Oregonians survived and thrived: some retained title to their lands and integrated into mainstream Oregon society, while others found ways to preserve their culture. Other peoples also protected their families and cultures by sustaining independent ethnic communities, such as Portland's three different Chinatowns or the Japanese schools that prospered in Salem, Hood River and elsewhere. Black communities thrived with independent civic organizations, churches, and businesses, and they advocated for equality through such means as the Advocate newspaper and the Portland National Association for the Advancement of Colored People (NAACP) — the first NAACP chapter west of the Mississippi River. Oregonians also made two symbolic yet important political steps toward equality: in 1926, they repealed the section of the state constitution that excluded Blacks from Oregon, and in 1927, they overturned the state constitution's prohibition of Black and Chinese suffrage.

By the late 1920s, Oregon had transformed in ways that could seem contradictory. Reformers had created the Oregon System and passed hundreds of initiatives and laws that sought to improve state society and environments. But those efforts only went so far. Many Oregonians rejected not only radicalism and reform, but also ethnic groups and communities that some White, Protestant Oregonians believed too foreign, strange, or unassimilable. Oregon's landscapes bore the marks of this exclusion, such as the limits on Japanese ownership of land. Environmental conservation efforts also revealed other contradictory characteristics of these reforms. For example, Oregon established its first state park in 1922 and Oregon's senior U.S. senator, Charles McNary, co-sponsored a federal act in 1924 that encouraged forest fire protection and reforestation. But McNary's bill also avoided federal regulation of private harvesting practices, leaving timber companies in Oregon essentially free to cut as much as they wanted wherever they wanted. And the state park system had its origins in the State Highway Commission, whose central purpose was to build more, better, faster roads that cut through forests and farmlands. For Oregonians in the 1920s, these did not seem like contradictions, but rather evidence that they could and should reform, improve and control Oregon's social and natural environments.

Confidence Amidst the Crises of Depression and World War II

Oregonians' confidence in and enthusiasm for control of nature continued even as the world crashed into economic catastrophe and global conflict. The Great Depression was particularly obvious and severe in Oregon's cities, with massive unemployment in manufacturing and the service industries and the appearance of "Hoovervilles" in Portland's Sullivan Gulch and the "Hotel de Minto," a shelter for young unemployed men on the top floor of Salem's city hall. The Depression hit rural areas, too, as prices, production and employment crashed in Oregon's forests, mills, farms, fisheries and ranches. In Mill City, for example, the A.B. Hammond Timber Company mills quickly cut back the work week to 20 hours, then 10 hours, and finally shut down operations in 1935. Oregonians showed remarkable resilience and confidence in the face of this economic catastrophe. In rural areas, they turned to Oregon's rich environments, relying on subsistence farming, fishing, hunting, and gathering and creating bartering economies that supported their communities. In towns and cities, municipal governments, civic organizations and other groups provided food and relief work for the unemployed. But the depth and severity of the Depression overwhelmed such noble efforts.

At the urgent demand of many Oregonians, the federal government stepped in with the New Deal, which provided relief, assistance, and action. The government encouraged workers to join unions and provided assistance to farmers through the Soil Conservation Service and the Rural Electrification Administration. Some federal programs were directed at Native peoples. The Indian Reorganization Act of 1934 halted the allotment of reservation land, provided credit opportunities and funds for the purchase of additional lands, and provided a path toward federally-recognized self-government and economic development, like that followed by the Warm Springs tribes, which incorporated as the Confederated Tribes of the Warm Springs Reservation in 1937. Native Oregonians also participated in federal work programs including the Civilian Conservation Corps (CCC), the Works Progress Administration (WPA) and the Public Works Administration (PWA). These and many other agencies provided paychecks and left a permanent mark on Oregon's society and landscape. The CCC built trails, fire lookouts, warming shelters and more in Oregon's forests; the WPA constructed Timberline Lodge on Mount Hood, hired artists and writers for cultural projects and created other employment opportunities; and the PWA built parks, schools, and government buildings,

constructed bridges connecting Highway 101 on the coast and added other infrastructure throughout the state. Some of these federal projects radically changed Oregon's environments, especially Bonneville Dam, funded by the PWA and built by the Army Corps of Engineers between 1933 and 1938. Bonneville Dam created a 48-mile-long reservoir on the Columbia River, improved navigation, and generated electricity, but it also damaged salmon habitats. Water projects bloomed during the New Deal: the Bureau of Reclamation completed the Vale-Owhyee Project in the mid-1930s, creating more than 24,000 acres of irrigable farmland by the end of the decade, and federal studies of the Columbia River and its tributaries promised more river development for irrigation, hydropower, flood control and more. These studies, projects and programs represented an optimistic confidence that by transforming and controlling nature, Oregonians could overcome any obstacle, even the Great Depression.

The Isaac Lee Patterson Bridge over the Rogue River at Gold Beach is one of several coastal bridges built during the 1930s. (Oregon State Archives scenic photo)

The Depression was eclipsed by the even greater cataclysm of World War II, which ended the economic catastrophe and impacted Oregonians in a variety of ways. More than 2,800 Oregonians died and 5,000 were wounded in the line of duty, and six people died when a balloon bomb floated over the Pacific Ocean from Japan and exploded in Bly in May 1945. The U.S. military built training camps and facilities throughout the state, including Camp Adair north of Corvallis, Camp White near Medford and Camp Abbott (which later became the resort village of Sunriver). Oregonians rationed food and fuel, staffed lookouts to protect forest resources, bought war bonds, saved and recycled metal and rubber and mobilized into civilian defense and air patrol units. They also worked long hours producing war materiel in existing factories, like the Thomas Kay Woolen Mill in Salem that ran three shifts to make Army blankets, and in brand-new facilities, including the Kaiser shipyards in Portland, which produced 455 ships and employed tens of thousands of workers during the war.

The war presented both opportunities and challenges to women and minorities in Oregon. The Bracero program brought more than 15,000 Mexican contract laborers to Oregon to plant, weed and harvest crops. Although they generally received better wages than in Mexico, Bracero workers faced racism, poor working and living conditions, and broken promises that they would be paid when they returned home. Thousands of Blacks came to work in Portland, where they found discrimination and an acute housing crisis. These problems were only partially alleviated by the rapid construction of Vanport, which provided homes, schools, nurseries and other services to 35,000 residents, 35 percent of whom were Black, and all of whom lived directly in the path of the Columbia River, which flooded and destroyed the city in 1948. Women also found work at the Kaiser shipyards, the Kay Woolen Mill and other manufacturers supplying the war effort. Despite persistent sexual harassment and unequal treatment — at the end of the war, they were the first to be fired — women proved the value of their work to themselves and to others.

Oregonians of Japanese descent endured particularly tragic discrimination during World War II. Beginning in April 1942, Japanese Oregonians — both immigrants who were prohibited by federal law from American citizenship as well as their children, who were birthright citizens of the United States — were forcibly evacuated from their homes in Portland, Hood River and throughout western Oregon, crowded into unsanitary transfer facilities, and sent to concentration camps in California, Idaho and Tule Lake, just across the southern Oregon border in California. At the same time, hundreds of Japanese Oregonians enlisted and served in the armed forces. When the camps closed and the war ended in 1945, Japanese Oregonians found themselves unwelcomed in their former homes, and many decided they could not return. But almost 70 percent did go back, because they — like Latino and Latinas, Blacks, women and everyone who had helped Oregon prosper during the war — rightfully called Oregon home.

All Oregonians lived and worked in landscapes that had radically transformed in just a few decades. A single generation had seen wagon trails turned into railroads, animal power replaced by mechanized farm equipment, rivers dammed and rerouted, deserts irrigated, swamps drained, and astonishing quantities of lumber, food crops, livestock, fish and minerals produced from Oregon's environments. Forests, fields, rangelands and waterways had industrialized, and Oregon more generally urbanized: in 1870, more than 90 percent of Oregonians lived in rural areas, but by 1930, the numbers of urban and rural residents were about equal. Oregonians knew that such transformations could have negative effects, but they were confident they could minimize such consequences through reform and management. For example, in 1941, the state legislature passed the Oregon Forest Conservation Act, which required commercial logging operations to leave enough trees standing and/or plant new trees to maintain forest growth. Such efforts seemed to show Oregonians that not only could they overcome natural obstacles, but they could control and eliminate those obstacles. The end of economic depression and the war unleashed this confidence, and Oregonians found new and dramatic ways to assert control over nature. But such efforts, they soon learned, also had dramatic consequences.

Section III: Pursuing Growth and Sustainability

Postwar Boom

Although confident that they could and should control Oregon's environments, Oregonians also were anxious that the years after World War II might bring a return to the Great Depression or some other calamity. Just the opposite, it turned out: Oregon's population and economy, like the rest of the nation, boomed. In 1940, the federal census counted 1,089,684 people in Oregon; by 1960, 1,768,687 people called Oregon home. Between 1945 and 1965, Oregon's per capita income more than doubled and Oregonians cashed in their paychecks, war bonds and savings to buy cars, radios, refrigerators, washing machines, and, most importantly, houses. Real estate developers and home builders went on a construction spree, expanding cities, towns, and suburbs. Eugene, for instance, added 4,717 acres between 1950 and 1960, and Corvallis grew by more than 3,000 acres in that same decade. An increasingly dense network of roads and highways, including Interstate 5, connected these places and facilitated economic growth.

The smooth asphalt freeways and freshly-painted housing developments suggested that all Oregonians shared in and enthusiastically embraced this growth. But this appearance of consensus was forced upon some Native Oregonians through a process called tribal termination, by which the federal government sought to eliminate its trusteeship of Native lands and force the assimilation of Native peoples. Beginning in 1953, the U.S. Congress passed a series of laws that effectively ended federal recognition of tribal sovereignty and terminated the federal government's responsibility to oversee and protect the lands, resources and interests of the Klamath and all Native groups west of the Cascades (the Warm Springs and Umatilla Reservations successfully prevented termination). The laws brought disastrous results: reservation lands were sold off, private speculators swindled Natives out of their land and property, Natives lost all services (such as health and education) formerly provided by the federal government, tribal governments disbanded, and Native communities scattered. The problems with termination suggested tension and trouble under the surface of Oregon's postwar growth and confidence.

The Dalles Dam on the Columbia River is one of many projects intended to harness the power of Oregon rivers in the postwar era. (Oregon State Archives scenic photo)

Pursuing broader economic growth and inspired by new technologies, Oregonians expanded and intensified their efforts to master Oregon's rivers, fields and forests in the two decades after World War II. The U.S. Army Corps of Engineers, Bureau of Reclamation, and local utility companies built dozens of dams, from massive structures like the 260-foot-high concrete The Dalles Dam on the Columbia to smaller projects like the 78-foot-high earthen fill Keene Creek Dam on the Rogue River. Oregon's farmers, chambers of commerce and civic groups cheered these river development projects, which promised flood control, improved navigation, inexpensive electricity, pollution mitigation, recreational opportunities and irrigation. While irrigation allowed farmers to control the timing, quantity and distribution of water in their fields, new chemical herbicides helped them manage weeds, and powerful insecticides effectively eliminated — for a short time — grasshoppers and other pests. These technologies, along with field burning, fertilizers, new tractors and combines and other investments, produced impressive results: for example, between 1945 and 1965, Oregon yields of field crops (barley, corn, hay, hops, oats, peas, rye, sugar beets and wheat) increased by 65 percent and production grew by 50 percent. Oregon timber production also increased: from 6,046 million board-feet in 1945 to 9,394 million board-feet 20 years later. Chainsaws, diesel-powered tractors and trucks and improved mill technology and processes facilitated this leap in production, as independent loggers and timber companies large and small supplied local, national, and international lumber markets. While technology increased efficiency, increased production also required the labor of tens of thousands of workers in forests, fields and pastures. In 1959, the U.S. Census of Agriculture counted 16,332 hired farm workers in Oregon, more than half of whom worked as seasonal labor.

These efforts to master nature produced worrisome consequences for both Oregon's environments and its peoples. As the growth in timber production began to exhaust the supply of timber on private lands, logging shifted to federal Forest Service and Bureau of Land Management public lands. Old growth forests were to be "converted" into tree farms and accessed by thousands of miles of logging roads; a 1956 forestry report called for nearly 15,000 miles of new access roads in Oregon's national forests. Such practices produced unsightly landscapes, upset complex ancient forest ecosystems and damaged fish habitat in streams and rivers. On Oregon's rivers, dams blocked salmon migrating to and from the Pacific Ocean, and fish hatcheries, fish ladders and other technical solutions only partially mitigated the loss in salmon populations. Dams slowed and warmed rivers — another problem for salmon — and inundated some communities and fishing sites with water; the most infamous example is Celilo Falls, drowned by The Dalles Dam in 1957.

Changes in Oregon's agricultural landscapes revealed other problematic consequences — political and cultural, as well as environmental — from the transformations of the post-war period. While farm production and yields increased, the state's agricultural character underwent a fundamental shift: by 1970, only 5 percent of Oregonians were farmers, as more people moved to Oregon's towns and cities for work. This change was particularly obvious west of the Cascades and especially in the Willamette Valley, which lost 20 percent of its farmland to residential, commercial and industrial development between 1950 and 1965. Such development gobbled up farmland and other open spaces, overwhelmed sewer and water systems, and polluted Oregon's water and soil with sewage and industrial contaminants. Changes to farming also raised concerns in the 1960s about the efficacy and safety of pesticides, herbicides and other chemicals that had been used to increase agricultural production. Moreover, these shifts in Oregon's economic and demographic character revealed increasing concentration in the Willamette Valley not just of Oregon's population, but also political and economic power. Oregon's urban and rural environments were undergoing a remarkable transformation, and not always for the best.

The Oregon Story and Other Narratives

These problems attracted the attention of a growing number of Oregonians, including some in positions of power, who supported a series of innovative and landmark environmental protection initiatives. Pollution was a particularly visible problem on the Willamette River, where industrial pollutants, sewage, and other contaminants led to unsafe water quality, especially during drier months. During the 1960s and 1970s, the Oregon State Sanitary Authority and its successor, the Department of Environmental Quality (established in 1969), strengthened and enforced efforts to limit pollution from Willamette River cities and industries, especially pulp and paper mills. By 1972, all municipalities and all but one pulp and paper mill met pollution treatment requirements. The state also sought to reduce other kinds of waste and encourage conservation: the "Bottle Bill" of 1971 established a deposit and return system for beverage containers; the "Bicycle Bill" (also 1971) required jurisdictions building roads, streets, or highways to also include facilities for bicycles and pedestrians; and state agencies, as well as some private businesses, implemented a variety of energy conservation measures.

Other environmental protection efforts of the time sought to preserve open spaces for public enjoyment and recreation. In 1967, the "Beach Bill" established that all of Oregon's beaches, from the water to the dunes, were open to the public and were not for private ownership and development, expanding and strengthening existing protections established in 1913. Six years later, Oregon established a groundbreaking statewide land-use planning system that required all cities and counties to create zoning ordinance and long-range land-use plans. These plans established urban growth boundaries to regulate sprawl and set goals in 19 areas, including energy conservation, preservation of agricultural and forest lands, and air, water and land resource quality. Taken together, these and other environmental protection initiatives represented what then-Governor Tom McCall called "The Oregon Story": a belief that Oregonians should take innovative action to improve the quality of life in their state.

A 1973 statewide land use planning system law aimed to regulate sprawl and protect farmland, such as in the Willamette Valley. (Oregon State Archives scenic photo)

Other Oregon Stories also were being written during the 1960s and 1970s, as minorities, women and other marginalized groups continued to assert their power and equality. The ongoing women's rights movement secured significant political victories, including the state legislature's vote to ratify the federal Equal Rights Amendment, the election of the first woman to statewide office (Norma Paulus, elected Secretary of State in 1977), and

state legislation that prohibited discrimination against women in employment and retirement, removed marital status or cohabitation as a defense against rape, and more. Blacks in Oregon had achieved important political victories in the two decades after World War II, including state laws prohibiting discrimination in housing, employment and public accommodations. That political work continued through the following decades, along with protests, community organization and activism in groups like the Black United Front. Such activism confronted school segregation, police brutality, and other persistent forms of discrimination, including issues of environmental justice. Black Oregonians resisted "urban renewal" projects that destroyed Black homes and businesses, and they fought back against disproportionate levels of pollution in Black communities – for example, the high loads of toxins in Portland's Columbia Slough, a waterway generally neglected by Oregon environmentalists focused on more "natural" rivers and streams.

Native Oregonians, too, fought back against discrimination and marginalization through activist groups, in tribal communities, and individually. East of the Cascades, the Warm Springs tribes developed successful timber operations and the Kah-Nee-Ta Resort, and the Burns Paiute Tribe secured federal recognition and reservation lands in 1972. Over the next two decades, the terminated tribes west of the Cascades successfully campaigned to restore federal recognition of tribal sovereignty: Siletz (1977), Cow Creek (1982), Grand Ronde (1983), Coos, Lower Umpqua, and Siuslaw (1984), Klamath (1986), and Coquille (1989). Latino communities in Oregon continued to grow, developing a variety of cultural, educational, and political organizations, including Pro Fiestas Mexicanas, the Valley Migrant League, and Colegio César Chávez. By 1980, 5.4 percent of Oregon's population was nonwhite, compared to 1.2 percent 40 years earlier. Through political activism, community organization and evolving cultural heritage, these communities contributed their own narratives to an increasingly diverse Oregon Story.

Much of that Oregon Story was being written in, by, and for the urban residents of the Willamette Valley, the center of the state's political and economic power. But the narrative looked different in rural parts of Oregon. While urban areas grew and diversified, the rural population of the state remained relatively homogenous: only 20 percent of the Oregon's nonwhite population in 1980 lived in rural areas. The Willamette Valley's enthusiasm for environmental protection certainly affected rural Oregon communities, but those communities expressed far less enthusiasm for such regulations. Timber production remained vitally important, providing not only jobs in the woods and in the mills, but also revenue from federal timber sales to pay for schools and other public services. Although Oregon passed a comprehensive Forest Practices Act in 1971 that sought to protect soil, air, water and wildlife on both public and private land, the timber industry, state and federal regulatory agencies, and politicians alike continued to support the lucrative practice of clearcutting old growth forests. Land use planning found strong opposition in rural communities east of the Cascades and in southern Oregon. Voters in timber-dependent and ranching communities supported initiatives in 1976, 1978 and 1983 that would have rolled back Oregon's comprehensive land use planning laws, but they were outnumbered by Willamette Valley opponents to the initiatives. By the 1980s, rural and urban Oregonians often were deeply divided over the meaning of The Oregon Story.

The Gaps Widen

In the 1980s and 1990s, the divisions among Oregonians seemed to widen, including differences in perceptions and uses of Oregon's environments. The divisions became most obvious in fights over Oregon's old growth forests. An economic recession in the early 1980s, coupled with the introduction of labor-saving computerized technology, led to mill closures and layoffs; in 1982, forest work employed 20 percent fewer people than just 10 years before. Some of those jobs returned in the mid-1980s as the economy improved, demand for timber increased, and logging on federal lands, especially in old growth forests, jumped to record levels. This raised worries among some scientists and others concerned about the loss of wildlife and old growth forests. The controversy crystalized around the northern spotted owl, whose population serves as an indicator for the ecological health and complexity of the old growth forests where it lives. In 1990, the owl was listed as a threatened species under the 1973 Endangered Species Act, requiring action to protect the owl and its habitat. Four years later, the federal government adopted the Northwest Forest Plan, which significantly reduced logging on federal lands. The management plan contributed to ongoing job loss in the timber industry, where the workforce already was shrinking due to logging and milling technology.

Oregonians also saw more conflicts over dams, irrigation projects, and other river development schemes that negatively affected fish habitat. In the 1990s, a variety of salmon populations were designated as threatened or endangered, leading to more regulations on fishing, hydroelectric power generation, and irrigation, and affecting the management of the Columbia and other Oregon rivers. In the news media and often on the ground, it appeared that such measures pitted rural Oregonians, whose communities depended on farming, logging and other forms of natural resource extraction, against urban Oregonians, who generally supported efforts to preserve the state's environments for wildlife and recreation.

Divisions among Oregonians became even more pronounced around other transformations in Oregon society. As it had throughout its history, Oregon

attracted new immigrants from different backgrounds, and the state's population continued to diversify, with 7 percent of Oregonians identifying as nonwhite in the 1990 census, compared to 5.4 percent 10 years before. Minorities in Oregon achieved important measures of progress in the 1980s and 1990s, from the election of the first Blacks to the state legislature and statewide offices to the establishment of Pineros y Campesinos Unidos del Noroeste (PCUN), a Latino forest- and farm-worker union. But minority populations continued to experience discrimination, marginalization and even hatred. Racist skinhead groups developed in some Oregon communities, including Portland, where a skinhead murdered Ethiopian exchange student Mulugeta Seraw in 1988. Skinheads also murdered two Salem residents in an apartment firebombing in 1992: Hattie Mae Cohens, a 29-year-old Black lesbian, and Brian Mock, a 45-year-old gay man.

These murders occurred within the context of a conservative backlash against the gay and lesbian rights' movement, which had secured notable victories in the 1970s and 1980s, including limited anti-discrimination laws in Portland (1974), Eugene (1977), and at the state level (1987). Some Oregonians opposed such developments and presented voters with anti-gay rights ballot measures: in 1988, voters repealed the state's efforts to prohibit discrimination against gays in state employment, but in 1992, 1994 and 2000, Oregonians rejected ballot measures that sought to restrict civil rights protection based on sexual orientation and, more generally, discourage homosexuality. Most of the opposition to these initiatives came from urban areas, while more voters in rural Oregon supported them and passed local anti-gay rights ordinances. The state legislature and court system overturned these city and county measures — another example, some rural Oregonians said, of the increasing cultural and political chasm between the urban Willamette Valley and the rest of the state.

Oregonians also divided over public spending, taxes, and economic differences more generally in the 1980s and 1990s. Following a national trend that started in the late 1970s and continued into the 1980s, a fiscally-conservative anti-tax movement developed in Oregon that focused especially on cutting property taxes. Such taxes supported schools, social services and state programs directed at the conservation of Oregon's environments, but many Oregonians regarded their contribution as too onerous, especially in Portland, where property values and taxes had increased rapidly in the 1980s. By 1989, Oregon property taxes were the 7th highest per capita in the United States. In 1990, voters approved Measure 5, an initiative that constitutionally limited property taxes; seven years later, voters approved Measure 50, which capped annual increases on property taxes. Together, these initiatives decreased how much of their personal income Oregonians paid to state and local taxes (from 12.1 percent in 1989 to 10.5 percent in 1999) and shifted the burden for paying for schools from local property taxes to the state general fund, which relied more and more on income taxes. Oregon voters also overwhelmingly defeated sales tax initiatives in 1985, 1986 and 1993, leaving the state dependent on income taxes to fund education, environmental conservation and preservation programs and other government functions.

Those taxes came from vastly different income levels that largely fell along an urban/rural divide. The historic concentration of wealth in the Willamette Valley was well established by 1970, when the Portland area had the highest median income level, while the seven counties with the lowest levels were located outside the Valley. That division remained firmly in place 30 years later: Washington, Clackamas and Yamhill counties had the three highest median income levels, while Wheeler, Lake and Curry counties had the three lowest. At the end of the 20th century, it seemed that Oregon's people were as divided in economic, political and cultural issues as they were in their perceptions and uses of Oregon's environments.

Bridges and Divides

Those differences in income levels reflected deeper changes to Oregon's economy, which increasingly shifted away from logging, farming, ranching and other ways of working directly in Oregon's environments. By the end of the 20th century, the technology industry was booming in Washington County and a few other spots in the state, collectively called the "Silicon Forest." Some of these companies were homegrown, such as Electro Scientific Industries and Tektronix in the Portland area and Entek International in Lebanon. But Oregon's technology sector really took off with the arrival of out-of-state businesses, including Hewlett-Packard and Intel in 1976 to Corvallis and Portland, respectively. The Silicon Forest grew as other companies such as Japan's Fujitsu and Epson arrived in Oregon and smaller companies spun off from Intel, Tektronix and other established businesses. By 2005, nearly 20 percent of Oregon's economy came from the technology sector. Reflecting the shift from environmental extraction to environmental recreation, a thriving sportswear industry also developed in Oregon, building on the legacy of Jantzen (established 1916), Columbia (1937) and Nike (1984), as well as Germany-based Adidas. These companies maintained corporate offices and design departments (but not manufacturing facilities) in the Portland area. The Great Recession of 2008 slowed this economic growth — unemployment almost hit 12 percent in April 2009 — but the economic transformations continued, as many other technology, service and consumer-oriented businesses moved to the state and especially to Portland, which grew in national and international popularity as a fashionable place to work, live and play.

The large Nike campus in Beaverton anchors Oregon's thriving sportswear industry in the Portland area. (Oregon State Archives scenic photo)

In many ways, Oregon's environments made such growth possible: cheap and abundant water and electricity attracted technology firms, and Oregon's reputation as a mecca for outdoor recreation drew many other businesses and workers. Building on this reputation as a "Pacific Wonderland" — a license plate slogan originally used in 1959 and reissued in 2010 — Oregon's tourism industry grew dramatically at the end of the 20th and beginning of the 21st century. In 2003, the state legislature created the Oregon Tourism Commission, also known as Travel Oregon, to advertise the state to the nation and world: from adventure-based activities such as mountain biking and windsurfing to more easily accessible car camping at state parks and motorized boating on reservoirs created by river development projects. Other tourist attractions included Oregon's flourishing wine and craft beer industries, whale-watching and other activities at the Oregon Coast, and shopping, including the Woodburn Premium Outlets, which became a top tourist destination. The growth of tourism represented not only a significant shift in Oregon's economy, but also in the way that Oregonians perceived and interacted with their environments.

The tourism industry included the state's casinos, all owned by Oregon tribes — which, like other minorities and women, continued to assert their power and equality in the state's economy, politics and society. Following the passage of the federal Indian Gaming Regulatory Act in 1988, all nine federally-recognized tribes in Oregon built casinos, beginning with Seven Feathers Hotel and Casino Resort, owned by the Cow Creek Band of Umpqua Tribe of Indians. While paling in comparison to the revenue generated by the state-run Oregon Lottery system, these casinos not only brought tourists and their dollars to the state, but also created employment for local economies, provided funds for charitable work, contributed funds for road and highway improvements and generated revenue and services, including health and educational programs. Such transformations contributed to ongoing efforts to preserve and cultivate Native culture, society, and governance, and the 2010 census counted more than 53,000 American Indians and Alaska Natives in Oregon.

Other minority populations in Oregon also grew: nonwhites accounted for 12 percent of Oregon's population in 2010, nearly double the percentage of just 20 years before. With a population of more than 450,000 in 2010, Latinx made up the largest minority population in Oregon and played an increasingly important role in state culture and politics. In 1997, Susan Castillo became the first Latina to serve in the state legislature; five years later, she became Oregon superintendent of schools, the first Latina elected to a statewide office. Castillo joined other Oregon women winning important elected offices: Barbara Roberts served as governor from 1991–95, Ellen Rosenblum became the state's first female attorney general in 2002, and in 2015, Kate Brown became the state's second female governor and the first openly bisexual governor in the nation. Brown's ascendancy to the governorship represented in some ways the success of the gay and lesbian rights movement. In 2004, Oregon voters approved Measure 36, which defined marriage as a union between man and woman. But in 2007, the state legislature passed bills permitting same-sex couples to adopt children and prohibiting discrimination based on sexual orientation and gender identity. Measure 36 was reversed in 2015, when the U.S. Supreme Court ruled that bans on same-sex marriage were unconstitutional. Despite this victory for lesbian, gay, bisexual, transgender and queer and/or questioning (LGBTQ) people, minorities and women continued to face discrimination and prejudice in 21st century Oregon. The forces of gentrification in increasingly hip and expensive Portland, as well as neighborhoods in other Oregon cities, priced many Blacks out of their homes, and a vigorous effort in 2020 for racial justice during the Black Lives Matter movement met with a more vigorous police and federal law enforcement response, as well as disdain from some rural residents who imagined lawlessness and anarchy in Oregon's largest city.

While the state's demographics changed, Oregonians continued to grapple with the fundamental question of how they ought to interact with Oregon's environments. Even with the growth of technology, tourism and other newer sectors of Oregon's economy, many Oregonians still made their living working directly with Oregon's fields and forests. In 2015, nearly 35,000 Oregon farms and ranches occupied about 16 million acres and produced more than $5 billion in agricultural products, from the cattle, hay and wheat often grown east of the Cascades to the more specialized products of western Oregon, including filberts, hops, grass seed, landscaping plants, berries, grapes for wine and much more. Although timber production did not reach the historic high levels of the 1960s and 1970s, logging continued and even stabilized to some degree, averaging 4,250 million board-feet between 2000 and 2015, with a notable drop to 2,748 million board-feet in 2009 during the Great Recession. At the same time, the push to preserve and protect Oregon's environments also continued, driven by the state's reputation as environmentally-friendly, urban Oregonians' desire to recreate in non-urban settings, and, for some people, a deeper sense of the intrinsic value of nature. These different ways of interacting with Oregon's environments produced plenty of tension at the beginning of the 21st century. A particularly heated conflict erupted in the Klamath Basin in 2001, when the Bureau of Reclamation shut off Klamath project irrigation water in an effort to save endangered Coho salmon and two species of sucker fish valued by the Klamath Tribes. This led to a series of public and dangerous confrontations between farmers, federal officials, environmentalists, and tribal members. But the confrontations eventually gave way to conversations and, by 2010, an agreement was made not only to share the Klamath River's water, but also to remove four older dams to help restore fish habitat. Although the potential for conflict remained, much of the heat of the confrontation dissipated as Oregonians from diverse backgrounds tried to reconcile their different views of Oregon's environments.

The Potential for Conflict and Pragmatic Compromise

At the dawn of the 21st century, wolves returned to Oregon, sparking conversations that revealed both change and continuity in the complex relationships between Oregon's peoples and Oregon's environments. When settlers gathered at the Wolf Meetings of 1843, they created a proto-government to issue bounties on wolves and other predators, a century-long effort that eliminated grey wolves from Oregon by the mid-1940s. When wolves reappeared in northeastern Oregon in 1999, 25 years after being listed as an endangered species, they inspired a different set of responses. Oregon environmentalists rejoiced in the wolves' return, embracing the animals as a symbol of wildness and pointing to the role played by predators in the landscapes of northeastern Oregon — concepts that would have been totally foreign to the settlers who gathered at the Wolf Meetings of 1843. In contrast, cattle ranchers saw wolves as predators that destroyed valuable livestock, echoing the arguments of the Wolf Meetings. But by the 21st century, there were no serious suggestions to exterminate wolves. Instead, the Oregon Fish and Wildlife Commission created the Oregon Wolf Conservation and Management Plan (adopted in 2005; revised in 2010; updated in 2019) with the objective of both protecting livestock and recovering a "self-sustaining population" of grey wolves. Town hall meetings, legislative and court hearings, and other public fora about the wolf plan generated plenty of controversy and conflict, particularly when the Commission removed wolves from the state's endangered species list in 2016. Nevertheless, both environmentalists and ranchers insisted on the need for cooperation as they discussed new approaches to the 150-year-old question of wolves and their place in Oregon.

A rustic old barn on the Birdseye Ranch in Jackson County near the Rogue River. The ranch was founded in 1853. (Oregon State Archives scenic photo)

Such conversations and openness to cooperation will be crucial as Oregonians continue to face complex challenges in the 21st century. Economic, social, and cultural differences between rural and urban communities will continue to divide Oregonians on a variety of political issues, from tax policy, public services, and racial justice to land use planning and environmental regulations. Demographic changes will accelerate, producing even more diverse communities that will enrich the state and challenge Oregon's legacy of homogeneity. Climate change will produce unprecedented environmental transformations in every corner of the state, including rising sea levels, decreased snowpack, unpredictable precipitation, intense droughts and storms, more wildfires and floods, and a host of other dangers. These challenges surely will prompt conflict, as Oregonians confront their different and evolving ways of interacting with their environments. But such challenges will also prompt conversations that may lead to pragmatic compromise and cooperation — an important and defining characteristic of the history of Oregon's people and environments.

Further Reading

This brief survey cannot adequately address the many people, events, themes and analytical approaches that make up Oregon's history. Readers are encouraged to explore the books and websites listed below, which represent only a sampling of recent scholarship that has inspired this essay and which continues to expand and deepen as Oregon's history evolves.

Barber, Katrine. *Death of Celilo Falls*. Seattle: University of Washington Press, 2005.

Beckham, Stephen Dow. *Oregon Indians: Voices from Two Centuries*. Corvallis: Oregon State University Press, 2006.

Berg, Laura, ed. *The First Oregonians*. Portland: Oregon Council for the Humanities, 2007.

Boag, Peter. *Same-Sex Affairs: Constructing and Controlling Homosexuality in the Pacific Northwest*. Berkeley: University of California Press, 2003.

Cox, Thomas. *The Other Oregon: People, Environment, and History East of the Cascades*. Corvallis: Oregon State University Press, 2019.

Eisenberg, Ellen. *Embracing a Western Identity: Jewish Oregonians, 1849-1950*. Corvallis: Oregon State University Press, 2015.

Gamboa, Erasmo and Carolyn M. Buan, eds. Nosotros: *The Hispanic People of Oregon: Essays and Recollections*. Portland: Oregon Council for the Humanities, 1995.

Jensen, Kimberly. *Oregon's Doctor to the World: Esther Pohl Lovejoy and a Life in Activism*. Seattle: University of Washington Press, 2012.

Jetté, Melinda Marie. *At the Hearth of the Crossed Races: A French-Indian Community in Nineteenth-Century Oregon, 1812-1859*. Corvallis: Oregon State University Press, 2015.

"Oregon Women's History Consortium." http://www.oregonwomenshistory.org/.

Peterson del Mar, David. *Oregon's Promise: An Interpretive History*. Corvallis: Oregon State University Press, 2003.

Robbins, William G. *Landscapes of Conflict: The Oregon Story, 1940-2000*. Seattle: University of Washington Press, 2004.

— — —. Oregon: *This Storied Land*. Portland: Oregon Historical Society Press, 2005.

Robbins, William G. Landscapes of Promise: The Oregon Story, 1800-1940. Seattle: University of Washington Press, 1999.

Tamura, Linda. *The Hood River Issei: An Oral History of Japanese Settlers in Oregon's Hood River Valley*. Urbana: University of Illinois Press, 1993.

Taylor, Joseph E. *Persistent Callings: Seasons of Work and Identity on the Oregon Coast*. Corvallis: Oregon State University Press, 2019.

"The Oregon Encyclopedia." https://oregonencyclopedia.org/.

Whaley, Gray H. *Oregon and the Collapse of Illahee: U.S. Empire and the Transformation of an Indigenous World, 1792-1859*. Chapel Hill: University of North Carolina Press, 2010.

ACT OF CONGRESS ADMITTING OREGON INTO THE UNION

Preamble

Whereas the people of Oregon have framed, ratified and adopted a constitution of state government which is republican in form, and in conformity with the Constitution of the United States and have applied for admission into the Union on an equal footing with the other states; therefore —

1. Admission of State—Boundaries

That Oregon be, and she is hereby, received into the Union on an equal footing with the other states in all respects whatever, with the following boundaries: In order that the boundaries of the state may be known and established, it is hereby ordained and declared that the State of Oregon shall be bounded as follows, to wit: Beginning one marine league at sea, due west from the point where the forty-second parallel of north latitude intersects the same, thence northerly, at the same distance from the line of the coast lying west and opposite the state, including all islands within the jurisdiction of the United States, to a point due west and opposite the middle of the north ship channel of the Columbia River; thence easterly, to and up the middle channel of said river, and, where it is divided by islands, up the middle and widest channel thereof, to a point near Fort Walla Walla, where the forty-sixth parallel of north latitude crosses said river, thence east, on said parallel, to the middle of the main channel of the Shoshone or Snake River; thence up the middle of the main channel of said river, to the mouth of the Owyhee River; thence due south, to the parallel of latitude forty-two degrees north; thence west, along said parallel, to the place of beginning, including jurisdiction in civil and criminal cases upon the Columbia River and Snake River, concurrently with states and territories of which those rivers form a boundary in common with this state.

2. Concurrent Jurisdiction on Columbia & Other Rivers—Navigable Waters to be Common Highways

The said State of Oregon shall have concurrent jurisdiction on the Columbia and all other rivers and waters bordering on the said State of Oregon, so far as the same shall form a common boundary to said state, and any other state or states now or hereafter to be formed or bounded by the same; and said rivers and waters, and all the navigable waters of said state, shall be common highways and forever free, as well as to the inhabitants of said state as to all other citizens of the United States, without any tax, duty & impost, or toll thereof.

3. Representation in Congress

Until the next census and apportionment of representatives, the State of Oregon shall be entitled to one representative in the Congress of the United States.

4. Propositions Submitted to People of State

The following propositions be and the same are hereby offered to the said people of Oregon for their free acceptance or rejection, which, if accepted, shall be obligatory on the United States and upon the said State of Oregon, to wit:

School Lands

First, that sections numbered sixteen and thirty-six in every township of public lands in said state, and where either of said sections, or any part thereof, has been sold or otherwise disposed of, other lands equivalent thereto, and as contiguous as may be, shall be granted to said state for the use of schools.

University Lands

Second, the seventy-two sections of land shall be set apart and reserved for the use and support of a state university, to be selected by the Governor of said state, subject to the approval of the Commissioner of the General Land Office, and to be appropriated and applied in such manner as the legislature of said state may prescribe for the purpose aforesaid, but for no other purpose.

Lands For Public Buildings

Third, that ten entire sections of land, to be selected by the Governor of said state, in legal subdivisions, shall be granted to said state for the purpose of completing the public buildings, or for the erection of others at the seat of government, under the direction of the legislature thereof.

Salt Springs & Contiguous Lands

Fourth, that all salt springs within said state, not exceeding twelve in number, with six sections of land adjoining, or as contiguous as may be to each, shall be granted to said state for its use, the same to be selected by the Governor thereof within one year after the admission of said state, and when so selected, to be used or disposed of on such terms, conditions and regulations as the legislature shall direct; provided, that no salt spring or land, the right whereof is now vested in any individual or individuals, or which may be hereafter confirmed or adjudged to any individual or individuals, shall by this article be granted to said state.

Percentage on Land Sales

Fifth, that 5 per centum of the net proceeds of sales of all public lands lying within said state which shall be sold by Congress after the admission of said state into the Union, after deducting all the expenses incident to the same, shall be paid to said state, for the purpose of making public roads and internal improvements, as the legislature shall direct; provided, that the foregoing propositions, hereinbefore offered, are on the condition that the people of Oregon shall provide by an ordinance, irrevocable without the consent of the United States, that said state shall never interfere with the primary disposal of the soil within the same by the United States, or with any regulations Congress may find necessary for securing the title in said soil to bona fide purchasers thereof; and that in no case shall nonresident proprietors be taxed higher than residents.

Conditions on Which Propositions Are Offered

Sixth, and that the state shall never tax the lands or the property of the United States in said state; provided, however, that in case any of the lands herein granted to the State of Oregon have heretofore been confirmed to the Territory of Oregon for the purposes specified in this act, the amount so confirmed shall be deducted from the quantity specified in this act.

5. Residue of Territory

Until Congress shall otherwise direct, the residue of the Territory of Oregon shall be and is hereby incorporated into and made a part of the Territory of Washington.

Approved February 14, 1859. Proposition of Congress accepted by the Legislative Assembly of the State of Oregon on June 3, 1859.

MONUMENTAL PLACES: NATIONAL MONUMENTS IN THE CULTURE AND HERITAGE OF OREGON'S TRIBES

Written by Douglas Deur

Newberry, John Day, Cascade-Siskiyou and Oregon Caves: all of Oregon's national monuments hold special significance to Native American tribes. Among the state's most distinctive, beautiful and resource-rich landscapes, these places have stood apart, inspiring people across generations. In the high mountains of Oregon's southwest and in high deserts east of the Cascades, these have long been places to live, harvest, pray and celebrate among Oregon's tribal communities.

Newberry National Volcanic Monument is a place of exceptionally ancient significance. Over 10,000 years ago, this was the site of village settlements and camps, as well as important hunting grounds. Across time, the spring waters that bubbled to the surface here, and the lakes of Newberry Crater—Paulina and East Lake—sustained residents and visitors alike. Yet, this landscape stood apart for other reasons as this was among the Northwest's most important places to quarry obsidian, which occasionally erupted from the ground, flowed downslope and hardened into ridges of glassy black rock stretching across the volcanic landscape. Reflecting this remarkable antiquity of human use, tribal oral tradition speaks of the place as a center of settlement and obsidian gathering since the beginning of remembered time. Archaeologists also attest to the depth of human connections to this place, uncovering settlements and quarries buried below deep ash from Mount Mazama, which erupted and collapsed some 7,700 years ago to form Crater Lake.

Some of Newberry's obsidian flows long predated human settlement while others emerged anew during eruptions witnessed by tribal ancestors. In the oral traditions handed down across generations, these obsidian deposits are described as a gift from the Creator, delivered for the benefit of humanity. From Newberry obsidian, traditional craftspeople fashioned arrowheads, spears, scrapers, knives and tools for many other purposes. Each flow had distinct properties. In one place, people might find simple black obsidian of remarkable strength, useful for constructing arrowheads, spearheads and other tools for hunting game. Said to "crave blood," the ancestors treated this kind of rock with caution and respect. In other places, less durable obsidian, marked with vivid colors or patterns, could be fashioned into items for ceremonial and ornamental use. Each flow was known and visited in turn, depending on the need. At one time, trails radiated out in every direction from these deposits like spokes of a wheel, marked by the debris from ancient traders and toolmakers who occasionally chipped away at the stone as they traveled. In turn, these trails intersected with major trade routes that ran north-south along the approximate route of today's Highway 97, connecting the people of south and central Oregon with the major fishing stations and trade centers on the Columbia—at Celilo Falls and The Dalles—where this obsidian was in high demand.

As settlers and the U.S. military entered central Oregon in the mid-19th century, the landscape took on additional layers of significance. The Paiute band led by Chief Paulina, for example, visited this spiritually-potent place and used it as a hideout while resisting relocation to the Klamath Reservation in the 1860s. By the time central Oregon's "Indian wars" were over a decade later, the people who lived near Newberry had been relocated to the Klamath Reservation, the nearby Warm Springs Reservation and other tribal reservations and communities such as Burns Paiute east of the Cascades. The Monument remains significant to these tribes today—and to many others across the region, reflecting the celebrated significance of Newberry Crater obsidian. Certain tribes still visit, occasionally gathering obsidian for use by tribal youth in summertime "culture camps" that teach obsidian toolmaking and other traditional crafts of enduring cultural significance.

More so than in other Oregon monuments, **John Day Fossil Beds National Monument** was an everyday home to many people. Today's Monument has three distinct units: the famously fossil-rich Sheep Rock and Clarno Units and the spectacularly scenic Painted Hills. Each of these places was well known to the Native people long before contact, especially the Umatilla, Northern Paiute, Tenino, Cayuse and other tribes whose traditional lands converged in the John Day Basin. Their settlements and camps once lined the John Day River and its fish-bearing tributaries that wend through and alongside the Monument's lands. Semi-subterranean houses were home to entire extended families here, while camps, located at seasonal harvest sites featured small structures walled with mats—woven from plants such as cattail or tule and placed over frames of wood. Major landmarks throughout the John Day Basin have long served as focal points of oral traditions and keystone cultural teachings. Place names of the area, recalled by modern tribal elders—Ákakpa—"Canada goose place," Xúlxuli—"[place with] small fish/trout," Íišnima—"river with cow parsnip"—still allow us to hear the words

The layers seen at the John Day Fossil Beds National Monument Painted Hills Unit offer spectacular views and clues to our past. (Oregon State Archives scenic photo)

of the ancestors and appreciate what they saw and valued while living and traveling on the land. Amidst the rugged geology of the John Day Basin are stone quarries, places for gathering pigments, and many spiritual places. Picture Gorge, along the John Day River, is named for pictographs protected within the Monument and remains significant to tribal members today.

Each year, the harvest of food followed familiar patterns. In spring, families living in and near the Monument traveled to rich patches of biscuitroot (Lomatium spp.) and other plant foods, which they harvested, dried and stockpiled for later use. By May, the salmon arrived, bringing intensive harvests—as well as social gatherings at fishing stations. Along the John Day River and its tributaries, residents could fish for salmon, steelhead and lamprey, as well as trout and other freshwater fish. With spears, natural fiber nets, woven fish traps and piled rock dams, residents fished together while their families processed and preserved fish on the adjacent banks—each community showing their respect for the fish through annual "first fish" ceremonies and by myriad other means.

The lands in and around the Monument have been celebrated as good elk hunting territory, and by late spring, some traditionally traveled to the hills around the monument to hunt elk and mule deer. Even buffalo and bighorn sheep could be hunted nearby. Then there are pronghorn antelope. Oregon's pronghorns can reach astonishing speeds, over 55 miles per hour, the posted speed limit for most of the state's highways. This is perhaps the legacy of countless generations outpacing fast-running predators like the American cheetah that are now gone, seen only in fossil form below the ground. Undeterred, the pronghorn still run at highway speeds. Native hunters devised ways to catch such fast-moving game—building blinds or chutes of stone, or ambushing the pronghorn during their relatively slow and inelegant river crossings. While men especially hunted, women continued to focus on plant food harvests—digging camas in moist meadows, for example, during hunts. Especially in late summer, some families have traditionally traveled into nearby mountains for huckleberry gathering and other harvests linked to unique montane habitats–including biscuitroot, bitterroot, wild carrot and chokecherries, as well as beaver and other small game. As people travel through this landscape, they also gather medicinal plants; plants for tool use such as juniper, prized for crafting bows, digging sticks and other tools; or plants such as willow for use in baskets and many other traditional tools and crafts. With each harvest, the elders have advised that people show thanks, honor each species harvested, and take other steps to ensure abundance into future times. Honoring the obligations between humankind and the plants and animals of this land—enhancing some species, showing restraint in the harvest of others – traditional resource managers ensured the wellbeing of future generations of each, far into the imaginable future. When horses arrived in the generations leading up to direct Euro-American contact, the tribes living near the monument gained newfound mobility—with families from much larger constellations of villages able to gather at John Day fishing stations, to make more expansive treks into the mountains, and to travel for social, subsistence and ceremonial events far away.

A series of 19th century treaties sought to open these lands to non-Native settlers and to remove the Native people of the John Day Basin to distant reservations. The lands encompassing John Day Fossil Beds were lost under the terms of the Warm Springs treaty, and many living near the Monument moved to that reservation in time; others found their way to the Umatilla and short-lived Malheur Reservations to the east, and a small number joined Paiute kin in the Klamath Reservation to the south. Mining districts, large ranches and non-Native settlements soon reoccupied many places of traditional significance. In spite of their forced displacement, many families held on—still returning to lands near the Monument to sustain seasonal camps for hunting and other purposes on traditional resource lands, a practice that continued into recent times. And tribes continue to reconnect and show their respect for these places in other ways: Warm Springs has acquired lands near the Monument for economic purposes, for example, as well as the active restoration of plants, fish, animals, and the protection of culturally important places. Elders from Umatilla and other tribes also hold rich oral traditions of this special place and work to sustain the lands and resources of this part of their traditional homeland.

Many tribes' traditional lands have also converged in the mountainous lands now managed as part of the **Cascade-Siskiyou National Monument**, near the crest of Oregon's southern Cascade Range. Shastas, Takelmas and Klamaths have considered parts of the Monument home, though the lands also sit within close proximity to other tribes of the Rogue and Klamath Basins who often visited this part of the Cascade crest. For most, this was a place visited seasonally. As these mountains are much cooler than the lowlands, people living in the valleys traditionally ascended into the mountains as snow retreated and summer approached; in lands now managed as part of Cascade-Siskiyou, families held seasonal camps and relied on the many mountain streams for water (only much later would some of these streams be dammed, creating present-day reservoirs). These communities knew when to begin their annual ascent into the mountains by

Cascade Siskiyou's incredible biodiversity provides a home to plant and animal species not normally seen in such close proximity. (Oregon State Archives scenic photo)

observing the seasonal choreographies of plants, animals, and even insects in the lowlands, and by tracking the snowline's gradual ascent up to the mountaintops. They traveled along major trails, linking various places in the mountains with the large lowland settlements of the Bear Creek Valley (modern Ashland-Medford), the middle Klamath River of California and the upper Klamath Basin near modern-day Klamath Falls. As they traveled in these mountains, they encountered special sites visited for social but also ceremonial purposes, their significance elevated further by occasional views of distant peaks—such as Mount Shasta or Crater Lake—that hold central significance in Native oral traditions.

The remarkable botanical diversity that led to the creation of Cascade-Siskiyou National Monument in 2000 was deeply important to these tribes as well, and a major motivation for their annual trek. The mountains contain hundreds of species with known traditional uses—some utilized while people

camped on site and others brought to the lowlands for later use. Acorns from Oregon, white and California black oaks, carefully processed to leach their tannins, could be formed into edible meals, soups, breads and other foods. Pines in these mountains have edible inner "cambium" bark—used in times of scarcity, but also considered a delicacy in its own right. Saps from these trees can be used in medicine, gum, sealants and for many other purposes. In some places, the ancestors found sugar pine (Pinus lambertiana), the world's tallest pine with the world's longest cones. As with other pines, the seeds of sugar pine are gathered, sometimes by knocking them to the ground with long poles, and eaten. Edible berries abound: manzanita berries, gooseberries, chokecherries, serviceberries, huckleberries, elderberries, thimbleberries, wild blackberries and many others could be harvested in this place. Tarweed and grasses provide edible seeds. Edible greens abound, as do many showy flowers with edible bulbs such as camas, brodiaeas, fawn lilies, fritillaries and wild onions that are traditionally harvested in these mountains too. Tribes also traditionally gather basketry materials in these mountains, which contain a remarkable variety of sedges and rushes, and special plants such as beargrass (Xerophyllum tenax), a species used to produce the white ornamentation on most traditional Oregon baskets. Here and there, in damp places, tribal harvesters found the yellow pond lily—the seeds being roasted and consumed as a staple by some area tribes (people have also harvested insects, such as grasshoppers, crickets and yellow jacket larvae where they could be found). Tribal ancestors managed the productivity of these plant habitats in many ways—especially through the use of fire, which also opened meadows for hunting deer and other species, served to keep trails and campsites open, and reduced the risk of catastrophic forest fires. Traces of their traditional management can still be seen there, inscribed on the land.

Much the same can be said of **Oregon Caves National Monument**, which sits on a high mountain ridge only 30 miles to the west of Cascade-Siskiyou. Many tribes, Athabaskan communities such as the Dakubetede, Takelmas and even Shastas and Karuks from the middle Klamath River—have traditional lands intersecting in these high mountains. Here, the forest is somewhat wetter than Cascade-Siskiyou, with dense conifer forests of Douglas fir and other species, the highest lands dotted by montane meadows and rocky ridgetops. The astonishing botanical diversity of southwest Oregon's high mountain ridges extends to this Monument too, the area abounding in plants used for food, medicines and materials, and for all manner of other cultural and spiritual purposes. Small camas prairies and patches of beargrass are found in these high mountains, apparently sustained and tended over generations—the camas producing edible bulbs that, when roasted, contributed to the diet even during extended stays in the high country. In drier scrub forests downslope, acorn-bearing oaks were once abundant on the forest-meadow margin, with acorn grinding stones still hidden alongside long-standing harvesting sites.

The mountains are more jagged here, with deep river and stream valleys below. Historically, trails crisscrossed these mountains, often following ridgelines to avoid the deeply-dissected terrain. They are echoed somewhat by modern park trails. Precontact trails linked the densely-settled valleys, but also led to major sites in the mountains: berry patches, places for harvesting basket materials, hunting sites and camas meadows. As one modern elder asserts "almost everything you needed was along that trail." So too, traditional spiritual practitioners have ascended these trails, viewing culturally-significant peaks in the distance and showing respect to the terrain and its many inhabitants as they go.

The tribes traditionally held gatherings in the valleys far below, often at settlements near falls and fishing riffles. Taking place in these settlements were large dances, uniting people far and wide to trade, visit, carry out ceremonies, fish and feast. At these events, young people met those they would marry from other tribes and villages—families intentionally marrying their young people into other communities, helping to sustain social, economic and strategic ties across this mountainous and culturally variegated corner of the state. People from the Klamath River might travel through the mountains near Oregon Caves to visit tribes in the Illinois and Applegate River Basins – carrying dentalium money shells, tobacco grown in small cultivated plots, or pine nut beads, for example, to trade for camas, acorns and many other goods with local tribes. As they traveled through these montane trails, people often camped in places where they could find protection from the wind and sun of the high country, often visiting springs issuing cold water even in the hottest times of the year.

Among the tribes of the state, caves hold many kinds of significance: as places to seek temporary shelter, to pray, to store or chill foods, to hunt and to do many other things. Tribal oral traditions speak of elaborate caves on the mountain ridges near Oregon Caves, though they reveal little of what the ancestors knew of them. Some note the presence of caves linked to networks even more elaborate than scientists recognize. Common narratives of the "discovery" of these caves by non-Native settler Elijah Davidson in 1874 ring hollow, as the cave Davidson encountered already contained subtle but unambiguous evidence of Native use. Every part of the southwestern Oregon landscape was traveled and known intimately across countless generations, and Oregon Caves was no exception.

The peoples of both Cascade-Siskiyou and Oregon Caves shared similar fates in the 19th century. Soon after the California Gold Rush, miners streamed into the valleys and by the early 1850s, the region was awash in bloodshed. United States forces and militias sought to relocate, contain, or exterminate many of these communities as part of what became known as the "Rogue Indian Wars." The tribes of the area, unified by marriage, trade and other alliances came to aid one another, but were doomed by the seemingly limitless population and resources of U.S. forces. Many retreated into California or the Upper Klamath Basin to hide among other tribes, though most were taken by force to Oregon's Coast Reservation—later becoming part of the confederated tribes of Siletz and Grand Ronde. Some families instead persisted as part of the Cow Creek, Klamath, Shasta, Karuk and other tribal communities. In spite of many obstacles, some tribal families have returned to these two

The historic Oregon Caves Chateau was built in the 1930s and is now a national landmark. It's undergoing extensive renovation and is expected to reopen for the 2024-2025 season. (Oregon State Archives scenic photo)

Monuments—sustaining or often rediscovering relationships their ancestors have long held with these lands.

Newberry, John Day, Cascade-Siskiyou and Oregon Caves: all these places are still known and valued by Oregon's tribes—even by tribes beyond the borders of our state. Many tribal members still visit these places, wishing to see the landscape as the ancestors once saw it, with many sustaining oral traditions and practices that ensure the culture is kept alive, passing place-based knowledge from older to younger members of the tribes. Since the mid-19th century and often into present day, access to these places has been a challenge for tribal members. And while treaties protect traditional resource harvests in some places, in others no protections exist. Still, today tribes and the managers of these monuments have active conversations. They continue to work out longstanding problems and to discuss the long-term future of these special places, both parties wishing to protect these places for the benefit of future generations. The sites are still in some important ways "tribal lands," though they are now part of a shared heritage linking Native and non-Native peoples. Do visit. Make these places part of your own personal geography. Yet, tribal elders ask: please show the deepest respect. For these are lands that have been respected and visited for countless generations before us. Every

History

part of these Monuments' natural landscape is eminently worthy of respect. The care of the lands now falls into the hands of our present generation, including both Native and non-Native peoples. Soon enough, we all must hand them on to the next generation, intact, along with the knowledge and concern to preserve them. In a fundamental way, these Monuments and the knowledge of how to care for them, is part of our shared inheritance as Oregonians.

Professor Douglas Deur is an associate research professor of anthropology at Portland State University and an adjunct professor of environmental studies at the University of Victoria. Dr. Deur holds advanced degrees in both geography and anthropology, and his writings are frequently coauthored with Native American scholars and elders.

A BRIEF ACCOUNT OF A LONG GEOLOGIC HISTORY IN OREGON'S FOUR NATIONAL MONUMENTS

Written by Jason D. McClaughrey

Introduction

Geology is a historical science that describes the evolution of the three-dimensional Earth with the addition of a fourth dimension: time. The approximately 4.6-billion-year natural history of Earth is told by geologists, who unravel a complex past through careful observation and study of clues written into the rock record. These clues urge geologists to ask questions about "how?", "why?" and "when?". The answers and hypotheses they develop from such questions help bring long-vanished landscapes and environments back into view. They add context to the nature of both the Earth's slow incremental changes as well as of its major catastrophes.

Thomas Condon, a 19th century minister and Oregon's first State Geologist, held that "In prying apart the stone layers of the rocks the scientist is in reality opening the leaves of the past history of our world, and that in these buried leaves of sand stone and mud deposits of seas and lakes of former ages, he is uncovering not only the real shells and bones of the life of the period, but even the ripple marks of the water that once covered them." But what is the critical importance of seeking answers about our geologic past? Like Thomas Condon, it is now widely understood that the dynamic nature of the geologic past and present is the key to our future. These keys unlock more accurate predictions of what lies ahead so we might become more resilient to future geologic change.

Oregon is a land of natural geologic wonder, with a rock history verified back some 400 million years. The rocks tell a story of a region shaped by long-lived plate tectonic interactions between the western edge of the North American Plate and the plates that underlie the ancestral and modern Pacific Ocean. Dynamic processes of plate-to-plate collisions, interaction with a mantle plume, volcanic activity, earthquakes, faulting and folding, erosion, and sedimentation have all contributed to the formation of Oregon's familiar landscapes. Landscapes in the Klamath Mountains, Coast Range, Willamette Valley, Columbia River Gorge, Cascade Range, Blue Mountains, High Lava Plains, Basin and Range, and Owyhee Uplands all provide an account of Oregon's long geologic history. How did these landscapes come to be as we see them now?

Newberry National Volcanic Monument is home to Paulina Lake and East Lake. Each offers recreational opportunities for anglers, picnickers, hikers and campers. (Oregon State Archives scenic photo)

Oregon's National Monuments

National monuments celebrate and protect parts of our collective human and natural history. They focus on areas that commemorate a prehistoric or historic event, honor an individual or group of people, or preserve a site that has exceptional public or scientific interest. National monuments can be created in two different ways as defined by the Antiquities Act of 1906, either by Presidential Proclamation or by an act of Congress. One-hundred twenty-nine national monuments have been designated for protection in the United States. The first in 1906 and the most recent in 2021.

Oregon has four national monuments, including Newberry National Volcanic Monument, John Day Fossil Beds National Monument, Oregon Caves National Monument and Preserve, and Cascade-Siskiyou National Monument. They were designated as national monuments primarily because of their importance to our geologic, natural, and cultural heritage. All contain a rich history of geologic features whose scientific importance overlaps with the cultural, ecological, educational, aesthetic, and recreational values of the State of Oregon.

Newberry National Volcanic Monument

Newberry National Volcanic Monument is in Deschutes County near Bend in central Oregon, 40 miles east of the Cascade Range crest. The monument boundary includes 54,822 acres of lava flows, cinder cones and lakes between the Deschutes River and Newberry Volcano. Congress designated the unique volcanic landscape in the Deschutes National Forest as a national monument in 1990, to preserve and protect Newberry's remarkable geologic landforms, plant and animal communities, scenery and opportunities for recreation.

Managed by the Deschutes National Forest, Newberry National Volcanic Monument provides visitors with opportunities to explore an active volcano and wander through part of the vast lava lands of central Oregon. High ground located atop volcanic vents offer stunning panoramic views of the Cascade Range, the High Desert and Newberry Volcano itself. The Lava Lands visitor center at Lava Butte showcases and explains the features that make Newberry National Volcanic Monument unique. Over sixty miles of hiking trails wind through the monument, ranging from short roadside interpretive paths to the 21-mile Crater Rim trail.

The central focus of the monument is Newberry Volcano, named in honor of Dr. John S. Newberry, a naturalist attached to a mid-19th century U.S. Army expeditionary force. Newberry Volcano is a broad shield of basaltic lava flows, with early activity dating back about 400,000 years. It is the largest volcano in the Cascade Range. The main volcano covers an area of 500 square miles. More far-reaching lava flows expand the volcanic footprint to 1,150 square miles. Newberry Volcano rises about 0.5 miles above the surrounding terrain and encompasses a 4- by 5-mile-wide summit caldera. Paulina Peak, at an elevation of 7,984 feet, is the highest point on the caldera rim; it formed as a rhyolite lava flow about 83,000 years ago. Between 300,000 and 75,000 years ago, major explosive eruptions at Newberry Volcano generated several large, hot flows of ash and rock. Subsequent collapse of eruptive vents such as the one for Newberry produced the modern summit caldera, whose crest was from 500 to 1,000 feet higher than present-day Paulina Peak.

The most recent volcanic activity at Newberry Volcano is concentrated within the summit caldera and along its northwest rift zone, reaching from the volcano summit northwest to the Deschutes River. More than 400 cinder cones, spatter cones, fissure vents and lava flows dot the flanks of Newberry Volcano and the northwest rift zone. These volcanoes grew and died in the last 12,000 years, with at least 12 lava flows erupting within the northwest rift zone as late as 7,000 years ago. The largest of these lava flows came from Lava Butte along U.S. Highway 97. As this lava flowed downslope to the Deschutes River, it pushed the river channel west to its present location. The floor of Newberry caldera is filled with many volcanic features erupted in the last 7,700 years, including obsidian lava flows and tuff or pumice cones. The youngest lava within the national monument is the Big Obsidian Flow, which was erupted within the caldera about 1,300 years ago. The caldera itself is partially filled by Paulina and East lakes; features separated from one another by the Central Pumice Cone.

John Day Fossil Beds National Monument

John Day Fossil Beds National Monument is in Wheeler and Grant Counties in north-central Oregon, at the western end of the Blue Mountains. Established by Congress in 1974, the monument covers 14,062 acres. It is managed by the National Park Service and is arranged into three administrative units: Clarno, Painted Hills and Sheep Rock. These units were each set aside to protect one of the world's most complete, diverse and well-preserved fossil records of Cenozoic land-based plants and animals. The fossils, combined with their relative stratigraphic positions within many well-dated volcanic units, offer a rare opportunity to unravel a very precise history of regional volcanic activity, changing landscapes, climate fluctuations, and evolving plant and animal life.

Rocks and fossils found in the John Day Basin have been the focus of geologic investigations for 160 years, starting with those led by Dr. Thomas Condon. Visitors to the John Day Fossil Beds National Monument today experience a journey through time, where the rocks and fossils provide details about how life evolved in this area over the past 45 million years. The monument challenges visitors to imagine the landscape of eastern Oregon as it was millions of years ago, when palm trees grew, sheep-like oreodonts and rhinos roamed, and volcanic eruptions periodically devastated the landscape and its ecosystems. Much of this story is told through detailed exhibits, educational programs, and ongoing scientific research at the Thomas Condon Paleontology Center in the Sheep Rock unit. The natural marvels of the park can also be experienced simply by taking a walk. By doing so visitors will find evidence of 45-to 7-million-year-old landscapes shaped and reshaped by volcanic activity and climatic fluctuations. From oldest to youngest, this history is preserved within the rocks of the Clarno and John Day formations, Columbia River Basalt and the Mascall and Rattlesnake formations. All units of the monument have short and easy interpretive trails to more challenging adventures that pass by fossil-rich areas or allow access to multicolored hillsides, castle-like cliffs and deep canyons.

The time between 45 and 25 million years ago, when the Clarno and John Day formations were deposited, corresponds with a time when volcanic fields expanded across the Blue Mountains. Within these volcanic fields, broad shield volcanoes, smaller domes and dome fields, and larger eruptive centers such as the 40-milion-year-old Wildcat Mountain, 32-milion-year-old Tower Mountain, and 29.5-milion-year-old Crooked River calderas grew. The great volumes of volcanic ash erupted from the calderas sped along in hot ash clouds that hugged the landscape or fell as ash-falls that blanketed the terrain. One of these is the 28.7-million-year-old Picture Gorge ash flow that likely erupted from the Crooked River caldera. The remnant of this ash flow now forms prominent ledges that are a distinctive part of the John Day Formation in the monument. Located between and draining these volcanic fields, were broad basins that accumulated lava flows, volcanic mudflows, thick layers of ash, and stream, lake, and marsh deposits of the Clarno and John Day formations. Fossils within the John Day Fossil Beds are often preserved in fine-grained sedimentary rocks produced from the weathering and erosion of volcanic materials.

Ash-derived sediment within the Clarno and John Day formations locally entombed and spectacularly preserved an array of ancient soils and now-extinct animals and plants as fossils. Many fossils have been found in the approximately 29-million-year-old Turtle Cove Member of the John Day Formation. Fossils found of now-extinct mammals include fragments of mouse-deer, sheep-like oreodonts, rhinoceros, and giant, hog-like entelodonts. Together, these soils and fossils indicate a very wet subtropical greenhouse-like climate between 45 and 33 million years ago. Fossil evidence after 33 million years ago indicates there was a dramatic shift in climate to cooler and drier conditions. Wooded areas became like today's eastern United States. Deciduous forests grew in the lowlands and coniferous forests grew at higher elevations.

Starting around 17 million years ago the relatively fluid lava flows of the Picture Gorge Basalt flooded the older volcanic landscape developed on the Clarno and John Day formations. These lava flows are part of the Columbia River Basalt Group and erupted from a series of fissures east of Sheep Rock. South of Sheep Rock, the Picture Gorge Basalt is buried by ash-rich sedimentary rocks and tuff of the Mascall and Rattlesnake formations. Between 16 and 13 million years ago fine-grained tuff, siltstone and ancient soils of the Mascall Formation accumulated in low-gradient rivers, lakes and marshes. Volcanic ash erupted at this time from several volcanic sources across southeast Oregon, including the Castle Rock and Ironside Mountain calderas. Ancient soils and an array of plant and

animal fossils in the Mascall Formation suggest a humid and temperate climate with open grasslands and forested areas. Mastodons, horses, camels, rabbits, burrowing ground squirrels, and gophers roamed these areas. The Rattlesnake Formation is the youngest geologic unit in the monument, including sedimentary rocks deposited in river and alluvial fan environments. It also includes the 7-million-year-old Rattlesnake Tuff, a large ash flow erupted from a caldera near Burns in southeast Oregon.

Oregon Caves National Monument and Preserve

Oregon Caves National Monument and Preserve is an often-overlooked jewel located southeast of Cave Junction in Josephine County. It is within the Rogue River-Siskiyou National Forest and managed by the National Park Service. The Oregon Caves and a surrounding area of about 484 acres were originally recognized and designated as a national monument by Presidential executive order in 1909. A complex geology, rich biodiversity and one of only a few large marble caves in the Pacific Northwest combine to make this place of national scientific and public significance. A 4,070-acre national preserve was added to the monument in 2014 by Congress. The preserve protects the surrounding watershed that supports the caves, as well as old-growth mixed coniferous and deciduous forests.

Rocks of the Rattlesnake terrane, now part of the Siskiyou Mountains, were formed well offshore 200 million years ago as volcanic seamounts and seafloors. Limestones were likely reefs that formed next to the volcanic seamounts. The collection of rocks that hosts the limestone in the Rattlesnake Creek terrane is believed by many geologists to represent the remains of ancient submarine landslides or may have formed through faulting within a subduction zone as the terrane formed together and grew. All these features merged and were ultimately attached to western Oregon as plates underlying the Pacific Ocean collided with the North American Plate. About 160 million years ago, molten material of the Grayback pluton pushed into rocks of the Rattlesnake Creek terrane. The combination of the terrane coming together around 170 million years ago and intrusion of the Grayback pluton about 160 million years ago changed the limestone to marble.

Oregon Caves began to form only about 1.7 million years ago when marble was near the surface and fractures formed in the rock. The caves grew as rainwater fell on the mountainous forests, percolated down through fractures and the marble was dissolved by slightly acidic groundwater. This dissolution created the large underground passageways and rooms while the bedrock was beneath the water table. Oregon Caves contains a variety of cave formations which grow from the cave ceiling, walls, or floor as calcite minerals precipitate from water seeping through fractures. Calcite builds up over time to form cave formations like floor-rooted stalagmites and ceiling-hanging stalactites. The oldest of these cave formations, a flowstone from Neptune's Grotto, is 370,000 years old.

Paleontologists examining sediment in the Oregon Caves have recognized many fossils of scientific importance. Remains of a 38,000-year-old jaguar, black bear and 50,000-year-old grizzly bear have all been found. Cave sediments, with an abundance of fossilized remains, range in age from less than 10,000 years old to at least 120,000 years old; some may be as old as 1.5 million years.

Cascade-Siskiyou National Monument

Cascade-Siskiyou National Monument straddles the Oregon-California border near Ashland in Jackson County. This 114,000-acre national monument was established by Presidential proclamation in 2000 in recognition of the area's remarkable ecology and to protect its diverse range of biological, geological, aquatic, archeological and historic resources. The monument area was expanded to 170,686 acres in 2017 and includes the Soda Mountain Wilderness. It is managed by the Bureau of Land Management.

Cascade-Siskiyou National Monument is in an area where the Great Basin meets two geologically distinct mountain ranges: the Siskiyou and the Cascades. It is a place of complex geology, steep rock canyons, towering fir forests, sunlit oak groves and wildflower-strewn meadows. Visitors explore the monument via a network of trails, including 19 miles of the Pacific Crest National Scenic Trail. Hyatt Lake Recreation Area, in the northeast part of the monument, is a popular site for boating and camping.

Most of the Cascade-Siskiyou National Monument is part of the Cascade Range and thus is volcanic in origin; however, much older terrane rocks do crop out along the western edge of the Siskiyou Mountains. Geologic distinctions in the dominantly

The beautiful Pilot Rock is one of the most recognizable features at Cascade Siskiyou National Monument. (Oregon State Archives scenic photo)

volcanic rocks of the Cascades and older terrane rocks underlying the Siskiyou range have produced a highly varied landscape marked by differences in topography, climate and biology. The early geologic history in this part of the Siskiyou Mountains is related to formation of the Applegate terrane. Rocks of the Applegate terrane record a history of ocean sediments filling a basin near a chain of volcanoes between 212 and 192 million years ago. After merging with other Klamath Mountains terranes and docking with southwestern Oregon, magma invaded the Applegate terrane, cooled, and formed the Ashland pluton 160 million years ago. This was part of a larger magmatic event that also formed the Grayback pluton in Oregon Caves National Monument around the same time.

Starting about 100 million years ago, muddy, sandy and gravelly sediments were being deposited along Oregon's ancient Pacific coastline. This coastline was different than the north to south one we know today. One hundred million years ago the ocean was further inland with a coastline stretching northeast across the state from Medford to Pendleton. Rock remnants of this coastline are now preserved in sedimentary rocks of the Hornbrook Formation in the Klamath Mountains and in similar formations cropping out at the west end of the Blue Mountains. These rocks were deposited in what geologists refer to as a forearc basin. The basin was located between an oceanward subduction zone on the west and a large chain of volcanoes that existed in central Idaho during this time.

Rocks of the Payne Cliffs Formation were deposited across the Hornbrook Formation by a large river system draining a broad, flat plain between 50 and 40 million years ago. The Early Western and High Cascades Mountains were built by volcanic activity across older river deposits of the Payne Cliffs. Since 34 million years ago, persistent volcanic activity in this part of the Cascade Range has built and erased many individual volcanoes and deposited a wide array of vent rocks, lava flows, mudflows and falls and flows of ash. Pilot Rock, a prominent 25.6-million-year-old volcanic intrusion, is part of this volcanic sequence in the monument. Uplift of the Klamath Mountains, starting about 20 million years ago, resulted in eastward tilting of all rocks in the monument.

Oregon's Geologic Future

Oregon's national monuments are natural laboratories of high-societal value, protecting and preserving evidence of our geologic past. They provide both for scientific insight and opportunities for public education into long- and short-term climate change, evolution of plant and animal life, the relationships between rocks, landscapes, soils, and ecology, and geologic hazards. Geologists play an integral role in the study of Oregon's national monuments, discovering the details of our past and providing all of us a toolbox to be resilient to future geologic change.

Jason McClaughry is a Registered Professional Geologist and is the Eastern Oregon Regional Geologist and Program Manager for the Geological Survey and Services Program at the Oregon Department of Geology and Mineral Industries (DOGAMI). He holds an M.S. degree in Geology from Washington State University and a B.S. degree in Geology from the University of Puget Sound.

This fire tower and overlook at Lava Butte in the Newberry National Volcanic Monument offers a spectacular view of monument and the Cascade Range. (Oregon State Archives scenic photo)

CHRONOLOGICAL HISTORY OF OREGON

Oregon's history contains many more significant dates than space will permit, but this list may prove helpful to those embarking on a study of the state.

Oregon Country 1543–1847

1543—Bartolome Ferrelo sails north as far as the southwest coast of Oregon

1565—Manila Galleon trade route opens across North Pacific

1579—Sir Francis Drake allegedly visits Oregon

1603—Martin d-Aguilar sails along the Pacific Coast, sighting and naming Cape Blanco and reaching Coos Bay and possibly sighting the Columbia River

1707—*San Francisco Xavier* probably wrecks at Nehalem

1738—Pierre Gaultier de la Verendrye leads first expedition into Oregon

1765—First use of word "Ouragon" in Maj. Robert Rogers' petition to explore American West

1774—Spanish explorer Capt. Juan Perez sails to Northwest Coast

1775—Capt. Bruno Heceta sees mouth of Columbia River and names it Rio San Roque

1775–1780—First smallpox outbreak among Oregon's indigenous people

1778—Capt. James Cook makes landfall at Cape Foulweather and discovers fur wealth of Northwest Coast

1788—Capt. Robert Gray trades with tribes in Tillamook Bay; Markus Lopius, Black African traveling with Gray, probably killed at Tillamook

1792—Capt. Robert Gray enters and names the Columbia River; Capt. George Vancouver expedition charts Columbia estuary; Lt. William E. Broughton names Mount Hood after British naval officer Alexander Arthur Hood

1801–1802—Second smallpox outbreak among Oregon's Tribes

1803—Louisiana Purchase extends United States to Rocky Mountains

1804—President Thomas Jefferson dispatches Lewis and Clark Expedition

1805—Lewis and Clark Expedition explores lower Snake and Columbia Rivers and establishes Fort Clatsop

1806—Lewis and Clark Expedition returns to the United States

1811—John Jacob Astor's Pacific Fur Company establishes Fort Astoria

1812—Overland Astorians discover South Pass in Wyoming, later route of Oregon Trail

1813—North West Company, a British enterprise, purchases Fort Astoria and names it Fort George

1814—First white woman to arrive in Oregon County, Jane Barnes, arrives at Fort George on North West Company's ship; First domestic livestock imported by sea from California

1817—William Cullen Bryant refers to "Oregon" in poem "Thanatopsis"

1818—North West Company establishes Fort Nez Perce; James Biddle and John Prevost assert United States interests in Oregon; United States and Great Britain agree to "joint occupancy" of Oregon

1819—Adams-Onis Treaty cedes Spain's discovery rights north of 42 degrees to the U.S.

1821—Hudson's Bay Company subsumes North West Company

1824—U.S. and Russia agree to 50 degrees latitude as southern boundary of Russian interests; Dr. John McLoughlin begins long tenure as Chief Factor for Hudson's Bay Company

1825—Workmen build Fort Vancouver on Columbia River

1827—First sawmill begins cutting lumber near Fort Vancouver

1828—Jedediah Smith's party travels overland from California; First grist mill starts making flour at Fort Vancouver

1829—Dr. John McLoughlin establishes claim at Willamette Falls, later Oregon City

1830—Fever pandemic begins calamitous death toll of tribes

1832—Newspapers report four Indians from Pacific Northwest in St. Louis seeking missionaries; Capt. B. L. E. Bonneville arrives overland to trap and trade for furs on Columbia Plateau; Hudson's Bay Company establishes Fort Umpqua at Elkton

1833—First school opens at Fort Vancouver; First lumber exports by Hudson's Bay Company to China

1834—Jason Lee's party establishes Methodist Mission near Wheatland

1836—First steamship *Beaver* begins service for Hudson's Bay Company on the Columbia River; Lt. William Slacum mounts reconnaissance of western Oregon; Whitman-Spalding mission party arrives overland via Oregon Trail; Washington Irving publishes *Astoria*

1838—Willamette Cattle Company drives livestock overland from California; Priests Blanchet and Demers arrive overland from Canada and celebrate first Catholic mass in the Pacific Northwest

1839—Catholics establish mission at St. Paul; First printing press in the Northwest brought to Lapwai (now Idaho) from Honolulu and used to print a Nez Perce primer, the first book produced in the Pacific Northwest

1841—Ewing Young's death leads to public meetings; First Catholic boys' school founded at Saint Paul; First ship, *Star of Oregon,* built by settlers

1842—Methodist missionaries found the Oregon Institute in Salem, a predecessor to Willamette University; First brick building, a house, erected by George Gay in Polk County

1843—First large migration of over 900 immigrants arrives via Oregon Trail; Lt. John C. Fremont mounts reconnaissance of Oregon Trail; "Wolf Meetings" lead to Provisional Government; Oregonians submit petition to Senate seeking U.S. jurisdiction

1844—First town plat surveyed at Oregon City; First Catholic girls' school founded at Saint Paul; Acts to prohibit slavery and exclude blacks and mulattoes from Oregon Territory were passed and the "Lash Law" enacted requiring Blacks – "be they free or slave – be whipped twice a year until he or she shall quit the territory"

1845—Meek Cutoff opens as alleged short cut to Oregon Trail; Estimated 3,000 overland immigrants arrive; Oregonians petition Congress

for federal services; First Provisional governor, George Abernethy, elected; Francis Pettygrove and A. L. Lovejoy name Portland and commence plat of city

1846—Barlow Road opens as toll route; Applegate Trail, alternative to Oregon Trail, opens; Oregon Treaty affirms U.S. sovereignty to Pacific Northwest; First newspaper on the west coast, *Oregon Spectator,* founded in Oregon City

1847—First Indian war, the Cayuse War begins at Waiilatpu (also known as the Witman Massacre); First postmaster, John Shively, named at Astoria; First English book, a *Blue Back Speller,* printed in Oregon City

Oregon Territory 1848–1858

1848—Joseph Meek carries petition east seeking federal "patronage"; Organic Act creates Oregon Territory; James Marshall discovers gold in California; First U.S. Customs Service office opens in Astoria

1849—First territorial governor, Joseph Lane, assumes duties; First Mounted Riflemen of U.S. Army arrive overland; First "Beaver" gold coins minted in Oregon City

1850—Congress passes Oregon Donation Land Act; First capital punishment—five Cayuse are hanged in Oregon City; Investors start printing *The Oregonian* in Portland

1851—First General Land Office opens in Oregon City; Willamette Valley Treaty Commission negotiates treaties; Teamsters discover gold in Rogue River Valley; Anson Dart convenes Tansy Point Treaty Council at mouth of Columbia River; First U.S. Army post, Fort Orford, built at Port Orford; U.S. Coast Survey begins charting shoreline; First Chinese immigrant, Mr. Sung Sung establishes the Sung boarding house and restaurant on Portland's Second Avenue

1852—U.S. Army establishes Fort Dalles on Oregon Trail; Congress names Salem capital of Oregon Territory

1853—Territorial legislature adopts Oregon law code; U.S. Army establishes Fort Lane in Rogue River Valley; Territorial legislature publishes *Oregon Archives*; Congress funds Scottsburg-Myrtle Creek Wagon Road; Cow Creek and Rogue River Tribes negotiate treaties with U.S.; Oregon Institute becomes Willamette University; Congress carves Washington Territory out of Oregon Territory; First coal exports begin on southwest Oregon coast; The Typographical Society, Oregon's first labor union is organized

1854—Volunteers massacre Coquille Indians; Legislature prohibits sale of ardent spirits, arms and ammunition to tribes; Legislature bars testimony of "Negroes, mulattoes, and Indians, or persons one half or more of Indian blood" in proceedings involving a white person

History

1855—Umatilla, Nez Perce, Warm Springs and Walla Walla tribes sign treaties reserving land and rights to food resources; Rogue River Indian War and Yakima Indian War begin; President James Buchanan creates Siletz Reservation; Territorial Capitol burns in Salem

1856—U.S. Army establishes Forts Umpqua, Hoskins and Yamhill; President James Buchanan creates Grand Ronde Reservation; U.S. Army orders closure of settlement east of Cascades because of warfare with tribes

The TriMet MAX light rail system began service in the Portland metropolitan area in 1986. (Oregon State Archives scenic photo)

1857—Constitutional Convention meets in Salem; Draft constitution bans slavery and bars African-Americans from residency and decides that voting will be for white male citizens only; Aaron Meier and Emil Frank found Meier & Frank Department Store

1858—First election selects state officials

State of Oregon 1859–Present

1859—Congress grants Oregon statehood on February 14, becoming only state admitted to Union with exclusion laws in their constitution; First bank established by Ladd & Tilton in Portland; First elected governor of state, John Whiteaker, inaugurated

1860—Oregon Steam Navigation Company begins service; First daily stage operates between Portland and Sacramento

1861—First Oregon State Fair held at Oregon City

1862—Congress passes Homestead Act; First Oregon Cavalry raises six companies; Gold Rush begins in Blue Mountains; First portage railroad completed at Cascades; Laws passed banning interracial marriages and requiring Blacks, Chinese, Hawaiians (Kanakas) and Mulattos to pay annual $5 tax – those not able to pay required to perform road maintenance

1863—U.S. Army establishes Fort Klamath

1864—Treaty creates Klamath Reservation; Telegraph line connects Portland-Sacramento; Popular vote approves Salem as state capital

1865—Long Tom Rebellion confirms pro-southern sympathies

1866—First lighthouse, Cape Arago, illuminates light signal; Married Women's Property Act protects women's rights

1867—U.S. Army establishes Fort Harney; first Chinese temple or "Joss House" was built at corner of Portland's Oak St. and SW 2nd Ave.

1868—Oregon State Agricultural College opens (later becomes Oregon State University)

1869—Direct export of wheat to Europe begins

1870—First woman suffrage organizations form in Albany and Salem; Despite failing in Oregon election, U.S. Constitution adds 15th Amendment, granting African-American men the right to vote

1871—Susan B. Anthony and Abigail Scott Duniway advocate women's rights in Pacific Northwest; Duniway launches women's rights newspaper *The New Northwest*

1872—Oregon & California Railroad completes line to Roseburg; Modoc Indian War begins

1873—Oregon Patrons of Husbandry (Grange) forms chapters; Modoc tribesmen face trial and execution at Fort Klamath; Oregon Pioneer Association forms; Great fire destroys much of downtown Portland; Oregon State Equal Suffrage Association formed

1875—First U.S. Life-Saving Service station opens near Coos Bay

1876—University of Oregon opens; Robert D. Hume builds salmon cannery on Rogue River

1877—Nez Perce Indian War involves Chief Joseph's band; Congress passes Desert Land Act

1878—High schools authorized for districts with 1,000 students; Bannock-Paiute Indian War sweeps into southeastern Oregon; Some women gain right to vote in school elections

1879—BIA Indian Training School opens in Forest Grove, third boarding school of its type, designed to assimilate tribal children into white culture and teach vocational skills

1880—Great Gale snow and wind storm devastates parts of Oregon and Washington; O. R. & N. Company begins railroad through Gorge; first person/woman of Japanese ancestry settles in Oregon, near Gresham

1882—Normal schools open in Monmouth, Ashland and Drain to train teachers

1883—O. R. & N. Company railroad reaches Umatilla, providing transcontinental links

1884—Oregon Short Line railroad extends to Huntington

1885—Mary Leonard first female lawyer in Oregon; Bureau of Indian Affairs moves Forest Grove boarding school to Salem, later renamed Chemawa Indian School

1886—Oregon Supreme Court admits Oregon's first female lawyer, Mary Gysin Leonard, to the state bar; Chief Joseph's Nez Perce band locates on Colville Reservation

1887—Locals rob and massacre 34 Chinese gold miners at Deep Creek in Hells Canyon; General Allotment Act assaults tribal lands on reservations; Cranberry harvests begin; First state to make Labor Day a holiday

1888—First Agricultural Experiment Station opens at Corvallis

1890—Congress passes Oregon Indian Depredation Claims Act; Chinese Consolidated Benevolent Association founded

1891—Congress passes Forest Reserve Act

1892—Congress authorizes Columbia River Lightship No. 50

1894—Mazama Club forms to promote outdoor adventure

1896—Workmen complete Cascade Locks

1897—Holdup of 1897 blocks state legislature

1898—Oregon Historical Society receives charter; Oregon National Guard soldiers first to arrive in Manila at Spanish-American War's start

1900—Workmen complete Yamhill River Locks

1902—Crater Lake National Park opens; Congress passes Federal Reclamation Act; Voters amend Constitution for Initiative and Referendum, allowing citizens to propose new laws and constitutional amendments

1903—Heppner Flood kills 225 people; First *Voters' Pamphlet* published

1904—Direct primary law passes; First African-American, George Hardin, named officer in Portland Police Bureau

1905—Lewis and Clark Centennial Exposition commemorates the 100th anniversary of the Lewis and Clark Expedition; Klamath Irrigation Project begins; Oregon land fraud trials pursue wrongdoers

1906—City home rule law approved, allowing extensive city lawmaking authority; Indictment by grand jury law approved; Taxes begin on telephone, telegraph and railroads; First meeting of Association of Oregon Counties

1907—President Theodore Roosevelt creates "Midnight Reserves," setting aside millions of acres of national forests

1908—Constitution amended for Recall provision; First woman, Lola Baldwin, named head of Women's Division, Portland Police

1909—State's Central Fish Hatchery opens at Bonneville; Oregon Caves National Monument created; Pendleton Round-Up begins; Congress passes Enlarged Homestead Act; Carolyn B. Shelton served as acting governor when Governor Chamberlain resigned to be sworn in as U.S. Senator. She served in this capacity for 48 hours, becoming Oregon's first female governor

1910—Three-fourths verdict in civil cases approved; Employers' Liability Act approved

1911—Columbia River Gorge Highway construction begins; First U.S. primary elections held in Oregon; Oregon Trunk Railroad completes line to Bend

1912—Women's suffrage approved; Prohibition of private convict labor approved; Eight-hour day on public works approved; First U.S. minimum wage law approved

1913—Presidential preference primary law approved; Governor Oswald West declares beaches open to public

1914—Death penalty abolished; Prohibition approved; Eight-hour day approved for women; Congress revests O & C Railroad land grant; Marian B. Towne elected as first woman to serve in Oregon's House of Representatives; Legislature requires publication of *Oregon Blue Book*

1915—Kathryn Clarke wins Douglas County special election to serve as first woman in the Oregon Senate

1916—Workmen complete Celilo Locks and Canal; Congress passes Stock-Raising Homestead Act

1917—U.S. Army Spruce Production Division begins logging

1918—Influenza pandemic kills hundreds; Emergency Fleet Corporation contracts for ships; Oregonians enlist to serve in World War I

1919—First state gasoline tax in U.S. authorized to fund highways

1920—Death penalty reinstated; Oregon League of Women Voters founded

1921—Ku Klux Klan organizes chapters; Hurricane hits Oregon and Washington; ballot measure allowing women to serve as jurors passes

1922—First state park opened by Oregon Highway Commission south of Monmouth, named for Sarah Helmick; Compulsory School Act approved, outlawing private and parochial schools and requiring children aged 8 to 18 to attend public school; First African-American woman, Beatrice Cannady, graduates from Lewis & Clark Law School; Japanese-American Citizens' League founded

1923—Alien Land Law approved, preventing first generation Japanese-Americans from owning or leasing land; Alien Business Restriction Law approved, denying business licenses to first generation Japanese-Americans; Prohibition of sectarian garb in schools approved

1924—Congress extends citizenship to Native Americans; Compulsory School Act held unconstitutional; Mary Jane Spurlin first female judge in Oregon; Clarke-McNary Act aids federal-state forest fire protection

1925 — State parks and waysides authorized; League of Oregon Cities founded

1926 — Fishwheels abolished; Astor Column completed; Exclusion of African-Americans clause removed from Constitution

1927 — State Constitution amended to remove voting restrictions against African and Chinese Americans

1929 — State Park Commission created

1930 — Vale Irrigation Project begins water delivery; First Oregon woman judge, Mary Jane Spurlin, appointed to Multnomah County District Court

1933 — Tillamook Burn destroys 350,000 acres of old growth timber; Civilian Conservation Corps and Works Projects Administration start projects

1934 — First grazing district under Taylor Grazing Act forms at Bonanza

1935 — Congress authorizes Bonneville Dam; Fire destroys State Capitol

1936 — 11 die as Bandon Fire destroys town; Nan Wood Honeyman is First Oregon woman elected to U.S. House of Representatives; Five major bridges are completed on Highway 101

1937 — President Franklin D. Roosevelt dedicates Timberline Lodge and Bonneville Dam; Gas chamber built at Oregon State Penitentiary for capital punishment; Oregon Shakespeare Festival forms in Ashland; Congress creates Bonneville Power Administration; Bankhead-Jones Act authorizes buyout of homesteaders

1938 — 544 Report approved for Willamette River flood control; Bonneville Dam completed

1939 — Second Tillamook Burn destroys 310,000 forest acres; State capitol completed in Salem

1941 — Oregonians enlist to serve in World War II

1942 — Executive Order 9066 authorizes removal of Japanese-Americans to internment camps; Japanese submarine shells Fort Stevens; Siskiyou National Forest firebombed by Japanese; U.S. Army builds Camp Adair and Camp Abbot; U.S. Navy builds Tillamook and Tongue Point Naval Air Stations; Vanport founded to house wartime workers

1945 — Six Oregonians die in explosion of Japanese incendiary balloon near Bly; Third Tillamook Burn destroys 125,000 forest acres; Supplement to 1923 Alien Land Law passes

1946 — Portland State University (PSU) founded; Rural School Law encourages consolidation of districts

1947 — Plane crash kills Governor Snell, Secretary of State Farrell, and others

1948 — Columbia River Flood destroys Vanport; Vollum and Murdock found Tektronix

1949 — State Department of Forestry begins replanting Tillamook Burn; Fair Labor Practices

Commission established; State Supreme Court invalidates 1923 and 1945 Alien Land acts; First woman, Dorothy McCullough Lee, elected Portland mayor

1951 — Law prohibiting interracial marriges repealed; Fourth Tillamook Burn destroys 130,000 forest acres

1952 — Constitution amended to provide for equal representation in state legislature

1953 — Public Accommodations Law prohibits racial discrimination by businesses

1954 — Congress terminates Western Oregon tribes; Supreme Court upholds *Brown v. Board of Education of Topeka*, abolishing segregated schools

1956 — Congress authorizes Interstate freeway system; Congress terminates Klamath Tribe

1957 — Oregon Fair Housing Act passes

1959 — Oregon ratifies 15th Amendment to the U.S. Constitution, granting African-American men the right to vote, 89 years after its adoption; First *Oregon Bulletin* published

1960 — Congress passes Multiple Use-Sustained Yield Act for management of national forests; Mercedes Deiz first African American female lawyer in Oregon; First female U.S. Senator from Oregon, Maurine Neuberger, elected

1962 — Columbus Day Storm causes major damage in Western Oregon; Oregon State University football player, Terry Baker, (QB) becomes state's first Heisman Trophy winner

1964 — Death penalty abolished; National Civil Rights Act outlaws unequal voter registation requirements and racial segregation in schools, the workplace and public places

1965 — Congress passes Voting Rights Act, prohibiting qualifications or prerequisites to voting

1966 — Workmen complete Astoria-Megler Bridge spanning Columbia River estuary; I-5 affords non-stop driving through Oregon

1967 — Beach Bill approved, ensuring public access to all of Oregon's coastal beaches; Racial tensions escalate into riots in Portland

1969 — Federal District Court in *Sohappy v. Smith* affirms tribal treaty fishing rights in Columbia River

1971 — Bottle Bill approved; Congress confirms Burns Paiute Reservation

1973 — Statewide major land use planning legislation approved; Public Meetings Law approved; Public Records Law for access approved; Tillamook State Forest created; Congress approves Endangered Species Act; Oregon ratifies U.S. Equal Rights Amendment

1974 — Congress creates John Day Fossil Beds National Monument; Oregon Health Sciences University forms out of mergers; Governor Tom McCall sets odd/even gasoline refueling days

1975—Congress creates Hells Canyon National Recreation Area

1976—First woman, Norma Paulus, elected secretary of state; Trojan, Oregon's first nuclear power plant built near Saint Helens

1977—Oregon first state to ban aerosol sprays by law; Congress restores Confederated Tribes of Siletz; First woman Betty Roberts appointed to Oregon Court of Appeals; Portland Trail Blazers win NBA Championship

1978—Death penalty reinstated

1979—Federal District Court in *Kimball v. Callahan* affirms Klamath tribal hunting and fishing rights within former reservation; Portland-area voters create "Metro," the first elective metropolitan council in the U.S.

1980—Congress creates new Siletz Reservation; Mount Saint Helens eruption disrupts ship traffic on Columbia River

1981—Bhagwan Shree Rajneesh establishes Rajneeshpuram near Antelope

1982—Congress restores Cow Creek Band of Umpqua Tribe; First woman, Betty Roberts, appointed justice of Oregon Supreme Court

1983—Congress restores Confederated Tribes of Grand Ronde

1984—Congress restores Confederated Tribes of Coos, Lower Umpqua and Siuslaw; First Oregon lottery ratified by voters; First African-American woman, Margaret Carter, elected to state legislature

1985—Bhagwan Shree Rajneesh deported and fined $400,000; First woman, Vera Katz, selected speaker of Oregon House

1986—Congress restores Klamath Tribe; Metropolitan Area Express (MAX) begins light-rail service in Portland

1988—Congress creates Grand Ronde Reservation; Congress approves Civil Liberties Act paying $20,000 to each surviving interned Japanese-American; Ballot Measure 8 bans discrimination based on sexual orientation

1989—Congress restores Coquille Tribe; African exchange student, Mulugeta Seraw, killed by racist skinheads in Portland

1990—Ballot Measure 5 limits property taxes to support schools and government; U.S. Department of Fish and Wildlife lists Northern Spotted Owl as endangered

1991—First woman, Barbara Roberts, elected governor

1992—First African-American, James A. Hill, Jr., elected to statewide office as state treasurer; First gaming compact for casinos signed with Cow Creek and Umpqua Tribes

1993—First statewide vote-by-mail election held in U.S.

1994—First Death With Dignity Act approved, permitting doctor-assisted suicide

1995—Beverly Clarno becomes first woman to serve as speaker of the Oregon's House of Representatives

1996—First vote-by-mail election for federal office held

1999—*New Carissa,* freighter runs aground near Coos Bay; U.S. Department of Fish and Wildlife lists several salmon species from Columbia and Willamette Rivers as endangered

2002—Susan Castillo, first Hispanic woman elected to statewide office as school superintendent; Forest fires leave nearly 100,000 acres burned; Measure requiring removal of racist language from state Constitution passes

2003—Oregon begins ten-year plan to fix deteriorating bridges

2004—Trojan, Oregon's only nuclear power plant, decommissioned; L. L. Stub Stewart State Park opens, Oregon's first new state park campground in more than 30 years

2005—Oregon State Quarter released with design featuring Crater Lake

2006—Trojan, Oregon's decommissioned nuclear power plant, imploded

2007—Oregon's constitution 150 years old; Sandy River's Marmot Dam, built in 1912, removed; Oregon Equality Act passes

2008—*New Carissa,* freighter that ran aground on Coos Bay beach in 1999, dismantled and removed

2009—Oregon celebrates its sesquicentennial on February 14, 2009; Oregon unemployment rate tops 12% amid recession

2010—Governor's panel predicts 10 years of state budget deficits

2012—Oregon legislature begins annual sessions with the even-numbered years having a month-long session in February

2013—Klamath Tribes' senior water rights in Upper Klamath Basin reaffirmed by courts; Drought and lightning produced most expensive wildfire season on record, leave over 100,000 acres burned; Josephine County's last sawmill closes for lack of logs

2014—U.S. District court strikes down same-sex marriage ban; Voters approve recreational marijuana use; Equal Rights for Women in Oregon Constitution; University of Oregon football quarterback Marcus Mariota, wins the Heisman Trophy

2015—Governor John Kitzhaber resigns Feb. 18, 2015 and Secretary of State Kate Brown becomes governor according to the order of succession required by the Oregon Constitution; Minoru Yasui, Hood River Attorney, posthumously awarded the Presidential Medal of Freedom in recognition of his challenge of a military curfew placed on Japanese-Americans during World War II and for his lifetime of civil rights work.

2016—Armed militants seize and occupy the headquarters of Harney County's Malheur National Wildlife Refuge for 41 days

2017—Total solar eclipse across Oregon on August 21, 2017, the Path of totality includes Lincoln City, Newport, Salem, Albany, Madras, Baker City and Ontario; Senate Bill 13, the "Tribal History/Shared History" law is enacted, directing the Oregon Department of Education to create a K-12 Native American curriculum for inclusion in Oregon's public schools; Oregon's 158-year-old Constitution is professionally restored and put on display

2018—Justice Adrienne C. Nelson is appointed to the Oregon Supreme Court, making her the first African American to sit on the state's highest court; Oregonian Colin O'Brady first to traverse Antarctica solo and unaided

2019—The Devil's Staircase in the Oregon Coast Range designated a federal Wilderness Area; Blockbuster Video in Bend, Oregon becomes the world's last Blockbuster movie rental store

2020—National racial unrest spurs spring/summer protests around the state; Governor Brown invokes the Emergency Conflagration Act as fires threaten structures in nine Oregon counties; A Washington County man is Oregon's first diagnosed COVID-19 case on February 28, 2020; A Multnomah County man is Oregon's first reported COVID-19 death on March 14, 2020; Oregon gave its first COVID-19 vaccines in four Oregon hospitals

2021— Juneteenth and Indigenous Peoples' Day become state of Oregon holidays; In June, Oregon saw three consecutive days of record-breaking heat across the state, tying the statewide all-time high temperature of 119°F in Jefferson County; Oregon receives a sixth Congressional district and completes redistricting

2022—Three women are on the ballot to become Oregon's next governor; In July, the World Athletic Championships are held in Eugene, bringing together the world's best track and field athletes

CONSTITUTION OF OREGON
2021 EDITION

The Oregon Constitution was framed by a convention of 60 delegates chosen by the people. The convention met on the third Monday in August 1857 and adjourned on September 18 of the same year. On November 9, 1857, the Constitution was approved by vote of the people of the Oregon Territory. The Act of Congress admitting Oregon into the Union was approved February 14, 1859, and on that date the Constitution went into effect.

The Constitution is here published as it is in effect following the approval of amendments and revisions on November 3, 2020. The text of the original signed copy of the Constitution filed in the office of the Secretary of State is retained unless it has been repealed or superseded by amendment or revision. Where the original text has been amended or revised or where a new provision has been added to the original Constitution, the source of the amendment, revision or addition is indicated in the source note immediately following the text of the amended, revised or new section. Notations also have been made setting out the history of repealed sections.

Unless otherwise specifically noted, the leadlines for the sections have been supplied by the Office of the Legislative Counsel.

PREAMBLE

We the people of the State of Oregon to the end that Justice be established, order maintained, and liberty perpetuated, do ordain this Constitution. —

ARTICLE I
BILL OF RIGHTS

Section 1. Natural rights inherent in people. We declare that all men, when they form a social compact are equal in right: that all power is inherent in the people, and all free governments are founded on their authority, and instituted for their peace, safety, and happiness; and they have at all times a right to alter, reform, or abolish the government in such manner as they may think proper.—

Section 2. Freedom of worship. All men shall be secure in the Natural right, to worship Almighty God according to the dictates of their own consciences.—

Section 3. Freedom of religious opinion. No law shall in any case whatever control the free exercise, and enjoyment of religeous [sic] opinions, or interfere with the rights of conscience.—

Section 4. No religious qualification for office. No religious test shall be required as a qualification for any office of trust or profit.—

Section 5. No money to be appropriated for religion. No money shall be drawn from the Treasury for the benefit of any religeous [sic], or theological institution, nor shall any money be appropriated for the payment of any religeous [sic] services in either house of the Legislative Assembly.—

Section 6. No religious test for witnesses or jurors. No person shall be rendered incompetent as a witness, or juror in consequence of his opinions on matters of religeon [sic]; nor be questioned in any Court of Justice touching his religeous [sic] belief to affect the weight of his testimony.—

Section 7. Manner of administering oath or affirmation. The mode of administering an oath, or affirmation shall be such as may be most consistent with, and binding upon the conscience of the person to whom such oath or affirmation may be administered.—

Section 8. Freedom of speech and press. No law shall be passed restraining the free expression of opinion, or restricting the right to speak, write, or print freely on any subject whatever; but every person shall be responsible for the abuse of this right.—

Section 9. Unreasonable searches or seizures. No law shall violate the right of the people to be secure in their persons, houses, papers, and effects, against unreasonable search, or seizure; and no warrant shall issue but upon probable cause, supported by oath, or affirmation, and particularly describing the place to be searched, and the person or thing to be seized.—

Section 10. Administration of justice. No court shall be secret, but justice shall be administered, openly and without purchase, completely and without delay, and every man shall have remedy by due course of law for injury done him in his person, property, or reputation.—

Section 11. Rights of Accused in Criminal Prosecution. In all criminal prosecutions, the accused shall have the right to public trial by an impartial jury in the county in which the offense shall have been committed; to be heard by himself and counsel; to demand the nature and cause of the accusation against him, and to have a copy thereof; to meet the witnesses face to face, and to have compulsory process for obtaining witnesses in his favor; provided, however, that any accused person, in other than capital cases, and with the consent of the trial judge, may elect to waive trial by jury and consent to be tried by the judge of the court alone, such election to be in writing; provided, however, that in the circuit court ten members of the jury may render a verdict of guilty or not guilty, save and except a verdict of guilty of first degree murder, which shall be found only by a unanimous verdict, and not otherwise; provided further, that the existing laws and constitutional provisions relative to criminal prosecutions shall be continued and remain in effect as to all prosecutions for crimes committed before the taking effect of this amendment. [Constitution of 1859; Amendment proposed by S.J.R. 4, 1931, and adopted by the people Nov. 8, 1932; Amendment proposed by S.J.R. 4, 1931 (2d s.s.), and adopted by the people May 18, 1934]

Note: The leadline to section 11 was a part of the measure submitted to the people by S.J.R. 4, 1931.

Section 12. Double jeopardy; compulsory self-incrimination. No person shall be put in jeopardy twice for the same offence [sic], nor be compelled in any criminal prosecution to testify against himself.—

Section 13. Treatment of arrested or confined persons. No person arrested, or confined in jail, shall be treated with unnecessary rigor.—

Section 14. Bailable offenses. Offences [sic], except murder, and treason, shall be bailable by sufficient sureties.

Murder or treason, shall not be bailable, when the proof is evident, or the presumption strong.—

Section 15. Foundation principles of criminal law. Laws for the punishment of crime shall be founded on these principles: protection of society, personal responsibility, accountability for one's actions and reformation. [Constitution of 1859; Amendment proposed by S.J.R. 32, 1995, and adopted by the people Nov. 5, 1996]

Section 16. Excessive bail and fines; cruel and unusual punishments; power of jury in criminal case. Excessive bail shall not be required, nor excessive fines imposed. Cruel and unusual punishments shall not be inflicted, but all penalties shall be proportioned to the offense.—In all criminal cases whatever, the jury shall have the right to determine the law, and the facts under the direction of the Court as to the law, and the right of new trial, as in civil cases.

Section 17. Jury trial in civil cases. In all civil cases the right of Trial by Jury shall remain inviolate.—

Section 18. Private property or services taken for public use. Private property shall not be taken for public use, nor the particular services of any man be demanded, without just compensation; nor except in the case of the state, without such compensation first assessed and tendered; provided, that the use of all roads, ways and waterways necessary to promote the transportation of the raw products of mine or farm or forest or water for beneficial use or drainage is necessary to the development and welfare of the state and is declared a public use. [Constitution of 1859; Amendment proposed by S.J.R. 17, 1919, and adopted by the people May 21, 1920; Amendment proposed by S.J.R. 8, 1923, and adopted by the people Nov. 4, 1924]

Section 19. Imprisonment for debt. There shall be no imprisonment for debt, except in case of fraud or absconding debtors.—

Section 20. Equality of privileges and immunities of citizens. No law shall be passed granting to any citizen or class of citizens privileges, or immunities, which, upon the same terms, shall not equally belong to all citizens.—

Section 21. Ex-post facto laws; laws impairing contracts; laws depending on authorization in order to take effect; laws submitted to electors. No ex-post facto law, or law impairing the obligation of contracts shall ever be passed, nor shall any law be passed, the taking effect of which shall be made to depend upon any authority, except as provided in this Constitution; provided, that laws locating the Capitol of the State, locating County Seats, and submitting town, and corporate acts, and other local, and Special laws may take effect, or not, upon a vote of the electors interested.—

Section 22. Suspension of operation of laws. The operation of the laws shall never be suspended, except by the Authority of the Legislative Assembly.

Section 23. Habeas corpus. The privilege of the writ of habeas corpus shall not be suspended unless in case of rebellion, or invasion the public safety require it.—

Section 24. Treason. Treason against the State shall consist only in levying war against it, or adhering to its enemies, giving them aid or comfort.—No person shall be convicted of treason unless on the testimony of two witnesses to the same overt act, or confession in open Court.—

Section 25. Corruption of blood or forfeiture of estate. No conviction shall work corruption of blood, or forfeiture of estate.—

Section 26. Assemblages of people; instruction of representatives; application to legislature. No law shall be passed restraining any of the inhabitants of the State from assembling together in a peaceable manner to consult for their common good; nor from instructing their representatives; nor from applying to the Legislature for redress of grievances [sic].—

Section 27. Right to bear arms; military subordinate to civil power. The people shall have the right to bear arms for the defence [sic] of themselves, and the State, but the Military shall be kept in strict subordination to the civil power[.]

Section 28. Quartering soldiers. No soldier shall, in time of peace, be quartered in any house, without the consent of the owner, nor in time of war, except in the manner prescribed by law.

Section 29. Titles of nobility; hereditary distinctions. No law shall be passed granting any title of Nobility, or conferring hereditary distinctions.—

Section 30. Emigration. No law shall be passed prohibiting emigration from the State.—

Section 31. Rights of aliens; immigration to state. [Constitution of 1859; repeal proposed by H.J.R. 16, 1969, and adopted by the people May 26, 1970]

Section 32. Taxes and duties; uniformity of taxation. No tax or duty shall be imposed without the consent of the people or their representatives in the Legislative Assembly; and all taxation shall be uniform on the same class of subjects within the territorial limits of the authority levying the tax. [Constitution of 1859; Amendment proposed by H.J.R. 16, 1917, and adopted by the people June 4, 1917]

Section 33. Enumeration of rights not exclusive. This enumeration of rights, and privileges shall not be construed to impair or deny others retained by the people.—

Section 34. Slavery or involuntary servitude. There shall be neither slavery, nor involuntary servitude in the State, otherwise than as a punishment for crime, whereof the party shall have been duly convicted.— [Added to Bill of Rights as unnumbered section by vote of the people at time of adoption of the Oregon Constitution in accordance with section 4 of Article XVIII thereof]

Section 35. Restrictions on rights of certain persons. [Added to Bill of Rights as unnumbered section by vote of the people at time of adoption of the Oregon Constitution in accordance with Section 4 of Article XVIII thereof; Repeal proposed by H.J.R. 8, 1925, and adopted by the people Nov. 2, 1926]

Section 36. Liquor prohibition. [Created through initiative petition filed July 1, 1914, and adopted by the people Nov. 3, 1914; Repeal proposed by initiative petition filed March 20, 1933, and adopted by the people July 21, 1933]

Section 36. Capital punishment abolished. [Created through initiative petition filed July 2, 1914, and adopted by the people Nov. 3, 1914; Repeal proposed by S.J.R. 8, 1920 (s.s.), and adopted by the people May 21, 1920, as Const. Art. I, §38]

Note: At the general election in 1914 two sections, each designated as section 36, were created and added to the Constitution by separate initiative petitions. One of these sections was the prohibition section and the other abolished capital punishment.

Section 36a. Prohibition of importation of liquors. [Created through initiative petition filed July 6, 1916, and adopted by the people Nov. 7, 1916; Repeal proposed by initiative petition filed March 20, 1933, and adopted by the people July 21, 1933]

Section 37. Penalty for murder in first degree. [Created through S.J.R. 8, 1920, and adopted by the people May 21, 1920; Repeal proposed by S.J.R. 3, 1963, and adopted by the people Nov. 3, 1964]

Section 38. Laws abrogated by amendment abolishing death penalty revived. [Created through S.J.R. 8, 1920, and adopted by the people May 21, 1920; Repeal proposed by S.J.R. 3, 1963, and adopted by the people Nov. 3, 1964]

Constitution

Section 39. Sale of liquor by individual glass. The State shall have power to license private clubs, fraternal organizations, veterans' organizations, railroad corporations operating interstate trains and commercial establishments where food is cooked and served, for the purpose of selling alcoholic liquor by the individual glass at retail, for consumption on the premises, including mixed drinks and cocktails, compounded or mixed on the premises only. The Legislative Assembly shall provide in such detail as it shall deem advisable for carrying out and administering the provisions of this amendment and shall provide adequate safeguards to carry out the original intent and purpose of the Oregon Liquor Control Act, including the promotion of temperance in the use and consumption of alcoholic beverages, encourage the use and consumption of lighter beverages and aid in the establishment of Oregon industry. This power is subject to the following:

(1) The provisions of this amendment shall take effect and be in operation sixty (60) days after the approval and adoption by the people of Oregon; provided, however, the right of a local option election exists in the counties and in any incorporated city or town containing a population of at least five hundred (500). The Legislative Assembly shall prescribe a means and a procedure by which the voters of any county or incorporated city or town as limited above in any county, may through a local option election determine whether to prohibit or permit such power, and such procedure shall specifically include that whenever fifteen per cent (15%) of the registered voters of any county in the state or of any incorporated city or town as limited above, in any county in the state, shall file a petition requesting an election in this matter, the question shall be voted upon at the next regular November biennial election, provided said petition is filed not less than sixty (60) days before the day of election.

(2) Legislation relating to this matter shall operate uniformly throughout the state and all individuals shall be treated equally; and all provisions shall be liberally construed for the accomplishment of these purposes. [Created through initiative petition filed July 2, 1952, and adopted by the people Nov. 4, 1952]

Section 40. Penalty for aggravated murder. Notwithstanding sections 15 and 16 of this Article, the penalty for aggravated murder as defined by law shall be death upon unanimous affirmative jury findings as provided by law and otherwise shall be life imprisonment with minimum sentence as provided by law. [Created through initiative petition filed July 6, 1983, and adopted by the people Nov. 6, 1984]

Section 41. Work and training for corrections institution inmates; work programs; limitations; duties of corrections director. (1) Whereas the people of the state of Oregon find and declare that inmates who are confined in corrections institutions should work as hard as the taxpayers who provide for their upkeep; and whereas the people also find and declare that inmates confined within corrections institutions must be fully engaged in productive activity if they are to successfully re-enter society with practical skills and a viable work ethic; now, therefore, the people declare:

(2) All inmates of state corrections institutions shall be actively engaged full-time in work or on-the-job training. The work or on-the-job training programs shall be established and overseen by the corrections director, who shall ensure that such programs are cost-effective and are designed to develop inmate motivation, work capabilities and cooperation. Such programs may include boot camp prison programs. Education may be provided to inmates as part of work or on-the-job training so long as each inmate is engaged at least half-time in hands-on training or work activity.

(3) Each inmate shall begin full-time work or on-the-job training immediately upon admission to a corrections institution, allowing for a short time for administrative intake and processing. The specific quantity of hours per day to be spent in work or on-the-job training shall be determined by the corrections director, but the overall time spent in work or training shall be full-time. However, no inmate has a legally enforceable right to a job or to otherwise participate in work, on-the-job training or educational programs or to compensation for work or labor performed while an inmate of any state, county or city corrections facility or institution. The corrections director may reduce or exempt participation in work or training programs by those inmates deemed by corrections officials as physically or mentally disabled, or as too dangerous to society to engage in such programs.

(4) There shall be sufficient work and training programs to ensure that every eligible inmate is productively involved in one or more programs. Where an inmate is drug and alcohol addicted so as to prevent the inmate from effectively participating in work or training programs, corrections officials shall provide appropriate drug or alcohol treatment.

(5) The intent of the people is that taxpayer-supported institutions and programs shall be free to benefit from inmate work. Prison work programs shall be designed and carried out so as to achieve savings in government operations, so as to achieve a net profit in private sector activities or so as to benefit the community.

(6) The provisions of this section are mandatory for all state corrections institutions. The provisions of this section are permissive for county or city corrections facilities. No law, ordinance or charter shall prevent or restrict a county or city governing body from implementing all or part of the provisions of this section. Compensation, if any, shall be determined and established by the governing body of the county or city which chooses to engage in prison work programs, and the governing body may choose to adopt any power or exemption allowed in this section.

(7) The corrections director shall contact public and private enterprises in this state and seek proposals to use inmate work. The corrections director may: (a) install and equip plants in any state corrections institution, or any other location, for the employment or training of any of the inmates therein; or (b) purchase, acquire, install, maintain and operate materials, machinery and appliances necessary to the conduct and operation of such plants. The corrections director shall use every effort to enter into contracts or agreements with private business concerns or government agencies to accomplish the production or marketing of products or services produced or performed by inmates. The corrections director may carry out the director's powers and duties under this section by delegation to others.

(8) Compensation, if any, for inmates who engage in prison work programs shall be determined and established by the corrections director. Such compensation shall not be subject to existing public or private sector minimum or prevailing wage laws, except where required to comply with federal law. Inmate compensation from enterprises entering into agreements with the state shall be exempt from unemployment compensation taxes to the extent allowed under federal law. Inmate injury or disease attributable to any inmate work shall be covered by a corrections system inmate injury fund rather than the workers compensation law. Except as otherwise required by federal law to permit transportation in interstate commerce of goods, wares or merchandise manufactured, produced or mined, wholly or in part by inmates or except as otherwise required by state law, any compensation earned through prison work programs shall only be used for the following purposes: (a) reimbursement for all or a portion of the costs

of the inmate's rehabilitation, housing, health care, and living costs; (b) restitution or compensation to the victims of the particular inmate's crime; (c) restitution or compensation to the victims of crime generally through a fund designed for that purpose; (d) financial support for immediate family of the inmate outside the corrections institution; and (e) payment of fines, court costs, and applicable taxes.

(9) All income generated from prison work programs shall be kept separate from general fund accounts and shall only be used for implementing, maintaining and developing prison work programs. Prison industry work programs shall be exempt from statutory competitive bid and purchase requirements. Expenditures for prison work programs shall be exempt from the legislative appropriations process to the extent the programs rely on income sources other than state taxes and fees. Where state taxes or fees are the source of capital or operating expenditures, the appropriations shall be made by the legislative assembly. The state programs shall be run in a businesslike fashion and shall be subject to regulation by the corrections director. Expenditures from income generated by state prison work programs must be approved by the corrections director. Agreements with private enterprise as to state prison work programs must be approved by the corrections director. The corrections director shall make all state records available for public scrutiny and the records shall be subject to audit by the Secretary of State.

(10) Prison work products or services shall be available to any public agency and to any private enterprise of any state, any nation or any American Indian or Alaskan Native tribe without restriction imposed by any state or local law, ordinance or regulation as to competition with other public or private sector enterprises. The products and services of corrections work programs shall be provided on such terms as are set by the corrections director. To the extent determined possible by the corrections director, the corrections director shall avoid establishing or expanding for-profit prison work programs that produce goods or services offered for sale in the private sector if the establishment or expansion would displace or significantly reduce preexisting private enterprise. To the extent determined possible by the corrections director, the corrections director shall avoid establishing or expanding prison work programs if the establishment or expansion would displace or significantly reduce government or nonprofit programs that employ persons with developmental disabilities. However, the decision to establish, maintain, expand, reduce or terminate any prison work program remains in the sole discretion of the corrections director.

(11) Inmate work shall be used as much as possible to help operate the corrections institutions themselves, to support other government operations and to support community charitable organizations. This work includes, but is not limited to, institutional food production; maintenance and repair of buildings, grounds, and equipment; office support services, including printing; prison clothing production and maintenance; prison medical services; training other inmates; agricultural and forestry work, especially in parks and public forest lands; and environmental clean-up projects. Every state agency shall cooperate with the corrections director in establishing inmate work programs.

(12) As used throughout this section, unless the context requires otherwise: "full-time" means the equivalent of at least forty hours per seven day week, specifically including time spent by inmates as required by the Department of Corrections, while the inmate is participating in work or on-the-job training, to provide for the safety and security of the public, correctional staff and inmates; "corrections director" means the person in charge of the state corrections system.

(13) This section is self-implementing and supersedes all existing inconsistent statutes. This section shall become effective April 1, 1995. If any part of this section or its application to any person or circumstance is held to be invalid for any reason, then the remaining parts or applications to any persons or circumstances shall not be affected but shall remain in full force and effect. [Created through initiative petition filed Jan. 12, 1994, and adopted by the people Nov. 8, 1994; Amendment proposed by H.J.R. 2, 1997, and adopted by the people May 20, 1997; Amendment proposed by H.J.R. 82, 1999, and adopted by the people Nov. 2, 1999]

Note: Added to Article I as unnumbered section by initiative petition (Measure No. 17, 1994) adopted by the people Nov. 8, 1994.

Note: An initiative petition (Measure No. 40, 1996) proposed adding a new section relating to crime victims' rights to the Oregon Constitution. That section, appearing as section 42 of Article I in previous editions of this Constitution, was declared void for not being enacted in compliance with section 1, Article XVII of this Constitution. See Armatta v. Kitzhaber, 327 Or. 250, 959 P.2d 49 (1998).

Section 42. Rights of victim in criminal prosecutions and juvenile court delinquency proceedings. (1) To preserve and protect the right of crime victims to justice, to ensure crime victims a meaningful role in the criminal and juvenile justice systems, to accord crime victims due dignity and respect and to ensure that criminal and juvenile court delinquency proceedings are conducted to seek the truth as to the defendant's innocence or guilt, and also to ensure that a fair balance is struck between the rights of crime victims and the rights of criminal defendants in the course and conduct of criminal and juvenile court delinquency proceedings, the following rights are hereby granted to victims in all prosecutions for crimes and in juvenile court delinquency proceedings:

(a) The right to be present at and, upon specific request, to be informed in advance of any critical stage of the proceedings held in open court when the defendant will be present, and to be heard at the pretrial release hearing and the sentencing or juvenile court delinquency disposition;

(b) The right, upon request, to obtain information about the conviction, sentence, imprisonment, criminal history and future release from physical custody of the criminal defendant or convicted criminal and equivalent information regarding the alleged youth offender or youth offender;

(c) The right to refuse an interview, deposition or other discovery request by the criminal defendant or other person acting on behalf of the criminal defendant provided, however, that nothing in this paragraph shall restrict any other constitutional right of the defendant to discovery against the state;

(d) The right to receive prompt restitution from the convicted criminal who caused the victim's loss or injury;

(e) The right to have a copy of a transcript of any court proceeding in open court, if one is otherwise prepared;

(f) The right to be consulted, upon request, regarding plea negotiations involving any violent felony; and

(g) The right to be informed of these rights as soon as practicable.

(2) This section applies to all criminal and juvenile court delinquency proceedings pending or commenced on or after the effective date of this section. Nothing in this section reduces a criminal defendant's rights under the Constitution of the United States. Except as otherwise specifically provided, this section supersedes any conflicting section of this Constitution. Nothing in this section is intended to create any cause of action for compensation or damages nor may this section be used to invalidate an accusatory instrument, conviction or adjudication or otherwise terminate any criminal or juvenile delinquency

Constitution

proceedings at any point after the case is commenced or on appeal. Except as otherwise provided in subsections (3) and (4) of this section, nothing in this section may be used to invalidate a ruling of a court or to suspend any criminal or juvenile delinquency proceedings at any point after the case is commenced.

(3)(a) Every victim described in paragraph (c) of subsection (6) of this section shall have remedy by due course of law for violation of a right established in this section.

(b) A victim may assert a claim for a right established in this section in a pending case, by a mandamus proceeding if no case is pending or as otherwise provided by law.

(c) The Legislative Assembly may provide by law for further effectuation of the provisions of this subsection, including authorization for expedited and interlocutory consideration of claims for relief and the establishment of reasonable limitations on the time allowed for bringing such claims.

(d) No claim for a right established in this section shall suspend a criminal or juvenile delinquency proceeding if such a suspension would violate a right of a criminal defendant guaranteed by this Constitution or the Constitution of the United States.

(4) Upon the victim's request, the prosecuting attorney, in the attorney's discretion, may assert and enforce a right established in this section.

(5) Upon the filing by the prosecuting attorney of an affidavit setting forth cause, a court shall suspend the rights established in this section in any case involving organized crime or victims who are minors.

(6) As used in this section:

(a) "Convicted criminal" includes a youth offender in juvenile court delinquency proceedings.

(b) "Criminal defendant" includes an alleged youth offender in juvenile court delinquency proceedings.

(c) "Victim" means any person determined by the prosecuting attorney or the court to have suffered direct financial, psychological or physical harm as a result of a crime and, in the case of a victim who is a minor, the legal guardian of the minor.

(d) "Violent felony" means a felony in which there was actual or threatened serious physical injury to a victim or a felony sexual offense.

(7) In the event that no person has been determined to be a victim of the crime, the people of Oregon, represented by the prosecuting attorney, are considered to be the victims. In no event is it intended that the criminal defendant be considered the victim. [Created through H.J.R. 87, 1999, and adopted by the people Nov. 2, 1999; Amendment proposed by H.J.R. 49, 2007, and adopted by the people May 20, 2008]

Note: The effective date of House Joint Resolutions 87, 89, 90 and 94, compiled as sections 42, 43, 44 and 45, Article I, is Dec. 2, 1999.

Note: Sections 42, 43, 44 and 45, were added to Article I as unnumbered sections by the amendments proposed by House Joint Resolutions 87, 89, 90 and 94, 1999, and adopted by the people Nov. 2, 1999.

Section 43. Rights of victim and public to protection from accused person during criminal proceedings; denial of pretrial release. (1) To ensure that a fair balance is struck between the rights of crime victims and the rights of criminal defendants in the course and conduct of criminal proceedings, the following rights are hereby granted to victims in all prosecutions for crimes:

(a) The right to be reasonably protected from the criminal defendant or the convicted criminal throughout the criminal justice process and from the alleged youth offender or youth offender throughout the juvenile delinquency proceedings.

(b) The right to have decisions by the court regarding the pretrial release of a criminal defendant based upon the principle of reasonable protection of the victim and the public, as well as the likelihood that the criminal defendant will appear for trial. Murder, aggravated murder and treason shall not be bailable when the proof is evident or the presumption strong that the person is guilty. Other violent felonies shall not be bailable when a court has determined there is probable cause to believe the criminal defendant committed the crime, and the court finds, by clear and convincing evidence, that there is danger of physical injury or sexual victimization to the victim or members of the public by the criminal defendant while on release.

(2) This section applies to proceedings pending or commenced on or after the effective date of this section. Nothing in this section abridges any right of the criminal defendant guaranteed by the Constitution of the United States, including the rights to be represented by counsel, have counsel appointed if indigent, testify, present witnesses, cross-examine witnesses or present information at the release hearing. Nothing in this section creates any cause of action for compensation or damages nor may this section be used to invalidate an accusatory instrument, conviction or adjudication or otherwise terminate any criminal or juvenile delinquency proceeding at any point after the case is commenced or on appeal. Except as otherwise provided in paragraph (b) of subsection (4) of this section and in subsection (5) of this section, nothing in this section may be used to invalidate a ruling of a court or to suspend any criminal or juvenile delinquency proceedings at any point after the case is commenced. Except as otherwise specifically provided, this section supersedes any conflicting section of this Constitution.

(3) As used in this section:

(a) "Victim" means any person determined by the prosecuting attorney or the court to have suffered direct financial, psychological or physical harm as a result of a crime and, in the case of a victim who is a minor, the legal guardian of the minor.

(b) "Violent felony" means a felony in which there was actual or threatened serious physical injury to a victim or a felony sexual offense.

(4)(a) The prosecuting attorney is the party authorized to assert the rights of the public established by this section.

(b) Upon the victim's request, the prosecuting attorney, in the attorney's discretion, may assert and enforce a right established in this section.

(5)(a) Every victim described in paragraph (a) of subsection (3) of this section shall have remedy by due course of law for violation of a right established in this section.

(b) A victim may assert a claim for a right established in this section in a pending case, by a mandamus proceeding if no case is pending or as otherwise provided by law.

(c) The Legislative Assembly may provide by law for further effectuation of the provisions of this subsection, including authorization for expedited and interlocutory consideration of claims for relief and the establishment of reasonable limitations on the time allowed for bringing such claims.

(d) No claim for a right established in this section shall suspend a criminal or juvenile delinquency proceeding if such a suspension would violate a right of a criminal defendant or alleged youth offender guaranteed by this Constitution or the Constitution of the United States.

(6) In the event that no person has been determined to be a victim of the crime, the people of Oregon, represented by the prosecuting attorney, are considered to be the victims. In no event is it intended that the criminal defendant be considered the victim. [Created through H.J.R. 90, 1999,

and adopted by the people Nov. 2, 1999; Amendment proposed by H.J.R. 50, 2007, and adopted by the people May 20, 2008]

Note: See notes under section 42 of this Article.

Section 44. Term of imprisonment imposed by court to be fully served; exceptions. (1)(a) A term of imprisonment imposed by a judge in open court may not be set aside or otherwise not carried out, except as authorized by the sentencing court or through the subsequent exercise of:

(A) The power of the Governor to grant reprieves, commutations and pardons; or

(B) Judicial authority to grant appellate or post-conviction relief.

(b) No law shall limit a court's authority to sentence a criminal defendant consecutively for crimes against different victims.

(2) This section applies to all offenses committed on or after the effective date of this section. Nothing in this section reduces a criminal defendant's rights under the Constitution of the United States. Except as otherwise specifically provided, this section supersedes any conflicting section of this Constitution. Nothing in this section creates any cause of action for compensation or damages nor may this section be used to invalidate an accusatory instrument, ruling of a court, conviction or adjudication or otherwise suspend or terminate any criminal or juvenile delinquency proceedings at any point after the case is commenced or on appeal.

(3) As used in this section, "victim" means any person determined by the prosecuting attorney to have suffered direct financial, psychological or physical harm as a result of a crime and, in the case of a victim who is a minor, the legal guardian of the minor. In the event no person has been determined to be a victim of the crime, the people of Oregon, represented by the prosecuting attorney, are considered to be the victims. In no event is it intended that the criminal defendant be considered the victim. [Created through H.J.R. 94, 1999, and adopted by the people Nov. 2, 1999]

Note: See notes under section 42 of this Article.

Section 45. Person convicted of certain crimes not eligible to serve as juror on grand jury or trial jury in criminal case. (1) In all grand juries and in all prosecutions for crimes tried to a jury, the jury shall be composed of persons who have not been convicted:

(a) Of a felony or served a felony sentence within the 15 years immediately preceding the date the persons are required to report for jury duty; or

(b) Of a misdemeanor involving violence or dishonesty or served a sentence for a misdemeanor involving violence or dishonesty within the five years immediately preceding the date the persons are required to report for jury duty.

(2) This section applies to all criminal proceedings pending or commenced on or after the effective date of this section, except a criminal proceeding in which a jury has been impaneled and sworn on the effective date of this section. Nothing in this section reduces a criminal defendant's rights under the Constitution of the United States. Except as otherwise specifically provided, this section supersedes any conflicting section of this Constitution. Nothing in this section is intended to create any cause of action for compensation or damages nor may this section be used to disqualify a jury, invalidate an accusatory instrument, ruling of a court, conviction or adjudication or otherwise suspend or terminate any criminal proceeding at any point after a jury is impaneled and sworn or on appeal. [Created through H.J.R. 89, 1999, and adopted by the people Nov. 2, 1999]

Note: See notes under section 42 of this Article.

Section 46. Prohibition on denial or abridgment of rights on account of sex. (1) Equality of rights under the law shall not be denied or abridged by the State of Oregon or by any political subdivision in this state on account of sex.

(2) The Legislative Assembly shall have the power to enforce, by appropriate legislation, the provisions of this section.

(3) Nothing in this section shall diminish a right otherwise available to persons under section 20 of this Article or any other provision of this Constitution. [Created through initiative petition filed Oct. 24, 2013, and adopted by the people Nov. 4, 2014]

ARTICLE II
SUFFRAGE AND ELECTIONS

Section 1. Elections free. All elections shall be free and equal.—

Section 2. Qualifications of electors. (1) Every citizen of the United States is entitled to vote in all elections not otherwise provided for by this Constitution if such citizen:

(a) Is 18 years of age or older;

(b) Has resided in this state during the six months immediately preceding the election, except that provision may be made by law to permit a person who has resided in this state less than 30 days immediately preceding the election, but who is otherwise qualified under this subsection, to vote in the election for candidates for nomination or election for President or Vice President of the United States or elector of President and Vice President of the United States; and

(c) Is registered not less than 20 calendar days immediately preceding any election in the manner provided by law.

(2) Provision may be made by law to require that persons who vote upon questions of levying special taxes or issuing public bonds shall be taxpayers. [Constitution of 1859; Amendment proposed by initiative petition filed Dec. 20, 1910, and adopted by the people Nov. 5, 1912; Amendment proposed by S.J.R. 6, 1913, and adopted by the people Nov. 3, 1914; Amendment proposed by S.J.R. 6, 1923, and adopted by the people Nov. 4, 1924; Amendment proposed by H.J.R. 7, 1927, and adopted by the people June 28, 1927; Amendment proposed by H.J.R. 5, 1931, and adopted by the people Nov. 8, 1932; Amendment proposed by H.J.R. 26, 1959, and adopted by the people Nov. 8, 1960; Amendment proposed by H.J.R. 41, 1973, and adopted by the people Nov.

5, 1974; Amendment proposed by initiative petition filed July 20, 1986, and adopted by the people Nov. 4, 1986; Amendment proposed by H.J.R. 4, 2007, and adopted by the people Nov. 4, 2008]

Note: The leadline to section 2 was a part of the measure submitted to the people by initiative petition (Measure No. 13, 1986) and adopted by the people Nov. 4, 1986.

Section 3. Rights of certain electors. A person suffering from a mental handicap is entitled to the full rights of an elector, if otherwise qualified, unless the person has been adjudicated incompetent to vote as provided by law. The privilege of an elector, upon conviction of any crime which is punishable by imprisonment in the penitentiary, shall be forfeited, unless otherwise provided by law. [Constitution of 1859; Amendment proposed by S.J.R. 9, 1943, and adopted by the people Nov. 7, 1944; Amendment proposed by S.J.R. 26, 1979, and adopted by the people Nov. 4, 1980]

Section 4. Residence. For the purpose of voting, no person shall be deemed to have gained, or lost a residence, by reason of his presence, or absence while employed in the service of the United States, or of this State; nor while engaged in the navigation of the waters of this State, or of the United States, or of the high seas; nor while a student of any Seminary of Learning; nor while kept at any alms house, or other assylum [sic], at public expence [sic]; nor while confined in any public prison.—

Section 5. Soldiers, seamen and marines; residence; right to vote. No soldier, seaman, or marine in the Army, or Navy of the United States, or of their allies, shall be deemed to have acquired a residence in the state, in consequence of having been stationed within the same; nor shall any such soldier, seaman, or marine have the right to vote.—

Section 6. Right of suffrage for certain persons. [Constitution of 1859; Repeal proposed by H.J.R. 4, 1927, and adopted by the people June 28, 1927]

Section 7. Bribery at elections. Every person shall be disqualified from holding office, during the term for which he may have been elected, who shall have given, or offered a bribe, threat, or reward to procure his election.—

Section 8. Regulation of elections limits on contributions and expenditures; required disclosures. (1) The Legislative Assembly shall enact laws to support the privilege of free suffrage, prescribing the manner of regulating, and conducting elections, and prohibiting under adequate penalties, all undue influence therein, from power, bribery, tumult, and other improper conduct.

(2) The Legislative Assembly, the governing body of a city, county, municipality or district empowered by law or by this Constitution to enact legislation, or the people through the initiative process, may enact laws or ordinances within its jurisdiction that:

(a) Limit contributions made in connection with political campaigns or to influence the outcome of any election in a manner that does not prevent candidates and political committees from gathering the resources necessary for effective advocacy;

(b) Require the disclosure of contributions or expenditures made in connection with political campaigns or to influence the outcome of any election;

(c) Require that an advertisement made in connection with a political campaign or to influence the outcome of any election identify the persons or entities that paid for the advertisement; and

(d) Limit expenditures made in connection with political campaigns or to influence the outcome of any election to the extent permitted under the Constitution of the United States.

(3) Subsection (2) of this section applies to laws and ordinances enacted by the Legislative Assembly or the governing body of a city, county, municipality or district, or enacted or approved by the people through the initiative process, on or after January 1, 2016. [Constitution of 1859; Amendment proposed by S.J.R. 18, 2019, and adopted by the people Nov. 3, 2020]

Section 9. Penalty for dueling. Every person who shall give, or accept a challenge to fight a duel, or who shall knowingly carry to another person such challenge, or who shall agree to go out of the State to fight a duel, shall be ineligible to any office of trust, or profit.—

Section 10. Lucrative offices; holding other offices forbidden. No person holding a lucrative office, or appointment under the United States, or under this State, shall be eligible to a seat in the Legislative Assembly; nor shall any person hold more than one lucrative office at the same time, except as in this Constition [sic] expressly permitted; Provided, that Officers in the Militia, to which there is attached no annual salary, and the Office of Post Master, where the compensation does not exceed One Hundred Dollars per annum, shall not be deemed lucrative.—

Section 11. When collector or holder of public moneys ineligible to office. No person who may hereafter be a collector, or holder of public moneys, shall be eligible to any office of trust or profit, until he shall have accounted for, and paid over according to law, all sums for which he may be liable.—

Section 12. Temporary appointments to office. In all cases, in which it is provided that an office shall not be filled by the same person, more than a certain number of years continuously, an appointment pro tempore shall not be reckoned a part of that term.—

Section 13. Privileges of electors. In all cases, except treason, felony, and breach of the peace, electors shall be free from arrest in going to elections, during their attendance there, and in returning from the same; and no elector shall be obliged to do duty in the Militia on any day of election, except in time of war, or public danger.—

Section 14. Time of holding elections and assuming duties of office. The regular general biennial election in Oregon for the year A. D. 1910 and thereafter shall be held on the first Tuesday after the first Monday in November. All officers except the Governor, elected for a six year term in 1904 or for a four year term in 1906 or for a two year term in 1908 shall continue to hold their respective offices until the first Monday in January, 1911; and all officers, except the Governor elected at any regular general biennial election after the adoption of this amendment shall assume the duties of their respective offices on the first Monday in January following such election. All laws pertaining to the nomination of candidates, registration of voters and all other things incident to the holding of the regular biennial election shall be enforced and be effected the same number of days before the first Tuesday after the first Monday in November that they have heretofore been before the first Monday in June biennially, except as may hereafter be provided by law. [Constitution of 1859; Amendment proposed by H.J.R. 7, 1907, and adopted by the people June 1, 1908]

Section 14a. Time of holding elections in incorporated cities and towns. Incorporated cities and towns shall hold their nominating and regular elections for their several elective officers at the same time that the primary and general biennial elections for State and county officers are held, and the election precincts and officers shall be the same for all elections held at the same time. All provisions of the charters and ordinances of incorporated cities and towns pertaining to the holding of elections shall continue in full force and effect except so far as they relate to the time of holding such elections. Every officer who, at the time of the adoption of this amendment, is the duly qualified incumbent of an elective office of an incorporated city or town shall hold his office for the term for which he was elected and until his successor is elected and qualified. The Legislature, and cities and towns, shall enact such supplementary legislation as may be necessary to carry the provisions of this amendment into effect. [Created through H.J.R. 22, 1917, and adopted by the people June 4, 1917]

Section 15. Method of voting in legislature. In all elections by the Legislative Assembly, or by either branch thereof, votes shall be given openly or viva voce, and not by ballot, forever; and in all elections by the people, votes shall be given openly, or viva voce, until the Legislative Assembly shall otherwise direct.—

Section 16. Election by plurality; proportional representation. In all elections authorized by this constitution until otherwise provided by law, the person or persons receiving the highest number of votes shall be declared elected, but provision may be made by law for elections by equal proportional representation of all the voters for every office which is filled by the election of two or more persons whose official duties, rights and powers are equal and concurrent. Every qualified elector resident in his precinct and registered as may be required by law, may vote for one person under the title for each office. Provision may be made by law for the voter's direct or indirect expression of his first, second or additional choices among the candidates for any office. For an office which is filled by the election of one person it may be required by law that the person elected shall be the final choice of a majority of the electors voting for candidates for that office. These principles may be applied by law to nominations by political parties and organizations. [Constitution of 1859; Amendment proposed by initiative petition filed Jan. 29, 1908, and adopted by the people June 1, 1908]

Section 17. Place of voting. All qualified electors shall vote in the election precinct in the County where they may reside, for County Officers, and in any County in the State for State Officers, or in any County of a Congressional District in which such electors may reside, for Members of Congress.—

Section 18. Recall; meaning of words "the legislative assembly shall provide." (1) Every public officer in Oregon is subject, as herein provided, to recall by the electors of the state or of the electoral district from which the public officer is elected.

(2) Fifteen per cent, but not more, of the number of electors who voted for Governor in the officer's electoral district at the most recent election at which a candidate for Governor was elected to a full term, may be required to file their petition demanding the officer's recall by the people.

(3) They shall set forth in the petition the reasons for the demand.

(4) If the public officer offers to resign, the resignation shall be accepted and take effect on the day it is offered, and the vacancy shall be filled as may be provided by law. If the public officer does not resign within five days after the petition is filed, a special election shall be ordered to be held within 35 days in the electoral district to determine whether the people will recall the officer.

(5) On the ballot at the election shall be printed in not more than 200 words the reasons for demanding the recall of the officer as set forth in the recall petition, and, in not more than 200 words, the officer's justification of the officer's course in office. The officer shall continue to perform the duties of office until the result of the special election is officially declared. If an officer is recalled from any public office the vacancy shall be filled immediately in the manner provided by law for filling a vacancy in that office arising from any other cause.

(6) The recall petition shall be filed with the officer with whom a petition for nomination to such office should be filed, and the same officer shall order the special election when it is required. No such petition shall be circulated against any officer until the officer has actually held the office six months, save and except that it may be filed against a senator or representative in the legislative assembly at any time after five days from the beginning of the first session after the election of the senator or representative.

(7) After one such petition and special election, no further recall petition shall be filed against the same officer during the term for which the officer was elected unless such further petitioners first pay into the public treasury which has paid such special election expenses, the whole amount of its expenses for the preceding special election.

(8) Such additional legislation as may aid the operation of this section shall be provided by the legislative assembly, including provision for payment by the public treasury of the reasonable special election campaign expenses of such officer. But the words, "the legislative assembly shall provide," or any similar or equivalent words in this constitution or any amendment thereto, shall not be construed to grant to the legislative assembly any exclusive power of lawmaking nor in any way to limit the initiative and referendum powers reserved by the people. [Created through initiative petition filed Jan. 29, 1908, and adopted by the people June 1, 1908; Amendment proposed by S.J.R. 16, 1925, and adopted by the people Nov. 2, 1926; Amendment proposed by H.J.R. 1, 1983, and adopted by the people Nov. 6, 1984]

Note: "Recall." constituted the leadline to section 18 and was a part of the measure submitted to the people by S.J.R. 16, 1925.

Note: An initiative petition (Measure No. 3, 1992) proposed adding new sections relating to term limits to the Oregon Constitution. Those sections, appearing as sections 19, 20 and 21 of Article II in previous editions of this Constitution, were declared void for not being enacted in compliance with section 1, Article XVII of this Constitution. See Lehman v. Bradbury, 333 Or. 231, 37 P.3d 989 (2002).

Section 22. Political campaign contribution limitations. Section (1) For purposes of campaigning for an elected public office, a candidate may use or direct only contributions which originate from individuals who at the time of their donation were residents of the electoral district of the public office sought by the candidate, unless the contribution consists of volunteer time, information provided to the candidate, or funding provided by federal, state, or local government for purposes of campaigning for an elected public office.

Section (2) Where more than ten percent (10%) of a candidate's total campaign funding is in violation of Section (1), and0 the candidate is subsequently elected, the elected official shall forfeit the office and shall not hold a subsequent elected public office for a period equal to twice the tenure of the office sought. Where more than ten percent (10%) of a candidate's total campaign funding is in violation of Section (1) and the candidate is not elected, the unelected candidate shall not hold a subsequent elected public office for a period equal to twice the tenure of the office sought.

Section (3) A qualified donor (an individual who is a resident within the electoral district of the office sought by the candidate) shall not contribute to a candidate's campaign any restricted contributions of Section (1) received from an unqualified donor for the purpose of contributing to a candidate's campaign for elected public office. An unqualified donor (an entity which is not an individual and who is not a resident of the electoral district of the office sought by the candidate) shall not give any restricted con-

Constitution

tributions of Section (1) to a qualified donor for the purpose of contributing to a candidate's campaign for elected public office.

Section (4) A violation of Section (3) shall be an unclassified felony. [Created through initiative petition filed Jan. 25, 1993, and adopted by the people Nov. 8, 1994]

Note: An initiative petition (Measure No. 6, 1994) adopted by the people Nov. 8, 1994, proposed a constitutional amendment as an unnumbered section. Section 22 sections (1), (2), (3) and (4) were designated in the proposed amendment as "SECTION 1.," "SECTION 2." "SECTION 3." and "SECTION 4.," respectively.

Section 23. Approval by more than majority required for certain measures submitted to people. (1) Any measure that includes any proposed requirement for more than a majority of votes cast by the electorate to approve any change in law or government action shall become effective only if approved by at least the same percentage of voters specified in the proposed voting requirement.

(2) For the purposes of this section, "measure" includes all initiatives and all measures referred to the voters by the Legislative Assembly.

(3) The requirements of this section apply to all measures presented to the voters at the November 3, 1998 election and thereafter.

(4) The purpose of this section is to prevent greater-than-majority voting requirements from being imposed by only a majority of the voters. [Created through initiative petition filed Jan. 15, 1998, and adopted by the people Nov. 3, 1998]

Note: Added as unnumbered section to the Constitution but not to any Article therein by initiative petition (Measure No. 63, 1998) adopted by the people Nov. 3, 1998.

Note: An initiative petition (Measure No. 62, 1998) proposed adding new sections and a subsection relating to political campaigns to the Oregon Constitution. Those sections, appearing as sections 24 to 32 of Article II and sections 1 (6), 1b and 1c of Article IV in previous editions of this Constitution, were declared void for not being enacted in compliance with section 1, Article XVII of this Constitution. See Swett v. Bradbury, 333 Or. 597, 43 P.3d 1094 (2002).

Section 24. Death of candidate prior to election. When any vacancy occurs in the nomination of a candidate for elective public office in this state, and the vacancy is due to the death of the candidate, the Legislative Assembly may provide by law that:

(1) The regularly scheduled election for that public office may be postponed;

(2) The public office may be filled at a subsequent election; and

(3) Votes cast for candidates for the public office at the regularly scheduled election may not be considered. [Created through S.J.R. 19, 2003, and adopted by the people Nov. 2, 2004]

ARTICLE III
DISTRIBUTION OF POWERS

Section 1. Separation of powers. The powers of the Government shall be divided into three separate branches, the Legislative, the Executive, including the administrative, and the Judicial; and no person charged with official duties under one of these branches, shall exercise any of the functions of another, except as in this Constitution

expressly provided. [Constitution of 1859; Amendment proposed by H.J.R. 44, 2011, and adopted by the people Nov. 6, 2012]

Section 2. Budgetary control over executive and administrative officers and agencies. The Legislative Assembly shall have power to establish an agency to exercise budgetary control over all executive and administrative state officers, departments, boards, commissions and agencies of the State Government. [Created through S.J.R. 24, 1951, and adopted by the people Nov. 4, 1952]

Note: Section 2 was designated as "Sec. 1" by S.J.R. 24, 1951, and adopted by the people Nov. 4, 1952.

Section 3. Joint legislative committee to allocate emergency fund appropriations and to authorize expenditures beyond budgetary limits. (1) The Legislative Assembly is authorized to establish by law a joint committee composed of members of both houses of the Legislative Assembly, the membership to be as fixed by law, which committee may exercise, during the interim between sessions of the Legislative Assembly, such of the following powers as may be conferred upon it by law:

(a) Where an emergency exists, to allocate to any state agency, out of any emergency fund that may be appropriated to the committee for that purpose, additional funds beyond the amount appropriated to the agency by the Legislative Assembly, or funds to carry on an activity required by law for which an appropriation was not made.

(b) Where an emergency exists, to authorize any state agency to expend, from funds dedicated or continuously appropriated for the uses and purposes of the agency, sums in excess of the amount of the budget of the agency as approved in accordance with law.

(c) In the case of a new activity coming into existence at such a time as to preclude the possibility of submitting a budget to the Legislative Assembly for approval, to approve, or revise and approve, a budget of the money appropriated for such new activity.

(d) Where an emergency exists, to revise or amend the budgets of state agencies to the extent of authorizing transfers between expenditure classifications within the budget of an agency.

(2) The Legislative Assembly shall prescribe by law what shall constitute an emergency for the purposes of this section.

(3) As used in this section, "state agency" means any elected or appointed officer, board, commission, department, institution, branch or other agency of the state government.

(4) The term of members of the joint committee established pursuant to this section shall run from the adjournment of one odd-numbered year regular session to the organization of the next odd-numbered year regular session. No member of a committee shall cease to be such member solely by reason of the expiration of his term of office as a member of the Legislative Assembly. [Created through S.J.R. 24, 1951, and adopted by the people Nov. 4, 1952; Amendment proposed by S.J.R. 41, 2010, and adopted by the people Nov. 2, 2010]

Note: Section 3 was designated as "Sec. 2" by S.J.R. 24, 1951, and adopted by the people Nov. 4, 1952.

Section 4. Senate confirmation of executive appointments. (1) The Legislative Assembly in the manner provided by law may require that all appointments and reappointments to state public office made by the Governor shall be subject to confirmation by the Senate.

(2) The appointee shall not be eligible to serve until confirmed in the manner required by law and if not confirmed in that manner, shall not be eligible to serve in the public office.

(3) In addition to appointive offices, the provisions of this section shall apply to any state elective office when the Governor is authorized by law or this Constitution to fill any vacancy therein, except the office of judge of any court, United States Senator or Representative and a district, county or precinct office. [Created through S.J.R. 20, 1977, and adopted by the people Nov. 7, 1978]

ARTICLE IV
LEGISLATIVE BRANCH

Section 1. Legislative power; initiative and referendum. (1) The legislative power of the state, except for the initiative and referendum powers reserved to the people, is vested in a Legislative Assembly, consisting of a Senate and a House of Representatives.

(2)(a) The people reserve to themselves the initiative power, which is to propose laws and amendments to the Constitution and enact or reject them at an election independently of the Legislative Assembly.

(b) An initiative law may be proposed only by a petition signed by a number of qualified voters equal to six percent of the total number of votes cast for all candidates for Governor at the election at which a Governor was elected for a term of four years next preceding the filing of the petition.

(c) An initiative amendment to the Constitution may be proposed only by a petition signed by a number of quali-

fied voters equal to eight percent of the total number of votes cast for all candidates for Governor at the election at which a Governor was elected for a term of four years next preceding the filing of the petition.

(d) An initiative petition shall include the full text of the proposed law or amendment to the Constitution. A proposed law or amendment to the Constitution shall embrace one subject only and matters properly connected therewith.

(e) An initiative petition shall be filed not less than four months before the election at which the proposed law or amendment to the Constitution is to be voted upon.

(3)(a) The people reserve to themselves the referendum power, which is to approve or reject at an election any Act, or part thereof, of the Legislative Assembly that does not become effective earlier than 90 days after the end of the session at which the Act is passed.

(b) A referendum on an Act or part thereof may be ordered by a petition signed by a number of qualified voters equal to four percent of the total number of votes cast for all candidates for Governor at the election at which a Governor was elected for a term of four years next preceding the filing of the petition. A referendum petition shall be filed not more than 90 days after the end of the session at which the Act is passed.

(c) A referendum on an Act may be ordered by the Legislative Assembly by law. Notwithstanding section 15b, Article V of this Constitution, bills ordering a referendum and bills on which a referendum is ordered are not subject to veto by the Governor.

(4)(a) Petitions or orders for the initiative or referendum shall be filed with the Secretary of State. The Legislative Assembly shall provide by law for the manner in which the Secretary of State shall determine whether a petition contains the required number of signatures of qualified voters. The Secretary of State shall complete the verification process within the 30-day period after the last day on which the petition may be filed as provided in paragraph (e) of subsection (2) or paragraph (b) of subsection (3) of this section.

(b) Initiative and referendum measures shall be submitted to the people as provided in this section and by law not inconsistent therewith.

(c) All elections on initiative and referendum measures shall be held at the regular general elections, unless otherwise ordered by the Legislative Assembly.

(d) Notwithstanding section 1, Article XVII of this Constitution, an initiative or referendum measure becomes effective 30 days after the day on which it is enacted or approved by a majority of the votes cast thereon. A referendum ordered by petition on a part of an Act does not delay the remainder of the Act from becoming effective.

(5) The initiative and referendum powers reserved to the people by subsections (2) and (3) of this section are further reserved to the qualified voters of each municipality and district as to all local, special and municipal legislation of every character in or for their municipality or district. The manner of exercising those powers shall be provided by general laws, but cities may provide the manner of exercising those powers as to their municipal legislation. In a city, not more than 15 percent of the qualified voters may be required to propose legislation by the initiative, and not more than 10 percent of the qualified voters may be required to order a referendum on legislation. [Created through H.J.R. 16, 1967, and adopted by the people May 28, 1968 (this section adopted in lieu of former sections 1 and 1a of this Article); Amendment proposed by S.J.R. 27, 1985, and adopted by the people May 20, 1986; Amendment proposed by S.J.R. 3, 1999, and adopted by the people May 16, 2000]

Note: An initiative petition (Measure No. 62, 1998) proposed adding new sections and a subsection relating to political campaigns to the Oregon Constitution. Those sections, appearing as sections 24 to 32 of Article II and sections 1 (6), 1b and 1c of Article IV in previous editions of this Constitution, were declared void for not being enacted in compliance with section 1, Article XVII of this Constitution. See Swett v. Bradbury, 333 Or. 597, 43 P.3d 1094 (2002).

Section 1. Legislative authority vested in assembly; initiative and referendum; style of bills. [Constitution of 1859; Amendment proposed by H.J.R. 1, 1901, and adopted by the people June 2, 1902; Amendment proposed by S.J.R. 6, 1953, and adopted by the people Nov. 2, 1954; Repeal proposed by H.J.R. 16, 1967, and adopted by the people May 28, 1968 (present section 1 of this Article adopted in lieu of this section)]

Section 1a. Initiative and referendum on parts of laws and on local, special and municipal laws. [Created through initiative petition filed Feb. 3, 1906, and adopted by the people June 4, 1906; Repeal proposed by H.J.R. 16, 1967, and adopted by the people May 28, 1968 (present section 1 of this Article adopted in lieu of this section)]

Note: Section 1b as submitted to the people was preceded by the following:

To protect the integrity of initiative and referendum petitions, the People of Oregon add the following provisions to the Constitution of the State of Oregon:

Section 1b. Payment for signatures. It shall be unlawful to pay or receive money or other thing of value based on the number of signatures obtained on an initiative or referendum petition. Nothing herein prohibits payment for signature gathering which is not based, either directly or indirectly, on the number of signatures obtained. [Created through initiative petition filed Nov. 7, 2001, and adopted by the people Nov. 5, 2002]

Note: Added as unnumbered section to the Constitution but not to any Article therein by initiative petition (Measure No. 26, 2002) adopted by the people Nov. 5, 2002.

Section 1d. Effective date of amendment to section 1, Article IV, by S.J.R. 3, 1999. [Created through S.J.R. 3, 1999, and adopted by the people May 16, 2000; Repealed Dec. 31, 2002, as specified in text of section adopted by the people May 16, 2000]

Section 2. Number of Senators and Representatives. The Senate shall consist of sixteen, and the House of Representatives of thirty four members, which number shall not be increased until the year Eighteen Hundred and Sixty, after which time the Legislative Assembly may increase the number of Senators and Representatives, always keeping as near as may be the same ratio as to the number of Senators, and Representatives: Provided that the Senate shall never exceed thirty and the House of Representatives sixty members.—

Section 3. How Senators and Representatives chosen; filling vacancies; qualifications. (1) The senators and representatives shall be chosen by the electors of the respective counties or districts or subdistricts within a county or district into which the state may from time to time be divided by law.

(2)(a) If a vacancy occurs in the office of senator or representative from any county or district or subdistrict, the vacancy shall be filled as may be provided by law.

(b) Except as provided in paragraph (c) of this subsection, a person who is appointed to fill a vacancy in the office of senator or representative must be an inhabitant of the district the person is appointed to represent for at least one year next preceding the date of the appointment.

(c) For purposes of an appointment occurring during the period beginning on January 1 of the year a reapportionment becomes operative under section 6 of this Article, the person must have been an inhabitant of the district for one year next preceding the date of the appointment or from

January 1 of the year the reapportionment becomes operative to the date of the appointment, whichever is less. [Constitution of 1859; Amendment proposed by S.J.R. 20, 1929, and adopted by the people Nov. 4, 1930; Amendment proposed by H.J.R. 20, 1953, and adopted by the people Nov. 2, 1954; Amendment proposed by S.J.R. 14, 1995, and adopted by the people May 16, 1995; Amendment proposed by H.J.R. 31, 2007, and adopted by the people Nov. 4, 2008]

Section 3a. Applicability of qualifications for appointment to legislative vacancy. [Section 3a was designated section 1b, which was created by S.J.R. 14, 1995, and adopted by the people May 16, 1995; Repealed Dec. 31, 1999, as specified in text of section adopted by the people May 16, 1995]

Section 4. Term of office of legislators; classification of Senators. (1) The Senators shall be elected for the term of four years, and Representatives for the term of two years. The term of each Senator and Representative shall commence on the second Monday in January following his election, and shall continue for the full period of four years or two years, as the case may be, unless a different commencing day for such terms shall have been appointed by law.

(2) The Senators shall continue to be divided into two classes, in accordance with the division by lot provided for under the former provisions of this Constitution, so that one-half, as nearly as possible, of the number of Senators shall be elected biennially.

(3) Any Senator or Representative whose term, under the former provisions of this section, would have expired on the first Monday in January 1961, shall continue in office until the second Monday in January 1961. [Constitution of 1859; Amendment proposed by S.J.R. 23, 1951, and adopted by the people Nov. 4, 1952; Amendment proposed by S.J.R. 28, 1959, and adopted by the people Nov. 8, 1960]

Section 5. Census. [Constitution of 1859; Repeal proposed by H.J.R. 16, 1971, and adopted by the people May 23, 1972]

Section 6. Apportionment of Senators and Representatives. [Constitution of 1859; Amendment proposed by initiative petition filed July 3, 1952, and adopted by the people Nov. 4, 1952; Repeal proposed by H.J.R. 6, 1985, and adopted by the people Nov. 4, 1986 (present section 6 of this Article adopted in lieu of this section)]

Section 6. Apportionment of Senators and Representatives; operative date. (1) At the odd-numbered year regular session of the Legislative Assembly next following an enumeration of the inhabitants by the United States Government, the number of Senators and Representatives shall be fixed by law and apportioned among legislative districts according to population. A senatorial district shall consist of two representative districts. Any Senator whose term continues through the next odd-numbered year regular legislative session after the operative date of the reapportionment shall be specifically assigned to a senatorial district. The ratio of Senators and Representatives, respectively, to population shall be determined by dividing the total population of the state by the number of Senators and by the number of Representatives. A reapportionment by the Legislative Assembly becomes operative as described in subsection (6) of this section.

(2) This subsection governs judicial review and correction of a reapportionment enacted by the Legislative Assembly.

(a) Original jurisdiction is vested in the Supreme Court, upon the petition of any elector of the state filed with the Supreme Court on or before August 1 of the year in which the Legislative Assembly enacts a reapportionment, to review any reapportionment so enacted.

(b) If the Supreme Court determines that the reapportionment thus reviewed complies with subsection (1) of this section and all law applicable thereto, it shall dismiss the petition by written opinion on or before September 1 of the same year and the reapportionment becomes operative as described in subsection (6) of this section.

(c) If the Supreme Court determines that the reapportionment does not comply with subsection (1) of this section and all law applicable thereto, the reapportionment shall be void. In its written opinion, the Supreme Court shall specify with particularity wherein the reapportionment fails to comply. The opinion shall further direct the Secretary of State to draft a reapportionment of the Senators and Representatives in accordance with the provisions of subsection (1) of this section and all law applicable thereto. The Supreme Court shall file its order with the Secretary of State on or before September 15. The Secretary of State shall conduct a hearing on the reapportionment at which the public may submit evidence, views and argument. The Secretary of State shall cause a transcription of the hearing to be prepared which, with the evidence, shall become part of the record. The Secretary of State shall file the corrected reapportionment with the Supreme Court on or before November 1 of the same year.

(d) On or before November 15, the Supreme Court shall review the corrected reapportionment to assure its compliance with subsection (1) of this section and all law applicable thereto and may further correct the reapportionment if the court considers correction to be necessary.

(e) The corrected reapportionment becomes operative as described in subsection (6) of this section.

(3) This subsection governs enactment, judicial review and correction of a reapportionment if the Legislative Assembly fails to enact any reapportionment by July 1 of the year of the odd-numbered year regular session of the Legislative Assembly next following an enumeration of the inhabitants by the United States Government.

(a) The Secretary of State shall make a reapportionment of the Senators and Representatives in accordance with the provisions of subsection (1) of this section and all law applicable thereto. The Secretary of State shall conduct a hearing on the reapportionment at which the public may submit evidence, views and argument. The Secretary of State shall cause a transcription of the hearing to be prepared which, with the evidence, shall become part of the record. The reapportionment so made shall be filed with the Supreme Court by August 15 of the same year. The reapportionment becomes operative as described in subsection (6) of this section.

(b) Original jurisdiction is vested in the Supreme Court upon the petition of any elector of the state filed with the Supreme Court on or before September 15 of the same year to review any reapportionment and the record made by the Secretary of State.

(c) If the Supreme Court determines that the reapportionment thus reviewed complies with subsection (1) of this section and all law applicable thereto, it shall dismiss the petition by written opinion on or before October 15 of the same year and the reapportionment becomes operative as described in subsection (6) of this section.

(d) If the Supreme Court determines that the reapportionment does not comply with subsection (1) of this section and all law applicable thereto, the reapportionment shall be void. The Supreme Court shall return the reapportionment by November 1 to the Secretary of State accompanied by a written opinion specifying with particularity wherein the reapportionment fails to comply. The opinion shall further direct the Secretary of State to correct the reapportionment in those particulars, and in no others, and

file the corrected reapportionment with the Supreme Court on or before December 1 of the same year.

(e) On or before December 15, the Supreme Court shall review the corrected reapportionment to assure its compliance with subsection (1) of this section and all law applicable thereto and may further correct the reapportionment if the court considers correction to be necessary.

(f) The reapportionment becomes operative as described in subsection (6) of this section.

(4) Any reapportionment that becomes operative as provided in this section is a law of the state except for purposes of initiative and referendum.

(5) Notwithstanding section 18, Article II of this Constitution, after the convening of the next odd-numbered year regular legislative session following the reapportionment, a Senator whose term continues through that legislative session is subject to recall by the electors of the district to which the Senator is assigned and not by the electors of the district existing before the latest reapportionment. The number of signatures required on the recall petition is 15 percent of the total votes cast for all candidates for Governor at the most recent election at which a candidate for Governor was elected to a full term in the two representative districts comprising the senatorial district to which the Senator was assigned.

(6)(a) Except as provided in paragraph (b) of this subsection, a reapportionment made under this section becomes operative on the second Monday in January of the next odd-numbered year after the applicable deadline for making a final reapportionment under this section.

(b) For purposes of electing Senators and Representatives to the next term of office that commences after the applicable deadline for making a final reapportionment under this section, a reapportionment made under this section becomes operative on January 1 of the calendar year next following the applicable deadline for making a final reapportionment under this section. [Created through H.J.R. 6, 1985, and adopted by the people Nov. 4, 1986 (this section adopted in lieu of former section 6 of this Article); Amendment proposed by H.J.R. 31, 2007, and adopted by the people Nov. 4, 2008; Amendment proposed by S.J.R. 41, 2010, and adopted by the people Nov. 2, 2010]

Section 7. Senatorial districts; senatorial and representative subdistricts. A senatorial district, when more than one county shall constitute the same, shall be composed of contiguous counties, and no county shall be divided in creating such senatorial districts. Senatorial or representative districts comprising not more than one county may be divided into subdistricts from time to time by law. Subdistricts shall be composed of contiguous territory within the district; and the ratios to population of senators or representatives, as the case may be, elected from the subdistricts, shall be substantially equal within the district. [Constitution of 1859; Amendment proposed by H.J.R. 20, 1953, and adopted by the people Nov. 2, 1954]

Section 8. Qualification of Senators and Representatives; effect of felony conviction. (1)(a) Except as provided in paragraph (b) of this subsection, a person may not be a Senator or Representative if the person at the time of election:

(A) Is not a citizen of the United States; and

(B) Has not been for one year next preceding the election an inhabitant of the district from which the Senator or Representative may be chosen.

(b) For purposes of the general election next following the applicable deadline for making a final apportionment under section 6 of this Article, the person must have been an inhabitant of the district from January 1 of the year following the applicable deadline for making the final reapportionment to the date of the election.

(2) Senators and Representatives shall be at least twenty one years of age.

(3) A person may not be a Senator or Representative if the person has been convicted of a felony during:

(a) The term of office of the person as a Senator or Representative; or

(b) The period beginning on the date of the election at which the person was elected to the office of Senator or Representative and ending on the first day of the term of office to which the person was elected.

(4) A person is not eligible to be elected as a Senator or Representative if that person has been convicted of a felony and has not completed the sentence received for the conviction prior to the date that person would take office if elected. As used in this subsection, "sentence received for the conviction" includes a term of imprisonment, any period of probation or post-prison supervision and payment of a monetary obligation imposed as all or part of a sentence.

(5) Notwithstanding sections 11 and 15, Article IV of this Constitution:

(a) The office of a Senator or Representative convicted of a felony during the term to which the Senator or Representative was elected or appointed shall become vacant on the date the Senator or Representative is convicted.

(b) A person elected to the office of Senator or Representative and convicted of a felony during the period beginning on the date of the election and ending on the first day of the term of office to which the person was elected shall be ineligible to take office and the office shall become vacant on the first day of the next term of office.

(6) Subject to subsection (4) of this section, a person who is ineligible to be a Senator or Representative under subsection (3) of this section may:

(a) Be a Senator or Representative after the expiration of the term of office during which the person is ineligible; and

(b) Be a candidate for the office of Senator or Representative prior to the expiration of the term of office during which the person is ineligible.

(7)(a) Except as provided in paragraph (b) of this subsection, a person may not be a Senator or Representative if the person at all times during the term of office of the person as a Senator or Representative is not an inhabitant of the district from which the Senator or Representative may be chosen or which the Senator or Representative has been appointed to represent. A person does not lose status as an inhabitant of a district if the person is absent from the district for purposes of business of the Legislative Assembly.

(b) Following the applicable deadline for making a final apportionment under section 6 of this Article, until the expiration of the term of office of the person, a person may be an inhabitant of any district. [Constitution of 1859; Amendment proposed by H.J.R. 6, 1985, and adopted by the people Nov. 4, 1986; Amendment proposed by S.J.R. 33, 1993, and adopted by the people Nov. 8, 1994; Amendment proposed by S.J.R. 14, 1995, and adopted by the people May 16, 1995; Amendment proposed by H.J.R. 31, 2007, and adopted by the people Nov. 4, 2008]

Section 8a. Applicability of qualification for legislative office. [Created by S.J.R. 14, 1995, and adopted by the people May 16, 1995; Repealed Dec. 31, 1999, as specified in text of section adopted by the people May 16, 1995]

Section 9. Legislators free from arrest and not subject to civil process in certain cases; words uttered in debate. Senators and Representatives in all cases, except for treason, felony, or breaches of the peace, shall be privileged from arrest during the session of the Legislative Assembly, and in going to and returning from the same;

and shall not be subject to any civil process during the session of the Legislative Assembly, nor during the fifteen days next before the commencement thereof: Nor shall a member for words uttered in debate in either house, be questioned in any other place.—

Section 10. Annual regular sessions of the Legislative Assembly; organizational session; extension of regular sessions. (1) The Legislative Assembly shall hold annual sessions at the Capitol of the State. Each session must begin on the day designated by law as the first day of the session. Except as provided in subsection (3) of this section:

(a) A session beginning in an odd-numbered year may not exceed 160 calendar days in duration; and

(b) A session beginning in an even-numbered year may not exceed 35 calendar days in duration.

(2) The Legislative Assembly may hold an organizational session that is not subject to the limits of subsection (1) of this section for the purposes of introducing measures and performing the duties and effecting the organization described in sections 11 and 12 of this Article. The Legislative Assembly may not undertake final consideration of a measure or reconsideration of a measure following a gubernatorial veto when convened in an organizational session.

(3) A regular session, as described in subsection (1) of this section, may be extended for a period of five calendar days by the affirmative vote of two-thirds of the members of each house. A session may be extended more than once. An extension must begin on the first calendar day after the end of the immediately preceding session or extension except that if the first calendar day is a Sunday, the extension may begin on the next Monday. [Constitution of 1859; Amendment proposed by S.J.R. 41, 2010, and adopted by the people Nov. 2, 2010]

Section 10a. Emergency sessions of the Legislative Assembly. In the event of an emergency the Legislative Assembly shall be convened by the presiding officers of both Houses at the Capitol of the State at times other than required by section 10 of this Article upon the written request of the majority of the members of each House to commence within five days after receipt of the minimum requisite number of requests. [Created through H.J.R. 28, 1975, and adopted by the people Nov. 2, 1976]

Section 11. Legislative officers; rules of proceedings; adjournments. Each house when assembled, shall choose its own officers, judge of the election, qualifications, and returns of its own members; determine its own rules of proceeding, and sit upon its own adjournments; but neither house shall without the concurrence of the other, adjourn for more than three days, nor to any other place than that in which it may be sitting.—

Section 12. Quorum; failure to effect organization. Two thirds of each house shall constitute a quorum to do business, but a smaller number may meet; adjourn from day to day, and compel the attendance of absent members. A quorum being in attendance, if either house fail to effect an organization within the first five days thereafter, the members of the house so failing shall be entitled to no compensation from the end of the said five days until an organization shall have been effected.—

Section 13. Journal; when yeas and nays to be entered. Each house shall keep a journal of its proceedings.—The yeas and nays on any question, shall at the request of any two members, be entered, together with the names of the members demanding the same, on the journal; provided that on a motion to adjourn it shall require one tenth of the members present to order the yeas, and nays.

Section 14. Deliberations to be open; rules to implement requirement. The deliberations of each house, of committees of each house or joint committees and of committees of the whole, shall be open. Each house shall adopt rules to implement the requirement of this section and the houses jointly shall adopt rules to implement the requirements of this section in any joint activity that the two houses may undertake. [Constitution of 1859; Amendment proposed by S.J.R. 36, 1973, and adopted by the people Nov. 5, 1974; Amendment proposed by H.J.R. 29, 1977, and adopted by the people May 23, 1978]

Section 15. Punishment and expulsion of members. Either house may punish its members for disorderly behavior, and may with the concurrence of two thirds, expel a member; but not a second time for the same cause.—

Section 16. Punishment of nonmembers. Either house, during its session, may punish by imprisonment, any person, not a member, who shall have been guilty of disrespect to the house by disorderly or contemptious [sic] behavior in its presence, but such imprisonment shall not at any time, exceed twenty [sic] twenty four hours.—

Section 17. General powers of Legislative Assembly. Each house shall have all powers necessary for a chamber of the Legislative Branch, of a free, and independent State. [Constitution of 1859; Amendment proposed by H.J.R. 44, 2011, and adopted by the people Nov. 6, 2012]

Section 18. Where bills to originate. Bills may originate in either house, but may be amended, or rejected in the other; except that bills for raising revenue shall originate in the House of Representatives.—

Section 19. Reading of bills; vote on final passage. Every bill shall be read by title only on three several days, in each house, unless in case of emergency two-thirds of the house where such bill may be pending shall, by a vote of yeas and nays, deem it expedient to dispense with this rule; provided, however, on its final passage such bill shall be read section by section unless such requirement be suspended by a vote of two-thirds of the house where such bill may be pending, and the vote on the final passage of every bill or joint resolution shall be taken by yeas and nays. [Constitution of 1859; Amendment proposed by S.J.R. 15, 1945, and adopted by the people Nov. 5, 1946]

Section 20. Subject and title of Act. Every Act shall embrace but one subject, and matters properly connected therewith, which subject shall be expressed in the title. But if any subject shall be embraced in an Act which shall not be expressed in the title, such Act shall be void only as to so much thereof as shall not be expressed in the title.

This section shall not be construed to prevent the inclusion in an amendatory Act, under a proper title, of matters otherwise germane to the same general subject, although the title or titles of the original Act or Acts may not have been sufficiently broad to have permitted such matter to have been so included in such original Act or Acts, or any of them. [Constitution of 1859; Amendment proposed by S.J.R. 41, 1951, and adopted by the people Nov. 4, 1952]

Section 21. Acts to be plainly worded. Every act, and joint resolution shall be plainly worded, avoiding as far as practicable the use of technical terms.—

Section 22. Mode of revision and amendment. No act shall ever be revised, or amended by mere reference to its title, but the act revised, or section amended shall be set forth, and published at full length. However, if, at any session of the Legislative Assembly, there are enacted two or more acts amending the same section, each of the acts shall be given effect to the extent that the amendments do not conflict in purpose. If the amendments conflict in purpose, the act last signed by the Governor shall control. [Constitution of 1859; Amendment proposed by S.J.R. 28, 1975, and adopted by the people Nov. 2, 1976]

Section 23. Certain local and special laws prohibited. The Legislative Assembly, shall not pass special or local laws, in any of the following enumerated cases, that is to say:—

Regulating the jurisdiction, and duties of justices of the peace, and of constables;

For the punishment of Crimes, and Misdemeanors;

Regulating the practice in Courts of Justice;

Providing for changing the venue in civil, and Criminal cases;

Granting divorces;

Changing the names of persons;

For laying, opening, and working on highways, and for the election, or appointment of supervisors;

Vacating roads, Town plats, Streets, Alleys, and Public squares;

Summoning and empanneling [sic] grand, and petit jurors;

For the assessment and collection of Taxes, for State, County, Township, or road purposes;

Providing for supporting Common schools, and for the preservation of school funds;

In relation to interest on money;

Providing for opening, and conducting the elections of State, County, and Township officers, and designating the places of voting;

Providing for the sale of real estate, belonging to minors, or other persons laboring under legal disabilities, by executors, administrators, guardians, or trustees.—

Section 24. Suit against state. Provision may be made by general law, for bringing suit against the State, as to all liabilities originating after, or existing at the time of the adoption of this Constitution; but no special act authorizeing [sic] such suit to be brought, or making compensation to any person claiming damages against the State, shall ever be passed.—

Section 25. Majority necessary to pass bills and resolutions; special requirements for bills raising revenue; signatures of presiding officers required. (1) Except as otherwise provided in subsection (2) of this section, a majority of all the members elected to each House shall be necessary to pass every bill or Joint resolution.

(2) Three-fifths of all members elected to each House shall be necessary to pass bills for raising revenue.

(3) All bills, and Joint resolutions passed, shall be signed by the presiding officers of the respective houses. [Constitution of 1859; Amendment proposed by H.J.R. 14, 1995, and adopted by the people May 21, 1996]

Section 26. Protest by member. Any member of either house, shall have the right to protest, and have his protest, with his reasons for dissent, entered on the journal.—

Section 27. All statutes public laws; exceptions. Every Statute shall be a public law, unless otherwise declared in the Statute itself.—

Section 28. When Act takes effect. No act shall take effect, until ninety days from the end of the session at which the same shall have been passed, except in case of emergency; which emergency shall be declared in the preamble, or in the body of the law.

Section 29. Compensation of members. The members of the Legislative Assembly shall receive for their services a salary to be established and paid in the same manner as the salaries of other elected state officers and employes. [Constitution of 1859; Amendment proposed by S.J.R. 3, 1941, and adopted by the people Nov. 3, 1942; Amendment proposed by H.J.R. 5, 1949, and adopted by the people Nov. 7, 1950; Amendment proposed by H.J.R. 8, 1961, and adopted by the people May 18, 1962]

Section 30. Members not eligible to other offices. No Senator or Representative shall, during the time for which he may have been elected, be eligible to any office the election to which is vested in the Legislative Assembly; nor shall be appointed to any civil office of profit which shall have been created, or the emoluments of which shall have been increased during such term; but this latter provision shall not be construed to apply to any officer elective by the people.—

Section 31. Oath of members. The members of the Legislative Assembly shall before they enter on the duties of their respective offices, take and subscribe the following oath or affirmation;—I do solemnly swear (or affirm as the case may be) that I will support the Constitution of the United States, and the Constitution of the State of Oregon, and that I will faithfully discharge the duties of Senator (or Representative as the case may be) according to the best of my Ability, And such oath may be administered by the Govenor [sic], Secretary of State, or a judge of the Supreme Court.—

Section 32. Income tax defined by federal law; review of tax laws required. Notwithstanding any other provision of this Constitution, the Legislative Assembly, in any law imposing a tax or taxes on, in respect to or measured by income, may define the income on, in respect to or by which such tax or taxes are imposed or measured, by reference to any provision of the laws of the United States as the same may be or become effective at any time or from time to time, and may prescribe exceptions or modifications to any such provisions. At each regular session the Legislative Assembly shall, and at any special session may, provide for a review of the Oregon laws imposing a tax upon or measured by income, but no such laws shall be amended or repealed except by a legislative Act. [Created through H.J.R. 3, 1969, and adopted by the people Nov. 3, 1970]

Section 33. Reduction of criminal sentences approved by initiative or referendum process. Notwithstanding the provisions of section 25 of this Article, a two-thirds vote of all the members elected to each house shall be necessary to pass a bill that reduces a criminal sentence approved by the people under section 1 of this Article. [Created through initiative petition filed Nov. 16, 1993, and adopted by the people Nov. 8, 1994]

ARTICLE V
EXECUTIVE BRANCH

Section 1. Governor as chief executive; term of office; period of eligibility. The cheif [sic] executive power of the State, shall be vested in a Governor, who shall hold his office for the term of four years; and no person shall be eligible to such office more than Eight, in any period of twelve years.—

Section 2. Qualifications of Governor. No person except a citizen of the United States, shall be eligible to the Office of Governor, nor shall any person be eligible to that office who shall not have attained the age of thirty years, and who shall not have been three years next preceding his election, a resident within this State. The minimum age requirement of this section does not apply to a person who succeeds to the office of Governor under section 8a of this Article. [Constitution of 1859; Amendment proposed by H.J.R. 52, 1973, and adopted by the people Nov. 5, 1974]

Section 3. Who not eligible. No member of Congress, or person holding any office under the United States, or under this State, or under any other power, shall fill the Office of Governor, except as may be otherwise provided in this Constitution.—

Section 4. Election of Governor. The Governor shall be elected by the qualified Electors of the State at the times, and places of choosing members of the Legislative Assembly; and the returns of every Election for Governor, shall be sealed up, and transmitted to the Secretary of State; directed to the Speaker of the House of Representatives, who shall open, and publish them in the presence of both houses of the Legislative Assembly.—

Section 5. Greatest number of votes decisive; election by legislature in case of tie. The person having the highest number of votes for Governor, shall be elected; but in case two or more persons shall have an equal and the highest number of votes for Governor, the two houses of the Legislative Assembly at the next regular session thereof, shall forthwith by joint vote, proceed to elect one of the said persons Governor.—

Section 6. Contested elections. Contested Elections for Governor shall be determined by the Legislative Assembly in such manner as may be prescribed by law.—

Section 7. Term of office. The official term of the Governor shall be four years; and shall commence at such times as may be prescribed by this constitution, or prescribed by law.—

Section 8. Vacancy in office of Governor. [Constitution of 1859; Amendment proposed by S.J.R. 10, 1920 (s.s.), and adopted by the people May 21, 1920; Amendment proposed by S.J.R. 8, 1945, and adopted by the people Nov. 5, 1946; Repeal proposed by initiative petition filed July 7, 1972, and adopted by the people Nov. 7, 1972 (present section 8a of this Article adopted in lieu of this section)]

Section 8a. Vacancy in office of Governor. In case of the removal from office of the Governor, or of his death, resignation, or disability to discharge the duties of his office as prescribed by law, the Secretary of State; or if there be none, or in case of his removal from office, death, resignation, or disability to discharge the duties of his office as prescribed by law, then the State Treasurer; or if there be none, or in case of his removal from office, death, resignation, or disability to discharge the duties of his office as prescribed by law, then the President of the Senate; or if there be none, or in case of his removal from office, death, resignation, or disability to discharge the duties of his office as prescribed by law, then the Speaker of the House of Representatives, shall become Governor until the disability be removed, or a Governor be elected at the next general biennial election. The Governor elected to fill the vacancy shall hold office for the unexpired term of the outgoing Governor. The Secretary of State or the State Treasurer shall appoint a person to fill his office until the election of a Governor, at which time the office so filled by appointment shall be filled by election; or, in the event of a disability of the Governor, to be Acting Secretary of State or Acting State Treasurer until the disability be removed. The person so appointed shall not be eligible to succeed to the office of Governor by automatic succession under this section during the term of his appointment. [Created through initiative petition filed July 7, 1972, and adopted by the people Nov. 7, 1972 (this section adopted in lieu of former section 8 of this Article)]

Section 9. Governor as commander in chief of state military forces. The Governor shall be commander in chief [sic] of the military, and naval forces of this State, and may call out such forces to execute the laws, to suppress insurrection [sic], or to repel invasion.

Section 10. Governor to see laws executed. He shall take care that the Laws be faithfully executed.—

Section 11. Recommendations to legislature. He shall from time to time give to the Legislative Assembly information touching the condition of the State, and reccomend [sic] such measures as he shall judge to be expedient[.]

Section 12. Governor may convene legislature. He may on extraordinary occasions convene the Legislative Assembly by proclamation, and shall state to both houses when assembled, the purpose for which they shall have been convened.—

Section 13. Transaction of governmental business. He shall transact all necessary business with the officers of government, and may require information in writing from the offices of the Administrative, and Military Departments upon any subject relating to the duties of their respective offices.—

Section 14. Reprieves, commutations and pardons; remission of fines and forfeitures. He shall have power to grant reprieves, commutations, and pardons, after conviction, for all offences [sic] except treason, subject to such regulations as may be provided by law. Upon conviction for treason he shall have power to suspend the execution of the sentence until the case shall be reported to the Legislative Assembly, at its next meeting, when the Legislative Assembly shall either grant a pardon, commute the sentence, direct the execution of the sentence, or grant a farther [sic] reprieve.—

He shall have power to remit fines, and forfeitures, under such regulations as may be prescribed by law; and shall report to the Legislative Assembly at its next meeting each case of reprieve, commutation, or pardon granted, and the reasons for granting the same; and also the names of all persons in whose favor remission of fines, and forfeitures shall have been made, and the several amounts remitted[.]

Section 15. [This section of the Constitution of 1859 was redesignated as section 15b by the amendment proposed by S.J.R. 12, 1915, and adopted by the people Nov. 7, 1916]

Section 15a. Single item and emergency clause veto. The Governor shall have power to veto single items in appropriation bills, and any provision in new bills declaring an emergency, without thereby affecting any other provision of such bill. [Created through S.J.R. 12, 1915, and adopted by the people Nov. 7, 1916; Amendment proposed by S.J.R. 13, 1921, and adopted by the people June 7, 1921]

Section 15b. Legislative enactments; approval by Governor; notice of intention to disapprove; disapproval and reconsideration by legislature; failure of Governor to return bill. (1) Every bill which shall have passed the Legislative Assembly shall, before it becomes a law, be presented to the Governor; if the Governor

approve, the Governor shall sign it; but if not, the Governor shall return it with written objections to that house in which it shall have originated, which house shall enter the objections at large upon the journal and proceed to reconsider it.

(2) If, after such reconsideration, two-thirds of the members present shall agree to pass the bill, it shall be sent, together with the objections, to the other house, by which it shall likewise be reconsidered, and, if approved by two-thirds of the members present, it shall become a law. But in all such cases, the votes of both houses shall be determined by yeas and nays, and the names of the members voting for or against the bill shall be entered on the journal of each house respectively.

(3) If any bill shall not be returned by the Governor within five days (Saturdays and Sundays excepted) after it shall have been presented to the Governor, it shall be a law without signature, unless the general adjournment shall prevent its return, in which case it shall be a law, unless the Governor within thirty days next after the adjournment (Saturdays and Sundays excepted) shall file such bill, with written objections thereto, in the office of the Secretary of State, who shall lay the same before the Legislative Assembly at its next session in like manner as if it had been returned by the Governor.

(4) Before filing a bill after adjournment with written objections, the Governor must announce publicly the possible intention to do so at least five days before filing the bill with written objections. However, nothing in this subsection requires the Governor to file any bill with objections because of the announcement. [Created through S.J.R. 12, 1915, and adopted by the people Nov. 7, 1916; Amendment proposed by H.J.R. 9, 1937, and adopted by the people Nov. 8, 1938; Amendment proposed by S.J.R. 4, 1987, and adopted by the people Nov. 8, 1988]

Note: See note at section 15, Article V.

Section 16. Governor to Fill Vacancies by Appointment. When during a recess of the legislative assembly a vacancy occurs in any office, the appointment to which is vested in the legislative assembly, or when at any time a vacancy occurs in any other state office, or in the office of judge of any court, the governor shall fill such vacancy by appointment, which shall expire when a successor has been elected and qualified. When any vacancy occurs in any elective office of the state or of any district or county thereof, the vacancy shall be filled at the next general election, provided such vacancy occurs more than sixty-one (61) days prior to such general election. [Constitution of 1859; Amendment proposed by H.J.R. 5, 1925, and adopted by the people Nov. 2, 1926; Amendment proposed by H.J.R. 30, 1985, and adopted by the people May 20, 1986; Amendment proposed by S.J.R. 4, 1993, and adopted by the people Nov. 8, 1994]

Note: The leadline to section 16 was a part of the measure submitted to the people by H.J.R. 5, 1925.

Section 17. Governor to issue writs of election to fill vacancies in legislature. He shall issue writs of Election to fill such vacancies as may have occured [sic] in the Legislative Assembly.

Section 18. Commissions. All commissions shall issue in the name of the State; shall be signed by the Govenor [sic], sealed with the seal of the State, and attested by the Secretary of State.—

ARTICLE VI
ADMINISTRATIVE DEPARTMENT

Constitution

Section 1. Election of Secretary and Treasurer of state; terms of office; period of eligibility. There shall be elected by the qualified electors of the State, at the times and places of choosing Members of the Legislative Assembly, a Secretary, and Treasurer of State, who shall severally hold their offices for the term of four years; but no person shall be eligible to either of said offices more than Eight in any period of Twelve years.—

Section 2. Duties of Secretary of State. The Secretary of State shall keep a fair record of the official acts of the Legislative Assembly, and Executive Branch; and shall when required lay the same, and all matters relative thereto before either chamber of the Legislative Assembly. The Secretary of State shall be by virtue of holding the office, Auditor of Public Accounts, and shall perform such other duties as shall be assigned to the Secretary of State by law. [Constitution of 1859; Amendment proposed by H.J.R. 44, 2011, and adopted by the people Nov. 6, 2012]

Section 3. Seal of state. There shall be a seal of State, kept by the Secretary of State for official purposes, which shall be called "The seal of the State of Oregon".—

Section 4. Powers and duties of Treasurer. The powers, and duties of the Treasurer of State shall be such as may be prescribed by law.—

Section 5. Offices and records of executive officers. The Governor, Secretary of State, and Treasurer of State shall severally keep the public records, books and papers at the seat of government in any manner relating to their respective offices. [Constitution of 1859; Amendment proposed by S.J.R. 13, 1985, and adopted by the people Nov. 4, 1986]

Section 6. County Officers: There shall be elected in each county by the qualified electors thereof at the time of holding general elections, a county clerk, treasurer and sheriff who shall severally hold their offices for the term of four years. [Constitution of 1859; Amendment proposed by initiative petition filed June 9, 1920, and adopted by the people Nov. 2, 1920; Amendment proposed by H.J.R. 7, 1955, and adopted by the people Nov. 6, 1956]

Note: The deadline to section 6 was a part of the measure proposed by initiative petition filed June 9, 1920, and adopted by the people Nov. 2, 1920.

Section 7. Other officers. Such other county, township, precinct, and City officers as may be necessary, shall be elected, or appointed in such manner as may be prescribed by law.—

Section 8. County officers' qualifications; location of offices of county and city officers; duties of such officers. Every county officer shall be an elector of the county, and the county assessor, county sheriff, county coroner and county surveyor shall possess such other qualifications as may be prescribed by law. All county and city officers shall keep their respective offices at such places therein, and perform such duties, as may be prescribed by law. [Constitution of 1859; Amendment proposed by H.J.R. 7, 1955, and adopted by the people Nov. 6, 1956; Amendment proposed by H.J.R. 42, 1971, and adopted by the people Nov. 7, 1972; Amendment proposed by H.J.R. 22, 1973, and adopted by the people Nov. 5, 1974]

Section 9. Vacancies in county, township, precinct and city offices. Vacancies in County, Township, precinct and City offices shall be filled in such manner as may be prescribed by law.—

Section 9a. County manager form of government. [Created through H.J.R. 3, 1943, and adopted by the people Nov. 7, 1944; Repeal proposed by H.J.R. 22, 1957, and adopted by the people Nov. 4, 1958]

Section 10. County home rule under county charter. The Legislative Assembly shall provide by law a method whereby the legal voters of any county, by majority vote of such voters voting thereon at any legally called election, may adopt, amend, revise or repeal a county charter. A county charter may provide for the exercise by the county of authority over matters of county concern. Local improvements shall be financed only by taxes, assessments or charges imposed on benefited property, unless otherwise provided by law or charter. A county charter shall prescribe the organization of the county government and shall provide directly, or by its authority, for the number, election or appointment, qualifications, tenure, compensation, powers and duties of such officers as the county deems necessary. Such officers shall among them exercise all the powers and perform all the duties, as distributed by the county charter or by its authority, now or hereafter, by the Constitution or laws of this state, granted to or imposed upon any county officer. Except as expressly provided by general law, a county charter shall not affect the selection, tenure, compensation, powers or duties prescribed by law for judges in their judicial capacity, for justices of the peace or for district attorneys. The initiative and referendum powers reserved to the people by this Constitution hereby are further reserved to the legal voters of every county relative to the adoption, amendment, revision or repeal of a county charter and to legislation passed by counties which have adopted such a charter; and no county shall require that referendum petitions be filed less than 90 days after the provisions of the charter or the legislation proposed for referral is adopted by the county governing body. To be circulated, referendum or initiative petitions shall set forth in full the charter or legislative provisions proposed for adoption or referral. Referendum petitions shall not be required to include a ballot title to be circulated. In a county a number of signatures of qualified voters equal to but not greater than four percent of the total number of all votes cast in the county for all candidates for Governor at the election at which a Governor was elected for a term of four years next preceding the filing of the petition shall be required for a petition to order a referendum on county legislation or a part thereof. A number of signatures equal to but not greater than six percent of the total number of votes cast in the county for all candidates for Governor at the election at which a Governor was elected for a term of four years next preceding the filing of the petition shall be required for a petition to propose an initiative ordinance. A number of signatures equal to but not greater than eight percent of the total number of votes cast in the county for all candidates for Governor at the election at which a Governor was elected for a term of four years next preceding the filing of the petition shall be required for a petition to propose a charter amendment. [Created through H.J.R. 22, 1957, and adopted by the people Nov. 4, 1958; Amendment proposed by S.J.R. 48, 1959, and adopted by the people Nov. 8, 1960; Amendment proposed by H.J.R. 21, 1977, and adopted by the people May 23, 1978]

ARTICLE VII (Amended)
THE JUDICIAL BRANCH

Section 1. Courts; election of judges; term of office; compensation. The judicial power of the state shall be vested in one supreme court and in such other courts as may from time to time be created by law. The judges of the supreme and other courts shall be elected by the legal voters of the state or of their respective districts for a term of six years, and shall receive such compensation as may be provided by law, which compensation shall not be diminished during the term for which they are elected. [Created through initiative petition filed July 7, 1910, and adopted by the people Nov. 8, 1910]

Section 1a. Retirement of judges; recall to temporary active service. Notwithstanding the provisions of section 1, Article VII (Amended) of this Constitution, a judge of any court shall retire from judicial office at the end of the calendar year in which he attains the age of 75 years. The Legislative Assembly or the people may by law:

(1) Fix a lesser age for mandatory retirement not earlier than the end of the calendar year in which the judge attains the age of 70 years;

(2) Provide for recalling retired judges to temporary active service on the court from which they are retired; and

(3) Authorize or require the retirement of judges for physical or mental disability or any other cause rendering judges incapable of performing their judicial duties.

This section shall not affect the term to which any judge shall have been elected or appointed prior to or at the time of approval and ratification of this section. [Created through S.J.R. 3, 1959, and adopted by the people Nov. 8, 1960]

Section 2. Amendment's effect on courts, jurisdiction and judicial system; Supreme Court's original jurisdiction. The courts, jurisdiction, and judicial system of Oregon, except so far as expressly changed by this amendment, shall remain as at present constituted until otherwise provided by law. But the supreme court may, in its own discretion, take original jurisdiction in mandamus, quo warranto and habeas corpus proceedings. [Created through initiative petition filed July 7, 1910, and adopted by the people Nov. 8, 1910]

Section 2a. Temporary appointment and assignment of judges. The Legislative Assembly or the people may by law empower the Supreme Court to:

(1) Appoint retired judges of the Supreme Court or judges of courts inferior to the Supreme Court as temporary members of the Supreme Court.

(2) Appoint members of the bar as judges pro tempore of courts inferior to the Supreme Court.

(3) Assign judges of courts inferior to the Supreme Court to serve temporarily outside the district for which they were elected.

A judge or member of the bar so appointed or assigned shall while serving have all the judicial powers and duties of a regularly elected judge of the court to which he is assigned or appointed. [Created through S.J.R. 30, 1957, and adopted by the people Nov. 4, 1958]

Section 2b. Inferior courts may be affected in certain respects by special or local laws. Notwithstanding the provisions of section 23, Article IV of this Constitution, laws creating courts inferior to the Supreme Court or prescribing and defining the jurisdiction of such courts or the manner in which such jurisdiction may be exercised, may be made applicable:

(1) To all judicial districts or other subdivisions of this state; or

(2) To designated classes of judicial districts or other subdivisions; or

(3) To particular judicial districts or other subdivisions. [Created through S.J.R. 34, 1961, and adopted by the people Nov. 6, 1962]

Section 3. Jury trial; re-examination of issues by appellate court; record on appeal to Supreme Court; affirmance notwithstanding error; determination of case by Supreme Court. In actions at law, where the value in controversy shall exceed $750, the right of trial by jury shall be preserved, and no fact tried by a jury shall be otherwise re-examined in any court of this state, unless the court can affirmatively say there is no evidence to support the verdict. Until otherwise provided by law, upon appeal of any case to the supreme court, either party may have attached to the bill of exceptions the whole testimony, the instructions of the court to the jury, and any other matter material to the decision of the appeal. If the supreme court shall be of opinion, after consideration of all the matters thus submitted, that the judgment of the court appealed from was such as should have been rendered in the case, such judgment shall be affirmed, notwithstanding any error committed during the trial; or if, in any respect, the judgment appealed from should be changed, and the supreme court shall be of opinion that it can determine what judgment should have been entered in the court below, it shall direct such judgment to be entered in the same manner and with like effect as decrees are now entered in equity cases on appeal to the supreme court. Provided, that nothing in this section shall be construed to authorize the supreme court to find the defendant in a criminal case guilty of an offense for which a greater penalty is provided than that of which the accused was convicted in the lower court. [Created through initiative petition filed July 7, 1910, and adopted by the people Nov. 8, 1910; Amendment proposed by H.J.R. 71, 1973, and adopted by the people Nov. 5, 1974; Amendment proposed by H.J.R. 47, 1995, and adopted by the people May 21, 1996]

Section 4. Supreme Court; terms; statements of decisions of court. The terms of the supreme court shall be appointed by law; but there shall be one term at the seat of government annually. At the close of each term the judges shall file with the secretary of state concise written statements of the decisions made at that term. [Created through initiative petition filed July 7, 1910, and adopted by the people Nov. 8, 1910]

Section 5. Juries; indictment; information. [Created through initiative petition filed July 7, 1910, and adopted by the people Nov. 8, 1910; Amendment proposed by S.J.R. 23, 1957, and adopted by the people Nov. 4, 1958; Repeal proposed by S.J.R. 1, 1973, and adopted by the people Nov. 5, 1974 (present section 5 of this Article adopted in lieu of this section)]

Section 5. Juries; indictment; information; verdict in civil cases. (1) The Legislative Assembly shall provide by law for:

(a) Selecting juries and qualifications of jurors;

(b) Drawing and summoning grand jurors from the regular jury list at any time, separate from the panel of petit jurors;

(c) Empaneling more than one grand jury in a county; and

(d) The sitting of a grand jury during vacation as well as session of the court.

(2) A grand jury shall consist of seven jurors chosen by lot from the whole number of jurors in attendance at the court, five of whom must concur to find an indictment.

(3) Except as provided in subsections (4) and (5) of this section, a person shall be charged in a circuit court with the commission of any crime punishable as a felony only on indictment by a grand jury.

(4) The district attorney may charge a person on an information filed in circuit court of a crime punishable as a felony if the person appears before the judge of the circuit court and knowingly waives indictment.

(5) The district attorney may charge a person on an information filed in circuit court if, after a preliminary hearing before a magistrate, the person has been held to answer upon a showing of probable cause that a crime punishable as a felony has been committed and that the person has committed it, or if the person knowingly waives preliminary hearing.

(6) An information shall be substantially in the form provided by law for an indictment. The district attorney may file an amended indictment or information whenever, by ruling of the court, an indictment or information is held to be defective in form.

(7) In civil cases three-fourths of the jury may render a verdict. [Created through S.J.R. 1, 1973, and adopted by the people Nov. 5, 1974 (this section adopted in lieu of former section 5 of this Article)]

Section 6. Incompetency or malfeasance of public officer. Public officers shall not be impeached; but incompetency, corruption, malfeasance or delinquency in office may be tried in the same manner as criminal offenses, and judgment may be given of dismissal from office, and such further punishment as may have been prescribed by law. [Created through initiative petition filed July 7, 1910, and adopted by the people Nov. 8, 1910]

Section 7. Oath of office of Judges of Supreme Court. Every judge of the supreme court, before entering upon the duties of his office, shall take and subscribe, and transmit to the secretary of state, the following oath:

"I, _____, do solemnly swear (or affirm) that I will support the constitution of the United States, and the constitution of the State of Oregon, and that I will faithfully and impartially discharge the duties of a judge of the supreme court of this state, according to the best of my ability, and that I will not accept any other office, except judicial offices, during the term for which I have been elected." [Created through initiative petition filed July 7, 1910, and adopted by the people Nov. 8, 1910]

Section 8. Removal, suspension or censure of judges.
(1) In the manner provided by law, and notwithstanding section 1 of this Article, a judge of any court may be removed or suspended from his judicial office by the Supreme Court, or censured by the Supreme Court, for:

(a) Conviction in a court of this or any other state, or of the United States, of a crime punishable as a felony or a crime involving moral turpitude; or

(b) Wilful misconduct in a judicial office where such misconduct bears a demonstrable relationship to the effective performance of judicial duties; or

(c) Wilful or persistent failure to perform judicial duties; or

(d) Generally incompetent performance of judicial duties; or

(e) Wilful violation of any rule of judicial conduct as shall be established by the Supreme Court; or

(f) Habitual drunkenness or illegal use of narcotic or dangerous drugs.

(2) Notwithstanding section 6 of this Article, the methods provided in this section, section 1a of this Article and in section 18, Article II of this Constitution, are the exclusive methods of the removal, suspension, or censure of a judge. [Created through S.J.R. 9, 1967, and adopted by the people Nov. 5, 1968; Amendment proposed by S.J.R. 48, 1975, and adopted by the people May 25, 1976]

Section 9. Juries of less than 12 jurors. Provision may be made by law for juries consisting of less than 12 but not less than six jurors. [Created through S.J.R. 17, 1971, and adopted by the people Nov. 7, 1972]

ARTICLE VII (Original)
THE JUDICIAL BRANCH

Note: Original Article VII, compiled below, has been supplanted in part by amended Article VII and in part by statutes enacted by the Legislative Assembly. The provisions of original Article VII relating to courts, jurisdiction and the judicial system, by the terms of section 2 of amended Article VII, are given the status of a statute and are subject to change by statutes enacted by the Legislative Assembly, except so far as changed by amended Article VII.

Sec. 1. Courts in which judicial power vested
2. Supreme Court
3. Terms of office of Judges
4. Vacancy
5. Chief Justice
6. Jurisdiction
7. Term of Supreme Court; statements of decisions of court
8. Circuit court
9. Jurisdiction of circuit courts
10. Supreme and circuit judges; election in classes
11. County judges and terms of county courts
12. Jurisdiction of county courts; county commissioners
13. Writs granted by county judge; habeas corpus proceedings
14. Expenses of court in certain counties
15. County clerk; recorder
16. Sheriff
17. Prosecuting attorneys
19. Official delinquencies
20. Removal of Judges of Supreme Court and prosecuting attorneys from office
21. Oath of office of Supreme Court Judges

Section 1. Courts in which judicial power vested. The Judicial power of the State shall be vested in a Suprume [sic] Court, Circuits [sic] Courts, and County Courts, which shall be Courts of Record having general jurisdiction, to be defined, limited, and regulated by law in accordance with this Constitution.— Justices of the Peace may also be invested with limited Judicial powers, and Municipal Courts may be created to administer the regulations of incorporated towns, and cities. —

Section 2. Supreme Court. The Supreme Court shall consist of Four Justices to be chosen in districts by the electors thereof, who shall be citizens of the United States, and who shall have resided in the State at least three years next preceding their election, and after their election to reside in their respective districts: The number of Justices, the Districts may be increased, but shall never exceed seven; and the boundaries of districts may be changed, but no Change of Districts, shall have the effect to remove a Judge from office, or require him to change his residence without his consent. [Constitution of 1859; Amendment proposed by S.J.R. 7, 2001, and adopted by the people Nov. 5, 2002]

Section 3. Terms of office of Judges. The Judges first chosen under this Constitution shall allot among themselves, their terms of office, so that the term of one of them shall expire in Two years, one in Four years, and Two in

Six years, and thereafter, one or more shall be chosen every Two years to serve for the term of Six years. —

Section 4. Vacancy. Every vacancy in the office of Judge of the Supreme Court shall be filled by election for the remainder of the vacant term, unless it would expire at the next election, and until so filled, or when it would so expire, the Governor shall fill the vacancy by appointment. —

Section 5. Chief Justice. The Judge who has the shortest term to serve, or the oldest of several having such shortest term, and not holding by appointment shall be the Chief [sic] Justice. —

Section 6. Jurisdiction. The Supreme Court shall have jurisdiction only to revise the final decisions of the Circuit Courts, and every cause shall be tried, and every decision shall be made by those Judges only, or a majority of them, who did not try the cause, or make the decision in the Circuit Court. —

Section 7. Term of Supreme Court; statements of decisions of court. The terms of the Supreme Court shall be appointed by Law; but there shall be one term at the seat of Government annually: —

And at the close of each term the Judges shall file with the Secretary of State, Concise written Statements of the decisions made at that term. —

Note: Section 7 is in substance the same as section 4 of amended Article VII.

Section 8. Circuit court. The Circuits [sic] Courts shall be held twice at least in each year in each County organized for judicial purposes, by one of the Justices of the Supreme Court at times to be appointed by law; and at such other times as may be appointed by the Judges severally in pursuance of law. —

Section 9. Jurisdiction of circuit courts. All judicial power, authority, and jurisdiction not vested by this Constitution, or by laws consistent therewith, exclusively in some other Court shall belong to the Circuit Courts, and they shall have appellate jurisdiction, and supervisory control over the County Courts, and all other inferior Courts, Officers, and tribunals. —

Section 10. Supreme and circuit judges; election in classes. The Legislative Assembly, may provide for the election of Supreme, and Circuit Judges, in distinct classes, one of which classes shall consist of three Justices of the Supreme Court, who shall not perform Circuit duty, and the other class shall consist of the necessary number of Circuit Judges, who shall hold full terms without allotment, and who shall take the same oath as the Supreme Judges. [Constitution of 1859; Amendment proposed by S.J.R. 7, 2001, and adopted by the people Nov. 5, 2002]

Section 11. County judges and terms of county courts. There shall be elected in each County for the term of Four years a County Judge, who shall hold the County Court at times to be regulated by law. —

Section 12. Jurisdiction of county courts; county commissioners. The County Court shall have the jurisdiction pertaining to Probate Courts, and boards of County Commissioners, and such other powers, and duties, and such civil Jurisdiction, not exceeding the amount or value of five hundred dollars, and such criminal jurisdiction not extending to death or imprisonment in the penitentiary, as may be prescribed by law. — But the Legislative Assembly may provide for the election of Two Commissioners to sit with the County Judge whilst transacting County business, in any, or all of the Counties, or may provide a seperate [sic] board for transacting such business. —

Section 13. Writs granted by county judge; habeas corpus proceedings. The County Judge may grant preliminary injuctions [sic], and such other writs as the Legislative Assembly may authorize him to grant, return-able to the Circuit Court, or otherwise as may be provided by law; and may hear, and decide questions arising upon habeas corpus; provided such decision be not against the authority, or proceedings of a Court, or Judge of equal, or higher jurisdiction. —

Section 14. Expenses of court in certain counties. The Counties having less than ten thousand inhabitants, shall be reimbursed wholly or in part for the salary, and expenses of the County Court by fees, percentage, & other equitable taxation, of the business done in said Court & in the office of the County Clerk. [Constitution of 1859; Amendment proposed by S.J.R. 7, 2001, and adopted by the people Nov. 5, 2002]

Section 15. County clerk; recorder. A County Clerk shall be elected in each County for the term of Two years, who shall keep all the public records, books, and papers of the County; record conveyances, and perform the duties of Clerk of the Circuit, and County Courts, and such other duties as may be prescribed by law: — But whenever the number of voters in any County shall exceed Twelve Hundred, the Legislative Assembly may authorize the election of one person as Clerk of the Circuit Court, one person as Clerk of the County Court, and one person Recorder of conveyances. —

Section 16. Sheriff. A sheriff shall be elected in each County for the term of Two years, who shall be the ministerial officer of the Circuit, and County Courts, and shall perform such other duties as may be prescribed by law.—

Section 17. Prosecuting attorneys. There shall be elected by districts comprised of one, or more counties, a sufficient number of prosecuting Attorneys, who shall be the law officers of the State, and of the counties within their respective districts, and shall perform such duties pertaining to the administration of Law, and general police as the Legislative Assembly may direct. —

Section 18. Verdict by Three-fourths Jury in Civil Cases; Jurors; Grand Jurors; Indictment May Be Amended, When. [Constitution of 1859; Amendment proposed by initiative petition filed Jan. 30, 1908, and adopted by the people June 1, 1908; Amendment proposed by H.J.R. 14, 1927, and adopted by the people June 28, 1927; Repeal proposed by S.J.R. 23, 1957, and adopted by the people Nov. 4, 1958]

Section 19. Official delinquencies. Public Officers shall not be impeached, but incompetency, corruption, malfeasance, or delinquency in office may be tried in the same manner as criminal offences [sic], and judgment may be given of dismissal from Office, and such further punishment as may have been prescribed by law. —

Note: Section 19 is the same as section 6 of amended Article VII.

Section 20. Removal of Judges of Supreme Court and prosecuting attorneys from office. The Govenor [sic] may remove from Office a Judge of the Supreme Court, or Prosecuting Attorney upon the Joint resolution of the Legislative Assembly, in which Two Thirds of the members elected to each house shall concur, for incompetency, Corruption, malfeasance, or delinquency in office, or other sufficient cause stated in such resolution. —

Section 21. Oath of office of Supreme Court Judges. Every judge of the Supreme Court before entering upon the duties of his office shall take, subscribe, and transmit to the Secretary of State the following oath. — I _____ do solemnly swear (or affirm) that I will support the Constitution of the United States, and the constitution of the State of Oregon, and that I will faithfully, and impartially discharge the duties of a Judge of the Supreme, and Circuits [sic] Courts of said State according to the best of my ability, and that I will not accept any other office, except Judicial offices during the term for which I have been elected. —

ARTICLE VIII
EDUCATION AND SCHOOL LANDS

Section 1. Superintendent of Public Instruction. The Governor shall be superintendent of public instruction, and his powers, and duties in that capacity shall be such as may be prescribed by law; but after the term of five years from the adoption of this Constitution, it shall be competent for the Legislative Assembly to provide by law for the election of a superintendent, to provide for his compensation, and prescribe his powers and duties.—

Section 2. Common School Fund. (1) The sources of the Common School Fund are:

(a) The proceeds of all lands granted to this state for educational purposes, except the lands granted to aid in the establishment of institutions of higher education under the Acts of February 14, 1859 (11 Stat. 383) and July 2, 1862 (12 Stat. 503).

(b) All the moneys and clear proceeds of all property which may accrue to the state by escheat.

(c) The proceeds of all gifts, devises and bequests, made by any person to the state for common school purposes.

(d) The proceeds of all property granted to the state, when the purposes of such grant shall not be stated.

(e) The proceeds of the five hundred thousand acres of land to which this state is entitled under the Act of September 4, 1841 (5 Stat. 455).

(f) The five percent of the net proceeds of the sales of public lands to which this state became entitled on her admission into the union.

(g) After providing for the cost of administration and any refunds or credits authorized by law, the proceeds from any tax or excise levied on, with respect to or measured by the extraction, production, storage, use, sale, distribution or receipt of oil or natural gas and the proceeds from any tax or excise levied on the ownership of oil or natural gas. However, the rate of such taxes shall not be greater than six percent of the market value of all oil and natural gas produced or salvaged from the earth or waters of this state as and when owned or produced. This paragraph does not include proceeds from any tax or excise as described in section 3, Article IX of this Constitution.

(2) All revenues derived from the sources mentioned in subsection (1) of this section shall become a part of the Common School Fund. The State Land Board may expend moneys in the Common School Fund to carry out its powers and duties under subsection (2) of section 5 of this Article. Unexpended moneys in the Common School Fund shall be invested as the Legislative Assembly shall provide by law and shall not be subject to the limitations of section 6, Article XI of this Constitution. The State Land Board may apply, as it considers appropriate, income derived from the investment of the Common School Fund to the operating expenses of the State Land Board in exercising its powers and duties under subsection (2) of section 5 of this Article. The remainder of the income derived from the investment of the Common School Fund shall be applied to the support of primary and secondary education as prescribed by law. [Constitution of 1859; Amendment proposed by H.J.R. 7, 1967, and adopted by the people May 28, 1968;

Amendment proposed by H.J.R. 6, 1979, and adopted by the people Nov. 4, 1980; Amendment to subsection (2) proposed by S.J.R. 1, 1987, and adopted by the people Nov. 8, 1988; Amendment to paragraph (b) of subsection (1) proposed by H.J.R. 3, 1989, and adopted by the people June 27, 1989]

Section 3. System of common schools. The Legislative Assembly shall provide by law for the establishment of a uniform, and general system of Common schools.

Section 4. Distribution of school fund income. Provision shall be made by law for the distribution of the income of the common school fund among the several Counties of this state in proportion to the number of children resident therein between the ages, four and twenty years.—

Section 5. State Land Board; land management. (1) The Governor, Secretary of State and State Treasurer shall constitute a State Land Board for the disposition and management of lands described in section 2 of this Article, and other lands owned by this state that are placed under their jurisdiction by law. Their powers and duties shall be prescribed by law.

(2) The board shall manage lands under its jurisdiction with the object of obtaining the greatest benefit for the people of this state, consistent with the conservation of this resource under sound techniques of land management. [Constitution of 1859; Amendment proposed by H.J.R. 7, 1967, and adopted by the people May 28, 1968]

Section 6. Qualifications of electors at school elections. [Created through initiative petition filed June 25, 1948, and adopted by the people Nov. 2, 1948; Repeal proposed by H.J.R. 4, 2007, and adopted by the people Nov. 4, 2008]

Note: The leadline to section 6 was a part of the measure proposed by initiative petition filed June 25, 1948, and adopted by the people Nov. 2, 1948.

Section 7. Prohibition of sale of state timber unless timber processed in Oregon. (1) Notwithstanding subsection (2) of section 5 of this Article or any other provision of this Constitution, the State Land Board shall not authorize the sale or export of timber from lands described in section 2 of this Article unless such timber will be processed in Oregon. The limitation on sale or export in this subsection shall not apply to species, grades or quantities of timber which may be found by the State Land Board to be surplus to domestic needs.

(2) Notwithstanding any prior agreements or other provisions of law or this Constitution, the Legislative Assembly shall not authorize the sale or export of timber from state lands other than those described in section 2 of this Article unless such timber will be processed in Oregon. The limitation on sale or export in this subsection shall not apply to species, grades or quantities of timber which may be found by the State Forester to be surplus to domestic needs.

(3) This section first becomes operative when federal law is enacted allowing this state to exercise such authority or when a court or the Attorney General of this state determines that such authority lawfully may be exercised. [Created through S.J.R. 8, 1989, and adopted by the people June 27, 1989]

Section 8. Adequate and Equitable Funding. (1) The Legislative Assembly shall appropriate in each biennium a sum of money sufficient to ensure that the state's system of public education meets quality goals established by law, and publish a report that either demonstrates the appropriation is sufficient, or identifies the reasons for the insufficiency, its extent, and its impact on the ability of the state's system of public education to meet those goals.

(2) Consistent with such legal obligation as it may have to maintain substantial equity in state funding, the Legislative Assembly shall establish a system of

Equalization Grants to eligible districts for each year in which the voters of such districts approve local option taxes as described in Article XI, section 11 (4)(a)(B) of this Constitution. The amount of such Grants and eligibility criteria shall be determined by the Legislative Assembly. [Created through initiative petition filed Oct. 22, 1999, and adopted by the people Nov. 7, 2000]

Note: Added to Article VIII as unnumbered section by initiative petition (Measure No. 1, 2000) adopted by the people Nov. 7, 2000.

Note: The leadline to section 8 was a part of the measure submitted to the people by Measure No. 1, 2000.

ARTICLE IX
FINANCE

Section 1. Assessment and taxation; uniform rules; uniformity of operation of laws. The Legislative Assembly shall, and the people through the initiative may, provide by law uniform rules of assessment and taxation. All taxes shall be levied and collected under general laws operating uniformly throughout the State. [Constitution of 1859; Amendment proposed by H.J.R. 16, 1917, and adopted by the people June 4, 1917]

Section 1a. Poll or head tax; declaration of emergency in tax laws. No poll or head tax shall be levied or collected in Oregon. The Legislative Assembly shall not declare an emergency in any act regulating taxation or exemption. [Created through initiative petition filed June 23, 1910, and adopted by the people Nov. 8, 1910; Amendment proposed by S.J.R. 10, 1911, and adopted by the people Nov. 5, 1912]

Section 1b. Ships exempt from taxation until 1935. All ships and vessels of fifty tons or more capacity engaged in either passenger or freight coasting or foreign trade, whose home ports of registration are in the State of Oregon, shall be and are hereby exempted from all taxes of every kind whatsoever, excepting taxes for State purposes, until the first day of January, 1935. [Created through S.J.R. 18, 1915, and adopted by the people Nov. 7, 1916]

Section 1c. Financing redevelopment and urban renewal projects. The Legislative Assembly may provide that the ad valorem taxes levied by any taxing unit, in which is located all or part of an area included in a redevelopment or urban renewal project, may be divided so that the taxes levied against any increase in the assessed value, as defined by law, of property in such area obtaining after the effective date of the ordinance or resolution approving the redevelopment or urban renewal plan for such area, shall be used to pay any indebtedness incurred for the redevelopment or urban renewal project. The legislature may enact such laws as may be necessary to carry out the purposes of this section. [Created through S.J.R. 32, 1959, and adopted by the people Nov. 8, 1960; Amendment proposed by H.J.R. 85, 1997, and adopted by the people May 20, 1997]

Section 2. Legislature to provide revenue to pay current state expenses and interest. The Legislative Assembly shall provide for raising revenue sufficiently to defray the expenses of the State for each fiscal year, and also a sufficient sum to pay the interest on the State debt, if there be any.—

Section 3. Laws imposing taxes; gasoline and motor vehicle taxes. [Constitution of 1859; Amendment proposed by S.J.R. 11, 1941, and adopted by the people Nov. 3, 1942; Repeal proposed by S.J.R. 7, 1979, and adopted by the people May 20, 1980]

Section 3. Tax imposed only by law; statement of purpose. No tax shall be levied except in accordance with law. Every law imposing a tax shall state distinctly the purpose to which the revenue shall be applied. [Created through S.J.R. 7, 1979, and adopted by the people May 20, 1980 (this section and section 3a adopted in lieu of former section 3 of this Article)]

Section 3a. Use of revenue from taxes on motor vehicle use and fuel; legislative review of allocation of taxes between vehicle classes. (1) Except as provided in subsection (2) of this section, revenue from the following shall be used exclusively for the construction, reconstruction, improvement, repair, maintenance, operation and use of public highways, roads, streets and roadside rest areas in this state:

(a) Any tax levied on, with respect to, or measured by the storage, withdrawal, use, sale, distribution, importation or receipt of motor vehicle fuel or any other product used for the propulsion of motor vehicles; and

(b) Any tax or excise levied on the ownership, operation or use of motor vehicles.

(2) Revenues described in subsection (1) of this section:

(a) May also be used for the cost of administration and any refunds or credits authorized by law.

(b) May also be used for the retirement of bonds for which such revenues have been pledged.

(c) If from levies under paragraph (b) of subsection (1) of this section on campers, motor homes, travel trailers, snowmobiles, or like vehicles, may also be used for the acquisition, development, maintenance or care of parks or recreation areas.

(d) If from levies under paragraph (b) of subsection (1) of this section on vehicles used or held out for use for commercial purposes, may also be used for enforcement of commercial vehicle weight, size, load, conformation and equipment regulation.

(3) Revenues described in subsection (1) of this section that are generated by taxes or excises imposed by the state shall be generated in a manner that ensures that the share of revenues paid for the use of light vehicles, including cars, and the share of revenues paid for the use of heavy vehicles, including trucks, is fair and proportionate to the costs incurred for the highway system because of each class of vehicle. The Legislative Assembly shall provide for a biennial review and, if necessary, adjustment, of rev-

enue sources to ensure fairness and proportionality. [Created through S.J.R. 7, 1979, and adopted by the people May 20, 1980 (this section and section 3 adopted in lieu of former section 3 of this Article); Amendment proposed by S.J.R. 44, 1999, and adopted by the people Nov. 2, 1999; Amendment proposed by S.J.R. 14, 2003, and adopted by the people Nov. 2, 2004]

Section 3b. Rate of levy on oil or natural gas; exception. Any tax or excise levied on, with respect to or measured by the extraction, production, storage, use, sale, distribution or receipt of oil or natural gas, or the ownership thereof, shall not be levied at a rate that is greater than six percent of the market value of all oil and natural gas produced or salvaged from the earth or waters of this state as and when owned or produced. This section does not apply to any tax or excise the proceeds of which are dedicated as described in sections 3 and 3a of this Article. [Created through H.J.R. 6, 1979, and adopted by the people Nov. 4, 1980]

Note: Section 3b was designated as "Section 3a" by H.J.R. 6, 1979, and adopted by the people Nov. 4, 1980.

Section 4. Appropriation necessary for withdrawal from treasury. No money shall be drawn from the treasury, but in pursuance of appropriations made by law.—

Section 5. Publication of accounts. An accurate statement of the receipts, and expenditures of the public money shall be published with the laws of each odd-numbered year regular session of the Legislative Assembly. [Constitution of 1859; Amendment proposed by S.J.R. 41, 2010, and adopted by the people Nov. 2, 2010]

Section 6. Deficiency of funds; tax levy to pay. Whenever the expenses, of any fiscal year, shall exceed the income, the Legislative Assembly shall provide for levying a tax, for the ensuing fiscal year, sufficient, with other sources of income, to pay the deficiency, as well as the estimated expense of the ensuing fiscal year.—

Section 7. Appropriation laws not to contain provisions on other subjects. Laws making appropriations, for the salaries of public officers, and other current expenses of the State, shall contain provisions upon no other subject.—

Section 8. Stationery for use of state. All stationary [sic] required for the use of the State shall be furnished by the lowest responsible bidder, under such regulations as may be prescribed by law. But no State Officer, or member of the Legislative Assembly shall be interested in any bid, or contract for furnishing such stationery.—

Section 9. Taxation of certain benefits prohibited. Benefits payable under the federal old age and survivors insurance program or benefits under section 3(a), 4(a) or 4(f) of the federal Railroad Retirement Act of 1974, as amended, or their successors, shall not be considered income for the purposes of any tax levied by the state or by a local government in this state. Such benefits shall not be used in computing the tax liability of any person under any such tax. Nothing in this section is intended to affect any benefits to which the beneficiary would otherwise be entitled. This section applies to tax periods beginning on or after January 1, 1986. [Created through H.J.R. 26, 1985, and adopted by the people May 20, 1986]

Section 10. Retirement plan contributions by governmental employees. (1) Notwithstanding any existing State or Federal laws, an employee of the State of Oregon or any political subdivision of the state who is a member of a retirement system or plan established by law, charter or ordinance, or who will receive a retirement benefit from a system or plan offered by the state or a political subdivision of the state, must contribute to the system or plan an amount equal to six percent of their salary or gross wage.

(2) On and after January 1, 1995, the state and political subdivisions of the state shall not thereafter contract or otherwise agree to make any payment or contribution to a retirement system or plan that would have the effect of relieving an employee, regardless of when that employee was employed, of the obligation imposed by subsection (1) of this section.

(3) On and after January 1, 1995, the state and political subdivisions of the state shall not thereafter contract or otherwise agree to increase any salary, benefit or other compensation payable to an employee for the purpose of offsetting or compensating an employee for the obligation imposed by subsection (1) of this section. [Created through initiative petition filed May 10, 1993, and adopted by the people Nov. 8, 1994]

Section 11. Retirement plan rate of return contract guarantee prohibited. (1) Neither the state nor any political subdivision of the state shall contract to guarantee any rate of interest or return on the funds in a retirement system or plan established by law, charter or ordinance for the benefit of an employee of the state or a political subdivision of the state. [Created through initiative petition filed May 10, 1993, and adopted by the people Nov. 8, 1994]

Section 12. Retirement not to be increased by unused sick leave. (1) Notwithstanding any existing Federal or State law, the retirement benefits of an employee of the state or any political subdivision of the state retiring on or after January 1, 1995, shall not in any way be increased as a result of or due to unused sick leave. [Created through initiative petition filed May 10, 1993, and adopted by the people Nov. 8, 1994]

Section 13. Retirement plan restriction severability. If any part of Sections 10, 11 or 12 of this Article is held to be unconstitutional under the Federal or State Constitution, the remaining parts shall not be affected and shall remain in full force and effect. [Created through initiative petition filed May 10, 1993, and adopted by the people Nov. 8, 1994]

Section 14. Revenue estimate; retention of excess corporate tax revenue in General Fund for public education funding; return of other excess revenue to taxpayers; legislative increase in estimate. (1) As soon as is practicable after adjournment sine die of an odd-numbered year regular session of the Legislative Assembly, the Governor shall cause an estimate to be prepared of revenues that will be received by the General Fund for the biennium beginning July 1. The estimated revenues from corporate income and excise taxes shall be separately stated from the estimated revenues from other General Fund sources.

(2) As soon as is practicable after the end of the biennium, the Governor shall cause actual collections of revenues received by the General Fund for that biennium to be determined. The revenues received from corporate income and excise taxes shall be determined separately from the revenues received from other General Fund sources.

(3) If the revenues received by the General Fund from corporate income and excise taxes during the biennium exceed the amount estimated to be received from corporate income and excise taxes for the biennium, by two percent or more, the total amount of the excess shall be retained in the General Fund and used to provide additional funding for public education, kindergarten through twelfth grade.

(4) If the revenues received from General Fund revenue sources, exclusive of those described in subsection (3) of this section, during the biennium exceed the amount estimated to be received from such sources for the biennium, by two percent or more, the total amount of the excess shall be returned to personal income taxpayers.

(5) The Legislative Assembly may enact laws:

(a) Establishing a tax credit, refund payment or other mechanism by which the excess revenues are returned to taxpayers, and establishing administrative procedures connected therewith.

(b) Allowing the excess revenues to be reduced by administrative costs associated with returning the excess revenues.

(c) Permitting a taxpayer's share of the excess revenues not to be returned to the taxpayer if the taxpayer's share is less than a de minimis amount identified by the Legislative Assembly.

(d) Permitting a taxpayer's share of excess revenues to be offset by any liability of the taxpayer for which the state is authorized to undertake collection efforts.

(6)(a) Prior to the close of a biennium for which an estimate described in subsection (1) of this section has been made, the Legislative Assembly, by a two-thirds majority vote of all members elected to each House, may enact legislation declaring an emergency and increasing the amount of the estimate prepared pursuant to subsection (1) of this section.

(b) The prohibition against declaring an emergency in an act regulating taxation or exemption in section 1a, Article IX of this Constitution, does not apply to legislation enacted pursuant to this subsection.

(7) This section does not apply:

(a) If, for a biennium or any portion of a biennium, a state tax is not imposed on or measured by the income of individuals.

(b) To revenues derived from any minimum tax imposed on corporations for the privilege of carrying on or doing business in this state that is imposed as a fixed amount and that is nonapportioned (except for changes of accounting periods).

(c) To biennia beginning before July 1, 2001. [Created through H.J.R. 17, 1999, and adopted by the people Nov. 7, 2000; Amendment proposed by S.J.R. 41, 2010, and adopted by the people Nov. 2, 2010; Amendment proposed by initiative petition filed Dec. 7, 2011, and adopted by the people Nov. 6, 2012]

Section 15. Prohibition on tax, fee or other assessment upon transfer of interest in real property; exception. The state, a city, county, district or other political subdivision or municipal corporation of this state shall not impose, by ordinance or other law, a tax, fee or other assessment upon the transfer of any interest in real property, or measured by the consideration paid or received upon the transfer of any interest in real property. This section does not apply to any tax, fee or other assessment in effect and operative on December 31, 2009. [Created through initiative petition filed March 4, 2010, and adopted by the people Nov. 6, 2012]

Note: Added to Article IX as unnumbered section by initiative petition (Measure No. 79, 2012) adopted by the people Nov. 6, 2012.

ARTICLE X
THE MILITIA

Section 1. State militia. The Legislative Assembly shall provide by law for the organization, maintenance and discipline of a state militia for the defense and protection of the State. [Constitution of 1859; Amendment proposed by H.J.R. 5, 1961, and adopted by the people Nov. 6, 1962]

Section 2. Persons exempt. Persons whose religious tenets, or conscientious scruples forbid them to bear arms shall not be compelled to do so. [Constitution of 1859;

Amendment proposed by H.J.R. 5, 1961, and adopted by the people Nov. 6, 1962]

Section 3. Officers. The Governor, in his capacity as Commander-in-Chief of the military forces of the State, shall appoint and commission an Adjutant General. All other officers of the militia of the State shall be appointed and commissioned by the Governor upon the recommendation of the Adjutant General. [Constitution of 1859; Amendment proposed by H.J.R. 5, 1961, and adopted by the people Nov. 6, 1962]

Section 4. Staff officers; commissions. [Constitution of 1859; Repeal proposed by H.J.R. 5, 1961, and adopted by the people Nov. 6, 1962]

Section 5. Legislature to make regulations for militia. [Constitution of 1859; Repeal proposed by H.J.R. 5, 1961, and adopted by the people Nov. 6, 1962]

Section 6. Continuity of government in event of enemy attack. [Created through H.J.R. 9, 1959, and adopted by the people Nov. 8, 1960; Repeal proposed by H.J.R. 24, 1975, and adopted by the people Nov. 2, 1976]

ARTICLE X-A
CATASTROPHIC DISASTERS

Section 1. Definitions; declaration of catastrophic disaster; convening of Legislative Assembly. (1) As used in this Article, "catastrophic disaster" means a natural or human-caused event that:

(a) Results in extraordinary levels of death, injury, property damage or disruption of daily life in this state; and

(b) Severely affects the population, infrastructure, environment, economy or government functioning of this state.

(2) As used in this Article, "catastrophic disaster" includes, but is not limited to, any of the following events if the event meets the criteria listed in subsection (1) of this section:

(a) Act of terrorism.

(b) Earthquake.

(c) Flood.

(d) Public health emergency.

(e) Tsunami.

(f) Volcanic eruption.

(g) War.

(3) The Governor may invoke the provisions of this Article if the Governor finds and declares that a catastrophic disaster has occurred. A finding required by this subsection shall specify the nature of the catastrophic disaster.

(4) At the time the Governor invokes the provisions of this Article under subsection (3) of this section, the Governor shall issue a proclamation convening the Legislative Assembly under section 12, Article V of this Constitution, unless:

(a) The Legislative Assembly is in session at the time the catastrophic disaster is declared; or

(b) The Legislative Assembly is scheduled to convene in regular session within 30 days after the date the catastrophic disaster is declared.

(5) If the Governor declares that a catastrophic disaster has occurred, the Governor shall manage the immediate response to the disaster. The actions of the Legislative Assembly under sections 3 and 4 of this Article are limited to actions necessary to implement the Governor's immediate response to the disaster and to actions necessary to aid recovery from the disaster. [Created through H.J.R. 7, 2011, and adopted by the people Nov. 6, 2012]

Section 2. Additional powers of Governor; use of General Fund moneys and lottery funds. (1) If the Governor declares that a catastrophic disaster has occurred, the Governor may:

(a) Use moneys appropriated from the General Fund to executive agencies for the current biennium to respond to the catastrophic disaster, regardless of the legislatively expressed purpose of the appropriation at the time the appropriation was made.

(b) Use lottery funds allocated to executive agencies for the current biennium to respond to the catastrophic disaster, regardless of the legislatively expressed purpose of the allocation at the time the allocation was made. The Governor may not reallocate lottery funds under this paragraph for purposes not authorized by section 4, Article XV of this Constitution.

(2) The authority granted to the Governor by this section terminates upon the taking effect of a law enacted after the declaration of a catastrophic disaster that specifies purposes for which appropriated General Fund moneys or allocated lottery funds may be used, or upon the date on which the provisions of sections 1 to 5 of this Article cease to be operative as provided in section 6 of this Article, whichever is sooner. [Created through H.J.R. 7, 2011, and adopted by the people Nov. 6, 2012]

Section 3. Procedural requirements for Legislative Assembly. If the Governor declares that a catastrophic disaster has occurred:

(1) Notwithstanding sections 10 and 10a, Article IV of this Constitution, the Legislative Assembly may convene in a place other than the Capitol of the State if the Governor or the Legislative Assembly determines that the Capitol is inaccessible.

(2) Notwithstanding section .12, Article IV of this Constitution, during any period of time when members of the Legislative Assembly are unable to compel the attendance of two-thirds of the members of each house because the catastrophic disaster has made it impossible to locate members or impossible for them to attend, two-thirds of the members of each house who are able to attend shall constitute a quorum to do business.

(3) In a session of the Legislative Assembly that is called because of the catastrophic disaster or that was imminent or ongoing at the time the catastrophic disaster was declared, the number of members of each house that constitutes a quorum under subsection (2) of this section may suspend the rule regarding reading of bills under the same circumstances and in the same manner that two-thirds of the members may suspend the rule under section 19, Article IV of this Constitution.

(4) Notwithstanding section 25, Article IV of this Constitution, during any period of time when members of the Legislative Assembly are unable to compel the attendance of two-thirds of the members of each house because the catastrophic disaster has made it impossible to locate members or impossible for them to attend, three-fifths of the members of each house who are able to attend a session described in subsection (3) of this section shall be necessary to pass every bill or joint resolution.

(5) Notwithstanding section 1a, Article IX of this Constitution, the Legislative Assembly may declare an emergency in any bill regulating taxation or exemption, including but not limited to any bill that decreases or suspends taxes or postpones the due date of taxes, if the Legislative Assembly determines that the enactment of the bill is necessary to provide an adequate response to the catastrophic disaster. [Created through H.J.R. 7, 2011, and adopted by the people Nov. 6, 2012]

Section 4. Additional powers of Legislative Assembly. (1) If the Governor declares that a catastrophic disaster has occurred:

(a) The Legislative Assembly may enact laws authorizing the use of revenue described in section 3a, Article IX of this Constitution, for purposes other than those described in that section.

(b) The Legislative Assembly may, by a vote of the number of members of each house that constitutes a quorum under subsection (2) of section 3 of this Article, appropriate moneys that would otherwise be returned to taxpayers under section 14, Article IX of this Constitution, to state agencies for the purpose of responding to the catastrophic disaster.

(c) Notwithstanding section 7, Article XI of this Constitution, the Legislative Assembly may lend the credit of the state or create debts or liabilities in an amount the Legislative Assembly considers necessary to provide an adequate response to the catastrophic disaster.

(d) The provisions of section 15, Article XI of this Constitution, do not apply to any law that is approved by three-fifths of the members of each house who are able to attend a session described in subsection (3) of section 3 of this Article.

(e) The Legislative Assembly may take action described in subsection (6) of section 15, Article XI of this Constitution, upon approval by three-fifths of the members of each house who are able to attend a session described in subsection (3) of section 3 of this Article.

(f) Notwithstanding section 4, Article XV of this Constitution, the Legislative Assembly may allocate proceeds from the State Lottery for any purpose and in any ratio the Legislative Assembly determines necessary to provide an adequate response to the catastrophic disaster.

(2) Nothing in this section overrides or otherwise affects the provisions of section 15b, Article V of this Constitution. [Created through H.J.R. 7, 2011, and adopted by the people Nov. 6, 2012]

Section 5. Participation in session of Legislative Assembly by electronic or other means. For purposes of sections 3 and 4 of this Article, a member of the Legislative Assembly who cannot be physically present at a session convened under section 1 of this Article shall be considered in attendance if the member is able to participate in the session through electronic or other means that enable the member to hear or read the proceedings as the proceedings are occurring and enable others to hear or read the member's votes or other contributions as the votes or other contributions are occurring. [Created through H.J.R. 7, 2011, and adopted by the people Nov. 6, 2012]

Section 6. Termination of operation of this Article; extension by Legislative Assembly; transition provisions; limitation on power of Governor to invoke this Article. (1) Except as provided in subsection (2) of this section, the provisions of sections 1 to 5 of this Article, once invoked, shall cease to be operative not later than 30 days following the date the Governor invoked the provisions of sections 1 to 5 of this Article, or on an earlier date recommended by the Governor and determined by the Legislative Assembly. The Governor may not recommend a date under this subsection unless the Governor finds and declares that the immediate response to the catastrophic disaster has ended.

(2) Prior to expiration of the 30-day limit established in subsection (1) of this section, the Legislative Assembly may extend the operation of sections 1 to 5 of this Article beyond the 30-day limit upon the approval of three-fifths of the members of each house who are able to attend a session described in subsection (3) of section 3 of this Article.

(3) The determination by the Legislative Assembly required by subsection (1) of this section or an extension described in subsection (2) of this section shall take the form of a bill. A bill that extends the operation of sections 1 to 5 of this Article shall establish a date upon which the provisions of sections 1 to 5 of this Article shall cease to be operative. A bill described in this subsection shall be presented to the Governor for action in accordance with section 15b, Article V of this Constitution.

(4) A bill described in subsection (3) of this section may include any provisions the Legislative Assembly considers necessary to provide an orderly transition to compliance with the requirements of this Constitution that have been overridden under this Article because of the Governor's declaration of a catastrophic disaster.

(5) The Governor may not invoke the provisions of sections 1 to 5 of this Article more than one time with respect to the same catastrophic disaster. A determination under subsection (1) of this section or an extension described in subsection (2) of this section that establishes a date upon which the provisions of sections 1 to 5 of this Article shall cease to be operative does not prevent invoking the provisions of sections 1 to 5 of this Article in response to a new declaration by the Governor that a different catastrophic disaster has occurred. [Created through H.J.R. 7, 2011, and adopted by the people Nov. 6, 2012]

ARTICLE XI
CORPORATIONS AND INTERNAL IMPROVEMENTS

Section 1. Prohibition of state banks. The Legislative Assembly shall not have the power to establish, or incorporate any bank or banking company, or monied [sic] institution whatever; nor shall any bank company, or instition [sic] exist in the State, with the privilege of making, issuing, or putting in circulation, any bill, check, certificate, prommisory [sic] note, or other paper, or the paper of any bank company, or person, to circulate as money. —

Note: The semicolon appearing in the signed Constitution after the word "whatever" in section 1 was not in the original draft reported to and adopted by the convention and is not part of the Constitution. State v. H.S. & L.A., 8 Or. 396, 401 (1880).

Section 2. Formation of corporations; municipal charters; intoxicating liquor regulation. Corporations may be formed under general laws, but shall not be created by the Legislative Assembly by special laws. The Legislative Assembly shall not enact, amend or repeal any charter or act of incorporation for any municipality, city or town. The legal voters of every city and town are hereby granted power to enact and amend their municipal charter, subject to the Constitution and criminal laws of the State of Oregon, and the exclusive power to license, regulate, control, or to suppress or prohibit, the sale of intoxicating liquors therein is vested in such municipality; but such municipality shall within its limits be subject to the provisions of the local option law of the State of Oregon. [Constitution of 1859; Amendment proposed by initiative petition filed Dec.13, 1905, and adopted by the people June 4, 1906; Amendment proposed by initiative petition filed June 23, 1910, and adopted by the people Nov. 8, 1910]

Section 2a. Merger of adjoining municipalities; county-city consolidation. (1) The Legislative Assembly, or the people by the Initiative, may enact a general law providing a method whereby an incorporated city or town or municipal corporation may surrender its charter and be merged into an adjoining city or town, provided a majority of the electors of each of the incorporated cities or towns or municipal corporations affected authorize the surrender or merger, as the case may be.

(2) In all counties having a city therein containing over 300,000 inhabitants, the county and city government thereof may be consolidated in such manner as may be provided by law with one set of officers. The consolidated county and city may be incorporated under general laws providing for incorporation for municipal purposes. The provisions of this Constitution applicable to cities, and also those applicable to counties, so far as not inconsistent or prohibited to cities, shall be applicable to such consolidated government. [Created through H.J.R. 10, 1913, and adopted by the people Nov. 3, 1914; Amendment proposed by S.J.R. 29, 1967, and adopted by the people Nov. 5, 1968]

Section 3. Liability of stockholders. The stockholders of all corporations and joint stock companies shall be liable for the indebtedness of said corporation to the amount of their stock subscribed and unpaid and no more, excepting that the stockholders of corporations or joint stock companies conducting the business of banking shall be individually liable equally and ratably and not one for another, for the benefit of the depositors of said bank, to the amount of their stock, at the par value thereof, in addition to the par value of such shares, unless such banking corporation shall have provided security through membership in the federal deposit insurance corporation or other instrumentality of the United States or otherwise for the benefit of the depositors of said bank equivalent in amount to such double liability of said stockholders. [Constitution of 1859; Amendment proposed by S.J.R. 13, 1911, and adopted by the people Nov. 5, 1912; Amendment proposed by H.J.R. 2, 1943, and adopted by the people Nov. 7, 1944]

Constitution

Section 4. Compensation for property taken by corporation. No person's property shall be taken by any corporation under authority of law, without compensation being first made, or secured in such manner as may be prescribed by law. —

Section 5. Restriction of municipal powers in Acts of incorporation. Acts of the Legislative Assembly, incorporating towns, and cities, shall restrict their powers of taxation, borrowing money, contracting debts, and loaning their credit. —

Section 6. State not to be stockholder in company; exceptions. (1) Except as provided in subsection (3) of this section, the state shall not subscribe to, or be interested in the stock of any company, association or corporation. However, as provided by law the state may hold and dispose of stock, including stock already received, that is donated or bequeathed; and may invest, in the stock of any company, association or corporation, any funds or moneys that:

(a) Are donated or bequeathed for higher education purposes;

(b) Are the proceeds from the disposition of stock that is donated or bequeathed for higher education purposes, including stock already received; or

(c) Are dividends paid with respect to stock that is donated or bequeathed for higher education purposes, including stock already received.

(2) Notwithstanding the limits contained in subsection (1) of this section, the state may hold and dispose of stock:

(a) Received in exchange for technology created in whole or in part by a public institution of post-secondary education; or

(b) Received prior to December 5, 2002, as a state asset invested in the creation or development of technology or resources within Oregon.

(3) Subsections (1) and (2) of this section do not apply to public universities. [Constitution of 1859; Amendment proposed by H.J.R. 11, 1955, and adopted by the people Nov. 6, 1956; Amendment proposed by H.J.R. 27, 1969, and adopted by the people Nov. 3, 1970; Amendment proposed by S.J.R. 17, 2001, and adopted by the people May 21, 2002; Amendment proposed by H.J.R. 203, 2016, and adopted by the people Nov. 8, 2016]

Note: H.J.R. 203, 2016, adopted by the people Nov. 8, 2016, did not properly indicate that the initial "the" should be printed lowercase.

Section 7. Credit of State Not to Be Loaned; Limitation Upon Power of Contracting Debts. The Legislative Assembly shall not lend the credit of the state nor in any manner create any debt or liabilities which shall singly or in the aggregate with previous debts or liabilities exceed the sum of fifty thousand dollars, except in case of war or to repel invasion or suppress insurrection or to build and maintain permanent roads; and the Legislative Assembly shall not lend the credit of the state nor in any manner create any debts or liabilities to build and maintain permanent roads which shall singly or in the aggregate with previous debts or liabilities incurred for that purpose exceed one percent of the true cash value of all the property of the state taxed on an ad valorem basis; and every contract of indebtedness entered into or assumed by or on behalf of the state in violation of the provisions of this section shall be void and of no effect. This section does not apply to any agreement entered into pursuant to law by the state or any agency thereof for the lease of real property to the state or agency for any period not exceeding 20 years and for a public purpose. [Constitution of 1859; Amendment proposed by initiative petition filed July 2, 1912, and adopted by the people Nov. 5, 1912; Amendment proposed by H.J.R.

11, 1920 (s.s.), and adopted by the people May 21, 1920; Amendment proposed by S.J.R. 4, 1961, and adopted by the people Nov. 6, 1962; Amendment proposed by S.J.R. 19, 1963, and adopted by the people Nov. 3, 1964]

Note: The leadline to section 7 was a part of the measure submitted to the people by H.J.R. 11, 1920 (s.s.).

Section 8. State not to assume debts of counties, towns or other corporations. The State shall never assume the debts of any county, town, or other corporation whatever, unless such debts, shall have been created to repel invasion, suppress insurrection, or defend the State in war. —

Section 9. Limitations on powers of county or city to assist corporations. (1) No county, city, town or other municipal corporation, by vote of its citizens, or otherwise, shall become a stockholder in any joint company, corporation or association, whatever, or raise money for, or loan its credit to, or in aid of, any such company, corporation or association.

(2) Notwithstanding subsection (1) of this section, any municipal corporation designated as a port under any general or special law of the state of Oregon may be empowered by statute to raise money and expend the same in the form of a bonus to aid in establishing water transportation lines between such port and any other domestic or foreign port or ports, and to aid in establishing water transportation lines on the interior rivers of this state, or on the rivers between Washington and Oregon, or on the rivers of Washington and Idaho reached by navigation from Oregon's rivers. Any debts of a municipality to raise money created for the aforesaid purpose shall be incurred only on approval of a majority of those voting on the question, and shall not, either singly or in the aggregate, with previous debts and liabilities incurred for that purpose, exceed one percent of the assessed valuation of all property in the municipality.

(3) The prohibitions and limitations set forth in subsection (1) of this section do not apply to the use by a county, city, town or other municipal corporation of bonded indebtedness that is payable from ad valorem taxes not subject to limitation under section 11 or 11b of this Article to finance capital costs of affordable housing, but only if:

(a) The bonded indebtedness is approved by the majority of voters voting on the measure authorizing the bonded indebtedness at an election that meets the requirements of subsection (8) of section 11 of this Article, as modified by section 11k of this Article;

(b) The measure authorizing the bonded indebtedness describes "affordable housing" for purposes of the measure;

(c) The jurisdiction authorizing the bonded indebtedness provides for annual audits of and public reporting on the expenditure of proceeds of the bonded indebtedness; and

(d) The principal amount of the jurisdiction's bonded indebtedness outstanding for such purpose does not exceed one-half of one percent of the real market value of all property in the jurisdiction. [Constitution of 1859; Amendment proposed by S.J.R. 13, 1917, and adopted by the people June 4, 1917; Amendment proposed by H.J.R. 201, 2018, and adopted by the people Nov. 6, 2018]

Section 10. County debt limitation. No county shall create any debt or liabilities which shall singly or in the aggregate, with previous debts or liabilities, exceed the sum of $5,000; provided, however, counties may incur bonded indebtedness in excess of such $5,000 limitation to carry out purposes authorized by statute, such bonded indebtedness not to exceed limits fixed by statute. [Constitution of 1859; Amendment proposed by initiative petition filed July 7, 1910, and adopted by the people Nov. 8,

1910; Amendment proposed by initiative petition filed July 2, 1912, and adopted by the people Nov. 5, 1912; Amendment proposed by S.J.R. 11, 1919, and adopted by the people June 3, 1919; Amendment proposed by H.J.R. 7, 1920 (s.s.), and adopted by the people May 21, 1920; Amendment proposed by S.J.R. 1, 1921 (s.s.), and adopted by the people Nov. 7, 1922; Amendment proposed by S.J.R. 5, 1921 (s.s.), and adopted by the people Nov. 7, 1922; Amendment proposed by H.J.R. 3, 1925, and adopted by the people Nov. 2, 1926; Amendment proposed by S.J.R. 18, 1925, and adopted by the people Nov. 2, 1926; Amendment proposed by H.J.R. 19, 1925, and adopted by the people Nov. 2, 1926; Amendment proposed by H.J.R. 21, 1957, and adopted by the people Nov. 4, 1958]

Section 11. Tax and indebtedness limitation. [Created through initiative petition filed July 6, 1916, and adopted by the people Nov. 7, 1916; Amendment proposed by H.J.R. 9, 1931, and adopted by the people Nov. 8, 1932; Amendment proposed by H.J.R. 9, 1951, and adopted by the people Nov. 4, 1952; Repeal proposed by S.J.R. 33, 1961, and adopted by the people Nov. 6, 1962 (second section 11 of this Article adopted in lieu of this section)]

Section 11. Tax base limitation. [Created through S.J.R. 33, 1961, and adopted by the people Nov. 6, 1962 (this section adopted in lieu of first section 11 of this Article); Amendment proposed by H.J.R. 28, 1985, and adopted by the people May 20, 1986; Repeal proposed by H.J.R. 85, 1997, and adopted by the people May 20, 1997 (present section 11 of this Article adopted in lieu of this section and sections 11a, 11f, 11g, 11h, 11i and 11j of this Article)]

Section 11. Property tax limitations on assessed value and rate of tax; exceptions. (1)(a) For the tax year beginning July 1, 1997, each unit of property in this state shall have a maximum assessed value for ad valorem property tax purposes that does not exceed the property's real market value for the tax year beginning July 1, 1995, reduced by 10 percent.

(b) For tax years beginning after July 1, 1997, the property's maximum assessed value shall not increase by more than three percent from the previous tax year.

(c) Notwithstanding paragraph (a) or (b) of this subsection, property shall be valued at the ratio of average maximum assessed value to average real market value of property located in the area in which the property is located that is within the same property class, if on or after July 1, 1995:

(A) The property is new property or new improvements to property;

(B) The property is partitioned or subdivided;

(C) The property is rezoned and used consistently with the rezoning;

(D) The property is first taken into account as omitted property;

(E) The property becomes disqualified from exemption, partial exemption or special assessment; or

(F) A lot line adjustment is made with respect to the property, except that the total assessed value of all property affected by a lot line adjustment shall not exceed the total maximum assessed value of the affected property under paragraph (a) or (b) of this subsection.

(d) Property shall be valued under paragraph (c) of this subsection only for the first tax year in which the changes described in paragraph (c) of this subsection are taken into account following the effective date of this section. For each tax year thereafter, the limits described in paragraph (b) of this subsection apply.

(e) The Legislative Assembly shall enact laws that establish property classes and areas sufficient to make a determination under paragraph (c) of this subsection.

(f) Each property's assessed value shall not exceed the property's real market value.

(g) There shall not be a reappraisal of the real market value used in the tax year beginning July 1, 1995, for purposes of determining the property's maximum assessed value under paragraph (a) of this subsection.

(2) The maximum assessed value of property that is assessed under a partial exemption or special assessment law shall be determined by applying the percentage reduction of paragraph (a) and the limit of paragraph (b) of subsection (1) of this section, or if newly eligible for partial exemption or special assessment, using a ratio developed in a manner consistent with paragraph (c) of subsection (1) of this section to the property's partially exempt or specially assessed value in the manner provided by law. After disqualification from partial exemption or special assessment, any additional taxes authorized by law may be imposed, but in the aggregate may not exceed the amount that would have been imposed under this section had the property not been partially exempt or specially assessed for the years for which the additional taxes are being collected.

(3)(a)(A) The Legislative Assembly shall enact laws to reduce the amount of ad valorem property taxes imposed by local taxing districts in this state so that the total of all ad valorem property taxes imposed in this state for the tax year beginning July 1, 1997, is reduced by 17 percent from the total of all ad valorem property taxes that would have been imposed under repealed sections 11 and 11a of this Article (1995 Edition) and section 11b of this Article but not taking into account Ballot Measure 47 (1996), for the tax year beginning July 1, 1997.

(B) The ad valorem property taxes to be reduced under subparagraph (A) of this paragraph are those taxes that would have been imposed under repealed sections 11 or 11a of this Article (1995 Edition) or section 11b of this Article, as modified by subsection (11) of this section, other than taxes described in subsection (4), (5), (6) or (7) of this section, taxes imposed to pay bonded indebtedness described in section 11b of this Article, as modified by paragraph (d) of subsection (11) of this section, or taxes described in section 1c, Article IX of this Constitution.

(C) It shall be the policy of this state to distribute the reductions caused by this paragraph so as to reflect:

(i) The lesser of ad valorem property taxes imposed for the tax year beginning July 1, 1995, reduced by 10 percent, or ad valorem property taxes imposed for the tax year beginning July 1, 1994;

(ii) Growth in new value under subparagraph (A), (B), (C), (D) or (E) of paragraph (c) of subsection (1) of this section, as added to the assessment and tax rolls for the tax year beginning July 1, 1996, or July 1, 1997 (or, if applicable, for the tax year beginning July 1, 1995); and

(iii) Ad valorem property taxes authorized by voters to be imposed in tax years beginning on or after July 1, 1996, and imposed according to that authority for the tax year beginning July 1, 1997.

(D) It shall be the policy of this state and the local taxing districts of this state to prioritize public safety and public education in responding to the reductions caused by this paragraph while minimizing the loss of decision-making control of local taxing districts.

(E) If the total value for the tax year beginning July 1, 1997, of additions of value described in subparagraph (A), (B), (C), (D) or (E) of paragraph (c) of subsection (1) of this section that are added to the assessment and tax rolls for the tax year beginning July 1, 1996, or July 1, 1997, exceeds four percent of the total assessed value of property statewide for the tax year beginning July 1, 1997 (before taking into account the additions of value described in subparagraph (A), (B), (C), (D) or (E) of paragraph (c) of subsection (1) of this section), then any ad valorem property taxes attributable to the excess above four percent shall reduce the dollar amount of the reduction described in subparagraph (A) of this paragraph.

(b) For the tax year beginning July 1, 1997, the ad valorem property taxes that were reduced under paragraph (a) of this subsection shall be imposed on the assessed value of property in a local taxing district as provided by law, and the rate of the ad valorem property taxes imposed under this paragraph shall be the local taxing district's permanent limit on the rate of ad valorem property taxes imposed by the district for tax years beginning after July 1, 1997, except as provided in subsection (5) of this section.

(c)(A) A local taxing district that has not previously imposed ad valorem property taxes and that seeks to impose ad valorem property taxes shall establish a limit on the rate of ad valorem property tax to be imposed by the district. The rate limit established under this subparagraph shall be approved by a majority of voters voting on the question. The rate limit approved under this subparagraph shall serve as the district's permanent rate limit under paragraph (b) of this subsection.

(B) The voter participation requirements described in subsection (8) of this section apply to an election under this paragraph.

(d) If two or more local taxing districts seek to consolidate or merge, the limit on the rate of ad valorem property tax to be imposed by the consolidated or merged district shall be the rate that would produce the same tax revenue as the local taxing districts would have cumulatively produced in the year of consolidation or merger, if the consolidation or merger had not occurred.

(e)(A) If a local taxing district divides, the limit on the rate of ad valorem property tax to be imposed by each local taxing district after division shall be the same as the local taxing district's rate limit under paragraph (b) of this subsection prior to division.

(B) Notwithstanding subparagraph (A) of this paragraph, the limit determined under this paragraph shall not be greater than the rate that would have produced the same amount of ad valorem property tax revenue in the year of division, had the division not occurred.

(f) Rates of ad valorem property tax established under this subsection may be carried to a number of decimal places provided by law and rounded as provided by law.

(g) Urban renewal levies described in this subsection shall be imposed as provided in subsections (15) and (16) of this section and may not be imposed under this subsection.

(h) Ad valorem property taxes described in this subsection shall be subject to the limitations described in section 11b of this Article, as modified by subsection (11) of this section.

(4)(a)(A) A local taxing district other than a school district may impose a local option ad valorem property tax that exceeds the limitations imposed under this section by submitting the question of the levy to voters in the local taxing district and obtaining the approval of a majority of the voters voting on the question.

(B) The Legislative Assembly may enact laws permitting a school district to impose a local option ad valorem property tax as otherwise provided under this subsection.

(b) A levy imposed pursuant to legislation enacted under this subsection may be imposed for no more than five years, except that a levy for a capital project may be imposed for no more than the lesser of the expected useful life of the capital project or 10 years.

(c) The voter participation requirements described in subsection (8) of this section apply to an election held under this subsection.

(5)(a) Any portion of a local taxing district levy shall not be subject to reduction and limitation under paragraphs (a) and (b) of subsection (3) of this section if that portion of the levy is used to repay:

(A) Principal and interest for any bond issued before December 5, 1996, and secured by a pledge or explicit commitment of ad valorem property taxes or a covenant to levy or collect ad valorem property taxes;

(B) Principal and interest for any other formal, written borrowing of moneys executed before December 5, 1996, for which ad valorem property tax revenues have been pledged or explicitly committed, or that are secured by a covenant to levy or collect ad valorem property taxes;

(C) Principal and interest for any bond issued to refund an obligation described in subparagraph (A) or (B) of this paragraph; or

(D) Local government pension and disability plan obligations that commit ad valorem property taxes and to ad valorem property taxes imposed to fulfill those obligations.

(b)(A) A levy described in this subsection shall be imposed on assessed value as otherwise provided by law in an amount sufficient to repay the debt described in this subsection. Ad valorem property taxes may not be imposed under this subsection that repay the debt at an earlier date or on a different schedule than established in the agreement creating the debt.

(B) A levy described in this subsection shall be subject to the limitations imposed under section 11b of this Article, as modified by subsection (11) of this section.

(c)(A) As used in this subsection, "local government pension and disability plan obligations that commit ad valorem property taxes" is limited to contractual obligations for which the levy of ad valorem property taxes has been committed by a local government charter provision that was in effect on December 5, 1996, and, if in effect on December 5, 1996, as amended thereafter.

(B) The rates of ad valorem property taxes described in this paragraph may be adjusted so that the maximum allowable rate is capable of raising the revenue that the levy would have been authorized to raise if applied to property valued at real market value.

(C) Notwithstanding subparagraph (B) of this paragraph, ad valorem property taxes described in this paragraph shall be taken into account for purposes of the limitations in section 11b of this Article, as modified by subsection (11) of this section.

(D) If any proposed amendment to a charter described in subparagraph (A) of this paragraph permits the ad valorem property tax levy for local government pension and disability plan obligations to be increased, the amendment must be approved by voters in an election. The voter participation requirements described in subsection (8) of this section apply to an election under this subparagraph. No amendment to any charter described in this paragraph may cause ad valorem property taxes to exceed the limitations of section 11b of this Article, as amended by subsection (11) of this section.

(d) If the levy described in this subsection was a tax base or other permanent continuing levy, other than a levy imposed for the purpose described in subparagraph (D) of paragraph (a) of this subsection, prior to the effective date of this section, for the tax year following the repayment of debt described in this subsection the local taxing district's rate of ad valorem property tax established under paragraph (b) of subsection (3) of this section shall be increased to the rate that would have been in effect had the levy not been excepted from the reduction described in subsection (3) of this section. No adjustment shall be made to the rate of ad valorem property tax of local taxing districts other than the district imposing a levy under this subsection.

(e) If this subsection would apply to a levy described in paragraph (d) of this subsection, the local taxing district imposing the levy may elect out of the provisions of this subsection. The levy of a local taxing district making the election shall be included in the reduction and ad valorem property tax rate determination described in subsection (3) of this section.

(6)(a) The ad valorem property tax of a local taxing district, other than a city, county or school district, that is used to support a hospital facility shall not be subject to the reduction described in paragraph (a) of subsection (3) of this section. The entire ad valorem property tax imposed under this subsection for the tax year beginning July 1, 1997, shall be the local taxing district's permanent limit on the rate of ad valorem property taxes imposed by the district under paragraph (b) of subsection (3) of this section.

(b) Ad valorem property taxes described in this subsection shall be subject to the limitations imposed under section 11b of this Article, as modified by subsection (11) of this section.

(7) Notwithstanding any other existing or former provision of this Constitution, the following are validated, ratified, approved and confirmed:

(a) Any levy of ad valorem property taxes approved by a majority of voters voting on the question in an election held before December 5, 1996, if the election met the voter participation requirements described in subsection (8) of this section and the ad valorem property taxes were first imposed for the tax year beginning July 1, 1996, or July 1, 1997. A levy described in this paragraph shall not be subject to reduction under paragraph (a) of subsection (3) of this section but shall be taken into account in determining the local taxing district's permanent rate of ad valorem property tax under paragraph (b) of subsection (3) of this section. This paragraph does not apply to levies described in subsection (5) of this section or to levies to pay bonded indebtedness described in section 11b of this Article, as modified by subsection (11) of this section.

(b) Any serial or one-year levy to replace an existing serial or one-year levy approved by a majority of the voters voting on the question at an election held after December 4, 1996, and to be first imposed for the tax year beginning July 1, 1997, if the rate or the amount of the levy approved is not greater than the rate or the amount of the levy replaced.

(c) Any levy of ad valorem property taxes approved by a majority of voters voting on the question in an election held on or after December 5, 1996, and before the effective date of this section if the election met the voter participation requirements described in subsection (8) of this section and the ad valorem property taxes were first imposed for the tax year beginning July 1, 1997. A levy described in this paragraph shall be treated as a local option ad valorem property tax under subsection (4) of this section. This paragraph does not apply to levies described in subsection (5) of this section or to levies to pay bonded indebtedness described in section 11b of this Article, as modified by subsection (11) of this section.

(8) An election described in subsection (3), (4), (5)(c)(D), (7)(a) or (c) or (11) of this section shall authorize the matter upon which the election is being held only if:

(a) At least 50 percent of registered voters eligible to vote in the election cast a ballot; or

(b) The election is a general election in an even-numbered year.

(9) The Legislative Assembly shall replace, from the state's General Fund, revenue lost by the public school system because of the limitations of this section. The amount of the replacement revenue shall not be less than the total replaced in fiscal year 1997-1998.

(10)(a) As used in this section:

(A) "Improvements" includes new construction, reconstruction, major additions, remodeling, renovation and rehabilitation, including installation, but does not include minor construction or ongoing maintenance and repair.

(B) "Ad valorem property tax" does not include taxes imposed to pay principal and interest on bonded indebtedness described in paragraph (d) of subsection (11) of this section.

(b) In calculating the addition to value for new property and improvements, the amount added shall be net of the value of retired property.

(11) For purposes of this section and for purposes of implementing the limits in section 11b of this Article in tax years beginning on or after July 1, 1997:

(a)(A) The real market value of property shall be the amount in cash that could reasonably be expected to be paid by an informed buyer to an informed seller, each acting without compulsion in an arm's length transaction occurring as of the assessment date for the tax year, as established by law.

(B) The Legislative Assembly shall enact laws to adjust the real market value of property to reflect a substantial casualty loss of value after the assessment date.

(b) The $5 (public school system) and $10 (other government) limits on property taxes per $1,000 of real market value described in subsection (1) of section 11b of this Article shall be determined on the basis of property taxes imposed in each geographic area taxed by the same local taxing districts.

(c)(A) All property taxes described in this section are subject to the limits described in paragraph (b) of this subsection, except for taxes described in paragraph (d) of this subsection.

(B) If property taxes exceed the limitations imposed under either category of local taxing district under paragraph (b) of this subsection:

(i) Any local option ad valorem property taxes imposed under this subsection shall be proportionally reduced by those local taxing districts within the category that is imposing local option ad valorem property taxes; and

(ii) After local option ad valorem property taxes have been eliminated, all other ad valorem property taxes shall be proportionally reduced by those taxing districts within the category, until the limits are no longer exceeded.

(C) The percentages used to make the proportional reductions under subparagraph (B) of this paragraph shall be calculated separately for each category.

(d) Bonded indebtedness, the taxes of which are not subject to limitation under this section or section 11b of this Article, consists of:

(A) Bonded indebtedness authorized by a provision of this Constitution;

(B) Bonded indebtedness issued on or before November 6, 1990; or

(C) Bonded indebtedness:

(i) Incurred for capital construction or capital improvements; and

(ii)(I) If issued after November 6, 1990, and approved prior to December 5, 1996, the issuance of which has been approved by a majority of voters voting on the question; or

(II) If approved by voters after December 5, 1996, the issuance of which has been approved by a majority of voters voting on the question in an election that is in compliance with the voter participation requirements in subsection (8) of this section.

(12) Bonded indebtedness described in subsection (11) of this section includes bonded indebtedness issued to refund bonded indebtedness described in subsection (11) of this section.

(13) As used in subsection (11) of this section, with respect to bonded indebtedness issued on or after December 5, 1996, "capital construction" and "capital improvements":

(a) Include public safety and law enforcement vehicles with a projected useful life of five years or more; and

(b) Do not include:

(A) Maintenance and repairs, the need for which could reasonably be anticipated.

(B) Supplies and equipment that are not intrinsic to the structure.

(14) Ad valorem property taxes imposed to pay principal and interest on bonded indebtedness described in section 11b of this Article, as modified by subsection (11) of this section, shall be imposed on the assessed value of the property determined under this section or, in the case of specially assessed property, as otherwise provided by law or as limited by this section, whichever is applicable.

(15) If ad valorem property taxes are divided as provided in section 1c, Article IX of this Constitution, in order to fund a redevelopment or urban renewal project, then notwithstanding subsection (1) of this section, the ad valorem property taxes levied against the increase shall be used exclusively to pay any indebtedness incurred for the redevelopment or urban renewal project.

(16) The Legislative Assembly shall enact laws that allow collection of ad valorem property taxes sufficient to pay, when due, indebtedness incurred to carry out urban renewal plans existing on December 5, 1996. These collections shall cease when the indebtedness is paid. Unless excepted from limitation under section 11b of this Article, as modified by subsection (11) of this section, nothing in this subsection shall be construed to remove ad valorem property taxes levied against the increase from the dollar limits in paragraph (b) of subsection (11) of this section.

(17)(a) If, in an election on November 5, 1996, voters approved a new tax base for a local taxing district under repealed section 11 of this Article (1995 Edition) that was not to go into effect until the tax year beginning July 1, 1998, the local taxing district's permanent rate limit under subsection (3) of this section shall be recalculated for the tax year beginning on July 1, 1998, to reflect:

(A) Ad valorem property taxes that would have been imposed had repealed section 11 of this Article (1995 Edition) remained in effect; and

(B) Any other permanent continuing levies that would have been imposed under repealed section 11 of this Article (1995 Edition), as reduced by subsection (3) of this section.

(b) The rate limit determined under this subsection shall be the local taxing district's permanent rate limit for tax years beginning on or after July 1, 1999.

(18) Section 32, Article I, and section 1, Article IX of this Constitution, shall not apply to this section.

(19)(a) The Legislative Assembly shall by statute limit the ability of local taxing districts to impose new or additional fees, taxes, assessments or other charges for the purpose of using the proceeds as alternative sources of funding to make up for ad valorem property tax revenue reductions caused by the initial implementation of this section, unless the new or additional fee, tax, assessment or other charge is approved by voters.

(b) This subsection shall not apply to new or additional fees, taxes, assessments or other charges for a government product or service that a person:

(A) May legally obtain from a source other than government; and

(B) Is reasonably able to obtain from a source other than government.

(c) As used in this subsection, "new or additional fees, taxes, assessments or other charges" does not include moneys received by a local taxing district as:

(A) Rent or lease payments;

(B) Interest, dividends, royalties or other investment earnings;

(C) Fines, penalties and unitary assessments;

(D) Amounts charged to and paid by another unit of government for products, services or property; or

(E) Payments derived from a contract entered into by the local taxing district as a proprietary function of the local taxing district.

(d) This subsection does not apply to a local taxing district that derived less than 10 percent of the local taxing district's operating revenues from ad valorem property taxes, other than ad valorem property taxes imposed to pay bonded indebtedness, during the fiscal year ending June 30, 1996.

(e) An election under this subsection need not comply with the voter participation requirements described in subsection (8) of this section.

(20) If any provision of this section is determined to be unconstitutional or otherwise invalid, the remaining provisions shall continue in full force and effect. [Created through H.J.R. 85, 1997, and adopted by the people May 20, 1997 (this section adopted in lieu of former sections 11, 11a, 11f, 11g, 11h, 11i and 11j of this Article)]

Note: The effective date of House Joint Resolution 85, 1997, is June 19, 1997.

Section 11a. School district tax levy. [Created through S.J.R. 3, 1987, and adopted by the people May 19, 1987; Repeal proposed by H.J.R. 85, 1997, and adopted by the people May 20, 1997 (present section 11 adopted in lieu of this section and sections 11, 11f, 11g, 11h, 11i and 11j of this Article)]

Section 11b. Property tax categories; limitation on categories; exceptions. (1) During and after the fiscal year 1991-92, taxes imposed upon any property shall be separated into two categories: One which dedicates revenues raised specifically to fund the public school system and one which dedicates revenues raised to fund government operations other than the public school system. The taxes in each category shall be limited as set forth in the table which follows and these limits shall apply whether the taxes imposed on property are calculated on the basis of the value of that property or on some other basis:

MAXIMUM ALLOWABLE TAXES

For Each $1000.00 of Property's Real Market Value

Fiscal Year	School System	Other than Schools
1991-1992	$15.00	$10.00
1992-1993	$12.50	$10.00
1993-1994	$10.00	$10.00
1994-1995	$ 7.50	$10.00
1995-1996	$ 5.00	$10.00
and thereafter		

Property tax revenues are deemed to be dedicated to funding the public school system if the revenues are to be used exclusively for educational services, including support services, provided by some unit of government, at any level from pre-kindergarten through post-graduate training.

(2) The following definitions shall apply to this section:

(a) "Real market value" is the minimum amount in cash which could reasonably be expected by an informed seller acting without compulsion, from an informed buyer acting without compulsion, in an "arms-length" transaction during the period for which the property is taxed.

(b) A "tax" is any charge imposed by a governmental unit upon property or upon a property owner as a direct consequence of ownership of that property except incurred charges and assessments for local improvements.

(c) "Incurred charges" include and are specifically limited to those charges by government which can be controlled or avoided by the property owner.

(i) because the charges are based on the quantity of the goods or services used and the owner has direct control over the quantity; or

(ii) because the goods or services are provided only on the specific request of the property owner; or

(iii) because the goods or services are provided by the governmental unit only after the individual property owner has failed to meet routine obligations of ownership and such action is deemed necessary to enforce regulations pertaining to health or safety. Incurred charges shall not exceed the actual costs of providing the goods or services.

(d) A "local improvement" is a capital construction project undertaken by a governmental unit

(i) which provides a special benefit only to specific properties or rectifies a problem caused by specific properties, and

(ii) the costs of which are assessed against those properties in a single assessment upon the completion of the project, and

(iii) for which the payment of the assessment plus appropriate interest may be spread over a period of at least ten years. The total of all assessments for a local improvement shall not exceed the actual costs incurred by the governmental unit in designing, constructing and financing the project.

(3) The limitations of subsection (1) of this section apply to all taxes imposed on property or property ownership except

(a) Taxes imposed to pay the principal and interest on bonded indebtedness authorized by a specific provision of this Constitution.

(b) Taxes imposed to pay the principal and interest on bonded indebtedness incurred or to be incurred for capital construction or improvements, provided the bonds are offered as general obligations of the issuing governmental unit and provided further that either the bonds were issued not later than November 6, 1990, or the question of the issuance of the specific bonds has been approved by the electors of the issuing governmental unit.

(4) In the event that taxes authorized by any provision of this Constitution to be imposed upon any property should exceed the limitation imposed on either category of taxing units defined in subsection (1) of this section, then, notwithstanding any other provision of this Constitution, the taxes imposed upon such property by the taxing units in that category shall be reduced evenly by the percentage necessary to meet the limitation for that category. The percentages used to reduce the taxes imposed shall be calculated separately for each category and may vary from property to property within the same taxing unit. The limitation imposed by this section shall not affect the tax base of a taxing unit.

(5) The Legislative Assembly shall replace from the State's general fund any revenue lost by the public school system because of the limitations of this section. The Legislative Assembly is authorized, however, to adopt laws which would limit the total of such replacement revenue plus the taxes imposed within the limitations of this section in any year to the corresponding total for the previous year plus 6 percent. This subsection applies only during fiscal years 1991-92 through 1995-96, inclusive. [Created through initiative petition filed May 8, 1990, and adopted by the people Nov. 6, 1990]

Section 11c. Limits in addition to other tax limits. The limits in section 11b of this Article are in addition to any limits imposed on individual taxing units by this Constitution. [Created through initiative petition filed May 8, 1990, and adopted by the people Nov. 6, 1990]

Section 11d. Effect of section 11b on exemptions and assessments. Nothing in sections 11b to 11e of this Article is intended to require or to prohibit the amendment of any current statute which partially or totally exempts certain classes of property or which prescribes special rules for assessing certain classes of property, unless such amendment is required or prohibited by the implementation of the limitations imposed by section 11b of this Article. [Created through initiative petition filed May 8, 1990, and adopted by the people Nov. 6, 1990]

Section 11e. Severability of sections 11b, 11c and 11d. If any portion, clause or phrase of sections 11b to 11e of this Article is for any reason held to be invalid or unconstitutional by a court of competent jurisdiction, the remaining portions, clauses and phrases shall not be affected but shall remain in full force and effect. [Created through initiative petition filed May 8, 1990, and adopted by the people Nov. 6, 1990]

Section 11f. School district tax levy following merger. [Created through H.J.R. 14, 1989, and adopted by the people Nov. 6, 1990; Repeal proposed by H.J.R. 85, 1997, and adopted by the people May 20, 1997 (present section 11 adopted in lieu of this section and sections 11, 11a, 11g, 11h, 11i and 11j of this Article)]

Note: Section 11f was designated as "Section 11b" by H.J.R. 14, 1989, and adopted by the people Nov. 6, 1990.

Section 11g. Tax increase limitation; exceptions. [Created through initiative petition filed Dec. 8, 1996, and adopted by the people Nov. 5, 1996; Repeal proposed by H.J.R. 85, 1997, and adopted by the people May 20, 1997 (present section 11 adopted in lieu of this section and sections 11, 11a, 11f, 11h, 11i and 11j of this Article)]

Section 11h. Voluntary contributions for support of schools or other public entities. [Created through initiative petition filed Dec. 8, 1995, and adopted by the people Nov. 5, 1996; Repeal proposed by H.J.R. 85, 1997, and adopted by the people May 20, 1997 (present section 11 adopted in lieu of this section and sections 11, 11a, 11f, 11g, 11i and 11j of this Article)]

Section 11i. Legislation to implement limitation and contribution provisions. [Created through initiative petition filed Dec. 8, 1995, and adopted by the people Nov. 5, 1996; Repeal proposed by H.J.R. 85, 1997, and adopted by the people May 20, 1997 (present section 11 adopted in lieu of this section and sections 11, 11a, 11f, 11g, 11h and 11j of this Article)]

Section 11j. Severability of sections 11g, 11h and 11i. [Created through initiative petition filed Dec. 8, 1995, and adopted by the people Nov. 5, 1996; Repeal proposed by H.J.R. 85, 1997, and adopted by the people May 20, 1997 (present section 11 adopted in lieu of this section and sections 11, 11a, 11f, 11g, 11h and 11i of this Article)]

Section 11k. Limitation on applicability of section 11 (8) voting requirements to elections on measures held in May or November of any year. Notwithstanding subsection (8) of section 11 of this Article, subsection (8) of section 11 of this Article does not apply to any measure voted on in an election held in May or November of any year. [Created through H.J.R. 15, 2007, and adopted by the people Nov. 4, 2008]

Section 11L. Limitation on applicability of sections 11 and 11b on bonded indebtedness to finance capital

costs. (1) The limitations of sections 11 and 11b of this Article do not apply to bonded indebtedness incurred by local taxing districts if the bonded indebtedness was incurred on or after January 1, 2011, to finance capital costs as defined in subsection (5) of this section.

(2) Bonded indebtedness described in subsection (1) of this section includes bonded indebtedness issued to refund bonded indebtedness described in subsection (1) of this section.

(3) Notwithstanding subsection (1) of this section, subsection (8) of section 11 of this Article, as limited by section 11k of this Article, applies to measures that authorize bonded indebtedness described in subsection (1) of this section.

(4) The weighted average life of bonded indebtedness incurred on or after January 1, 2011, to finance capital costs may not exceed the weighted average life of the capital costs that are financed with that indebtedness.

(5)(a) As used in this section, "capital costs" means costs of land and of other assets having a useful life of more than one year, including costs associated with acquisition, construction, improvement, remodeling, furnishing, equipping, maintenance or repair.

(b) "Capital costs" does not include costs of routine maintenance or supplies. [Created through H.J.R. 13, 2009, and adopted by the people May 18, 2010]

Section 12. People's utility districts. Peoples' [sic] Utility Districts may be created of territory, contiguous or otherwise, within one or more counties, and may consist of an incorporated municipality, or municipalities, with or without unincorporated territory, for the purpose of supplying water for domestic and municipal purposes; for the development of water power and/or electric energy; and for the distribution, disposal and sale of water, water power and electric energy. Such districts shall be managed by boards of directors, consisting of five members, who shall be residents of such districts. Such districts shall have power:

(a) To call and hold elections within their respective districts.

(b) To levy taxes upon the taxable property of such districts.

(c) To issue, sell and assume evidences of indebtedness.

(d) To enter into contracts.

(e) To exercise the power of eminent domain.

(f) To acquire and hold real and other property necessary or incident to the business of such districts.

(g) To acquire, develop, and/or otherwise provide for a supply of water, water power and electric energy.

Such districts may sell, distribute and/or otherwise dispose of water, water power and electric energy within or without the territory of such districts. The legislative assembly shall and the people may provide any legislation, that may be necessary, in addition to existing laws, to carry out the provisions of this section. [Created through initiative petition filed July 3, 1930, and adopted by the people Nov. 4, 1930]

Section 13. Interests of employes when operation of transportation system assumed by public body. Notwithstanding the provisions of section 20, Article I, section 10, Article VI, and sections 2 and 9, Article XI, of this Constitution, when any city, county, political subdivision, public agency or municipal corporation assumes responsibility for the operation of a public transportation system, the city, county, political subdivision, public agency or municipal corporation shall make fair and equitable arrangements to protect the interests of employes and retired employes affected. Such protective arrangements may include, without being limited to, such provisions as

may be necessary for the preservation of rights, privileges and benefits (including continuation of pension rights and payment of benefits) under existing collective bargaining agreements, or otherwise. [Created through H.J.R. 13, 1965, and adopted by the people Nov. 8, 1966]

Section 14. Metropolitan service district charter. (1) The Legislative Assembly shall provide by law a method whereby the legal electors of any metropolitan service district organized under the laws of this state, by majority vote of such electors voting thereon at any legally called election, may adopt, amend, revise or repeal a district charter.

(2) A district charter shall prescribe the organization of the district government and shall provide directly, or by its authority, for the number, election or appointment, qualifications, tenure, compensation, powers and duties of such officers as the district considers necessary. Such officers shall among them exercise all the powers and perform all the duties, as granted to, imposed upon or distributed among district officers by the Constitution or laws of this state, by the district charter or by its authority.

(3) A district charter may provide for the exercise by ordinance of powers granted to the district by the Constitution or laws of this state.

(4) A metropolitan service district shall have jurisdiction over matters of metropolitan concern as set forth in the charter of the district.

(5) The initiative and referendum powers reserved to the people by this Constitution hereby are further reserved to the legal electors of a metropolitan service district relative to the adoption, amendment, revision or repeal of a district charter and district legislation enacted thereunder. Such powers shall be exercised in the manner provided for county measures under section 10, Article VI of this Constitution. [Created by S.J.R. 2, 1989, and adopted by the people Nov. 6, 1990]

Section 15. Funding of programs imposed upon local governments; exceptions. (1) Except as provided in subsection (7) of this section, when the Legislative Assembly or any state agency requires any local government to establish a new program or provide an increased level of service for an existing program, the State of Oregon shall appropriate and allocate to the local government moneys sufficient to pay the ongoing, usual and reasonable costs of performing the mandated service or activity.

(2) As used in this section:

(a) "Enterprise activity" means a program under which a local government sells products or services in competition with a nongovernment entity.

(b) "Local government" means a city, county, municipal corporation or municipal utility operated by a board or commission.

(c) "Program" means a program or project imposed by enactment of the Legislative Assembly or by rule or order of a state agency under which a local government must provide administrative, financial, social, health or other specified services to persons, government agencies or to the public generally.

(d) "Usual and reasonable costs" means those costs incurred by the affected local governments for a specific program using generally accepted methods of service delivery and administrative practice.

(3) A local government is not required to comply with any state law or administrative rule or order enacted or adopted after January 1, 1997, that requires the expenditure of money by the local government for a new program or increased level of service for an existing program until the state appropriates and allocates to the local government reimbursement for any costs incurred to carry out the law, rule or order and unless the Legislative Assembly provides,

by appropriation, reimbursement in each succeeding year for such costs. However, a local government may refuse to comply with a state law or administrative rule or order under this subsection only if the amount appropriated and allocated to the local government by the Legislative Assembly for a program in a fiscal year:

(a) Is less than 95 percent of the usual and reasonable costs incurred by the local government in conducting the program at the same level of service in the preceding fiscal year; or

(b) Requires the local government to spend for the program, in addition to the amount appropriated and allocated by the Legislative Assembly, an amount that exceeds one-hundredth of one percent of the annual budget adopted by the governing body of the local government for that fiscal year.

(4) When a local government determines that a program is a program for which moneys are required to be appropriated and allocated under subsection (1) of this section, if the local government expended moneys to conduct the program and was not reimbursed under this section for the usual and reasonable costs of the program, the local government may submit the issue of reimbursement to nonbinding arbitration by a panel of three arbitrators. The panel shall consist of one representative from the Oregon Department of Administrative Services, the League of Oregon Cities and the Association of Oregon Counties. The panel shall determine whether the costs incurred by the local government are required to be reimbursed under this section and the amount of reimbursement. The decision of the arbitration panel is not binding upon the parties and may not be enforced by any court in this state.

(5) In any legal proceeding or arbitration proceeding under this section, the local government shall bear the burden of proving by a preponderance of the evidence that moneys appropriated by the Legislative Assembly are not sufficient to reimburse the local government for the usual and reasonable costs of a program.

(6) Except upon approval by three-fifths of the membership of each house of the Legislative Assembly, the Legislative Assembly shall not enact, amend or repeal any law if the anticipated effect of the action is to reduce the amount of state revenues derived from a specific state tax and distributed to local governments as an aggregate during the distribution period for such revenues immediately preceding January 1, 1997.

(7) This section shall not apply to:

(a) Any law that is approved by three-fifths of the membership of each house of the Legislative Assembly.

(b) Any costs resulting from a law creating or changing the definition of a crime or a law establishing sentences for conviction of a crime.

(c) An existing program as enacted by legislation prior to January 1, 1997, except for legislation withdrawing state funds for programs required prior to January 1, 1997, unless the program is made optional.

(d) A new program or an increased level of program services established pursuant to action of the Federal Government so long as the program or increased level of program services imposes costs on local governments that are no greater than the usual and reasonable costs to local governments resulting from compliance with the minimum program standards required under federal law or regulations.

(e) Any requirement imposed by the judicial branch of government.

(f) Legislation enacted or approved by electors in this state under the initiative and referendum powers reserved to the people under section 1, Article IV of this Constitution.

(g) Programs that are intended to inform citizens about the activities of local governments.

(8) When a local government is not required under subsection (3) of this section to comply with a state law or administrative rule or order relating to an enterprise activity, if a nongovernment entity competes with the local government by selling products or services that are similar to the products and services sold under the enterprise activity, the nongovernment entity is not required to comply with the state law or administrative rule or order relating to that enterprise activity.

(9) Nothing in this section shall give rise to a claim by a private person against the State of Oregon based on the establishment of a new program or an increased level of service for an existing program without sufficient appropriation and allocation of funds to pay the ongoing, usual and reasonable costs of performing the mandated service or activity.

(10) Subsection (4) of this section does not apply to a local government when the local government is voluntarily providing a program four years after the effective date of the enactment, rule or order that imposed the program.

(11) In lieu of appropriating and allocating funds under this section, the Legislative Assembly may identify and direct the imposition of a fee or charge to be used by a local government to recover the actual cost of the program. [Created through H.J.R. 2, 1995, and adopted by the people Nov. 5, 1996]

Section 15a. Subsequent vote for reaffirmation of section 15. [Created through H.J.R. 2, 1995, and adopted by the people Nov. 5, 1996; Repeal proposed by S.J.R. 39, 1999, and adopted by the people Nov. 7, 2000]

ARTICLE XI-A
RURAL CREDITS

[Created through initiative petition filed July 6, 1916, and adopted by the people Nov. 7, 1916; Repeal proposed by S.J.R. 1, 1941, and adopted by the people Nov. 3, 1942]

ARTICLE XI-A
FARM AND HOME LOANS TO VETERANS

Sec. 1. State empowered to make farm and home loans to veterans; standards and priorities for loans
2. Bonds
3. Eligibility to receive loans
4. Tax levy
5. Repeal of conflicting constitutional provisions
6. Refunding bonds

Section 1. State empowered to make farm and home loans to veterans; standards and priorities for loans. (1) Notwithstanding the limits contained in section 7, Article XI of this Constitution, the credit of the State of Oregon may be loaned and indebtedness incurred in an amount not to exceed eight percent of the true cash value of all the property in the state, for the purpose of creating a fund, to be known as the "Oregon War Veterans' Fund," to be advanced for the acquisition of farms and homes for the benefit of male and female residents of the State of Oregon who served in the Armed Forces of the United States. Secured repayment thereof shall be and is a prerequisite to the advancement of money from such fund, except that moneys in the Oregon War Veterans' Fund may also be appropriated to the Director of Veterans' Affairs to be expended, without security, for the following purposes:

(a) Aiding veterans' organizations in connection with their programs of service to veterans;

(b) Training service officers appointed by the counties to give aid as provided by law to veterans and their dependents;

(c) Aiding the counties in connection with programs of service to veterans;

(d) The duties of the Director of Veterans' Affairs as conservator of the estates of beneficiaries of the United States Veterans' Administration; and

(e) The duties of the Director of Veterans' Affairs in providing services to veterans, their dependents and survivors.

(2) The Director of Veterans' Affairs may establish standards and priorities with respect to the granting of loans from the Oregon War Veterans' Fund that, as determined by the director, best accomplish the purposes and promote the financial sustainability of the Oregon War Veterans' Fund, including, but not limited to, standards and priorities necessary to maintain the tax-exempt status of earnings from bonds issued under authority of this section and section 2 of this Article. [Created through H.J.R. 7, 1943, and adopted by the people Nov. 7, 1944; Amendment proposed by H.J.R. 1, 1949, and adopted by the people Nov. 7, 1950; Amendment proposed by H.J.R. 14, 1951, and adopted by the people Nov. 4, 1952; Amendment proposed by S.J.R. 14, 1959, and adopted by the people Nov. 8, 1960; Amendment proposed by H.J.R. 9, 1967, and adopted by the people Nov. 5, 1968; Amendment proposed by H.J.R. 33, 1969, and adopted by the people Nov. 3, 1970; Amendment proposed by H.J.R. 12, 1973, and adopted by the people May 28, 1974; Amendment proposed by H.J.R. 10, 1977, and adopted by the people May 17, 1977; Amendment proposed by S.J.R. 53, 1977, and adopted by the people May 17, 1977; Amendment proposed by S.J.R. 2, 1999, and adopted by the people Nov. 7, 2000; Amendment proposed by H.J.R. 7, 2009, and adopted by the people Nov. 2, 2010]

Section 2. Bonds. Bonds of the state of Oregon containing a direct promise on behalf of the state to pay the face value thereof, with the interest therein provided for, may be issued to an amount authorized by section 1 hereof for the purpose of creating said "Oregon War Veterans' Fund." Said bonds shall be a direct obligation of the state and shall be in such form and shall run for such periods of time and bear such rates of interest as provided by statute. [Created through H.J.R. 7, 1943, and adopted by the people Nov. 7, 1944; Amendment proposed by H.J.R. 1, 1949, and adopted by the people Nov. 7, 1950]

Section 3. Eligibility to receive loans. No person shall receive money from the Oregon War Veterans' Fund except the following:

(1) A person who:

(a) Resides in the State of Oregon at the time of applying for a loan from the fund;

(b) Is a veteran, as that term is defined by Oregon law;

(c) Served under honorable conditions on active duty in the Armed Forces of the United States; and

(d) Satisfies the requirements applicable to the funding source for the loan from the Oregon War Veterans' Fund.

(2)(a) The spouse of a person who is qualified to receive a loan under subsection (1) of this section but who has either been missing in action or a prisoner of war while on active duty in the Armed Forces of the United States even though the status of missing or being a prisoner occurred prior to completion of a minimum length of service or the person never resided in this state, provided the spouse resides in this state at the time of application for the loan.

(b) The surviving spouse of a person who was qualified to receive a loan under subsection (1) of this section but who died while on active duty in the Armed Forces of the United States even though the death occurred prior to completion of a minimum length of service or the person never resided in this state, provided the surviving spouse resides in this state at the time of application for the loan.

(c) The eligibility of a surviving spouse under this subsection shall terminate on the spouse's remarriage.

(3) As used in this section, "active duty" does not include attendance at a school under military orders, except schooling incident to an active enlistment or a regular tour of duty, or normal military training as a reserve officer or member of an organized reserve or National Guard unit. [Created through H.J.R. 7, 1943, and adopted by the people Nov. 7, 1944; Amendment proposed by H.J.R. 1, 1949, and adopted by the people Nov. 7, 1950; Amendment proposed by H.J.R. 14, 1951, and adopted by the people Nov. 4, 1952; Amendment proposed by S.J.R. 14, 1959, and adopted by the people Nov. 8, 1960; Amendment proposed by H.J.R. 9, 1967, and adopted by the people Nov. 5, 1968; Amendment proposed by S.J.R. 23, 1971, and adopted by the people Nov. 7, 1972; Amendment proposed by H.J.R. 23, 1975, and adopted by the people May 25, 1976; Amendment proposed by H.J.R. 23, 1979, and adopted by the people May 20, 1980; Amendment proposed by S.J.R. 3, 1995, and adopted by the people Nov. 5, 1996; Amendment proposed by S.J.R. 2, 1999, and adopted by the people Nov. 7, 2000; Amendment proposed by H.J.R. 7, 2009, and adopted by the people Nov. 2, 2010]

Section 4. Tax levy. There shall be levied each year, at the same time and in the same manner that other taxes are levied, a tax upon all property in the state of Oregon not exempt from taxation, not to exceed two (2) mills on each dollar valuation, to provide for the payment of principal and interest of the bonds authorized to be issued by this article. The two (2) mills additional tax herein provided for hereby is specifically authorized and said tax levy hereby authorized shall be in addition to all other taxes which may be levied according to law. [Created through H.J.R. 7, 1943, and adopted by the people Nov. 7, 1944; Amendment proposed by H.J.R. 85, 1997, and adopted by the people May 20, 1997]

Section 5. Repeal of conflicting constitutional provisions. The provisions of the constitution in conflict with this amendment hereby are repealed so far as they conflict herewith. [Created through H.J.R. 7, 1943, and adopted by the people Nov. 7, 1944]

Section 6. Refunding bonds. Refunding bonds may be issued and sold to refund any bonds issued under authority of sections 1 and 2 of this article. There may be issued and outstanding at any one time bonds aggregating the amount authorized by section 1 hereof, but at no time shall the total of all bonds outstanding, including refunding bonds, exceed the amount so authorized. [Created through H.J.R. 7, 1943, and adopted by the people Nov. 7, 1944]

ARTICLE XI-B
STATE PAYMENT OF IRRIGATION AND DRAINAGE DISTRICT INTEREST

[Created through H.J.R. 32, 1919, and adopted by the people June 3, 1919; Repeal proposed by H.J.R. 1, 1929, and adopted by the people Nov. 4, 1930]

ARTICLE XI-C
WORLD WAR VETERANS' STATE AID SINKING FUND

[Created through H.J.R. 12, 1921, and adopted by the people June 7, 1921; Amendment proposed by H.J.R. 7, 1923, and adopted by the people Nov. 4, 1924; Repeal proposed by S.J.R. 12, 1951, and adopted by the people Nov. 4, 1952]

ARTICLE XI-D
STATE POWER DEVELOPMENT

Sec. 1. State's rights, title and interest to water and waterpower sites to be held in perpetuity
   2. State's powers enumerated
   3. Legislation to effectuate article

4. Construction of article

Section 1. State's rights, title and interest to water and water-power sites to be held in perpetuity. The rights, title and interest in and to all water for the development of water power and to water power sites, which the state of Oregon now owns or may hereafter acquire, shall be held by it in perpetuity. [Created through initiative petition filed July 7, 1932, and adopted by the people Nov. 8, 1932]

Section 2. State's powers enumerated. The state of Oregon is authorized and empowered:

(1) To control and/or develop the water power within the state;

(2) To lease water and water power sites for the development of water power;

(3) To control, use, transmit, distribute, sell and/or dispose of electric energy;

(4) To develop, separately or in conjunction with the United States, or in conjunction with the political subdivisions of this state, any water power within the state, and to acquire, construct, maintain and/or operate hydroelectric power plants, transmission and distribution lines;(

(5) To develop, separately or in conjunction with the United States, with any state or states, or political subdivisions thereof, or with any political subdivision of this state, any water power in any interstate stream and to acquire, construct, maintain and/or operate hydroelectric power plants, transmission and distribution lines;

(6) To contract with the United States, with any state or states, or political subdivisions thereof, or with any political subdivision of this state, for the purchase or acquisition of water, water power and/or electric energy for use, transmission, distribution, sale and/or disposal thereof;

(7) To fix rates and charges for the use of water in the development of water power and for the sale and/or disposal of water power and/or electric energy;

(8) To loan the credit of the state, and to incur indebtedness in an amount not exceeding one and one-half percent of the true cash value of all the property in the state taxed on an ad valorem basis, for the purpose of providing funds with which to carry out the provisions of this article, notwithstanding any limitations elsewhere contained in this constitution;

(9) To do any and all things necessary or convenient to carry out the provisions of this article. [Created through initiative petition filed July 7, 1932, and adopted by the people Nov. 8, 1932; Amendment proposed by S.J.R. 6, 1961, and adopted by the people Nov. 6, 1962]

Section 3. Legislation to effectuate article. The legislative assembly shall, and the people may, provide any legislation that may be necessary in addition to existing laws, to carry out the provisions of this article; Provided, that any board or commission created, or empowered to administer the laws enacted to carry out the purposes of this article shall consist of three members and be elected without party affiliation or designation. [Created through initiative petition filed July 7, 1932, and adopted by the people Nov. 8, 1932]

Section 4. Construction of article. Nothing in this article shall be construed to affect in any way the laws, and the administration thereof, now existing or hereafter enacted, relating to the appropriation and use of water for beneficial purposes, other than for the development of water power. [Created through initiative petition filed July 7, 1932, and adopted by the people Nov. 8, 1932]

ARTICLE XI-E
STATE REFORESTATION

Section 1. State empowered to lend credit for forest rehabilitation and reforestation; bonds; taxation. The credit of the state may be loaned and indebtedness incurred in an amount which shall not exceed at any one time 3/16 of 1 percent of the true cash value of all the property in the state taxed on an ad valorem basis, to provide funds for forest rehabilitation and reforestation and for the acquisition, management, and development of lands for such purposes. So long as any such indebtedness shall remain outstanding, the funds derived from the sale, exchange, or use of said lands, and from the disposal of products therefrom, shall be applied only in the liquidation of such indebtedness. Bonds or other obligations issued pursuant hereto may be renewed or refunded. An ad valorem tax shall be levied annually upon all the property in the state of Oregon taxed on an ad valorem basis, in sufficient amount to provide for the payment of such indebtedness and the interest thereon. The legislative assembly may provide other revenues to supplement or replace the said tax levies. The legislature shall enact legislation to carry out the provisions hereof. This amendment shall supersede all constitutional provisions in conflict herewith. [Created through H.J.R. 24, 1947, and adopted by the people Nov. 2, 1948; Amendment proposed by S.J.R. 7, 1961, and adopted by the people Nov. 6, 1962; Amendment proposed by H.J.R. 85, 1997, and adopted by the people May 20, 1997]

ARTICLE XI-F(1)
HIGHER EDUCATION BUILDING PROJECTS

Sec. 1. State empowered to lend credit for higher education building projects
2. Limitation on authorization to incur indebtedness
3. Sources of revenue
4. Bonds
5. Legislation to effectuate Article

Section 1. State empowered to lend credit for higher education building projects. The credit of the state may be loaned and indebtedness incurred in an amount which shall not exceed at any one time three-fourths of one percent of the true cash value of all the taxable property in the state, as determined by law to provide funds with which to acquire, construct, improve, repair, equip and furnish buildings, structures, land and other projects, or parts thereof, that the legislative assembly determines will benefit higher education institutions or activities. [Created through H.J.R. 26, 1949, and adopted by the people Nov. 7, 1950; Amendment proposed by H.J.R. 12, 1959, and adopted by the people Nov. 8, 1960; Amendment proposed by H.J.R. 101, 2010, and adopted by the people May 18, 2010]

Section 2. Limitation on authorization to incur indebtedness. Indebtedness shall not be incurred to finance projects described in section 1 of this Article unless the constructing authority conservatively estimates that the constructing authority will have sufficient revenues to pay the indebtedness and operate the projects financed with the proceeds of the indebtedness. For purposes of this section, "revenues" includes all funds available to the constructing authority except amounts appropriated by the legislative assembly from the General Fund. [Created through H.J.R. 26, 1949, and adopted by the people Nov. 7, 1950; Amendment proposed by H.J.R. 101, 2010, and adopted by the people May 18, 2010]

Section 3. Sources of revenue. Ad valorem taxes shall be levied annually upon all the taxable property in the state of Oregon in sufficient amount, with the aforesaid revenues, to provide for the payment of such indebtedness and the interest thereon. The legislative assembly may provide other revenues to supplement or replace such tax levies. [Created through H.J.R. 26, 1949, and adopted by the people Nov. 7, 1950; Amendment proposed by H.J.R. 101, 2010, and adopted by the people May 18, 2010]

Section 4. Bonds. Bonds issued pursuant to this article shall be the direct general obligations of the state, and be in such form, run for such periods of time, and bear such rates of interest, as shall be provided by statute. Such bonds may be refunded with bonds of like obligation. Unless provided by statute, no bonds shall be issued pursuant to this article for the construction of buildings or other structures for higher education until after all of the aforesaid outstanding revenue bonds shall have been redeemed or refunded. [Created through H.J.R. 26, 1949, and adopted by the people Nov. 7, 1950]

Section 5. Legislation to effectuate Article. The legislative assembly shall enact legislation to carry out the provisions hereof. This article shall supersede all conflicting constitutional provisions. [Created through H.J.R. 26, 1949, and adopted by the people Nov. 7, 1950]

ARTICLE XI-F(2)
VETERANS' BONUS

Section 1. State empowered to lend credit to pay veterans' bonus; issuance of bonds. Notwithstanding the limitations contained in Section 7 of Article XI of the constitution, the credit of the State of Oregon may be loaned and indebtedness incurred to an amount not exceeding 5 percent of the assessed valuation of all the property in the state, for the purpose of creating a fund to be paid to residents of the State of Oregon who served in the armed forces of the United States between September 16, 1940, and June 30, 1946, and were honorably discharged from such service, which fund shall be known as the "World War II Veterans' Compensation Fund."

Bonds of the State of Oregon, containing a direct promise on behalf of the state to pay the face value thereof with the interest thereon provided for may be issued to an amount authorized in Section 1 hereof for the purpose of creating said World War II Veterans' Compensation Fund. Refunding bonds may be issued and sold to refund any bonds issued under authority of Section 1 hereof. There may be issued and outstanding at any one time bonds aggregating the amount authorized by Section 1, but at no time shall the total of all bonds outstanding, including refunding bonds, exceed the amount so authorized. Said bonds shall be a direct obligation of the State and shall be in such form and shall run for such periods of time and bear such rates of interest as shall be provided by statute. No person shall be eligible to receive money from said fund except the veterans as defined in Section 3 of this act [sic]. The legislature shall and the people may provide any additional legislation that may be necessary, in addition to existing laws, to carry out the provisions of this section. [Created through initiative petition filed June 30, 1950, and adopted by the people Nov. 7, 1950]

Section 2. Definitions. The following words, terms, and phrases, as used in this act [sic] shall have the following meaning unless the text otherwise requires:

(1) "Domestic service" means service within the continental limits of the United States, excluding Alaska, Hawaii, Canal Zone and Puerto Rico.

(2) "Foreign Service" means service in all other places, including sea duty.

(3) "Husband" means the unremarried husband, and "wife" means the unremarried wife.

(4) "Child or Children" means child or children of issue, child or children by adoption or child or children to whom the deceased person has stood in loco parentis for one year or more immediately preceding his death.

(5) "Parent or Parents" means natural parent or parents; parent or parents by adoption; or, person or persons, including stepparent or stepparents, who have stood in loco parentis to the deceased person for a period of one year or more immediately prior to entrance into the armed service of the United States.

(6) "Veterans" means any person who shall have served in active duty in the armed forces of the United States at any time between September 16, 1940, and June 30, 1946, both dates inclusive, and who, at the time of commencing such service, was and had been a bona fide resident of the State of Oregon for at least one year immediately preceding the commencement of such service, and who shall have been separated from such service under honorable conditions, or who is still in such service, or who has been retired. [Created through initiative petition filed June 30, 1950, and adopted by the people Nov. 7, 1950]

Section 3. Amount of bonus. Every veteran who was in such service for a period of at least 90 days shall be entitled to receive compensation at the rate of Ten Dollars ($10.00) for each full month during which such veteran was in active domestic service and Fifteen Dollars ($15.00) for each full month during which such veteran was in active foreign service within said period of time. Any veteran who was serving on active duty in the armed forces between September 16, 1940, and June 30, 1946, whose services were terminated by reason of service-connected disabilities, and who, upon filing a claim for disabilities with the United States Veterans' Administration within three months after separation from the armed service, was rated not less than 50% disabled as a result of such claim, shall be deemed to have served sufficient time to entitle him or her to the maximum payment under this act [sic] and shall be so entitled. The maximum amount of compensation payable under this act [sic] shall be six hundred dollars ($600.00) and no such compensation shall be paid to any veteran who shall have received from another state a bonus or compensation because of such military service. [Created through initiative petition filed June 30, 1950, and adopted by the people Nov. 7, 1950]

Section 4. Survivors of certain deceased veterans entitled to maximum amount. The survivor or survivors, of the deceased veteran whose death was caused or contributed to by a service-connected disease or disability incurred in service under conditions other than dishonorable, shall be entitled, in the order of survivorship provided in this act [sic], to receive the maximum amount of said compensation irrespective of the amount such deceased would have been entitled to receive if living. [Created through initiative petition filed June 30, 1950, and adopted by the people Nov. 7, 1950]

Section 5. Certain persons not eligible. No compensation shall be paid under this act [sic] to any veteran who, during the period of service refused on conscientious, political or other grounds to subject himself to full military discipline and unqualified service, or to any veteran for any periods of time spent under penal confinement during the period of active duty, or for service in the merchant marine: Provided, however, that for the purposes of this act [sic], active service in the chaplain corps, or medical corps shall be deemed unqualified service under full military discipline. [Created through initiative petition filed June 30, 1950, and adopted by the people Nov. 7, 1950]

Section 6. Order of distribution among survivors. The survivor or survivors of any deceased veteran who would have been entitled to compensation under this act [sic], other than those mentioned in Section 4 of this act [sic], shall be entitled to receive the same amount of compensation as said deceased veteran would have received, if living, which shall be distributed as follows:

(1) To the husband or wife, as the case may be, the whole amount.

(2) If there be no husband or wife, to the child or children, equally; and

(3) If there be no husband or wife or child or children, to the parent or parents, equally. [Created through initiative petition filed June 30, 1950, and adopted by the people Nov. 7, 1950]

Section 7. Bonus not saleable or assignable; bonus free from creditors' claims and state taxes. No sale or assignment of any right or claim to compensation under this act [sic] shall be valid, no claims of creditors shall be enforcible against rights or claims to or payments of such compensation, and such compensation shall be exempt from all taxes imposed by the laws of this state. [Created through initiative petition filed June 30, 1950, and adopted by the people Nov. 7, 1950]

Section 8. Administration of article; rules and regulations. The director of Veterans' Affairs, State of Oregon, referred to herein as the "director" hereby is authorized and empowered, and it shall be his duty, to administer the provisions of this act [sic], and with the approval of the veterans advisory committee may make such rules and regulations as are deemed necessary to accomplish the purpose hereof. [Created through initiative petition filed June 30, 1950, and adopted by the people Nov. 7, 1950]

Section 9. Applications. All applications for certificates under this act [sic] shall be made within two years from the effective date hereof and upon forms to be supplied by the director. Said applications shall be duly verified by the claimant before a notary public or other person authorized to take acknowledgments, and shall set forth applicant's name, residence at the time of entry into the service, date and place of enlistment, induction or entry upon active federal service, beginning and ending dates of foreign service, date of discharge, retirement or release from active federal service, statement of time lost by reason of penal confinement during the period of active duty; together with the applicant's original discharge, or certificate in lieu of lost discharge, or certificate of service, or if the applicant has not been released at the time of application, a statement by competent military authority that the applicant during the period for which compensation is claimed did not refuse to subject himself to full military discipline and unqualified service, and that the applicant has not been separated from service under circumstances other than honorable. The director may require such further information to be included in such application as deemed necessary to enable him to determine the eligibility of the applicant. Such applications, together with satisfactory evidence of honorable service, shall be filed with the director. The director shall make such reasonable requirements for applicants as may be necessary to prevent fraud or the payment of compensation to persons not entitled thereto. [Created through initiative petition filed June 30, 1950, and adopted by the people Nov. 7, 1950]

Section 10. Furnishing forms; printing, office supplies and equipment; employes; payment of expenses. The director shall furnish free of charge, upon request, the necessary forms upon which applications may be made and may authorize the county clerks, Veterans organizations and other organizations, and notaries public willing to assist veterans without charge, to act for him in receiving application under this act [sic], and shall furnish such clerks, organizations and notaries public, with the proper forms for such purpose. The director hereby is authorized and directed with the approval of the veterans' advisory committee, to procure such printing, office supplies and equipment and to employ such persons as may be necessary in order to properly carry out the provisions of this act [sic], and all expense incurred by him in the administration thereof shall be paid out of the World War II Veterans' Compensation Fund, in the manner provided by law for payment of claims from other state funds. [Created through initiative petition filed June 30, 1950, and adopted by the people Nov. 7, 1950]

ARTICLE XI-G
HIGHER EDUCATION INSTITUTIONS AND ACTIVITIES; COMMUNITY COLLEGES

Sec. 1. State empowered to lend credit for financing higher education institutions and activities, and community colleges
2. Bonds
3. Sources of revenue

Section 1. State empowered to lend credit for financing higher education institutions and activities, and community colleges. (1) Notwithstanding the limitations contained in section 7, Article XI of this Constitution, and in addition to other exceptions from the limitations of such section, the credit of the state may be loaned and indebtedness incurred in an amount not to exceed at any time three-fourths of one percent of the true cash value of all taxable property in the state, as determined by law.

(2) Proceeds from any loan authorized or indebtedness incurred under this section shall be used to provide funds with which to acquire, construct, improve, repair, equip and furnish buildings, structures, land and other projects, or parts thereof, that the Legislative Assembly determines will benefit higher education institutions or activities or community colleges authorized by law to receive state aid.

(3) The amount of any indebtedness incurred under this section in any biennium shall be matched by an amount that is at least equal to the amount of the indebtedness. The matching amount must be used for the same or similar purposes as the proceeds of the indebtedness and may consist of moneys appropriated from the General Fund or any other moneys available to the constructing authority for such purposes. However, the matching amount may not consist of proceeds of indebtedness incurred by the state under any other Article of this Constitution. Any matching amount appropriated from the General Fund to meet the requirements of this subsection must be specifically designated therefor by the Legislative Assembly.

(4) Nothing in this section prevents the financing of projects, or parts thereof, by a combination of the moneys available under this section, under Article XI-F(1) of this Constitution, and from other lawful sources. [Created through H.J.R. 8, 1963 (s.s.), and adopted by the people May 15, 1964; Amendment proposed by H.J.R. 2, 1967 (s.s.), and adopted by the people May 28, 1968; Amendment proposed by H.J.R. 101, 2010, and adopted by the people May 18, 2010]

Section 2. Bonds. Bonds issued pursuant to this Article shall be the direct general obligations of the state and shall be in such form, run for such periods of time, and bear such rates of interest as the Legislative Assembly provides. Such bonds may be refunded with bonds of like obligation. [Created through H.J.R. 8, 1963 (s.s.), and adopted by the people May 15, 1964]

Section 3. Sources of revenue. Ad valorem taxes shall be levied annually upon the taxable property within the State of Oregon in sufficient amount to provide for the prompt payment of bonds issued pursuant to this Article and the interest thereon. The Legislative Assembly may provide other revenues to supplement or replace, in whole or in part, such tax levies. [Created through H.J.R. 8, 1963 (s.s.), and adopted by the people May 15, 1964]

ARTICLE XI-H
POLLUTION CONTROL

Sec. 1. State empowered to lend credit for financing pollution control facilities or related activities
2. Only facilities 70 percent self-supporting and self-liquidating authorized; exceptions
3. Authority of public bodies to receive funds
4. Sources of revenue
5. Bonds
6. Legislation to effectuate Article

Section 1. State empowered to lend credit for financing pollution control facilities or related activities. In the manner provided by law and notwithstanding the limitations contained in sections 7 and 8, Article XI, of this Constitution, the credit of the State of Oregon may be loaned and indebtedness incurred in an amount not to exceed, at any one time, one percent of the true cash value of all taxable property in the state:

(1) To provide funds to be advanced, by contract, grant, loan or otherwise, to any municipal corporation, city, county or agency of the State of Oregon, or combinations thereof, for the purpose of planning, acquisition, construction, alteration or improvement of facilities for or activities related to, the collection, treatment, dilution and disposal of all forms of waste in or upon the air, water and lands of this state; and

(2) To provide funds for the acquisition, by purchase, loan or otherwise, of bonds, notes or other obligations of any municipal corporation, city, county or agency of the State of Oregon, or combinations thereof, issued or made for the purposes of subsection (1) of this section. [Created through H.J.R. 14, 1969, and adopted by the people May 26, 1970; Amendment proposed by S.J.R. 41, 1989, and adopted by the people May 22, 1990]

Section 2. Only facilities 70 percent self-supporting and self-liquidating authorized; exceptions. The facilities for which funds are advanced and for which bonds, notes or other obligations are issued or made and acquired pursuant to this Article shall be only such facilities as conservatively appear to the agency designated by law to make the determination to be not less than 70 percent self-supporting and self-liquidating from revenues, gifts, grants from the Federal Government, user charges, assessments and other fees. This section shall not apply to any activities for which funds are advanced and shall not apply to facilities for the collection, treatment, dilution, removal and disposal of hazardous substances. [Created through H.J.R. 14, 1969, and adopted by the people May 26, 1970; Amendment proposed by S.J.R. 41, 1989, and adopted by the people May 22, 1990]

Section 3. Authority of public bodies to receive funds. Notwithstanding the limitations contained in section 10, Article XI of this Constitution, municipal corporations, cities, counties, and agencies of the State of Oregon, or combinations thereof, may receive funds referred to in section 1 of this Article, by contract, grant, loan or otherwise and may also receive such funds through disposition

to the state, by sale, loan or otherwise, of bonds, notes or other obligations issued or made for the purposes set forth in section 1 of this Article. [Created through H.J.R. 14, 1969, and adopted by the people May 26, 1970]

Section 4. Sources of revenue. Ad valorem taxes shall be levied annually upon all taxable property within the State of Oregon in sufficient amount to provide, together with the revenues, gifts, grants from the Federal Government, user charges, assessments and other fees referred to in section 2 of this Article for the payment of indebtedness incurred by the state and the interest thereon. The Legislative Assembly may provide other revenues to supplement or replace such tax levies. [Created through H.J.R. 14, 1969, and adopted by the people May 26, 1970]

Section 5. Bonds. Bonds issued pursuant to section 1 of this Article shall be the direct obligations of the state and shall be in such form, run for such periods of time, and bear such rates of interest, as shall be provided by law. Such bonds may be refunded with bonds of like obligation. [Created through H.J.R. 14, 1969, and adopted by the people May 26, 1970]

Section 6. Legislation to effectuate Article. The Legislative Assembly shall enact legislation to carry out the provisions of this Article. This Article shall supersede all conflicting constitutional provisions and shall supersede any conflicting provision of a county or city charter or act of incorporation. [Created through H.J.R. 14, 1969, and adopted by the people May 26, 1970]

ARTICLE XI-I(1)
WATER DEVELOPMENT PROJECTS

Sec. 1. State empowered to lend credit to establish Water Development Fund; eligibility; use
2. Bonds
3. Refunding bonds
4. Sources of revenue
5. Legislation to effectuate Article

Section 1. State empowered to lend credit to establish Water Development Fund; eligibility; use. Notwithstanding the limits contained in sections 7 and 8, Article XI of this Constitution, the credit of the State of Oregon may be loaned and indebtedness incurred in an amount not to exceed one and one-half percent of the true cash value of all the property in the state for the purpose of creating a fund to be known as the Water Development Fund. The fund shall be used to provide financing for loans for residents of this state for construction of water development projects for irrigation, drainage, fish protection, watershed restoration and municipal uses and for the acquisition of easements and rights of way for water development projects authorized by law. Secured repayment thereof shall be and is a prerequisite to the advancement of money from such fund. As used in this section, "resident" includes both natural persons and any corporation or cooperative, either for profit or nonprofit, whose principal income is from farming in Oregon or municipal or quasi-municipal or other body subject to the laws of the State of Oregon. Not less than 50 percent of the potential amount available from the fund will be reserved for irrigation and drainage projects. For municipal use, only municipalities and communities with populations less than 30,000 are eligible for loans from the fund. [Created through S.J.R. 1, 1977, and adopted by the people Nov. 8, 1977; Amendment proposed by S.J.R. 6, 1981, and adopted by the people May 18, 1982; Amendment proposed by H.J.R. 45, 1987, and adopted by the people May 17, 1988]

Section 2. Bonds. Bonds of the State of Oregon containing a direct promise on behalf of the state to pay the face value thereof, with the interest therein provided for, may be issued to an amount authorized by section 1 of this

Article for the purpose of creating such fund. The bonds shall be a direct obligation of the state and shall be in such form and shall run for such periods of time and bear such rates of interest as provided by statute. [Created through S.J.R. 1, 1977, and adopted by the people Nov. 8, 1977]

Section 3. Refunding bonds. Refunding bonds may be issued and sold to refund any bonds issued under authority of sections 1 and 2 of this Article. There may be issued and outstanding at any time bonds aggregating the amount authorized by section 1 of this Article but at no time shall the total of all bonds outstanding, including refunding bonds, exceed the amount so authorized. [Created through S.J.R. 1, 1977, and adopted by the people Nov. 8, 1977]

Section 4. Sources of revenue. Ad valorem taxes shall be levied annually upon all the taxable property in the State of Oregon in sufficient amount to provide for the payment of principal and interest of the bonds issued pursuant to this Article. The Legislative Assembly may provide other revenues to supplement or replace, in whole or in part, such tax levies. [Created through S.J.R. 1, 1977, and adopted by the people Nov. 8, 1977]

Section 5. Legislation to effectuate Article. The Legislative Assembly shall enact legislation to carry out the provisions of this Article. This Article supersedes any conflicting provision of a county or city charter or act of incorporation. [Created through S.J.R. 1, 1977, and adopted by the people Nov. 8, 1977]

ARTICLE XI-I(2)
MULTIFAMILY HOUSING FOR ELDERLY AND DISABLED

Section 1. State empowered to lend credit for multifamily housing for elderly and disabled persons. In the manner provided by law and notwithstanding the limitations contained in section 7, Article XI of this Constitution, the credit of the State of Oregon may be loaned and indebtedness incurred in an amount not to exceed, at any one time, one-half of one percent of the true cash value of all taxable property in the state to provide funds to be advanced, by contract, grant, loan or otherwise, for the purpose of providing additional financing for multifamily housing for the elderly and for disabled persons. Multifamily housing means a structure or facility designed to contain more than one living unit. Additional financing may be provided to the elderly to purchase ownership interest in the structure or facility. [Created through H.J.R. 61, 1977, and adopted by the people May 23, 1978; Amendment proposed by S.J.R. 34, 1979, and adopted by the people May 20, 1980; Amendment proposed by H.J.R. 1, 1981, and adopted by the people May 18, 1982]

Section 2. Sources of revenue. The bonds shall be payable from contract or loan proceeds; bond reserves; other funds available for these purposes; and, if necessary, state ad valorem taxes. [Created through H.J.R. 61, 1977, and adopted by the people May 23, 1978]

Section 3. Bonds. Bonds issued pursuant to section 1 of this Article shall be the direct obligations of the state and shall be in such form, run for such periods of time and bear such rates of interest as shall be provided by law. The bonds may be refunded with bonds of like obligation. [Created through H.J.R. 61, 1977, and adopted by the people May 23, 1978]

Section 4. Legislation to effectuate Article. The Legislative Assembly shall enact legislation to carry out the provisions of this Article. This Article shall supersede

all conflicting constitutional provisions. [Created through H.J.R. 61, 1977, and adopted by the people May 23, 1978]

ARTICLE XI-J
SMALL SCALE LOCAL ENERGY LOANS

Section 1. State empowered to loan credit for small scale local energy loans; eligibility; use. Notwithstanding the limits contained in sections 7 and 8, Article XI of this Constitution, the credit of the State of Oregon may be loaned and indebtedness incurred in an amount not to exceed one-half of one percent of the true cash value of all the property in the state for the purpose of creating a fund to be known as the Small Scale Local Energy Project Loan Fund. The fund shall be used to provide financing for the development of small scale local energy projects. Secured repayment thereof shall be and is a prerequisite to the advancement of money from such fund. [Created through S.J.R. 24, 1979, and adopted by the people May 20, 1980]

Section 2. Bonds. Bonds of the State of Oregon containing a direct promise on behalf of the state to pay the face value thereof, with the interest therein provided for, may be issued to an amount authorized by section 1 of this Article for the purpose of creating such fund. The bonds shall be a direct obligation of the state and shall be in such form and shall run for such periods of time and bear such rates of interest as provided by statute. [Created through S.J.R. 24, 1979, and adopted by the people May 20, 1980]

Section 3. Refunding bonds. Refunding bonds may be issued and sold to refund any bonds issued under authority of sections 1 and 2 of this Article. There may be issued and outstanding at any time bonds aggregating the amount authorized by section 1 of this Article but at no time shall the total of all bonds outstanding including refunding bonds, exceed the amount so authorized. [Created through S.J.R. 24, 1979, and adopted by the people May 20, 1980]

Section 4. Sources of revenue. Ad valorem taxes shall be levied annually upon all the taxable property in the State of Oregon in sufficient amount to provide for the payment of principal and interest of the bonds issued pursuant to this Article. The Legislative Assembly may provide other revenues to supplement or replace, in whole or in part, such tax levies. [Created through S.J.R. 24, 1979, and adopted by the people May 20, 1980]

Section 5. Legislation to effectuate Article. The Legislative Assembly shall enact legislation to carry out the provisions of this Article. This Article supersedes any conflicting provision of a county or city charter or act of incorporation. [Created through S.J.R. 24, 1979, and adopted by the people May 20, 1980]

ARTICLE XI-K
GUARANTEE OF BONDED INDEBTEDNESS OF EDUCATION DISTRICTS

Section 1. State empowered to guarantee bonded indebtedness of education districts. To secure lower

Constitution

interest costs on the general obligation bonds of school districts, education service districts and community college districts, the State of Oregon may guarantee the general obligation bonded indebtedness of those districts as provided in sections 2 to 6 of this Article and laws enacted pursuant to this Article. [Created through H.J.R. 71, 1997, and adopted by the people Nov. 3, 1998]

Section 2. State empowered to lend credit for state guarantee of bonded indebtedness of education districts. In the manner provided by law and notwithstanding the limitations contained in sections 7 and 8, Article XI of this Constitution, the credit of the State of Oregon may be loaned and indebtedness incurred, in an amount not to exceed, at any one time, one-half of one percent of the true cash value of all taxable property in the state, to provide funds as necessary to satisfy the state guaranty of the bonded general obligation indebtedness of school districts, education service districts and community college districts that qualify, under procedures that shall be established by law, to issue general obligation bonds that are guaranteed by the full faith and credit of this state. The state may guarantee the general obligation debt of qualified school districts, education service districts and community college districts and may guarantee general obligation bonded indebtedness incurred to refund the school district, education service district or community college district general obligation bonded indebtedness. [Created through H.J.R. 71, 1997, and adopted by the people Nov. 3, 1998]

Section 3. Repayment by education districts. The Legislative Assembly may provide that reimbursement to the state shall be obtained from, but shall not be limited to, moneys that otherwise would be used for the support of the educational programs of the school district, the education service district or the community college district that incurred the bonded indebtedness with respect to which any payment under the state's guaranty is made. [Created through H.J.R. 71, 1997, and adopted by the people Nov. 3, 1998]

Section 4. Sources of revenue. The State of Oregon may issue bonds if and as necessary to provide funding to satisfy the state's guaranty obligations undertaken pursuant to this Article. In addition, notwithstanding anything to the contrary in Article VIII of this Constitution, the state may borrow available moneys from the Common School Fund if such borrowing is reasonably necessary to satisfy the state's guaranty obligations undertaken pursuant to this Article. The State of Oregon also may issue bonds if and as necessary to provide funding to repay the borrowed moneys, and any interest thereon, to the Common School Fund. The bonds shall be payable from any moneys reimbursed to the state under section 3 of this Article, from any moneys recoverable from the school district, the education service district or the community college district that incurred the bonded indebtedness with respect to which any payment under the state's guaranty is made, any other funds available for these purposes and, if necessary, from state ad valorem taxes. [Created through H.J.R. 71, 1997, and adopted by the people Nov. 3, 1998]

Section 5. Bonds. Bonds of the state issued pursuant to this Article shall be the direct obligations of the state and shall be in such form, run for such periods of time and bear such rates of interest as shall be provided by law. The bonds may be refunded with bonds of like obligation. [Created through H.J.R. 71, 1997, and adopted by the people Nov. 3, 1998]

Section 6. Legislation to effectuate Article. The Legislative Assembly shall enact legislation to carry out the provisions of this Article, including provisions that authorize the state's recovery, from any school district, education service district or community college district that incurred the bonded indebtedness with respect to which any payment under the state's guaranty is made, any

amounts necessary to make the state whole. This Article shall supersede all conflicting constitutional provisions and shall supersede any conflicting provision of any law, ordinance or charter pertaining to any school district, education service district or community college district. [Created through H.J.R. 71, 1997, and adopted by the people Nov. 3, 1998]

ARTICLE XI-L
OREGON HEALTH AND SCIENCE UNIVERSITY

Sec. 1. State empowered to lend credit for financing capital costs of Oregon Health and Science University; bonds
2. Sources of repayment
3. Refunding bonds
4. Legislation to effectuate Article
5. Relationship to conflicting provisions of Constitution

Section 1. State empowered to lend credit for financing capital costs of Oregon Health and Science University; bonds. (1) In the manner provided by law and notwithstanding the limitations contained in section 7, Article XI of this Constitution, the credit of the State of Oregon may be loaned and indebtedness incurred, in an aggregate outstanding principal amount not to exceed, at any one time, one-half of one percent of the real market value of all property in the state, to provide funds to finance capital costs of Oregon Health and Science University. Bonds issued under this section may not be paid from ad valorem property taxes.

(2) Any indebtedness incurred under this section shall be in the form of general obligation bonds of the State of Oregon containing a direct promise on behalf of the State of Oregon to pay the principal, premium, if any, and interest on such bonds, in an aggregate outstanding principal amount not to exceed the amount authorized in subsection (1) of this section. The bonds shall be the direct obligation of the State of Oregon and shall be in such form, run for such period of time, have such terms and bear such rates of interest as may be provided by statute. The full faith and credit and taxing power of the State of Oregon shall be pledged to the payment of the principal, premium, if any, and interest on such bonds provided, however, that the ad valorem taxing power of the State of Oregon may not be pledged to the payment of such bonds.

(3) The proceeds from bonds issued under this section shall be used to finance capital costs of Oregon Health and Science University and costs of issuing bonds pursuant to this Article. Bonds issued under this section to finance capital costs of Oregon Health and Science University shall be issued in an aggregate principal amount that produces net proceeds for the university in an amount that does not exceed $200 million.

(4) The proceeds from bonds issued under this section may not be used to finance operating costs of Oregon Health and Science University.

(5) As used in this Article, "bonds" means bonds, notes or other financial obligations of the State of Oregon issued under this section. [Created through H.J.R. 19, 2001, and adopted by the people May 21, 2002]

Section 2. Sources of repayment. The principal, premium, if any, interest and any other amounts payable with respect to bonds issued under section 1 of this Article shall be repaid as determined by the Legislative Assembly from the following sources:

(1) Amounts appropriated for such purpose by the Legislative Assembly from the General Fund, including any taxes levied to pay the bonds other than ad valorem property taxes;

(2) Amounts allocated for such purpose by the Legislative Assembly from the proceeds of the State Lottery or from the Master Settlement Agreement entered into on November 23, 1998, by the State of Oregon and leading United States tobacco product manufacturers; and

(3) Amounts appropriated or allocated for such purpose by the Legislative Assembly from other sources of revenue. [Created through H.J.R. 19, 2001, and adopted by the people May 21, 2002]

Section 3. Refunding bonds. Bonds issued under section 1 of this Article may be refunded with bonds of like obligation. [Created through H.J.R. 19, 2001, and adopted by the people May 21, 2002]

Section 4. Legislation to effectuate Article. The Legislative Assembly may enact legislation to carry out the provisions of this Article. [Created through H.J.R. 19, 2001, and adopted by the people May 21, 2002]

Section 5. Relationship to conflicting provisions of Constitution. This Article shall supersede all conflicting provisions of this constitution. [Created through H.J.R. 19, 2001, and adopted by the people May 21, 2002]

ARTICLE XI-M
SEISMIC REHABILITATION OF PUBLIC EDUCATION BUILDINGS

Sec. 1. State empowered to lend credit for seismic rehabilitation of public education buildings; bonds
2. Sources of repayment
3. Refunding bonds
4. Legislation to effectuate Article
5. Relationship to conflicting provisions of Constitution

Note: Article XI-M was designated as "Article XI-L" by S.J.R. 21, 2001, and adopted by the people Nov. 5, 2002.

Section 1. State empowered to lend credit for seismic rehabilitation of public education buildings; bonds. (1) In the manner provided by law and notwithstanding the limitations contained in section 7, Article XI of this Constitution, the credit of the State of Oregon may be loaned and indebtedness incurred, in an aggregate outstanding principal amount not to exceed, at any one time, one-fifth of one percent of the real market value of all property in the state, to provide funds for the planning and implementation of seismic rehabilitation of public education buildings, including surveying and conducting engineering evaluations of the need for seismic rehabilitation.

(2) Any indebtedness incurred under this section must be in the form of general obligation bonds of the State of Oregon containing a direct promise on behalf of the State of Oregon to pay the principal, premium, if any, interest and other amounts payable with respect to the bonds, in an aggregate outstanding principal amount not to exceed the amount authorized in subsection (1) of this section. The bonds are the direct obligation of the State of Oregon and must be in a form, run for a period of time, have terms and bear rates of interest as may be provided by statute. The full faith and credit and taxing power of the State of Oregon must be pledged to the payment of the principal, premium, if any, and interest on the general obligation bonds; however, the ad valorem taxing power of the State of Oregon may not be pledged to the payment of the bonds issued under this section.

(3) As used in this section, "public education building" means a building owned by the State Board of Higher Education, a school district, an education service district, a community college district or a community college service district. [Created through S.J.R. 21, 2001, and adopted by the people Nov. 5, 2002]

Section 2. Sources of repayment. The principal, premium, if any, interest and other amounts payable with

respect to the general obligation bonds issued under section 1 of this Article must be repaid as determined by the Legislative Assembly from the following sources:

(1) Amounts appropriated for the purpose by the Legislative Assembly from the General Fund, including taxes, other than ad valorem property taxes, levied to pay the bonds;

(2) Amounts allocated for the purpose by the Legislative Assembly from the proceeds of the State Lottery or from the Master Settlement Agreement entered into on November 23, 1998, by the State of Oregon and leading United States tobacco product manufacturers; and

(3) Amounts appropriated or allocated for the purpose by the Legislative Assembly from other sources of revenue. [Created through S.J.R. 21, 2001, and adopted by the people Nov. 5, 2002]

Section 3. Refunding bonds. General obligation bonds issued under section 1 of this Article may be refunded with bonds of like obligation. [Created through S.J.R. 21, 2001, and adopted by the people Nov. 5, 2002]

Section 4. Legislation to effectuate Article. The Legislative Assembly may enact legislation to carry out the provisions of this Article. [Created through S.J.R. 21, 2001, and adopted by the people Nov. 5, 2002]

Section 5. Relationship to conflicting provisions of Constitution. This Article supersedes conflicting provisions of this Constitution. [Created through S.J.R. 21, 2001, and adopted by the people Nov. 5, 2002]

ARTICLE XI-N
SEISMIC REHABILITATION OF EMERGENCY SERVICES BUILDINGS

Sec. 1. State empowered to lend credit for seismic rehabilitation of emergency services buildings; bonds
2. Sources of repayment
3. Refunding bonds
4. Legislation to effectuate Article
5. Relationship to conflicting provisions of Constitution

Note: Article XI-N was designated as "Article XI-L" by S.J.R. 22, 2001, and adopted by the people Nov. 5, 2002.

Section 1. State empowered to lend credit for seismic rehabilitation of emergency services buildings; bonds. (1) In the manner provided by law and notwithstanding the limitations contained in section 7, Article XI of this Constitution, the credit of the State of Oregon may be loaned and indebtedness incurred, in an aggregate outstanding principal amount not to exceed, at any one time, one-fifth of one percent of the real market value of all property in the state, to provide funds for the planning and implementation of seismic rehabilitation of emergency services buildings, including surveying and conducting engineering evaluations of the need for seismic rehabilitation.

(2) Any indebtedness incurred under this section must be in the form of general obligation bonds of the State of Oregon containing a direct promise on behalf of the State of Oregon to pay the principal, premium, if any, interest and other amounts payable with respect to the bonds, in an aggregate outstanding principal amount not to exceed the amount authorized in subsection (1) of this section. The bonds are the direct obligation of the State of Oregon and must be in a form, run for a period of time, have terms and bear rates of interest as may be provided by statute. The full faith and credit and taxing power of the State of Oregon must be pledged to the payment of the principal, premium, if any, and interest on the general obligation bonds; however, the ad valorem taxing power of the State of Oregon may not be pledged to the payment of the bonds issued under this section.

(3) As used in this section:

(a) "Acute inpatient care facility" means a licensed hospital with an organized medical staff, with permanent facilities that include inpatient beds, and with comprehensive medical services, including physician services and continuous nursing services under the supervision of registered nurses, to provide diagnosis and medical or surgical treatment primarily for but not limited to acutely ill patients and accident victims. "Acute inpatient care facility" includes the Oregon Health and Science University.

(b) "Emergency services building" means a public building used for fire protection services, a hospital building that contains an acute inpatient care facility, a police station, a sheriff's office or a similar facility used by a state, county, district or municipal law enforcement agency. [Created through S.J.R. 22, 2001, and adopted by the people Nov. 5, 2002]

Section 2. Sources of repayment. The principal, premium, if any, interest and other amounts payable with respect to the general obligation bonds issued under section 1 of this Article must be repaid as determined by the Legislative Assembly from the following sources:

(1) Amounts appropriated for the purpose by the Legislative Assembly from the General Fund, including taxes, other than ad valorem property taxes, levied to pay the bonds;

(2) Amounts allocated for the purpose by the Legislative Assembly from the proceeds of the State Lottery or from the Master Settlement Agreement entered into on November 23, 1998, by the State of Oregon and leading United States tobacco product manufacturers; and

(3) Amounts appropriated or allocated for the purpose by the Legislative Assembly from other sources of revenue. [Created through S.J.R. 22, 2001, and adopted by the people Nov. 5, 2002]

Section 3. Refunding bonds. General obligation bonds issued under section 1 of this Article may be refunded with bonds of like obligation. [Created through S.J.R. 22, 2001, and adopted by the people Nov. 5, 2002]

Section 4. Legislation to effectuate Article. The Legislative Assembly may enact legislation to carry out the provisions of this Article. [Created through S.J.R. 22, 2001, and adopted by the people Nov. 5, 2002]

Section 5. Relationship to conflicting provisions of Constitution. This Article supersedes conflicting provisions of this Constitution. [Created through S.J.R. 22, 2001, and adopted by the people Nov. 5, 2002]

ARTICLE XI-O
PENSION LIABILITIES

Sec. 1.   State empowered to lend credit for pension liabilities
2.   Refunding obligations
3.   Legislation to effectuate Article
4.   Relationship to conflicting provisions of Constitution

Section 1. State empowered to lend credit for pension liabilities. (1) In the manner provided by law and notwithstanding the limitations contained in section 7, Article XI of this Constitution, the credit of the State of Oregon may be loaned and indebtedness incurred to finance the State of Oregon's pension liabilities. Indebtedness authorized by this section also may be used to pay costs of issuing or incurring indebtedness under this section.

(2) Indebtedness incurred under this section is a general obligation of the State of Oregon and must contain a direct promise on behalf of the State of Oregon to pay the principal, premium, if any, and interest on that indebtedness. The State of Oregon shall pledge its full faith and credit and taxing power to pay that indebtedness; however, the ad val-

orem taxing power of the State of Oregon may not be pledged to pay that indebtedness. The amount of indebtedness authorized by this section and outstanding at any time may not exceed one percent of the real market value of all property in the state. [Created through H.J.R. 18, 2003, and adopted by the people Sept. 16, 2003]

Section 2. Refunding obligations. Indebtedness incurred under section 1 of this Article may be refunded with like obligations. [Created through H.J.R. 18, 2003, and adopted by the people Sept. 16, 2003]

Section 3. Legislation to effectuate Article. The Legislative Assembly may enact legislation to carry out the provisions of this Article. [Created through H.J.R. 18, 2003, and adopted by the people Sept. 16, 2003]

Section 4. Relationship to conflicting provisions of Constitution. This Article supersedes all conflicting provisions of this Constitution. [Created through H.J.R. 18, 2003, and adopted by the people Sept. 16, 2003]

ARTICLE XI-P
SCHOOL DISTRICT CAPITAL COSTS

Sec. 1.   State empowered to lend credit for grants or loans to school districts to finance capital costs; general obligation bond proceeds as matching funds
2.   Sources of repayment
3.   Refunding bonds
4.   School capital matching fund
5.   "Capital costs" defined
6.   Legislation to effectuate Article
7.   Relationship to conflicting provision of Constitution

Section 1. State empowered to lend credit for grants or loans to school districts to finance capital costs; general obligation bond proceeds as matching funds. (1) In the manner provided by law and notwithstanding the limitations contained in section 7, Article XI of this Constitution, the State of Oregon may loan its credit and incur indebtedness in an aggregate outstanding principal amount not to exceed, at any one time, one-half of one percent of the real market value of the real property in this state, to provide funds to be advanced by grant or loan to school districts to finance the capital costs of the school districts. Bonds issued under this section may not be paid from ad valorem property taxes.

(2) Indebtedness incurred under this section must be in the form of general obligation bonds of the State of Oregon containing a direct promise to pay the principal, interest and premium, if any, of the bonds in an aggregate outstanding principal amount not to exceed the amount authorized in subsection (1) of this section. The bonds are the direct obligation of the State of Oregon and must be in such form, run for such periods of time, have such terms and bear such rates of interest as may be provided by statute. The State of Oregon shall pledge its full faith and credit and taxing power to the payment of the principal, interest and premium, if any, of the bonds. However, the State of Oregon may not pledge its ad valorem taxing power to the payment of the bonds.

(3) The proceeds from bonds issued under this section may be used only to provide matching funds to finance the capital costs of school districts that have received voter approval for local general obligation bonds and to provide for the costs of issuing bonds and the payment of debt service.

(4) The proceeds from bonds issued under this section may not be used to finance the operating costs of school districts. [Created through H.J.R. 13, 2009, and adopted by the people May 18, 2010]

Section 2. Sources of repayment. The principal, interest and premium, if any, of the bonds issued under section

1 of this Article must be repaid as determined by the Legislative Assembly from the following sources:

(1) Amounts appropriated for repayment by the Legislative Assembly from the General Fund, including taxes levied to pay the bonds except ad valorem property taxes;

(2) Amounts appropriated or allocated for repayment by the Legislative Assembly from other sources of revenue; or

(3) Any other available moneys. [Created through H.J.R. 13, 2009, and adopted by the people May 18, 2010]

Section 3. Refunding bonds. Bonds issued under section 1 of this Article may be refunded with bonds of like obligation. [Created through H.J.R. 13, 2009, and adopted by the people May 18, 2010]

Section 4. School capital matching fund. (1) There is created a school capital matching fund. Moneys in the fund may be invested and the earnings shall be retained in the fund or expended as provided by the Legislative Assembly.

(2) The Legislative Assembly may by law appropriate, allocate or transfer moneys or revenue to the school capital matching fund.

(3) The Legislative Assembly may appropriate, allocate or transfer moneys in the school capital matching fund and earnings on moneys in the fund for the purposes of providing:

(a) State matching funds to school districts to finance capital costs; and

(b) Payment of debt service for general obligation bonds issued pursuant to this Article. [Created through H.J.R. 13, 2009, and adopted by the people May 18, 2010]

Section 5. "Capital costs" defined. As used in this Article, "capital costs" means costs of land and of other assets having a useful life of more than one year, including costs associated with acquisition, construction, improvement, remodeling, furnishing, equipping, maintenance or repair. [Created through H.J.R. 13, 2009, and adopted by the people May 18, 2010]

Section 6. Legislation to effectuate Article. The Legislative Assembly may enact legislation to carry out the provisions of this Article. [Created through H.J.R. 13, 2009, and adopted by the people May 18, 2010]

Section 7. Relationship to conflicting provision of Constitution. This Article supersedes any conflicting provision of this Constitution. [Created through H.J.R. 13, 2009, and adopted by the people May 18, 2010]

ARTICLE XI-Q
REAL OR PERSONAL PROPERTY
OWNED OR OPERATED BY STATE

Sec. 1. State empowered to lend credit for real or personal property to be owned or operated by state; refinancing authority
  2. Limit on indebtedness; general obligation of state
  3. Legislation to effectuate Article
  4. Relationship to conflicting provisions of Constitution

Note: Article XI-Q was designated as "Article XI-P" by S.J.R. 48, 2010, and adopted by the people Nov. 2, 2010.

Section 1. State empowered to lend credit for real or personal property to be owned or operated by state; refinancing authority. (1) In the manner provided by law and notwithstanding the limitations contained in section 7, Article XI of this Constitution, the credit of the State of Oregon may be loaned and indebtedness incurred to finance the costs of:

(a) Acquiring, constructing, remodeling, repairing, equipping or furnishing real or personal property that is or will be owned or operated by the State of Oregon, including, without limitation, facilities and systems;

(b) Infrastructure related to the real or personal property; or

(c) Indebtedness incurred under this subsection.

(2) In the manner provided by law and notwithstanding the limitations contained in section 7, Article XI of this Constitution, the credit of the State of Oregon may be loaned and indebtedness incurred to refinance:

(a) Indebtedness incurred under subsection (1) of this section.

(b) Borrowings issued before the effective date of this Article to finance or refinance costs described in subsection (1) of this section. [Created through S.J.R. 48, 2010, and adopted by the people Nov. 2, 2010]

Note: The effective date of Senate Joint Resolution 48, 2010, is Dec. 2, 2010.

Section 2. Limit on indebtedness; general obligation of state. (1) Indebtedness may not be incurred under section 1 of this Article if the indebtedness would cause the total principal amount of indebtedness incurred under section 1 of this Article and outstanding to exceed one percent of the real market value of the property in this state.

(2) Indebtedness incurred under section 1 of this Article is a general obligation of the State of Oregon and must contain a direct promise on behalf of the State of Oregon to pay the principal, premium, if any, and interest on the obligation. The full faith and credit and taxing power of the State of Oregon must be pledged to payment of the indebtedness. However, the State of Oregon may not pledge or levy an ad valorem tax to pay the indebtedness. [Created through S.J.R. 48, 2010, and adopted by the people Nov. 2, 2010]

Section 3. Legislation to effectuate Article. The Legislative Assembly may enact legislation to carry out the provisions of this Article. [Created through S.J.R. 48, 2010, and adopted by the people Nov. 2, 2010]

Section 4. Relationship to conflicting provisions of Constitution. This Article supersedes conflicting provisions of this Constitution. [Created through S.J.R. 48, 2010, and adopted by the people Nov. 2, 2010]

ARTICLE XII
STATE PRINTING

Section 1. State printing; State Printer. Laws may be enacted providing for the state printing and binding, and for the election or appointment of a state printer, who shall have had not less than ten years' experience in the art of printing. The state printer shall receive such compensation as may from time to time be provided by law. Until such laws shall be enacted the state printer shall be elected, and the printing done as heretofore provided by this constitution and the general laws. [Constitution of 1859; Amendment proposed by S.J.R. 1, 1901, and adopted by the people June 6, 1904; Amendment proposed by initiative petition filed Feb. 3, 1906, and adopted by the people June 4, 1906]

ARTICLE XIII
SALARIES

Section 1. Salaries or other compensation of state officers. [Constitution of 1859; Repeal proposed by S.J.R. 12, 1955, and adopted by the people Nov. 6, 1956]

ARTICLE XIV
SEAT OF GOVERNMENT

Sec. 1. Seat of government
  2. Erection of state house prior to 1865

Section 1. Seat of government. [Constitution of 1859; Repeal proposed by S.J.R. 41, 1957, and adopted by the peo-

Constitution

ple Nov. 4, 1958 (present section 1 and former 1958 section 3 of this Article adopted in lieu of this section and former original section 3 of this Article)]

Section 1. Seat of government. The permanent seat of government for the state shall be Marion County. [Created through S.J.R. 41, 1957, and adopted by the people Nov. 4, 1958 (this section and former 1958 section 3 of this Article adopted in lieu of former original sections 1 and 3 of this Article)]

Section 2. Erection of state house prior to 1865. No tax shall be levied, or money of the State expended, or debt contracted for the erection of a State House prior to the year eighteen hundred and sixty five. —

Section 3. Limitation on removal of seat of government; location of state institutions. [Constitution of 1859; Amendment proposed by S.J.R. 1, 1907, and adopted by the people June 1, 1908; Repeal proposed by S.J.R. 41, 1957, and adopted by the people Nov. 4, 1958 (present section 1 and former 1958 section 3 of this Article adopted in lieu of this section and former section 1 of this Article)]

Section 4. Location and use of state institutions. [Created through S.J.R. 41, 1957, and adopted by the people Nov. 4, 1958 (this section, designated as "Section 2" by S.J.R. 41, 1957, and present section 1 of this Article adopted in lieu of former original sections 1 and 3 of this Article); Repeal proposed by S.J.R. 9, 1971, and adopted by the people Nov. 7, 1972]

ARTICLE XV
MISCELLANEOUS

Section 1. Officers to hold office until successors elected; exceptions; effect on defeated incumbent.
(1) All officers, except members of the Legislative Assembly and incumbents who seek reelection and are defeated, shall hold their offices until their successors are elected, and qualified.

(2) If an incumbent seeks reelection and is defeated, he shall hold office only until the end of his term; and if an election contest is pending in the courts regarding that office when the term of such an incumbent ends and a successor to the office has not been elected or if elected, has not qualified because of such election contest, the person appointed to fill the vacancy thus created shall serve only until the contest and any appeal is finally determined notwithstanding any other provision of this constitution.

[Constitution of 1859; Amendment proposed by H.J.R. 51, 1969, and adopted by the people Nov. 3, 1970]

Section 2. Tenure of office; how fixed; maximum tenure. When the duration of any office is not provided for by this Constitution, it may be declared by law; and if not so declared, such office shall be held during the pleasure of the authority making the appointment. But the Legislative Assembly shall not create any office, the tenure of which shall be longer than four years.

Section 3. Oaths of office. Every person elected or appointed to any office under this Constitution, shall, before entering on the duties thereof, take an oath or affirmation to support the Constitution of the United States, and of this State, and also an oath of office. —

Note: The amendments to sections 4, 4a, 4b and 4c and the repeal of section 4d by Measure No. 76, 2010, as submitted to the people was preceded by a preamble that reads as follows:

PREAMBLE: The people of the State of Oregon find that renewing the current dedication in the Oregon Constitution of fifteen percent of lottery revenues to parks, water quality and fish and wildlife habitats will provide lasting social, economic, environmental and public health benefits. The people of the State of Oregon also find that renewal of the Parks and Natural Resources Fund will support voluntary efforts to:

(1) Protect and restore water quality, watersheds and habitats for native fish and wildlife that provide a healthy environment for current and future generations of Oregonians;

(2) Maintain and expand public parks, natural areas and recreation areas to meet the diverse needs of a growing population and to provide opportunities for [sic] to experience nature and enjoy outdoor recreation activities close to home and in the many special places throughout Oregon;

(3) Provide jobs and economic opportunities improving the health of our forests, prairies, lakes, streams, wetlands, rivers, and parks, including efforts to halt the spread of invasive species;

(4) Strengthen the audit and reporting requirements, identify desired outcomes and specify allowable uses of the fund in order to provide more strategic, accountable and efficient uses of the Parks and Natural Resources Fund; and

(5) Enhance the ability of public land managers, private organizations, individuals and businesses to work together in local, regional and statewide partnerships to expand recreation opportunities, improve water quality and conserve fish and wildlife habitat.

Section 4. Regulation of lotteries; state lottery; use of net proceeds from state lottery. (1) Except as provided in subsections (2), (3), (4), (8) and (9) of this section, lotteries and the sale of lottery tickets, for any purpose whatever, are prohibited, and the Legislative Assembly shall prevent the same by penal laws.

(2) The Legislative Assembly may provide for the establishment, operation, and regulation of raffles and the lottery commonly known as bingo or lotto by charitable, fraternal, or religious organizations. As used in this section, charitable, fraternal or religious organization means such organizations or foundations as defined by law because of their charitable, fraternal, or religious purposes. The regulations shall define eligible organizations or foundations, and may prescribe the frequency of raffles, bingo or lotto, set a maximum monetary limit for prizes and require a statement of the odds on winning a prize. The Legislative Assembly shall vest the regulatory authority in any appropriate state agency.

(3) There is hereby created the State Lottery Commission which shall establish and operate a State Lottery. All proceeds from the State Lottery, including

interest, but excluding costs of administration and payment of prizes, shall be used for any of the following purposes: creating jobs, furthering economic development, financing public education in Oregon or restoring and protecting Oregon's parks, beaches, watersheds and native fish and wildlife.

(4)(a) The State Lottery Commission shall be comprised of five members appointed by the Governor and confirmed by the Senate who shall serve at the pleasure of the Governor. At least one of the Commissioners shall have a minimum of five years experience in law enforcement and at least one of the Commissioners shall be a certified public accountant. The Commission is empowered to promulgate rules related to the procedures of the Commission and the operation of the State Lottery. Such rules and any statutes enacted to further implement this article shall insure the integrity, security, honesty, and fairness of the Lottery. The Commission shall have such additional powers and duties as may be provided by law.

(b) The Governor shall appoint a Director subject to confirmation by the Senate who shall serve at the pleasure of the Governor. The Director shall be qualified by training and experience to direct the operations of a state-operated lottery. The Director shall be responsible for managing the affairs of the Commission. The Director may appoint and prescribe the duties of no more than four Assistant Directors as the Director deems necessary. One of the Assistant Directors shall be responsible for a security division to assure security, integrity, honesty, and fairness in the operations and administration of the State Lottery. To fulfill these responsibilities, the Assistant Director for security shall be qualified by training and experience, including at least five years of law enforcement experience, and knowledge and experience in computer security.

(c) The Director shall implement and operate a State Lottery pursuant to the rules, and under the guidance, of the Commission. The State Lottery may operate any game procedure authorized by the commission, except parimutuel racing, social games, and the games commonly known in Oregon as bingo or lotto, whereby prizes are distributed using any existing or future methods among adult persons who have paid for tickets or shares in that game; provided that, in lottery games utilizing computer terminals or other devices, no coins or currency shall ever be dispensed directly to players from such computer terminals or devices.

(d) There is hereby created within the General Fund the Oregon State Lottery Fund which is continuously appropriated for the purpose of administering and operating the Commission and the State Lottery. The State Lottery shall operate as a self-supporting revenue-raising agency of state government and no appropriations, loans, or other transfers of state funds shall be made to it. The State Lottery shall pay all prizes and all of its expenses out of the revenues it receives from the sale of tickets or shares to the public and turnover the net proceeds therefrom to a fund to be established by the Legislative Assembly from which the Legislative Assembly shall make appropriations for the benefit of any of the following public purposes: creating jobs, furthering economic development, financing public education in Oregon or restoring and protecting Oregon's parks, beaches, watersheds and native fish and wildlife. Effective July 1, 1997, 15% of the net proceeds from the State Lottery shall be deposited, from the fund created by the Legislative Assembly under this paragraph, in an education stability fund. Effective July 1, 2003, 18% of the net proceeds from the State Lottery shall be deposited, from the fund created by the Legislative Assembly under this paragraph, in an education stability fund. Earnings on moneys in the education stability fund shall be retained in the fund or expended for the public purpose of financing

public education in Oregon as provided by law. Except as provided in subsection (6) of this section, moneys in the education stability fund shall be invested as provided by law and shall not be subject to the limitations of section 6, Article XI of this Constitution. The Legislative Assembly may appropriate other moneys or revenue to the education stability fund. The Legislative Assembly shall appropriate amounts sufficient to pay lottery bonds before appropriating the net proceeds from the State Lottery for any other purpose. At least 84% of the total annual revenues from the sale of all lottery tickets or shares shall be returned to the public in the form of prizes and net revenues benefiting the public purpose.

(5) Notwithstanding paragraph (d) of subsection (4) of this section, the amount in the education stability fund created under paragraph (d) of subsection (4) of this section may not exceed an amount that is equal to five percent of the amount that was accrued as revenues in the state's General Fund during the prior biennium. If the amount in the education stability fund exceeds five percent of the amount that was accrued as revenues in the state's General Fund during the prior biennium:

(a) Additional net proceeds from the State Lottery may not be deposited in the education stability fund until the amount in the education stability fund is reduced to less than five percent of the amount that was accrued as revenues in the state's General Fund during the prior biennium; and

(b) Fifteen percent of the net proceeds from the State Lottery shall be deposited into the school capital matching fund created under section 4, Article XI-P of this Constitution.

(6) The Legislative Assembly may by law appropriate, allocate or transfer any portion of the principal of the education stability fund created under paragraph (d) of subsection (4) of this section for expenditure on public education if:

(a) The proposed appropriation, allocation or transfer is approved by three-fifths of the members serving in each house of the Legislative Assembly and the Legislative Assembly finds one of the following:

(A) That the last quarterly economic and revenue forecast for a biennium indicates that moneys available to the state's General Fund for the next biennium will be at least three percent less than appropriations from the state's General Fund for the current biennium;

(B) That there has been a decline for two or more consecutive quarters in the last 12 months in seasonally adjusted nonfarm payroll employment; or

(C) That a quarterly economic and revenue forecast projects that revenues in the state's General Fund in the current biennium will be at least two percent below what the revenues were projected to be in the revenue forecast on which the legislatively adopted budget for the current biennium was based; or

(b) The proposed appropriation, allocation or transfer is approved by three-fifths of the members serving in each house of the Legislative Assembly and the Governor declares an emergency.

(7) The Legislative Assembly may by law prescribe the procedures to be used and identify the persons required to make the forecasts described in subsection (6) of this section.

(8) Effective July 1, 1999, 15% of the net proceeds from the State Lottery shall be deposited in a parks and natural resources fund created by the Legislative Assembly. Of the moneys in the parks and natural resources fund, 50% shall be deposited in a parks subaccount and distributed for the public purposes of financing the protection, repair, operation, and creation of state, regional and local public parks,

ocean shore and public beach access areas, historic sites and recreation areas, and 50% shall be deposited in a natural resources subaccount and distributed for the public purposes of financing the restoration and protection of native fish and wildlife, watersheds and water quality in Oregon. The Legislative Assembly shall not limit expenditures from the parks and natural resources fund, or from the parks or natural resources subaccounts. The Legislative Assembly may appropriate other moneys or revenue to the parks and natural resources fund.

(9) Only one State Lottery operation shall be permitted in the State.

(10) The Legislative Assembly has no power to authorize, and shall prohibit, casinos from operation in the State of Oregon. [Constitution of 1859; Amendment proposed by H.J.R. 14, 1975, and adopted by the people Nov. 2, 1976; Amendment proposed by initiative petition filed April 3, 1984, and adopted by the people Nov. 6, 1984 (paragraph designations in subsection (4) were not included in the petition); Amendment proposed by H.J.R. 20, 1985, and adopted by the people Nov. 4, 1986; Amendment proposed by H.J.R. 15, 1995, and adopted by the people May 16, 1995; Amendment proposed by initiative petition filed March 11, 1998, and adopted by the people Nov. 3, 1998; Amendment proposed by H.J.R. 80, 2002 (3rd s.s.), and adopted by the people Sept. 17, 2002; Revision proposed by H.J.R. 13, 2009, and adopted by the people May 18, 2010; Amendment proposed by initiative petition filed Dec. 22, 2009, and adopted by the people Nov. 2, 2010]

Note: The amendments to section 4, as adopted by the people in Measure No. 66, 1998, incorrectly set forth the text of section 4 as it existed at the time the measure was submitted to the people. The text of the measure, as approved by the voters, was printed here.

Note: The amendments to section 4, as adopted by the people in Measure No. 76, 2010, at the Nov. 2010 general election did not set forth the text of section 4 as it was revised by the people in Measure No. 68, 2010 (H.J.R. 13, 2009), at the May 2010 primary election. The text of section 4, as revised by Measure No. 68, 2010, and amended by Measure No. 76, 2010, is printed here.

Section 4a. Use of net proceeds from state lottery for parks and recreation areas. (1) In each biennium the Legislative Assembly shall appropriate all of the moneys in the parks subaccount of the parks and natural resources fund established under section 4 of this Article for the uses allowed in subsection (2) of this section, and to achieve all of the following:

(a) Provide additional public parks, natural areas or outdoor recreational areas to meet the needs of current and future residents of the State of Oregon;

(b) Protect natural, cultural, historic and outdoor recreational resources of state or regional significance;

(c) Manage public parks, natural areas and outdoor recreation areas to ensure their long-term ecological health and provide for the enjoyment of current and future residents of the State of Oregon; and

(d) Provide diverse and equitable opportunities for residents of the State of Oregon to experience nature and participate in outdoor recreational activities in state, regional, local or neighborhood public parks and recreation areas.

(2) The moneys in the parks subaccount shall be used only to:

(a) Maintain, construct, improve, develop, manage and operate state parks, ocean shores, public beach access areas, historic sites, natural areas and outdoor and recreation areas;

(b) Acquire real property, or interests therein, that has significant natural, scenic, cultural, historic or recreational values, for the creation or operation of state parks, ocean

shores, public beach access areas, outdoor recreation areas and historic sites;

(c) Provide grants to regional or local government entities to acquire property for public parks, natural areas or outdoor recreation areas, or to develop or improve public parks, natural areas or outdoor recreation areas.

(3) In each biennium the Legislative Assembly shall appropriate no less than twelve percent of the moneys in the parks subaccount for local and regional grants as authorized under paragraph (c) of subsection (2) of this section. However, if in any biennium the amount of net proceeds deposited in the parks and natural resources fund created under section 4 of this Article increases by more than fifty percent above the amount deposited in the 2009-2011 biennium, the Legislative Assembly shall appropriate no less than twenty-five percent of the moneys in the parks subaccount for local and regional grants as authorized under paragraph (c) of subsection (2) of this section. The grants shall be administered by a single state agency. The costs of the state agency in administering the grants shall not be paid out of the portion of the moneys in the parks subaccount appropriated for local and regional grants. [Created through initiative petition filed March 11, 1998, and adopted by the people Nov. 3, 1998; Amendment proposed by initiative petition filed Dec. 22, 2009, and adopted by the people Nov. 2, 2010]

Section 4b. Use of net proceeds from state lottery for fish and wildlife, watershed and habitat protection. (1) In each biennium the Legislative Assembly shall appropriate all of the moneys in the natural resources subaccount of the parks and natural resources fund established under section 4 of this Article for the uses allowed in subsections (2) and (3) of this section, and to accomplish all of the following:

(a) Protect and improve water quality in Oregon's rivers, lakes, and streams by restoring natural watershed functions or stream flows;

(b) Secure long-term protection for lands and waters that provide significant habitats for native fish and wildlife;

(c) Restore and maintain habitats needed to sustain healthy and resilient populations of native fish and wildlife;

(d) Maintain the diversity of Oregon's plants, animals and ecosystems;

(e) Involve people in voluntary actions to protect, restore and maintain the ecological health of Oregon's lands and waters; and

(f) Remedy the conditions that limit the health of fish and wildlife, habitats and watershed functions in greatest need of conservation.

(2) In each biennium the Legislative Assembly shall appropriate no less than sixty-five percent of the moneys in the natural resources subaccount to one state agency, and that agency shall distribute those moneys as grants to entities other than state or federal agencies for projects that achieve the outcomes specified in subsection (1) of this section. However, if in any biennium the amount of net proceeds deposited in the parks and natural resources fund created under section 4 of this Article increases by more than fifty percent above the amount deposited in the 2009-2011 biennium, the Legislative Assembly shall appropriate no less than seventy percent of the moneys in the natural resources subaccount to one state agency, and that agency shall distribute those moneys as grants to entities other than state or federal agencies for projects that achieve the outcomes specified in subsection (1) of this section. In addition, these moneys shall be used only to:

(a) Acquire from willing owners interests in land or water that will protect or restore native fish or wildlife habitats, which interests may include but are not limited to fee interests, conservation easements or leases;

(b) Carry out projects to protect or restore native fish or wildlife habitats;

(c) Carry out projects to protect or restore natural watershed functions to improve water quality or stream flows; and

(d) Carry out resource assessment, planning, design and engineering, technical assistance, monitoring and outreach activities necessary for projects funded under paragraphs (a) through (c) of this subsection.

(3) In each biennium the Legislative Assembly shall appropriate that portion of the natural resources subaccount not appropriated under subsection (2) of this section to support all of the following activities:

(a) Develop, implement or update state conservation strategies or plans to protect or restore native fish or wildlife habitats or to protect or restore natural watershed functions to improve water quality or stream flows;

(b) Develop, implement or update regional or local strategies or plans that are consistent with the state strategies or plans described in paragraph (a) of this subsection;

(c) Develop, implement or update state strategies or plans to prevent, detect, control or eradicate invasive species that threaten native fish or wildlife habitats or that impair water quality;

(d) Support local delivery of programs or projects, including watershed education activities, that protect or restore native fish or wildlife habitats or watersheds;

(e) Pay the state agency costs of administering subsection (2) of this section, which costs shall not be paid out of the moneys available for grants under subsection (2) of this section; and

(f) Enforce fish and wildlife and habitat protection laws and regulations. [Created through initiative petition filed March 11, 1998, and adopted by the people Nov. 3, 1998; Amendment proposed by initiative petition filed Dec. 22, 2009, and adopted by the people Nov. 2, 2010]

Section 4c. Audit of agency receiving certain net proceeds from state lottery. The Secretary of State shall regularly audit any state agency that receives moneys from the parks and natural resources fund established under section 4 of this Article to address the financial integrity, compliance with applicable laws, efficiency and effectiveness of the use of the moneys. The costs of the audit shall be paid from the parks and natural resources fund. However, such costs may not be paid from the portions of such fund, or the subaccounts of the fund, that are dedicated to grants. The audit shall be submitted to the Legislative Assembly as part of a biennial report to the Legislative Assembly. In addition, each agency that receives moneys from the parks and natural resources fund shall submit a biennial performance report [sic] the Legislature [sic] Assembly that describes the measurable biennial and cumulative results of activities and programs financed by the fund. [Created through initiative petition filed March 11, 1998, and adopted by the people Nov. 3, 1998; Amendment proposed by initiative petition filed Dec. 22, 2009, and adopted by the people Nov. 2, 2010]

Note: Added as section 4c to the Constitution but not to any Article therein by initiative petition (Measure No. 66, 1998) adopted by the people Nov. 3, 1998.

Section 4d. Subsequent vote for reaffirmation of sections 4a, 4b and 4c and amendment to section 4. [Created through initiative petition filed March 11, 1998, and adopted by the people Nov. 3, 1998; Repeal proposed by initiative petition filed Dec. 22, 2009, and adopted by the people Nov. 2, 2010]

Section 4e. Transfer of moneys in school capital matching subaccount to school capital matching fund

created under section 4, Article XI-P. [Created through H.J.R. 13, 2009, and adopted by the people May 18, 2010; Repealed Jan. 2, 2011, as specified in text of section adopted by the people May 18, 2010]

Section 4f. Percentage of lottery revenues to be expended for benefit of veterans. (1) Effective July 1, 2017, 1.5 percent of the net proceeds from the State Lottery shall be deposited, from the fund created by the Legislative Assembly under paragraph (d) of subsection (4) of section 4 of this Article, in a veterans' services fund created by the Legislative Assembly. The Legislative Assembly may appropriate other moneys or revenue to the veterans' services fund.

(2) The moneys in the veterans' services fund may be used only to provide services for the benefit of veterans. Such services may include, without limitation:

(a) Assistance for veterans with reintegration, employment, education benefits and tuition, housing, physical and mental health care and addiction treatment programs;

(b) Assistance for veterans, spouses of veterans or dependents of veterans in accessing state and federal benefits; and

(c) Funding services provided by county veterans' service officers, campus veterans' service officers or nonprofit or tribal veterans' service officers.

(3) As used in this section, "veteran" means a resident of the State of Oregon who served in the Armed Forces of the United States. [Created through H.J.R. 202, 2016, and adopted by the people Nov. 8, 2016]

Section 5. Property of married women not subject to debts of husband; registration of separate property. The property and pecuniary rights of every married woman, at the time of marriage or afterwards, acquired by gift, devise, or inheritance shall not be subject to the debts, or contracts of the husband; and laws shall be passed providing for the registration of the wife's seperate [sic] property.

Section 5a. Policy regarding marriage. It is the policy of Oregon, and its political subdivisions, that only a marriage between one man and one woman shall be valid or legally recognized as a marriage. [Created through initiative petition filed March 2, 2004, and adopted by the people Nov. 2, 2004]

Note: Added as unnumbered section to the Constitution but not to any Article therein by initiative petition (Measure No. 36, 2004) adopted by the people Nov. 2, 2004.

Section 6. Minimum area and population of counties. No county shall be reduced to an area of less than four hundred square miles; nor shall any new county be established in this State containing a less area, nor unless such new county shall contain a population of at least twelve hundred inhabitants.

Section 7. Officers not to receive fees from or represent claimants against state. No State officers, or members of the Legislative Assembly, shall directly or indirectly receive a fee, or be engaged as counsel, agent, or Attorney in the prosecution of any claim against this State.—

Section 8. Certain persons not to hold real estate or mining claims; working mining claims. [Constitution of 1859; Repeal proposed by S.J.R. 14, 1945, and adopted by the people Nov. 5, 1946]

Section 8. Persons eligible to serve in legislature; employment of judges by Oregon National Guard or public university. Notwithstanding the provisions of section 1, Article III and section 10, Article II of this Constitution:

(1) A person employed by any board or commission established by law to supervise and coordinate the activities of Oregon's institutions of post-secondary education, a

person employed by a public university as defined by law or a member or employee of any school board is eligible to serve as a member of the Legislative Assembly, and membership in the Legislative Assembly does not prevent the person from being employed by any board or commission established by law to supervise and coordinate the activities of Oregon's post-secondary institutions of education or by a public university as defined by law, or from being a member or employee of a school board.

(2) A person serving as a judge of any court of this state may be employed by the Oregon National Guard for the purpose of performing military service or may be employed by any public university as defined by law for the purpose of teaching, and the employment does not prevent the person from serving as a judge. [Created through initiative petition filed June 13, 1958, and adopted by the people Nov. 4, 1958; Amendment proposed by S.J.R. 203, 2014, and adopted by the people Nov. 4, 2014]

Section 8a. [Created through S.J.R. 203, 2014, and adopted by the people Nov. 4, 2014; Section not compiled because of its temporary nature]

Section 9. When elective office becomes vacant. The Legislative Assembly may provide that any elective public office becomes vacant, under such conditions or circumstances as the Legislative Assembly may specify, whenever a person holding the office is elected to another public office more than 90 days prior to the expiration of the term of the office he is holding. For the purposes of this section, a person elected is considered to be elected as of the date the election is held. [Created through S.J.R. 41, 1959, and adopted by the people Nov. 8, 1960]

Section 10. The Oregon Property Protection Act of 2000. (1) This section may be known and shall be cited as the "Oregon Property Protection Act of 2000."

(2) Statement of principles. The People, in the exercise of the power reserved to them under the Constitution of the State of Oregon, declare that:

(a) A basic tenet of a democratic society is that a person is presumed innocent and should not be punished until proven guilty;

(b) The property of a person generally should not be forfeited in a forfeiture proceeding by government unless and until that person is convicted of a crime involving the property;

(c) The value of property forfeited should be proportional to the specific conduct for which the owner of the property has been convicted; and

(d) Proceeds from forfeited property should be used for treatment of drug abuse unless otherwise specified by law for another purpose.

(3) Forfeitures prohibited without conviction. Except as provided in this section, a judgment of forfeiture of property in a civil forfeiture proceeding by the State or any of its political subdivisions may not be entered until and unless the person claiming the property is convicted of a crime in Oregon or another jurisdiction and the property:

(a) Constitutes proceeds of the crime for which the claimant has been convicted;

(b) Was instrumental in committing or facilitating the crime for which the claimant has been convicted;

(c) Constitutes proceeds of one or more other crimes similar to the crime for which the claimant was convicted; or

(d) Was instrumental in committing or facilitating one or more other crimes similar to the crime for which the claimant was convicted.

(4) Forfeiture based on similar crimes. Property may be forfeited under paragraph (c) or (d) of subsection (3) of this section only if the claimant is notified in writing of the

other crime or crimes claimed to be similar to the crime for which the claimant was convicted. The notice must be given at the time the claimant is given notice of the seizure of the property for forfeiture, and the claimant must have an opportunity to challenge the seizure and forfeiture of the property.

(5) Forfeiture without conviction of claimant. The property of a claimant who has not been convicted of a crime may be forfeited in a civil forfeiture proceeding only if the claimant consents to the forfeiture of the property or the forfeiting agency proves the property constitutes proceeds or an instrumentality of crime committed by another person as described in subsection (3) of this section and:

(a) The claimant took the property with the intent to defeat forfeiture of the property;

(b) The claimant knew or should have known that the property constituted proceeds or an instrumentality of criminal conduct; or

(c) The claimant acquiesced in the criminal conduct. A person shall be considered to have acquiesced in criminal conduct if the person knew of the criminal conduct and failed to take reasonable action under the circumstances to terminate the criminal conduct or prevent use of the property to commit or facilitate the criminal conduct.

(6) Standard of proof. (a) Except as provided in paragraph (b) of this subsection, if the property to be forfeited in a civil forfeiture action is personal property, the forfeiting agency must prove the elements specified in subsection (3) or (5) of this section by a preponderance of the evidence. If the property to be forfeited in a civil forfeiture action is real property, the forfeiting agency must prove the elements specified in subsection (3) or (5) of this section by clear and convincing evidence.

(b) If a forfeiting agency establishes in a forfeiture proceeding that cash, weapons or negotiable instruments were found in close proximity to controlled substances or to instrumentalities of criminal conduct, the burden is on any person claiming the cash, weapons or negotiable instruments to prove by a preponderance of the evidence that the cash, weapons or negotiable instruments are not proceeds of criminal conduct or an instrumentality of criminal conduct.

(7) Value of property forfeited. The value of the property forfeited under the provisions of this section may not be excessive and shall be substantially proportional to the specific conduct for which the owner of the property has been convicted. For purposes of this section, "property" means any interest in anything of value, including the whole of any lot or tract of land and tangible and intangible personal property, including currency, instruments or securities or any other kind of privilege, interest, claim or right whether due or to become due. Nothing in this section shall prohibit a person from voluntarily giving a judgment of forfeiture.

(8) Financial institutions. In a civil forfeiture proceeding, if a financial institution claiming an interest in the property demonstrates that it holds an interest, the financial institution's interest is not subject to forfeiture.

(9) Exception for unclaimed property and contraband. Notwithstanding the provisions of subsection (3) of this section, if, following notice to all persons known to have an interest or who may have an interest, no person claims an interest in the seized property or if the property is contraband, a judgment of forfeiture may be allowed and entered without a criminal conviction. For purposes of this subsection, "contraband" means personal property, articles or things, including but not limited to controlled substances or drug paraphernalia, that a person is prohibited by Oregon statute or local ordinance from producing, obtaining or possessing.

(10) Exception for forfeiture of animals. This section does not apply to the forfeiture of animals that have been abused, neglected or abandoned.

(11) Law enforcement seizures unaffected. Nothing in this section shall be construed to affect the temporary seizure of property for evidentiary, forfeiture, or protective purposes, or to alter the power of the Governor to remit fines or forfeitures under Article V, Section 14, of this Constitution.

(12) Disposition of property to drug treatment. Any sale of forfeited property shall be conducted in a commercially reasonable manner. Property forfeited in a civil forfeiture proceeding shall be distributed or applied in the following order:

(a) To the satisfaction of any foreclosed liens, security interests and contracts in the order of their priority;

(b) To the State or any of its political subdivisions for actual and reasonable expenses related to the costs of the forfeiture proceeding, including attorney fees, storage, maintenance, management, and disposition of the property incurred in connection with the sale of any forfeited property; and

(c) To the State or any of its political subdivisions to be used exclusively for drug treatment, unless another disposition is specially provided by law.

(13) Restrictions on State transfers. Neither the State of Oregon, its political subdivisions, nor any forfeiting agency shall transfer forfeiture proceedings to the federal government unless a state court has affirmatively found that:

(a) The activity giving rise to the forfeiture is interstate in nature and sufficiently complex to justify the transfer;

(b) The seized property may only be forfeited under federal law; or

(c) Pursuing forfeiture under state law would unduly burden the state forfeiting agencies.

(14) Penalty for violations. Any person acting under color of law, official title or position who takes any action intending to conceal, transfer, withhold, retain, divert or otherwise prevent any moneys, conveyances, real property, or any things of value forfeited under the law of this State or the United States from being applied, deposited or used in accordance with the requirements of this section shall be subject to a civil penalty in an amount treble the value of the forfeited property concealed, transferred, withheld, retained or diverted. Nothing in this subsection shall be construed to impair judicial immunity if otherwise applicable.

(15) Reporting requirement. All forfeiting agencies shall report the nature and disposition of all property seized for forfeiture or forfeited to a State asset forfeiture oversight committee that is independent of any forfeiting agency. The asset forfeiture oversight committee shall generate and make available to the public an annual report of the information collected. The asset forfeiture oversight committee shall also make recommendations to ensure that asset forfeiture proceedings are handled in a manner that is fair to innocent property owners and interest holders.

(16) Severability. If any part of this section or its application to any person or circumstance is held to be invalid for any reason, then the remaining parts or applications to any persons or circumstances shall not be affected but shall remain in full force and effect. [Created through initiative petition filed Jan. 5, 2000, and adopted by the people Nov. 7, 2000; Amendment proposed by S.J.R. 18, 2007, and adopted by the people May 20, 2008]

Note: The leadlines to section 10 and subsections (2), (3), (9) and (11) to (16) of section 10 were a part of the measure submitted by initiative petition (Measure No. 3, 2000) adopted by the people Nov. 7, 2000. The leadlines to subsections (4) to (8) and (10) of

section 10 were a part of S.J.R. 18, 2007, which was adopted by the people May 20, 2008.

Note: The text of section 11 (sections 1 to 3, Measure No. 99, 2000) as submitted to the people was preceded by a preamble that reads as follows:

WHEREAS, thousands of Oregon seniors and persons with disabilities live independently in their own homes, which they prefer and is less costly than institutional care (i.e. nursing homes), because over 10,000 home care workers, (also known as client employed providers), paid by the State of Oregon provide in-home support services;

WHEREAS, home care workers provide services that range from housekeeping, shopping, meal preparation, money management and personal care to medical care and treatment, but receive little, if any, training in those areas resulting in a detrimental impact on quality of care;

WHEREAS, the quality of care provided to seniors and people with disabilities is diminished when there is a lack of stability in the workforce which is the result of home care workers receiving low wages, minimal training and benefits;

WHEREAS, both home care workers and clients receiving home care services would benefit from creating an entity which has the authority to provide, and is held accountable for the quality of services provided in Oregon's in-home system of long-term care.

Section 11. Home Care Commission. (1) Ensuring High Quality Home Care Services: Creation and Duties of the Quality Home Care Commission. (a) The Home Care Commission is created as an independent public commission consisting of nine members appointed by the Governor.

(b) The duties and functions of the Home Care Commission include, but are not limited to:

(A) Ensuring that high quality, comprehensive home care services are provided to the elderly and people with disabilities who receive personal care services in their homes by home care workers hired directly by the client and financed by payments from the State or by payments from a county or other public agency which receives money for that purpose from the State;

(B) Providing routine, emergency and respite referrals of qualified home care providers to the elderly and people with disabilities who receive personal care services by home care workers hired directly by the client and financed in whole or in part by the State, or by payment from a county or other public agency which receives money for that purpose from the State;

(C) Provide training opportunities for home care workers, seniors and people with disabilities as consumers of personal care services;

(D) Establish qualifications for home care workers;

(E) Establish and maintain a registry of qualified home care workers;

(F) Cooperate with area agencies on aging and disability services and other local agencies to provide the services described and set forth in this section.

(2) Home Care Commission Operation/Selection. (a) The Home Care Commission shall be comprised of nine members. Five members of the Commission shall be current or former consumers of home care services for the elderly or people with disabilities. One member shall be a representative of the Oregon Disabilities Commission, (or a successor entity, for as long as a comparable entity exists). One member shall be a representative of the Governor's Commission on Senior Services, (or a successor entity, for as long as a comparable entity exists). One member shall be a representative of the Oregon Association of Area Agencies on Aging and Disabilities, (or a successor entity, for as long as a comparable entity exists). One member

shall be a representative of the Senior and Disabled Services Division, (or a successor entity, for as long as a comparable entity exists).

(b) The term of office of each member is three years, subject to confirmation by the Senate. If there is a vacancy for any cause, the Governor shall make an appointment to become immediately effective for the unexpired term. A member is eligible for reappointment and may serve no more than three consecutive terms. In making appointments to the Commission, the Governor may take into consideration any nominations or recommendations made by the representative groups or agencies.

(3) Other Provisions — Legal Duties and Responsibilities of the Commission. (a) The Home Care Commission shall, in its own name, for the purpose of carrying into effect and promoting its functions, have authority to contract, lease, acquire, hold, own, encumber, insure, sell, replace, deal in and with and dispose of real and personal property.

(b) When conducting any activities in this Section or in subsection (1) of this section, and in making decisions relating to those activities, the Home Care Commission shall first consider the effect of its activities and its decisions on improving the quality of service delivery and ensuring adequate hours of service are provided to clients who are served by home care workers.

(c) Clients of home care services retain their right to select the providers of their choice, including family members.

(d) Employees of the Commission are not employees of the State of Oregon for any purpose.

(e) Notwithstanding the provisions in paragraph (d) of this subsection, the State of Oregon shall be held responsible for unemployment insurance payments for home care workers.

(f) For purposes of collective bargaining, the Commission shall be the employer of record of home care workers hired directly by the client and paid by the State, or by a county or other public agency which receives money for that purpose from the State. Home care workers have the right to form, join and participate in the activities of labor organizations of their own choosing for the purpose of representation and collective bargaining with the Commission on matters concerning employment relations. These rights shall be exercised in accordance with the rights granted to public employees with mediation and interest arbitration as the method of concluding the collective bargaining process. Home care workers shall not have the right to strike.

(g) The Commission may adopt rules to carry out its functions. [Created through initiative petition filed Nov. 10, 1999, and adopted by the people Nov. 7, 2000]

Note: The leadlines to subsections (1), (2) and (3) of section 11, except the periods in subsections (2) and (3), were a part of the measure submitted to the people by initiative petition (Measure No. 99, 2000) and adopted by the people Nov. 7, 2000.

Note: Section 11 was submitted to the voters as sections 1, 2 and 3 and added to the Constitution but not to any Article therein by Measure No. 99, 2000.

Note: In Measure No. 99, 2000, subsection (1)(a) and (b)(A) to (F) were designated as section 1 (A) and (B)(1) to (6); subsection (2)(a) and (b) as section 2 (A) and (B); and subsection (3)(a) to (g) as section 3 (A) to (G). The reference to subsection (1) of this section was a reference to Section 1 above, and the reference to paragraph (d) of this subsection was a reference to subsection (D) of this section.

Note: In Measure No. 99, 2000, the period in subsection (1)(b)(F) appeared as a semicolon, and there was no period in subsection (3)(e).

ARTICLE XVI
BOUNDARIES

Section 1. State boundaries. The State of Oregon shall be bounded as provided by section 1 of the Act of Congress of February 1859, admitting the State of Oregon into the Union of the United States, until:

(1) Such boundaries are modified by appropriate interstate compact or compacts heretofore or hereafter approved by the Congress of the United States; or

(2) The Legislative Assembly by law extends the boundaries or jurisdiction of this state an additional distance seaward under authority of a law heretofore or hereafter enacted by the Congress of the United States. [Constitution of 1859; Amendment proposed by S.J.R. 4, 1957, and adopted by the people Nov. 4, 1958; Amendment proposed by H.J.R. 24, 1967, and adopted by the people Nov. 5, 1968]

ARTICLE XVII
AMENDMENTS AND REVISIONS

Sec. 1.   Method of amending Constitution
     2.   Method of revising Constitution

Section 1. Method of amending Constitution. Any amendment or amendments to this Constitution may be proposed in either branch of the legislative assembly, and if the same shall be agreed to by a majority of all the members elected to each of the two houses, such proposed amendment or amendments shall, with the yeas and nays thereon, be entered in their journals and referred by the secretary of state to the people for their approval or rejection, at the next regular general election, except when the legislative assembly shall order a special election for that purpose. If a majority of the electors voting on any such amendment shall vote in favor thereof, it shall thereby become a part of this Constitution. The votes for and against such amendment, or amendments, severally, whether proposed by the legislative assembly or by initiative petition, shall be canvassed by the secretary of state in the presence of the governor, and if it shall appear to the governor that the majority of the votes cast at said election on said amendment, or amendments, severally, are cast in favor thereof, it shall be his duty forthwith after such canvass, by his proclamation, to declare the said amendment, or amendments, severally, having received said majority of votes to have been adopted by the people of Oregon as part of the Constitution thereof, and the same shall be in effect as a part of the Constitution from the date of such proclamation. When two or more amendments shall be submitted in the manner aforesaid to the voters of this state at the same election, they shall be so submitted that each amendment shall be voted on separately. No convention shall be called to amend or propose amendments to this Constitution, or to propose a new Constitution, unless the law providing for such convention shall first be approved by the people on a referendum vote at a regular general election. This article shall not be construed to impair the right of the people to amend this Constitution by vote upon an initiative petition therefor. [Created through initiative petition filed Feb. 3, 1906, and adopted by the people June 4, 1906]

Note: The above section replaces sections 1 and 2 of Article XVII of the original Constitution.

Section 2. Method of revising Constitution. (1) In addition to the power to amend this Constitution granted by section 1, Article IV, and section 1 of this Article, a revision of all or part of this Constitution may be proposed in either house of the Legislative Assembly and, if the proposed revision is agreed to by at least two-thirds of all the members of each house, the proposed revision shall, with the yeas and nays thereon, be entered in their journals and referred by the Secretary of State to the people for their approval or rejection, notwithstanding section 1, Article IV of this Constitution, at the next regular state-wide primary election, except when the Legislative Assembly orders a special election for that purpose. A proposed revision may deal with more than one subject and shall be voted upon as one question. The votes for and against the proposed revision shall be canvassed by the Secretary of State in the presence of the Governor and, if it appears to the Governor that the majority of the votes cast in the election on the proposed revision are in favor of the proposed revision, he shall, promptly following the canvass, declare, by his proclamation, that the proposed revision has received a majority of votes and has been adopted by the people as the Constitution of the State of Oregon or as a part of the Constitution of the State of Oregon, as the case may be. The revision shall be in effect as the Constitution or as a part of this Constitution from the date of such proclamation.

(2) Subject to subsection (3) of this section, an amendment proposed to the Constitution under section 1, Article IV, or under section 1 of this Article may be submitted to the people in the form of alternative provisions so that one provision will become a part of the Constitution if a proposed revision is adopted by the people and the other provision will become a part of the Constitution if a proposed revision is rejected by the people. A proposed amendment submitted in the form of alternative provisions as authorized by this subsection shall be voted upon as one question.

(3) Subsection (2) of this section applies only when:

(a) The Legislative Assembly proposes and refers to the people a revision under subsection (1) of this section; and

(b) An amendment is proposed under section 1, Article IV, or under section 1 of this Article; and

(c) The proposed amendment will be submitted to the people at an election held during the period between the adjournment of the legislative session at which the proposed revision is referred to the people and the next regular legislative session. [Created through H.J.R. 5, 1959, and adopted by the people Nov. 8, 1960]

ARTICLE XVIII
SCHEDULE

Section 1. Election to accept or reject Constitution. For the purpose of taking the vote of the electors of the State, for the acceptance or rejection of this Constitution, an election shall be held on the second Monday of November, in the year 1857, to be conducted according to existing laws regulating the election of Delegates in Congress, so far as applicable, except as herein otherwise provided.

Section 2. Questions submitted to voters. Each elector who offers to vote upon this Constitution, shall be asked by the judges of election this question:

Do you vote for the Constitution? Yes, or No.

And also this question:

Do you vote for Slavery in Oregon? Yes, or No.

And in the poll books shall be columns headed respectively.

"Constitution, Yes."   "Constitution, No"
"Slavery, Yes."   "Slavery, No".

And the names of the electors shall be entered in the poll books, together with their answers to the said questions, under their appropriate heads. The abstracts of the votes transmitted to the Secretary of the Territory, shall be publicly opened, and canvassed by the Governor and Secretary, or by either of them in the absence of the other; and the Governor, or in his absence the Secretary, shall forthwith issue his proclamation, and publish the same in the several newspapers printed in this State, declaring the result of the said election upon each of said questions. [Constitution of 1859; Amendment proposed by S.J.R. 7, 2001, and adopted by the people Nov. 5, 2002]

Section 3. Majority of votes required to accept or reject Constitution. If a majority of all the votes given for, and against the Constitution, shall be given for the Constitution, then this Constitution shall be deemed to be approved, and accepted by the electors of the State, and shall take effect accordingly; and if a majority of such votes shall be given against the Constitution, then this Constitution shall be deemed to be rejected by the electors of the State, and shall be void.—

Section 4. Vote on certain sections of Constitution. If this Constitution shall be accepted by the electors, and a majority of all the votes given for, and against slavery, shall be given for slavery, then the following section shall be added to the Bill of Rights, and shall be part of this Constitution:

"Sec. ___ "Persons lawfully held as slaves in any State, Territory, or District of the United States, under the laws thereof, may be brought into this State, and such Slaves, and their descendants may be held as slaves within this State, and shall not be emancipated without the consent of their owners."

And if a majority of such votes shall be given against slavery, then the foregoing section shall not, but the following sections shall be added to the Bill of Rights, and shall be a part of this Constitution.

"Sec. ___ There shall be neither slavery, nor involuntary servitude in the State, otherwise than as a punishment for crime, whereof the party shall have been duly convicted." [Constitution of 1859; Amendment proposed by S.J.R. 7, 2001, and adopted by the people Nov. 5, 2002]

Note: See sections 34 and 35 of Article I, Oregon Constitution.

Section 5. Apportionment of Senators and Representatives. Until an enumeration of the inhabitants of the State shall be made, and the senators and representatives apportioned as directed in the Constitution, the County of Marion shall have two senators, and four representatives.

Linn two senators, and four representatives.

Lane two senators, and three representatives.

Clackamas and Wasco, one senator jointly, and Clackamas three representatives, and Wasco one representative.

Yamhill one senator, and two representatives.

Polk one senator, and two representatives.

Benton one senator, and two representatives.

Multnomah, one senator, and two representatives.

Washington, Columbia, Clatsop, and Tillamook one senator jointly, and Washington one representative, and Washington and Columbia one representative jointly, and Clatsop and Tillamook one representative jointly.

Douglas, one senator, and two representatives.

Jackson one senator, and three representatives.

Josephine one senator, and one representative.

Umpqua, Coos and Curry, one senator jointly, and Umpqua one representative, and Coos and Curry one representative jointly. [Constitution of 1859; Amendment proposed by S.J.R. 7, 2001, and adopted by the people Nov. 5, 2002]

Section 6. Election under Constitution; organization of state. If this Constitution shall be ratified, an election shall be held on the first Monday of June 1858, for the election of members of the Legislative Assembly, a Representative in Congress, and State and County officers, and the Legislative Assembly shall convene at the Capital on the first Monday of July 1858, and proceed to elect two senators in Congress, and make such further provision as may be necessary to the complete organization of a State government.—

Section 7. Former laws continued in force. All laws in force in the Territory of Oregon when this Constitution takes effect, and consistent therewith, shall continue in force until altered, or repealed.—

Section 8. Officers to continue in office. All officers of the Territory of Oregon, or under its laws, when this Constitution takes effect, shall continue in office, until superseded by the State authorities.—

Section 9. Crimes against territory. Crimes and misdemeanors committed against the Territory of Oregon shall be punished by the State, as they might have been punished by the Territory, if the change of government had not been made.—

Section 10. Saving existing rights and liabilities. All property and rights of the Territory, and of the several counties, subdivisions, and political bodies corporate, of, or in the Territory, including fines, penalties, forfeitures, debts and claims, of whatsoever nature, and recognizances, obligations, and undertakings to, or for the use of the Territory, or any county, political corporation, office, or otherwise, to or for the public, shall inure to the State, or remain to the county, local division, corporation, officer, or public, as if the change of government had not been made. And private rights shall not be affected by such change.—

Section 11. Judicial districts. Until otherwise provided by law, the judicial districts of the State, shall be constituted as follows: The counties of Jackson, Josephine, and Douglas, shall constitute the first district. The counties of Umpqua, Coos, Curry, Lane, and Benton, shall constitute the second district.—The counties of Linn, Marion, Polk, Yamhill and Washington, shall constitute the third district.—The counties of Clackamas, Multnomah, Wasco, Columbia, Clatsop, and Tillamook, shall constitute the fourth district—and the County of Tillamook shall be attached to the county of Clatsop for judicial purposes.—

Index

Alphabetization is letter-by-letter (e.g., "Landscape" precedes "Land use.")

Index

Veterans' Affairs, Advisory Committee to the Director of, 77
Workers' Compensation Management-Labor Advisory Committee, 33–34
Advocacy
  Advocacy Commissions Office, 26–27
  Child Advocacy Section (Justice Department), 19
  Governor's Advocacy Office (Department of Human Services), 54
  Office of the Public Records Advocate, 69–70
Aeronautics. *See* Airplanes and airports
Affordable housing, 52–54
Affordable Rental Housing Division (Housing and Community Services Department), 53
African Americans. *See also* Minorities
  Commission on Black Affairs, 26
  history of, in Oregon, 295, 297–298, 302, 304, 308, 309, 311
  Oregon Black Pioneers, 148
Aging, services for
  Aging Veterans' Services, 77
  federal retirement benefits, tax exemption, 352
  Governor's Commission on Senior Services (Department of Human Services), 55
  Home Care Commission, 379–380
  housing for, 369
  Medicaid Long-Term Care Quality and Reimbursement Advisory Council (Department of Human Services), 55
  Northwest Senior and Disability Services, 228
  Office of Aging and People with Disabilities (Department of Human Services), 54–55
Aging and Disability Resource Connection (ARCD), 54
Agriculture
  commodity commissions, 28–29
  Department of State Lands, 72–73
  economy, 295–296, 298–299, 307, 311
  hops production, 3
  irrigation, 301, 305, 307, 309, 368–369
  laborer regulation, 17
  State Board of, 27, 28
  State Department of, 27–29
  technological change, 307
  top 10 commodities, 156
  veterans, farm loans to, 363–364
  Water Right Services Division (Water Resources Department), 78
  wine production, 8
Air National Guard, Oregon, 62
Airplanes and airports
  Department of Aviation, 30
  Evergreen Aviation & Space Museum, 152
  Western Antique Aeroplane Museum, 148
Air quality program (Department of Environmental Quality), 42
Albacore Commission (Department of Agriculture), 28
Alberta Rose Theatre, 145

Alcoholic beverages and alcohol abuse
  Bill of Rights of Oregon, 331, 332
  craft breweries, 2
  hop production, 3
  Liquor and Cannabis Commission, 59–60
  municipal regulation, 355
  Oregon Hop Commission (Department of Agriculture), 29
  prohibition (1914), 302
  Wine Board, 79
  wine production, 8
  wineries and craft breweries, 310
Alfalfa Seed Commission (Department of Agriculture), 28
All Classical Public Media, Inc., 145
Almanac, 1–10
Alternative energy projects, 1
Altitude, 1
American beaver (state animal), 1
American Indians. *See* Indian tribes
Amusement parks, 1
Animals. *See also* Livestock; *headings starting with "Wildlife"*
  Animal Health Program (Department of Agriculture), 27
  hunting regulation, 43–44
  Oregon Zoo, 152
  state animal, 1
  Veterinary Medical Examining Board, Oregon State, 77–78
Antitrust, 18
Appeals
  Appellate Division (Justice Department), 19
  Appellate Settlement Conference Program, 82
  civil cases, 347
  Employment Appeals Board (Employment Department), 39
  Fair Dismissal Appeals Board (Department of Education), 38
  Land Use Board of Appeals, 58
  Oregon Court of Appeals, 82, 84–85, 278–280
  Oregon Supreme Court. *See* Supreme Court, Oregon
  workers' compensation, 34
Appellate Division (Justice Department), 19
Applegate Trail, 298
Apportionment, U.S. House of Representatives, 1, 381
Appraiser Certification and Licensure Board (ACLB), 29
Apprenticeship and Training Division (Bureau of Labor and Industries), 17
Aquariums
  Hatfield Marine Science Center, 152
  Oregon Coast Aquarium, 152
Architect Examiners, State Board of, 29–30
Archives Division (Secretary of State), 13
Army Corps of Engineers' projects, 303, 305, 307
Army National Guard, Oregon, 62

Index

Index

Index

Index

Index

best practices, 66
Board of Naturopathic Medicine, 63
coordinated care organizations (CCOs), 47, 50
Department of Corrections, 35
Department of Human Services, 54–57
Equity and Inclusion Office, 48
Health Care Interpreter program, 48
Health Licensing Office (Health Authority), 48–49
Health Policy and Analytics Division (Health Authority), 49
Hospital, Oregon State (Health Authority), 50
Long Term Care Administrators Board (Health Licensing Office), 49
Occupational Safety and Health Division (Department of Consumer and Business Services), 33
Oregon Health and Science University (OHSU), 370–371
Oregon Health & Science University (OHSU), 141
Oregon Health Policy Board, 47
Oregon State Hospital (Health Authority), 50
Paid Leave Oregon, 40
Patient Safety Commission, 66
Prescription Drug Affordability Board (Department of Consumer and Business Services), 34
Public Health Advisory Board (Health Authority), 50
Public Health Division (Health Authority), 50
State Board of Nursing, 63–64
Traditional Health Worker program, 48
Health, Housing, Educational and Cultural Facilities Authority (HHECFA). See now Oregon Facilities Authority
Health Licensing Office (Health Authority), 48–49
Health Policy and Analytics Division (Health Authority), 49
Health Policy Board (Health Authority), 47
Health Systems Division (Health Authority), 49–50
Hearing Aids, Advisory Council on (Health Licensing Office), 49
Heating fuel. See Energy
HECC (Higher Education Coordinating Commission), 50–52, 138
Hell's Canyon (deepest gorge), 3
Hemp, industrial program, 27
Hemp Commission (Department of Agriculture), 29
Heritage organizations, 147–152
Oregon Heritage Commission (State Parks and Recreation Department), 65
Heritage Station Museum, 151
High Desert Museum, 146
Higher education. See Colleges and universities
Higher Education Coordinating Commission (HECC), 50–52, 138
High schools. See Schools
High-tech industries, 310

Highways and roads, 3
Commerce and Compliance Division (Department of Transportation), 75
Delivery and Operations Division (Department of Transportation), 75
development, 299–300
Highway Cost Allocation Study, 26
Patrol Services Division (Department of State Police), 68
Hispanic Affairs, Commission on, 27
Hispanics and Latinx, 306, 309, 311. See also Minorities
Historical markers (Travel Information Council), 76
Historical Records Advisory Board, Archives Division (Secretary of State), 13
Historical Society, 148
Historic Cemeteries, Commission on, 65
Historic landmarks, national, 5–6
Historic preservation (State Parks and Recreation Department)
Oregon Commission on Historic Cemeteries, 65
Oregon Heritage Commission, 65
State Advisory Committee on Historic Preservation, 65
State Historic Preservation Office, 64–65
History, 291–328
agriculture, 295–296, 299, 307, 311
British settlement, 294
cattle and sheep business, 296, 299, 301, 311
chronological history by year, 322–328
Civil War, 298
Depression era, 304
discrimination, 295, 297–298, 302, 304, 308, 309
earliest authorities governing state, 269–270
economy, 301–302, 303–304, 309–310
environmental concerns, 291, 303–304, 307–308
evangelical movement and missionaries, 294–295
first natives, 291–293
fur trade, 294
geologic formation of Oregon, 291
gold mining, 298–299, 301
Great Recession, 310
Indian wars, 297, 317
industrialization and urbanization, 301–302, 306
minorities, 297–298, 300, 302, 306, 308, 309
national monument lands, geologic history of, 314–318
"The Oregon Story," 307–309
Oregon System, 302–303, 304
organizations, 147–152
populist movement, 302–303
post-WWII development, 306–307

Index

Index

Index

injured workers, 33
Office of the Long-Term Care Ombudsman, 60
transportation (AskODOT), 74
workers' compensation, 33
OMSI (Oregon Museum of Science and Industry), 152
Open burning, Smoke Management Advisory Committee (State Forestry Department), 46
Opera—Portland Opera, 147
Operations Department (Department of Transportation), 75
Operations Division (Department of Corrections), 35
Opportunity Grants (Office of Student Access and Completion), 52
Optometry, Oregon Board of, 64
Oregon ...

Note: Agencies names, etc., that begin with Oregon and that are not listed here are located in the index under the next word in the name.

Oregon ABLE (Achieving a Better Life Experience) Savings Plan, 16
Oregon Administrative Rules, 13
Oregon & California Railroad lands, 300, 303
Oregon Bach Festival, 146
Oregon Ballet Theatre, 146
Oregon Black Pioneers, 148
Oregon Cascades West Council of Governments, 228
Oregon Caves National Monument, 320–321
tribal culture and, 316–317
Oregon Children's Theatre Company, 146
Oregon Coast Aquarium, 152
Oregon Coast Community College, 140
Oregon College Savings Plan, 14, 16
Oregon Constitution. *See* Constitution of Oregon
Oregon Corrections Enterprises (Department of Corrections), 35
Oregon Cultural Trust, 145
Oregon Disabilities Commission, 55
Oregon Donation Land Law (1850), 296, 298, 299
Oregon Forest Conservation Act (1941), 306
Oregon grape (state flower), 2
Oregon hairy triton (state seashell), 7
Oregon Health & Science University (OHSU), 141, 148, 370–371
Oregon Health Plan, 47, 49
Oregon Humanities, 145
Oregon Institute of Technology (OIT), 141
Oregon Jewish Museum and Center for Holocaust Education, 148
Oregon Land Fraud trials (1904–1910), 303
Oregon (Walamet) Mission of the Methodist Episcopal Church, 269
Oregon Museum Association, 148
Oregon Museum of Science and Industry (OMSI), 152
"Oregon, My Oregon" (state song), 7

Oregon National Historic Trail, 148
Oregon Newspaper Publishers Association, 164
Oregon Opportunity Grants, 52
Oregon Promise Grants, 52
Oregon Rail Heritage Foundation, 148
OregonSaves, 16
Oregon Savings Network, 16
Oregon School for the Deaf, 38, 138
Oregon Shakespeare Festival, 146
Oregon Short Term Fund Board, 15
Oregon State Lottery. *See* Lottery, Oregon State
Oregon State University (OSU), 141
College of Agricultural Sciences, 27
Hatfield Marine Science Center, 152
"The Oregon Story," 307–309
Oregon sunstone (state gemstone), 3
Oregon Swallowtail Butterfly (state insect), 4
Oregon Symphony Association, 146
Oregon System, 302–303, 304. *See also* Initiative, referendum and recall
Oregon Territory, 296, 323–324
Oregon Trail, 295, 298
Interpretive Center, 148
Oregon Treaty (1846), 296
Oregon Zoo, 152
Organic Act (1848), 296
Organized crime, 20
ORVET Home Loan Program, 77
OSAC (Office of Student Access and Completion), 52
OSATC (Oregon State Apprenticeship and Training Council), 17
Osprey (state raptor), 2
Osteopathic medicine (Medical Board), 61
OSU. *See* Oregon State University
Outdoor pageant, state, 6
Outdoor Recreation Office (State Parks and Recreation Department), 65
Overtime regulation, 17

P

Pacific daylight time, 7–8
Pacific Fur Company, 269, 294
Pacific Maritime Heritage Center, 151
Pacific Northwest College of Art, 142
Pacific Ocean. *See* Coastline
Pacific standard time, 7–8
Pacific University, 142
Paid Leave Oregon, 40
Pandemic. *See* COVID-19 pandemic
Pardons (Constitution of Oregon), 345
Pari-mutuel racing (Oregon Racing Commission), 71
Parks. *See also specific parks*
lottery proceeds used for, 376
national, 6
state, 6, 64–65, 304
Parks and Recreation Department, State, 64–65

Index

Index

Savings and loan associations, Financial Regulation Division (Department of Consumer and Business Services), 33

Savings for college tuition. *See* Educational assistance

Savings Growth Plan Advisory Committee (Public Employees Retirement System), 69

Scenic areas, trails, etc. *See* National scenic areas

Schminck Memorial Museum, 150

Scholarships. *See* Educational assistance

Schools, 137–143
  Common School Fund, 14, 15, 73, 350
  Constitution of Oregon, 350–351
  districts, 7
  education district bonds, 369–370
  Educators Benefit Board, 48
  Fair Dismissal Appeals Board (Department of Education), 38
  "40-40-20" goal, 137
  funding, 73, 132, 134, 137–138, 157, 350–351, 360–361, 372–373
  seismic rehabilitation of buildings, 371
  State Board of Education, 37–38, 137–138
  State School Fund, 138
  student statistics, 7
  Superintendent of Public Instruction, 350

ScienceWorks Hands-On Museum, 152

Seal, state, 7, 346

Search and seizure (Oregon Bill of Rights), 330

Seashell, state, 7

Seaside Museum and Historical Society, 151

Secondary schools. *See* Schools

Second Great Awakening, 295

Secretary of State, 12–14
  Constitution of Oregon, 346
  list of, by date, 271–272

Secretary of the Senate, 107

Securities, Financial Regulation Division (Department of Consumer and Business Services), 33

Seeds
  Alfalfa Seed Commission (Department of Agriculture), 28
  Plant Protection and Conservation Programs (Department of Agriculture), 28
  Ryegrass Growers Seed Commission (Department of Agriculture), 29

Seismic rehabilitation of emergency services and public education buildings, 371–372

Sekerak, Timothy (Chief Clerk of the House of Representatives), 107

Self-incrimination, right against (Oregon Bill of Rights), 330

Self-Sufficiency Programs (Department of Human Services), 40, 56

Senate, State. *See* Legislative Assembly

Senators, U.S., 167, 285–287

Senior citizens. *See* Aging, services for

Senior judges, 82, 85–86

Seniors. *See* Aging, services for

Senior Services, Governor's Commission on (Department of Human Services), 55

Sentencing
  capital punishment (Oregon Bill of Rights), 331
  commutation by governor (Constitution of Oregon), 344
  Oregon Criminal Justice Commission, 37
  reduction of sentence, 344
  term to be served in full (Oregon Bill of Rights), 335

Separation of powers (Constitution of Oregon), 338

Settlement of Oregon, 295–297, 314–315

Sex offenders
  insanity defense, 68–69
  sex offender notification system, 66
  Sex Offender Registration Unit (State Police Department), 68
  Sex Offender Treatment Board (Health Licensing Office), 49

Sexual orientation discrimination, 309, 311

Shakespeare Festival, 146

Sheep. *See* Livestock

Sheep Commission (Department of Agriculture), 29

Sheriffs (Constitution of Oregon), 346

Sherman County, 224

Sherman County Historical Society and Museum, 151

Ships. *See* Boats and boating

Shoes, oldest, 7

Signs and markers (Travel Information Council), 76

Siletz Indians, Confederated Tribes of, 173, 176–177, 220

Silverton Country Historical Society, 151

Sisters Folk Festival, 147

Size of Oregon, 6

Slavery, 297–298
  Oregon Bill of Rights, 331

Small businesses
  Ombudsman for Workers' Compensation (Department of Consumer and Business Services), 33
  Small Business Assistance Office (Corporation Division, Secretary of State), 13

Small claims, 105

Smoke Management Advisory Committee (State Forestry Department), 46

Snake River Correctional Institution, 36

Social Equity Office (Department of Transportation), 76

Socialist Party, 303

Social Workers, State Board of Licensed, 72

Soil, state, 7

Soil Conservation Service, 305

Solar energy, 1

Song, state, 7

SOU (Southern Oregon University), 141

Southern Oregon Historical Society, 151

Index

Veterans' Affairs Director, Advisory Committee to, 77

Veterans' Home and Farm Loan Program, 363–364

Veterans' Services Division (Department of Veterans' Affairs), 77

Veterinary Medical Examining Board, Oregon State, 77–78

Veto, governor's, 11, 109–110, 344

Vice-President of the United States, 170

Victims of crime
    Crime Victim and Survivor Services Division (Justice Department), 19
    Crime Victim Assistance Program appeals (Workers' Compensation Board), 19
    rights of (Oregon Bill of Rights), 333–334

Violence. *See also* Child abuse
    Temporary Assistance for Domestic Violence Survivors, 56
    victims' rights, 334

Vocational rehabilitation
    program (Employment Department), 40
    State Independent Living Council, 56–57
    State Rehabilitation Council, 57
    Vocational Rehabilitation (Department of Human Services), 56–57

Volcanoes, 314, 319–321

Voter registration, 233–234

Voting. *See* Elections

W

Wage and Hour Division (Bureau of Labor and Industries), 16, 17

Wagering. *See* Gambling

Wages, 156–157
    Legislative Assembly, compensation of members, 343
    minimum wage, 17, 156
    Prevailing Wage Advisory Committee (Bureau of Labor and Industries), 17
    Public Officials Compensation Commission (Department of Administrative Services), 26
    Wage and Hour Division (Bureau of Labor and Industries), 16, 17
    Wage Security Fund, 16

Wage Security Fund, 16

Wagner, Rob (President of State Senate), 107, 117

Wagon road companies, 300

Wagon trains, 295

Walla Walla University, 142

Wallowa County, 226

Warm Springs, Museum at, 149

Warm Springs Reservation, Confederated Tribes of, 173, 177–178, 218, 226

Warner Creek Correctional Facility, 36

Warner Pacific University, 142

Wasco County, 226

Wasco County Museum, 151

Washington County, 227

Water. *See also Rivers; following headings starting with "Water"*
    Constitution of Oregon, 368–369
    Department of Environmental Quality (DEQ), 42
    Groundwater Advisory Committee (Water Resources Department), 78–79
    lakes, statistics on, 4
    Natural Resources Programs (Department of Agriculture), 28
    rainfall, 6–7
    tribal water rights, 78

Waterfalls, 8

Waterfront Blues Festival, 147

Water power. *See* Electricity

Water quality program (Department of Environmental Quality), 42

Water Resources Commission, 78

Water Resources Department, 78–79

Water resources development (Constitution of Oregon), 368–369

Water Right Services Division (Water Resources Department), 78

Watershed management. *See also* Natural resources
    Constitution of Oregon, 368–369
    Watershed Enhancement Board, Oregon (OWEB), 79

Water transportation, 300, 301

Waterways. *See also* Rivers
    Constitution of Oregon, 368–369
    Department of State Lands, 73

Ways and Means, Joint Committee on (Legislative Assembly), 113

Web sites
    URLs are given as part of addresses for state departments, agencies, officers, etc., in Executive and Legislative sections.

Weeds (Department of Agriculture), 28

Weights and Measures Program, 27–28

Welfare. *See also* Medical assistance
    Child Welfare Advisory Committee (Department of Human Services), 55
    Child Welfare Division (Department of Human Services), 55
    Indian Child Welfare Act Advisory Committee (Department of Human Services), 55
    Supplemental Nutritional Assistance Program, 56
    Temporary Assistance for Needy Families (TANF), 56

Wells (Groundwater Advisory Committee), 78–79

Western Antique Aeroplane & Automobile Museum, 148

Western Interstate Commission for Higher Education, 141–142

Western meadowlark (state songbird), 1–2

Western Oregon University (WOU), 141

Western Seminary, 142

Western University of Health Sciences, 142

Wetlands (Department of State Lands), 73

Index

Index